MODERN ENVIRONMENTAL LAW
CASES AND CONTEXTS

*****

James R. May, Esq.

Distinguished Professor of Law
Widener University Delaware Law School

For Kathy, Jameson and Isabella
With hope that environmental law keeps its promise.

PREFACE AND ACKNOWLEDGMENTS

Thank you for reading this book. The need for environmental protection is all around: air and water pollution; severe weather, sea level rise, loss of species, wetlands, glaciers and biodiversity; water and food shortages; pandemics. It's also close at hand: the water from the tap; the local air quality index; local land use and development; flooding and storm damage. "Environmental Law" examines signature federal, state, international and global laws that address environmental pollution, rights, protection, and governance; natural resources and conservation of species; energy and land use law; disproportionate effects of environmental policies; and more. Environmental Law also integrates many of the concepts you've already learned in other courses, such as Constitutional Law, Administrative Law, Property and Civil Procedure, with problems that affect modern society.

This book is an original work. I have done my level best to make it educationally efficient, cost-effective, and current about water quality and rights, air quality, species loss, climate change, and so many other issues torn from the headlines, including recent decisions from the 2021-2022 and 2022-23 Terms (e.g., *West Virginia v. EPA; Sackett v. EPA*). While the book covers a lot of ground, I have endeavored to strip it of extraneous citations, distracters, notes and all the rest that can overwhelm a casebook. For example, the case material within largely excludes internal citations, quotations, references, notes, "ids," "ibids," etc., denoted by "***". The same goes for article excerpts, the full copyrights to which are of course held by the authors and publishers. The full treatment for any of what's inside is always just a click away. That said, as with any early edition, it's likely to have mistakes, misses and miscues. Subsequent editions will benefit from your input.

Environmental Law is a fast-moving and changing educational target. Unlike many courses you may encounter in your law school career, the only constant here is change. And lots of it. To be sure, as I finish this text only weeks prior to teaching what's inside, there are certain to be important developments the book doesn't reach. It isn't possible for a casebook on environmental law to be all things to all people, to cover everything. "Modern Environmental Law" attempts to cover the most dynamic and durable aspects of the subject.

Allow me to outline what's inside. The introductory chapter aims to provide essentials about Environmental Law, including what it is (and isn't), where it comes from, and some of its strengths and shortcomings. Part I introduces you to the field of Environmental Law, including its eight 'rooms': common law, federal legislation, state law, environmental rights, water rights, international environmental law, environmental justice, and everything else. Part II focuses on the interrelationship between environmental law and constitutional law. As you'll see constitutional law plays an important role in understanding how environmental law works, and why it sometimes disappoints.

Chapter 1 covers how common law and the public trust doctrine address environmental challenges. As those causes of action are likely the subject of courses in Torts and Property Law, we'll focus on constitutional limitations to applying common law to some of the world's most wicked problems, including climate change. In Part I you'll learn about the "Displacement Doctrine" and read a case in which the Supreme Court of the United States (SCOTUS) held that pervasive federal regulation – such as under the Clean Air Act – 'displaces' federal common law and 'preempts' state common law to address climate change. Part II explains what the Public Trust Doctrine is and how it is reflected for the most part in constitutions *elsewhere* around the globe, with one exceptional case borne from a unique constitutional provision in Pennsylvania.

Chapter 2 covers the National Environmental Policy Act (NEPA). It's a remarkable piece of legislation that requires federal agencies to look before they leap (it doesn't prevent them from leaping, however) by assessing environmental impacts of federal actions, and then avoiding or mitigating significant harmful impacts. After Part I's introduction, Part II provides the statutory and regulatory language that makes NEPA hum. In Part III, we'll see how receptive the SCOTUS has been to NEPA, meaning hardly at all. It's a procedural drill, in the Court's view, as we'll see in the contexts of exclusions, consideration of alternatives and effects, and mitigation.

Chapter 3 turns to the federal Endangered Species Act (ESA), what some have called the "pit-bull" of all environmental laws. It is the book's longest chapter because the ESA is a good illustration of how laws are made, as well as how Congress can require agencies to act and forbid the rest of us from doing so in certain circumstances when necessary to conserve a species. After reading perhaps the most famous (if not infamous) case in the environmental law canon in Part I, we'll read what Congress expressed as to the ESA's purposes and objectives in Part II, before turning to important issues as to what species and habitats are protected (Part III), what listing means to federal agencies (consultation, Part IV) and everybody else (prohibited takings, Part V). We'll finish this chapter with related subjects of enforcement (Part VI), criminal activity (Part VII), and international trade (Part VIII).

Chapter 4 pivots to pollution control, and with it, the Clean Water Act (CWA). The CWA is or was perhaps the nation's greatest public works success story, helping to protect rivers, streams, and wetlands across the United States in ways common law cannot, as Part I details. The linchpin of regulation under the CWA is deceptively simple: You need a permit to discharge, the subject of Part II. The Permit must require technology-based controls that EPA has set for the type of discharger involved (Part III), plus any water-quality based controls based on water quality standards established by each state (Part IV). As you'll see, there is unfinished business here.

Chapter 5 turns to the CWA's messier cousin, the Clean Air Act (CAA). The CAA is sort of a box of chocolates, you never know what you're going to get in word or decision. That said, as Part I explains, it's been another widely successful federal law in improving public health throughout the nation. The CAA's primary objective is to achieve national "ambient air quality standards" designed to ensure that the air is safe to breathe for everyone, everywhere, as Part II explores. Like the CWA, the CAA has a permit requirement, although not for all emissions. Like the CWA, those who need a permit must also comply with technology-based controls that EPA establishes, and states implement (Part III), including for hazardous air pollutants (Part IV). One of the CAA's innovations is a market-based scheme to address acid deposition (Part V).

Chapter 6 extends our involvement with air pollution, this time specifically about climate change, or what is known as the "Anthropocene." Part I explores international and global regulation of climate change, and in particular the inroads of constitutionalizing climate change. Part II then examines the role of courts and constitutional law in addressing the subject, which is to say not in a good way, although we'll learn about a novel federal case and legal theory that look to provide a legal foothold.

Chapter 7 explains the role of environmental rights in environmental law. 'Rights' typically derive expressly or implicitly from constitutional text. As Parts I and II explain, many nations and some states afford or recognize a judicially cognizable right to a healthy environment. We'll then explore questions as to whether Nature (Part III) and other Animals (Part IV) have rights. Part V finishes by considering how constitutions can and do protect the right to participate in environmental policymaking.

Chapter 8 considers the related but different subject of water rights, which for the most part is about who has 'rights' to use or own it. It's another complicated area of law. Part I turns outward, surveying how constitutions the world over recognize a right to water. Part II chains inward with water rights in the United States, featuring the First State.

Chapter 9 describes international environmental law. Part I takes a 30,000-foot view of all of its manifestations, including treaties, customs and principles. Part II then focuses on the internationally accepted concept of sustainability, including how it is constitutionally recognized, and its relationship with protecting and promoting human rights, including to dignity.

Chapter 10 concludes the book with the concept of environmental justice, which explores the disproportionate effects of environmental policies, implementation, and enforcement on vulnerable communities, and features a recent resolution of the American Bar Association to advance environmental justice in its policies, practices and procedures throughout the practice of law.

I recommend two things at the start. The first is to page through the book to see what's inside. This can help to see the trees for the forest. The second is to enjoy the course. Environmental Law is a course that is fun, interesting, and meaningful.

This book is the product of decades of teaching, observing and practicing environmental law and related subjects. In that regard it owes a debt of gratitude to every student and colleague who has endured working together on them. I'd also like to thank Giulia Lima (L '24) for her assistance with proofreading and Dr. Kathleen A. Siren for pitching in.

I hope you find these materials to be helpful and welcome your comments and suggestions for improvement.

James R. May, Esq.
Distinguished Professor of Law
Widener University Delaware Law School
Wilmington, DE
July 2023
jrmay@widener.edu.

Table of Contents

INTRODUCTION: MODERN ENVIRONMENTAL LAW

"Why should I care about future generations? What have they ever done for me?"
— *Groucho Marx*

"Unless someone like you cares a whole awful lot,
Nothing is going to get better. It's not."
— *Dr. Seuss, from The Lorax*

"A clear conscience is usually the sign of a bad memory."
— *Steven Wright*

"Federal courts too often have been cautious and overly deferential in the arena of environmental law, and the world has suffered for it."
— *Hon. Ann Aiken, United States District Court Judge, Juliana v. U.S.*

The introductory chapter aims to provide essentials about environmental law, including what it is (an isn't), where it comes from, and some of its strengths and shortcomings. Part I introduces you to the field of environmental law, including its eight 'rooms': common law, federal legislation, state laws, international law, environmental rights, water rights, environmental justice, and everything else. Part II focuses on the interrelationship between environmental law and constitutional law. As you'll see constitutional law plays an important role in understanding how environmental law works, and why it sometimes disappoints.

I.   INTRODUCTION TO ENVIRONMENTAL LAW

The environment is, as they say, all around. It is air, water, wind, and fire and so much more. Suffice to say that human beings are inextricably intertwined with the environment. We can't and wouldn't exist without it.

"Environmental law" is the study of laws, regulations and policies that govern humanity's relationship with the environment. To some extent it reflects law and society over time, some key developments of which include:

- Late 18th - early 19th century - European explorers claimed new lands. Deforestation, farming, settlement and introduction of new plants, animals, and diseases.
- 19th century - Frontier moved ever westward with land development, growing population.
- Mid 19th century - Onset of industrialization, resource depletion, pollution; start of first environmental movements.
- 1930s - Conversion of large tracts of former prairie to farmland.; "Sod busting", dustbowl of the 1930s, and depletion of soil resources, spurred conservation movement.
- Early 1950s - Rapid industrialization, fast population growth ("baby boom"), cheap energy.

- ☐ 1960s - Viet Nam War, civil activism and environmental activism (Cuyahoga River fires, Rachel Carson's book '*Silent Spring*' 1962), development of environmental laws and regulations.
- ☐ 1970s-2000 – Refinement and expansion of environmental law. Climate change denial.
- ☐ 2000-present – The Anthropocene takes root.

Modern environmental law can be thought of as a house with eight rooms:

1. Common Law and Public Trust. This is where environmental law began. For our purposes we can think of common law (you know it as tort law) as affording a series of causes of action ordinarily for damages to address and redress environmental harm to an individual or community, including nuisance, trespass, and strict liability for abnormally dangerous activities. Common law is largely the product of state law. There is no federal common law. State common laws often derive from the Restatement of Torts, the Restatement of Judgments, etc., (there is no "Restatement of Environmental Law") and differ from state to state, if only marginally, regarding causes of action, liability, proof, statutes of limitations, and damages. Aside from public nuisance, most common law causes of action are brought by private parties for damages for specific environmental harms to property, say, for a contaminated well or poisoned livestock or diminution of property value. Common law, however, isn't designed to redress public health and welfare or to promote the public good. An iconic predicate to modern environmental law in the United States is the conflagration of the Cuyahoga River outside of Cleveland in 1952, caused by the common discharge of oil, grease and flammable chemicals directly into surface waters:

Unregulated water pollution also spread disease, like Typhoid Fever in St. Louis more than a century ago:

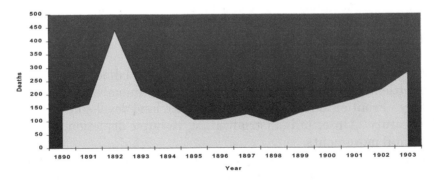

Unregulated air pollution was also rampant, causing "inversions" that killed hundreds in London, England and in Donora, Pennsylvania, near Pittsburgh:

BRIDGE OVER THE MONONGAHELA RIVER, PITTSBURG, PENN.

Moreover, thousands of chemicals wreak havoc with biodiversity, which Rachel Carson wrote about in her clarion call for action in 1962, "Silent Spring."

Relatedly, the public trust doctrine derives from the ancient notion that the sovereign holds certain natural resources and objects of nature in trust for the benefit of current and future generations. While the general rule in American law favors ownership of natural resources as private property, the public trust doctrine posits that some resources are subject to a perpetual trust that forecloses private exclusion rights. Yet the doctrine has gained little traction, except in the one state (Pennsylvania) that makes it a constitutional guarantee.

While common law and the public trust doctrine continue to provide a means for providing redress for environmental damages to private parties, their fundamental limitations led to the passage of wide-ranging legislation, discussed next.

2. Federal Law. Federal and state Legislatures can enact environmental laws to address environmental pollution or protection or promote species conservation. At the federal level, the

golden age of enactment ran from roughly 1969 to 1980, producing a series of environmental laws, covering everything from policy to pollution to species protection:

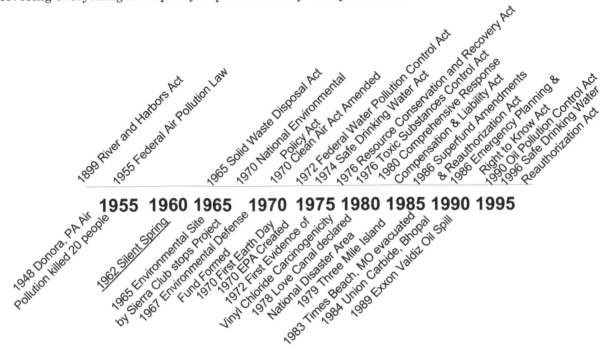

We can't cover all of them, so will focus here on these:

☐ National Environmental Policy Act (NEPA), <u>42 U.S.C. §4321, et seq.</u>

The passage of NEPA resulted in the creation of the Environmental Protection Agency. The "Congressional declaration of purpose" section at the beginning of the Act explains that NEPA's purpose is, "To declare a national policy which will encourage productive and enjoyable harmony between man and his environment; to promote efforts which will prevent or eliminate damage to the environment and biosphere and stimulate the health and welfare of man; to enrich the understanding of the ecological systems and natural resources important to the Nation; and to establish a Council on Environmental Quality." The <u>Council on Environmental Quality</u> establishes regulations and oversees NEPA's implementation across all federal agencies.

☐ Endangered Species Act (ESA) <u>16 U.S.C. §1531</u>

The ESA governs the conservation of fauna and flora in the United States. The "Policy" section of the ESA states that it is "the policy of Congress that all Federal departments and agencies shall seek to conserve endangered species and threatened species." The ESA only protects species that are "listed" as endangered or threatened by the U.S. Fish and Wildlife Service (a component of the Department of the Interior) or the National Marine Fisheries Service (Department of Commerce). All federal agencies must "consult" with these agencies before funding, authorizing or carrying out an activity to avoid harming listed species and critical habitats.

☐ Clean Water Act (CWA), <u>33 U.S.C. §1251, et seq.</u>

The CWA's "Congressional declaration of goals and policy" states that the "objective of this chapter is to restore and maintain the chemical, physical, and biological integrity of the Nation's waters." The act provides for research, enforcement, and state assistance in efforts to curb water pollution. The CWA is overseen by the federal Environmental Protection Agency, which Congress established in 1970. The CWA prohibits the discharge of pollutants without a permit issued by EPA or by states with delegated authority. Permits must comply with technological and water-quality based effluent limitations.

☐ Clean Air Act (CAA) <u>42 U.S.C.§7401, et seq.</u>

According to the "Congressional findings and declaration of purpose" of the CAA, the Act was designed to "protect and enhance the quality of the Nation's air resources" and to promote research and provide assistance to state and local governments in an effort to combat air pollution. The CAA is <u>overseen by the EPA</u>. The CAA requires a permit for emissions from major stationary sources. It also establishes tailpipe emission standards for vehicles and a "cap and trade" system to address acid deposition causes by large fossil-fuel burning powerplants.

<u>3. State Law</u>. Besides common law, all states and territories have their own environmental laws, regulations and agencies, and can differ widely if not dramatically. Check your local listings.

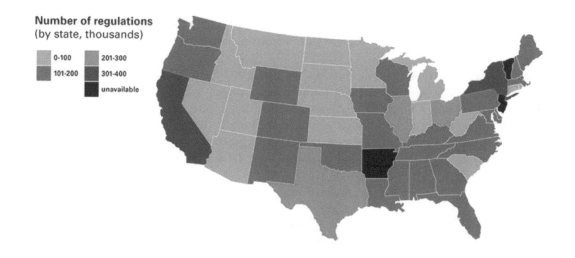

<u>4. Constitutional Law</u>. Much of constitutional law derives from lawsuits about the environment or the use of it, beginning perhaps with *Gibbons v. Ogden*, 22 U.S. 1 (1824), about Congress' authority to issue licenses to use waterways to ferry humans back and forth to Manhattan. Virtually every aspect of constitutional law impacts environmental law, including Due Process (is there a fundamental right to a stable climate?); Commerce Clause (can Congress protect endangered species that don't significantly affect interstate commerce?); Supremacy Clause (can states be stricter about the environment than Congress?); and the Takings Clause (can municipalities require homeowners and businesses to be environmentally responsible?).

In other words, he U.S. Supreme Court has played a huge role in the development of Environmental Law, some of which occurs through administrative law, next.

5. Administrative Law. Administrative law helps explain how environmental law is implemented (or isn't). Administrative law bisects constitutional issues concerning the President's authority to appoint and remove officers, Congress' authority to regulate, the federal courts' authority to adjudicate disputes involving public laws, a citizen's authority to challenge government action, and procedural due process. Administrative law also explores how the vast majority of our country's civil laws function, including agency rulemaking, adjudication, and enforcement.

Much of environmental law involves "rulemaking" the process of which looks something like:

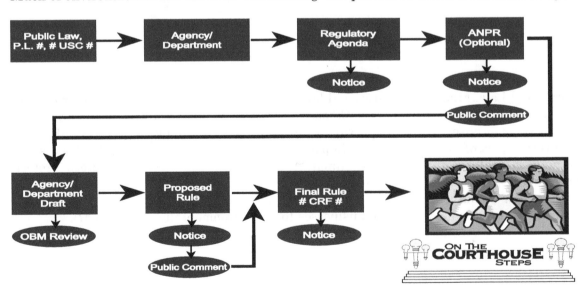

6. International Law. International law is the body of treaties, customs and principles recognized by cooperating nations. International law is largely soft law that requires party consent, protects sovereignty, and promotes cooperation. International "environmental" law has two flavors. The first stems from multilateral environmental agreements ("MEAs") among and between nations,

such as the 2015 Paris Accord on Climate Change. Most MEAs are negotiated by and through the United Nations Environment Programme in Nairobi, Kenya. The other stems from the recognition of the relationship between human rights and the environment, which is centered at the UN Human Rights Council in Geneva. The United Nations General Assembly also issues resolutions, such as in 2022 recognizing a basic right to a healthy environment, and the UN "Sustainable Development Goals":

7. Environmental Justice. "Environmental justice" means the just treatment and meaningful involvement of all people, regardless of income, race, color, national origin, Tribal affiliation, or disability, in agency decision-making and other federal activities that affect human health and the environment. The imbalances it seeks to address are the product of complex, interlocking systems including race, class, wealth, and colonization. Environmental justice embodies the principle that everyone, everywhere, enjoys equal worth, dignity, and access to a clean, healthful, and sustainable environment and that those most affected by environmental decisions should have the opportunity to have their voices heard and concerns taken seriously. But for a few exceptions at the subnational level in New York, New Jersey, California and elsewhere, environmental justice is largely a matter of policy and not positive law. Still, there is much activity afoot at the subnational level to advance environmental justice:

8. <u>Everything else</u>. Environmental law touches and concerns almost every area of law, including criminal (intentional endangerment); civil procedure (can a court exercise jurisdiction over a polluting company); property (does a regulation constitute an uncompensated taking of private property for public use); bankruptcy (are environmental penalties and damages dischargeable); real estate (what to do with contaminated land); and corporate and business law (to what extent are directors and officers liable or subject to derivate shareholder action for environmental harm). Additionally, there are economic conditions and pressures, especially in a capalistic system. Much environmental law is subject to cost/benefit analysis, where environmental costs (job losses and limitations on development) are monetized and exaggerated and environmental benefits (e.g., ecosystem services provided by wetlands and forests) are minimized and overlooked if not ignored, leading to distorted outcomes that frustrate a true assessment of costs and benefits.

How well does Environmental Law work? Given all the "law" above, one might think that the environment is safe and healthy. Yet we see otherwise as we look around (climate change; plastics; forever chemicals). What explains the lack of stronger environmental protection outcomes given the democracy-advancing attributes of U.S. law? First, there are several doctrines that prevent plaintiffs from enforcing federal environmental laws. To commence an action, the standing doctrine requires litigants to prove that they possess a concrete, specific and imminent injury to themselves and not solely to the public that is fairly traceable to the defendant's actions and that can be redressed by the federal court, such as an order for the defendant to comply with the relevant environmental law. This showing can be greater than that necessary to prove liability in the underlying case. Plaintiffs also cannot challenge an agency action until it is final and has legal consequences against the plaintiff, and the plaintiff has "exhausted" any available appeals before the agency that Congress has imposed.

The mootness doctrine then divests jurisdiction if at some point after a case is commenced the defendant comes into compliance, unless the plaintiff can demonstrate that the matter is "capable of repetition yet avoiding review."

Relatedly, the U.S. Supreme Court has been unwilling to afford more process in environmental matters than that which Congress specifically affords, for example, under the National Environmental Policy Act.

Second, structural imposts rooted in separation of powers can also prevent the enforcement of environmental laws. The political question doctrine relegates certain 'irksome issues' to the political branches and away from federal courts. Thus far, the Court has applied the doctrine in cases involving impeachment, constitutional qualifications, and foreign policy. Some lower courts have held it also applies in certain environmental matters, including climate change, and there is some suggestion that the Court is sympathetic to this point of view given its recent decision to stay a lower court case aiming to have the federal government establish national policies to address climate change.

The abstention doctrine has federal courts refrain from exercising jurisdiction if the case would intrude upon the powers of another court system. Some federal courts have invoked this doctrine to decline exercising jurisdiction in environmental cases subject to litigation in a state court or a judicial system in another country. A similar doctrine known as *forum non conveniens* permits state courts to dismiss claims deemed to be better litigated in a foreign jurisdiction, including claims for violation of environmental human rights.

The displacement doctrine has federal courts refrain from common law-based causes of action in those areas already addressed by a pervasive federal statutory law. For example, the Court has held that the federal Clean Air Act displaces federal common law causes of action, such as for public nuisance, to hold so-called 'climate majors' to account for their proportional contributions to climate change.

The federal government possesses limited authority to protect the environment. The Court has interpreted the Constitution as limiting federal and state authority to enact environmental laws in a variety of ways. Under the "Commerce Clause," Congress may only establish environmental laws to the extent that they are designed to address pollution or other challenges that have a "substantial affect" on interstate commerce. And it can only spend and tax in ways that promote the "general welfare." Moreover, federal agencies cannot regulate so-called 'major questions' without clear Congressional consent.

The Court has also held that Congress' constitutional capacity to enlist states to implement federal environmental policy is very limited. Under the 10th Amendment, Congress cannot require state governments or state officials to implement federal laws, including federal environmental programs. Moreover, Congress cannot threaten to withhold federal funding of such programs in ways that are 'coercive' to the states.

To protect the 'dignity' of the states, the Court has construed the 11th Amendment as granting states with 'sovereign immunity' from congressionally-created private causes of action, including for violating federal environmental laws, unless the state consents to being sued.

Third, despite the constitutional charge to "take care that laws are faithfully executed," the U.S. President has discretion to enforce federal environmental laws. The President also has authority to appoint the directors of federal environmental agencies with the advice and consent of the U.S. Senate, and nearly unbridled authority to remove constitutional officers overseeing environmental programs. The President also possesses unitary authority to establish foreign policy in environmental matters.

Fourth, while each state is a sovereign under a system known as "federalism," the Court has concluded that the U.S. Constitution limits progressive environmental policies from the states in several ways. The Court has held that the preemption doctrine under the Supremacy Clause prevents states from implementing environmental programs that would unduly interfere with or frustrate the implementation of federal environmental programs. It has also held that the negative implications of the Commerce Clause prevent states from enacting laws that favor conserving natural resources or promoting renewable energy if doing so would unduly impact interstate commerce. In addition, the Constitution forbids states from entering into treaties (called 'compacts') with foreign governments, such as those respecting climate change.

Moreover, the Court has construed the Takings Clause of the 5th Amendment to prevent state and local government authorities from restricting the use of private property so as to protect the environment in ways that "go too far" and amount to 'regulatory takings.'

Last, the Court has not construed the Bill of Rights of the U.S. Constitution to advance environmental protection. For example, the Court has been unwilling to recognize environmental rights as a liberty interest under the Due Process Clause, as a fundamental interest under the Equal Protection Clause, or as an unenumerated right under the 9th Amendment. And as mentioned, the Court recently granted an extraordinary stay of a lower court decision recognizing a constitutionally-protected life and liberty interest to a stable climate for present and future generations. Individual rights may also only be vindicated against federal or state government, and then only when there is a 'state action,' thus insulating private actors including corporations from constitutional claims. Private actors are also not generally subject to private causes of action for environmental harm committed outside the U.S. because the Court has established a presumption against extraterritorial application of U.S. laws and construed the Alien Tort Claims Act to apply in only very limited ways against U.S. corporations. Corporations are chartered under state law, most of which also serve for the most part to protect U.S. corporations from liability for environmental transgressions elsewhere. Finally, the Court has construed the Due Process Clause as limiting recovery of punitive damages in toxic tort actions to those that are deemed to be "proportional" to compensatory damages, that is, to no more than 4 or 5 times restitution. We'll explore these and additional concepts in the next part.

II.   THE INTERSECTION OF CONSTITUTIONAL AND ENVIRONMENTAL LAW

A good place to begin is to understand the various ways in which Constitutional Law affects Environmental Law, and with the following excerpt.

EXCERPT: JAMES R. MAY, INTRODUCTION TO CONSTITUTIONAL ENVIRONMENTAL LAW
Adapted from: Principles of Constitutional Environmental Law, James R. May (ed.) (ABA 2010)

For a featherweight 7,369 words the U.S. Constitution has a heavyweight impact on the arc of environmental law. Constitutional law doctrines often dictate what Congress, states, and individuals can and cannot do regarding the environment. From the nation's founding to about 1900, nearly all the U.S. Supreme Court cases involving environmental matters turned on either constitutional issues, such as the reach of the Commerce, Contract, Property, Enclave, Takings, and Due Process Clauses, or on legal theories such as the nondelegation and incorporation doctrines. From about 1900 until the dawn of the modern environmental era in about 1970, however, state and federal environmental protection laws seldom collided with constitutional principles because these laws were generally viewed as lying within legislative authority.

Since 1970, the sea has changed again, with constitutional issues often occupying center stage in federal and state efforts to protect land, air, water, species, and habitat, perhaps fueled by the U.S. Supreme Court's ambivalence about environmental protection and its renewed ambivalence about legislative authority generally. Indeed, from 2005 to 2010, more than 50 percent of the nearly four hundred federal cases yielding reported decisions involving environmental, natural resources, or energy law and policy turned on constitutional issues—including most often standing, sovereign immunity, takings, due process, and, with increasing frequency, political question, preemption, and federalism.

Most issues surrounding the extent to which Congress and the states can protect the environment arise in the crucible of federalism under our republican system that "split the atom of sovereignty." Accordingly, the subject of whether environmental protection is better served by federal or state authorities has been much debated. Suffice it to say that the Tenth Amendment provides states with wide latitude to regulate in spheres not withheld or retained. Yet there are substantial constitutional restraints on state authority, including the dormant Commerce Clause and the Supremacy and Takings Clauses.

This part provides a bird's-eye view of the constitutional features of environmental law. The first section examines the various constitutional law developments affecting the scope of Congress's power to regulate the environment. It focuses on the Commerce Clause and the concomitant extrinsic limits on such authority, including principles of federalism and the Tenth Amendment, as well as the diminished nondelegation doctrine. The second section does the same for state authority and the dormant Commerce Clause doctrine and the Supremacy Clause. The third section then examines two dynamic constitutional doctrines that tend to thwart the implementation of environmental laws—standing and political question, and interpretations of the Takings Clause and the Eleventh Amendment. The fourth section canvasses a variety of underutilized constitutional provisions and doctrines influencing the past and future development of natural resource policy, including the Treaty, Compact, General Welfare, Due Process, and Property Clauses; the First Amendment; and even less controversial provisions such as the Enclave Clause.

At bottom are questions of who decides who can do what, when, and where under the U.S. Constitution, that began soon after our nation's birth.

Most of these questions elude easy answers. After all, as Chief Justice John Marshall observed nearly two hundred years ago, "we must never forget that it is *a constitution* we are expounding." The legacy of jurisprudence from the Rehnquist Court and indications from the Roberts Court suggest that constitutional law will continue to exert a large amount of force on how environmental laws develop, suggesting a shade against environmental protection that is likely vestigial to the limited government, property rights, and federalism hues that imbue our founding document.

I.   Sources of and Limits to Federal Environmental Law

Most congressional authority to regulate natural resources, especially resources not found on federal lands, stems from the Commerce Clause, with some contributions from the Treaty, Spending, General Welfare, and Property Clauses. The Tenth Amendment and, to a lesser extent, the nondelegation doctrine have the potential to cabin the exercise of congressional authority over natural resources.

A. Congressional Authority

1. Commerce Clause

A majority of the nation's core environmental laws are founded on Congress's authority under the Commerce Clause. The Commerce Clause provides that "Congress shall have the power . . . [t]o regulate Commerce . . . among the several states." These laws include the National Environmental Policy Act (NEPA), the Clean Air Act (CAA), the Clean Water Act (CWA), the Endangered Species Act (ESA), the Resource Conservation and Recovery Act (RCRA), the Safe Drinking Water Act (SDWA), and the Comprehensive Environmental Response, Compensation, and Liability Act (CERCLA), to name but a few.

Commerce Clause jurisprudence has a long lineage. In 1824, the Supreme Court upheld Congress's broad Commerce Clause authority to regulate competing use of navigable waterways notwithstanding countervailing state laws. The Court found that Congress may regulate "those internal concerns which affect the States generally; but not to those which are completely within a particular State, which do not affect other States." Writing for the Court, Chief Justice Marshall maintained that in a representative democracy it is the voting public's job, and not the Court's, to curtail or redirect congressional action.

For about the next century, the Court rarely concluded that Congress exceeded its authority under the Commerce Clause, and when it did so, the cases did not involve the use and disposition of natural resources. But this changed during the throes of the industrial revolution, when the Court invalidated numerous congressional efforts to regulate natural resources under the Commerce Clause. The invalidated congressional acts attempted to control the use of natural resources at the point of manufacturing or production within a state. Examples include federal laws restricting monopolies in the sugar industry, limiting the extent to which children and sometimes women could work the fields and factories to convert natural resources into commercial products, setting prices in the coal and oil industries, or empowering coal and oil workers to engage in collective bargaining regarding maximum hours, minimum wages, pensions, and health care.

This trend reversed in 1937 when the Court, by a bare majority, upheld congressional authority under the Commerce Clause to regulate unfair labor practices in manufacturing and production in the steel industry, because it has a "close and substantial relation to interstate commerce." Four years later, the Court held that Congress's Commerce Clause authority extends to intrastate activities that have a "substantial effect" on interstate commerce. And the next year, the Court allowed Congress to regulate noncommercial use of natural resources, such as wheat grown for home consumption, if such individual activities could in the aggregate affect interstate commerce.

Given this expansive backdrop, for the next four decades natural resource laws were seldom subject to Commerce Clause challenges. When they were, the Court found Congress to have acted within its authority. For instance, in *Hodel v. Virginia Surface Mining & Reclamation Ass'n*, the Court held that the Commerce Clause provided Congress with authority under the Surface Mining Control and Reclamation Act (SMCRA) to require private mining companies to restore private lands located entirely within a state. The Court determined that the appropriate inquiry is whether Congress has a "rational basis" to find that a state activity substantially affects interstate commerce, not whether it actually does. Concurring, Justice Rehnquist ominously noted that Congress cannot regulate commerce "to the nth degree."

Recent Commerce Clause jurisprudence supports Rehnquist's limiting view of Congress's Commerce Clause authority. In *United States v. Lopez*, the Supreme Court held that the Commerce Clause permits Congress to regulate in three areas: channels of interstate commerce (such as navigable waters), instrumentalities of interstate commerce, and activities that "substantially affect" interstate commerce. Following *Lopez*, in *Morrison v. United States*, the Court described the substantially affects test as a function of whether (1) the underlying activity is "inherently economic," (2) Congress has made specific findings as to effect, (3) the law contains a jurisdictional element, and (4) the overall effects of the activity are actually substantial.

Lopez and *Morrison* have the potential to profoundly limit federal control over the environment, particularly such programs as the Endangered Species Act (ESA)—both because the survival of endangered species is often not inherently economic and because, even in the aggregate, endangered species do not necessarily have a substantial effect on interstate commerce. The lower courts, however, have so far not limited federal power in this way. For example, on the heels of *Lopez*, the D.C. Circuit decided that Congress has Commerce Clause authority under the ESA to protect an endangered fly that exists predominantly within a single state. Following *Morrison*, the Fourth Circuit held in *Gibbs v. Babbitt* that the ESA's prohibition on the "taking" of an individual endangered red wolf in North Carolina is within Congress's authority under the Commerce Clause. Over a stinging dissent, a majority of the court found that protecting endangered red wolves satisfies *Morrison* because tourism and the potential of a pelt market make regulation inherently economic in nature.

Likewise, the Fifth Circuit upheld Congress's Commerce Clause authority to apply the ESA to land development that would harm federally protected spiders and insects that neither inhabit nor cross state borders. In addition, the D.C. Circuit upheld Congress's authority to provide ESA protection to intrastate toads that do not facilitate economic opportunities like tourism. The Supreme Court denied petitions for certiorari each time they were sought in these cases, which might suggest the Court is not yet inclined to extend *Lopez* and *Morrison* to regulation of the environment.

A broader reading of the Commerce Clause was also suggested in *Gonzales v. Raich*. There, the Court upheld an aspect of the federal Controlled Substances Act, which prohibits in-state sale and distribution of marijuana notwithstanding state laws that permit in-state sale for medical purposes if prescribed by a physician. In a decision by Justice Stevens, the Court held that it was not necessary to decide "whether respondents' activities, taken in the aggregate, substantially affect interstate commerce in fact, but only whether a rational basis exists for so concluding."

Whether courts adopt the *Raich* or the *Lopez/Morrison* standard of review could profoundly impact environmental law. It is easier to show that Congress has Commerce Clause authority to protect species, habitat, and water quality under *Raich* than it is under *Lopez* and *Morrison*. For example, in *Alabama–Tombigbee Rivers Coalition v. Kempthorne*, the Eleventh Circuit upheld Congress's authority under the Commerce Clause to allow federal wildlife agencies to list as a protected species the last remaining population of the Alabama sturgeon, a noncommercial species that exists only within the state of Alabama. Applying *Raich*, the court maintained that "when a general regulatory statute bears a substantial relation to commerce, the *de minimis* character of individual instances arising under that statute is of no consequence." Notwithstanding the lack of an inherently economic activity and congressional findings of impact, the court easily held that Congress *could* have had a rational basis for concluding that protecting endangered species, in the aggregate, substantially affects interstate commerce. That the ESA bears a substantial relation to commerce, the court found, is reflected in the $5 to $6 billion spent annually on illegal trade in rare plants and animals; the "incalculable" value of genetic heritage; the unknown value of safeguarding species and genetic diversity for medical, agricultural, and aquacultural purposes; and the tens of billions of dollars in annual expenditures associated with hunting, fishing, birding, tourism, and other economic activities. Thus, the court concluded, "Congress was not constitutionally obligated to carve out an exception" for intrastate species or noncommercial species from the ESA's "comprehensive statutory scheme."

Some have also argued, based on *Lopez* and *Morrison*, that Congress lacks the authority to regulate waters that are not historically navigable-in-fact. But applying *Raich*, the Tenth Circuit found otherwise in *United States v. Hubenka*. There, the court held that the Commerce Clause authorizes the U.S. Army Corps of Engineers to regulate the dredging and filling of nonnavigable tributaries that flow downstream into navigable waters.

The record thus shows broad support among the federal appellate courts for congressional authority to regulate intrastate activities under the Commerce Clause. Nevertheless, the validity of congressional authority under the ESA and other federal natural resource acts is hardly secure. The composition of the Supreme Court has changed significantly since *Raich*. Justice O'Connor cast the deciding vote in *Raich*, but her successor, Justice Alito, seems inclined to view federal authority more narrowly. Moreover, Chief Justice Roberts, who was not involved in *Raich*, rather famously remarked in a circuit court dissent that the Commerce Clause does not provide Congress with authority to protect a "hapless toad that, for reasons of its own, lives its entire life in California."

In addition, context matters. The majority Justice Stevens mustered in *Raich*, involving controlled substances like marijuana, may not hold when the subject of regulation is a noncommercial, intrastate species with no inherent economic value, particularly when Congress has not made specific findings that loss of individual species has a "substantial effect" on interstate commerce. Finally, the Court has used *Lopez* and *Morrison*'s constrained view of Commerce Clause authority as a tool of statutory construction to limit the jurisdictional reach of other natural resources and environmental laws. For example, in *Solid Waste Agency of Northern Cook County (SWANCC) v. U.S. Army Corps of Engineers*, the Court passed on an opportunity to decide whether the Corps' and EPA's interpretation of the CWA as requiring a permit for discharge into an isolated, intrastate water not adjacent to a navigable waterway exceeds Congress's authority under the Commerce Clause. Instead, the Court invalidated the government's action as a matter of statutory interpretation, finding that the Corps' and EPA's use of the so-called migratory bird rule to establish jurisdiction exceeded the reach of the act's definition of "navigable waters." But the Court noted that a contrary interpretation would raise "significant constitutional questions" under the Commerce Clause.

The tenuous grip *Raich* has on Commerce Clause jurisprudence was on display again in *Rapanos v. United States*. Like *SWANCC*, *Rapanos* raised a question about the scope of the Corps' authority to regulate dredge and fill discharges. In *Rapanos*, the key discharges were on wetlands that were adjacent to nonnavigable tributaries of "navigable waters." Notably in *Rapanos*, Justice Kennedy's concurrence, which provided the key vote for remanding the case, relied on *Raich* for the proposition that "when a general regulatory statute bears a substantial relation to commerce, the de minimis character of individual instances arising under that statute is of no consequence." That is, in Justice Kennedy's view, Congress's Commerce Power extends to a class of activities that substantially affect interstate commerce, even when the individual activity being regulated itself has only a de minimis relationship to interstate commerce.

As recent cases under the Commerce Clause cast doubt about Congress's ability to protect the environment—particularly rare plants and animals, habitat, and water—the constitutionality of natural resource laws may hinge more frequently on other less prominent sources of congressional authority, like the Treaty, Spending, General Welfare, and Property Clauses, discussed below.

1.   Treaty Clause

The Treaty Clause is an underutilized source of congressional authority to enact environmental laws. It provides that the executive branch "shall have power, by and with the advice and consent of the Senate, to make Treaties, provided two thirds of the Senators present concur." After a treaty is approved, Congress has the power under the Necessary and Proper Clause "to make all laws which shall be necessary and proper for carrying into execution . . . all . . . powers vested by this Constitution in the Government of the United States." Because of the Supremacy Clause, these laws effectively preempt any conflicting laws enacted by states, although states are inclined to argue that the Tenth Amendment's reservation of power "to the states . . . or to the people" limits the federal reach of statutes on matters traditionally left to the states. Some jurisprudence suggests that the Treaty Clause invests Congress with the authority to force state adherence to federal natural resource laws enacted pursuant to validly ratified treaties, irrespective of the limitations otherwise imposed by the Tenth Amendment. The leading case involves the Migratory Bird Treaty Act (MBTA). Congress enacted the MBTA to facilitate enforcement of a treaty between the United States and Great Britain to protect a number of migratory birds in the United States and Canada. Missouri claimed the treaty infringed on rights reserved by the Tenth Amendment. The Supreme Court disagreed. In *Missouri v. Holland*, Justice Holmes, writing for the Court, upheld Congress's authority to enact legislation pursuant to a treaty that governed a traditional state function like hunting. The Court found that the Treaty Clause, when coupled with the Necessary and Proper Clause, provided Congress with authority to infringe on state sovereignty in ways it could not under the Commerce Clause alone. (The Tenth Amendment is discussed further below.)

The decision of *Missouri v. Holland* suggests that the Treaty and Necessary and Proper Clauses may offer better sources of constitutional authority for environmental laws enacted pursuant to an underlying treaty. The ESA, for example, which is subject to persistent Commerce Clause challenges, may be more constitutionally secure as an incident of Congress's Treaty Power, as it was enacted in part to implement aspects of the Convention on the International Trade in Endangered Species of Wild Fauna and Flora, and the Western Convention on Nature Protection and Wildlife Preservation. This also suggests a possible advantage for Senate ratification and congressional implementation of other treaties designed to level the playing field in the use of natural resources, such as the United Nations Convention on the Law of the Seas.

Bilateral treaties may also play a more substantial role in the future of water use and natural resources protection. In 1909, the United States and Canada entered into the International Boundary Waters Treaty, which established the International Joint Commission to help resolve disputes regarding waters shared by the two countries, including the Great Lakes. Disputes between the countries about water use could become more significant, particularly with a warming planet and the loss of the polar ice caps. Thus far, however, federal courts in the United States have declined to entertain disputes about boundary waters, finding such matters to be constitutionally committed to foreign policy and thus not justiciable.

3.   Spending and General Welfare Clauses

The Spending and General Welfare Clauses also provide potential bases for promoting natural resource values. In tandem, they permit Congress to tax and spend so as to "provide for the common defense and General Welfare of the United States," by attaching conditions to the receipt of federal funds, provided the conditions are not coercive.

The Land and Water Conservation Fund (LWCF) is a good example of a federal spending program that benefits natural resources. Established in 1964, the LWCF has provided hundreds of millions of dollars in grants to federal, state, and local governments to acquire land, water, and related resources for recreational, wildlife, and aesthetic purposes that benefit the public.

The General Welfare Clause's imprint on natural resources can also be problematic. This is perhaps best reflected by the work of the Bureau of Reclamation, which has sponsored many large water development projects throughout the western United States under the auspices of the General Welfare Clause and the Reclamation Act of 1902. Without the bureau, much of the western United States would still be undeveloped desert. Between 1902 and 1981, the federal government invested $7.3 billion in bureau projects to construct about 350 diversion dams, more than 15,000 miles of diversion canals, and about 50 hydroelectric plants, including the Hoover Dam.

4.   The Property Clause

The Property Clause authorizes Congress to make all "needful" rules concerning federal land, which constitutes about 28 percent of the country. In 1897, the Court analogized Congress's power under the Property Clause to state police power, lest federal property be at the mercy of the states. Since then, the Court has interpreted the scope of this authority to be "virtually without limitation." With this authority, Congress has enacted numerous laws allowing for development, use, and exploitation of natural resources on federal lands.

Other provisions of the Constitution have allowed Congress to exercise relatively unquestioned authority to protect natural resources on federal enclaves under the Enclave Clause. Congress also has authority to "acquiesce" to presidential power to "reserve" natural resources on federal land.

B.   Limits on Federal Authority

Federalism and the Tenth and Eleventh Amendments present the principal constraints on Congress's authority to enact environmental laws not exclusively designed to address activities on federal lands. The Tenth Amendment potentially limits the scope of federal legislation, while the Eleventh Amendment limits the federal government's ability to enforce its laws against the states in court. The largely defunct nondelegation doctrine and the First Amendment also influence federal authority to enact and implement environmental laws.

1.   Tenth Amendment

As mentioned below and discussed further in chapter 5, the Tenth Amendment supplies potential limits on Congress's authority to enact environmental laws, particularly in traditional areas of state and local authority, such as land use or public health. It preserves the "dignity" and sovereignty of the states by providing that "the powers not delegated to the United States by the Constitution, nor prohibited by it to the States, are reserved to the States."

Thus far, Tenth Amendment jurisprudence has curtailed environmental programs that upset political accountability and diminish state dignity. In *New York v. United States*, the Supreme Court held that Congress may not "commandeer" state political or personnel resources by requiring a state to "take title" of its own low-level radioactive waste even if it fails to arrange for proper disposal under federal law. Courts have been reluctant, however, to find that Congress has commandeered state resources under other circumstances. For example, a federal court rejected a state claim that the Magnuson-Stevens Fishery Conservation and Management Act violates the Tenth Amendment by compelling participation in a regional management council that set quotas on the seasonal catch of fish. Another court rejected a state's Tenth Amendment claim that the ESA commandeers state resources by requiring the state to engage in conservation efforts. Moreover, the Supreme Court held, by a slim majority, that the EPA's rejection of a state's determination of what constitutes "best available control technology" did not unduly infringe on state prerogatives under the CAA's system of cooperative federalism.

2.   Eleventh Amendment

Under the Eleventh Amendment, "[t]he Judicial power of the United States shall not be construed to extend to any suit in law or equity, commenced or prosecuted against one of the United States by Citizens of another State." Absent express consent, states are virtually immune from legal action in federal court, including lawsuits to force compliance with federal natural resource programs. The Eleventh Amendment clearly limits federal jurisdiction in actions based on diversity. A century ago, the Court extended this prohibition to federal court actions based on federal question jurisdiction. The Court has made clear that Congress may not subject states to federal question lawsuits without state consent, in federal court, in state court, or before federal agencies. In 1986, the Court upheld the constitutionality of the CERCLA insofar as it permits suits against the states for monetary damages in federal court, although the current Supreme Court majority has since become less tolerant even of lawsuits for money damages that would run against state treasuries.

This creates a potential obstacle to federal citizen suits seeking to redress violations of federal environmental laws by state agencies. For example, SMCRA allows citizens to sue state and federal mining agencies to enforce its provisions, including bonding provisions and requirements to protect water quality. Thus, in *Bragg v. West Virginia Coal Ass'n*, citizens brought an action to forestall the practice of filling valleys with excess spoil or waste rock from mountaintop mining. The citizens sued state and federal officials to enjoin them from issuing permits in the absence of the sufficient financial assurances SMCRA requires, including funding to protect affected streams. The Fourth Circuit dismissed the action. It held that SMCRA's "exclusive" delegation of permitting to a state transforms SMCRA requirements into state standards, which cannot be enforced in federal court. Notwithstanding the decision in this and subsequent cases, an argument remains that states waive their claim to immunity when they voluntarily seek approval to operate a program pursuant to a federal law like SMCRA.

The Court's Eleventh Amendment jurisprudence has also hampered implementation of federal whistleblower protection laws, designed to protect state employees who report a state agency's transgressions from federal environmental laws, including appropriations to states to administer federal natural resource programs. For example, in Rhode Island Department of Environmental Management v. United States, the First Circuit held that a state whistleblower could not bring an action against the state of Rhode Island before a federal administrative agency, alleging that he had been fired for reporting misappropriation of federal funds that were supposed to be used implement the Solid Waste Disposal Act.

State officials are still subject to federal causes of action for prospective injunctive relief, a tack left available under *Ex parte Young*. Thus, the Eleventh Amendment does not prevent a court from requiring a state official to comply with federal natural resource laws. Eleventh Amendment jurisprudence will likely continue to hamper efforts to enforce environmental laws against states. This is especially true insofar as it does not seem as though any of the newer members of the Court—Chief Justice Roberts and Associate Justices Alito, Kagan, and Sotomayor—share or emphasize Justice Rehnquist's solicitude for states' rights in this regard.

3. Nondelegation Doctrine

The nondelegation doctrine is rarely used, but it remains available as a limit on Congress's authority to vest administrative agencies with wide authority to implement environmental laws. The doctrine, described in greater detail in chapter 3, stems from Article I of the Constitution, which vests "all legislative" authority in Congress, and presumably not in agencies charged with implementing national policies. Nonetheless, while Congress may not "delegate" legislative authority to agencies that administer federal law, legislation that provides an "intelligible principle" to guide the exercise of agency discretion will be upheld. The relevance to environmental law is acute, as most federal pollution control laws contemplate agency implementation, and many federal programs governing the administration of public lands provide agencies with considerable discretion in managing those lands for the public interest or to achieve multiple, but possibly inconsistent, uses.

Other than in the midst of the New Deal in the 1930s, the Court has seldom found that Congress has failed to provide an "intelligible principle." Most recently, in 2001, the Court declined an opportunity to use the doctrine to strike a provision of the CAA that charges the EPA with the duty to set national ambient air quality standards as "requisite" to protect public health and welfare. In *Whitman v. American Trucking Ass'n*, the Court unanimously rejected the nondelegation challenge, holding that "requisite" falls "comfortably within" the Court's nondelegation jurisprudence.

It is risky, however, to think that the nondelegation doctrine—while in desuetude—is bereft of meaning. For example, Justice Thomas's concurrence in *American Trucking* all but invited a test case challenging other statutory provisions granting general authority to federal natural resource and environmental agencies. In addition, *American Trucking* reversed a contrary opinion from the D.C. Circuit Court of Appeals, usually the second most influential court in cases involving agency action and natural resources and environmental law. Moreover, the Court's newest appointees, Chief Justice Roberts and Associate Justices Alito, Sotomayor, and Kagan, have yet to weigh in on the nondelegation issue.

4. The First Amendment

The First Amendment protects "freedom of speech" and prohibits Congress from passing laws "respecting an establishment of religion, or prohibiting the free exercise thereof." In the environmental law context, First Amendment claims can arise in the context of public land management. In a leading case on the Free Exercise Clause, *Lyng v. Northwest Indian Cemetery Protective Ass'n*, various parties contested the U.S. Forest Service's plans to permit timber harvesting and road construction in an area of national forest that was traditionally used for religious purposes by members of three Native American tribes in northwestern California. The Court held that the Free Exercise Clause protects an individual from certain forms of governmental compulsion, but it does not give an individual a right to dictate government conduct, even if that conduct might significantly interfere with one's religious practices. Thus, the timber harvesting and road construction were allowed to go forward.

Unlike free exercise cases, Establishment Clause cases typically arise when the government seeks to protect resources of religious significance and someone objects to that protection on the ground that the government is promoting religion. For example, in *Mount Royal Joint Venture v. Kempthorne*, the Department of the Interior withdrew about 20,000 acres of public mineral estate from mineral location and entry, in part to protect areas of traditional spiritual importance to Native Americans. The court found that the secretary had also articulated secular purposes for the withdrawal, including the protection of aquifers and the environment. Consequently, the court concluded that the withdrawal did not primarily affect religious interests and thus did not foster excessive government entanglement with religion in a manner that would violate the Establishment Clause.

Recent limits on free speech rights of public employees may also have significant effects on putative whistleblowers. Under *Garcetti v. Ceballos*, government employees lose their First Amendment rights to speak out against government wrongdoing if they do so in the course of their employment. So, for instance, a government employee may be disciplined for speaking to a supervisor or writing an internal memo about an agency's wrongdoing. *Garcetti*, then, deters whistleblowing, even when the agency is violating environmental rules.

II.   Sources of and Limits to State Environmental Law

The Tenth Amendment generally provides the justification for state police power authority to regulate the use and disposition of natural resources on state or private land. The dormant Commerce Clause doctrine and the doctrine of federal preemption generally constrain such authority.

A.   Sources of State Authority
1. Tenth Amendment

As the Tenth Amendment "reserves" state authority in areas neither reserved for Congress nor withheld from the states, many states have adopted extensive laws governing the environment, especially when federal regulation has left gaps. Indeed, as chapter 5 explains, much environmental regulation is the product of federal-state cooperation, which is valid unless the federal government seems to be commandeering the states—that is, leaving them without a choice as to whether to comply—which, as discussed above, violates the Tenth Amendment.

2.   The Compact Clause

The Compact Clause of the U.S. Constitution provides that "no state shall, without the consent of Congress . . . enter into any agreement or compact with another state." States have entered into more than two hundred compacts, twenty-six of which involve allocating interstate waters.

Historically, water resource allocation has been the area where regional issues warranted an appreciation of the Compact Clause. For example, the Colorado River Compact of 1922—the first interstate water compact—includes seven states and has had a substantial influence on water resources allocation among those states. As our climate changes and demands for fresh water resources grow, disputes among states sharing waters are expected to increase dramatically. This is true even in areas that historically have had ample water supplies, such as the southeastern United States. Georgia, Florida, and Alabama, for example, have waged a pitched and unresolved battle over water rights to the Apalachicola-Chattahoochee-Flint River system for two decades.

The Supreme Court is generally loath to reach the merits of state disputes about water, pushing instead for interstate compacts. To aid in this effort, the Utton Transboundary Resources Center began work in 2004 to develop a Model Interstate Water Compact. Moreover, Tenth Amendment limitations apply to interstate compacts as well. As *New York v. United States* demonstrates, states cannot agree by interstate compact to allow Congress to commandeer their state environmental programs.

B.   Limits to State Authority

The dormant (or "negative") doctrine of the Commerce Clause and the Supremacy Clause most commonly limit state environmental laws.

1.   Dormant Commerce Clause

In the absence of federal laws, many states, counties, and municipalities have enacted legislation either to protect the environment from toxic wastes or to conserve resources for state purposes. Yet, the Supreme Court has invalidated many such efforts under a principle called the dormant or negative Commerce Clause. The idea that the Commerce Clause contains a dormant or negative aspect arguably originated in a natural resources case. Chief Justice John Marshall coined the phrase "dormant Commerce Clause" in *Willson v. Black-Bird Creek Marsh Co.*, a case that allowed Delaware to issue a license to block navigation of the Black-Bird Creek, absent a countervailing federal law.

Today, the phrase "dormant Commerce Clause" is most often used to describe limits on a state's authority to adopt laws or policies that discriminate against interstate commerce because they favor one state or impose an excessive burden on outsiders. The idea is that the United States constitutes a single economic market, and state laws regulating commerce cannot disadvantage economic activity from other states, just as interstate tariffs used to do. For example, the Court has struck down a ban on the importation of dangerous out-of-state waste, higher tipping fees or surcharges for wastes generated out of state, and waste flow control ordinances prohibiting landfill operators from accepting out-of-state waste or requiring all county waste be processed at the county's facility.

State efforts to sequester natural resources for the benefit of in-state residents are also vulnerable to dormant Commerce Clause objections. While several early cases upheld such state laws, the modern view is illustrated by such cases as *Hughes v. Oklahoma*, which overturned an Oklahoma law prohibiting the transport of minnows caught in the state for sale outside the state, and *Sporhase v. Nebraska*, which struck down a Nebraska statute that restricted withdrawal of groundwater from any well in the state for use in an adjoining state.

In similar fashion, the Court has also rejected state efforts to control commerce in energy and fuels. In 1982, for example, the Court struck down a state law that prohibited the export of energy generated within the state. It has also invalidated other state initiatives awarding tax credits for in-state ethanol production and requiring that in-state power plants burn in-state-mined coal.

Hughes establishes the general test for dormant Commerce Clause cases involving state regulation of the environment. First, the court asks "whether the challenged statute regulates evenhandedly with only 'incidental' effects on interstate commerce, or discriminates against interstate commerce. . . ." If the statute regulates evenhandedly, it is generally upheld unless the burden on commerce is excessive.

But when a statute discriminates, it is usually struck down unless the state can show that it is seeking to accomplish a legitimate local purpose that cannot be accomplished by less discriminatory means. For example, the Court upheld Maine's restrictions on the importation of bait fish when the state demonstrated that such fish might carry undetectable diseases that could adversely affect native fish species. By contrast, the Court struck down an additional fee that Alabama imposed for the disposal of hazardous waste generated outside the state on the ground that the fee discriminated against interstate commerce. The Court found that although the state may have had legitimate concerns about the amount of waste disposal in Alabama, less discriminatory means were available to address those concerns.

The Court has also recognized that when a state acts as a market participant rather than as a market regulator, the dormant Commerce Clause places no limits on state activities. But this exception does not allow the state to apply burdens on commerce beyond the market in which it participates. For example, Alaska was not allowed to claim the market participant exception for the sale of state timber that was subject to the requirement that the buyer partially process the timber prior to shipping it out of state.

Public facilities that regulate the environment for public benefit may enjoy wider latitude under the dormant Commerce Clause. In *United Haulers Ass'n v. Oneida-Herkimer Solid Waste Management Authority*, a plurality of the Court decided that a county's flow control ordinance that required that all solid waste generated within the county be delivered to the county's publicly owned solid waste processing facility does not violate the dormant Commerce Clause. Relying on *Pike v. Bruce Church, Inc.*, the plurality concluded that facilities operated by public hands for "public good" directed at goals other than mere protectionism have greater leeway to control the flow of wastes. Cases applying *United Haulers* thus far suggest that the constitutional prospects of local flow control regimes involving publicly owned facilities have been enhanced. *United Haulers* may also signal judicial receptivity to local flow control ordinances not involving "clearly public facilities." For example, relying on *United Haulers'* focus on safety, a federal district court in Georgia recognized broad state discretion to identify legitimate state ends respecting waste disposal.

The Supreme Court's skepticism toward state regulation of the flow of natural resources and energy is unlikely to change anytime soon and may become an even more problematic issue as states address climate change and the development of renewable energy sources. Only the late Chief Justice Rehnquist regularly dissented from the string of cases applying the dormant Commerce Clause to strike down state natural resource laws. He chided his colleagues for failing to "acknowledge that a safe and attractive environment is the commodity really at issue," reasoning that "[s]tates may take actions legitimately directed at the preservation of the State's natural resources, even if those actions incidentally work to disadvantage some out-of-state waste generators." Rehnquist also argued that federal courts should presume—as with quarantine laws—that state conservation laws are a rational means to achieve legitimate state ends that have but incidental effects on interstate commerce. Moreover, Rehnquist believed that federal courts should defer both to state legislative and judicial findings supportive of a nonprotectionist impetus behind state waste control laws. No current member of the Court seems to embrace Rehnquist's view of upholding state environmental laws in the face of challenges under the dormant Commerce Clause.

2.   Preemption

The Constitution's Supremacy Clause, provides that "[t]he Constitution and the Laws of the United States which shall be made in Pursuance thereof . . . shall be the Supreme Law of the Land." Thus, the Constitution authorizes federal environmental laws to displace inconsistent state laws. In 1819, in a case involving use of navigable waterways, the Court made its earliest pronouncement on the subject and held that federal law usurps inconsistent state laws that may "retard, impede, or burden" federal operations. Absent specific intent to preempt, the modern Court has held that Congress may preempt state law implicitly by "field" preemption, when Congress occupies a field of interest so pervasively that preemption is assumed, or when state law "conflicts" with federal law. Although the Court has held that a comprehensive regulatory scheme involving environmental protection may occupy the field and thus implicitly preempt federal common law, it has generally been receptive to state efforts to supply common law causes of action involving the use or protection of the environment.

Courts have been especially skeptical of claims that a federal law implicitly preempts state environmental laws. In *Exxon Shipping Co. v. Baker*, the Supreme Court held that the federal CWA does not preempt punitive damages under maritime law. Other courts have concluded that federal law does not expressly or impliedly preempt state-imposed fleet fuel efficiency requirements or tailpipe restrictions on greenhouse gas (GHG) emissions.

Moreover, the Court often tends to find that state actions concerning energy production, water allocation, and disposition of natural resources are not preempted absent an express preemption provision, a clear indication of a pervasive federal regime, or some actual federal-state conflict. In 1983, for example, the Court held that congressional regulation of the field of nuclear safety did not preempt California's moratorium on new nuclear power plants absent safe and reliable methods for disposal of high-level radioactive waste. And in 1978, the Court held that Congress did not intend to displace the application of state water law to the distribution of water behind a federally constructed dam.

On the other hand, state activities that impinge on federally occupied spheres of activity may be implicitly preempted. For example, the Court has held that federal legislation governing the issuance of fishing licenses preempts a state's effort to limit the ability of outsiders to fish in the state's territorial waters. And although the Court held that the Federal Power Act comprehensively regulates hydroelectric power and preempts a state's ability to set minimum stream flow requirements and protect fish populations, it nevertheless refused to cabin a state's effort to regulate hydroelectric development and protection of the environment when acting under the CWA.

The prospect of preemption continues, given the wide swath cut by federal environmental laws. Numerous state laws fill in both the wide and the interstitial fissures left by federal environmental law. Most states have myriad environmental laws that apply to activities that adversely affect ecosystems or diminish property values. Also, most states have comprehensive statutory programs that regulate water, air, and soil pollution; restrict the use of state natural resources such as wildlife, minerals, and forests; and use common or codified laws, such as nuisance, trespass, and negligence, to provide remedies for those harmed by excess pollution or imprudent land use resulting in injury to persons or property. Further, many local governments have laws governing the use of natural resources. Therefore, preemption issues will continue to influence the development of environmental laws at the state level.

2.   Displacement of Federal Common Law

The "displacement doctrine," is grounded in separation of powers. It stands for the proposition that federal law enacted by Congress or implemented by the Executive can displace the role that federal courts have to hear federal common law causes of action. In *American Electric Power Co. v. Connecticut* ("*AEP*"), the Court held that the discretionary authority that the Clean Air Act provides to EPA to regulate greenhouse gases under *Massachusetts v. EPA*, coupled with the corresponding regulatory actions EPA has taken since 2009, displaces the federal common law for public nuisance actions concerning climate change.

Writing for an 8-0 majority of the Court (Justice Sotomayor, recused), Justice Ginsburg was unwilling to vest federal judges with the task of performing what it viewed to be primarily regulatory roles subject to democratic processes:

> The judgments the plaintiffs would commit to federal judges, in suits that could be filed in any federal district, cannot be reconciled with the decisionmaking scheme Congress enacted. The Second Circuit erred, we hold, in ruling that federal judges may set limits on greenhouse gas emissions in face of a law empowering EPA to set the same limits, subject to judicial review only to ensure against action "arbitrary, capricious, . . . or otherwise not in accordance with law.

Thus, the Court concluded that "[a]ny such claim would be displaced by the federal legislation authorizing EPA to regulate carbon-dioxide emissions."

The Court's ruling in *Massachusetts* that the CAA provides EPA with discretionary authority to regulate greenhouse gases as "air pollutants" loomed large: "We hold that the Clean Air Act and the EPA actions it authorizes displace any federal common law right to seek abatement of carbon-dioxide emissions from fossil-fuel fired power plants. *Massachusetts* made plain that emissions of carbon dioxide qualify as air pollution subject to regulation under the Act. And we think it equally plain that the Act "speaks directly" to emissions of carbon dioxide from the defendants' plants."

The Court was unconvinced that federal courts should play a role in competing with EPA's regulatory authority: "It is altogether fitting that Congress designated an expert agency, here, EPA, as best suited to serve as primary regulator of greenhouse gas emissions. The expert agency is surely better equipped to do the job than individual district judges issuing ad hoc, case-by-case injunctions. Federal judges lack the scientific, economic, and technological resources an agency can utilize in coping with issues of this order."

The Court explained that its ruling does not affect *state* common law causes of action, which would be subject to a more exacting demonstration of congressional intent: "In light of our holding that the Clean Air Act displaces federal common law, the availability *vel non* of a state lawsuit depends, *inter alia*, on the preemptive effect of the federal Act." It noted that "[n]one of the parties have briefed preemption or otherwise addressed the availability of a claim under state nuisance law. We therefore leave the matter open for consideration on remand."

Four Justices – including Justice Kennedy – accepted that the states possess constitutional standing under *Massachusetts v. EPA*, suggesting that five members of the Court (including Justice Sotomayor) accept that position. No justice engaged either the political question or prudential standing arguments. Justices Alito (joined by Justice Thomas) issued a brief concurrence, it appears for no other reason than to question the outcome in *Massachusetts v. EPA* ("I agree with the Court's displacement analysis on the assumption (which I make for the sake of argument because no party contends otherwise) that the interpretation of the Clean Air Act, adopted by the majority in *Massachusetts* v. *EPA*, is correct.")

III.   Judicial Review

The two constitutional doctrines that most dramatically influence the prospects for judicial review are standing and political question.

A.   Standing

The doctrine of standing has had a pervasive and deeply imbedded influence on environmental law. The standing doctrine constrains the extent to which litigants can enforce federal environmental laws. Article III extends "judicial authority" to "Cases . . . and Controversies." In general, the Supreme Court has construed this provision to require that a plaintiff show a personal injury that can be traced to the defendant's conduct and redressed by a judicial remedy. In 1972, the Court recognized noneconomic, aesthetic, and environmental interests as legally cognizable "injuries" that can serve as a sufficient basis for constitutional standing under Article III. More recently, in *Friends of the Earth v. Laidlaw Environmental Services,* the Court made clear that it is injury to a person, and not the environment, that matters, thus obviating any need to show environmental degradation to support constitutional injury. An association has standing when (1) its members would otherwise have standing to sue in their own right, (2) the interests it seeks to protect are germane to the organization's purpose, and (3) neither the claim asserted nor the relief requested requires the participation of individual members in the lawsuit.

Despite these limits, standing doctrine should not prove an insurmountable bar to plaintiffs in environmental cases. For example, a federal appeals court found that a citizen group whose members regularly use Yellowstone National Park has constitutional standing to challenge construction of a coal-fired electric plant whose emissions reduce visibility. Others have found that plaintiffs concerned about the effects of climate change have standing to enforce compliance with the NEPA. And still others have shown receptivity to standing based on governmental failure to abide by statutorily required procedures in environmental laws.

However, a recent ruling from the Supreme Court suggests standing is still a real obstacle. In *Summers v. Earth Island Institute*, the plaintiffs contended that certain regulations established by the U.S. Forest Service are invalid because they were not preceded by advance notice and an opportunity for comment and administrative appeals as mandated by the Forest Service Decision Making and Appeals Reform Act. The Court held that Earth Island lacked standing to challenge the application of these regulations nationwide because it had voluntarily settled the portion of the lawsuit pertaining to its only member who suffered an actual injury-in-fact that was "concrete and particularized."

Regardless of how standing doctrine applies to organizations and individuals, states appear to enjoy wider latitude to demonstrate constitutional standing in cases involving environmental law. In *Massachusetts v. EPA*, the Court held that states are entitled to "special solicitude" in standing analysis in cases involving state efforts to protect natural resources. There, the Court recognized Massachusetts's potential shoreline loss as a legally cognizable injury in allowing it to challenge the EPA's failure to regulate GHG emissions. Individuals, on the other hand, must still show a tight "geographic nexus" between the claimed injury and the federal action. While standing jurisprudence can be both uncertain and fact-intensive, one sure bet is that it will continue to be a significant issue in the enforcement of environmental law.

B.   Political Question Doctrine

Although the political question doctrine has not traditionally impeded implementation of natural resource laws, recent decisions suggest it deserves to be watched closely in the future, at least concerning climate change. In *Marbury v. Madison*, Chief Justice Marshall lamented the "irksome" and "delicate" questions that are inherently political and out of reach to the judiciary. And in 1962, the Court held that matters demonstrably committed to a coordinate branch of government, or that lack ascertainable standards, or that could otherwise result in judicial embarrassment are nonjusticiable "political questions." For example, the Court has recognized that executive powers over foreign affairs, impeachment, and treaty abrogation are political questions into which courts "ought not . . . enter [the] political thicket."

The Court has declined to engage arguments inviting analysis under the political question doctrine in holding that the federal CAA provides the EPA with authority to regulate emissions of GHGs from new motor vehicles. Nonetheless, several federal courts have turned recently to the political question doctrine in deciding that cases involving climate change are nonjusticiable. For example, federal district courts in California, Louisiana, and New York have dismissed state public nuisance actions brought to address the effects of climate change against U.S. auto manufacturers, coal burning power plants, *and the oil and gas industry,* electing not to "enter the global warming thicket." Both cases reversed by federal courts are pending review before the U.S. Supreme Court.

IV. Individual Rights

Individual rights to private property, due process, and, to a lesser extent, a quality environment have profound impacts on environmental law.

A. Takings

The Fifth Amendment, which the Fourteenth Amendment incorporates to the states, forbids the government from "taking private property for public use without just compensation." The concept of "regulatory" takings first arose in *Pennsylvania Coal Co. v. Mahon*, which prohibited coal mining that might cause surface subsidence. Justice Holmes, writing for the Court, held that a state's regulation that goes "too far" could amount to a taking.

Determining whether a law constitutes a regulatory taking involves a balancing approach that turns on how closely the impact of the challenged regulation resembles a physical occupation of the regulated property. In *Penn Central Transportation Co. v. New York City*, the company argued that the New York City Landmarks Preservation Law of 1965 constituted a regulatory taking. The law allowed the city to designate structures and neighborhoods as "landmarks" or "landmark sites," thus preventing Penn Central from building a multistory office building atop Grand Central Terminal. The Court disagreed, finding that the city's restriction was substantially related to the general welfare of the city. In *Penn Central*, the Court weighed three factors to determine whether a government regulation triggers the obligation to compensate the property owners: (1) "the economic impact of the regulation on the claimant," (2) "the extent to which the regulation has interfered with distinct investment-backed expectations," and (3) the "character of the governmental action," that is, whether it amounts to a physical invasion or merely affects property interests through "some public program adjusting the benefits and burdens of economic life to promote the common good."

The Court has applied the *Penn Central* factors in a series of cases involving natural resources. A leading case is *Lucas v. South Carolina Coastal Council*. There, Lucas bought two beachfront residential lots on which he intended to build single-family homes. Shortly thereafter, the state enacted a law aimed to protect barrier islands that barred Lucas from erecting permanent residences. The Court held that depriving a landowner of all economically viable use of property goes too far and constitutes a regulatory taking per se, unless such use constitutes a nuisance under the state's traditional common law.

Even preexisting state laws can go too far and constitute a compensable taking. In *Palazzolo v. Rhode Island*, Anthony Palazzolo owned a waterfront parcel of land in Rhode Island, most of which was salt marsh subject to tidal flooding. State law enacted prior to his acquisition of the property designated state salt marshes as protected "coastal wetlands." Palazzolo claimed that the state's subsequent denial of his multiple requests to develop the property constituted a regulatory taking because it had deprived him of "all economically beneficial use" of his property. The Court upheld his claims, even though he acquired the property after the state law went into effect. Justice Kennedy, writing for the Court, held that a contrary ruling would "in effect, put an expiration date on the Takings Clause . . . [depriving] [f]uture generations [of] a right to challenge unreasonable limitations on the use and value of land."

Normal regulatory delays that temporarily deprive an owner of all economically beneficial use of property do not necessarily constitute a taking. In *Tahoe Sierra Preservation Council v. Tahoe Regional Planning Agency*, the government imposed two moratoria on development while it prepared a comprehensive land use plan. The moratoria lasted a total of about thirty-two months. The landowners claimed that during that time the moratoria constituted a deprivation of all economically viable use of land. The Court disagreed. Applying the *Penn Central* factors, it concluded that the delay did not constitute a taking, noting that a categorical rule that any temporary deprivation of all economic use constitutes a taking—no matter how brief—would impose unreasonable financial burdens due to normal, foreseeable delays in processing land use applications.

The Court has wrestled with how closely its takings jurisprudence ought to track substantive due process jurisprudence. In *Agins v. City of Tiburon*, the Court declared that government regulation of private property constitutes "a taking if it does not substantially advance legitimate state interests." This standard is analogous to the standard of review the Court uses in deciding whether a governmental law deprives one of a fundamental right to substantive due process.

After applying it for two decades, the Court subsequently abandoned the standard of review endorsed in *Agins*. In *Nollan v. California Coastal Commission*, the Court struck down a state requirement that certain beachfront property owners in California maintain along their property a public pathway that provided access to the beach. The Court held that while maintaining public access is a legitimate state interest, the means chosen did not substantially advance this end and constituted a compensable regulatory taking. Likewise, in *Dolan v. City of Tigard*, the Court rejected the City's effort to require Dolan to set aside part of her land for a greenway along a nearby creek to help alleviate surface runoff and for a pedestrian/bicycle path to relieve traffic congestion, in exchange for allowing her to expand her store and pave her parking lot. The Court held that the City had failed to show an "essential nexus" between the ends (reducing erosion and traffic) and the means chosen to achieve them.

More recently, in *Lingle v. Chevron U.S.A.*, the Court considered a takings challenge arising from a cap on the rent oil companies could charge dealers leasing company-owned service stations. Chevron and others argued the cap constituted a regulatory taking because the means chosen (limiting rent charges) did not "substantially advance" a legitimate state aim. Writing for a unanimous Court, Justice O'Connor denied the claim. In an effort to "correct course," the Court held that the "substantially advances" test announced in *Agins* is limited to substantive due process analysis and does not apply in the takings context. Instead, takings challenges should be assessed based on the severity of the burden caused by the regulation, not how well the regulation furthers governmental interests, which seems to make upholding regulation more likely.

Looking ahead, takings jurisprudence will continue to impact environmental law significantly, especially in constraining state actions. Government agencies are acutely aware of the potential to pay large compensatory awards for denying or delaying permission to develop property or for imposing conditions on property use. For example, the U.S. Court of Claims awarded $14 million to farmers who alleged that federal limits on water withdrawn from the Sacramento–San Joaquin Delta to conserve Chinook salmon and delta smelt and their habitat constituted a compensable regulatory taking. The same court, however, recently rejected a claim that prohibiting the development of jurisdictional wetlands constitutes a compensable taking of the most economically valuable use of the property.

. Many takings cases have been decided by a bare majority. Therefore, changes on the Supreme Court could substantially impact the Court's takings jurisprudence. Takings cases thus far from the Roberts Court suggest some hesitation to expand takings jurisprudence. In *John R. Sand & Gravel Co. v. United States*, the Court rejected claims that the EPA's installation and repositioning of fences around a contaminated site constituted a taking of the plaintiff's leasehold rights for its adjacent mining operation, although it did so on a technicality, finding that the claimant had failed to file the claim within the statute of limitations provided by federal law under the Tucker Act. Likewise, in *Wilkie v. Robbins*, it rejected a claim by a Wyoming ranch owner who asserted that the Bureau of Land Management's treatment of him following his refusal to grant the agency an easement across his property constituted a compensable taking. The Court found that alternate remedies were available and that it lacked standards for determining when the government's tactics "demanded too much and went too far."

B. Due Process

The Fifth Amendment, which applies to the federal government, and the Fourteenth Amendment, which applies to the states, provide that no individual "shall be deprived of . . . property without the due process of law." Due process, discussed more fully in chapter 11, generally protects only traditional property rights. Nonetheless, because environmental law frequently involves the issuance of permits and enforcement actions for violating permits or other legal requirements, due process rights abound. How much process is due varies with the scope of the right, but most federal and state agencies that regulate natural resources afford parties who are directly affected by agency decisions with procedural rights to contest those decisions. Less process is usually due when the use of natural resources poses a threat to health or safety.

In *Hodel v. Virginia Surface Mining & Reclamation Ass'n*, the Court upheld several provisions of SMCRA against procedural due process challenges. SMCRA permits the secretary of the interior to issue an order for immediate cessation of mining when he or she determines that conditions pose a serious threat to public health and safety or the environment. The Court held that this process did not violate the coal producers' procedural due process rights to an expedient hearing prior to issuance of the order.

Furthermore, failure to meet statutory requirements can extinguish a claim of deprivation of procedural due process. In *United States v. Locke*, the Court upheld the constitutionality of statutes providing for the automatic termination of vested property rights on the failure to comply with statutory conditions. The Federal Land Policy and Management Act requires mining claimants to rerecord claims every year with the Bureau of Land Management "*prior to* December 31" (emphasis added). When a mining claimant rerecorded a claim *on* December 31, the owner lost the claim that he had worked for more than twenty years. The Court held that no further process is required.

A. Rights to a Healthy Environment

The federal Constitution does not explicitly address environmental concerns. To the extent it reaches environmental issues implicitly or indirectly, it tends to hamper state efforts to operate as laboratories of innovative environmental policy or causes of action, in the ways described throughout this book. Yet the U.S. Constitution is not the sole source of constitutional influence on the practice of environmental law. State and national constitutions worldwide have been specially crafted to address local environmental concerns, be they preservation, redevelopment, sustainability, pollution abatement, climate change, energy reform, or environmental rights. These have the potential to provide additional avenues for influencing environmental law.

1. State Constitutional Law

More than one-third of U.S. states explicitly recognize environmental concerns as an overarching state policy or purport to provide a basic civil right to a quality environment. These subnational constitutional attributes have untapped potential to shape environmental law. Indeed, about twenty-one states have constitutions that address parochial environmental and natural resource issues. Some constitutions express a general policy of preserving natural areas and controlling pollution. For instance, Alabama's constitution says that it is "necessary and desirable" to conserve land for ecological value. Other state constitutions declare state authority to manage state resources. For example, Idaho's declares that "[t]he use of all waters . . . [is] subject to the regulations and control of the state in the manner prescribed by law."

Some state constitutions are directed at protecting those natural resources especially important to that particular state. California's, for example, provides a right to "reasonable" access to, and use of, the state's limited water resources. Some state constitutions expressly recognize a right to environmental quality as a basic civil right, including Hawaii, Illinois, Massachusetts, Montana, New York and Pennsylvania. Amid the myriad manifestations of constitutionally embedded environmental provisions, one commonality stands out: They are seldom subject to substantive interpretation, leaving some dormant and awaiting implementation through advocacy. This dearth in applicable jurisprudence is due to judicial concerns about recognizing and enforcing emerging constitutional features, to restraining economic development and property rights, to entering what are often political thickets, and to providing causes of action that may displace other legislative prerogatives granted to affected persons, as may be the case with state citizen suits to enforce state pollution control requirements.

1. Global Constitutional Laws

Constitutional provisions from roughly five dozen countries embed individualized rights to some form of healthy, adequate, or quality environment. Foreign domestic courts and international tribunals are enforcing constitutionally enshrined environmental rights with growing frequency, recognizing basic human rights to clean water, air, and land, and environmental opportunity. As chapter 13 describes, these provisions are inherently complex for five reasons involving form, scope, parties, remedies, and justiciability.

First, does the constitution embed an environmental right? While the constitutions of some countries do so explicitly, other provisions, such as a "right to life," have been read to confer similar rights implicitly. Second, there are issues of scope. Not only is the scope of the interest ill defined, but the very content of the right has no clear boundaries or definition. This leaves open questions, such as what is environment and what does it mean to have a "right" to a clean environment? Third, who possesses and who is obligated to respect environmental rights? Fourth, courts face significant challenges in fashioning and enforcing remedies for environmental harms. Last, particularly in constitutional democracies, under what conditions should courts enter the fray of vindicating generalized grievances of environmental harm or claims whose remedies have wide-ranging political consequences?

Domestic constitutions tend to reflect environmental principles in one of four ways: (1) as a policy directive, (2) as a procedural right or duty, (3) as an explicit substantive right, or (4) as an implicit substantive right derived from another enumerated right, such as a "right to life." Policy directives are generally not directly judicially enforceable, but they are intended to influence governmental decision making and can therefore be instrumental in providing environmental norms that guide policy makers. Environmental procedural rights normally involve requirements for environmental assessment, access to information, or rights to petition or participate. While procedural rights can be enforceable, they do not impart a substantive right to a quality environment. About 130 countries have constitutional provisions that reflect policy directives and/or procedural rights.

About [84] countries have included or added constitutional provisions that expressly recognize a substantive right to a quality environment. Two recent examples of these are Kenya, which in 2010 amended its constitution to provide that "[e]very person has the right to a clean and healthy environment," and Ecuador, which in 2007 amended its constitution to impart a basic "[r]ight to live in an environment that is healthy and ecologically balanced."

Environmental rights have been read into constitutions even when they are not explicitly mentioned or when judicial enforcement has been withheld. Courts in southern Asia, for instance, have inferred environmental rights from other constitutionally entrenched rights, most commonly a "right to life." Most notably, the highest courts in India, Pakistan, Bangladesh, and Nepal have each read a constitutional "right to life" in tandem with directive principles aimed at promoting environmental policy to embody substantive environmental rights.

Constitutional law represents the foundation on which modern environmental law is built. It provides the sources of and limits to federal and state environmental laws. Under the Commerce, Spending, General Welfare, Treaty and Property Clauses, and the Eleventh Amendment, it outlines the extent to with Congress may enact laws and agencies promulgate regulations that govern environmental protection. Under the nondelegation doctrine, and the Take Care Clause and Unitary Executive theory, it specifies the role of the President and his adjuncts to implement environmental laws. The Tenth Amendment and the dormant Commerce Clause help delineate what states can and can't do. The Due Process Clause, and the standing and political question doctrines guide courts in matters involving jurisdiction, process, and whether a case is justicable, The First and Fifth Amendments, and countless constitutional provisions at the subnational level in the U.S. and around the globe provide explicit environmental rights, many of which have yet to be tested.

***

As the pages that follow show, Constitutional Law will continue to be of primary importance to Environmental Law, it appears, for as long as Environmental Law exists. Our first case underscores this relationship, in which a federal judge for the first time recognized that the federal Due Process Clause affords a right to a stable climate. The case has the virtue of addressing many other aspects of Constitutional Law that can arise in Environmental Law, such as standing, equal protection, and the political question doctrine. (We'll return to this case later in the book.)

JULIANA V. UNITED STATES
217 F. Supp. 3d 1224 (2016)

AIKEN, JUDGE:

Plaintiffs in this civil rights action are a group of young people between the ages of eight and nineteen ("youth plaintiffs"); Earth Guardians, an association of young environmental activists; and Dr. James Hansen, acting as guardian for future generations. Plaintiffs filed this action against defendants the United States, President Barack Obama, and numerous executive agencies. Plaintiffs allege defendants have known for more than fifty years that the carbon dioxide ("CO_2") produced by burning fossil fuels was destabilizing the climate system in a way that would "significantly endanger plaintiffs, with the damage persisting for millenia." Despite that knowledge, plaintiffs assert defendants, "[b]y their exercise of sovereign authority over our country's atmosphere and fossil fuel resources, ... permitted, encouraged, and otherwise enabled continued exploitation, production, and combustion of fossil fuels, ... deliberately allow[ing] atmospheric CO_2 concentrations to escalate to levels unprecedented in human history[.]"Although many different entities contribute to greenhouse gas emissions, plaintiffs aver defendants bear "a higher degree of responsibility than any other individual, entity, or country" for exposing plaintiffs to the dangers of climate change. Plaintiffs argue defendants' actions violate their substantive due process rights to life, liberty, and property, and that defendants have violated their obligation to hold certain natural resources in trust for the people and for future generations.

Plaintiffs assert there is a very short window in which defendants could act to phase out fossil fuel exploitation and avert environmental catastrophe. They seek (1) a declaration their constitutional and public trust rights have been violated and (2) an order enjoining defendants from violating those rights and directing defendants to develop a plan to reduce CO_2 emissions.

Defendants moved to dismiss this action for lack of subject matter jurisdiction and failure to state a claim. * * * After oral argument, Magistrate Judge Coffin issued his Findings and Recommendation ("F & R") and recommended denying the motions to dismiss. Judge Coffin then referred the matter to me for review pursuant to 28 U.S.C. § 636 and Federal Rule of Civil Procedure 72. Doc. 69. Defendants and intervenors filed objections, and on September 13, 2016, this Court heard oral argument.

For the reasons set forth below, I adopt Judge Coffin's F & R as elaborated in this opinion and deny the motions to dismiss.

BACKGROUND

This is no ordinary lawsuit. Plaintiffs challenge the policies, acts, and omissions of the President of the United States, the Council on Environmental Quality, the Office of Management and Budget, the Office of Science and Technology Policy, the Department of Energy, the

Department of the Interior, the Department of Transportation ("DOT"), the Department of Agriculture, the Department of Commerce, the Department of Defense, the Department of State, and the Environmental Protection Agency ("EPA"). This lawsuit challenges decisions defendants have made across a vast set of topics—decisions like whether and to what extent to regulate CO_2 emissions from power plants and vehicles, whether to permit fossil fuel extraction and development to take place on federal lands, how much to charge for use of those lands, whether to give tax breaks to the fossil fuel industry, whether to subsidize or directly fund that industry, whether to fund the construction of fossil fuel infrastructure such as natural gas pipelines at home and abroad, whether to permit the export and import of fossil fuels from and to the United States, and whether to authorize new marine coal terminal projects. Plaintiffs assert defendants' decisions on these topics have substantially caused the planet to warm and the oceans to rise. They draw a direct causal line between defendants' policy choices and floods, food shortages, destruction of property, species extinction, and a host of other harms.

This lawsuit is not about proving that climate change is happening or that human activity is driving it. For the purposes of this motion, those facts are undisputed. The questions before the Court are whether defendants are responsible for some of the harm caused by climate change, whether plaintiffs may challenge defendants' climate change policy in court, and whether this Court can direct defendants to change their policy without running afoul of the separation of powers doctrine.

* * *

Under Federal Rule of Civil Procedure 12(b)(6), a complaint is construed in favor of the plaintiff, and its factual allegations are taken as true. However, the court need not accept as true "conclusory" allegations or unreasonable inferences. Thus, "for a complaint to survive a motion to dismiss, the non-conclusory factual content, and reasonable inferences from that content, must be plausibly suggestive of a claim entitling the plaintiff to relief." "A claim has facial plausibility when the plaintiff pleads factual content that allows the court to draw the reasonable inference that the defendant is liable for the misconduct alleged." "[O]nce a claim has been stated adequately, it may be supported by showing any set of facts consistent with the allegations in the complaint."

DISCUSSION

Judge Coffin recommended denying defendants' and intervenors' motions to dismiss and holding that plaintiffs' public trust and due process claims may proceed. * * * I first address the threshold challenges to jurisdiction, and then proceed to address the viability of plaintiffs' due process and public trust claims.

I. *Political Question*

If a case presents a political question, federal courts lack subject matter jurisdiction to decide that question. The political question doctrine is "primarily a function of the separation of powers."

* * *

In *Baker*, the Supreme Court identified six criteria, each of which could individually signal the presence of a political question:

> [(1) A] textually demonstrable constitutional commitment of the issue to a

coordinate political department; [(2)] a lack of judicially discoverable and manageable standards for resolving it; [(3)] the impossibility of deciding without an initial policy determination of a kind clearly for nonjudicial discretion; [(4)] the impossibility of a court's undertaking independent resolution without expressing lack of the respect due coordinate branches of government; [(5)] an unusual need for unquestioning adherence to a political decision already made; or [(6)] the potentiality of embarrassment from multifarious pronouncements by various departments on one question.

* * *

Climate change, energy policy, and environmental regulation are certainly "political" in the sense that they have "motivated partisan and sectional debate during important portions of our history." But a case does not present a political question merely because it "raises an issue of great importance to the political branches." Instead, dismissal on political question grounds is appropriate only if one of the *Baker* considerations is "inextricable" from the case. As a result, federal courts regularly adjudicate claims that arise in connection with politically charged issues.

* * *

D. *Summary: This Case Does Not Raise a Nonjusticiable Political Question*

There is no need to step outside the core role of the judiciary to decide this case. At its heart, this lawsuit asks this Court to determine whether defendants have violated plaintiffs' constitutional rights. That question is squarely within the purview of the judiciary. * * *

* * *

II. *Standing to Sue*

"A threshold question in every federal case is ... whether at least one plaintiff has standing." Standing requires a plaintiff to allege "such a personal stake in the outcome of the controversy as to warrant [the] invocation of federal-court jurisdiction and to justify exercise of the court's remedial powers[.]" To demonstrate standing, a plaintiff must show (1) she suffered an injury in fact that is concrete, particularized, and actual or imminent; (2) the injury is fairly traceable to the defendant's challenged conduct; and (3) the injury is likely to be redressed by a favorable court decision, *Lujan v. Defenders of Wildlife*, 504 U.S. 555, 560 (1992). A plaintiff must support each element of the standing test "with the manner and degree of evidence required at the successive stages of the litigation." *Id.* at 561. Accordingly, at the motion to dismiss stage "general allegations" suffice to establish standing because those allegations are presumed to "embrace those specific facts that are necessary to support the claim." *Id.* (citation and quotation marks omitted).

A. *Injury in Fact*

In an environmental case, a plaintiff cannot demonstrate injury in fact merely by alleging injury to the environment; there must be an allegation that the challenged conduct is harming (or imminently will harm) the plaintiff. * * *

Plaintiffs adequately allege injury in fact. Lead plaintiff Kelsey Juliana alleges algae blooms harm the water she drinks, and low water levels caused by drought kill the wild salmon she eats.

Plaintiff Xiuhtezcatl Roske–Martinez alleges increased wildfires and extreme flooding jeopardize his personal safety. Plaintiff Alexander Loznak alleges record-setting temperatures harm the health of the hazelnut orchard on his family farm, an important source of both revenue and food for him and his family. Plaintiff Jacob Lebel alleges drought conditions required his family to install an irrigation system at their farm. Plaintiff Zealand B. alleges he has been unable to ski during the winter as a result of decreased snowpack. Plaintiff Sahara V. alleges hot, dry conditions caused by forest fires aggravate her asthma.

* * *

That leaves imminence. Plaintiffs must demonstrate standing for each claim they seek to press and for each form of relief sought. Because plaintiffs seek injunctive relief, they must show their injuries are "ongoing or likely to recur." They have met this requirement. The complaint alleges that "[t]he present level of CO_2 and its warming, both realized and latent, are already in the zone of danger." It also alleges that "our country is now in a period of carbon overshoot, with early consequences that are already threatening and that will, in the short term, rise to unbearable unless Defendants take immediate action[.]" Youth plaintiffs each allege harm that is ongoing and likely to continue in the future. This is sufficient to satisfy the imminence requirement.

By alleging injuries that are concrete, particularized, and actual or imminent, plaintiffs have satisfied the first prong of the standing test.

B. *Causation*

The second requirement of standing is causation. A plaintiff must show the injury alleged is "fairly traceable" to the challenged action of the defendant and not the result of "the independent action of some third party not before the court." *Lujan*, 504 U.S. at 560 (citation and quotation marks omitted). Although a defendant's action need not be the sole source of injury to support standing, "[t]he line of causation between the defendant's action and the plaintiff's harm must be more than attenuated," However, a "causal chain does not fail simply because it has several links, provided those links are not hypothetical or tenuous and remain plausible."

* * *

The causal chain alleged by plaintiffs here is conclusory, but that is because they have not yet had the opportunity to present evidence. And * * * plaintiffs' causation allegations are not vague. At oral argument, plaintiffs explained that their theory of causation has two components. The first relates to defendants' affirmative acts. Specifically, plaintiffs allege that fossil fuel combustion accounts for approximately ninety-four percent of United States CO_2 emissions. Defendants lease public lands for oil, gas, and coal production; undercharge royalties in connection with those leases; provide tax breaks to companies to encourage fossil fuel development; permit the import and export of fossil fuels; and incentivize the purchase of sport utility vehicles. Here, the chain of causation is: fossil fuel combustion accounts for the lion's share of greenhouse gas emissions produced in the United States; defendants have the power to increase or decrease those emissions; and defendants use that power to engage in a variety of activities that actively cause and promote higher levels of fossil fuel combustion.

The second component of plaintiffs' causation theory involves defendants' failure to act in areas where they have authority to do so. Plaintiffs allege that together, power plants and transportation produce nearly two-thirds of CO_2 emissions in the United States. Plaintiffs also allege DOT and EPA have broad power to set emissions standards in these sectors. So the chain of causation is: DOT and EPA have jurisdiction over sectors producing sixty-four percent of United States emissions, which in turn constitute roughly fourteen percent of emissions worldwide; they allow high emissions levels by failing to set demanding standards; high emissions levels cause climate change; and climate change causes plaintiffs' injuries.

Each link in these causal chains may be difficult to prove, but the "spectre of difficulty down the road does not inform [the] justiciability determination at this early stage of the proceedings." At the pleading stage, plaintiffs have adequately alleged a causal link between defendants' conduct and the asserted injuries.

C. Redressability

The final prong of the standing inquiry is redressability. The causation and redressability prongs of the standing inquiry "overlap and are two facets of a single causation requirement." They are distinct in that causation "examines the connection between the alleged misconduct and injury, whereas redressability analyzes the connection between the alleged injury and requested judicial relief." A plaintiff need not show a favorable decision is certain to redress his injury, but must show a substantial likelihood it will do so. It is sufficient for the redressability inquiry to show that the requested remedy would "slow or reduce" the harm, *Massachusetts*, 549 U.S. at 525, 127 S. Ct. 1438 (citing *Larson v. Valente*, 456 U.S. 228, 243 n.15 (1982)).

The declaratory and injunctive relief plaintiffs request meets this standard. Most notably, plaintiffs ask this Court to "[o]rder Defendants to prepare and implement an enforceable national remedial plan to phase out fossil fuel emissions and draw down excess atmospheric CO_2[.]"If plaintiffs can show, as they have alleged, that defendants have control over a quarter of the planet's greenhouse gas emissions, and that a reduction in those emissions would reduce atmospheric CO_2 and slow climate change, then plaintiffs' requested relief would redress their injuries.

* * *

Redressability in this case is scientifically complex, particularly in light of the specter of "irreversible climate change," wherein greenhouse gas emissions above a certain level push the planet past "points of no return, beyond which irreversible consequences become inevitable, out of humanity's control." This raises a host of questions, among them: What part of plaintiffs' injuries are attributable to causes beyond this Court's control? Even if emissions increase elsewhere, will the magnitude of plaintiffs' injuries be less if they obtain the relief they seek in this lawsuit? When would we reach this point of no return, and do defendants have it within their power to avert reaching it even without cooperation from third parties? All of these questions are inextricably bound up in the causation inquiry, and none of them can be answered at the motion to dismiss stage.

Plaintiffs ask this Court to "order Defendants to cease their permitting, authorizing, and subsidizing of fossil fuels and, instead, move to swiftly phase out CO_2 emissions, as well as take such other action necessary to ensure that atmospheric CO_2 is no more concentrated than 350 ppm by 2100, including to develop a national plan to restore Earth's energy balance, and implement that national plan so as to stabilize the climate system." Construing the complaint in plaintiffs' favor, they allege that this relief would at least partially redress their asserted injuries. Youth plaintiffs have adequately alleged they have standing to sue.

III. *Due Process Claims*

The Due Process Clause of the Fifth Amendment to the United States Constitution bars the federal government from depriving a person of "life, liberty, or property" without "due process of law." U.S. CONST. amend. V. Plaintiffs allege defendants have violated their due process rights by "directly caus[ing] atmospheric CO_2 to rise to levels that dangerously interfere with a stable climate system required alike by our nation and Plaintiffs"; "knowingly endanger[ing] Plaintiffs' health and welfare by approving and promoting fossil fuel development, including exploration, extraction, production, transportation, importation, exportation, and combustion"; and, "[a]fter knowingly creating this dangerous situation for Plaintiffs, ... continu[ing] to knowingly enhance that danger by allowing fossil fuel production, consumption, and combustion at dangerous levels."

* * *

A. *Infringement of a Fundamental Right*

When a plaintiff challenges affirmative government action under the due process clause, the threshold inquiry is the applicable level of judicial scrutiny. The default level of scrutiny is rational basis, which requires a reviewing court to uphold the challenged governmental action so long as it "implements a rational means of achieving a legitimate governmental end[.]" When the government infringes a "fundamental right," however, a reviewing court applies strict scrutiny. Substantive due process "forbids the government to infringe certain 'fundamental' liberty interests *at all*, no matter what process is provided, unless the infringement is narrowly tailored to serve a compelling state interest." It appears undisputed by plaintiffs, and in any event is clear to this Court, that defendants' affirmative actions would survive rational basis review. Resolution of this part of the motions to dismiss therefore hinges on whether plaintiffs have alleged infringement of a fundamental right.

Fundamental liberty rights include both rights enumerated elsewhere in the Constitution and rights and liberties which are either (1) "deeply rooted in this Nation's history and tradition" or (2) "fundamental to our scheme of ordered liberty[.]" The Supreme Court has cautioned that federal courts must "exercise the utmost care whenever we are asked to break new ground in this field, lest the liberty protected by the Due Process Clause be subtly transformed into" judicial policy preferences.

This does not mean that "new" fundamental rights are out of bounds, though. When the Supreme Court broke new legal ground by recognizing a constitutional right to same-sex marriage, Justice Kennedy wrote that

> The nature of injustice is that we may not always see it in our own times. The generations that wrote and ratified the Bill of Rights ... did not presume to know the extent of freedom in all its dimensions, and so they entrusted to future generations a charter protecting the right of all persons to enjoy liberty as we learn its meaning. When new insight reveals discord between the Constitution's central protections and a received legal stricture, a claim to liberty must be addressed.

Obergefell v. Hodges, —— U.S. ——, 135 S. Ct. 2584, 2598 (2015). Thus, "[t]he identification and protection of fundamental rights is an enduring part of the judicial duty to interpret the Constitution ... [that] has not been reduced to any formula." *Id.* (citation and quotation marks omitted). In determining whether a right is fundamental, courts must exercise "reasoned judgment," keeping in mind that "[h]istory and tradition guide and discipline this inquiry but do not set its outer boundaries." *Id.* The genius of the Constitution is that its text allows "future generations [to] protect ... the right of all persons to enjoy liberty as we learn its meaning," *Id.*

* * *

Exercising my "reasoned judgment," I have no doubt that the right to a climate system capable of sustaining human life is fundamental to a free and ordered society. Just as marriage is the "foundation of the family," a stable climate system is quite literally the foundation "of society, without which there would be neither civilization nor progress."

* * *

In framing the fundamental right at issue as the right to a climate system capable of sustaining human life, I intend to strike a balance and to provide some protection against the constitutionalization of all environmental claims. On the one hand, the phrase "capable of sustaining human life" should not be read to require a plaintiff to allege that governmental action will result in the extinction of humans as a species. On the other hand, acknowledgment of this fundamental right does not transform any minor or even moderate act that contributes to the warming of the planet into a constitutional violation. In this opinion, this Court simply holds that where a complaint alleges governmental action is affirmatively and substantially damaging the climate system in a way that will cause human deaths, shorten human lifespans, result in widespread damage to property, threaten human food sources, and dramatically alter the planet's ecosystem, it states a claim for a due process violation. To hold otherwise would be to say that the Constitution affords no protection against a government's knowing decision to poison the air its citizens breathe or the water its citizens drink. Plaintiffs have adequately alleged infringement of a fundamental right.

* * *

IV. *Public Trust Claims*

In its broadest sense, the term "public trust" refers to the fundamental understanding that no government can legitimately abdicate its core sovereign powers. The public trust doctrine rests on the fundamental principle that "[e]very succeeding legislature possesses the same jurisdiction and power with respect to [the public interest] as its predecessors." The doctrine conceives of certain powers and obligations—for example, the police power—as inherent aspects of sovereignty. Permitting the government to permanently give one of these powers to another entity runs afoul of the public trust doctrine because it diminishes the power of future legislatures to promote the general welfare.

Plaintiffs' public trust claims arise from the particular application of the public trust doctrine to essential natural resources. With respect to these core resources, the sovereign's public trust obligations prevent it from "depriving a future legislature of the natural resources necessary to provide for the well-being and survival of its citizens." Application of the public trust doctrine to natural resources predates the United States of America. Its roots are in the Institutes of Justinian, part of the Corpus Juris Civilis, the body of Roman law that is the "foundation for modern civil law systems." The Institutes of Justinian declared "the following things are by natural law common to all—the air, running water, the sea, and consequently the seashore." The doctrine made its way to the United States through the English common law.

* * *

The seminal United States Supreme Court case on the public trust is *Illinois Central Railroad Company v. Illinois*, 146 U.S. 387 (1892). The Illinois legislature had conveyed to the Illinois Central Railroad Company title to part of the submerged lands beneath the harbor of Chicago, with the intent to give the company control over the waters above the submerged lands "against any future exercise of power over them by the state." *Id.* at 452, 13 S. Ct. 110. The Supreme Court held the legislature's attempt to give up its title to lands submerged beneath navigable waters was either void on its face or always subject to revocation. *Id.* at 453, 13 S. Ct. 110. "The state can no more abdicate its trust over property in which the whole people are interested, like navigable waters and soils under them ... than it can abdicate its police powers in the administration of government and the preservation of the peace." *Id.* In light of the "immense value" the harbor of Chicago carried for the people of Illinois, the "idea that its legislature can deprive the state of control over its bed and waters, and place the same in the hands of a private corporation" could not "be defended." *Id.* at 454, 13 S. Ct. 110.

The natural resources trust operates according to basic trust principles, which impose upon the trustee a fiduciary duty to "protect the trust property against damage or destruction." The trustee owes this duty equally to both current and future beneficiaries of the trust. In natural resources cases, the trust property consists of a set of resources important enough to the people to warrant public trust protection. The government, as trustee, has a fiduciary duty to protect the trust assets from damage so that current and future trust beneficiaries will be able to enjoy the benefits of the trust. The public trust doctrine is generally thought to impose three types of restrictions on governmental authority:

> [F]irst, the property subject to the trust must not only be used for a public purpose, but it must be held available for use by the general public; second, the property may not be sold, even for a fair cash equivalent; and third, the property must be maintained for particular types of uses.

Joseph L. Sax, *The Public Trust Doctrine in Natural Resource Law: Effective Judicial Intervention*, 68 MICH. L. REV. 471, 477 (1970).

This lawsuit is part of a wave of recent environmental cases asserting state and national governments have abdicated their responsibilities under the public trust doctrine. These lawsuits depart from the "traditional" public trust litigation model, which generally centers on the second restriction, the prohibition against alienation of a public trust asset. Instead, plaintiffs assert defendants have violated their duties as trustees by nominally retaining control over trust assets while actually allowing their depletion and destruction, effectively violating the first and third restrictions by excluding the public from use and enjoyment of public resources.

Defendants and intervenors argue the public trust doctrine has no application in this case. They advance four arguments: (1) the atmosphere, the central natural resource at issue in this lawsuit, is not a public trust asset; (2) the federal government, unlike the states, has no public trust obligations; (3) any common-law public trust claims have been displaced by federal statutes; and (4) even if there is a federal public trust, plaintiffs lack a right of action to enforce it. I address each contention in turn.

A. *Scope of Public Trust Assets*

The complaint alleges defendants violated their duties as trustees by failing to protect the atmosphere, water, seas, seashores, and wildlife. Defendants and intervenors argue plaintiffs' public trust claims fail because the complaint focuses on harm to the atmosphere, which is not a public trust asset. I conclude that it is not necessary at this stage to determine whether the atmosphere is a public trust asset because plaintiffs have alleged violations of the public trust doctrine in connection with the territorial sea.

The federal government holds title to the submerged lands between three and twelve miles from the coastlines of the United States. Time and again, the Supreme Court has held that the public trust doctrine applies to "lands beneath tidal waters." Because a number of plaintiffs' injuries relate to the effects of ocean acidification and rising ocean temperatures, they have adequately alleged harm to public trust assets.

* * *

The federal government, like the states, holds public assets—at a minimum, the territorial seas—in trust for the people. Plaintiffs' federal public trust claims are cognizable in federal court.

C. *Displacement of Public Trust Claims*

Defendants and intervenors next argue that any common-law public trust claims have been displaced by a variety of acts of Congress, including the Clean Air Act and the Clean Water Act. For this proposition, they rely on *American Electric Power Company, Inc. v. Connecticut*, 564 U.S. 410 (2011) ("*AEP*"). * * *

* * *

* * * In *AEP*, the Court did not have public trust claims before it and so it had no cause to consider the differences between public trust claims and other types of claims. Public trust claims are unique because they concern inherent attributes of sovereignty. The public trust imposes on the government an obligation to protect the *res* of the trust. A defining feature of that obligation is that it cannot be legislated away, Because of the nature of public trust claims, a displacement analysis simply does not apply.

* * *

D. *Enforceability of Public Trust Obligations in Federal Court*

As a final challenge to plaintiffs' public trust claims, defendants contend that even if the public trust doctrine applies to the federal government, plaintiffs lack a cause of action to enforce the public trust obligations. Relatedly, defendants argue that creation of a right of action to permit plaintiffs to assert their claims in federal court would be an exercise in federal common law-making subject to the same statutory displacement arguments outlined above.

In order to evaluate the merits of these arguments, I must first locate the source of plaintiffs' public trust claims. I conclude plaintiffs' public trust rights both predated the Constitution and are secured by it.

The public trust doctrine defines inherent aspects of sovereignty. The Social Contract theory, which heavily influenced Thomas Jefferson and other Founding Fathers, provides that people possess certain inalienable lights and that governments were established by consent of the governed for the purpose of securing those rights. Accordingly, the Declaration of Independence and the Constitution did not *create* the rights to life, liberty, or the pursuit of happiness—the documents are, instead, vehicles for protecting and promoting those already-existing rights. Governments, in turn, possess certain powers that permit them to safeguard the rights of the people; these powers are inherent in the authority to govern and cannot be sold or bargained away. One example is the police power. Another is the status as trustee pursuant to the public trust doctrine.

Although the public trust predates the Constitution, plaintiffs' right of action to enforce the government's obligations as trustee arises from the Constitution. I agree with Judge Coffin that plaintiffs' public trust claims are properly categorized as substantive due process claims. * * * But it is the Fifth Amendment that provides the right of action.

Plaintiffs' claims rest "directly on the Due Process Clause of the Fifth Amendment." They may, therefore, be asserted in federal court.

CONCLUSION

Throughout their objections, defendants and intervenors attempt to subject a lawsuit alleging constitutional injuries to case law governing statutory and common-law environmental claims. They are correct that plaintiffs likely could not obtain the relief they seek through citizen suits brought under the Clean Air Act, the Clean Water Act, or other environmental laws. But that argument misses the point. This action is of a different order than the typical environmental case. It alleges that defendants' actions and inactions—whether or not they violate any specific statutory duty—have so profoundly damaged our home planet that they threaten plaintiffs' fundamental constitutional rights to life and liberty.

* * *

Federal courts too often have been cautious and overly deferential in the arena of environmental law, and the world has suffered for it.

* * *

"A strong and independent judiciary is the cornerstone of our liberties." These words, spoken by Oregon Senator Mark O. Hatfield, are etched into the walls of the Portland United States courthouse for the District of Oregon. The words appear on the first floor, a daily reminder that it is "emphatically the province and duty of the judicial department to say what the law is." Even when a case implicates hotly contested political issues, the judiciary must not shrink from its role as a coequal branch of government.

I ADOPT Judge Coffin's Findings & Recommendation, as elaborated in this opinion. Defendants' Motion to Dismiss (doc. 27) and Intervenors' Motion to Dismiss (doc. 19) are DENIED.

IT IS SO ORDERED.

***

QUESTIONS

1. What happened in this case?
2. What were the issues?

3. How did the Court resolve them, and why?
4. What are the strengths and weaknesses in the Court's reasoning?

The chapters that follow address the ways in which Environmental Law has been realized, including common law and public trust, the Clean Water Act, the Clean Air Act, climate change and the anthropocene, environmental rights, water rights, international environmental law, and environmental justice.

I suggest three basic questions as you work your way through these materials.

1. What does the law say?
2. How is the law interpreted?
3. What are the law's strengths and weaknesses?

Also, be sure to be able to answer at least these questions about any case:

1. What happened in this case?
2. What were the issues?
3. How did the Court resolve them, and why?
4. What are the strengths and weaknesses in the Court's reasoning?

As you'll see, Environmental Law is interesting and complex. It reflects both the hope for and limitations of the rule of law across the federal, subnational and international legal order. I hope that this book helps you to make both sense of and the most of it in your legal careers.

***

CHAPTER 1: COMMON LAW AND PUBLIC TRUST

"The Commonwealth's obligations as trustee to conserve and maintain the public natural resources for the benefit of the people, including generations yet to come, create a right in the people to seek to enforce the obligations. ... We recognize that, along with articulating the people's rights as beneficiaries of the public trust, the Environmental Rights Amendment also encourages the General Assembly to exercise its trustee powers to enact environmental legislation that serves the purposes of the trust."

--Hon. Justice Castille, *Robinson Township v. Commonwealth of Pennsylvania*, Pa. Sup. Ct. (2013)

Chapter 1 covers how common law and the public trust doctrine address environmental challenges. As those causes of action are likely the subject of courses in Torts and Property Law, we'll focus on constitutional limitations to applying common law to some of the world's most wicked problems, including climate change. In Part I you'll learn about the "Displacement Doctrine" and read a case in which the Supreme Court of the United States (SCOTUS) held that pervasive federal regulation – such as under the Clean Air Act – 'displaces' federal common law and 'preempts' state common law to address climate change. Part II explains what the Public Trust Doctrine is and how it is reflected for the most part in constitutions *elsewhere* around the globe, with one exceptional case borne from rare constitutional provision in Pennsylvania.

I.   COMMON LAW ENVIRONMENTAL ACTIONS

Common law is where environmental law began. For our purposes we can think of common law (you know it as tort law) as affording a series of causes of action ordinarily for damages to address and redress environmental harm to an individual or community, including nuisance, trespass, and strict liability for abnormally dangerous activities. Common law is largely the product of state law. There is no federal common law. State common laws often derive from the Restatement of Torts, the Restatement of Judgments, etc., and differ from state to state, if only marginally, regarding causes of action, liability, proof, statutes of limitations, and damages. There is no "Restatement of Environmental Law." Aside from public nuisance, most common law causes of action are brought by private parties for damages for specific environmental harms to property, say, for a contaminated well or poisoned livestock or diminution of property value. Yet most common law isn't designed to redress public health and welfare.

Most federal environmental laws contain "savings clauses" that contemplate the continuing role of common law in addressing environmental harms. For example, the Clean Air Act's *savings clause* states that:

> "Nothing in this section shall restrict any right which any person (or class of persons) may have under any statute or common law to seek enforcement an any emission standard or limitation or to seek any other relief (including relief against the Administrator or a State agency)."

Thus, lacking federal or state legislation, some states have turned to public nuisance law – that is, an unreasonable interference with a right common to the public – to reach some environmental challenges, including climate change, forever chemicals, and interstate air and water pollution. Yet the U.S. Supreme Court has held that federal law can "displace" federal common law and "preempt" state law, discussed below.

A. DISPLACEMENT DOCTRINE

AMERICAN ELECTRIC POWER CO., INC. V. CONNECTICUT
564 U.S. 410 (2011)

JUSTICE GINSBURG delivered the opinion of the Court, in which CHIEF JUSTICE ROBERTS and JUSTICES SCALIA, KENNEDY, BREYER, and KAGAN joined. JUSTICE ALITO filed an opinion concurring in part and concurring in the judgment, in which JUSTICE THOMAS joined. JUSTICE SOTOMAYOR took no part in the consideration or decision of the case.

We address in this opinion the question whether the plaintiffs (several States, the city of New York, and three private land trusts) can maintain federal common law public nuisance claims against carbon-dioxide emitters (four private power companies and the federal Tennessee Valley Authority). As relief, the plaintiffs ask for a decree setting carbon-dioxide emissions for each defendant at an initial cap, to be further reduced annually. The Clean Air Act and the Environmental Protection Agency action the Act authorizes, we hold, displace the claims the plaintiffs seek to pursue.

I

In *Massachusetts v. EPA*, 549 U.S. 497 (2007), this Court held that the Clean Air Act, 42 U.S.C. § 7401 *et seq.*, authorizes federal regulation of emissions of carbon dioxide and other greenhouse gases. "[N]aturally present in the atmosphere and ... also emitted by human activities," greenhouse gases are so named because they "trap ... heat that would otherwise escape from the [Earth's] atmosphere, and thus form the greenhouse effect that helps keep the Earth warm enough for life." 74 Fed. Reg. 66499 (2009). *Massachusetts* held that the Environmental Protection Agency (EPA) had misread the Clean Air Act when it denied a rulemaking petition seeking controls on greenhouse gas emissions from new motor vehicles. 549 U.S., at 510–511. Greenhouse gases, we determined, qualify as "air pollutant[s]" within the meaning of the governing Clean Air Act provision, *id.* at 528-529 (quoting § 7602(g)); they are therefore within EPA's regulatory ken. Because EPA had authority to set greenhouse gas emission standards and had offered no "reasoned explanation" for failing to do so, we concluded that the agency had not acted "in accordance with law" when it denied the requested rulemaking. *Id.* at 534-535 (quoting § 7607(d)(9)(A)).

Responding to our decision in *Massachusetts,* EPA undertook greenhouse gas regulation. In December 2009, the agency concluded that greenhouse gas emissions from motor vehicles "cause, or contribute to, air pollution which may reasonably be anticipated to endanger public health or welfare," the Act's regulatory trigger. § 7521(a)(1); 74 Fed. Reg. 66496. The agency observed that "atmospheric greenhouse gas concentrations are now at elevated and essentially unprecedented levels," almost entirely "due to anthropogenic emissions," mean global temperatures, the agency continued, demonstrate an "unambiguous warming trend over the last 100 years," and particularly "over the past 30 years." Acknowledging that not all scientists agreed on the causes and consequences of the rise in global temperatures, EPA concluded that "compelling" evidence supported the "attribution of observed climate change to anthropogenic" emissions of greenhouse gases. Consequent dangers of greenhouse gas emissions, EPA determined, included increases in heat-related deaths; coastal inundation and erosion caused by melting icecaps and rising sea levels; more frequent and intense hurricanes, floods, and other "extreme weather events" that cause death and destroy infrastructure; drought due to reductions in mountain snowpack and shifting precipitation patterns; destruction of ecosystems supporting animals and plants; and potentially "significant disruptions" of food production.

EPA and the Department of Transportation subsequently issued a joint and initiated a joint rulemaking covering medium- and heavy-duty vehicles. EPA also began phasing in requirements that new or modified "[m]ajor [greenhouse gas] emitting facilities" use the "best available control technology." § 7475(a)(4). Finally, EPA commenced a rulemaking under § 111 of the Act, 42 U.S.C. § 7411, to set limits on greenhouse gas emissions from new, modified, and existing fossil-fuel fired power plants. Pursuant to a settlement finalized in March 2011, EPA has committed to issuing a proposed rule by July 2011, and a final rule by May 2012.

II

The lawsuits we consider here began well before EPA initiated the efforts to regulate greenhouse gases just described. In July 2004, two groups of plaintiffs filed separate complaints in the Southern District of New York against the same five major electric power companies. The first group of plaintiffs included eight States and New York City, the second joined three nonprofit land trusts; both groups are respondents here. The defendants, now petitioners, are four private companies and the Tennessee Valley Authority, a federally owned corporation that operates fossil-fuel fired power plants in several States. According to the complaints, the defendants "are the five largest emitters of carbon dioxide in the United States." Their collective annual emissions of 650 million tons constitute 25 percent of emissions from the domestic electric power sector, 10 percent of emissions from all domestic human activities and 2.5 percent of all anthropogenic emissions worldwide.

By contributing to global warming, the plaintiffs asserted, the defendants' carbon-dioxide emissions created a "substantial and unreasonable interference with public rights," in violation of the federal common law of interstate nuisance, or, in the alternative, of state tort law. The States and New York City alleged that public lands, infrastructure, and health were at risk from climate change. The trusts urged that climate change would destroy habitats for animals and rare species of trees and plants on land the trusts owned and conserved. All plaintiffs sought injunctive relief requiring each defendant "to cap its carbon dioxide emissions and then reduce them by a specified percentage each year for at least a decade."

The District Court dismissed both suits as presenting non-justiciable political questions, citing *Baker v. Carr,* 369 U.S. 186 (1962), but the Second Circuit reversed, 582 F.3d 309 (2009). On the threshold questions, the Court of Appeals held that the suits were not barred by the political question doctrine and that the plaintiffs had adequately alleged Article III standing.

* * *

We granted certiorari.

III

The petitioners contend that the federal courts lack authority to adjudicate this case. Four members of the Court would hold that at least some plaintiffs have Article III standing under *Massachusetts,* which permitted a State to challenge EPA's refusal to regulate greenhouse gas emissions, and, further, that no other threshold obstacle bars review. Four members of the Court, adhering to a dissenting opinion in *Massachusetts,* 549 U.S., at 535, or regarding that decision as distinguishable, would hold that none of the plaintiffs have Article III standing. We therefore affirm, by an equally divided Court, the Second Circuit's exercise of jurisdiction and proceed to the merits.

IV

A

"There is no federal general common law," *Erie R. Co. v. Tompkins,* 304 U.S. 64, 78 (1938), famously recognized. In the wake of *Erie,* however, a keener understanding developed. *Erie* "le[ft] to the states what ought be left to them," and thus required "federal courts [to] follow state decisions on matters of substantive law appropriately cognizable by the states." *Erie* also sparked "the emergence of a federal decisional law in areas of national concern." The "new" federal common law addresses "subjects within national legislative power where Congress has so directed" or where the basic scheme of the Constitution so demands. Environmental protection is undoubtedly an area "within national legislative power," one in which federal courts may fill in "statutory interstices," and, if necessary, even "fashion federal law." As the Court stated in *Milwaukee I* : "When we deal with air and water in their ambient or interstate aspects, there is a federal common law."

Decisions of this Court predating *Erie,* but compatible with the distinction emerging from that decision between "general common law" and "specialized federal common law," Friendly, *supra,* at 405, have approved federal common law suits brought by one State to abate pollution emanating from another State. See, *e.g., Missouri v. Illinois,* 180 U.S. 208, 241–243 (1901) (permitting suit by Missouri to enjoin Chicago from discharging untreated sewage into interstate waters); *New Jersey v. City of New York,* 283 U.S. 473, 477, 481–483 (1931) (ordering New York City to stop dumping garbage off New Jersey coast); *Georgia v. Tennessee Copper Co.,* 240 U.S. 650 (1916) (ordering private copper companies to curtail sulfur-dioxide discharges in Tennessee that caused harm in Georgia). The plaintiffs contend that their right to maintain this suit follows inexorably from that line of decisions.

Recognition that a subject is [meant] for federal law governance, however, does not necessarily mean that federal courts should create the controlling law. Absent a demonstrated need for a federal rule of decision, the Court has taken "the prudent course" of "adopt[ing] the readymade body of state law as the federal rule of decision until Congress strikes a different accommodation." *United States v. Kimbell Foods, Inc.,* 440 U.S. 715, 740 (1979). And where, as here, borrowing the law of a particular State would be inappropriate, the Court remains mindful that it does not have creative power akin to that vested in Congress.

In the cases on which the plaintiffs heavily rely, States were permitted to sue to challenge activity harmful to their citizens' health and welfare. We have not yet decided whether private citizens (here, the land trusts) or political subdivisions (New York City) of a State may invoke the federal common law of nuisance to abate out-of-state pollution. Nor have we ever held that a State may sue to abate any and all manner of pollution originating outside its borders.

The defendants argue that considerations of scale and complexity distinguish global warming from the more bounded pollution giving rise to past federal nuisance suits. Greenhouse gases once emitted "become well mixed in the atmosphere," emissions in New Jersey may contribute no more to flooding in New York than emissions in China. The plaintiffs, on the other hand, contend that an equitable remedy against the largest emitters of carbon dioxide in the United States is in order and not beyond judicial competence. And we have recognized that public nuisance law, like common law generally, adapts to changing scientific and factual circumstances.

We need not address the parties' dispute in this regard. For it is an academic question whether, in the absence of the Clean Air Act and the EPA actions the Act authorizes, the plaintiffs could state a federal common law claim for curtailment of greenhouse gas emissions because of their contribution to global warming. Any such claim would be displaced by the federal legislation authorizing EPA to regulate carbon-dioxide emissions.

B

"[W]hen Congress addresses a question previously governed by a decision rested on federal common law," the Court has explained, "the need for such an unusual exercise of law-making by federal courts disappears." *Milwaukee II*, 451 U.S., at 314 (holding that amendments to the Clean Water Act displaced the nuisance claim recognized in *Milwaukee I*). Legislative displacement of federal common law does not require the "same sort of evidence of a clear and manifest [congressional] purpose" demanded for preemption of state law. *Id.,* at 317. " '[D]ue regard for the presuppositions of our embracing federal system ... as a promoter of democracy,' " *id.,* at 316 (quoting *San Diego Building Trades Council v. Garmon,* 359 U.S. 236, 243 (1959)), does not enter the calculus, for it is primarily the office of Congress, not the federal courts, to prescribe national policy in areas of special federal interest. *TVA v. Hill,* 437 U.S. 153, 194 (1978). The test for whether congressional legislation excludes the declaration of federal common law is simply whether the statute "speak[s] directly to [the] question" at issue.

We hold that the Clean Air Act and the EPA actions it authorizes displace any federal common law right to seek abatement of carbon-dioxide emissions from fossil-fuel fired power plants. *Massachusetts* made plain that emissions of carbon dioxide qualify as air pollution subject to regulation under the Act. And we think it equally plain that the Act "speaks directly" to emissions of carbon dioxide from the defendants' plants.

Section 111 of the Act directs the EPA Administrator to list "categories of stationary sources" that "in [her] judgment ... caus[e], or contribut[e] significantly to, air pollution which may reasonably be anticipated to endanger public health or welfare." § 7411(b)(1)(A). Once EPA lists a category, the agency must establish standards of performance for emission of pollutants from new or modified sources within that category. § 7411(b)(1)(B); see also § 7411(a)(2). And, most relevant here, § 7411(d) then requires regulation of existing sources within the same category. For existing sources, EPA issues emissions guidelines, see 40 C.F.R. § 60.22, .23 (2009); in compliance with those guidelines and subject to federal oversight, the States then issue performance standards for stationary sources within their jurisdiction, § 7411(d)(1).

The Act provides multiple avenues for enforcement. EPA may delegate implementation and enforcement authority to the States, § 7411(c)(1), (d)(1), but the agency retains the power to inspect and monitor regulated sources, to impose administrative penalties for noncompliance, and to commence civil actions against polluters in federal court. §§ 7411(c)(2), (d)(2), 7413, 7414. In specified circumstances, the Act imposes criminal penalties on any person who knowingly violates emissions standards issued under § 7411. See § 7413(c). And the Act provides for private enforcement. If States (or EPA) fail to enforce emissions limits against regulated sources, the Act permits "any person" to bring a civil enforcement action in federal court. § 7604(a).

If EPA does not *set* emissions limits for a particular pollutant or source of pollution, States and private parties may petition for a rulemaking on the matter, and EPA's response will be reviewable in federal court. See § 7607(b)(1). As earlier noted, EPA is currently engaged in a § 7411 rulemaking to set standards for greenhouse gas emissions from fossil-fuel fired power plants. To settle litigation brought under § 7607(b) by a group that included the majority of the plaintiffs in this very case, the agency agreed to complete that rulemaking by May 2012. The Act itself thus provides a means to seek limits on emissions of carbon dioxide from domestic power plants—the same relief the plaintiffs seek by invoking federal common law. We see no room for a parallel track.

C

The plaintiffs argue, as the Second Circuit held, that federal common law is not displaced until EPA actually exercises its regulatory authority, *i.e.,* until it sets standards governing emissions from the defendants' plants. We disagree.

The sewage discharges at issue in *Milwaukee II,* we do not overlook, were subject to effluent limits set by EPA; under the displacing statute, "[e]very point source discharge" of water pollution was "prohibited unless covered by a permit." 451 U.S., at 318-320 (emphasis deleted). As *Milwaukee*

II made clear, however, the relevant question for purposes of displacement is "whether the field has been occupied, not whether it has been occupied in a particular manner." *Id.,* at 324. Of necessity, Congress selects different regulatory regimes to address different problems. Congress could hardly preemptively prohibit every discharge of carbon dioxide unless covered by a permit. After all, we each emit carbon dioxide merely by breathing.

The Clean Air Act is no less an exercise of the legislature's "considered judgment" concerning the regulation of air pollution because it permits emissions *until* EPA acts. The critical point is that Congress delegated to EPA the decision whether and how to regulate carbon-dioxide emissions from power plants; the delegation is what displaces federal common law. Indeed, were EPA to decline to regulate carbon-dioxide emissions altogether at the conclusion of its ongoing § 7411 rulemaking, the federal courts would have no warrant to employ the federal common law of nuisance to upset the agency's expert determination.

EPA's judgment, we hasten to add, would not escape judicial review. Federal courts, we earlier observed, can review agency action (or a final rule declining to take action) to ensure compliance with the statute Congress enacted. As we have noted, the Clean Air Act directs EPA to establish emissions standards for categories of stationary sources that, "in [the Administrator's] judgment," "caus[e], or contribut[e] significantly to, air pollution which may reasonably be anticipated to endanger public health or welfare." § 7411(b)(1)(A). "[T]he use of the word 'judgment,'" we explained in *Massachusetts,* "is not a roving license to ignore the statutory text." 549 U.S., at 533. "It is but a direction to exercise discretion within defined statutory limits." *Ibid.* EPA may not decline to regulate carbon-dioxide emissions from power plants if refusal to act would be "arbitrary, capricious, an abuse of discretion, or otherwise not in accordance with law." § 7607(d)(9)(A). If the plaintiffs in this case are dissatisfied with the outcome of EPA's forthcoming rulemaking, their recourse under federal law is to seek Court of Appeals review, and, ultimately, to petition for certiorari in this Court.

Indeed, this prescribed order of decisionmaking—the first decider under the Act is the expert administrative agency, the second, federal judges—is yet another reason to resist setting emissions standards by judicial decree under federal tort law. The appropriate amount of regulation in any particular greenhouse gas-producing sector cannot be prescribed in a vacuum: as with other questions of national or international policy, informed assessment of competing interests is required. Along with the environmental benefit potentially achievable, our Nation's energy needs and the possibility of economic disruption must weigh in the balance.

The Clean Air Act entrusts such complex balancing to EPA in the first instance, in combination with state regulators. Each "standard of performance" EPA sets must "tak[e] into account the cost of achieving [emissions] reduction and any nonair quality health and environmental impact and energy requirements." § 7411(a)(1), (b)(1)(B), (d)(1); see also 40 C.F.R. § 60.24(f) (EPA may permit state plans to deviate from generally applicable emissions standards upon demonstration that costs are "[u]nreasonable"). EPA may "distinguish among classes, types, and sizes" of stationary sources in apportioning responsibility for emissions reductions. § 7411(b)(2), (d); see also 40 C.F.R. § 60.22(b)(5). And the agency may waive compliance with emission limits to permit a facility to test drive an "innovative technological system" that has "not [yet] been adequately demonstrated." § 7411(j)(1)(A). The Act envisions extensive cooperation between federal and state authorities, see § 7401(a), (b), generally permitting each State to take the first cut at determining how best to achieve EPA emissions standards within its domain, see § 7411(c)(1), (d)(1)-(2).

It is altogether fitting that Congress designated an expert agency, here, EPA, as best suited to serve as primary regulator of greenhouse gas emissions. The expert agency is surely better equipped to do the job than individual district judges issuing ad hoc, case-by-case injunctions. Federal judges lack the scientific, economic, and technological resources an agency can utilize in coping with issues of this order. See generally *Chevron U.S.A. Inc. v. Natural Resources Defense*

Council, Inc., 467 U.S. 837, 865–866 (1984). Judges may not commission scientific studies or convene groups of experts for advice, or issue rules under notice-and-comment procedures inviting input by any interested person, or seek the counsel of regulators in the States where the defendants are located. Rather, judges are confined by a record comprising the evidence the parties present. Moreover, federal district judges, sitting as sole adjudicators, lack authority to render precedential decisions binding other judges, even members of the same court.

Notwithstanding these disabilities, the plaintiffs propose that individual federal judges determine, in the first instance, what amount of carbon-dioxide emissions is "unreasonable," and then decide what level of reduction is "practical, feasible and economically viable." These determinations would be made for the defendants named in the two lawsuits launched by the plaintiffs. Similar suits could be mounted, counsel for the States and New York City estimated, against "thousands or hundreds or tens" of other defendants fitting the description "large contributors" to carbon-dioxide emissions.

The judgments the plaintiffs would commit to federal judges, in suits that could be filed in any federal district, cannot be reconciled with the decisionmaking scheme Congress enacted. The Second Circuit erred, we hold, in ruling that federal judges may set limits on greenhouse gas emissions in face of a law empowering EPA to set the same limits, subject to judicial review only to ensure against action "arbitrary, capricious, ... or otherwise not in accordance with law." § 7607(d)(9).

V

The plaintiffs also sought relief under state law, in particular, the law of each State where the defendants operate power plants. The Second Circuit did not reach the state law claims because it held that federal common law governed. In light of our holding that the Clean Air Act displaces federal common law, the availability *vel non* of a state lawsuit depends, *inter alia,* on the preemptive effect of the federal Act. None of the parties have briefed preemption or otherwise addressed the availability of a claim under state nuisance law. We therefore leave the matter open for consideration on remand.

* * *

For the reasons stated, we reverse the judgment of the Second Circuit and remand the case for further proceedings consistent with this opinion.

It is so ordered.

QUESTIONS

1. What happened in this case?
2. What was/were the issue/issues?
3. How did the Court resolve it/them, and why?
4. What are the strengths and weaknesses in the Court's reasoning?

B. PREEMPTION

So what of the last question the Court left unanswered: To what extent does federal law preempt state state (common) laws?

EXCERPT: JAMES R. MAY, OF HAPPY INCIDENTS, CLIMATE, FEDERALISM, AND PREEMPTION

17 Temp. Pol. & Civ. Rts. L. Rev. 465 (2008)

Climate change ... is literally everywhere. Even the Supreme Court has taken note, observing that "[t]he harms associated with climate change are serious and well recognized," and potentially include "a precipitate rise in sea levels by the end of the century," "irreversible changes to natural ecosystems," "a significant reduction in water storage in winter snowpack in mountainous regions," and an "increase in the spread of disease."

A rising sea level helps to buoy a rising tide of legal and policy responses to climate change. These responses are guided by two polestars. The first is the Framer's invention of dual sovereignty; the second Congressional notions of cooperative federalism. Elemental to both is federal and state participation. Yet federal action on climate change long trails the states. The U.S. Senate never ratified the Kyoto Protocol. Executive response to climate change has been defined by disbelief. Congress has deferred meaningful measures, paralyzed by political performance anxiety. Federal agencies have denied authority to do much of anything, leading to a dizzying array of well intentioned though inert initiatives.

Hence, states have assumed the wheel. Supremely (sorry) situated to think globally and act locally, east to west, north to south, states are fast fulfilling federalism fantasies of being laboratories for legal and policy responses to climate change. States that step into the breach, however, are subject to bruising constitutional battles, including those under the political question doctrine, standing, and the Supremacy, dormant Commerce and Foreign Relations, Compact and Treaty clauses, Federalism is the common denominator to all of these.

First and necessarily foremost among these is preemption. The issue of whether federal law—or even the absence of it—keeps the states from taking action to address climate change is this article's aim.

* * *

One thing is for certain: the old rules no longer apply. Federal leadership long lacking, states have been busy drawing up the new rules.

* * *

I. FEDERALISM AND CLIMATE CHANGE

It is well accepted that the global dimensions of climate change pose special challenges for states. For example, the rising sea level would inundate the "East Coast of the United States, including most of Florida." Local effects in states such as Vermont include threats to the continued survival of maple trees, foliage and the ski industry. Massachusetts concluded that climate change will cost its taxpayers $1.8 billion annually due to increased flooding, loss of shoreline, and water borne diseases. Regional climate effects include extreme weather events and more significant droughts, floods, and fires.

States, then, understandably lead the charge against climate change. Led by California, many Atlantic and Pacific seaboard states have adopted tailpipe emission standards to limit emissions of greenhouse gases (GHGs) from new motor vehicles. States from the upper northeast to the lower southwest have plans to develop markets in renewable fuels and alternative, renewable energy. A group of eastern states have entered into a "Regional Greenhouse Gas Initiative" (RGGI) to participate in emerging international and domestic GHG credit-trading markets. Governors of some western states have entered into a comparable "Western Climate Initiative." Governor Schwarzenegger of California signed a cooperative arrangement with Great Britain to share information and markets in GHG credits. Governor Sebelius of Kansas rejected a proposal for a new coal-fired power station due to concerns about climate change. Delaware may soon approve the nation's first off-shore wind energy farm. Even the country's "red" center has state governors, legislatures, agencies and citizens poised for action. Across the country states improvise, ruminate and conjoin.

Is it constitutional for states to serve as the front line of defense against climate change? The Framers of the Constitution "split the atom of sovereignty." One end of the atom affords Congress enumerated powers to achieve specific ends. Among these powers, Congress may regulate commerce "among the several states," and implement the implied "necessary and proper" means for achieving those ends.

On the other end of the atom, the Constitution "reserves" for states the authority over matters neither enumerated for Congress nor withheld from the states. Historically, regulating pollution of any sort was solely a state function, a fundamentally "local" pursuit.

Federalism in its purest form promotes participatory democracy and state experimentation with social challenges: "there must be power in the states ... to remould, through experimentation, our economic practices and institutes to meet changing social and economic needs." It is a device for elevating, not suppressing, sovereigns. It reflects that "there must be power in the states ... to remould, through experimentation, our economic practices and institutes to meet changing social and economic needs."

B. Preemption

A question remains as to whether state responses to climate change are constitutional. The Constitution provides that federal law – the Constitution itself, Congressional enactments, and treaties – are the "supreme Law of the Land," thereby displacing competing state law. In its earliest pronouncement on the subject, in 1824, the United States Supreme Court held that federal law usurps inconsistent state laws that may "retard, impede, or burden" federal operations. More recently the Supreme Court has declared that the Supremacy Clause "invalidates state laws that 'interfere with, or are contrary to,' federal law." Thus, auto makers and others have claimed that federal law preempts states from taking action to address climate change, including by establishing GHG emission standards for new motor vehicles, because such actions interfere with, or are contrary to, federal law.

These claims contend that Congress has implicitly preempted state action. Preemption has two prongs, explicit and implicit. Explicit preemption occurs when Congress expresses a "clear and manifest" statement of intent to preempt state law. State law is implicitly preempted in one of two ways. Implicit "field" preemption occurs when federal law occupies a field of interest so pervasively that preemption is assumed ("field" preemption). Implicit "conflict" preemption occurs when it would be either impossible to comply with both federal and state law or when complying with state law would frustrate federal objectives.

There is a presumption against preemption, particularly when Congress has not evinced a clear intent to preempt state action. The Court generally upholds state action concerning matters traditionally under state control, such as energy and pollution control. This includes whether to allow construction of a new nuclear power plant, water allocation and use, and common law causes of action for environmental nuisance or negligence.

These cases reveal a reluctance to preempt state pollution control regulation – even in the face of existing federal law in the field – unless Congress explicitly intends that result. This is especially poignant with transboundary pollution, and doubly so with air pollution subject to the Clean Air Act. Lower courts have upheld state efforts to curb transboundary emissions of pollutants from coal-fired power plants, and state-imposed, fleet-fuel efficiency requirements for trucks. Yet a federal court held that federal law preempted a state law prohibiting New York utilities from selling sulfur dioxide "allowances" given the pervasive regulatory nature of Title IV of the CAA.

The Supreme Court has readily found state laws concerning environmental matters traditionally under federal control and subject to federal legislation, such as wildlife management, navigation, and use of waterways, to be preempted. For example, the Court held that federal legislation governing the issuance of fishing licenses preempts a state's effort to limit the ability of outsiders to fish in the state's territorial waters. It decided that the Federal Power Act preempts state minimum stream flow requirements for federally licensed dams. It held that federal and international law preempts state laws designed to make oil spills less likely because the laws reach activities in open waters or subject to international agreement. Recently, lower courts have held that the Atomic Energy Act preempts state efforts to respond to releases of radioactive materials, that states may not subject federal officers monitoring endangered wolf populations under the Endangered Species Act (ESA) to state law claims for trespass, and that the ESA preempts a state law banning leg-hold traps for catching protected species.

Federal law does not explicitly preempt state regulation of the precursors to climate change. The Clean Air Act, however, preempts states from adopting "any standard relating to the control of emissions from new motor vehicles or new motor vehicle engines."

The CAA, though, reflects federalism by providing a measure for state innovation. The CAA allows California to achieve a "waiver" from federal standards provided the State first finds that its own standards "will be, in the aggregate, at least as protective of public health and welfare as applicable Federal standards." EPA then must determine that the state standards are (1) not "arbitrary and capricious" considering feasibility and costs; (2) not inconsistent with federal tailpipe emission standards under section 202; and (3) needed to meet a local "compelling condition." If EPA grants the waiver request, other states are free to adopt them as well.

In 2005 California asked EPA to waive federal standards to permit it to adopt the CARB standards. Other states then adopted the CARB standards, pending EPA's decision on California's petition. Vermont was one of the first states to adopt the CARB standards. It adopted the CARB standards as part of a strategy to reduce its state's GHG emissions from vehicles by forty-five percent as a means of complying with RGGI. As the Supreme Court notes, Vermont and other states see the CARB standards as a means to an end, and not an end in itself.

With the waiver requests pending, the CARB standards were soon subject to challenge on preemption grounds. There are two cases that give weight to the idea that courts may be receptive to state efforts to address greenhouse gases, at least from new motor vehicles, under the cooperative federalism embodied in the Clean Air Act.

A leading case is *Green Mountain Chrysler Plymouth Dodge Jeep v. Crombie*, in which the plaintiffs, a consortium of new car dealers, automobile manufacturers and auto trade associations argued that federal law preempts Vermont's regulations adopting California's automobile GHG emission standards. The plaintiffs maintained that California's—and by extension Vermont's—standards are either expressly or impliedly preempted, either by the Supremacy or the Foreign Relations Clauses.

The plaintiffs claim that the Energy Policy and Conservation Act (EPCA) preempts the CARB standards. EPCA regulates *fuel efficiency*, not emissions. Congress enacted EPCA in response to the energy crisis of the 1970s. Its aim is to "provide for improved energy efficiency of motor vehicles." It requires the Department of Transportation (and its assignee, the National Highway Safety Transportation Agency, or the NHTSA) to set "corporate average fuel efficiency" (CAFÉ) standards for passenger cars based upon miles driven per gallon (mpg).

When Congress enacted EPCA in 1975, CAFÉ standards stood at roughly fourteen mpg. The EPCA required CAFÉ standards to achieve eighteen mpg by 1978, and further improve to 27.5 mpg by 1985, roughly doubling fuel efficiency fleet-wide. EPCA authorizes the NHTSA to adopt different standards thereafter. EPCA provides that when "deciding maximum feasible average fuel economy under this section, [NHTSA] shall consider technological feasibility, economic practicability, the effect of other motor vehicle standards of the Government on fuel economy, and the need of the United States to conserve energy." According to NHTSA, "economic practicality," includes consumer choice, economic hardship on the auto industry, and vehicle safety.

Plaintiffs claim that the CARB standards really govern efficiency – not emissions. GHG emissions are closely related to fuel efficiency. Burning fuel more efficiently means releasing less carbon along geometric lines. Stoichiometrically speaking, combusting a gallon of gasoline releases almost twenty pounds of carbon into the atmosphere. Thus, a gasoline-powered car that gets twenty mpg produces fifty percent more GHGs than one that achieves thirty mpg. Simply, reducing emissions necessarily means increasing fuel efficiency. Thus, goes the argument, while ostensibly about GHG emissions, the CARB standard actually regulates fuel efficiency. While the CARB standards do not overtly address fuel efficiency, auto manufacturers have calculated that they result in an equivalent mpg for passenger cars and small light-duty trucks at 43.7 and 27 mpg. This is different from, and thereby preempted by EPCA, which sets the comparative mpg at 35 and 23.5 by 2010.

The trouble is that EPCA specifically preempts state from adopting or enforcing fuel efficiency standards. It provides that:

[w]hen an average fuel economy standard prescribed under this chapter is in effect, a State or a political subdivision of a State may not adopt or enforce a law or regulation related to fuel economy standards or average fuel economy standards for automobiles covered by an average fuel economy standard under this chapter.

Unlike with emissions under the CAA, EPCA does not allow California to vary from the federal CAFÉ standards. It does not allow other states to adopt identical standards to those set by California. Auto makers thus maintain the EPCA preempts states from establishing tailpipe emission standards for GHGs.

The court in *Green Mountain* rejected the argument that EPCA preempts the CARB standards. After a sixteen-day trial, the court, per Chief Judge Sessions, issued a 244-page opinion that rejected all of the auto maker's preemption arguments.

The court's threshold finding was that preemption does not apply. It reasoned that given the legislative history of the CAA and EPCA, Congress intended California emissions standards to constitute "other motor vehicle standards of the Government" that the Department of Transportation must consider when establishing CAFÉ standards under EPCA section 502. The court reasoned that if California receives a waiver under the Clean Air Act, then its standards have "the same stature as a federal regulation." It thus concluded that "[t]he Supremacy Clause is not implicated when federal laws conflict or appear to conflict with one another." Hence, the court found that California's standards—once EPA grants a waiver under section 209(b)—cannot be preempted by the Supremacy Clause. Accordingly, while the California emission standards might "overlap" with EPCA, they cannot conflict with it.

Alternatively, assuming the California standards constitute state (and not federal) law, the court engaged in a tripartite analysis and found no express, field, or conflict preemption with respect to the Supremacy or Foreign Relations Clauses. First, it determined that EPCA does not explicitly preempt the California standards. It found that Congress did not intend that EPCA would stop states from having emission standards. The court held that while Congress meant to preempt state action to set fuel efficiency standards, it found no "clear and manifest" statement of congressional intent to prohibit states from regulating in traditional state areas, which the court concluded includes setting tailpipe emission standards.

Furthermore, it held that EPCA's preemption of state standards that "relate to" fuel efficiency did not apply given Congress' requirement in the EPCA that the NHTSA "consider" federal standards, which, in the court's view, include California's standards once EPA approves a waiver request. Therefore, because the California standards encompass emission standards not "related to fuel economy," California's standards are not fuel efficiency standards "cloaked in" emission standards and, are not expressly preempted by EPCA.

Second, the court held that EPCA does not implicitly preempt California's GHG emission standards based on field preemption. It reasoned that with EPCA Congress did not intend to "occupy the field" of tailpipe emission standards. To the contrary, the CAA's statutory scheme suggests otherwise because while CAA section 209(a) preempts state tailpipe emission standards, section 209(b) expressly permits California to promulgate more stringent standards that EPA can allow California to implement, and other states to adopt under section 177. It also held that while California's emission standards and the EPCA's assignment of fuel economy standards to the U.S. Department of Transportation (and it to the NHTSA) overlapped, the California standards do not "conflict" with EPCA.

Third, the court held that allowing states to adopt emission standards for GHGs would not "frustrate" or serve as an "obstacle to" implementation of EPCA. In particular, the court held that the California standards are not an obstacle to EPCA's requirement that the NHTSA consider technological feasibility and costs, including consumer choice, employment and safety. With regard to technological feasibility, the court was convinced that automakers have at their disposal a host of innovations available to help make motor vehicles from twenty-five to fifty percent more fuel-efficient notwithstanding emission requirements. These technical improvements include those to the power train, and use of alternate fuels, including diesel, ethanol blends, hydrogen and plug-in hybrids.

The court was not persuaded by any of the auto maker's arguments that they could not meet the CARB standards without increasing fuel economy. The court determined that fuel efficiency standards could be achieved with multifarious available design modifications, including gasoline derived injection, camless valve actuation, rolling resistance improvement, reduction in drag coefficient, continuous variable transmission, electronic power steering, improvements to the air conditioning system, emission credits, and other efforts.

Regarding costs, the court was not convinced that California's tailpipe emission standards for GHGs would diminish consumer choice or safety, or lead to product withdrawal.

Finally, the court rejected the automaker's two-fold foreign policy preemption arguments. First, it held that the California standards do not "conflict" with federal foreign policy concerning GHG emissions due to the lack of any such discernible policy. Second, it held that federal foreign policy does not "occupy the field" of GHG approaches. If anything, the court maintained, state standards assist the federal government to adhere to existing international requirements. It took notice of a myriad of Congressional and executive statements extolling the country's commitment to reducing GHG levels. Thus, the court concludes, the auto makers "have not shown that Congress exhibited a clear and manifest intent to render the regulation of carbon dioxide emissions from motor vehicles exclusively a federal domain."

The court's opinion in *Green Mountain* is clearly informed by notions of federalism. The court for one is not convinced that global climate change is solely a state concern: "regulation of greenhouse gases from new motor vehicles cannot clearly be categorized as either an area of traditional state regulation." The court maintains that "the states and federal government have overlapping spheres of authority, and regulate concurrently."

A few months after *Green Mountain* a district court in California rejected nearly identical preemption arguments in *Central Valley Chrysler-Jeep, Inc. v. Goldstene*. In *Central Valley*, a different coalition of automotive dealers and manufacturers challenged California's GHG tailpipe emission standards using the same preemption arguments as those dispensed in *Green Mountain*. While the court in *Central Valley* held that EPCA does not preempt California's GHG tailpipe emission standards, it disagreed with *Green Mountain*'s threshold decision that California standards constitute "federal standards" that cannot be preempted by federal law. It disagreed with *Green Mountain*'s reasoning that a waiver would "federalize" California's standards, leading to "a conclusion of non-conflict" with the EPCA. Instead, it found that the EPCA only preempts those state regulations "explicitly aimed at the establishment of fuel economy standards." Given that California's standards included air conditioning offsets, credits for hybrid vehicles and up-stream carbon offsets for alternative fuels, the court reasoned that the California regulations are much broader than EPCA and only have "incidental" effect on fuel economy.

***

II.   PUBLIC TRUST DOCTRINE

The following sections provide background to the public trust concepts, constitutionalization, and adjudication.

A. BACKGROUND

The public trust doctrine derives from the ancient notion that the sovereign holds certain natural resources and objects of nature in trust for the benefit of current and future generations. The doctrine is "rooted in the precept that some resources are so central to the well-being of the community that they must be protected by distinctive, judge-made principles."

The public trust doctrine is controversial. The general rule in American law favors ownership of natural resources as private property. The public trust doctrine, a jarring exception of uncertain dimensions, posits that some resources are subject to a perpetual trust that forecloses private exclusion rights. For environmentalists and preservationists who view private ownership as a source of the degradation of our natural and historical resources, the public trust doctrine holds out the hope of salvation through what amounts to a judicially enforced inalienability rule that locks resources into public ownership. For those who view private property as the bulwark of the free enterprise system and constitutional liberty, the doctrine looms as a vague threat.

B. CONSTITUTIONALIZATION

Environmental constitutionalism often reflects public trust notions. The constitutions of about one-half dozen countries reference holding or protecting resources for the 'public trust' or some variation of that terminology. These tend to impose a trust responsibility upon policy makers, rulers, or citizens to hold resources in trust for current or future generations. Some specify trust responsibilities as a general governing norm. For example, the Ugandan Constitution provides that "the Government or a local government as determined by Parliament by law, shall hold in trust for the people and protect, natural lakes, rivers, wetlands, forest reserves, game reserves, national parks and any land to be reserved for ecological and touristic purposes for the common good of all citizens." And the Constitution of Ethiopia provides that "The natural resources in the waters, forests, land, air lakes, rivers, and ports of the Empire are a sacred trust for the benefit of present and succeeding generations of the Ethiopian people." The Constitution of Papua New Guinea calls for "wise use to be made of our natural resources and the environment in and on the land or seabed, in the sea, under the land, and in the air, in the interests of our development and in trust for future generations." Many of the constitutional provisions that protect water, including those that assert sovereign jurisdictional control, also embody the public trust doctrine.

Reflecting traditional views of sovereignty, some constitutions invest public trust in a supreme leader. The Constitution of Swaziland, for example, provides that "all land (including any existing concessions) in Swaziland, save privately held title-deed land, shall continue to vest in iNgwenyama in trust for the Swazi Nation" and "all minerals and mineral oils in, under or upon any land in Swaziland shall, after the commencement of the Constitution, continue to vest in iNgwenyama in trust for the Swazi Nation." (iNgwenyama is the title of the male ruler or king of Swaziland.) And Ghana's constitution provides that "All public lands in Ghana shall be vested in the President on behalf of, and in trust for, the people of Ghana," and "every mineral in its natural state in, under or upon any land in Ghana, rivers, streams, water courses throughout Ghana, the exclusive economic zone and any area covered by the territorial sea or continental shelf is the property of the Republic of Ghana and shall be vested in the President on behalf of, and in trust for the people of Ghana."

Some constitutional provisions hold citizens accountable to hold resources in trust for future generations. For example, Tanzania's constitution provides "that all citizens together possess all the natural resources of the country in trust for their descendants." The Bhutanese constitution provides that "Every Bhutanese is a trustee of the Kingdom's natural resources and environment for the benefit of the present and future generations and it is the fundamental duty of every citizen to contribute to the protection of the natural environment."

Whether and the extent to which courts engage federal constitutional environmental public trust provisions remains to be seen, although ... several courts especially those on the Indian subcontinent, have constitutionalized the public trust doctrine despite the absence of any textual basis. In fact, because these textual provisions are largely unenforceable, it seems more likely that a court would import the public trust doctrine from the common law or even from widely accepted principles of international law than enforce one of these provisions in a case for injunctive relief or damages.

C. JUDICIAL RECEPTIVITY

Although proponents and detractors of the public trust doctrine dispute much, all agree that the leading case establishing the doctrine in the United States—the "lodestar" of the modern public trust doctrine is the United States Supreme Court's 1892 decision in Illinois Central Railroad Company v Illinois, 146 U.S. 387 (1892) The decision arose out of a dispute over control of the bed of Lake Michigan east of downtown Chicago. Four contestants wrangled over this resource: the Illinois Central Railroad Company, the City of Chicago, the State of Illinois, and the United States government. Each had a plausible legal theory supporting its claims, and each had reason to fear the consequences should another gain supremacy over development of the lakefront. Their struggle, beginning in the late 1860s, resulted in the enactment of the Lake Front Act by the Illinois legislature in 1869, which awarded the Illinois Central both a portion of the lakeshore for a new depot and more than one thousand acres of submerged land for the development of an outer harbor for Chicago. Just four years later, however, during the populist agitation known as the Granger Movement, the grant was repealed. For this and other reasons the legal dispute continued, leading to the litigation that eventually worked its way to the Supreme Court in 1892, which held that each state in its sovereign capacity holds title to all submerged lands within its borders and holds these lands in public trust.

The doctrine lives most vibrantly in jurisdictions with constitutions that recognize the right. Pennsylvania's, for example, provides: "Pennsylvania's public natural resources are the common property of all the people, including generations yet to come. As trustee of these resources, the Commonwealth shall conserve and maintain them for the benefit of all the people." Art. I Sec. 27. This provision has garnered attention, as we'll see in *Robinson Township*, next.

ROBINSON TOWNSHIP (AND DELAWARE RIVERKEEPER) V. COMMONWEALTH OF PENNSYLVANIA
83 A.3d 901, 623 Pa. 564 (Pa. Dec. 19. 2013)

CHIEF JUSTICE CASTILLE.

II. *The Second and Third Clauses of Section 27—The Public Trust*

The second right reserved by Section 27 is the common ownership of the people, including future generations, of Pennsylvania's public natural resources. On its terms, the second clause of Section 27 applies to a narrower category of "public" natural resources than the first clause of the provision. The drafters, however, left unqualified the phrase public natural resources, suggesting that the term fairly implicates relatively broad aspects of the environment, and is amenable to change over time to conform, for example, with the development of related legal and societal concerns. *Accord* 1970 Pa. Legislative Journal–House at 2274. At present, the concept of public natural resources includes not only state-owned lands, waterways, and mineral reserves, but also resources that implicate the public interest, such as ambient air, surface and ground water, wild flora, and fauna (including fish) that are outside the scope of purely private property. ...

The legislative history of the amendment supports this plain interpretation. In its original draft, the second clause of the proposed Environmental Rights Amendment included an enumeration of the public natural resources to be protected. The resources named were "the air, waters, fish, wildlife, and the public lands and property of the Commonwealth...." But, after members of the General Assembly expressed disquietude that the enumeration of resources would be interpreted "to limit, rather than expand, [the] basic concept" of public natural resources, Section 27 was amended and subsequently adopted in its existing, unrestricted, form. The drafters seemingly signaled an intent that the concept of public natural resources would be flexible to capture the full array of resources implicating the public interest, as these may be defined by statute or at common law.

The third clause of Section 27 establishes the Commonwealth's duties with respect to Pennsylvania's commonly-owned public natural resources, which are both negative (*i.e.,* prohibitory) and affirmative (*i.e.,* implicating enactment of legislation and regulations). The provision establishes the public trust doctrine with respect to these natural resources (the corpus of the trust), and designates "the Commonwealth" as trustee and the people as the named beneficiaries. *Payne,* 361 A.2d at 272. The terms of the trust are construed according to the intent of the settlor which, in this instance, is "the people."

"Trust" and "trustee" are terms of art that carried legal implications well developed at Pennsylvania law at the time the amendment was adopted. ... The statement offered in the General Assembly in support of the amendment explained the distinction between the roles of proprietor and trustee in these terms:

Under the proprietary theory, government deals at arms['] length with its citizens, measuring its gains by the balance sheet profits and appreciation it realizes from its resources operations. Under the trust theory, it deals with its citizens as a fiduciary, measuring its successes by the benefits it bestows upon all its citizens in their utilization of natural resources under law.

1970 Pa. Legislative Journal–House at 2273. *See also Nat'l Audubon Soc'y v. Superior Court,* 33 Cal.3d 419, 189 Cal.Rptr. 346, 658 P.2d 709, 724 (1983) ("[P]ublic trust is more than an affirmation of state power to use public property for public purposes. It is an affirmation of the duty of the state to protect the people's common heritage of streams, lakes, marshlands and tidelands, surrendering that right of protection only in rare cases when the abandonment of that right is consistent with the purposes of the trust."). The trust relationship does not contemplate a settlor placing blind faith in the uncontrolled discretion of a trustee; the settlor is entitled to maintain some control and flexibility, exercised by granting the trustee considerable discretion to accomplish the purposes of the trust. An exposition here is not necessary on all the ramifications that the term trustee may have in the context of Section 27. As in our discussion of the Environmental Rights Amendment generally, we merely outline foundational principles relevant to our disposition of this matter.

This environmental public trust was created by the people of Pennsylvania, as the common owners of the Commonwealth's public natural resources; this concept is consistent with the ratification process of the constitutional amendment delineating the terms of the trust. The Commonwealth is named trustee and, notably, duties and powers attendant to the trust are not vested exclusively in any single branch of Pennsylvania's government. The plain intent of the provision is to permit the checks and balances of government to operate in their usual fashion for the benefit of the people in order to accomplish the purposes of the trust. This includes local government.

As trustee, the Commonwealth is a fiduciary obligated to comply with the terms of the trust and with standards governing a fiduciary's conduct. The explicit terms of the trust require the government to "conserve and maintain" the corpus of the trust. *See* PA. CONST. art. I, § 27. The plain meaning of the terms conserve and maintain implicates a duty to prevent and remedy the degradation, diminution, or depletion of our public natural resources. As a fiduciary, the Commonwealth has a duty to act toward the corpus of the trust—the public natural resources—with prudence, loyalty, and impartiality. ...

As the parties here illustrate, two separate Commonwealth obligations are implicit in the nature of the trustee-beneficiary relationship. The first obligation arises from the prohibitory nature of the constitutional clause creating the trust, and is similar to other negative rights articulated in the Declaration of Rights. Stated otherwise, the Commonwealth has an obligation to refrain from performing its trustee duties respecting the environment unreasonably, including via legislative enactments or executive action. As trustee, the Commonwealth has a duty to refrain from permitting or encouraging the degradation, diminution, or depletion of public natural resources, whether such degradation, diminution, or depletion would occur through direct state action or indirectly, *e.g.*, because of the state's failure to restrain the actions of private parties. In this sense, the third clause of the Environmental Rights Amendment is complete because it establishes broad but concrete substantive parameters within which the Commonwealth may act. *Compare* PA. CONST. art. I, § 27 *with, e.g.,* PA. CONST. art. I, § 28. This Court perceives no impediment to citizen beneficiaries enforcing the constitutional prohibition in accordance with established principles of judicial review....

The second obligation peculiar to the trustee is, as the Commonwealth recognizes, to act affirmatively to protect the environment, via legislative action. Accord Geer, 161 U.S. 534 (trusteeship for benefit of state's people implies legislative duty "to enact such laws as will best preserve the subject of the trust, and secure its beneficial use in the future to the people of the state"). The General Assembly has not shied from this duty; it has enacted environmental statutes, most notably the Clean Streams Act, see 35 P.S. § 691.1 *et seq.;* the Air Pollution Control Act, see 35 P.S. § 4001 *et seq.;* and the Solid Waste Management Act, see 35 P.S. § 6018.101 *et seq.* As these statutes (and related regulations) illustrate, legislative enactments serve to define regulatory powers and duties, to describe prohibited conduct of private individuals and entities, to provide procedural safeguards, and to enunciate technical standards of environmental protection. These administrative details are appropriately addressed by legislation because, like other "great ordinances" in our Declaration of Rights, the generalized terms comprising the Environmental Rights Amendment do not articulate them. The call for complementary legislation, however, does not override the otherwise plain conferral of rights upon the people.

Of course, the trust's express directions to conserve and maintain public natural resources do not require a freeze of the existing public natural resource stock; rather, as with the rights affirmed by the first clause of Section 27, the duties to conserve and maintain are tempered by legitimate development tending to improve upon the lot of Pennsylvania's citizenry, with the evident goal of promoting sustainable development. *Accord* 1970 Pa. Legislative Journal–House at 2273; *Nat'l Audubon Soc'y,* 189 Cal.Rptr. 346, 658 P.2d at 727–29 (public trust doctrine permits sovereign to utilize trust resources required for prosperity and habitability of state, even if uses harm trust corpus; but, before state courts and agencies approve use of trust resources, they must consider effect of use upon public trust interests and attempt, so far as feasible, to avoid or minimize any harm to those interests; in that dispute, absence of "objective study" of impact on natural resource was deemed to hamper proper decision).

Within the public trust paradigm of Section 27, the beneficiaries of the trust are "all the people" of Pennsylvania, including generations yet to come. The trust's beneficiary designation has two obvious implications: first, the trustee has an obligation to deal impartially with all beneficiaries and, second, the trustee has an obligation to balance the interests of present and future beneficiaries. Dealing impartially with all beneficiaries means that the trustee must treat all equitably in light of the purposes of the trust. Here, the duty of impartiality implicates questions of access to and distribution of public natural resources, including consumable resources such as water, fish, and game. *See* Dernbach, 104 Dickinson L. Rev. at 14. The second, cross-generational dimension of Section 27 reinforces the conservation imperative: future generations are among the beneficiaries entitled to equal access and distribution of the resources, thus, the trustee cannot be shortsighted. *Accord* 1970 Pa. Legislative Journal–House at 2273 ("[s]ince the public trust doctrine would implicitly preclude the wasting of resources, the explicit inclusion of future generations as part of the relevant public might be considered superfluous," although situations may arise where such inclusion may prove wise). Moreover, this aspect of Section 27 recognizes the practical reality that environmental changes, whether positive or negative, have the potential to be incremental, have a compounding effect, and develop over generations. The Environmental Rights Amendment offers protection equally against actions with immediate severe impact on public natural resources and against actions with minimal or insignificant present consequences that are actually or likely to have significant or irreversible effects in the short or long term.

5. Other Considerations

Section 27 is explicit regarding the respective rights of the people and obligations of the Commonwealth, and considerations upon which we typically rely in statutory construction confirm our development of the basic principles enunciated by its drafters. Among the relevant considerations are the occasion and necessity for the constitutional provision, the legislative history and circumstances of enactment and ratification, the mischief to be remedied and the object to be attained.

It is not a historical accident that the Pennsylvania Constitution now places citizens' environmental rights on par with their political rights. Approximately three and a half centuries ago, white pine, Eastern hemlock, and mixed hardwood forests covered about 90 percent of the Commonwealth's surface of over 20 million acres. The Pennsylvania Lumber Museum, *History*, online at www.lumbermuseum.org/history.php (last accessed on May 23, 2013). Two centuries later, the state experienced a lumber harvesting industry boom that, by 1920, had left much of Pennsylvania barren. "Loggers moved to West Virginia and to the lake states, leaving behind thousands of devastated treeless acres," abandoning sawmills and sounding the death knell for once vibrant towns. Regeneration of our forests (less the diversity of species) has taken decades.

* * *

The third environmental event of great note was the industrial exploitation of Pennsylvania's coalfields from the middle of the nineteenth well into the twentieth century. During that time, the coal industry and the steel industry it powered were the keystone of Pennsylvania's increasingly industrialized economy. ... The two industries provided employment for large numbers of people and delivered tremendous opportunities for small and large investors. "[W]hen coal was a reigning monarch," the industry operated "virtually unrestricted" by either the state or federal government. The result, in the opinion of many, was devastating to the natural environment of the coal-rich regions of the Commonwealth, with long-lasting effects on human health and safety, and on the esthetic beauty of nature. These negative effects include banks of burning or non-burning soft sooty coal and refuse; underground mine fires; pollution of waters from acid mine drainage; subsidence of the soil; and landscapes scarred with strip mining pits and acid water impoundments. *See id.* In the mid–1960s, the Commonwealth began a massive undertaking to reclaim over 250,000 acres of abandoned surface mines and about 2,400 miles of streams contaminated with acid mine drainage, which did not meet water quality standards. The cost of projects to date has been in the hundreds of millions of dollars, and the Department of Environmental Protection has predicted that an estimated 15 billion dollars is in fact necessary to resolve the problem of abandoned mine reclamation alone.

The overwhelming tasks of reclamation and regeneration of the Commonwealth's natural resources, along with localized environmental incidents (such as the 1948 Donora smog tragedy in which twenty persons died of asphyxiation and 7,000 persons were hospitalized because of corrosive industrial smoke; the 1959 Knox Mine disaster in which the Susquehanna River disappeared into the Pittston Coal Vein; the 1961 Glen Alden mine water discharge that killed more than 300,000 fish; and the Centralia mine fire that started in 1962, is still burning, and led to the relocation of all residents in 1984) has led to the gradual enactment of statutes protecting our environment. The drafters of the Environmental Rights Amendment recognized and acknowledged the shocks to our environment and quality of life:

We seared and scarred our once green and pleasant land with mining operations. We polluted our rivers and our streams with acid mine drainage, with industrial waste, with sewage. We poisoned our 'delicate, pleasant and wholesome' air with the smoke of steel mills and coke ovens and with the fumes of millions of automobiles. We smashed our highways through fertile fields and thriving city neighborhoods. We cut down our trees and erected eyesores along our roads. We uglified our land and we called it progress.

1970 Pa. Legislative Journal–House at 2270 (quoting anonymous 1698 description of Penn's Woods air).

With these events in the recent collective memory of the General Assembly, the proposed Environmental Rights Amendment received the unanimous assent of both chambers during both the 1969–1970 and 1971–1972 legislative sessions. Pennsylvania voters ratified the proposed amendment of the citizens' Declaration of Rights on May 18, 1971, with a margin of nearly four to one, receiving 1,021,342 votes in favor and 259,979 opposed. Dernbach, 103 Dickinson L.Rev. at 695 n.2 (citing Franklin L. Kury, The Environmental Amendment to the Pennsylvania Constitution: Twenty Years Later and Largely Untested, 1 Vill. Envtl. L.J. 123, 123 (1990)).

The decision to affirm the people's environmental rights in a Declaration or Bill of Rights, alongside political rights, is relatively rare in American constitutional law. In addition to Pennsylvania, Montana and Rhode Island are the only other states of the Union to do so. *See* PA. CONST. art. I, § 27 (1971); MT. CONST. art. II, § 3 (1889); R.I. CONST. art. I, § 17 (1970). Three other states—Hawaii, Illinois, and Massachusetts—articulate and protect their citizens' environmental rights in separate articles of their charters. *See* HI. CONST. art. XI, §§ 1, 9 (1978); ILL. CONST. art. XI, §§ 1, 2 (1971–72); MA. CONST. amend. 49 (1972). Of these three states, Hawaii and Illinois, unlike Pennsylvania, expressly require further legislative action to vindicate the rights of the people. By comparison, other state charters articulate a "public policy" and attendant directions to the state legislatures to pass laws for the conservation or protection of either all or enumerated natural resources. *See, e.g.,* AK. CONST. art. VIII, §§ 1–18 (1959); COLO. CONST. art. XXVII, § 1 (1993); LA. CONST. art. IX, § 1 (1974); N.M. CONST. art. XX, § 21 (1971); N.Y. CONST. art. XIV, §§ 1–5 (1941); TX. CONST. art. XVI, § 59 (1917); VA. CONST. art. XI, §§ 1–4 (1971). Some charters address the people's rights to fish and hunt, often qualified by the government's right to regulate these activities for the purposes of conservation. *See, e.g.,* KY. CONST. § 255A (2012); VT. CONST. Ch. II, § 67 (1777); WI. CONST. art. I, § 26 (2003). Still other state constitutions simply authorize the expenditure of public money for the purposes of targeted conservation efforts. *See, e.g.,* OR. CONST. art. IX–H, §§ 1–6 (1970); W.V. CONST. art. VI, §§ 55, 56 (1996). Finally, many of the remaining states do not address natural resources in their organic charters at all. *See, e.g.,* NV. CONST. art. I, § 1 *et seq.*

That Pennsylvania deliberately chose a course different from virtually all of its sister states speaks to the Commonwealth's experience of having the benefit of vast natural resources whose virtually unrestrained exploitation, while initially a boon to investors, industry, and citizens, led to destructive and lasting consequences not only for the environment but also for the citizens' quality of life. Later generations paid and continue to pay a tribute to early uncontrolled and unsustainable development financially, in health and quality of life consequences, and with the relegation to history books of valuable natural and esthetic aspects of our environmental inheritance. The drafters and the citizens of the Commonwealth who ratified the Environmental Rights Amendment, aware of this history, articulated the people's rights and the government's duties to the people in broad and flexible terms that would permit not only reactive but also anticipatory protection of the environment for the benefit of current and future generations. Moreover, public trustee duties were delegated concomitantly to all branches and levels of government in recognition that the quality of the environment is a task with both local and statewide implications, and to ensure that all government neither infringed upon the people's rights nor failed to act for the benefit of the people in this area crucial to the well-being of all Pennsylvanians.

6. Existing Jurisprudence Regarding Article I, Section 27

For the most part, to date, the promise of the Environmental Rights Amendment to protect and conserve the quality of our environment has been realized via legislative enactments and executive agency action. The question of how Article I, Section 27 obligations restrain the exercise of police power by the government (*e.g.*, to regulate an industry), although a significant matter, has not presented itself for judicial resolution and this Court has had no opportunity to address the original understanding of the constitutional provision in this context until now. Subsequent to ratification, the Court entertained claims regarding the application of Section 27 in factual scenarios that generally fell within two categories: (1) challenges to specific private or governmental development projects, which implicated alleged violations of constitutional environmental rights and (2) challenges to local or statewide environmental quality laws, which implicated alleged violations of constitutional property rights. In light of the challenges, precedent has tended to define the broad constitutional rights in terms of compliance with various statutes and, as a result, to minimize the constitutional import of the Environmental Rights Amendment. Moreover, existing precedent has failed to differentiate between challenges based on whether they implicated the people's rights under the first or second clauses of Section 27, or the Commonwealth's trustee duties under the second and third clauses, or both. Courts seemingly applied the same analytical scheme to both types of challenges, which introduced additional confusion for the bench and bar and, as a practical matter, has impeded efforts to develop a coherent environmental rights jurisprudence.

I. Environmental Challenges to Development Projects

The leading cases in the first category of decisions are the 1973 decision in *Gettysburg, supra,* and the 1975–76 Commonwealth Court and Supreme Court opinions in *Payne, supra*. In *Gettysburg,* Commonwealth parties sought to enjoin the construction of an observation tower on private property neighboring the Gettysburg Battlefield, in Cumberland Township, Adams County. The Commonwealth parties alleged that the proposed construction disrupted the skyline, dominated the setting, and eroded and despoiled the natural beauty and historic environment of the site. Cumberland Township and Adams County, the affected local governments, had no land use legislation to restrict the development, however, and, as a result, the Commonwealth sought relief only under Article I, Section 27 of the Constitution. This Court affirmed the lower court's denial of relief. The decision of the Court was deeply divided: Messrs. Justice O'Brien and Pomeroy would have held that the Environmental Rights Amendment was not self-executing and because, in their view, the Commonwealth could not bring suit absent legislation implementing the amendment, the action had to be dismissed without reaching its merits; ... Mr. Justice Nix concurred in the result with no opinion; Messrs. Justice Roberts and Manderino, who did not specifically address the question of self-execution, would have reached the merits of the Commonwealth's claim and would have affirmed, finding no error with the lower courts' conclusion that the Commonwealth had not carried its burden of proof, and finally, Mr. Chief Justice Jones and Mr. Justice Eagen would have held that Section 27 was self-executing and would have reversed on the merits, concluding that the evidence of record did not support the lower court's decision, Because no majority rule or reasoning emerged from the several opinions, the *Gettysburg* decision offered little guidance regarding the standards applicable in deciding an Article I, Section 27 challenge.

The Court's next opportunity to address the substantive standards of proof required to obtain relief under Section 27 likewise offered little guidance. In *Payne,* residents of the City of Wilkes–Barre sought to enjoin the plan of the Pennsylvania Department of Transportation to widen River Street at the expense of one-half acre of the River Common, a local park; the project also required removal of several large trees and the elimination of a pedestrian walk. The residents/challengers argued that the Commonwealth violated its duties as trustee of Pennsylvania's public natural resources by approving the River Street project. In affirming the Commonwealth Court's denial of relief, this Court held, that the residents had not met their burden of proof. According to the Court, the residents were seeking automatic relief by merely asserting a common right to a protected value under the trusteeship of the state. But, the Court stated, the proper approach was to balance interests in conservation of natural resources and maintenance of an adequate highway system, a task that the legislation pursuant to which the River Street project had been approved, Act 120 of 1970, already accomplished. The residents, therefore, were not entitled to relief under Section 27. Notably, however, the Court directed that in its role as trustee, the Commonwealth (via agency action) had an obligation to avoid any environmental harm if possible but, absent a feasible alternative to the proposed development, had to permit the land use "in such a way as to minimize the environmental or ecological impact of the use."

The *Payne* Court also addressed a three-part test, which the Commonwealth Court had adopted to explicate the residents' burden of proof under Section 27. The Court did not adopt that test but noted that the standard was equivalent to appellate review of the agency's River Street project decision under Act 120. *Eagle Envtl. II,* 884 A.2d at 879 (although recognizing that balancing must take place, *Payne* Court did not require any specific balancing test between Commonwealth's duty to protect environment and other duties to public).

The Commonwealth Court in *Payne,* acting *en banc* and in its original jurisdiction, had dismissed the matter and entered a decree *nisi. Payne v. Kassab,* 11 Pa.Cmwlth. 14, 312 A.2d 86, 97 (1973). Notably, the court held that Section 27 was intended to allow "controlled development of resources rather than no development," and rejected the residents' argument that Section 27 had to be read in absolute terms so as to require an injunction any time a historical area was affected by a proposed development. In the court's formulation, relief under Section 27 required consideration of the following factors: "(1) Was there compliance with all applicable statutes and regulations relevant to the protection of the Commonwealth's public natural resources? (2) Does the record demonstrate a reasonable effort to reduce the environmental incursion to a minimum? (3) Does the environmental harm which will result from the challenged decision or action so clearly outweigh the benefits to be derived therefrom that to proceed further would be an abuse of discretion? Applying the test it devised, the Commonwealth Court concluded that the River Street project was constitutionally permissible. Subsequently, the court entered a final decree upon its earlier decision, *Payne v. Kassab,* 14 Pa.Cmwlth. 491, 323 A.2d 407 (1974); that decision was appealed by the residents and, as explained, our Court affirmed without elaborating further on the applicable substantive standards for obtaining Section 27 relief.

In subsequent cases implicating Section 27 challenges, the Commonwealth Court has generally applied its *Payne* test to a wide array of factual circumstances. ... Notably, although the test was developed in the context of a challenge pursuant to the second and third clauses of Section 27 (implicating trustee duties), the Commonwealth Court has applied it irrespective of the type of environmental rights claim raised.

More importantly, the *Payne* test appears to have become, for the Commonwealth Court, the benchmark for Section 27 decisions in lieu of the constitutional text. In its subsequent applications, the Commonwealth Court has indicated that the viability of constitutional claims premised upon the Environmental Rights Amendment was limited by whether the General Assembly had acted and by the General Assembly's policy choices, rather than by the plain language of the amendment. ... *See, e.g., Larwin Multihousing Pa. Corp. v. Com.*, 19 Pa.Cmwlth. 181, 343 A.2d 83, 89 n. 9 (1975) ("It is difficult to understand what protections are afforded by [Section 27] not already supplied by the township zoning ordinance and the comprehensive statutes of the Commonwealth concerning streams, air pollution and sewage disposal."). But, while the *Payne* test may have answered a call for guidance on substantive standards in this area of law and may be relatively easy to apply, the test poses difficulties both obvious and critical. First, the *Payne* test describes the Commonwealth's obligations—both as trustee and under the first clause of Section 27—in much narrower terms than the constitutional provision. Second, the test assumes that the availability of judicial relief premised upon Section 27 is contingent upon and constrained by legislative action. And, finally, the Commonwealth Court's *Payne* decision and its progeny have the effect of minimizing the constitutional duties of executive agencies and the judicial branch, and circumscribing the abilities of these entities to carry out their constitutional duties independent of legislative control. *Accord* Fernandez, 17 Harv. Envtl. L. Rev. at 358 ("When a state court declines to enforce a constitutional provision on the ground that it is not self-executing, it restricts its own role in the governing process."); ... The branches of government have independent constitutional duties pursuant to the Environmental Rights Amendment, as these duties are interpreted by the judicial branch and this Court in particular. Because of these critical difficulties, we conclude that the non-textual Article I, Section 27 test established in *Payne* and its progeny is inappropriate to determine matters outside the narrowest category of cases, *i.e.*, those cases in which a challenge is premised simply upon an alleged failure to comply with statutory standards enacted to advance Section 27 interests.

II. *Challenges that Implicate a Balancing of Article I Rights*

In a second line of decisions, our Court has addressed challenges to environmental legislation intended to protect the rights articulated in the Environmental Rights Amendment. In these matters, the Court has generally cited Section 27 as stating a public policy favoring environmental interests which the legislation sought to implement. *See, e.g., Nat'l Wood Preservers, Inc., supra,* 489 Pa. 221, 414 A.2d 37. In *National Wood Preservers,* owners leased a property for use by a business interest using chemicals to preserve wood. The business disposed of waste liquids containing toxic chemicals by discharging them into a well, which drained into the groundwater beneath the property and then into a nearby stream. Following an investigation, the-then Department of Environmental Resources ordered the owners and the business enterprise to abate the harmful condition, pursuant to Section 316 of the Clean Streams Law. *Id.* at 39–40 (citing 35 P.S. § 691.1). On appeal, this Court held that the agency orders were appropriate under Section 316. The Court, *inter alia,* rejected the appellants' argument that Section 316 was an impermissible exercise of police power, holding that enforcement of the provision did not constitute a taking under Article I, Section 10 of the Pennsylvania Constitution and the Fourteenth Amendment of the U.S. Constitution. According to the Court, in adopting the provision, the General Assembly acted in the interest of the public because "maintenance of the environment is a fundamental objective of state power," and a duty imposed upon the Commonwealth. *Id.* at 44 (citing PA. CONST. art. I, § 27). The Court also rejected the argument that Section 316 was an oppressive exercise of the police power, and held that ownership or occupancy were sufficient predicates for requiring corrective orders under the circumstances: "[t]he notion of fault is least functional ... when balancing the interests of a state in the exercise of its police power, because the beneficiary is not an individual but the community." ...

In 1993, the Court rejected another challenge to the constitutionality of legislation adopted to vindicate Section 27 rights. Appellant, the owner of the Boyd Theater in Philadelphia, challenged the historic landmark designation of the interior and exterior of the theater as a violation of the takings clauses of the Pennsylvania and U.S. Constitutions. On appeal, this Court vacated the historical designation order because the City had exceeded the scope of its statutory authority by designating the interior of the theater historic. In doing so, the Court nevertheless expressly upheld the constitutionality of the local ordinance, holding that the ordinance did not constitute a taking under either the U.S. Constitution or the Pennsylvania Constitution. The Court also rejected the contention that the Pennsylvania Constitution guaranteed more expansive rights than its federal counterpart with respect to governmental takings. In undertaking its analysis under the then-recent decision in *Edmunds, supra,* which reinvigorated Pennsylvania constitutional law, the Court noted that Section 27 "reflects a state policy encouraging the preservation of historic and aesthetic resources" and that the local ordinance was consistent with the policy.

Generally, litigation efforts of private interests to limit the exercise of the General Assembly's police power to protect the environment by asserting competing constitutional rights have been unsuccessful, in recognition of the Section 27 imperative. This second line of precedents is consistent with an interpretation of the Environmental Rights Amendment as encompassing a duty of the General Assembly to act in a manner that protects Pennsylvania's public natural resources from degradation and diminution.

III. *The Limitations of Existing Decisional Law in Light of the Present Dispute*

Nothing in this Court's precedent offers substantive and controlling guidance with respect to the type of claims that the citizens assert in this matter. The two lines of cases described above illustrate simply that the legislative and executive branches have taken the initiative in adding substance to the rights guaranteed by Section 27, as the drafters of the constitutional provision anticipated. Contrary to the same drafters' expectations, however, the provision has not yet led to the development of an environmental rights jurisprudence comparable to the tradition of political rights jurisprudence. The absence of such jurisprudence, however, does nothing to diminish the textual, organic rights. ... In any event, this Court has an obligation to vindicate the rights of its citizens where the circumstances require it and in accordance with the plain language of the Constitution.

B. The Relevant Provisions of Act 13

The adoption of Act 13 by the General Assembly accomplished the first major overhaul in nearly three decades of Title 58 of the Pennsylvania Consolidated Statutes, the Oil and Gas Act. The General Assembly declared its intent to permit optimal development of the Commonwealth's oil and gas resources, to protect the safety of personnel and facilities in covered industries, to protect the safety and property rights of persons residing in areas hosting oil and gas operations, and to protect natural resources, environmental rights and values secured by the Constitution of Pennsylvania. *See* 58 Pa.C.S. § 3202 (Declaration of purpose of chapter). Act 13 was initially introduced in the House of Representatives (House Bill 1950), where it was adopted on November 17, 2011, by a vote of 107 to 76. On December 14, 2011, the Senate adopted an amended bill by a vote of 28 to 22. Because the House did not concur in the amendments and the Senate insisted on the amendments, House Bill 1950 was sent to a conference committee on February 6, 2012. The conference committee adopted its report the same day and presented it to the two legislative houses on February 7, 2012. Against some protests that the call for votes did not permit further debate and amendment (*see, e.g.,* 2012 Pa. Legislative Journal—Senate 105, 108), the Senate adopted the conference committee's report on February 7, 2012, by a vote of 31 to 19, and the House adopted the same report on February 8, 2012, by a vote of 101 to 90. The General Assembly sent the bill to Governor Corbett on February 10, 2012, and the Governor signed it on February 14, 2012.

On appeal to this Court, the citizens request that we declare Act 13 unconstitutional in its entirety. This request for relief is premised primarily upon claims that discrete provisions central to Act 13 are unconstitutional: Sections 3303, 3304, and 3215(b)(4) and (d); but, the citizens also address other provisions, *i.e.,* Sections 3305 through 3309. 58 Pa.C.S. §§ 3303–3309; 3215(b), (d).

The Chapter 33 provisions—Sections 3303 through 3309—address local ordinances relating to oil and gas operations. Section 3303 states that "environmental acts are of Statewide concern and, to the extent that they regulate oil and gas operations, occupy the entire field of regulation, to the exclusion of all local ordinances." The General Assembly's stated intent in Act 13 is to preempt and supersede "local regulation of oil and gas operations regulated by the [statewide] environmental acts, as provided in this chapter [, Chapter 33]."

In addition, Section 3304 institutes uniformity among local ordinances Commonwealth-wide, to allow, as stated, for "the reasonable development of oil and gas resources," by both precluding local governments from acting in certain ways, and then requiring local government to take certain dictated actions while approving and permitting oil and gas operations within the parameters articulated by the provision. Section 3304 thus commands that all political subdivisions:

(1) Shall allow well and pipeline location assessment operations, including seismic operations and related activities conducted in accordance with all applicable Federal and State laws and regulations relating to the storage and use of explosives throughout every local government.

(2) May not impose conditions, requirements or limitations on the construction of oil and gas operations that are more stringent than conditions, requirements or limitations imposed on construction activities for other industrial uses within the geographic boundaries of the local government.

(3) May not impose conditions, requirements or limitations on the heights of structures, screening and fencing, lighting or noise relating to permanent oil and gas operations that are more stringent than the conditions, requirements or limitations imposed on other industrial uses or other land development within the particular zoning district where the oil and gas operations are situated within the local government.

(4) Shall have a review period for permitted uses that does not exceed 30 days for complete submissions or that does not exceed 120 days for conditional uses.

(5) Shall authorize oil and gas operations, other than activities at impoundment areas, compressor stations and processing plants, as a permitted use in all zoning districts.

(5.1) Notwithstanding section 3215 (relating to well location restrictions), may prohibit, or permit only as a conditional use, wells or well sites otherwise permitted under paragraph (5) within a residential district if the well site cannot be placed so that the wellhead is at least 500 feet from any existing building. In a residential district, all of the following apply:

(i) A well site may not be located so that the outer edge of the well pad is closer than 300 feet from an existing building.
(ii) Except as set forth in paragraph (5) and this paragraph, oil and gas operations, other than the placement, use and repair of oil and gas pipelines, water pipelines, access roads or security facilities, may not take place within 300 feet of an existing building.

(6) Shall authorize impoundment areas used for oil and gas operations as a permitted use in all zoning districts, provided that the edge of any impoundment area shall not be located closer than 300 feet from an existing building.

(7) Shall authorize natural gas compressor stations as a permitted use in agricultural and industrial zoning districts and as a conditional use in all other zoning districts, if the natural gas compressor building meets the following standards:

(i) is located 750 feet or more from the nearest existing building or 200 feet from the nearest lot line, whichever is greater, unless waived by the owner of the building or adjoining lot; and

(ii) the noise level does not exceed a noise standard of 60dbA at the nearest property line or the applicable standard imposed by Federal law, whichever is less.

(8) Shall authorize a natural gas processing plant as a permitted use in an industrial zoning district and as conditional uses in agricultural zoning districts if all of the following apply:

(i) The natural gas processing plant building is located at the greater of at least 750 feet from the nearest existing building or at least 200 feet from the nearest lot line unless waived by the owner of the building or adjoining lot.

(ii) The noise level of the natural gas processing plant building does not exceed a noise standard of 60dbA at the nearest property line or the applicable standard imposed by Federal law, whichever is less.

(9) Shall impose restrictions on vehicular access routes for overweight vehicles only as authorized under 75 Pa.C.S. (relating to vehicles) or the MPC.

(10) May not impose limits or conditions on subterranean operations or hours of operation of compressor stations and processing plants or hours of operation for the drilling of oil and gas wells or the assembly and disassembly of drilling rigs.

(11) May not increase setback distances set forth in Chapter 32 (relating to development) or this chapter. A local ordinance may impose setback distances that are not regulated by or set forth in Chapter 32 or this chapter if the setbacks are no more stringent than those for other industrial uses within the geographic boundaries of the local government.

58 Pa.C.S. § 3304.

Reviewing the amended Act, few could seriously dispute how remarkable a revolution is worked by this legislation upon the existing zoning regimen in Pennsylvania, including residential zones. In short, local government is required to authorize oil and gas operations, impoundment areas, and location assessment operations (including seismic testing and the use of explosives) as permitted uses in all zoning districts throughout a locality. Local government is also required to authorize natural gas compressor stations as permitted uses in agricultural and industrial districts, and as conditional uses in all other zoning districts. Local governments are also commanded to authorize natural gas processing plants as permitted uses in industrial districts and as conditional uses in agricultural districts. Moreover, Section 3304 limits local government to imposing conditions: on construction of oil and gas operations only as stringent as those on construction activities for industrial uses; and on heights of structures, screening and fencing, lighting and noise only as stringent as those imposed on other land development within the same zoning district. Local government is also simply prohibited from limiting subterranean operations and hours of operation for assembly and disassembly of drilling rigs, and for operation of oil and gas wells, compressor stations, or processing plants. Localities also may not increase setbacks from uses related to the oil and gas industry beyond those articulated by Act 13. In addition, the dictated approach to setbacks focuses only on "existing buildings," offering residents and property owners no setback protections should they desire to develop further their own properties. That local government's zoning role is reduced to *pro forma* accommodation is confirmed by the fact that review under local ordinances of proposed oil and gas-related uses must be completed in 30 days for permitted uses, and in 120 days for conditional uses. The displacement of prior planning, and derivative expectations, regarding land use, zoning, and enjoyment of property is unprecedented.

* * *

A failure to comply with Act 13's requirements that local government act swiftly to accommodate Act 13's new regimen has significant financial consequences for local government as well. Section 3307(a) authorizes the shifting of attorneys' fees and costs to local government, if the court determines that "local government enacted or enforced a local ordinance with willful or reckless disregard" of Act 13. Section 3308 also deems a municipality ineligible to receive unconventional gas well fees if the Public Utility Commission, the Commonwealth Court, or this Court issues an order that a local ordinance violated Act 13. Under Section 3309, local government has but a 120–day grace period following the effective date of Act 13 in which to take action to overturn the locality's prior land use planning scheme and to bring existing local ordinances into compliance with the new regime.

In Chapter 32, Section 3215 imposes modest oil and gas well location restrictions in reference to sensitive water resources, as follows:
(b) Limitation.—(1) No well site may be prepared or well drilled within 100 feet or, in the case of an unconventional well, 300 feet from the vertical well bore or 100 feet from the edge of the well site, whichever is greater, measured horizontally from any solid blue lined stream, spring or body of water as identified on the most current 7 1/2 minute topographic quadrangle map of the United States Geological Survey.

(2) The edge of the disturbed area associated with any unconventional well site must maintain a 100–foot setback from the edge of any solid blue lined stream, spring or body of water as identified on the most current 7 1/2 minute topographic quadrangle map of the United States Geological Survey.

(3) No unconventional well may be drilled within 300 feet of any wetlands greater than one acre in size, and the edge of the disturbed area of any well site must maintain a 100–foot setback from the boundary of the wetlands.

58 Pa.C.S. § 3215(b)(1)-(3). However, even these modest restrictions can be averted by the gas industry, with the Pennsylvania Department of Environmental Protection given considerable authority under the Act to grant waivers of setbacks:

(4) The department shall waive the distance restrictions upon submission of a plan identifying additional measures, facilities or practices to be employed during well site construction, drilling and operations necessary to protect the waters of this Commonwealth. The waiver, if granted, shall include additional terms and conditions required by the department necessary to protect the waters of this Commonwealth. Notwithstanding section 3211(e), if a waiver request has been submitted, the department may extend its permit review period for up to 15 days upon notification to the applicant of the reasons for the extension.

In short, notwithstanding the purported protection of sensitive waters via setbacks, pursuant to Section 3215(b)(4), oil and gas operators are entitled to automatic waivers of setbacks "upon submission of a plan identifying the additional measures, facilities or practices as prescribed by the [Department of Environmental Protection] to be employed during well site construction, drilling and operations." A waiver "shall include additional terms and conditions required by the [D]epartment necessary to protect the waters of this Commonwealth," consistent with regulations that "shall" be developed by the Environmental Quality Board. Remarkably, if a drilling permit that contains Department-imposed conditions is appealed, it is not the industry, but the Department, that "has the burden of proving that the conditions were necessary to protect against a probable harmful impact of [sic] the public resources." 58 Pa.C.S. § 3215(e)(2).

In a further blanket accommodation of industry and development, Section 3215(d) limits the ability of local government to have any meaningful say respecting drilling permits and well locations in their jurisdictions. Under Act 13, a municipality in which an unconventional gas well is proposed may submit written comments "describing local conditions or circumstances" which the municipality would like the Department of Environmental Protection to consider. But, the Department is not obligated to act upon local comments, although it may do so. In another remarkable provision, the Act further provides that, "[n]otwithstanding any other law, no municipality ... shall have a right of appeal or other form of review from the [D]epartment's decision." 58 Pa.C.S. § 3215(d).

C. Article I, Section 27 Rights in Application

We underscore that the citizens raise claims which implicate primarily the Commonwealth's duties as trustee under the Environmental Rights Amendment. The Commonwealth's position on the municipalities' role following Act 13's land use revolution respecting oil and gas operations is similar to its stance regarding the authority of the judiciary to entertain and decide this dispute: in the Commonwealth's view, there is no role. According to the Commonwealth, the question here is strictly one of policy, which only the General Assembly may formulate pursuant to its police powers and authority as trustee of Pennsylvania's public natural resources. By the Commonwealth's reasoning, municipalities have no authority to articulate or implement a different policy, and they have no authority even to claim that the General Assembly's policy violates the Commonwealth's organic charter. The Commonwealth suggests that Act 13 is an enactment based on valid legislative objectives and, therefore, falls properly within its exclusive discretionary policy judgment.

In contrast, the citizens construe the Environmental Rights Amendment as protecting individual rights and devolving duties upon various actors within the political system; and they claim that breaches of those duties or encroachments upon those rights is, at a minimum, actionable. According to the citizens, this dispute is not about municipal power, statutory or otherwise, to develop local policy, but it is instead about compliance with constitutional duties. Unless the Declaration of Rights is to have no meaning, the citizens are correct.

In relevant part, as we have explained previously, the Environmental Rights Amendment to the Pennsylvania Constitution delineates limitations on the Commonwealth's power to act as trustee of the public natural resources. It is worth reiterating that, insofar as the Amendment's prohibitory trustee language is concerned, the constitutional provision speaks on behalf of the people, to the people directly, rather than through the filter of the people's elected representatives to the General Assembly. *See* PA. CONST. art. I, §§ 25, 27.

The Commonwealth's obligations as trustee to conserve and maintain the public natural resources for the benefit of the people, including generations yet to come, create a right in the people to seek to enforce the obligations. *See Commonwealth ex rel. Logan v. Hiltner,* 307 Pa. 343, 161 A. 323, 325 (1932) ("It is a settled rule of constitutional construction that prohibitive and restrictive provisions are self[-]executing and may be enforced by the courts independently of any legislative action."); *accord Payne,* 361 A.2d at 272 (Environmental Rights Amendment creates public trust and names Commonwealth trustee; "[n]o implementing legislation is needed to enunciate these broad purposes and establish these relationships; the amendment does so by its own *Ipse dixit*."). This view is not an outlier. *Washingtonian Home of Chicago v. City of Chicago,* 157 Ill. 414, 41 N.E. 893, 896 (1895) ("[W]here [constitutional] provisions are negative or prohibitory in their character, they execute themselves. Where [the Constitution] limits the power of either of the departments of the government, or where it prohibits the performance of any act by an officer or person, none would contend that the power might be exercised or the act performed until prohibited by the general assembly. The constitution undeniably has as much vigor in prohibiting the exercise of power or the performance of an act as the general assembly."); Fernandez, 17 Harv. Envtl. L. Rev. at 353–54 ("If, despite the absence of a remedy, a provision directly vests a right on a party, the court may declare the provision to be self-executing and fashion a remedy itself."). Statutes and regulations addressing the right are "subordinate to the enjoyment of the right, the exercise of which is regulated. It must be regulation purely, not destruction." *Page v. Allen,* 58 Pa. 338, 1868 WL 7243, at *8 (Pa.1868). As a corollary, the Legislature may not abridge, add to, or alter the constitutional qualification of a right by statute.

We recognize that, along with articulating the people's rights as beneficiaries of the public trust, the Environmental Rights Amendment also encourages the General Assembly to exercise its trustee powers to enact environmental legislation that serves the purposes of the trust. But, in this litigation, the citizens' constitutional challenge is not to the General Assembly's power to enact such legislation; that is a power the General Assembly unquestionably possesses. The question arising from the Commonwealth's litigation stance is whether the General Assembly can perform the legislative function in a manner inconsistent with the constitutional mandate.

Act 13 is not generalized environmental legislation, but is instead a statute that regulates a single, important industry—oil and gas extraction and development. Oil and gas resources are both privately owned and partly public, *i.e.,* insofar as they are on public lands. Act 13 does not remotely purport to regulate simply those oil and gas resources that are part of the public trust corpus, but rather, it addresses the exploitation of all oil and gas resources throughout Pennsylvania. Act 13's primary stated purpose is not to effectuate the constitutional obligation to protect and preserve Pennsylvania's natural environment. Rather, the purpose of the statute is to provide a maximally favorable environment for industry operators to exploit Pennsylvania's oil and natural gas resources, including those in the Marcellus Shale Formation. *See* 58 Pa.C.S. § 3202 (primary purpose is to permit "optimal development of oil and gas resources"). The authority to regulate the oil and gas industry in this context derives, therefore, from the General Assembly's plenary power to enact laws for the purposes of promoting the general welfare, including public convenience and general prosperity, rather than from its corresponding duties as trustee of Pennsylvania's public natural resources. The public natural resources implicated by the "optimal" accommodation of industry here are resources essential to life, health, and liberty: surface and ground water, ambient air, and aspects of the natural environment in which the public has an interest. As the citizens illustrate, development of the natural gas industry in the Commonwealth unquestionably has and will have a lasting, and undeniably detrimental, impact on the quality of these core aspects of Pennsylvania's environment, which are part of the public trust.

As we have explained, Pennsylvania has a notable history of what appears retrospectively to have been a shortsighted exploitation of its bounteous environment, affecting its minerals, its water, its air, its flora and fauna, and its people. The lessons learned from that history led directly to the Environmental Rights Amendment, a measure which received overwhelming support from legislators and the voters alike. When coal was "King," there was no Environmental Rights Amendment to constrain exploitation of the resource, to protect the people and the environment, or to impose the sort of specific duty as trustee upon the Commonwealth as is found in the Amendment. Pennsylvania's very real and mixed past is visible today to anyone travelling across Pennsylvania's spectacular, rolling, varied terrain. The forests may not be primordial, but they have returned and are beautiful nonetheless; the mountains and valleys remain; the riverways remain, too, not as pure as when William Penn first laid eyes upon his colonial charter, but cleaner and better than they were in a relatively recent past, when the citizenry was less attuned to the environmental effects of the exploitation of subsurface natural resources. But, the landscape bears visible scars, too, as reminders of the past efforts of man to exploit Pennsylvania's natural assets. Pennsylvania's past is the necessary prologue here: the reserved rights, and the concomitant duties and constraints, embraced by the Environmental Rights Amendment, are a product of our unique history.

The type of constitutional challenge presented today is as unprecedented in Pennsylvania as is the legislation that engendered it. But, the challenge is in response to history seeming to repeat itself: an industry, offering the very real prospect of jobs and other important economic benefits, seeks to exploit a Pennsylvania resource, to supply an energy source much in demand. The political branches have responded with a comprehensive scheme that accommodates the recovery of the resource. By any responsible account, the exploitation of the Marcellus Shale Formation will produce a detrimental effect on the environment, on the people, their children, and future generations, and potentially on the public purse, perhaps rivaling the environmental effects of coal extraction. The litigation response was not available in the nineteenth century, since there was no Environmental Rights Amendment. The response is available now.

The challenge here is premised upon that part of our organic charter that now explicitly guarantees the people's right to an environment of quality and the concomitant expressed reservation of a right to benefit from the Commonwealth's duty of management of our public natural resources. The challengers here are citizens—just like the citizenry that reserved the right in our charter. They are residents or members of local legislative and executive bodies, and several localities directly affected by natural gas development and extraction in the Marcellus

Shale Formation. Contrary to the Commonwealth's characterization of the dispute, the citizens seek not to expand the authority of local government but to vindicate fundamental constitutional rights that, they say, have been compromised by a legislative determination that violates a public trust. The Commonwealth's efforts to minimize the import of this litigation by suggesting it is simply a dispute over public policy voiced by a disappointed minority requires a blindness to the reality here and to Pennsylvania history, including Pennsylvania constitutional history; and, the position ignores the reality that Act 13 has the potential to affect the reserved rights of every citizen of this Commonwealth now, and in the future. We will proceed now to the merits.

1. Section 3303

We begin by addressing the citizens' claims regarding the constitutionality of Section 3303 of Act 13.

***

With respect to the public trust, Article I, Section 27 of the Pennsylvania Constitution names not the General Assembly but "the Commonwealth" as trustee. We have explained that, as a result, all existing branches and levels of government derive constitutional duties and obligations with respect to the people. The municipalities affected by Act 13 all existed before that Act was adopted; and most if not all had land use measures in place. Those ordinances necessarily addressed the environment, and created reasonable expectations in the resident citizenry. To put it succinctly, our citizens buying homes and raising families in areas zoned residential had a reasonable expectation concerning the environment in which they were living, often for years or even decades. Act 13 fundamentally disrupted those expectations, and ordered local government to take measures to effect the new uses, irrespective of local concerns. The constitutional command respecting the environment necessarily restrains legislative power with respect to political subdivisions that have acted upon their Article I, Section 27 responsibilities: the General Assembly can neither offer political subdivisions purported relief from obligations under the Environmental Rights Amendment, nor can it remove necessary and reasonable authority from local governments to carry out these constitutional duties. Indeed, if the General Assembly had subsumed local government entirely by Act 13—it did not, instead it required local government essentially to be complicit in accommodating a new environmental regime irrespective of the character of the locale—the General Assembly could not eliminate the commands of Article I, Section 27. Rather, the General Assembly would simply have shifted the constitutional obligations onto itself. And those obligations include the duty to "conserve and maintain" the public natural resources, including clean air and pure water, "for the benefit of all the people." The Commonwealth, by the General Assembly, declares in Section 3303 that environmental obligations related to the oil and gas industries are of statewide concern and, on that basis, the Commonwealth purports to preempt the regulatory field to the exclusion of all local environmental legislation that might be perceived as affecting oil and gas operations. Act 13 thus commands municipalities to ignore their obligations under Article I, Section 27 and further directs municipalities to take affirmative actions to undo existing protections of the environment in their localities. The police power, broad as it may be, does not encompass such authority to so fundamentally disrupt these expectations respecting the environment. Accordingly, we are constrained to hold that, in enacting this provision of Act 13, the General Assembly transgressed its delegated police powers which, while broad and flexible, are nevertheless limited by constitutional commands, including the Environmental Rights Amendment.

2. Section 3304

Next, we address the Commonwealth's claims regarding the constitutionality of Section 3304, a provision that elaborates upon local regulation of oil and gas development in Pennsylvania. In regulating the oil and gas industry, the General Assembly exercises its constitutional police powers (to promote general welfare, convenience, and prosperity) but it must also exercise its discretion as trustee of the public natural resources (to "conserve and maintain" public natural resources for the benefit of the people), permitting changes to the corpus of the trust to encourage sustainable development where appropriate. *See Payne,* 361 A.2d at 273 ("[i]t is manifest that a balancing must take place...."). Discretion, in the trustee context, equates to a legal discretion cabined by the language of the trust and the trustee's fiduciary duties, rather than to mere subjective judgment. ... Proper exercise of a trustee's discretion is measured by benefits "bestow[ed] upon all [the Commonwealth's] citizens in their utilization of natural resources" rather than "by the balance sheet profits and appreciation [the trustee] realizes from its resources operations." *See* 1970 Pa. Legislative Journal–House at 2273; *id.* at 2270 ("[T]he measure of our progress is not just what we have but how we live...."). In this sense, the trustee may use the assets of the trust only for purposes authorized by the trust or necessary for the preservation of the trust; other uses are beyond the scope of the discretion conferred, even where the trustee claims to be acting solely to advance other discrete interests of the beneficiaries.

With respect to Act 13, the General Assembly certainly recognized, among other things, its twin constitutional duties to provide for the general welfare and prosperity by "permit[ting] optimal development of oil and gas resources of this Commonwealth," and for the protection of "natural resources, environmental rights and values secured by the Constitution of Pennsylvania." 58 Pa.C.S. § 3202. A declaration of intent, regardless of its validity or its beneficence, is neither dispositive nor is it even particularly probative of whether the means articulated in the legislative enactment, by which the intent is pursued, are constitutional. We pass upon a constitutional challenge to the legislative enactment not by measuring the wisdom of the means chosen by the General Assembly to pursue its policy, but by measuring the enactment against the relevant constitutional command.

We have explained that, among other fiduciary duties under Article I, Section 27, the General Assembly has the obligation to prevent degradation, diminution, and depletion of our public natural resources, which it may satisfy by enacting legislation that adequately restrains actions of private parties likely to cause harm to protected aspects of our environment. We are constrained to hold that Section 3304 falls considerably short of meeting this obligation for two reasons.

First, a new regulatory regime permitting industrial uses as a matter of right in every type of pre-existing zoning district is incapable of conserving or maintaining the constitutionally-protected aspects of the public environment and of a certain quality of life. In Pennsylvania, terrain and natural conditions frequently differ throughout a municipality, and from municipality to municipality. As a result, the impact on the quality, quantity, and well-being of our natural resources cannot reasonably be assessed on the basis of a statewide average. Protection of environmental values, in this respect, is a quintessential local issue that must be tailored to local conditions. Moreover, the Commonwealth is now over three centuries old, and its citizens settled the territory and built homes and communities long before the exploitation of natural gas in the Marcellus Shale Formation became economically feasible. Oil and gas operations do not function autonomously of their immediate surroundings. Act 13 emerged upon this complex background of settled habitability and ownership interests and expectations.

Despite this variety in the existing environmental and legislative landscape, Act 13 simply displaces development guidelines, guidelines which offer strict limitations on industrial uses in sensitive zoning districts; instead, Act 13 permits industrial oil and gas operations as a use "of right" in every zoning district throughout the Commonwealth, including in residential, commercial, and agricultural districts. Insofar as Section 3304 permits the fracking operations and exploitation of the Marcellus Shale at issue here, the provision compels exposure of otherwise protected areas to environmental and habitability costs associated with this particular industrial use: air, water, and soil pollution; persistent noise, lighting, and heavy vehicle traffic; and the building of facilities incongruous with the surrounding landscape. The entirely new legal regimen alters existing expectations of communities and property owners and substantially diminishes natural and esthetic values of the local environment, which contribute significantly to a quality of environmental life in Pennsylvania. Again, protected by their organic charter, these communities and property owners could reasonably rely upon the zoning schemes that municipalities designed at the General Assembly's prompt, schemes in which participation was mandatory and which imposed costs (for example, land use restrictions) upon participants, in addition to benefits. The costs, under the local schemes, presumably were rationally related to the scheme's benefits. For communities and property owners affected by Act 13, however, the General Assembly has effectively disposed of the regulatory structures upon which citizens and communities made significant financial and quality of life decisions, and has sanctioned a direct and harmful degradation of the environmental quality of life in these communities and zoning districts. In constitutional terms, the Act degrades the corpus of the trust. ...

A second difficulty arising from Section 3304's requirement that local government permit industrial uses in all zoning districts is that some properties and communities will carry much heavier environmental and habitability burdens than others. ... This disparate effect is irreconcilable with the express command that the trustee will manage the corpus of the trust for the benefit of "all the people." PA. CONST. art. I, § 27. A trustee must treat all beneficiaries equitably in light of the purposes of the trust. Again, we do not quarrel with the fact that competing constitutional commands may exist, that sustainable development may require some degradation of the corpus of the trust, and that the distribution of valuable resources may mean that reasonable distinctions are appropriate. But, Act 13's blunt approach fails to account for this constitutional command at all and, indeed, exacerbates the problem by offering minimal statewide protections while disabling local government from mitigating the impact of oil and gas development at a local level. Section 3304 requires either that no "conditions, requirements or limitations" be imposed on certain aspects of oil and gas location or operations or that such conditions, requirements, or limitations be no "more stringent" than those imposed on other industrial uses in the municipality (relating to construction activities) or other land development in the zoning district (relating to heights of structures, screening and fencing, lighting or noise). Remarkably, Section 3304 then goes even further, as it prohibits local government from tailoring protections for water and air quality (*e.g.*, through increased setbacks) and for the natural, scenic, and esthetic characteristics of the environment (*e.g.*, through increased setbacks, screening, fencing, reduced hours of operation requirements) in the affected areas within a municipality. Imposing statewide environmental and habitability standards appropriate for the heaviest of industrial areas in sensitive zoning districts lowers environmental and habitability protections for affected residents and property owners below the existing threshold and permits significant degradation of public natural resources. The outright ban on local regulation of oil and gas operations (such as ordinances seeking to conform development to local conditions) that would mitigate the effect, meanwhile, propagates serious detrimental and disparate effects on the corpus of the trust.

To be sure, the Commonwealth and its *amici* make compelling policy arguments that Pennsylvania's populace will benefit from the exploitation of the natural gas found in the Marcellus Shale Formation. Shale gas, according to the Commonwealth and its *amici*, has the potential to be a long-term source of energy that is cheap to transport to large metropolitan centers and businesses on the East Coast, and that can provide a welcome source of tax and other income for the Commonwealth and local communities. The Commonwealth offers that it has devised the best means by which to take advantage of Pennsylvania's rich shale gas resources, including by anticipating what it believes would be local efforts to derail industry development and by preventing what it says would be a "balkanization" of legal regimes with which the industry would have to comply.

If economic and energy benefits were the only considerations at issue, this particular argument would carry more weight. But, the Constitution constrains this Court not to be swayed by counter-policy arguments where the constitutional command is clear. In this sense, the Commonwealth fails to respond in any meaningful way to the citizens' claims that Act 13 falls far short of providing adequate protection to existing environmental and habitability features of neighborhoods in which they have established homes, schools, businesses that produce or sell food and provide healthcare, and other ventures, which ensure a quality of human life. In our view, the framers and ratifiers of the Environmental Rights Amendment intended the constitutional provision as a bulwark against enactments, like Act 13, which permit development with such an immediate, disruptive effect upon how Pennsylvanians live their lives. To comply with the constitutional command, the General Assembly must exercise its police powers to foster sustainable development in a manner that respects the reserved rights of the people to a clean, healthy, and esthetically-pleasing environment. ...

For these reasons, we are constrained to hold that the degradation of the corpus of the trust and the disparate impact on some citizens sanctioned by Section 3304 of Act 13 are incompatible with the express command of the Environmental Rights Amendment. We recognize the importance of this legislation, and do not question the intentions behind it; we recognize, too, the urgency with which the political branches believe they must act to secure the benefits of developing the unconventional natural gas industry. By any measure, this legislation is of sweeping import. But, in that urgency, it is apparent that the Article I, Section 27 constitutional commands have been swept aside. Act 13's unauthorized use of the public trust assets is unprecedented and constitutionally infirm, even assuming that the trustee believes it is acting solely and in good faith to advance the economic interests of the beneficiaries.

3. Section 3215(b)

Finally, we address the Commonwealth's claims regarding the constitutionality of Section 3215(b)(4). At the outset, we agree with the Commonwealth that Section 3215(b)(4) cannot be considered in isolation, and that we must review the entire decisional process regarding the protection of certain bodies of water described in Section 3215(b) to render a proper decision. Even placed into this broad context, the Commonwealth's characterization of the provision is, nevertheless, unpersuasive.

Section 3215(b) states mandatory setbacks for the gas industry but, even then, the provision also requires the Department of Environmental Protection to waive the setbacks on condition that the permit applicant submit "a plan" to protect Commonwealth waters. The Act requires the Department to articulate protective terms and conditions it deems "necessary," but upon appeal by the applicant, the Department has the burden to justify these conditions. In the process of granting these permits, the Act empowers the Department to "consider" local comments, but it is not required to act upon local concerns. Unlike the industry, local government may not seek review of permit decisions. *See* 58 Pa.C.S. § 3215(b), (d)-(e); *see also* 58 Pa.C.S. § 3212.1(b). Section 3215(b) presents twin difficulties.

Initially, neither Section 3215(b), nor any other provision of Act 13, describes what additional measures are "necessary" for a waiver of setbacks to be appropriate. The Commonwealth insists that Act 13 impliedly creates a floor and a ceiling on the type of conditions the Department may impose on a permit applicant. In the Commonwealth's view, the Department's discretion is limited by Act 13's express intent and by the Commonwealth's various existing environmental statutes. But, predictably enough given the broad language of Section 3215, the Commonwealth fails to identify any actual substantive conditions that may be deemed necessary for the purposes of Act 13. Rather, the necessary protections are determined according to criteria that the Environmental Quality Board shall articulate, which are to account for the impact on public natural resources of oil and gas operations; notably, those criteria must ensure optimal development of the industry. The direction to the Department of Environmental Protection then is merely "to consider" the Environmental Quality Board's criteria in granting well permits. At that point, again, review is limited to industry challenges. Neither local government nor affected citizens may pursue an appeal.

Even accounting for all elements of the statutory scheme in a manner most deferential to Act 13's statutory purpose, we are constrained to conclude that what the crucial term "necessary" entails in the context of Section 3215(b) remains malleable and unpredictable. The statute does not provide any ascertainable standards by which public natural resources are to be protected if an oil and gas operator seeks a waiver of the Section 3215(b) setbacks. The statement of legislative intent, which simply articulates broad principles, offers no additional clarification regarding the environmental standard governing either the applicant or the Department of Environmental Protection. Moreover, Act 13 offers no reference, however oblique, to any requirement that the Department is obligated to consider the Commonwealth's environmental statutes in rendering its permit decisions or imposing well permit conditions under Act 13. Section 3257 of Act 13, for example, which the Commonwealth cites as incorporating standards of environmental statutes into the Section 3215(b) decision, declares as a general matter (while offering specific examples) merely that Chapter 32 of Act 13 "provide[s] additional and cumulative remedies to control activities related to drilling for or production of oil and gas in this Commonwealth, and nothing contained in this chapter abridges or alters rights of action or remedies existing, or which existed previously, in equity or under common or statutory law, criminal or civil." 58 Pa.C.S. § 3257. The provision makes no reference to whether or how substantive standards of existing environmental acts enter into a well permit determination, let alone into a Section 3215(b)(4) decision. Considered in its totality, the Section 3215(b) scheme lacks identifiable and readily-enforceable environmental standards for granting well permits or setback waivers, which yields at best arbitrary terms and conditions and, at worst, wholly ineffective protections for the waters of the Commonwealth. In this sense, the Act has failed to ensure compliance with the express command of the Environmental Rights Amendment that the Commonwealth trustee "conserve and maintain," *inter alia*, the waters of the Commonwealth.

To exacerbate this problem, the decisional process of Section 3215 creates incentives to define "necessary" conditions by nominal standards, and invites arbitrary decision-making with a disparate impact on trust beneficiaries. From the outset, Section 3215(b) appears to provide for nothing more than a set of voluntary setbacks or, as an alternative, the opportunity for a permit applicant to negotiate with the Department of Environmental Protection the terms or conditions of its oil or natural gas well permit. If an applicant appeals permit terms or conditions—and only the applicant can appeal—Section 3215 remarkably places the burden on the Department to "prov[e] that the conditions were necessary to protect against a probable harmful impact of [sic] the public resources." 58 Pa.C.S. § 3215(e). Viewed in terms of the constitutional mandates, this is topsy-turvy: Act 13 places on the Department the burden of proof and persuasion, and the people are allocated thereby the risk of an erroneous decision by the Environmental Quality Board.. This naturally invites the Department to articulate "necessary" conditions as minimal standards that an applicant would accept without litigation. The scheme also provides the oil and gas operator leverage in the first instance to negotiate permit terms and conditions to optimize industrial development, even at the expense of protected environmental and habitability concerns. The statutory scheme overall dilutes the Department's authority to regulate and enforce adequate environmental standards, and fosters departures from the goal of sustainable development.

Finally, Section 3215(d) marginalizes participation by residents, business owners, and their elected representatives with environmental and habitability concerns, whose interests Section 3215 ostensibly protects. *See* 58 Pa.C.S. § 3202 (Declaration of purpose of chapter). The result is that Section 3215 fosters decisions regarding the environment and habitability that are non-responsive to local concerns; and, as with the uniformity requirement of Section 3304, the effect of failing to account for local conditions causes a disparate impact upon beneficiaries of the trust. Moreover, insofar as the Department of Environmental Protection is not required, but is merely permitted, to account for local concerns in its permit decisions, Section 3215(d) fails to ensure that any disparate effects are attenuated. Again, inequitable treatment of trust beneficiaries is irreconcilable with the trustee duty of impartiality.

Calling upon agency expertise to make permit decisions that comply with the Commonwealth's trustee obligations does not dissipate the structural difficulties with a statutory scheme that fails both to ensure conservation of the quality and quantity of the Commonwealth's waters and to treat all beneficiaries equitably in light of the purposes of the trust. In these respects, we are constrained to conclude that Act 13 has failed to properly discharge the Commonwealth's duties as trustee of the public natural resources.

4. Mandate

For these reasons, we agree with the citizens that, as an exercise of police power, Sections 3215(b)(4) and (d), 3303, and 3304 are incompatible with the Commonwealth's duty as trustee of Pennsylvania's public natural resources. Accordingly, we hold that these provisions are unconstitutional. Because we find that Sections 3215(b)(4) and 3304 violate the Environmental Rights Amendment, we do not address the related claims that these provisions violate, respectively, the separation of powers doctrine and the due process clauses of the Pennsylvania Constitution and the U.S. Constitution.

The Commonwealth Court's decision is affirmed in part, albeit on different grounds, and reversed in part.

· ·

QUESTIONS

1. What is the "public trust doctrine"?
2. How has it been recognized internationally?
3. How about constitutionally?
4. How has it fared in courts around the globe, and in the U.S.?
5. What role did it play in *Robinson Township*?

CHAPTER 2: NATIONAL ENVIRONMENTAL POLICY ACT

Chapter 2 covers the National Environmental Policy Act (NEPA). It's a remarkable piece of legislation that requires federal agencies to look before they leap (it doesn't prevent them from leaping, however) by assessing environmental impacts of federal actions, and then avoiding or mitigating significant harmful impacts. After Part I's introduction, Part II provides the statutory and regulatory language that makes NEPA hum. In Part III, we'll see how receptive the SCOTUS has been to NEPA, meaning hardly at all. It's a procedural drill, in the Court's view, as we'll see in the contexts of exclusions, consideration of alternatives and effects, and mitigation.

I.   INTRODUCTION TO NEPA

Environmental impact analysis ('EIA") is the process whereby an agency evaluates the environmental impacts of a proposed action, determines which impacts are unavoidable, and then provides for planning to avoid, mitigate or compensate for them.

The National Environmental Policy Act, 42 U.S.C. § 4321 et seq., ('NEPA') enshrines EIA at the federal level in the United States. NEPA was the nation's first real environmental law, and there was nothing else like it upon enactment in 1970. It's a remarkable legislative accomplishment. It combines federal land use planning and environmental protection. On the land use side, it requires federal agencies to work cooperatively to assess the short and long-term consequences of their actions to authorize (say, a highway), fund (say, for urban housing), or carry out (say, develop a plan for managing federal forests). On the environmental side, it requires the 'lead' agency to evaluate the extent of the project's adverse environmental impact to determine whether it is "significant," by issuing an "environmental assessment," or "EA." Thus, NEPA potentially reaches tens of thousands of federal actions every year.

When the agency by virtue of an EA determines that a project may have "significant" adverse environmental impacts, NEPA has it prepare a "detailed statement," commonly known as an "environmental impact statement," or "EIS." The EIS examines the extent of the project's adverse environmental effects and how to mitigate them, whether there are less harmful alternatives, and which impacts are irreversible. The EIS process is public and much like that which you learned about in Administrative Law for informal rulemaking under Section 553 of the Administrative Procedure Act: the lead agency publishes a notice of action in the Federal Register, issues a "Draft EIS," invites public comment, holds informal public hearings, and issues a final EIS with an explanatory record of decision. And as in Administrative Law, the final decision may be subject to judicial review by a federal court.

While it passed both houses of Congress overwhelmingly, and was the brainchild of the Nixon Administration, NEPA quickly became and has remained controversial. On the one hand, there is no question that it has improved outcomes in some if not many situations. Federal agencies have issued hundreds of thousands of EAs and thousands of EISs. For example, a NEPA process preceded the construction, expansion, and maintenance of every federal highway in the country, including on and off ramps and service and rest areas. The same can be said for many state roads for which federal funding is involved, as well as rail lines, many hiking paths, walkways, etc. Chances are that no matter how you made your way to school, NEPA was lurking all around, unbeknownst to you. For these and thousands of other federal-related actions, NEPA has facilitated transparency, coordination and participation.

On the other hand, NEPA is little more than a paper tiger. The U.S. Supreme Court has issued a string of cases that emphasize NEPA's procedural strictures to consider environmental impacts but render toothless its substantive objectives, which are to "encourage productive and enjoyable harmony between man and his environment; to promote efforts which will prevent or eliminate damage to the environment and biosphere and stimulate the health and welfare of man; to enrich the understanding of the ecological systems and natural resources important to the Nation." By and large, the SCOTUS has sided with the more narrow reading of NEPA 17 times and all but once over more than 40 years, in fact.

NEPA has also been widely influential. About three-fourths of the nations on the planet have enacted laws or constitutional provisions that require environmental assessment to some degree, sometimes even more than does NEPA. Moreover, a handful of states have also enacted "little NEPAs" that require state agencies to evaluate the environmental impacts of state projects that would otherwise fall outside NEPA's purview.

The following reading explores these notions in greater detail.

EXCERPT: RICHARD LAZARUS, THE NATIONAL ENVIRONMENTAL POLICY ACT IN THE U.S. SUPREME COURT: A REAPPRAISAL AND A PEEK BEHIND THE CURTAINS
100 Geo. L.J. 1507 (2012)

Copyright © 2012 by Georgetown University and The Georgetown Law Journal; Richard Lazarus

The National Environmental Policy Act of 1969 (NEPA) has long been trumpeted as environmental law's "Magna Carta" in the United States, with its sweeping declarations about the need to safeguard the natural environment for future generations. NEPA requires federal agencies to prepare environmental impact statements (EISs) whenever they propose major federal actions that would significantly affect the quality of the human environment. NEPA's simple admonishment that government planners should in effect "look before they leap" has prompted the preparation of approximately 34,000 draft and final EISs and successfully prevented at least hundreds, and likely thousands, of actions from causing unnecessary damage to the nation's environment. As many as half of the states have, in turn, enacted their own NEPA programs modeled upon the federal statute. And approximately 160 other countries have done the same, making NEPA the nation's most successful international export in the field of environmental protection law.

NEPA's reception before the United States Supreme Court, however, tells a different story. The Supreme Court has decided seventeen NEPA cases on the merits since the statute's enactment. In all seventeen cases, NEPA plaintiffs had won in the lower courts and opposed High Court review. The federal government petitioned for review in fifteen of the cases and industry alone petitioned in the other two, with the government filing in support of industry on the merits after the Court granted the industry petition. The Court has not once granted a petition filed by a NEPA plaintiff and then heard the case on the merits. Instead, in every one of the 111 occasions when NEPA plaintiffs have sought the Court's review of a lower court loss, the Court has ultimately denied plenary review.[9] By contrast, the Court has denied federal government NEPA petitions only three times in more than forty years.

Even more strikingly, the federal government has won every single NEPA case the Court has decided. It has a perfect 17-0 record. Indeed, until environmentalists lost Winter v. Natural Resources Defense Council, Inc. in 2008, NEPA plaintiffs had not received a single vote in their favor in more than thirty years in any of the NEPA cases decided after plenary review on the merits. And, the only Justice dissenting before 1976 was Justice William Douglas, in two NEPA cases. But even that sole dissent can fairly be discounted. Justice Douglas always voted for environmentalists, sometimes seemingly regardless of the actual merits.

***

I. NEPA: ORIGINS, SIGNIFICANCE, AND THE SUPREME COURT
NEPA is a fascinating law, but this is not the occasion to repeat in full its rich and unlikely history. Instead, this section reviews the statute's history only insofar as it is necessary for the topic at hand. This discussion includes NEPA's unlikely origins, its transformation by lower federal courts into a much more significant law than its original sponsors anticipated, and, finally, the law's far different treatment by the Supreme Court.

A. NEPA'S ORIGINS
NEPA resulted from a confluence of environmental visionaries, ranging from members of Congress to academic scholars. Senator Henry "Scoop" Jackson and his committee staff are widely credited for promoting the central insight that better environmental results could be achieved by merging the holistic teachings of what was then dubbed "ecosystem ecology" with "systems analysis" for more rational, systematic governmental decision making. By focusing on the need for federal legislation that emphasized planning and conceived of the natural environment as a complex, integrated system, Jackson famously clashed with another environmental political icon of that era, Senator Edmund Muskie, who sought to craft legislation that addressed pollution through a series of distinct, focused regulatory regimes organized by specific environmental media such as air and water.

We now know, of course, that Congress ultimately embraced both approaches in a series of ambitious legislative enactments during the 1970s, some of which trumpeted planning and others media-specific, pollution-control regulation. But Jackson's NEPA was where the modern era of environmental law began, signed into law with great fanfare by President Richard Nixon on January 1, 1970. Much of NEPA's greatness is reflected in the soaring rhetoric found in its first section, extolling the nation to move in bold new directions. Section 101 of NEPA formally "declares that it is the continuing policy of the Federal Government ... to use all practicable means and measures ... to create and maintain conditions under which man and nature can exist in productive harmony ...." The Act announces that it is the "continuing responsibility of the Federal Government to use all practicable means[] consistent with other essential considerations of national policy" to achieve a series of stated objectives, including to "fulfill the responsibilities of each generation as trustee of the environment for succeeding generations," to "assure for all Americans safe, healthful, productive, and esthetically and culturally pleasing surroundings," and to "attain the widest range of beneficial uses of the environment without degradation [or] risk to health or safety ...."

Section 102, however, is where NEPA finds its potential substantive and procedural bite. NEPA's potential substantive mandate is contained within the few words set forth in § 102(1), where "Congress authorizes and directs that, to the fullest extent possible ... the policies, regulations, and public laws of the United States shall be interpreted and administered in accordance with the policies set forth in [NEPA]." The next clause, § 102(2), contains NEPA's procedural mandate and limits that mandate to agencies of the federal government. It directs that, "to the fullest extent possible, ... all agencies of the Federal Government" must prepare what have come to be known as "environmental impact statements" "in every recommendation or report on proposals for legislation and other major Federal actions significantly affecting the quality of the human environment ...."

NEPA's procedural mandate has its own fascinating history. It was the brainchild of Dr. Lynton Keith Caldwell, a political scientist from Indiana University and a formal consultant to Senator Jackson's Senate committee whose salary was paid for by an environmental think tank, the Conservation Foundation. In his testimony before the Senate Committee, Caldwell explained why he thought it was essential for NEPA to be more than merely hortatory and have "an action-forcing, operational aspect," such as a formal requirement that federal agencies consider the environmental impacts of their actions as part of their planning process: "For example, it seems to me that a statement of policy by the Congress should at least consider measures to require the Federal agencies, in submitting proposals, to contain within the proposals an evaluation of the effect of these proposals upon the state of the environment." As a direct result of Caldwell's recommendation, NEPA § 102, as ultimately enacted, included the formal requirement that agencies prepare EISs for major federal actions significantly affecting the quality of the human environment.

What was noticeably missing from NEPA's language, however, was any suggestion that its mandate was subject to judicial enforcement through litigation. NEPA contains no hint of such an enforcement mechanism in either the language of the law or its accompanying legislative history. There is no direct reference to the availability of a private right of action to enforce NEPA or even any indirect reference that might suggest that Congress had at least contemplated the possibility. NEPA's drafters, including Caldwell, apparently believed that the primary enforcement mechanism of NEPA's EIS requirement would not be lawsuits but dialogues among agencies within the executive branch or between the executive branch and Congress. Congress does not appear to have contemplated the kind of heightened judicial role in the enforcement of NEPA subsequently embraced by the federal judiciary.

Precisely because Congress apparently never contemplated a significant role for NEPA in litigation, the dramatic rise of NEPA in the courts in the early 1970s was a surprise to many, including its principal legislative sponsor, Senator Jackson. Some commentators have suggested that Jackson may well have even regretted his sponsorship of NEPA as a result of the unexpected way that NEPA became the basis of so many lawsuits against the federal government. ...

[NEPA led to] an explosion of federal court litigation, especially because many federal agencies, like the AEC, that had historically paid little attention to environmental considerations, delayed before deciding to take seriously Calvert Cliffs' admonition of strict procedural compliance. No doubt because of Wright's characterization of NEPA's procedural mandate as inflexible, other courts looked mostly to those procedural requirements rather than trying to ground their rulings in the statute's substantive provisions. Accordingly, courts reversed federal agency decisions not to prepare EISs at all, rejecting agency claims that their actions were not major, federal, or lacked significant environmental impacts. Courts also faulted federal agencies for failing to take seriously NEPA's requirement that agencies consider a range of alternatives to their proposed actions. The courts created, in effect, a virtual "common law" of detailed NEPA procedural requirements, remarkable for its lack of direct ties to § 102(2)'s specific statutory language.

The President's Council on Environmental Quality (CEQ), which was created by NEPA and charged with its administration, emboldened NEPA further by promulgating a comprehensive set of regulations that effectively codified the demanding set of detailed procedural requirements originally established by the federal courts, frequently beyond the statutory language. The CEQ regulations "became the bible for the federal establishment and for reviewing courts. They became NEPA." CEQ, therefore, undermined the efforts of federal agencies that were skeptical, or even hostile, to NEPA's procedural mandate. Moreover, CEQ's formal action undercut the argument that NEPA's requirements were merely the product of unchecked judicial activism by giving them the imprimatur of the Executive Office of the President.

As NEPA entered its second decade during the 1980s, commentators began to debate the practical reach of NEPA's procedural requirements, but it was clear that NEPA was now significant and settled law. Federal agencies routinely began to complete EISs, preparing 17,714 draft and final EISs from 1970 through 1979.

The EISs themselves were significant. They provided nongovernmental organizations with information on agency actions they never could have produced on their own. Based on that new information, environmentalists could determine what restrictions other environmental-protection laws might impose on the proposed federal agency activity and notify agency officials of the need for compliance with those restrictions. Moreover, NEPA's procedural requirement that EISs be prepared for major federal actions significantly affecting the human environment has had at least two significant substantive-- even if indirect--effects on agency action. First, agencies can seek to avoid preparing an EIS by agreeing to mitigate environmental impacts as necessary to reduce the impact of the proposed action below the "significant" threshold. Agencies prepare approximately 50,000 environmental assessments each year. Although no EIS results, the environmental impact is reduced, which is NEPA's ultimate goal. This has been dubbed the "tourniquet effect." Second, the process of preparing EISs can itself change agency behavior. It is one thing to resist expending resources to acquire information about adverse environmental impacts. It is quite another to ignore such information once it is available and part of the decision-making record. It is the rare government official who would do the latter, especially because NEPA also had the effect of prompting agencies to change the background and expertise of those hired and appointed to include agency personnel more knowledgeable about environmental impact. In many respects, therefore, it is "the NEPA process that makes a difference, far more than the NEPA documents themselves."

Nor is NEPA's sphere of influence limited to the actions of federal agencies, even though NEPA by its own terms is so limited. Inspired by the federal example, as many as thirty-two states have enacted their own state NEPA, known as "SEPAs," some of which are broader than the federal law insomuch as they extend to private action significantly affecting the environment and include a substantive mandate. NEPA had a similar effect internationally. Although early efforts to apply NEPA extraterritorially fell short, other nations have enacted their own environmental-assessment laws, modeled largely after NEPA. At present, approximately 160 countries have such laws, as do international organizations such as the World Bank. Indeed, commentators have sometimes described NEPA as this nation's most significant environmental law export. NEPA's transformative legacy is the product of far more than its statutory language: ambitious early judicial rulings provided the trigger, detailed agency regulations codified and furthered those rulings, and state legislatures and other countries ultimately magnified NEPA's reach by applying its teachings to their own respective jurisdictions.

***

QUESTIONS

1. What is 'environmental impact analysis?'
2. What are some of its advantages?

3. Disadvantages?
4. What do you make of Professor Lazarus' observation: "In many respects, therefore, it is 'the NEPA process that makes a difference, far more than the NEPA documents themselves.'" What does this mean?
5. If you were to craft a statute governing EIA, what would it entail?

II.   STATUTORY LANGUAGE

With that backdrop, let's now turn to NEPA's language. NEPA is an extraordinarily brief and elegant statute. It is in fact the shortest major federal environmental law Congress has ever enacted. Here we focus on NEPA's most important provisions concerning (1) purpose, (2) policies and goals, and (3) cooperation and reports, provided below.

NATIONAL ENVIRONMENTAL POLICY ACT,

PURPOSE, 42 USC 4321

Sec 2. The purposes of this Act are: To declare a national policy which will encourage productive and enjoyable harmony between man and his environment; to promote efforts which will prevent or eliminate damage to the environment and biosphere and stimulate the health and welfare of man; to enrich the understanding of the ecological systems and natural resources important to the Nation; and to establish a Council on Environmental Qualify.

TITLE I - POLICIES AND GOALS: CONGRESSIONAL DECLARATION OF NATIONAL ENVIRONMENTAL POLICY, 42 USC 4331

Sec 101.

(a) The Congress, recognizes the profound impact of man's activity on the interrelations of all components of the natural environment, particularly the profound influences of population. growth, high-density urbanization, industrial expansion, resource exploitation, and new and expanding technological advances and recognizes further the critical importance of restoring and maintaining environmental quality to the overall welfare and development of man, declares that it is the continuing policy of the Federal Government, in cooperation with State and local governments, and other concerned public and private organizations, to use all practicable means and measures, including financial and technical assistance, in a manner calculated to foster and promote the general welfare, to create and maintain conditions under which man and nature can exist in productive harmony, and fulfill the social economic, and other requirements of present and future generations of Americans.

(b) In order to carry out the policy set forth in this Act, it is the continuing responsibility of the Federal Government to use all practicable means, consistent with other essential considerations of national policy, to improve and coordinate Federal plans, functions, programs, and resources to the end that the Nation may—

(1) fulfill the responsibilities of each generation as trustee of the environment for succeeding generations:

(2) assure for all Americans safe, healthful, productive and esthetically and culturally pleasing. surroundings;

(3) attain the widest range of beneficial uses of the environment without degradation, risk to health of safety, or other undesirable and unintended consequences;

(4) preserve important historic, cultural, and natural aspects of our national heritage, and maintain wherever possible, an environment which supports diversity and variety of individual choice;

(5) achieve a balance between population and resource use which will permit high standards of living and a wide sharing of life's amenities; and

(6) Enhance the quality of renewable resources and approach the maximum attainable recycling of depletable resources.

(c) The Congress recognizes that each person should enjoy a healthful environment and that each person has a responsibility to contribute to the preservation and enhancement of the environment.

COOPERATION OF AGENCIES, REPORTS, AVAILABILITY OF INFORMATION-, RECOMMENDATIONS; INTERNATIONAL AND NATIONAL COORDINATION OF EFFORTS, 42 USC 4332

Sec. 102. The Congress authorizes and directs that, to the fullest extent possible:

(1) the policies, regulations, and public laws of the United States shall be interpreted and administered in accordance with the policies set forth in this Act, and (2) all agencies of the Federal Government shall--

(A) utilize a systematic, interdisciplinary approach which will insure the integrated use of the natural and social sciences and the environmental design arts in planning and in decisionmaking which may have an impact on man's environment;

(B) identify and develop methods and procedures, in consultation with the
Council on Environmental Quality established by title II of this Act, which will insure that presently unquantified environmental amenities and values may be given appropriate consideration in decisionmaking along with economic and technical considerations;

(C) Include in every recommendation or report on proposals for legislation and other major Federal actions significantly affecting the quality of the human environment, a detailed statement by the responsible official on—

(i) the environmental impact of the proposed action,
(ii) any adverse environmental effects which cannot be avoided should the proposal be implemented,
(iii) alternatives to the proposed action,
(iv) the relationship between local short-term uses of man's environment and the maintenance and enhancement of long-term productivity, and
(v) any irreversible and irretrievable commitments of resources which would be involved in the proposed action should it be implemented.

Prior to making any detailed statement, the responsible Federal official shall consult with and obtain the comments of any Federal agency which has jurisdiction by law or special expertise with respect to any environmental impact Involved. Copies of such statement and the comments and views of the appropriate Federal, State, and local agencies, which are authorized to develop and enforce environmental standards, shall be made available to the President, the Council on Environmental Quality and to the public as provided by section 552 of title 5, United States Code, and shall accompany the proposal through the existing agency review process.

***

(E) study, develop, and describe appropriate alternatives to recommended courses of action in any proposal which involves unresolved conflicts concerning alternative uses of available resources;

(F) recognize the worldwide and long-range character of environmental problems and, where consistent with the foreign policy of the United States, lend appropriate support to initiatives, resolutions, and programs designed to maximize international cooperation in anticipating and preventing a decline in the quality of mankind's world environment;

(G) make available to States, counties, municipalities, institutions, and individuals, advice and information useful in restoring, maintaining, and enhancing the quality of the environment;

(H) initiate and utilize ecological information in the planning and development of resource-oriented projects; and

(I) assist the Council on Environmental Quality established by title II of this Act.

QUESTIONS

1. What are NEPA's purposes?
2. What were Congress' objectives in enacting NEPA?
3. What is NEPA's 'action-forcing' provision?
4. What are the 'ABC's' of NEPA?
5. Under what circumstances does NEPA require preparation of a "detailed statement?"
6. What is another name for "detailed statement?"
7. What kind of action does NEPA require, and under what circumstances?

III. NEPA (CEQ) REGULATIONS

Curiously, NEPA does not define its key terms. Congress left that to the NEPA-established Council on Environmental Quality, or 'CEQ.' The CEQ serves two primary roles. The first is to advise the President about environmental policy. These days, the CEQ seldom performs this function. The second is to establish regulations to implement NEPA, which are found at 40 C.F.R. Part 1500 et seq., and provided in part below.

NATIONAL ENVIRONMENTAL POLICY ACT (NEPA)
TITLE: 40 -- Protection of Environment
PART 1500 -- PURPOSE, POLICY, AND MANDATE
1500.1 Purpose.

(a) The National Environmental Policy Act (NEPA) is our basic national charter for protection of the environment. It establishes policy, sets goals (section 101), and provides means (section 102) for carrying out the policy. Section 102(2) contains ``action-forcing'' provisions to make sure that federal agencies act according to the letter and spirit of the Act. The regulations that follow implement section 102(2). Their purpose is to tell federal agencies what they must do to comply with the procedures and achieve the goals of the Act. The President, the federal agencies, and the courts share responsibility for enforcing the Act so as to achieve the substantive requirements of section 101.

(b) NEPA procedures must insure that environmental information is available to public officials and citizens before decisions are made and before actions are taken. The information must be of high quality. Accurate scientific analysis, expert agency comments, and public scrutiny are essential to implementing NEPA. Most important, NEPA documents must concentrate on the issues that are truly significant to the action in question, rather than amassing needless detail.

(c) Ultimately, of course, it is not better documents but better decisions that count. NEPA's purpose is not to generate paperwork -even excellent paperwork -- but to foster excellent action. The NEPA process is intended to help public officials make decisions that are based on understanding of environmental consequences, and take actions that protect, restore, and enhance the environment. These regulations provide the direction to achieve this purpose.

1500.2 Policy.
Federal agencies shall to the fullest extent possible:

(a) Interpret and administer the policies, regulations, and public laws of the United States in accordance with the policies set forth in the Act and in these regulations.

(b) Implement procedures to make the NEPA process more useful to decisionmakers and the public; to reduce paperwork and the accumulation of extraneous background data; and to emphasize real environmental issues and alternatives. Environmental impact statements shall be concise, clear, and to the point, and shall be supported by evidence that agencies have made the necessary environmental analyses.

(c) Integrate the requirements of NEPA with other planning and environmental review procedures required by law or by agency practice so that all such procedures run concurrently rather than consecutively.

(d) Encourage and facilitate public involvement in decisions which affect the quality of the human environment.

(e) Use the NEPA process to identify and assess the reasonable alternatives to proposed actions that will avoid or minimize adverse effects of these actions upon the quality of the human environment.

(f) Use all practicable means, consistent with the requirements of the Act and other essential considerations of national policy, to restore and enhance the quality of the human environment and avoid or minimize any possible adverse effects of their actions upon the quality of the human environment.

All agencies of the Federal Government shall comply with these regulations. It is the intent of these regulations to allow each agency flexibility in adapting its implementing procedures authorized by 1507.3 to the requirements of other applicable laws.

1507.2 Agency capability to comply.

Each agency shall be capable (in terms of personnel and other resources) of complying with the requirements enumerated below. Such compliance may include use of other's resources, but the using agency shall itself have sufficient capability to evaluate what others do for it. Agencies shall:

(a) Fulfill the requirements of section 102(2)(A) of the Act to utilize a systematic, interdisciplinary approach which will insure the integrated use of the natural and social sciences and the environmental design arts in planning and in decisionmaking which may have an impact on the human environment. Agencies shall designate a person to be responsible for overall review of agency NEPA compliance.

(b) Identify methods and procedures required by section 102(2)(B) to insure that presently unquantified environmental amenities and values may be given appropriate consideration.

(c) Prepare adequate environmental impact statements pursuant to section 102(2)(C) and comment on statements in the areas where the agency has jurisdiction by law or special expertise or is authorized to develop and enforce environmental standards.

(d) Study, develop, and describe alternatives to recommended courses of action in any proposal which involves unresolved conflicts concerning alternative uses of available resources. This requirement of section 102(2)(E) extends to all such proposals, not just the more limited scope of section 102(2)(C)(iii) where the discussion of alternatives is confined to impact statements.

(e) Comply with the requirements of section 102(2)(H) that the agency initiate and utilize ecological information in the planning and development of resource-oriented projects.

(f) Fulfill the requirements of sections 102(2)(F), 102(2)(G), and 102(2)(I), of the Act ...

1506.11 Emergencies.
(a) Where emergency circumstances make it necessary to take an action with significant environmental impact without observing the provisions of these regulations, the Federal agency taking the action should consult with the Council about alternative arrangements. Agencies and the Council will limit such arrangements to actions necessary to control the immediate impacts of the emergency. Other actions remain subject to NEPA review.

1507.3 Agency procedures.
(a) Not later than eight months after publication of these regulations as finally adopted in the Federal Register, or five months after the establishment of an agency, whichever shall come later, each agency shall as necessary adopt procedures to supplement these regulations. ...

(b) Agency procedures shall comply with these regulations except where compliance would be inconsistent with statutory requirements and shall include:
(1) Those procedures required by 1501.2(d), 1502.9(c)(3), 1505.1, 1506.6(e), and 1508.4.
(2) Specific criteria for and identification of those typical classes of action:
(i) Which normally do require environmental impact statements.
(ii) Which normally do not require either an environmental impact statement or an environmental assessment (categorical exclusions (1508.4)).
(iii) Which normally require environmental assessments but not necessarily environmental impact statements.

(c) Agency procedures may include specific criteria for providing limited exceptions to the provisions of these regulations for classified proposals. They are proposed actions which are specifically authorized under criteria established by an Executive Order or statute to be kept secret in the interest of national defense or foreign policy and are in fact properly classified pursuant to such Executive Order or statute. Environmental assessments and environmental impact statements which address classified proposals may be safeguarded and restricted from public dissemination in accordance with agencies' own regulations applicable to classified information. These documents may be organized so that classified portions can be included as annexes, in order that the unclassified portions can be made available to the public.

PART 1508 -- TERMINOLOGY AND INDEX

1508.3 ``Affecting" means will or may have an effect on.

1508.4 ``Categorical exclusion" means a category of actions which do not individually or cumulatively have a significant effect on the human environment and which have been found to have no such effect in procedures adopted by a Federal agency in implementation of these regulations (1507.3) and for which, therefore, neither an environmental assessment nor an environmental impact statement is required. An agency may decide in its procedures or otherwise, to prepare environmental assessments for the reasons stated in 1508.9 even though it is not required to do so. Any procedures under this section shall provide for extraordinary circumstances in which a normally excluded action may have a significant environmental effect.

1508.5 ``Cooperating agency" means any Federal agency other than a lead agency which has jurisdiction by law or special expertise with respect to any environmental impact involved in a proposal (or a reasonable alternative) for legislation or other major Federal action significantly affecting the quality of the human environment. The selection and responsibilities of a cooperating agency are described in 1501.6. A State or local agency of similar qualifications or, when the effects are on a reservation, an Indian Tribe, may by agreement with the lead agency become a cooperating agency.

1508.6 ``Council" means the Council on Environmental Quality established by title II of the Act.

1508.7 ``Cumulative impact" is the impact on the environment which results from the incremental impact of the action when added to other past, present, and reasonably foreseeable future actions regardless of what agency (Federal or non-Federal) or person undertakes such other actions. Cumulative impacts can result from individually minor but collectively significant actions taking place over a period of time.

1508.8 ``Effects" include:
(a) Direct effects, which are caused by the action and occur at the same time and place.
(b) Indirect effects, which are caused by the action and are later in time or farther removed in distance, but are still reasonably foreseeable. Indirect effects may include growth inducing effects and other effects related to induced changes in the pattern of land use, population density or growth rate, and related effects on air and water and other natural systems, including ecosystems.

Effects and impacts as used in these regulations are synonymous. Effects includes ecological (such as the effects on natural resources and on the components, structures, and functioning of affected ecosystems), aesthetic, historic, cultural, economic, social, or health, whether direct, indirect, or cumulative. Effects may also include those resulting from actions which may have both beneficial and detrimental effects, even if on balance the agency believes that the effect will be beneficial.

1508.9 ``Environmental assessment":

(a) Means a concise public document for which a Federal agency is responsible that serves to:

(1) Briefly provide sufficient evidence and analysis for determining whether to prepare an environmental impact statement or a finding of no significant impact.

(2) Aid an agency's compliance with the Act when no environmental impact statement is necessary.

(3) Facilitate preparation of a statement when one is necessary.

(b) Shall include brief discussions of the need for the proposal, of alternatives as required by section 102(2)(E), of the environmental impacts of the proposed action and alternatives, and a listing of agencies and persons consulted.

1508.10 ``Environmental document" includes the documents specified in 1508.9 (environmental assessment), 1508.11 (environmental impact statement), 1508.13 (finding of no significant impact), and 1508.22 (notice of intent).

1508.11 ``Environmental impact statement" means a detailed written statement as required by section 102(2)(C) of the Act.

1508.12 ``Federal agency" means all agencies of the Federal Government. It does not mean the Congress, the Judiciary, or the President, including the performance of staff functions for the President in his Executive Office. It also includes for purposes of these regulations States and units of general local government and Indian tribes assuming NEPA responsibilities under section 104(h) of the Housing and Community Development Act of 1974.

1508.13 ``Finding of no significant impact" means a document by a Federal agency briefly presenting the reasons why an action, not otherwise excluded (1508.4), will not have a significant effect on the human environment and for which an environmental impact statement therefore will not be prepared. It shall include the environmental assessment or a summary of it and shall note any other environmental documents related to it (1501.7(a)(5)). If the assessment is included, the finding need not repeat any of the discussion in the assessment but may incorporate it by reference.

1508.14 ``Human environment" shall be interpreted comprehensively to include the natural and physical environment and the relationship of people with that environment. (See the definition of ``effects" (1508.8).) This means that economic or social effects are not intended by themselves to require preparation of an environmental impact statement. When an environmental impact statement is prepared and economic or social and natural or physical environmental effects are interrelated, then the environmental impact statement will discuss all of these effects on the human environment.

1508.15 "Jurisdiction by law" means agency authority to approve, veto, or finance all or part of the proposal.

1508.16 ``Lead agency" means the agency or agencies preparing or having taken primary responsibility for preparing the environmental impact statement.

1508.17 Legislation. [Omitted]

1508.18 ``Major Federal action'' includes actions with effects that may be major and which are potentially subject to Federal control and responsibility. Major reinforces but does not have a meaning independent of significantly (1508.27). Actions include the circumstance where the responsible officials fail to act and that failure to act is reviewable by courts or administrative tribunals under the Administrative Procedure Act or other applicable law as agency action.

(a) Actions include new and continuing activities, including projects and programs entirely or partly financed, assisted, conducted, regulated, or approved by federal agencies; new or revised agency rules, regulations, plans, policies, or procedures; and legislative proposals (1506.8, 1508.17). Actions do not include funding assistance solely in the form of general revenue sharing funds, distributed under the State and Local Fiscal Assistance Act of 1972, 31 U.S.C. 1221 et seq., with no Federal agency control over the subsequent use of such funds. Actions do not include bringing judicial or administrative civil or criminal enforcement actions.

(b) Federal actions tend to fall within one of the following categories:

 (1) Adoption of official policy, such as rules, regulations, and interpretations adopted pursuant to the Administrative Procedure Act, 5 U.S.C. 551 et seq.; treaties and international conventions or agreements; formal documents establishing an agency's policies which will result in or substantially alter agency programs.
 (2) Adoption of formal plans, such as official documents prepared or approved by federal agencies which guide or prescribe alternative uses of Federal resources, upon which future agency actions will be based.
 (3) Adoption of programs, such as a group of concerted actions to implement a specific policy or plan; systematic and connected agency decisions allocating agency resources to implement a specific statutory program or executive directive.
 (4) Approval of specific projects, such as construction or management activities located in a defined geographic area. Projects include actions approved by permit or other regulatory decision as well as federal and federally assisted activities.

1508.19 ``Matter'' [Omitted]

1508.20 ``Mitigation'' includes:
(a) Avoiding the impact altogether by not taking a certain action or parts of an action.

(b) Minimizing impacts by limiting the degree or magnitude of the action and its implementation.

(c) Rectifying the impact by repairing, rehabilitating, or restoring the affected environment.

(d) Reducing or eliminating the impact over time by preservation and maintenance operations during the life of the action.

(e) Compensating for the impact by replacing or providing substitute resources or environments.

1508.21``NEPA process'' means all measures necessary for compliance with the requirements of section 2 and title I of NEPA.

1508.22 Notice of intent [Omitted]
1508.23 Proposal [Omitted]
1508.24 Referring agency [Omitted]

1508.25 Scope. Scope consists of the range of actions, alternatives, and impacts to be considered in an environmental impact statement. The scope of an individual statement may depend on its relationships to other statements (1502.20 and 1508.28). To determine the scope of environmental impact statements, agencies shall consider 3 types of actions, 3 types of alternatives, and 3 types of impacts. They include:

(a) Actions (other than unconnected single actions) which may be:
(1) Connected actions, which means that they are closely related and therefore should be discussed in the same impact statement. Actions are connected if they:
(i) Automatically trigger other actions which may require environmental impact statements.
(ii) Cannot or will not proceed unless other actions are taken previously or simultaneously.
(iii) Are interdependent parts of a larger action and depend on the larger action for their justification.
(2) Cumulative actions, which when viewed with other proposed actions have cumulatively significant impacts and should therefore be discussed in the same impact statement.
(3) Similar actions, which when viewed with other reasonably foreseeable or proposed agency actions, have similarities that provide a basis for evaluating their environmental consequences together, such as common timing or geography. An agency may wish to analyze these actions in the same impact statement. It should do so when the best way to assess adequately the combined impacts of similar actions or reasonable alternatives to such actions is to treat them in a single impact statement.

(b) Alternatives, which include:
(1) No action alternative.
(2) Other reasonable courses of actions.
(3) Mitigation measures (not in the proposed action).

(c) Impacts, which may be: (1) Direct; (2) indirect; (3) cumulative.

1508.26 Special expertise. ``Special expertise'' means statutory responsibility, agency mission, or related program experience.

1508.27 Significantly. ``Significantly'' as used in NEPA requires considerations of both context and intensity:

(a) Context. This means that the significance of an action must be analyzed in several contexts such as society as a whole (human, national), the affected region, the affected interests, and the locality. Significance varies with the setting of the proposed action. For instance, in the case of a site-specific action, significance would usually depend upon the effects in the locale rather than in the world as a whole. Both short- and long-term effects are relevant.

(b) Intensity. This refers to the severity of impact. Responsible officials must bear in mind that more than one agency may make decisions about partial aspects of a major action. The following should be considered in evaluating intensity:
(1) Impacts that may be both beneficial and adverse. A significant effect may exist even if the Federal agency believes that on balance the effect will be beneficial.
(2) The degree to which the proposed action affects public health or safety.
(3) Unique characteristics of the geographic area such as proximity to historic or cultural resources, park lands, prime farmlands, wetlands, wild and scenic rivers, or ecologically critical areas.

(4) The degree to which the effects on the quality of the human environment are likely to be highly controversial.

(5) The degree to which the possible effects on the human environment are highly uncertain or involve unique or unknown risks.

(6) The degree to which the action may establish a precedent for future actions with significant effects or represents a decision in principle about a future consideration.

(7) Whether the action is related to other actions with individually insignificant but cumulatively significant impacts. Significance exists if it is reasonable to anticipate a cumulatively significant impact on the environment. Significance cannot be avoided by terming an action temporary or by breaking it down into small component parts.

(8) The degree to which the action may adversely affect districts, sites, highways, structures, or objects listed in or eligible for listing in the National Register of Historic Places or may cause loss or destruction of significant scientific, cultural, or historical resources.

(9) The degree to which the action may adversely affect an endangered or threatened species or its habitat that has been determined to be critical under the Endangered Species Act of 1973.

(10) Whether the action threatens a violation of Federal, State, or local law or requirements imposed for the protection of the environment.

1508.28 Tiering. ``Tiering'' refers to the coverage of general matters in broader environmental impact statements (such as national program or policy statements) with subsequent narrower statements or environmental analyses (such as regional or basinwide program statements or ultimately site-specific statements) incorporating by reference the general discussions and concentrating solely on the issues specific to the statement subsequently prepared. Tiering is appropriate when the sequence of statements or analyses is:

(a) From a program, plan, or policy environmental impact statement to a program, plan, or policy statement or analysis of lesser scope or to a site-specific statement or analysis.

(b) From an environmental impact statement on a specific action at an early stage (such as need and site selection) to a supplement (which is preferred) or a subsequent statement or analysis at a later stage (such as environmental mitigation). Tiering in such cases is appropriate when it helps the lead agency to focus on the issues which are ripe for decision and exclude from consideration issues already decided or not yet ripe.

***

The NEPA process can be imagined with the following diagram:

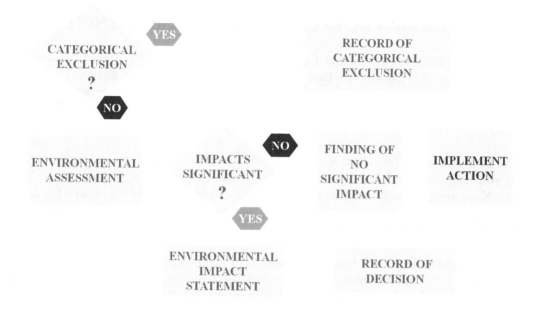

PROPOSED
ACTION

CATEGORICAL
EXCLUSION
?

YES

RECORD OF
CATEGORICAL
EXCLUSION

NO

ENVIRONMENTAL
ASSESSMENT

IMPACTS
SIGNIFICANT
?

NO

FINDING OF
NO
SIGNIFICANT
IMPACT

IMPLEMENT
ACTION

YES

ENVIRONMENTAL
IMPACT
STATEMENT

RECORD OF
DECISION

See if you can connect the lines between the figures in the diagram above.

QUESTIONS

1. Who wrote the NEPA regulations? Who or what is the CEQ?
2. What is the purpose of these regulations?
3. What is a "categorical exclusion," and when is it used?
4. What is an "environmental assessment," and what is its purpose?
5. What is a "major federal action?"
6. What is "major"?
7. What is a "federal"
8. What is "action"?
9. What is "significant"
10. What is "affecting?"
11. What is/are "effects?"
12. What is "human environment?"
13. What "impacts" are considered in determining whether an impact is significant?
14. What are "alternatives?"
15. What is "mitigation," and when is it used?
16. What is "tiering"?

IV.   NEPA IN THE U.S. SUPREME COURT

The SCOTUS has taken an unusual interest in NEPA through the years. To be sure, it has issued opinions in 19 cases in a little more than 50 years, that is, about one major NEPA decision every other year. The "environment" lost in all but one of them, including when agencies can ignore or evade NEPA (depends); whether federal courts can require more process than NEPA does (no); whether "significant" includes psychological effects (no); whether agencies must consider the "worst case scenario" (no); whether and the extent to which agencies must consider indirect (off-site) impacts (depends); and when an agency must supplement an existing EIS to account for a change in circumstances (depends). Questions follow each case.

A. CATEGORICAL EXCLUSIONS AND EMERGENCIES

In Winter v. Natural Resources Defense Council ("NRDC"), 129 S. Ct. (2009), the SCOTUS reversed the U.S. Court of Appeals for the Ninth Circuit and ruled 5-4 that the U.S. Navy's interests in security and military preparedness outweighs the plaintiffs' interest in protecting whales and other marine mammals from acoustic harm caused by submarine seeking sonar devices.

In Winter, the Court voted to lift a "narrowly tailored" preliminary injunction to enjoin the U.S. Navy's use of mid-frequency active sonar off the southern California coast, known as the "SOCAL exercise." The Navy regards mid-frequency active sonar as the sole effective means for detecting and tracking enemy diesel-electric submarines. The Navy's sonar, however, also disrupts marine mammals that rely upon their own sonar.

The Natural Resources Defense Council challenged the Navy's failure to perform an environmental impact statement under the National Environmental Policy Act ("NEPA") and attached other claims under the Coastal Zone Management Act ("CZMA") and the Endangered Species Act.

Finding the "possibility" of causing irreparable environmental harm, the district court issued a preliminary injunction requiring, inter alia, the Navy to "power down" (1) completely if marine mammals were spotted within 2,200-yards of Navy vessels ships or (2) by 75 percent in the presence of other significant "surface ducting" conditions.

Following the initial grant of preliminary injunction, the Bush administration then identified the SOCAL exercise to be of "paramount interest to the United States" and granted the Navy a waiver from the CZMA. Correspondingly, the White House Council on Environmental Quality granted the Navy's request for "alternative arrangements for compliance with" NEPA due to a national "emergency."

Thereafter, the Navy appealed the lower court's injunction to the Ninth Circuit. Rather than lift the injunction, the Ninth Circuit remanded to have the district court weigh the exemption's impacts on the injunction.

On remand the lower court threw out the "emergency" premise behind the Council on Environmental Quality's "alternative arrangements" decision. While finding it "constitutionally suspicious," the lower court did not rule on the legality of the waiver of CZMA requirements. The Ninth Circuit affirmed, finding the lower court had not abused its discretion in issuing the limited preliminary injunction. The Ninth Circuit stayed the injunction's "power down" provisions, however, allowing the Navy to appeal the case to the Supreme Court. The Navy still would be subject to the injunction's four less restrictive conditions that the Navy did not appeal, including a 12 nautical-mile no-sonar zone along the California coast and enhanced monitoring requirements.

Writing for the majority, Chief Justice Roberts reversed the Ninth Circuit 5-4 and vacated the injunction and its "power down" requirements on two grounds. First, the majority held that the lower courts' preliminary injunction analysis applied an incorrect standard that did not require a sufficient showing of harm. It held that the lower court should have asked whether the SOCAL exercise would result in the "likelihood" rather than the "possibility" of irreparable harm, because the "possibility" standard is "too lenient." Second, it determined the lower courts had given short shrift to the Navy's interests in security and preparedness.

Turning to the merits, the Court held first that respondents had not met their burden of showing irreparable harm. The Court reached this conclusion notwithstanding the Navy's own countervailing data, which while both lower courts found to be "cursory, unsupported by evidence [and] unconvincing," still revealed that sonar training had resulted in 564 physical injuries and 170,000 behavioral disturbances of marine mammals. The environmental respondents also argued that countless other reported and undetected mass strandings of marine animals had been "associated" with sonar training. Instead, the Court concluded that the Navy had been conducting sonar training for 40 years without documented cases of irreparable harm.

Next, the majority concluded that, properly balanced, the Navy's military interests far outweighed respondents' interest in protecting and observing marine mammals. It reasoned that balancing the public interest supporting the Navy's national security and military preparedness against NRDC's public interest in protecting marine mammals for observation and education "does not strike us as a close question." Disagreeing with the lower courts, the majority found the equities tipped strongly in the Navy's favor: "To be prepared for war is one of the most effectual means of preserving peace." The majority noted that the president deemed active sonar as "essential to national security" because adversaries possess 300 submarines. Mid-frequency active sonar, the Navy argued, is "the most effective technology" for "antisubmarine warfare, a top war-fighting priority for the Pacific Fleet." Citing senior naval officers, the majority observed the importance of training ship crews with all possible war stressors occurring simultaneously, thus making mid-frequency active sonar "mission critical" for training. The imposition of the mitigating regulations would require the Navy "to deploy an inadequately trained submarine force," which would in turn jeopardize the safety of the fleet. Imposition of other mitigating factors, the majority held, could decrease the overall effectiveness of sonar training generally. On the other hand, "[f]or the plaintiffs, the most serious possible injury would be harm to an unknown number of the marine mammals that they study and observe..." in contrast, forcing the Navy to deploy an inadequately trained antisubmarine force jeopardizes the safety of the fleet." The majority concluded that the "public interest in conducting training exercises with active sonar under realistic conditions plainly outweighs the interests advanced by the plaintiffs."

Thus the majority found the district court had applied the incorrect standard and abused its discretion on the merits. Finding in favor of the Navy, the court reversed the decisions below and did not impose the lower court's "power down" requirements.

While the majority did not engage sustainability principles at all, the dissent concerned itself with just how the SOCAL exercise affected marine mammals. Justice Ruth Bader Ginsburg, joined by Justice David Souter, dissented: "In light of the likely, substantial harm to the environment, NRDC's almost inevitable success on the merits of its claim that NEPA required the Navy to prepare an EIS, the history of this litigation, and the public interest, I cannot agree that the mitigation measures the District Court imposed signal an abuse of discretion."

In particular, Justice Ginsburg had no trouble finding irreparable harm, and thus, diminution of sustainability. She was dismayed about how the Court could overlook "170,000 behavioral disturbances, including 8,000 instances of temporary hearing loss; and 564 Level A harms, including 436 injuries to a beaked whale population numbering only 1,121." She also observed that, "sonar is linked to mass strandings of marine mammals, hemorrhaging around the brain and ears, acute spongiotic changes in the central nervous system, and lesions in vital organs." On balancing the competing interests of the parties, Ginsburg concluded that these injuries "cannot be lightly dismissed, even in the face an alleged risk to the effectiveness of the [Navy's training exercises.]"

Charting a more solicitous course, Justice John Paul Stevens, joining Justice Stephen G. Breyer, concurred in part and dissented in part. They would have found that neither court below adequately explained why the balance of equities favored the two specific mitigation measures being challenged over the Navy's assertions that it could not effectively conduct its exercises subject to the conditions. They would have remanded for a more narrowly tailored injunction, but continued the Ninth Circuit's stay conditions as the status quo until the completion of the SOCAL exercise, thus promoting sustainability to some extent.

The postscript is that the Navy concluded its SOCAL exercise and completed its NEPA environmental impact statement for the SOCAL exercise in January 2009.

QUESTIONS
1. Why is it important that NEPA provide for exclusions?
2. How do the NEPA regulations address categorical exclusions? Emergencies?
3. What happened in Winters?
4. How did the SCOTUS rule, and why?
5. Do you agree or disagree? Explain.
6. Do you agree or disagree with the dissent? Explain.

B. ADDITIONAL PROCESS

VERMONT YANKEE V. NRDC
98 S.Ct. 1197 (1978)

Mr. Justice REHNQUIST delivered the opinion of the Court.

In 1946, Congress enacted the Administrative Procedure Act, which as we have noted elsewhere was not only "a new, basic and comprehensive regulation of procedures in many agencies," but was also a legislative enactment which settled "long-continued and hard-fought contentions, and enacts a formula upon which opposing social and political forces have come to rest."[The APA addresses insofar as with] rulemaking, requires in subsection (b) that "notice of proposed rule making shall be published in the Federal Register . . .," describes the contents of that notice, and goes on to require in subsection (c) that after the notice the agency "shall give interested persons an opportunity to participate in the rule making through submission of written data, views, or arguments with or without opportunity for oral presentation. After consideration of the relevant matter presented, the agency shall incorporate in the rules adopted a concise general statement of their basis and purpose." Interpreting this provision of the Act in United States v. Allegheny-Ludlum Steel Corp., and United States v. Florida East Coast R. Co., we held that generally speaking this section of the Act established the maximum procedural requirements which Congress was willing to have the courts impose upon agencies in conducting rulemaking procedures. Agencies are free to grant additional procedural rights in the exercise of their discretion, but reviewing courts are generally not free to impose them if the agencies have not chosen to grant them. This is not to say necessarily that there are no circumstances which would ever justify a court in overturning agency action because of a failure to employ procedures beyond those required by the statute. But such circumstances, if they exist, are extremely rare.

We [] conclude that the court improperly intruded into the agency's decision making process, making it necessary for us to reverse and remand with respect to this part of the cases also.

I.

A

Under the Atomic Energy Act of 1954, The Atomic Energy Commission was given broad regulatory authority over the development of nuclear energy. Under the terms of the Act, a utility seeking to construct and operate a nuclear power plant must obtain a separate permit or license at both the construction and the operation stage of the project. In order to obtain the construction permit, the utility must file a preliminary safety analysis report, an environmental report, and certain information regarding the antitrust implications of the proposed project. This application then undergoes exhaustive review by the Commission's staff and by the Advisory Committee on Reactor Safeguards (ACRS), a group of distinguished experts in the field of atomic energy. Both groups submit to the Commission their own evaluations, which then become part of the record of the utility's application. The Commission staff also undertakes the review required by the National Environmental Policy Act of 1969 (NEPA), 42 U.S.C. § 4321 et seq., and prepares a draft environmental impact statement, which, after being circulated for comment, is revised and becomes a final environmental impact statement. Thereupon a three-member Atomic Safety and Licensing Board conducts a public adjudicatory hearing, and reaches a decision4 which can be appealed to the Atomic Safety and Licensing Appeal Board, and currently, in the Commission's discretion, to the Commission itself. The final agency decision may be appealed to the courts of appeals. The same sort of process occurs when the utility applies for a license to operate the plant, except that a hearing need only be held in contested cases and may be limited to the matters in controversy.

***

D

With respect to the challenge of Vermont Yankee's license, the court first ruled that in the absence of effective rulemaking proceedings, the Commission must deal with the environmental impact of fuel reprocessing and disposal in individual licensing proceedings. The court then examined the rulemaking proceedings and, despite the fact that it appeared that the agency employed all the procedures required by 5 U.S.C. § 553 (1976 ed.) and more, the court determined the proceedings to be inadequate and overturned the rule. Accordingly, the Commission's determination with respect to Vermont Yankee's license was also remanded for further proceedings.

With respect to the permit to Consumers Power, the court first held that the environmental impact statement for construction of the Midland reactors was fatally defective for failure to examine energy conservation as an alternative to a plant of this size. ...

A

Petitioner Vermont Yankee first argues that the Commission may grant a license to operate a nuclear reactor without any consideration of waste disposal and fuel reprocessing. We find, however, that this issue is no longer presented by the record in this case. The Commission does not contend that it is not required to consider the environmental impact of the spent fuel processes when licensing nuclear power plants. Indeed, the Commission has publicly stated subsequent to the Court of Appeals' decision in the instant case that consideration of the environmental impact of the back end of the fuel cycle in "the environmental impact statements for individual LWR's [light-water power reactors] would represent a full and candid assessment of costs and benefits consistent with the legal requirements and spirit of NEPA." Even prior to the Court of Appeals decision the Commission implicitly agreed that it would consider the back end of the fuel cycle in all licensing proceedings: It indicated that it was not necessary to reopen prior licensing proceedings because "the environmental effects of the uranium fuel cycle have been shown to be relatively insignificant," and thus incorporation of those effects into the cost-benefit analysis would not change the results of such licensing proceedings. Thus, at this stage of the proceedings the only question presented for review in this regard is whether the Commission may consider the environmental impact of the fuel processes when licensing nuclear reactors. In addition to the weight which normally attaches to the agency's determination of such a question, other reasons support the Commission's conclusion.

Vermont Yankee will produce annually well over 100 pounds of radioactive wastes, some of which will be highly toxic. The Commission itself, in a pamphlet published by its information office, clearly recognizes that these wastes "pose the most severe potential health hazard . . . ." U.S. Atomic Energy Commission, Radioactive Wastes 12 (1965). Many of these substances must be isolated for anywhere from 600 to hundreds of thousands of years. It is hard to argue that these wastes do not constitute "adverse environmental effects which cannot be avoided should the proposal be implemented," or that by operating nuclear power plants we are not making " irreversible and irretrievable commitments of resources." 42 U.S.C. §§ 4332(2)(C)(ii), (v). As the Court of Appeals recognized, the environmental impact of the radioactive wastes produced by a nuclear power plant is analytically indistinguishable from the environmental effects of "the stack gases produced by a coal-burning power plant." For these reasons we hold that the Commission acted well within its statutory authority when it considered the back end of the fuel cycle in individual licensing proceedings.

B

But this much is absolutely clear. Absent constitutional constraints or extremely compelling circumstances the "administrative agencies 'should be free to fashion their own rules of procedure and to pursue methods of inquiry capable of permitting them to discharge their multitudinous duties.' " Indeed, our cases could hardly be more explicit in this regard. The Court has, as we noted in FCC v. Schreiber, upheld this principle in a variety of applications, including that case where the District Court, instead of inquiring into the validity of the Federal Communications Commission's exercise of its rulemaking authority, devised procedures to be followed by the agency on the basis of its conception of how the public and private interest involved could best be served. Examining § 4(j) of the Communications Act of 1934, the Court unanimously held that the Court of Appeals erred in upholding that action. And the basic reason for this decision was the Court of Appeals' serious departure from the very basic tenet of administrative law that agencies should be free to fashion their own rules of procedure.

***

"At least in the absence of substantial justification for doing otherwise, a reviewing court may not, after determining that additional evidence is requisite for adequate review, proceed by dictating to the agency the methods, procedures, and time dimension of the needed inquiry and ordering the results to be reported to the court without opportunity for further consideration on the basis of the new evidence by the agency. Such a procedure clearly runs the risk of 'propel[ling] the court into the domain which Congress has set aside exclusively for the administrative agency.' SEC v. Chenery Corp., 332 U.S. 194, 196, 67 (1947)."

***

Respondent NRDC also argues that the fact that the Commission's inquiry was undertaken in the context of NEPA somehow permits a court to require procedures beyond those specified in § 4 of the APA when investigating factual issues through rulemaking. The Court of Appeals was apparently also of this view, indicating that agencies may be required to "develop new procedures to accomplish the innovative task of implementing NEPA through rulemaking." But we search in vain for something in NEPA which would mandate such a result. We have before observed that "NEPA does not repeal by implication any other statute." In fact, just two Terms ago, we emphasized that the only procedural requirements imposed by NEPA are those stated in the plain language of the Act. Thus, it is clear NEPA cannot serve as the basis for a substantial revision of the carefully constructed procedural specifications of the APA.

In short, nothing in the APA, NEPA, the circumstances of this case, the nature of the issues being considered, past agency practice, or the statutory mandate under which the Commission operates permitted the court to review and overturn the rulemaking proceeding on the basis of the procedural devices employed (or not employed) by the Commission so long as the Commission employed at least the statutory minima, a matter about which there is no doubt in this case.

***

The court should engage in this kind of review and not stray beyond the judicial province to explore the procedural format or to impose upon the agency its own notion of which procedures are "best" or most likely to further some vague, undefined public good.

***

QUESTIONS

1. Are agencies generally free to afford more process than required? Courts?
2. What happened in Vermont Yankee?
3. What was at issue?
4. How did the SCOTUS decide the issue?
5. Do you agree or disagree? Explain.

C. ALTERNATIVES

STRYCKER'S BAY NEIGHBORHOOD COUNCIL V. KARLEN
100 S.Ct. 497 (1980)

PER CURIAM.
The protracted nature of this litigation is perhaps best illustrated by the identity of the original federal defendant, "George Romney, Secretary of the Department of Housing and Urban Development." At the center of this dispute is the site of a proposed low-income housing project to be constructed on Manhattan's Upper West Side. In 1962, the New York City Planning Commission (Commission), acting in conjunction with the United States Department of Housing and Urban Development (HUD), began formulating a plan for the renewal of 20 square blocks known as the "West Side Urban Renewal Area" (WSURA) through a joint effort on the part of private parties and various government agencies. As originally written, the plan called for a mix

of 70% middle-income housing and 30% low-income housing and designated the site at issue here as the location of one of the middle-income projects. In 1969, after substantial progress toward completion of the plan, local agencies in New York determined that the number of low-income units proposed for WSURA would be insufficient to satisfy an increased need for such units. In response to this shortage the Commission amended the plan to designate the site as the future location of a high-rise building containing 160 units of low-income housing. HUD approved this amendment in December 1972.

Meanwhile, in October 1971, the Trinity Episcopal School Corp. (Trinity), which had participated in the plan by building a combination school and middle-income housing development at a nearby location, sued in the United States District Court for the Southern District of New York to enjoin the Commission and HUD from constructing low-income housing on the site. The present respondents, Roland N. Karlen, Alvin C. Hudgins, and the Committee of Neighbors To Insure a Normal Urban Environment (CONTINUE), intervened as plaintiffs, while petitioner Strycker's Bay Neighborhood Council, Inc., intervened as a defendant.

The District Court entered judgment in favor of petitioners. It concluded, inter alia, that petitioners had not violated the National Environmental Policy Act of 1969 (NEPA).

On respondents' appeal, the Second Circuit affirmed all but the District Court's treatment of the NEPA claim. While the Court of Appeals agreed with the District Court that HUD was not required to prepare a full-scale environmental impact statement under § 102(2)(C) of NEPA, it held that HUD had not complied with § 102(2)(E), which requires an agency to "study, develop, and describe appropriate alternatives to recommended courses of action in any proposal which involves unresolved conflicts concerning alternative uses of available resources."According to the Court of Appeals, any consideration by HUD of alternatives to placing low-income housing on the site "was either highly limited or nonexistent." Citing the "background of urban environmental factors" behind HUD's decision, the Court of Appeals remanded the case, requiring HUD to prepare a "statement of possible alternatives, the consequences thereof and the facts and reasons for and against . . . ." The statement was not to reflect "HUD's concept or the Housing Authority's views as to how these agencies would choose to resolve the city's low income group housing situation," but rather was to explain "how within the framework of the Plan its objective of economic integration can best be achieved with a minimum of adverse environmental impact." The Court of Appeals believed that, given such an assessment of alternatives, "the agencies with the cooperation of the interested parties should be able to arrive at an equitable solution."

On remand, HUD prepared a lengthy report entitled Special Environmental Clearance (1977). After marshaling the data, the report asserted that, "while the choice of Site 30 for development as a 100 percent low-income project has raised valid questions about the potential social environmental impacts involved, the problems associated with the impact on social fabric and community structures are not considered so serious as to require that this component be rated as unacceptable." The last portion of the report incorporated a study wherein the Commission evaluated nine alternative locations for the project and found none of them acceptable. While HUD's report conceded that this study may not have considered all possible alternatives, it credited the Commission's conclusion that any relocation of the units would entail an unacceptable delay of two years or more. According to HUD, "[m]easured against the environmental costs associated with the minimum two-year delay, the benefits seem insufficient to justify a mandated substitution of sites."

After soliciting the parties' comments on HUD's report, the District Court again entered judgment in favor of petitioners. The court was "impressed with [HUD's analysis] as being thorough and exhaustive," and found that "HUD's consideration of the alternatives was neither arbitrary nor capricious"; on the contrary, "[i]t was done in good faith and in full accordance with the law."

On appeal, the Second Circuit vacated and remanded again. The appellate court focused upon that part of HUD's report where the agency considered and rejected alternative sites, and in particular upon HUD's reliance on the delay such a relocation would entail. The Court of Appeals purported to recognize that its role in reviewing HUD's decision was defined by the Administrative Procedure Act (APA), 5 U.S.C. § 706(2)(A), which provides that agency actions should be set aside if found to be "arbitrary, capricious, an abuse of discretion, or otherwise not in accordance with law . . . ." Additionally, however, the Court of Appeals looked to "[t]he provisions of NEPA" for "the substantive standards necessary to review the merits of agency decisions . . . ." The Court of Appeals conceded that HUD had "given 'consideration' to alternatives" to redesignating the site. Nevertheless, the court believed that " 'consideration' is not an end in itself." Concentrating on HUD's finding that development of an alternative location would entail an unacceptable delay, the appellate court held that such delay could not be "an overriding factor" in HUD's decision to proceed with the development. According to the court, when HUD considers such projects, "environmental factors, such as crowding low-income housing into a concentrated area, should be given determinative weight." The Court of Appeals therefore remanded the case to the District Court, instructing HUD to attack the shortage of low-income housing in a manner that would avoid the "concentration" of such housing on Site 30.

In Vermont Yankee Nuclear Power Corp. v. NRDC, 435 U.S. 519, 558 (1978), we stated that NEPA, while establishing "significant substantive goals for the Nation," imposes upon agencies duties that are "essentially procedural." As we stressed in that case, NEPA was designed "to insure a fully informed and well-considered decision," but not necessarily "a decision the judges of the Court of Appeals or of this Court would have reached had they been members of the decisionmaking unit of the agency." Vermont Yankee cuts sharply against the Court of Appeals' conclusion that an agency, in selecting a course of action, must elevate environmental concerns over other appropriate considerations. On the contrary, once an agency has made a decision subject to NEPA's procedural requirements, the only role for a court is to insure that the agency has considered the environmental consequences; it cannot " 'interject itself within the area of discretion of the executive as to the choice of the action to be taken.' " Kleppe v. Sierra Club, 427 U.S. 390, 410, n. 21 (1976).

In the present litigation there is no doubt that HUD considered the environmental consequences of its decision to redesignate the proposed site for low-income housing. NEPA requires no more. The petitions for certiorari are granted, and the judgment of the Court of Appeals is therefore

Reversed.

Mr. Justice MARSHALL, dissenting.

The issue raised by these cases is far more difficult than the per curiam opinion suggests. The Court of Appeals held that the Secretary of Housing and Urban Development (HUD) had acted arbitrarily in concluding that prevention of a delay in the construction process justified the selection of a housing site which could produce adverse social environmental effects, including racial and economic concentration. Today the majority responds that "once an agency has made a decision subject to NEPA's procedural requirements, the only role for a court is to insure that the agency has considered the environmental consequences," and that in this case "there is no doubt that HUD considered the environmental consequences of its decision to redesignate the proposed site for low-income housing. NEPA requires no more." The majority finds support for this conclusion in the closing paragraph of our decision in Vermont Yankee Nuclear Power Corp. v. NRDC, 435 U.S. 519, 558 (1978).

Vermont Yankee does not stand for the broad proposition that the majority advances today. The relevant passage in that opinion was meant to be only a "further observation of some relevance to this case," that "observation" was a response to this Court's perception that the Court of Appeals in that case was attempting "under the guise of judicial review of agency action" to assert its own policy judgment as to the desirability of developing nuclear energy as an energy source for this Nation, a judgment which is properly left to Congress. The Court of Appeals had remanded the case to the agency because of "a single alleged oversight on a peripheral issue, urged by parties who never fully cooperated or indeed raised the issue below," It was in this context that the Court remarked that "NEPA does set forth significant substantive goals for the Nation, but its mandate to the agencies is essentially procedural." (emphasis supplied). Accordingly, "[a]dministrative decisions should be set aside in this context, as in every other, only for substantial procedural or substantive reasons as mandated by statute," (emphasis supplied). Thus Vermont Yankee does not stand for the proposition that a court reviewing agency action under NEPA is limited solely to the factual issue of whether the agency "considered" environmental consequences. The agency's decision must still be set aside if it is "arbitrary, capricious, an abuse of discretion, or otherwise not in accordance with law," 5 U.S.C. § 706(2)(A), and the reviewing court must still insure that the agency "has taken a 'hard look' at environmental consequences," Kleppe v. Sierra Club, 427 U.S. 390, 410, n. 21 (1976).

In the present case, the Court of Appeals did not "substitute its judgment for that of the agency as to the environmental consequences of its actions," for HUD in its special Environmental Clearance Report acknowledged the adverse environmental consequences of its proposed action: "the choice of Site 30 for development as a 100 percent low-income project has raised valid questions about the potential social environmental impacts involved." These valid questions arise from the fact that 68% of all public housing units would be sited on only one crosstown axis in this area of New York City. As the Court of Appeals observed, the resulting high concentration of low-income housing would hardly further racial and economic integration. The environmental "impact ... on social fabric and community structures" was given a B rating in the report, indicating that from this perspective the project is "questionable" and ameliorative measures are "mandated." The report lists 10 ameliorative measures necessary to make the project acceptable. The report also discusses two alternatives, Sites 9 and 41, both of which are the appropriate size for the project and require "only minimal" amounts of relocation and clearance. Concerning Site 9 the report explicitly concludes that "[f]rom the standpoint of social environmental impact, this location would be superior to Site 30 for the development of low-rent public housing." The sole reason for rejecting the environmentally superior site was the fact that if the location were shifted to Site 9, there would be a projected delay of two years in the construction of the housing.

The issue before the Court of Appeals, therefore, was whether HUD was free under NEPA to reject an alternative acknowledged to be environmentally preferable solely on the ground that any change in sites would cause delay. This was hardly a "peripheral issue" in the case. Whether NEPA, which sets forth "significant substantive goals," Vermont Yankee Nuclear Power Corp. v. NRDC, 435 U.S., at 558, permits a projected two-year time difference to be controlling over environmental superiority is by no means clear. Resolution of the issue, however, is certainly within the normal scope of review of agency action to determine if it is arbitrary, capricious, or an abuse of discretion. The question whether HUD can make delay the paramount concern over environmental superiority is essentially a restatement of the question whether HUD in considering the environmental consequences of its proposed action gave those consequences a "hard look," which is exactly the proper question for the reviewing court to ask. Kleppe v. Sierra Club, 427 U.S., at 410, n. 21.

The issue of whether the Secretary's decision was arbitrary or capricious is sufficiently difficult and important to merit plenary consideration in this Court. Further, I do not subscribe to the Court's apparent suggestion that Vermont Yankee limits the reviewing court to the essentially mindless task of determining whether an agency "considered" environmental factors even if that agency may have effectively decided to ignore those factors in reaching its conclusion. Indeed, I cannot believe that the Court would adhere to that position in a different factual setting. Our cases establish that the arbitrary-or-capricious standard prescribes a "searching and careful" judicial inquiry designed to ensure that the agency has not exercised its discretion in an unreasonable manner. Citizens To Preserve Overton Park, Inc. v. Volpe, 401 U.S. 402, 416 (1971). Believing that today's summary reversal represents a departure from that principle, I respectfully dissent.

It is apparent to me that this is not the type of case for a summary disposition. We should at least have a plenary hearing.

***

QUESTIONS

1. Why are alternatives important to NEPA?
2. How do the NEPA regulations address alternatives?
3. What happened in Karlen?
4. What was the alternative at issue in Karlen?
5. What did the majority of the SCOTUS decide, and why?
6. Do you agree or disagree? Explain.
7. What was Justice Marshall's point? Do you agree or disagree? Explain.

D. EFFECTS

METROPOLITAN EDISON CO. V. PEOPLE AGAINST NUCLEAR ENERGY (PANE)
103 S. Ct. 1556 (1983)

Justice REHNQUIST delivered the opinion of the Court.

The issue in these cases is whether petitioner Nuclear Regulatory Commission (NRC) complied with the National Environmental Policy Act, 42 U.S.C. § 4321 et seq. (NEPA), when it considered whether to permit petitioner Metropolitan Edison Co. to resume operation of the Three Mile Island Unit 1 nuclear power plant (TMI-1). The Court of Appeals for the District of Columbia Circuit held that the NRC improperly failed to consider whether the risk of an accident at TMI-1 might cause harm to the psychological health and community well-being of residents of the surrounding area. We reverse.

Metropolitan owns two nuclear power plants at Three Mile Island near Harrisburg, Pennsylvania. Both of these plants were licensed by the NRC after extensive proceedings, which included preparation of Environmental Impact Statements (EIS). On March 28, 1979, TMI-1 was not operating; it had been shut down for refueling. TMI-2 was operating, and it suffered a serious accident that damaged the reactor.[1] Although, as it turned out, no dangerous radiation was released, the accident caused widespread concern. The Governor of Pennsylvania recommended an evacuation of all pregnant women and small children, and many area residents did leave their homes for several days.

After the accident, the NRC ordered Metropolitan to keep TMI-1 shut down until it had an opportunity to determine whether the plant could be operated safely. The NRC then published a notice of hearing specifying several safety related issues for consideration. The notice stated that the Commission had not determined whether to consider psychological harm or other indirect effects of the accident or of renewed operation of TMI-1. It invited interested parties to submit briefs on this issue.

Petitioner People Against Nuclear Energy (PANE), intervened and responded to this invitation. PANE is an association of residents of the Harrisburg area who are opposed to further operation of either TMI reactor. PANE contended that restarting TMI-1 would cause both severe psychological health damage to persons living in the vicinity, and serious damage to the stability, cohesiveness, and well-being of the neighboring communities.[2]

The NRC decided not to take evidence concerning PANE's contentions. PANE filed a petition for review in the Court of Appeals, contending that both NEPA and the Atomic Energy Act, 42 U.S.C. § 2011 et seq., require the NRC to address its contentions. Metropolitan intervened on the side of the NRC.

The Court of Appeals concluded that the Atomic Energy Act does not require the NRC to address PANE's contentions. It did find, however, that NEPA requires the NRC to evaluate "the potential psychological health effects of operating" TMI-1 which have arisen since the original EIS was prepared. It also held that, if the NRC finds that significant new circumstances or information exist on this subject, it shall prepare a "supplemental [EIS] which considers not only the effects on psychological health but also effects on the well being of the communities surrounding Three Mile Island." We granted certiorari.

All the parties agree that effects on human health can be cognizable under NEPA, and that human health may include psychological health. The Court of Appeals thought these propositions were enough to complete a syllogism that disposes of the case: NEPA requires agencies to consider effects on health. An effect on psychological health is an effect on health. Therefore, NEPA requires agencies to consider the effects on psychological health asserted by PANE. PANE, using similar reasoning, contends that because the psychological health damage to its members would be caused by a change in the environment (renewed operation of TMI-1), NEPA requires the NRC to consider that damage. Although these arguments are appealing at first glance, we believe they skip over an essential step in the analysis. They do not consider the closeness of the relationship between the change in the environment and the "effect" at issue.

Section 102(C) of NEPA, 42 U.S.C. 4332(C), directs all federal agencies to
"include in every recommendation or report on proposals for legislation and other major Federal actions significantly affecting the quality of the human environment, a detailed statement by the responsible official on-
(i) the environmental impact of the proposed action, [and]
(ii) any adverse environmental effects which cannot be avoided should the proposal be implemented ...."

To paraphrase the statutory language in light of the facts of this case, where an agency action significantly affects the quality of the human environment, the agency must evaluate the "environmental impact" and any unavoidable adverse environmental effects of its proposal. The theme of § 102 is sounded by the adjective "environmental": NEPA does not require the agency to assess every impact or effect of its proposed action, but only the impact or effect on the environment. If we were to seize the word "environmental" out of its context and give it the broadest possible definition, the words "adverse environmental effects" might embrace virtually any consequence of a governmental action that some one thought "adverse." But we think the context of the statute shows that Congress was talking about the physical environment-the world around us, so to speak. NEPA was designed to promote human welfare by alerting governmental actors to the effect of their proposed actions on the physical environment.

The statements of two principal sponsors of NEPA, explaining to their colleagues the Conference Report that was ultimately enacted, illustrate this point:

> "What is involved [in NEPA] is a declaration that we do not intend as a government or as a people to initiate actions which endanger the continued existence or the health of mankind: That we will not intentionally initiate actions which do irreparable damage to the air, land and water which support life on earth." 115 Cong.Rec. 40416 (1969) (Remarks of Sen. Jackson) (emphasis supplied).

> "[W]e can now move forward to preserve and enhance our air, aquatic, and terrestrial environments ... to carry out the policies and goals set forth in the bill to provide each citizen of this great country a healthful environment." 115 Cong.Rec. 40924 (1969) (Remarks of Rep. Dingell) (emphasis supplied).

Thus, although NEPA states its goals in sweeping terms of human health and welfare, these goals are ends that Congress has chosen to pursue by means of protecting the physical environment.

To determine whether § 102 requires consideration of a particular effect, we must look at the relationship between that effect and the change in the physical environment caused by the major federal action at issue. For example, if the Department of Health and Human Services were to implement extremely stringent requirements for hospitals and nursing homes receiving federal funds, many perfectly adequate hospitals and homes might be forced out of existence. The remaining facilities might be so limited or so expensive that many ill people would be unable to afford medical care and would suffer severe health damage. Nonetheless, NEPA would not require the Department to prepare an EIS evaluating that health damage because it would not be proximately related to a change in the physical environment.

Some effects that are "caused by" a change in the physical environment in the sense of "but for" causation, will nonetheless not fall within § 102 because the causal chain is too attenuated. For example, residents of the Harrisburg area have relatives in other parts of the country. Renewed operation of TMI-1 may well cause psychological health problems for these people. They may suffer "anxiety, tension and fear, a sense of helplessness," and accompanying physical disorders, because of the risk that their relatives may be harmed in a nuclear accident. However, this harm is simply too remote from the physical environment to justify requiring the NRC to evaluate the psychological health damage to these people that may be caused by renewed operation of TMI-1.

Our understanding of the congressional concerns that led to the enactment of NEPA suggests that the terms "environmental effect" and "environmental impact" in § 102 be read to include a requirement of a reasonably close causal relationship between a change in the physical environment and the effect at issue. This requirement is like the familiar doctrine of proximate cause from tort law. See generally W. Prosser, Law of Torts ch. 7 (4th ed. 1971). The issue before us, then, is how to give content to this requirement. This is a question of first impression in this Court.

The federal action that affects the environment in this case is permitting renewed operation of TMI-1. The direct effects on the environment of this action include release of low-level radiation, increased fog in the Harrisburg area (caused by operation of the plant's cooling towers), and the release of warm water into the Susquehanna River. The NRC has considered each of these effects in its EIS, and again in the EIA. Another effect of renewed operation is a risk of a nuclear accident. The NRC has also considered this effect.

PANE argues that the psychological health damage it alleges "will flow directly from the risk of [a nuclear] accident." But a risk of an accident is not an effect on the physical environment. A risk is, by definition, unrealized in the physical world. In a causal chain from renewed operation of TMI-1 to psychological health damage, the element of risk and its perception by PANE's members are necessary middle links. We believe that the element of risk lengthens the causal chain beyond the reach of NEPA.

Risk is a pervasive element of modern life; to say more would belabor the obvious. Many of the risks we face are generated by modern technology, which brings both the possibility of major accidents and opportunities for tremendous achievements. Medical experts apparently agree that risk can generate stress in human beings, which in turn may rise to the level of serious health damage. For this reason among many others, the question whether the gains from any technological advance are worth its attendant risks may be an important public policy issue. Nonetheless, it is quite different from the question whether the same gains are worth a given level of alteration of our physical environment or depletion of our natural resources. The latter question rather than the former is the central concern of NEPA.

Time and resources are simply too limited for us to believe that Congress intended to extend NEPA as far as the Court of Appeals has taken it. See Vermont Yankee Nuclear Power Corp. v. NRDC, 435 U.S. 519, 551 (1978). The scope of the agency's inquiries must remain manageable if NEPA's goal of "ensur[ing] a fully informed and well considered decision is to be accomplished.

If contentions of psychological health damage caused by risk were cognizable under NEPA, agencies would, at the very least, be obliged to expend considerable resources developing psychiatric expertise that is not otherwise relevant to their congressionally assigned functions. The available resources may be spread so thin that agencies are unable adequately to pursue protection of the physical environment and natural resources. As we said in another context, "[w]e cannot attribute to Congress the intention to ... open the door to such obvious incongruities and undesireable possibilities."

This case bears strong resemblance to other cases in which plaintiffs have sought to require agencies to evaluate the risk of crime from the operation of a jail or other public facility in their neighborhood. The plaintiffs in these cases could have alleged that the risk of crime (or their dislike of the occupants of the facility) would cause severe psychological health damage. The operation of the facility is an event in the physical environment, but the psychological health damage to neighboring residents resulting from unrealized risks of crime is too far removed from that event to be covered by NEPA. The psychological health damage alleged by PANE is no closer to an event in the environment or to environmental concerns.

The Court of Appeals thought that PANE's contentions are qualitatively different from the harm at issue in the cases just described. It thought PANE raised an issue of health damage, while those cases presented questions of fear or policy disagreement. We do not believe this line is so easily drawn. Anyone who fears or dislikes a project may find himself suffering from "anxiety, tension, fear, [and] a sense of helplessness." Neither the language nor the history of NEPA suggest that it was intended to give citizens a general opportunity to air their policy objections to proposed federal actions. The political process, and not NEPA, provides the appropriate forum in which to air policy disagreements.

We do not mean to denigrate the fears of PANE's members, or to suggest that the psychological health damage they fear could not, in fact, occur. Nonetheless, it is difficult for us to see the differences between someone who dislikes a government decision so much that he suffers anxiety and stress, someone who fears the effects of that decision so much that he suffers similar anxiety and stress, and someone who suffers anxiety and stress that "flow directly," from the risks associated with the same decision. It would be extraordinarily difficult for agencies to differentiate between "genuine" claims of psychological health damage and claims that are grounded solely in disagreement with a democratically adopted policy. Until Congress provides a more explicit statutory instruction than NEPA now contains, we do not think agencies are obliged to undertake the inquiry.

The Court of Appeals' opinion seems at one point to acknowledge the force of these arguments, but seeks to distinguish the situation suggested by the related cases. First, the Court of Appeals thought the harm alleged by PANE is far more severe than the harm alleged in other cases. It thought the severity of the harm is relevant to whether NEPA requires consideration of an effect. This cannot be the case. NEPA addresses environmental effects of federal actions. The gravity of harm does not change its character. If a harm does not have a sufficiently close connection to the physical environment, NEPA does not apply.

Second, the Court of Appeals noted that PANE's claim was made "in the wake of a unique and traumatic nuclear accident." We do not understand how the accident at TMI-2 transforms PANE's contentions into "environmental effects." The Court of Appeals "cannot believe that the psychological aftermath of the March 1979 accident falls outside" NEPA. On the contrary, NEPA is not directed at the effects of past accidents and does not create a remedial scheme for past federal actions. It was enacted to require agencies to assess the future effects of future actions. There is nothing in the language or the history of NEPA to suggest that its scope should be expanded "in the wake of" any kind of accident.

For these reasons, we hold that the NRC need not consider PANE's contentions. NEPA does not require agencies to evaluate the effects of risk, qua risk. The judgment of the Court of Appeals is reversed, and the case is remanded with instructions to dismiss the petition for review.

It is so ordered.

Justice BRENNAN, concurring.

I join the opinion of the Court. There can be no doubt that psychological injuries are cognizable under NEPA. As the Court points out, however, the particular psychological injury alleged in this case did not arise, for example, out of the direct sensory impact of a change in the physical environment, but out of a perception of risk. In light of the history and policies underlying NEPA, I agree with the Court that this crucial distinction "lengthens the causal chain beyond the reach" of the statute.

QUESTIONS

1. Why is ascertaining effects important to NEPA?
2. How do the NEPA regulations address "effects"?
3. What happened in PANE?
4. What was/were the issue/issues before the SCOTUS?
5. What did the court rule?
6. Do you agree or disagree? Explain.

E. MITIGATION AND WORST CASE SCENERIO

ROBERTSON V. METHOW VALLEY CITIZENS COALITION
109 S.Ct. 1835 (1989)

Justice STEVENS delivered the opinion of the Court.

We granted certiorari to decide two questions of law. As framed by petitioners, they are:

"1. Whether the National Environmental Policy Act requires federal agencies to include in each environmental impact statement: (a) a fully developed plan to mitigate environmental harm; and (b) a 'worst case' analysis of potential environmental harm if relevant information concerning significant environmental effects is unavailable or too costly to obtain.
....

Concluding that the Court of Appeals for the Ninth Circuit misapplied the National Environmental Policy Act of 1969 (NEPA), 83 Stat. 852, 42 U.S.C. § 4321 et seq., and gave inadequate deference to the Forest Service's interpretation of its own regulations, we reverse and remand for further proceedings.

I

The Forest Service is authorized by statute to manage the national forests for "outdoor recreation, range, timber, watershed, and wildlife and fish purposes."Pursuant to that authorization, the Forest Service has issued "special use" permits for the operation of approximately 170 Alpine and Nordic ski areas on federal lands.

The Forest Service permit process involves three separate stages. The Forest Service first examines the general environmental and financial feasibility of a proposed project and decides whether to issue a special use permit. Because that decision is a "major Federal action" within the meaning of NEPA, it must be preceded by the preparation of an Environmental Impact Statement (EIS). If the Service decides to issue a permit, it then proceeds to select a developer, formulate the basic terms of the arrangement with the selected party, and issue the permit.[2] The special use permit does not, however, give the developer the right to begin construction. In a final stage of review, the Service evaluates the permittee's "master plan" for development, construction, and operation of the project. Construction may begin only after an additional environmental analysis (although it is not clear that a second EIS need always be prepared) and final approval of the developer's master plan. This case arises out of the Forest Service's decision to issue a special use permit authorizing the development of a major destination Alpine ski resort at Sandy Butte in the North Cascade Mountains.

Sandy Butte is a 6,000-foot mountain located in the Okanogan National Forest in Okanogan County, Washington. At present Sandy Butte, like the Methow Valley it overlooks, is an unspoiled, sparsely populated area that the District Court characterized as "pristine." In 1968, Congress established the North Cascades National Park and directed the Secretaries of the Interior and Agriculture to agree on the designation of areas within, and adjacent to, the park for public uses, including ski areas. A study conducted by the Forest Service pursuant to this congressional directive identified Sandy Butte as having the highest potential of any site in the State of Washington for development as a major downhill ski resort.[3]

In 1978, Methow Recreation, Inc. (MRI), applied for a special use permit to develop and operate its proposed "Early Winters Ski Resort" on Sandy Butte and an 1,165-acre parcel of land it had acquired adjacent to the National Forest. The proposed development would make use of approximately 3,900 acres of Sandy Butte; would entice visitors to travel long distances to stay at the resort for several days at a time; and would stimulate extensive commercial and residential growth in the vicinity to accommodate both vacationers and staff.

In response to MRI's application, the Forest Service, in cooperation with state and county officials, prepared an EIS known as the Early Winters Alpine Winter Sports Study (Early Winters Study or Study). The stated purpose of the EIS was "to provide the information required to evaluate the potential for skiing at Early Winters" and "to assist in making a decision whether to issue a Special Use Permit for downhill skiing on all or a portion of approximately 3900 acres of National Forest System land." A draft of the Study was completed and circulated in 1982, but release of the final EIS was delayed as Congress considered including Sandy Butte in a proposed wilderness area. When the Washington State Wilderness Act of 1984 was passed, however, Sandy Butte was excluded from the wilderness designation, and the EIS was released.

The Early Winters Study is a printed document containing almost 150 pages of text and 12 appendices. It evaluated five alternative levels of development of Sandy Butte that might be authorized, the lowest being a "no action" alternative and the highest being development of a 16-lift ski area able to accommodate 10,500 skiers at one time. The Study considered the effect of each level of development on water resources, soil, wildlife, air quality, vegetation, and visual quality, as well as land use and transportation in the Methow Valley, probable demographic shifts, the economic market for skiing and other summer and winter recreational activities in the Valley, and the energy requirements for the ski area and related developments. The Study's discussion of possible impacts was not limited to on-site effects, but also, as required by Council on Environmental Quality (CEQ) regulations, see 40 CFR § 1502.16(b) (1987), addressed "off-site impacts that each alternative might have on community facilities, socio-economic and other environmental conditions in the Upper Methow Valley." As to off-site effects, the Study explained that "due to the uncertainty of where other public and private lands may become developed," it is difficult to evaluate off-site impacts, and thus the document's analysis is necessarily "not site-specific." Finally, the Study outlined certain steps that might be taken to mitigate adverse effects, both on Sandy Butte and in the neighboring Methow Valley, but indicated that these proposed steps are merely conceptual and "will be made more specific as part of the design and implementation stages of the planning process."

The effects of the proposed development on air quality and wildlife received particular attention in the Study. In the chapter on "Environmental Consequences," the first subject discussed is air quality. As is true of other subjects, the discussion included an analysis of cumulative impacts over several years resulting from actions on other lands as well as from the development of Sandy Butte itself. The Study concluded that although the construction, maintenance, and operation of the proposed ski area "will not have a measurable effect on existing or future air quality," the off-site development of private land under all five alternatives-including the "no action" alternative- "will have a significant effect on air quality during severe meteorological inversion periods." The burning of wood for space heat, the Study explained, would constitute the primary cause of diminished air quality, and the damage would increase incrementally with each of the successive levels of proposed development. The Study cautioned that without efforts to mitigate these effects, even under the "no action" alternative, the increase in automobile, fireplace, and wood stove use would reduce air quality below state standards, but added that "[t]he numerous mitigation measures discussed" in the Study "will greatly reduce the impacts presented by the model."

In its discussion of air-quality mitigation measures, the EIS identified actions that could be taken by the county government to mitigate the adverse effects of development, as well as those that the Forest Service itself could implement at the construction stage of the project. The Study suggested that Okanogan County develop an air quality management plan, requiring weatherization of new buildings, limiting the number of wood stoves and fireplaces, and adopting monitoring and enforcement measures.[5] In addition, the Study suggested that the Forest Service require that the master plan include procedures to control dust and to comply with smoke management practices.

In its discussion of adverse effects on area wildlife, the EIS concluded that no endangered or threatened species would be affected by the proposed development and that the only impact on sensitive species was the probable loss of a pair of spotted owls and their progeny. With regard to other wildlife, the Study considered the impact on 75 different indigenous species and predicted that within a decade after development vegetational change and increased human activity would lead to a decrease in population for 31 species, while causing an increase in population for another 24 species on Sandy Butte. Two species, the pine marten and nesting goshawk, would be eliminated altogether from the area of development.

In a comment in response to the draft EIS, the Washington Department of Game voiced a special concern about potential losses to the State's largest migratory deer herd, which uses the Methow Valley as a critical winter range and as its migration route. The state agency estimated that the total population of mule deer in the area most likely to be affected was "better than 30,000 animals" and that "the ultimate impact on the Methow deer herd could exceed a 50 percent reduction in numbers." The agency asserted that "Okanogan County residents place a great deal of importance on the area's deer herd." In addition, it explained that hunters had "harvested" 3,247 deer in the Methow Valley area in 1981, and that, since in 1980 hunters on average spent $1,980 for each deer killed in Washington, they had contributed over $6 million to the State's economy in 1981. Because the deer harvest is apparently proportional to the size of the herd, the state agency predicted that "Washington business can expect to lose over $3 million annually from reduced recreational opportunity." The Forest Service's own analysis of the impact on the deer herd was more modest. It first concluded that the actual operation of the ski hill would have only a "minor" direct impact on the herd,[7] but then recognized that the off-site effect of the development "would noticeably reduce numbers of deer in the Methow [Valley] with any alternative." Although its estimate indicated a possible 15 percent decrease in the size of the herd, it summarized the State's contrary view in the text of the EIS, and stressed that off-site effects are difficult to estimate due to uncertainty concerning private development.

As was true of its discussion of air quality, the EIS also described both on-site and off-site mitigation measures. Among possible on-site mitigation possibilities, the Study recommended locating runs, ski lifts, and roads so as to minimize interference with wildlife, restricting access to selected roads during fawning season, and further examination of the effect of the development on mule deer migration routes.[8] Off-site options discussed in the Study included the use of zoning and tax incentives to limit development on deer winter range and migration routes, encouragement of conservation easements, and acquisition and management by local government of critical tracts of land.[9] As with the measures suggested for mitigating the off-site effects on air quality, the proposed options were primarily directed to steps that might be taken by state and local government.

Ultimately, the Early Winters Study recommended the issuance of a permit for development at the second highest level considered-a 16-lift ski area able to accommodate 8,200 skiers at one time. On July 5, 1984, the Regional Forester decided to issue a special use permit as recommended by the Study.In his decision, the Regional Forester found that no major adverse effects would result directly from the federal action, but that secondary effects could include a degradation of existing air quality and a reduction of mule deer winter range. He therefore directed the supervisor of the Okanogan National Forest, both independently and in cooperation with local officials, to identify and implement certain mitigating measures.

Four organizations (respondents) opposing the decision to issue a permit appealed the Regional Forester's decision to the Chief of the Forest Service. After a hearing, he affirmed the Regional Forester's decision. Stressing that the decision, which simply approved the general concept of issuing a 30-year special use permit for development of Sandy Butte, did not authorize construction of a particular ski area and, in fact, did not even act on MRI specific permit application, he concluded that the EIS's discussion of mitigation was "adequate for this stage in the review process."

Thereafter, respondents brought this action under the Administrative Procedure Act, 5 U.S.C. §§ 701-706, to obtain judicial review of the Forest Service's decision. Their principal claim was that the Early Winters Study did not satisfy the requirements of NEPA, 42 U.S.C. § 4332. With the consent of the parties, the case was assigned to a United States Magistrate. After a trial, the Magistrate filed a comprehensive written opinion and concluded that the EIS was adequate. Specifically, he found that the EIS had adequately disclosed the adverse impacts on the mule deer herd and on air quality and that there was no duty to prepare a "worst case analysis" because the relevant information essential to a reasoned decision was available. In concluding that the discussion of off-site, or secondary, impacts was adequate, the Magistrate stressed that courts apply a "rule of reason" in evaluating the adequacy of an EIS and "take the uncertainty and speculation involved with secondary impacts into account in passing on the adequacy of the discussion of secondary impacts." On the subject of mitigation, he explained that "[m]ere listing ... is generally inadequate to satisfy the CEQ regulations," but found that "in this EIS there is more-not much more-but more than a mere listing of mitigation measures." Moreover, emphasizing the tiered nature of the Forest Service's decisional process, the Magistrate noted that additional mitigation strategies would be included in the master plan, that the Forest Service continues to develop mitigation plans as further information becomes available, and that the Regional Forester's decision conditioned issuance of the special use permit on execution of an agreement between the Forest Service, the State of Washington, and Okanogan County concerning mitigation.

Concluding that the Early Winters Study was inadequate as a matter of law, the Court of Appeals reversed. The court held that the Forest Service could not rely on " 'the implementation of mitigation measures' " to support its conclusion that the impact on the mule deer would be minor, "since not only has the effectiveness of these mitigation measures not yet been assessed, but the mitigation measures themselves have yet to be developed." It then added that if the agency had difficulty obtaining adequate information to make a reasoned assessment of the environmental impact on the herd, it had a duty to make a so-called "worst case analysis." Such an analysis is " 'formulated on the basis of available information, using reasonable projections of the worst possible consequences of a proposed action.'

The court found a similar defect in the EIS' treatment of air quality. Since the EIS made it clear that commercial development in the Methow Valley will result in violations of state air-quality standards unless effective mitigation measures are put in place by the local governments and the private developer, the Court of Appeals concluded that the Forest Service had an affirmative duty to "develop the necessary mitigation measures before the permit is granted." The court held that this duty was imposed by both the Forest Service's own regulations and § 102 of NEPA. It read the statute as imposing a substantive requirement that " 'action be taken to mitigate the adverse effects of major federal actions.' For this reason, it concluded that "an EIS must include a thorough discussion of measures to mitigate the adverse environmental impacts of a proposed action." The Court of Appeals concluded by quoting this paragraph from an opinion it had just announced:

" 'The importance of the mitigation plan cannot be overestimated. It is a determinative factor in evaluating the adequacy of an environmental impact statement. Without a complete mitigation plan, the decisionmaker is unable to make an informed judgment as to the environmental impact of the project-one of the main purposes of an environmental impact statement.' "

II

Section 101 of NEPA declares a broad national commitment to protecting and promoting environmental quality. To ensure that this commitment is "infused into the ongoing programs and actions of the Federal Government, the act also establishes some important 'action-forcing' procedures." Section 102 thus, among other measures
"directs that, to the fullest extent possible ... all agencies of the Federal Government shall-

"(C) include in every recommendation or report on proposals for legislation and other major Federal actions significantly affecting the quality of the human environment, a detailed statement by the responsible official on-
"(i) the environmental impact of the proposed action,
"(ii) any adverse environmental effects which cannot be avoided should the proposal be implemented,
"(iii) alternatives to the proposed action,
"(iv) the relationship between local short-term uses of man's environment and the maintenance and enhancement of long-term productivity, and
"(v) any irreversible and irretrievable commitments of resources which would be involved in the proposed action should it be implemented."

The statutory requirement that a federal agency contemplating a major action prepare such an environmental impact statement serves NEPA's "action-forcing" purpose in two important respects. It ensures that the agency, in reaching its decision, will have available, and will carefully consider, detailed information concerning significant environmental impacts; it also guarantees that the relevant information will be made available to the larger audience that may also play a role in both the decisionmaking process and the implementation of that decision.

Simply by focusing the agency's attention on the environmental consequences of a proposed project, NEPA ensures that important effects will not be overlooked or underestimated only to be discovered after resources have been committed or the die otherwise cast. Moreover, the strong precatory language of § 101 of the Act and the requirement that agencies prepare detailed impact statements inevitably bring pressure to bear on agencies "to respond to the needs of environmental quality."

Publication of an EIS, both in draft and final form, also serves a larger informational role. It gives the public the assurance that the agency "has indeed considered environmental concerns in its decisionmaking process," and, perhaps more significantly, provides a springboard for public comment. Thus, in this case the final draft of the Early Winters Study reflects not only the work of the Forest Service itself, but also the critical views of the Washington State Department of Game, the Methow Valley Citizens Council, and Friends of the Earth, as well as many others, to whom copies of the draft Study were circulated. Moreover, with respect to a development such as Sandy Butte, where the adverse effects on air quality and the mule deer herd are primarily attributable to predicted off-site development that will be subject to regulation by other governmental bodies, the EIS serves the function of offering those bodies adequate notice of the expected consequences and the opportunity to plan and implement corrective measures in a timely manner.

The sweeping policy goals announced in § 101 of NEPA are thus realized through a set of "action-forcing" procedures that require that agencies take a " 'hard look' at environmental consequences," and that provide for broad dissemination of relevant environmental information. Although these procedures are almost certain to affect the agency's substantive decision, it is now well settled that NEPA itself does not mandate particular results, but simply prescribes the necessary process. If the adverse environmental effects of the proposed action are adequately identified and evaluated, the agency is not constrained by NEPA from deciding that other values outweigh the environmental costs. In this case, for example, it would not have violated NEPA if the Forest Service, after complying with the Act's procedural prerequisites, had decided that the benefits to be derived from downhill skiing at Sandy Butte justified the issuance of a special use permit, notwithstanding the loss of 15 percent, 50 percent, or even 100 percent of the mule deer herd. Other statutes may impose substantive environmental obligations on federal agencies, but NEPA merely prohibits uninformed-rather than unwise-agency action.

To be sure, one important ingredient of an EIS is the discussion of steps that can be taken to mitigate adverse environmental consequences. The requirement that an EIS contain a detailed discussion of possible mitigation measures flows both from the language of the Act and, more expressly, from CEQ's implementing regulations. Implicit in NEPA's demand that an agency prepare a detailed statement on "any adverse environmental effects which cannot be avoided should the proposal be implemented," is an understanding that the EIS will discuss the extent to which adverse effects can be avoided. More generally, omission of a reasonably complete discussion of possible mitigation measures would undermine the "action-forcing" function of NEPA. Without such a discussion, neither the agency nor other interested groups and individuals can properly evaluate the severity of the adverse effects. An adverse effect that can be fully remedied by, for example, an inconsequential public expenditure is certainly not as serious as a similar effect that can only be modestly ameliorated through the commitment of vast public and private resources. Recognizing the importance of such a discussion in guaranteeing that the agency has taken a "hard look" at the environmental consequences of proposed federal action, CEQ regulations require that the agency discuss possible mitigation measures in defining the scope of the EIS, in discussing alternatives to the proposed action, § 1502.14(f), and consequences of that action, § 1502.16(h), and in explaining its ultimate decision, § 1505.2(c).

There is a fundamental distinction, however, between a requirement that mitigation be discussed in sufficient detail to ensure that environmental consequences have been fairly evaluated, on the one hand, and a substantive requirement that a complete mitigation plan be actually formulated and adopted, on the other. In this case, the off-site effects on air quality and on the mule deer herd cannot be mitigated unless nonfederal government agencies take appropriate action. Since it is those state and local governmental bodies that have jurisdiction over the area in which the adverse effects need be addressed and since they have the authority to mitigate them, it would be incongruous to conclude that the Forest Service has no power to act until the local agencies have reached a final conclusion on what mitigating measures they consider necessary. Even more significantly, it would be inconsistent with NEPA's reliance on procedural mechanisms-as opposed to substantive, result-based standards-to demand the presence of a fully developed plan that will mitigate environmental harm before an agency can act. ("NEPA does not require agencies to adopt any particular internal decisionmaking structure").

We thus conclude that the Court of Appeals erred, first, in assuming that "NEPA requires that 'action be taken to mitigate the adverse effects of major federal actions,' and, second, in finding that this substantive requirement entails the further duty to include in every EIS "a detailed explanation of specific measures which will be employed to mitigate the adverse impacts of a proposed action."

III

The Court of Appeals also concluded that the Forest Service had an obligation to make a "worst case analysis" if it could not make a reasoned assessment of the impact of the Early Winters project on the mule deer herd. Such a "worst case analysis" was required at one time by CEQ regulations, but those regulations have since been amended. Moreover, although the prior regulations may well have expressed a permissible application of NEPA, the Act itself does not mandate that uncertainty in predicting environmental harms be addressed exclusively in this manner. Accordingly, we conclude that the Court of Appeals also erred in requiring the "worst case" study.

In 1977, President Carter directed that CEQ promulgate binding regulations implementing the procedural provisions of NEPA. Pursuant to this Presidential order, CEQ promulgated implementing regulations. Under § 1502.22 of these regulations-a provision which became known as the "worst case requirement"-CEQ provided that if certain information relevant to the agency's evaluation of the proposed action is either unavailable or too costly to obtain, the agency must include in the EIS a "worst case analysis and an indication of the probability or improbability of its occurrence." In 1986, however, CEQ replaced the "worst case" requirement with a requirement that federal agencies, in the face of unavailable information concerning a reasonably foreseeable significant environmental consequence, prepare "a summary of existing credible scientific evidence which is relevant to evaluating the ... adverse impacts" and prepare an "evaluation of such impacts based upon theoretical approaches or research methods generally accepted in the scientific community." 40 CFR § 1502.22(b) (1987). The amended regulation thus "retains the duty to describe the consequences of a remote, but potentially severe impact, but grounds the duty in evaluation of scientific opinion rather than in the framework of a conjectural 'worst case analysis.' ".

The Court of Appeals recognized that the "worst case analysis" regulation has been superseded, yet held that "[t]his rescission ... does not nullify the requirement ... since the regulation was merely a codification of prior NEPA case law." 833 F.2d, at 817, n. 11. This conclusion, however, is erroneous in a number of respects. Most notably, review of NEPA case law reveals that the regulation, in fact, was not a codification of prior judicial decisions. The cases cited by the Court of Appeals ultimately rely on the Fifth Circuit's decision in Sierra Club v. Sigler, 695 F.2d 957 (1983). Sigler, however, simply recognized that the "worst case analysis" regulation codified the "judicially created principl[e]" that an EIS must "consider the probabilities of the occurrence of any environmental effects it discusses." As CEQ recognized at the time it superseded the regulation, case law prior to the adoption of the "worst case analysis" provision did require agencies to describe environmental impacts even in the face of substantial uncertainty, but did not require that this obligation necessarily be met through the mechanism of a "worst case analysis." CEQ's abandonment of the "worst case analysis" provision, therefore, is not inconsistent with any previously established judicial interpretation of the statute.

Nor are we convinced that the new CEQ regulation is not controlling simply because it was preceded by a rule that was in some respects more demanding. In Andrus v. Sierra Club, we held that CEQ regulations are entitled to substantial deference. In that case we recognized that although less deference may be in order in some cases in which the " 'administrative guidelines' " conflict " 'with earlier pronouncements of the agency,' " substantial deference is nonetheless appropriate if there appears to have been good reason for the change, Here, the amendment only came after the prior regulation had been subjected to considerable criticism.[17] Moreover, the amendment was designed to better serve the twin functions of an EIS-requiring agencies to take a "hard look" at the consequences of the proposed action and providing important information to other groups and individuals. CEQ explained that by requiring that an EIS focus on reasonably foreseeable impacts, the new regulation "will generate information and discussion on those consequences of greatest concern to the public and of greatest relevance to the agency's decision,", rather than distorting the decisionmaking process by overemphasizing highly speculative harms. In light of this well-considered basis for the change, the new regulation is entitled to substantial deference. Accordingly, the Court of Appeals erred in concluding that the Early Winters Study is inadequate because it failed to include a "worst case analysis."

IV

The Court of Appeals also held that the Forest Service's failure to develop a complete mitigation plan violated the agency's own regulations. Those regulations require that an application for a special use permit include "measures and plans for the protection and rehabilitation of the environment during construction, operation, maintenance, and termination of the project,", and that "[e]ach special use authorization ... contain ... [t]erms and conditions which will ... minimize damage to scenic and esthetic values and fish and wildlife habitat and otherwise protect the environment,". Applying those regulations, the Court of Appeals concluded that "[s]ince the mitigation 'plan' here at issue is so vague and undeveloped as to be wholly inadequate, ... the Regional Forester's decision to grant the special use permit could be none other than arbitrary, capricious and an abuse of discretion." We disagree.

The Early Winters Study made clear that on-site effects of the development will be minimal and will be easily mitigated. For example, the Study reported that "[i]mpacts from construction, maintenance and operation of the proposed 'hill' development on National Forest land will not have a measurable effect on existing or future air quality," and that "[t]he effect development and operation of the ski hill would have on deer migration should be minor." Given the limited on-site effects of the proposed development, the recommended ameliorative steps-which, for example, called for "prompt revegetation of all disturbed areas," and suggested locating "new service roads away from water resources and fawning cover," cannot be deemed overly vague or underdeveloped.

The Court of Appeals' conclusion that the Early Winters Study's treatment of possible mitigation measures is inadequate apparently turns on the court's review of the proposed off-site measures. Although NEPA and CEQ regulations require detailed analysis of both on-site and off-site mitigation measures, there is no basis for concluding that the Forest Service's own regulations must also be read in all cases to condition issuance of a special use permit on consideration (and implementation) of off-site mitigation measures. The Forest Service regulations were promulgated pursuant to a broad grant of authority "to permit the use and occupancy of suitable areas of land within the national forests ... for the purpose of constructing or maintaining hotels, resorts, and any other structures or facilities necessary or desirable for recreation, public convenience, or safety," and were not based on the more direct congressional concern for environmental quality embodied in NEPA. As is clear from the text of the permit issued to MRI, the Forest Service has decided to implement its mitigation regulations by imposing appropriate controls over MRI's actual development and operation during the term of the permit. It was surely not unreasonable for the Forest Service in this case to have construed those regulations as not extending to actions that might be taken by Okanogan County or the State of Washington to ameliorate the off-site effects of the Early Winters project on air quality and the mule deer herd. This interpretation of the agency's own regulation is not "plainly erroneous or inconsistent with the regulation," and is thus controlling.

V

In sum, we conclude that NEPA does not require a fully developed plan detailing what steps will be taken to mitigate adverse environmental impacts and does not require a "worst case analysis." In addition, we hold that the Forest Service has adopted a permissible interpretation of its own regulations. The judgment of the Court of Appeals is accordingly reversed, and the case is remanded for further proceedings consistent with this opinion.

It is so ordered.

Justice BRENNAN, concurring.

I write separately to highlight the Court's observation that "one important ingredient of an EIS is the discussion of steps that can be taken to mitigate adverse environmental consequences."

QUESTIONS

1. Why is mitigation important to NEPA?
2. How do the NEPA regulations define "mitigation?"
3. What is "tiering," and how does it relate to mitigation?
4. According to Methow Valley, does NEPA impose a substantive duty on agencies to mitigate adverse environmental effects or to include in each EIS a fully developed mitigation plan? Why or why not?
5. According to Methow Valley, does NEPA impose a duty on an agency to make a "worst case analysis" in its EIS if it cannot make a reasoned assessment of a proposed project's environmental impact?
6. According to Methow Valley, was it unreasonable for the Forest Service to decline to consider off-site mitigation efforts that might be taken by state and local authorities?
7. Do you agree or disagree with the outcome? Explain.

CHAPTER 3: CONSERVING ENDANGERED AND THREATENED SPECIES

Chapter 3 turns to the federal Endangered Species Act (ESA), what some have called the "pit-bull" of all environmental laws. It is the book's longest chapter because the ESA is helping to see how laws are made, as well as how Congress can require agencies to act and forbid the rest of us from doing so in certain circumstances when necessary to conserve a species. After reading perhaps the most famous (if not infamous) case in the environmental law canon in Part I, we'll read what Congress expressed as to the ESA's purposes and objectives in Part II, before turning to important issues as to what species and habitats are protected (Part III), what listing means to federal agencies (consultation, Part IV) and everybody else (prohibited takings, Part V). We'll finish this chapter with related subjects of enforcement (Part VI), criminal activity (Part VII), and international trade (Part VIII).

I. ESA BACKGROUND

Human-induced loss of biodiversity – including the slow-motion extirpation of plant and animal species via hunting, poaching, illegal trade, habitat disruption, and climate change – is an intractable domestic and international problem, something the noted humanist and botanist E.O. Wilson has termed the fifth great "epoch" in species transformation that the Earth has experienced over 5 billion years.

The ESA is the most effective natural resources statute the nation has seen. It has been instrumental in conserving innumerable species threatened with extinction, and with protecting critical habitat. It has had other salutatory effects, including energizing the U.S. Fish and Wildlife Service and the National Marine Fisheries Services, providing means to list and conserve T/E species, providing millions of dollars in funding, giving the federal government authority to appropriate land to protect species, instituting a program to assist states with species protection, and implementing international accords concerning trade in protected species.

At its core, the ESA has two principal thrusts. The first stems from Section 7, which requires federal agencies to "consult" with the USFWS or the NMFS prior to authorizing, engaging in, or funding federal action. The consultation process serves to ensure that the action will not "jeopardize" the continued existence of any listed T/E species. In this regard, think of Section 7 as NEPA for species protection. The second is grounded in Section 9, which is more direct and prescriptive: it criminalizes the "taking" of threatened or endangered plant or animal species or their habitat. The ESA, in turn, defines "taking" very broadly to include any action that kills, harms, or even disrupts. In this regard, the ESA has been called the "pit bull" of federal natural resources law.

The ESA is also a story told through the lens of legislative history and through the eyes of an intrepid and idealistic young law professor at the University of Tennessee fifty years ago. More on that later.

Congress enacted the original federal "Endangered Species Act" (ESA) in 1966. The 1966 ESA had three principal attributes. First, it charged the Secretary of Interior with listing the names of threatened "native fish and wildlife." Second, it allowed the Secretary to purchase land to conserve, protect or restore "selected species." Last, it required all federal agencies both to protect these species and "insofar as is practicable and consistent with the[ir] primary purposes," "preserve the habitats of such threatened species on lands under their jurisdiction." And even on these lands, the Secretary could permit the hunting and fishing of endangered species. Accordingly, given its limited reach and scope, the 1966 ESA did little to protect species from extinction. In 1969, Congress turned outward by amending the ESA to prohibit the importation of species "threatened with worldwide extinction" and to ban on the transportation and sale of wildlife taken in violation of any federal, state, or foreign law.

A U.S. – led multilateral effort to address trade in wild and exotic species eventually contributed to a strengthening of the ESA. In 1972, the U.S. State Department under the Nixon Administration (again, who would have thought?) helped to negotiate the International Convention on Trade in Threatened and Endangered Species (CITES). (CITES is the subject of an upcoming module.) The U.S. Senate ratified CITES nearly unanimously. Congress then turned to enacting domestic legislation to implement it.

What happened next was extraordinary. In 1973 the U.S. House of Representatives and the U.S. Senate negotiated and passed a multifaceted and intricate statute to "conserve" threatened and endangered species and their habitat, still known as the "Endangered Species Act." Noted Natural Resources Law Professor George C. Coggins summed up goings-on in Congress as follows:

"The dominant theme pervading all Congressional discussion of the proposed [Endangered Species Act of 1973] was the overriding need *to devote whatever effort and resources were necessary* to avoid further diminution of national and worldwide wildlife resources. Much of the testimony at the hearings and much debate was devoted to the biological problem of extinction. Senators and Congressmen uniformly deplored the irreplaceable loss to aesthetics, science, ecology, and the national heritage should more species disappear."

Coggins, *Conserving Wildlife Resources: An Overview of the Endangered Species Act of 1973*, 51 N.D.L.Rev. 315, 321 (1975). (Emphasis added.)

The ESA enjoyed wide and bipartisan political and public support. President Nixon signed into law in 1974, prior to his resignation associated with the Watergate fiasco.

The ESA made an immediate splash in the following decision. Even forty years on, *TVA v. Hill* stands as perhaps the most influential judicial rendering ever about species protection in particular, and the role of natural resources law in general.

TVA V. HILL
437 U.S. 153 (1978)

Mr. Chief Justice BURGER delivered the opinion of the Court.

The questions presented in this case are (a) whether the Endangered Species Act of 1973 requires a court to enjoin the operation of a virtually completed federal dam—which had been authorized prior to 1973—when, pursuant to authority vested in him by Congress, the Secretary of the Interior has determined that operation of the dam would eradicate an endangered species; and (b) whether continued congressional appropriations for the dam after 1973 constituted an implied repeal of the Endangered Species Act, at least as to the particular dam.

I

The Little Tennessee River originates in the mountains of northern Georgia and flows through the national forest lands of North Carolina into Tennessee, where it converges with the Big Tennessee River near Knoxville. The lower 33 miles of the Little Tennessee takes the river's clear, free-flowing waters through an area of great natural beauty. Among other environmental amenities, this stretch of river is said to contain abundant trout. Considerable historical importance attaches to the areas immediately adjacent to this portion of the Little Tennessee's banks. To the south of the river's edge lies Fort Loudon, established in 1756 as England's southwestern outpost in the French and Indian War. Nearby are also the ancient sites of several native American villages, the archeological stores of which are to a large extent unexplored. These include the Cherokee towns of Echota and Tennase, the former being the sacred capital of the Cherokee Nation as early as the 16th century and the latter providing the linguistic basis from which the State of Tennessee derives its name.

In this area of the Little Tennessee River the Tennessee Valley Authority, a wholly owned public corporation of the United States, began constructing the Tellico Dam and Reservoir Project in 1967, shortly after Congress appropriated initial funds for its development. Tellico is a multipurpose regional development project designed principally to stimulate shoreline development, generate sufficient electric current to heat 20,000 homes, and provide flatwater recreation and flood control, as well as improve economic conditions in "an area characterized by underutilization of human resources and outmigration of young people." Of particular relevance to this case is one aspect of the project, a dam which TVA determined to place on the Little Tennessee, a short distance from where the river's waters meet with the Big Tennessee. When fully operational, the dam would impound water covering some 16,500 acres—much of which represents valuable and productive farmland—thereby converting the river's shallow, fast-flowing waters into a deep reservoir over 30 miles in length.

The Tellico Dam has never opened, however, despite the fact that construction has been virtually completed and the dam is essentially ready for operation. Although Congress has appropriated monies for Tellico every year since 1967, progress was delayed, and ultimately stopped, by a tangle of lawsuits and administrative proceedings. After unsuccessfully urging TVA to consider alternatives to damming the Little Tennessee, local citizens and national conservation groups brought suit in the District Court, claiming that the project did not conform to the requirements of the National Environmental Policy Act of 1969. After finding TVA to be in violation of NEPA, the District Court enjoined the dam's completion pending the filing of an appropriate environmental impact statement. The injunction remained in effect until late 1973, when the District Court concluded that TVA's final environmental impact statement for Tellico was in compliance with the law.

A few months prior to the District Court's decision dissolving the NEPA injunction, a discovery was made in the waters of the Little Tennessee which would profoundly affect the Tellico Project. Exploring the area around Coytee Springs, which is about seven miles from the mouth of the river, a University of Tennessee ichthyologist, Dr. David A. Etnier, found a previously unknown species of perch, the snail darter, or *Percina (Imostoma) tanasi*. This three-inch, tannish-colored fish, whose numbers are estimated to be in the range of 10,000 to 15,000, would soon engage the attention of environmentalists, the TVA, the Department of the Interior, the Congress of the United States, and ultimately the federal courts, as a new and additional basis to halt construction of the dam.

Until recently the finding of a new species of animal life would hardly generate a cause célèbre. This is particularly so in the case of darters, of which there are approximately 130 known species,

8 to 10 of these having been identified only in the last five years. The moving force behind the snail darter's sudden fame came some four months after its discovery, when the Congress passed the Endangered Species Act of 1973 (Act). This legislation, among other things, authorizes the Secretary of the Interior to declare species of animal life "endangered" and to identify the "critical habitat" of these creatures. When a species or its habitat is so listed, the following portion of the Act—relevant here—becomes effective:

"The Secretary [of the Interior] shall review other programs administered by him and utilize such programs in furtherance of the purposes of this chapter. All other Federal departments and agencies shall, in consultation with and with the assistance of the Secretary, utilize their authorities in furtherance of the purposes of this chapter by carrying out programs for the conservation of endangered species and threatened species listed pursuant to section 1533 of this title and *by taking such action necessary to insure that actions authorized, funded, or carried out by them do not jeopardize the continued existence of such endangered species and threatened species or result in the destruction or modification of habitat of such species* which is determined by the Secretary, after consultation as appropriate with the affected States, to be critical." 16 U.S.C. § 1536 (1976 ed.) (emphasis added).

In January 1975, the respondents in this case and others petitioned the Secretary of the Interior to list the snail darter as an endangered species. After receiving comments from various interested parties, including TVA and the State of Tennessee, the Secretary formally listed the snail darter as an endangered species on October 8, 1975. In so acting, it was noted that "the snail darter is a living entity which is genetically distinct and reproductively isolated from other fishes." More important for the purposes of this case, the Secretary determined that the snail darter apparently lives only in that portion of the Little Tennessee River which would be completely inundated by the reservoir created as a consequence of the Tellico Dam's completion. The Secretary went on to explain the significance of the dam to the habitat of the snail darter:

"[T]he snail darter occurs only in the swifter portions of shoals over clean gravel substrate in cool, low-turbidity water. Food of the snail darter is almost exclusively snails which require a clean gravel substrate for their survival. *The proposed impoundment of water behind the proposed Tellico Dam would result in total destruction of the snail darter's habitat.*"

Subsequent to this determination, the Secretary declared the area of the Little Tennessee which would be affected by the Tellico Dam to be the "critical habitat" of the snail darter. Using these determinations as a predicate, and notwithstanding the near completion of the dam, the Secretary declared that pursuant to § 7 of the Act, "all Federal agencies must take such action as is necessary to insure that actions authorized, funded, or carried out by them do not result in the destruction or modification of this critical habitat area." This notice, of course, was pointedly directed at TVA and clearly aimed at halting completion or operation of the dam.

During the pendency of these administrative actions, other developments of relevance to the snail darter issue were transpiring. Communication was occurring between the Department of the Interior's Fish and Wildlife Service and TVA with a view toward settling the issue informally. These negotiations were to no avail, however, since TVA consistently took the position that the only available alternative was to attempt relocating the snail darter population to another suitable location. To this end, TVA conducted a search of alternative sites which might sustain the fish, culminating in the experimental transplantation of a number of snail darters to the nearby Hiwassee River. However, the Secretary of the Interior was not satisfied with the results of these efforts, finding that TVA had presented "little evidence that they have carefully studied the Hiwassee to determine whether or not" there were "biological and other factors in this river that [would] negate a successful transplant."

Meanwhile, Congress had also become involved in the fate of the snail darter. Appearing before a Subcommittee of the House Committee on Appropriations in April 1975—some seven months before the snail darter was listed as endangered—TVA representatives described the discovery of the fish and the relevance of the Endangered Species Act to the Tellico Project. At that time TVA presented a position which it would advance in successive forums thereafter, namely, that the Act did not prohibit the completion of a project authorized, funded, and substantially constructed before the Act was passed. TVA also described its efforts to transplant the snail darter, but contended that the dam should be finished regardless of the experiment's success. Thereafter, the House Committee on Appropriations, in its June 20, 1975, Report, stated the following in the course of recommending that an additional $29 million be appropriated for Tellico:

"The *Committee* directs that the project, for which an environmental impact statement has been completed and provided the Committee, should be completed as promptly as possible . . . ."

Congress then approved the TVA general budget, which contained funds for continued construction of the Tellico Project. In December 1975, one month after the snail darter was declared an endangered species, the President signed the bill into law.

In February 1976, pursuant to § 11(g) of the Endangered Species Act, respondents filed the case now under review, seeking to enjoin completion of the dam and impoundment of the reservoir on the ground that those actions would violate the Act by directly causing the extinction of the species *Percina (Imostoma) tanasi*. The District Court denied respondents' request for a preliminary injunction and set the matter for trial. Shortly thereafter the House and Senate held appropriations hearings which would include discussions of the Tellico budget.

At these hearings, TVA Chairman Wagner reiterated the agency's position that the Act did not apply to a project which was over 50% finished by the time the Act became effective and some 70% to 80% complete when the snail darter was officially listed as endangered. It also notified the Committees of the recently filed lawsuit's status and reported that TVA's efforts to transplant the snail darter had "been very encouraging."

Trial was held in the District Court on April 29 and 30, 1976, and on May 25, 1976, the court entered its memorandum opinion and order denying respondents their requested relief and dismissing the complaint. The District Court found that closure of the dam and the consequent impoundment of the reservoir would "result in the adverse modification, if not complete destruction, of the snail darter's critical habitat," making it "highly probable" that "the continued existence of the snail darter" would be "jeopardize [d]." Despite these findings, the District Court declined to embrace the plaintiffs' position on the merits: that once a federal project was shown to jeopardize an endangered species, a court of equity is compelled to issue an injunction restraining violation of the Endangered Species Act.

In reaching this result, the District Court stressed that the entire project was then about 80% complete and, based on available evidence, "there [were] no alternatives to impoundment of the reservoir, short of scrapping the entire project." The District Court also found that if the Tellico Project was permanently enjoined, "[s]ome $53 million would be lost in nonrecoverable obligations," meaning that a large portion of the $78 million already expended would be wasted. The court also noted that the Endangered Species Act of 1973 was passed some seven years after construction on the dam commenced and that Congress had continued appropriations for Tellico, with full awareness of the snail darter problem. Assessing these various factors, the District Court concluded:

"At some point in time a federal project becomes so near completion and so incapable of modification that a court of equity should not apply a statute enacted long after inception of the project to produce an unreasonable result. . . . Where there has been an irreversible and irretrievable commitment of resources by Congress to a project over a span of almost a decade, the Court should proceed with a great deal of circumspection."

To accept the plaintiffs' position, the District Court argued, would inexorably lead to what it characterized as the absurd result of requiring "a court to halt impoundment of water behind a fully completed dam if an endangered species were discovered in the river on the day before such impoundment was scheduled to take place. We cannot conceive that Congress intended such a result."

Less than a month after the District Court decision, the Senate and House Appropriations Committees recommended the full budget request of $9 million for continued work on Tellico. In its Report accompanying the appropriations bill, the Senate Committee stated:

"During subcommittee hearings, TVA was questioned about the relationship between the Tellico project's completion and the November 1975 listing of the snail darter (a small 3-inch fish which was discovered in 1973) as an endangered species under the Endangered Species Act. TVA informed the Committee that it was continuing its efforts to preserve the darter, while working towards the scheduled 1977 completion date. TVA repeated its view that the Endangered Species Act did not prevent the completion of the Tellico project, which has been under construction for nearly a decade. The subcommittee brought this matter, as well as the recent U. S. District Court's decision upholding TVA's decision to complete the project, to the attention of the full Committee. *The Committee does not view* the Endangered Species Act as prohibiting the completion of the Tellico project at its advanced stage and directs that this project be completed as promptly as possible in the public interest."

On June 29, 1976, both Houses of Congress passed TVA's general budget, which included funds for Tellico; the President signed the bill on July 12, 1976.

Thereafter, in the Court of Appeals, respondents argued that the District Court had abused its discretion by not issuing an injunction in the face of "a blatant statutory violation." The Court of Appeals agreed, and on January 31, 1977, it reversed, remanding "with instructions that a permanent injunction issue halting all activities incident to the Tellico Project which may destroy or modify the critical habitat of the snail darter." The Court of Appeals directed that the injunction "remain in effect until Congress, by appropriate legislation, exempts Tellico from compliance with the Act or the snail darter has been deleted from the list of endangered species or its critical habitat materially redefined."

The Court of Appeals accepted the District Court's finding that closure of the dam would result in the known population of snail darters being "significantly reduced if not completely extirpated." TVA, in fact, had conceded as much in the Court of Appeals, but argued that "closure of the Tellico Dam, as the last stage of a ten-year project, falls outside the legitimate purview of the Act if it is rationally construed." Disagreeing, the Court of Appeals held that the record revealed a prima facie violation of § 7 of the Act, namely that TVA had failed to take "such action . . . necessary to insure" that its "actions" did not jeopardize the snail darter or its critical habitat.

The reviewing court thus rejected TVA's contention that the word "actions" in § 7 of the Act was not intended by Congress to encompass the terminal phases of ongoing projects. Not only could the court find no "positive reinforcement" for TVA's argument in the Act's legislative history, but also such an interpretation was seen as being "inimical to . . . its objectives." By way of illustration, that court pointed out that "the detrimental impact of a project upon an endangered species may not always be clearly perceived before construction is well underway." Given such a likelihood, the Court of Appeals was of the opinion that TVA's position would require the District Court, sitting as a chancellor, to balance the worth of an endangered species against the value of an ongoing public works measure, a result which the appellate court was not willing to accept. Emphasizing the limits on judicial power in this setting, the court stated:

"Current project status cannot be translated into a workable standard of judicial review. Whether a dam is 50% or 90% completed is irrelevant in calculating the social and scientific costs attributable to the disappearance of a unique form of life. Courts are ill-equipped to calculate how many dollars must be invested before the value of a dam exceeds that of the endangered species. Our responsibility under § 1540(g)(1)(A) is merely to preserve the status quo where endangered species are threatened, thereby guaranteeing the legislative or executive branches sufficient opportunity to grapple with the alternatives."

As far as the Court of Appeals was concerned, it made no difference that Congress had repeatedly approved appropriations for Tellico, referring to such legislative approval as an "advisory opinio[n]" concerning the proper application of an existing statute. In that court's view, the only relevant legislation was the Act itself, "[t]he meaning and spirit" of which was "clear on its face."

Turning to the question of an appropriate remedy, the Court of Appeals ruled that the District Court had erred by not issuing an injunction. While recognizing the irretrievable loss of millions of dollars of public funds which would accompany injunctive relief, the court nonetheless decided that the Act explicitly commanded precisely that result:

"It is conceivable that the welfare of an endangered species may weigh more heavily upon the public conscience, as expressed by the final will of Congress, than the write off of those millions of dollars already expended for Tellico in excess of its present salvageable value."

Following the issuance of the permanent injunction, members of TVA's Board of Directors appeared before Subcommittees of the House and Senate Appropriations Committees to testify in support of continued appropriations for Tellico. The Subcommittees were apprised of all aspects of Tellico's status, including the Court of Appeals' decision. TVA reported that the dam stood "ready for the gates to be closed and the reservoir filled," Hearings on Public Works for Water and Power Development and Energy Research Appropriation Bill, 1978, before a Subcommittee of the House Committee on Appropriations, and requested funds for completion of certain ancillary parts of the project, such as public use areas, roads, and bridges. As to the snail darter itself, TVA commented optimistically on its transplantation efforts, expressing the opinion that the relocated fish were "doing well and ha[d] reproduced."

Both Appropriations Committees subsequently recommended the full amount requested for completion of the Tellico Project. In its June 2, 1977, Report, the House Appropriations Committee stated:

"It is *the Committee's view* that the Endangered Species Act was not intended to halt projects such as these in their advanced stage of completion, and [the Committee] strongly recommends that these projects not be stopped because of misuse of the Act."

As a solution to the problem, the House Committee advised that TVA should cooperate with the Department of the Interior "to relocate the endangered species to another suitable habitat so as to permit the project to proceed as rapidly as possible." Toward this end, the Committee recommended a special appropriation of $2 million to facilitate relocation of the snail darter and other endangered species which threatened to delay or stop TVA projects. Much the same occurred on the Senate side, with its Appropriations Committee recommending both the amount requested to complete Tellico and the special appropriation for transplantation of endangered species. Reporting to the Senate on these measures, the Appropriations Committee took a particularly strong stand on the snail darter issue:

"This *committee has not viewed* the Endangered Species Act as preventing the completion and use of these projects which were well under way at the time the affected species were listed as endangered. If the act has such an effect which is contrary to *the Committee's understanding* of the intent of Congress in enacting the Endangered Species Act, funds should be appropriated to allow these projects to be completed and their benefits realized in the public interest, the Endangered Species Act notwithstanding."

TVA's budget, including funds for completion of Tellico and relocation of the snail darter, passed both Houses of Congress and was signed into law on August 7, 1977.

We granted certiorari, to review the judgment of the Court of Appeals.

II

We begin with the premise that operation of the Tellico Dam will either eradicate the known population of snail darters or destroy their critical habitat. Petitioner does not now seriously dispute this fact. In any event, under § 4(a)(1) of the Act, The Secretary of the Interior is vested with exclusive authority to determine whether a species such as the snail darter is "endangered" or "threatened" and to ascertain the factors which have led to such a precarious existence. By § 4(d) Congress has authorized—indeed commanded—the Secretary to "issue such regulations as he deems necessary and advisable to provide for the conservation of such species." As we have seen, the Secretary promulgated regulations which declared the snail darter an endangered species whose critical habitat would be destroyed by creation of the Tellico Dam. Doubtless petitioner would prefer not to have these regulations on the books, but there is no suggestion that the Secretary exceeded his authority or abused his discretion in issuing the regulations. Indeed, no judicial review of the Secretary's determinations has ever been sought and hence the validity of his actions are not open to review in this Court.

Starting from the above premise, two questions are presented: (a) Would TVA be in violation of the Act if it completed and operated the Tellico Dam as planned? (b) If TVA's actions would offend the Act, is an injunction the appropriate remedy for the violation? For the reasons stated hereinafter, we hold that both questions must be answered in the affirmative.

(A)

It may seem curious to some that the survival of a relatively small number of three-inch fish among all the countless millions of species extant would require the permanent halting of a virtually completed dam for which Congress has expended more than $100 million. The paradox is not minimized by the fact that Congress continued to appropriate large sums of public money for the project, even after congressional Appropriations Committees were apprised of its apparent impact upon the survival of the snail darter. We conclude, however, that the explicit provisions of the Endangered Species Act require precisely that result.

One would be hard pressed to find a statutory provision whose terms were any plainer than those in § 7 of the Endangered Species Act. Its very words affirmatively command all federal agencies "to *insure* that actions *authorized, funded,* or *carried out* by them do not *jeopardize* the continued existence" of an endangered species or "*result* in the destruction or modification of habitat of such species . . . ." 16 U.S.C. § 1536 (1976 ed.). (Emphasis added.) This language admits of no exception. Nonetheless, petitioner urges, as do the dissenters, that the Act cannot reasonably be interpreted as applying to a federal project which was well under way when Congress passed the Endangered Species Act of 1973. To sustain that position, however, we would be forced to ignore the ordinary meaning of plain language. It has not been shown, for example, how TVA can close the gates of the Tellico Dam without "carrying out" an action that has been "authorized" and "funded" by a federal agency. Nor can we understand how such action will "*insure* " that the snail darter's habitat is not disrupted.[18] Accepting the Secretary's determinations, as we must, it is clear that TVA's proposed operation of the dam will have precisely the opposite effect, namely the *eradication* of an endangered species.

Concededly, this view of the Act will produce results requiring the sacrifice of the anticipated benefits of the project and of many millions of dollars in public funds. But examination of the language, history, and structure of the legislation under review here indicates beyond doubt that Congress intended endangered species to be afforded the highest of priorities.

The legislative proceedings in 1973 are, in fact, replete with expressions of concern over the risk that might lie in the loss of *any* endangered species.[23] Typifying these sentiments is the Report of the House Committee on Merchant Marine and Fisheries on H.R. 37, a bill which contained the essential features of the subsequently enacted Act of 1973; in explaining the need for the legislation, the Report stated:
"As we homogenize the habitats in which these plants and animals evolved, and as we increase the pressure for products that they are in a position to supply (usually unwillingly) we threaten their—and our own—genetic heritage.
"The value of this genetic heritage is, quite literally, incalculable.

"From the most narrow possible point of view, *it is in the best interests of mankind to minimize the losses of genetic variations.* The reason is simple: they are potential resources. They are keys to puzzles which we cannot solve, and may provide answers to questions which we have not yet learned to ask.

"To take a homely, but apt, example: one of the critical chemicals in the regulation of ovulations in humans was found in a common plant. Once discovered, and analyzed, humans could duplicate it synthetically, but had it never existed—or had it been driven out of existence before we knew its potentialities—we would never have tried to synthesize it in the first place.

"Who knows, or can say, what potential cures for cancer or other scourges, present or future, may lie locked up in the structures of plants which may yet be undiscovered, much less analyzed? . . . Sheer self-interest impels us to be cautious.

"*The institutionalization of that caution* lies at the heart of H.R. 37 . . . ." H.R.Rep.No.93–412, pp. 4–5 (1973). (Emphasis added.)

As the examples cited here demonstrate, Congress was concerned about the *unknown* uses that endangered species might have and about the *unforeseeable* place such creatures may have in the chain of life on this planet.

As it was finally passed, the Endangered Species Act of 1973 represented the most comprehensive legislation for the preservation of endangered species ever enacted by any nation. Its stated purposes were "to provide a means whereby the ecosystems upon which endangered species and threatened species depend may be conserved," and "to provide a program for the conservation of such . . . species . . . ." 16 U.S.C. § 1531(b) (1976 ed.). In furtherance of these goals, Congress expressly stated in § 2(c) that "all Federal departments and agencies *shall* seek *to conserve endangered species* and threatened species . . . ." 16 U.S.C. § 1531(c) (1976 ed.). (Emphasis added.) Lest there be any ambiguity as to the meaning of this statutory directive, the Act specifically defined "conserve" as meaning "to use and the use of *all methods and procedures which are necessary* to bring *any endangered species or threatened species* to the point at which the measures provided pursuant to this chapter are no longer necessary." § 1532(2). (Emphasis added.) Aside from § 7, other provisions indicated the seriousness with which Congress viewed this issue: Virtually all dealings with endangered species, including taking, possession, transportation, and sale, were prohibited, 16 U.S.C. § 1538 (1976 ed.), except in extremely narrow circumstances, see § 1539(b). The Secretary was also given extensive power to develop regulations and programs for the preservation of endangered and threatened species.[25] § 1533(d). Citizen involvement was encouraged by the Act, with provisions allowing interested persons to petition the Secretary to list a species as endangered or threatened, § 1533(c)(2), and bring civil suits in United States district courts to force compliance with any provision of the Act, §§ 1540(c) and (g).

Section 7 of the Act, which of course is relied upon by respondents in this case, provides a particularly good gauge of congressional intent. As we have seen, this provision had its genesis in the Endangered Species Act of 1966, but that legislation qualified the obligation of federal agencies by stating that they should seek to preserve endangered species only "*insofar as is practicable and consistent with the[ir] primary purposes . . . .*" Likewise, every bill introduced in 1973 contained a qualification similar to that found in the earlier statutes. Exemplary of these was the administration bill, H.R. 4758, which in § 2(b) would direct federal agencies to use their authorities to further the ends of the Act "*insofar as is practicable and consistent with the[ir] primary purposes . . . .*" (Emphasis added.) Explaining the idea behind this language, an administration spokesman told Congress that it "would further signal to all . . . agencies of the Government that this is the *first priority, consistent with their primary objectives.*" 1973 House Hearings 213 (statement of Deputy Assistant Secretary of the Interior). (Emphasis added.)

****

It is against this legislative background that we must measure TVA's claim that the Act was not intended to stop operation of a project which, like Tellico Dam, was near completion when an endangered species was discovered in its path. While there is no discussion in the legislative history of precisely this problem, the totality of congressional action makes it abundantly clear that the result we reach today is wholly in accord with both the words of the statute and the intent of Congress. The plain intent of Congress in enacting this statute was to halt and reverse the trend toward species extinction, whatever the cost. This is reflected not only in the stated policies of the Act, but in literally every section of the statute. All persons, including federal agencies, are specifically instructed not to "take" endangered species, meaning that no one is "to harass, harm,[30] pursue, hunt, shoot, wound, kill, trap, capture, or collect" such life forms. 16 U.S.C. §§ 1532(14), 1538(a)(1)(B) (1976 ed.). Agencies in particular are directed by §§ 2(c) and 3(2) of the Act to "use . . . *all methods* and procedures which are necessary" to preserve endangered

---

species. 16 U.S.C. §§ 1531(c), 1532(2) (emphasis added) (1976 ed.). In addition, the legislative history undergirding § 7 reveals an explicit congressional decision to require agencies to afford first priority to the declared national policy of saving endangered species. The pointed omission of the type of qualifying language previously included in endangered species legislation reveals a conscious decision by Congress to give endangered species priority over the "primary missions" of federal agencies.

It is not for us to speculate, much less act, on whether Congress would have altered its stance had the specific events of this case been anticipated. In any event, we discern no hint in the deliberations of Congress relating to the 1973 Act that would compel a different result than we reach here. Indeed, the repeated expressions of congressional concern over what it saw as the potentially enormous danger presented by the eradication of *any* endangered species suggest how the balance would have been struck had the issue been presented to Congress in 1973.

Furthermore, it is clear Congress foresaw that § 7 would, on occasion, require agencies to alter ongoing projects in order to fulfill the goals of the Act. [An] example is provided by the House Committee Report:

"Under the authority of [§ 7], the Director of the Park Service would be required *to conform the practices of his agency* to the need for protecting the rapidly dwindling stock of grizzly bears within Yellowstone Park. These bears, which may be endangered, and are undeniably threatened, should at least be protected by supplying them with carcasses from excess elk within the park, *by curtailing the destruction of habitat by clearcutting National Forests surrounding the Park*, and by preventing hunting until their numbers have recovered sufficiently to withstand these pressures." H.R.Rep.No.93–412, p. 14 (1973). (Emphasis added.)

One might dispute the applicability of these examples to the Tellico Dam by saying that in this case the burden on the public through the loss of millions of unrecoverable dollars would greatly outweigh the loss of the snail darter. But neither the Endangered Species Act nor Art. III of the Constitution provides federal courts with authority to make such fine utilitarian calculations. On the contrary, the plain language of the Act, buttressed by its legislative history, shows clearly that Congress viewed the value of endangered species as "incalculable." Quite obviously, it would be difficult for a court to balance the loss of a sum certain—even $100 million—against a congressionally declared "incalculable" value, even assuming we had the power to engage in such a weighing process, which we emphatically do not.

In passing the Endangered Species Act of 1973, Congress was also aware of certain instances in which exceptions to the statute's broad sweep would be necessary. Thus, § 10, 16 U.S.C. § 1539 (1976 ed.), creates a number of limited "hardship exemptions," none of which would even remotely apply to the Tellico Project. In fact, there are no exemptions in the Endangered Species Act for federal agencies, meaning that under the maxim *expressio unius est exclusio alterius*, we must presume that these were the only "hardship cases" Congress intended to exempt.

Notwithstanding Congress' expression of intent in 1973, we are urged to find that the continuing appropriations for Tellico Dam constitute an implied repeal of the 1973 Act, at least insofar as it applies to the Tellico Project. In support of this view, TVA points to the statements found in various House and Senate Appropriations Committees' Reports; as described in Part I, *supra*, those Reports generally reflected the attitude of the *Committees* either that the Act did not apply to Tellico or that the dam should be completed regardless of the provisions of the Act. Since we are unwilling to assume that these latter Committee statements constituted advice to ignore the provisions of a duly enacted law, we assume that these Committees believed that the Act simply was not applicable in this situation. But even under this interpretation of the Committees' actions, we are unable to conclude that the Act has been in any respect amended or repealed.

There is nothing in the appropriations measures, as passed, which states that the Tellico Project was to be completed irrespective of the requirements of the Endangered Species Act. These appropriations, in fact, represented relatively minor components of the lump-sum amounts for the *entire* TVA budget. To find a repeal of the Endangered Species Act under these circumstances would surely do violence to the "'cardinal rule . . . that repeals by implication are not favored.'" [] In practical terms, this "cardinal rule" means that "[i]n the absence of some affirmative showing of an intention to repeal, the only permissible justification for a repeal by implication is when the earlier and later statutes are irreconcilable." The doctrine disfavoring repeals by implication "applies with full vigor when . . . the subsequent legislation is an *appropriations* measure." []

[Remainder of this portion of the opinion disfavoring repeals by implication is omitted.]

(B)

Having determined that there is an irreconcilable conflict between operation of the Tellico Dam and the explicit provisions of § 7 of the Endangered Species Act, we must now consider what remedy, if any, is appropriate. It is correct, of course, that a federal judge sitting as a chancellor is not mechanically obligated to grant an injunction for every violation of law. This Court made plain ... that "[a] grant of *jurisdiction* to issue compliance orders hardly suggests an absolute duty to do so under any and all circumstances." As a general matter it may be said that "[s]ince all or almost all equitable remedies are discretionary, the balancing of equities and hardships is appropriate in almost any case as a guide to the chancellor's discretion."[]

But these principles take a court only so far. Our system of government is, after all, a tripartite one, with each branch having certain defined functions delegated to it by the Constitution. While "[i]t is emphatically the province and duty of the judicial department to say what the law is," *Marbury v. Madison*, 1 Cranch 137, 177, 2 L.Ed. 60 (1803), it is equally—and emphatically —the exclusive province of the Congress not only to formulate legislative policies and mandate programs and projects, but also to establish their relative priority for the Nation. Once Congress, exercising its delegated powers, has decided the order of priorities in a given area, it is for the Executive to administer the laws and for the courts to enforce them when enforcement is sought.

Here we are urged to view the Endangered Species Act "reasonably," and hence shape a remedy "that accords with some modicum of common sense and the public weal." But is that our function? We have no expert knowledge on the subject of endangered species, much less do we have a mandate from the people to strike a balance of equities on the side of the Tellico Dam. Congress has spoken in the plainest of words, making it abundantly clear that the balance has been struck in favor of affording endangered species the highest of priorities, thereby adopting a policy which it described as "institutionalized caution."

Our individual appraisal of the wisdom or un-wisdom of a particular course consciously selected by the Congress is to be put aside in the process of interpreting a statute. Once the meaning of an enactment is discerned and its constitutionality determined, the judicial process comes to an end. We do not sit as a committee of review, nor are we vested with the power of veto. The lines ascribed to Sir Thomas More by Robert Bolt are not without relevance here:

"The law, Roper, the law. I know what's legal, not what's right. And I'll stick to what's legal. . . . I'm *not* God. The currents and eddies of right and wrong, which you find such plain-sailing, I can't navigate, I'm no voyager. But in the thickets of the law, oh there I'm a forester. . . . What would you do? Cut a great road through the law to get after the Devil? . . . And when the last law was down, and the Devil turned round on you—where would you hide, Roper, the laws all being flat? . . . This country's planted thick with laws from coast to coast—Man's laws, not God's—and if you cut them down . . . d'you really think you could stand upright in the winds that would blow then? . . . Yes, I'd give the Devil benefit of law, for my own safety's sake." R. Bolt, A Man for All Seasons, Act I, p. 147 (Three Plays, Heinemann ed. 1967).

We agree with the Court of Appeals that in our constitutional system the commitment to the separation of powers is too fundamental for us to pre-empt congressional action by judicially decreeing what accords with "common sense and the public weal." Our Constitution vests such responsibilities in the political branches.

Affirmed.

Mr. Justice POWELL, with whom Mr. Justice BLACKMUN joins, dissenting.

The Court today holds that § 7 of the Endangered Species Act requires a federal court, for the purpose of protecting an endangered species or its habitat, to enjoin permanently the operation of any federal project, whether completed or substantially completed. This decision casts a long shadow over the operation of even the most important projects, serving vital needs of society and national defense, whenever it is determined that continued operation would threaten extinction of an endangered species or its habitat. This result is said to be required by the "plain intent of Congress" as well as by the language of the statute.

In my view § 7 cannot reasonably be interpreted as applying to a project that is completed or substantially completed[1] when its threat to an endangered species is discovered. Nor can I believe that Congress could have intended this Act to produce the "absurd result"—in the words of the District Court—of this case. If it were clear from the language of the Act and its legislative history that Congress intended to authorize this result, this Court would be compelled to enforce it. It is not our province to rectify policy or political judgments by the Legislative Branch, however egregiously they may disserve the public interest. But where the statutory language and legislative history, as in this case, need not be construed to reach such a result, I view it as the duty of this Court to adopt a permissible construction that accords with some modicum of common sense and the public weal.

[Remainder of dissent by Justices Powell and Blackmun omitted]

Mr. Justice REHNQUIST, dissenting.

In the light of my Brother POWELL's dissenting opinion, I am far less convinced than is the Court that the Endangered Species Act of 1973, 16 U.S.C. § 1531 *et seq.* (1976 ed.), was intended to prohibit the completion of the Tellico Dam. But the very difficulty and doubtfulness of the correct answer to this legal question convinces me that the Act did *not* prohibit the District Court from refusing, in the exercise of its traditional equitable powers, to enjoin petitioner from completing the Dam. ...

Since equity is "the instrument for nice adjustment and reconciliation between the public interest and private needs," a decree in one case will seldom be the exact counterpart of a decree in another. The District Court recognized that Congress, when it enacted the Endangered Species Act, made the preservation of the habitat of the snail darter an important public concern. But it concluded that this interest on one side of the balance was more than outweighed by other equally significant factors. These factors, further elaborated in the dissent of my Brother POWELL, satisfy me that the District Court's refusal to issue an injunction was not an abuse of its discretion. I therefore dissent from the Court's opinion holding otherwise.

QUESTIONS

1. According to the SCOTUS in *TVA v. Hill*, How did the ESA come about?
2. What happened in *TVA v. Hill?*
3. How did the SCOTUS rule, and why?
4. What did the SCOTUS make of the government's argument that an appropriation measure repealed portions of the ESA for this project?
5. Do you agree or disagree with the outcome?
6. Judging solely by this opinion, what do you think the impact of the ESA would be going forward?

The purpose of the ESA is to "conserve" some of the last remaining plants and animals on the planet, the value of which as the SCOTUS has noted are "incalculable."

II.   TEXTUAL ENDANGERED SPECIES ACT

A. ESA PURPOSES

The ESA's findings, purposes and policies are rather breathtaking, especially from the mouths of federal legislators. As with NEPA, the ESA is its own best evidence of what it means and aspires to do. In pertinent part, it provides:

16 USCA § 1531 (ESA Section 2): Congressional findings and declaration of purposes and policy

(a) Findings
 The Congress finds and declares that--
(1) various species of fish, wildlife, and plants in the United States have been rendered extinct as a consequence of economic growth and development untempered by adequate concern and conservation;
(2) other species of fish, wildlife, and plants have been so depleted in numbers that they are in danger of or threatened with extinction;
(3) these species of fish, wildlife, and plants are of esthetic, ecological, educational, historical, recreational, and scientific value to the Nation and its people;
(4) the United States has pledged itself as a sovereign state in the international community to conserve to the extent practicable the various species of fish or wildlife and plants facing extinction, pursuant to--
(A) migratory bird treaties with Canada and Mexico;
(B) the Migratory and Endangered Bird Treaty with Japan;
 (C) the Convention on Nature Protection and Wildlife Preservation in the Western Hemisphere;
(D) the International Convention for the Northwest Atlantic Fisheries;
(E) the International Convention for the High Seas Fisheries of the North Pacific Ocean;
(F) the Convention on International Trade in Endangered Species of Wild Fauna and Flora; and
(G) other international agreements; and
(5) encouraging the States and other interested parties, through Federal financial assistance and a system of incentives, to develop and maintain conservation programs which meet national and

international standards is a key to meeting the Nation's international commitments and to better safeguarding, for the benefit of all citizens, the Nation's heritage in fish, wildlife, and plants.

(b) Purposes

The purposes of this chapter are to provide a means whereby the ecosystems upon which endangered species and threatened species depend may be conserved, to provide a program for the conservation of such endangered species and threatened species, and to take such steps as may be appropriate to achieve the purposes of the treaties and conventions set forth in subsection (a) of this section.

(c) Policy

(1) It is further declared to be the policy of Congress that all Federal departments and agencies shall seek to conserve endangered species and threatened species and shall utilize their authorities in furtherance of the purposes of this chapter.

(2) It is further declared to be the policy of Congress that Federal agencies shall cooperate with State and local agencies to resolve water resource issues in concert with conservation of endangered species.

QUESTIONS

1. What findings did Congress make in the wake of the ESA?
2. What are the ESA's purposes?
3. What are the policies behind the ESA?
4. What is the relationship between the ESA and international law?

B. ESA DEFINITIONS

The ESA defines most of its key terms, including "species," "threatened," "endangered," "critical habitat," "plant," "animal," and "conservation." Study these definitions carefully, as they delineate the ESA's scope and are often determinative in resolving disputes in courts and before relevant agencies. I don't say this that often, but under the ESA, Congress knew what it was doing, said what it meant, and meant what it said, for the most 'part' (which is an inside joke in and of itself). Here you go:

§ 1532. Definitions (ESA Section 3)

For the purposes of this chapter--

(1) The term "alternative courses of action" means all alternatives and thus is not limited to original project objectives and agency jurisdiction.

(2) The term "commercial activity" means all activities of industry and trade, including, but not limited to, the buying or selling of commodities and activities conducted for the purpose of facilitating such buying and selling: *Provided, however,* That it does not include exhibition of commodities by museums or similar cultural or historical organizations.

(3) The terms "conserve", "conserving", and "conservation" mean to use and the use of all methods and procedures which are necessary to bring any endangered species or threatened species to the point at which the measures provided pursuant to this chapter are no longer necessary. Such methods and procedures include, but are not limited to, all activities associated with scientific resources management such as research, census, law enforcement, habitat acquisition and

maintenance, propagation, live trapping, and transplantation, and, in the extraordinary case where population pressures within a given ecosystem cannot be otherwise relieved, may include regulated taking.

(4) The term "Convention" means the Convention on International Trade in Endangered Species of Wild Fauna and Flora, signed on March 3, 1973, and the appendices thereto.

(5)(A) The term "critical habitat" for a threatened or endangered species means--
(i) the specific areas within the geographical area occupied by the species, at the time it is listed in accordance with the provisions of section 1533 of this title, on which are found those physical or biological features (I) essential to the conservation of the species and (II) which may require special management considerations or protection; and
(ii) specific areas outside the geographical area occupied by the species at the time it is listed in accordance with the provisions of section 1533 of this title, upon a determination by the Secretary that such areas are essential for the conservation of the species.
(B) Critical habitat may be established for those species now listed as threatened or endangered species for which no critical habitat has heretofore been established as set forth in subparagraph (A) of this paragraph.
(C) Except in those circumstances determined by the Secretary, critical habitat shall not include the entire geographical area which can be occupied by the threatened or endangered species.

(6) The term "endangered species" means any species which is in danger of extinction throughout all or a significant portion of its range other than a species of the Class Insecta determined by the Secretary to constitute a pest whose protection under the provisions of this chapter would present an overwhelming and overriding risk to man.

(7) The term "Federal agency" means any department, agency, or instrumentality of the United States.

(8) The term "fish or wildlife" means any member of the animal kingdom, including without limitation any mammal, fish, bird (including any migratory, nonmigratory, or endangered bird for which protection is also afforded by treaty or other international agreement), amphibian, reptile, mollusk, crustacean, arthropod or other invertebrate, and includes any part, product, egg, or offspring thereof, or the dead body or parts thereof.

(9) The term "foreign commerce" includes, among other things, any transaction--
(A) between persons within one foreign country;
(B) between persons in two or more foreign countries;
(C) between a person within the United States and a person in a foreign country; or
(D) between persons within the United States, where the fish and wildlife in question are moving in any country or countries outside the United States.

(10) The term "import" means to land on, bring into, or introduce into, or attempt to land on, bring into, or introduce into, any place subject to the jurisdiction of the United States, whether or not such landing, bringing, or introduction constitutes an importation within the meaning of the customs laws of the United States.

(12) The term "permit or license applicant" means, when used with respect to an action of a Federal agency for which exemption is sought under section 1536 of this title, any person whose application to such agency for a permit or license has been denied primarily because of the application of section 1536(a) of this title to such agency action.

(13) The term "person" means an individual, corporation, partnership, trust, association, or any other private entity; or any officer, employee, agent, department, or instrumentality of the Federal Government, of any State, municipality, or political subdivision of a State, or of any foreign government; any State, municipality, or political subdivision of a State; or any other entity subject to the jurisdiction of the United States.

(14) The term "plant" means any member of the plant kingdom, including seeds, roots and other parts thereof.

(15) The term "Secretary" means, except as otherwise herein provided, the Secretary of the Interior or the Secretary of Commerce as program responsibilities are vested pursuant to the provisions of Reorganization Plan Numbered 4 of 1970; except that with respect to the enforcement of the provisions of this chapter and the Convention which pertain to the importation or exportation of terrestrial plants, the term also means the Secretary of Agriculture.

(16) The term "species" includes any subspecies of fish or wildlife or plants, and any distinct population segment of any species of vertebrate fish or wildlife which interbreeds when mature.

(17) The term "State" means any of the several States, the District of Columbia, the Commonwealth of Puerto Rico, American Samoa, the Virgin Islands, Guam, and the Trust Territory of the Pacific Islands.

(18) The term "State agency" means any State agency, department, board, commission, or other governmental entity which is responsible for the management and conservation of fish, plant, or wildlife resources within a State.

(19) The term "take" means to harass, harm, pursue, hunt, shoot, wound, kill, trap, capture, or collect, or to attempt to engage in any such conduct.

(20) The term "threatened species" means any species which is likely to become an endangered species within the foreseeable future throughout all or a significant portion of its range.

(21) The term "United States", when used in a geographical context, includes all States.

QUESTIONS

1. The ESA's purpose is to "conserve" T&E species. Does the ESA define that term, and if so, how?
2. What is a "species" under the ESA?
3. Same, for "endangered."
4. Same for "threatened."
5. The ESA protects both T&E "fish and wildlife" species. Does it define that term, and if so, how?
6. Same, for "plant."
7. The ESA prevents "persons" from "taking" T&E species. Does the ESA define those term, and if so, how?
8. Why is the role of identifying "critical habitat"? Does the ESA define that term, and if so, how?
9.

III.   LISTING PROTECTED SPECIES AND HABITAT

Not all biological species that are biologically threatened with extinction fall under the ESA. Only those "listed," along with their "critical habitat," under Section 4 fall within the auspices of the ESA. As we shall see, Congress went out of its way to specify what it takes to earn federal protection, and how such recognition occurs. We will begin with statutory language, followed by a case that shows how Section 4 works in context.

A. STATUTORY LANGUAGE

We will begin this section by reading Section 4 of the ESA. It governs the procedural and substantive regarding identifying T&E species and their critical habitat. The spacing is a challenge (for me, too). Persevere. Questions follow.

16 U.S.C.A. § 1533 (ESA Section 4): Determination of endangered species and threatened species

(a) Generally

(1) The Secretary shall by regulation promulgated in accordance with subsection (b) of this section determine whether any species is an endangered species or a threatened species because of any of the following factors:
(A) the present or threatened destruction, modification, or curtailment of its habitat or range;
(B) overutilization for commercial, recreational, scientific, or educational purposes;
(C) disease or predation;
(D) the inadequacy of existing regulatory mechanisms; or
(E) other natural or manmade factors affecting its continued existence.

(2) With respect to any species over which program responsibilities have been vested in the Secretary of Commerce pursuant to Reorganization Plan Numbered 4 of 1970--
(A) in any case in which the Secretary of Commerce determines that such species should--
(i) be listed as an endangered species or a threatened species, or
(ii) be changed in status from a threatened species to an endangered species,
he shall so inform the Secretary of the Interior, who shall list such species in accordance with this section;
(B) in any case in which the Secretary of Commerce determines that such species should--
(i) be removed from any list published pursuant to subsection (c) of this section, or
(ii) be changed in status from an endangered species to a threatened species,
he shall recommend such action to the Secretary of the Interior, and the Secretary of the Interior, if he concurs in the recommendation, shall implement such action; and
(C) the Secretary of the Interior may not list or remove from any list any such species, and may not change the status of any such species which are listed, without a prior favorable determination made pursuant to this section by the Secretary of Commerce.

(3)(A) The Secretary, by regulation promulgated in accordance with subsection (b) of this section and to the maximum extent prudent and determinable--
(i) shall, concurrently with making a determination under paragraph (1) that a species is an endangered species or a threatened species, designate any habitat of such species which is then considered to be critical habitat; and
(ii) may, from time-to-time thereafter as appropriate, revise such designation.

(B)   (i) The Secretary shall not designate as critical habitat any lands or other geographical areas owned or controlled by the Department of Defense, or designated for its use, that are subject to an integrated natural resources management plan prepared under section 670a of this title, if the Secretary determines in writing that such plan provides a benefit to the species for which critical habitat is proposed for designation.

(ii) Nothing in this paragraph affects the requirement to consult under section 1536(a)(2) of this title with respect to an agency action (as that term is defined in that section).

(iii) Nothing in this paragraph affects the obligation of the Department of Defense to comply with section 1538 of this title, including the prohibition preventing extinction and taking of endangered species and threatened species.

(b) Basis for determinations

(1)   (A) The Secretary shall make determinations required by subsection (a) (1) of this section solely on the basis of the best scientific and commercial data available to him after conducting a review of the status of the species and after taking into account those efforts, if any, being made by any State or foreign nation, or any political subdivision of a State or foreign nation, to protect such species, whether by predator control, protection of habitat and food supply, or other conservation practices, within any area under its jurisdiction, or on the high seas.

(B) In carrying out this section, the Secretary shall give consideration to species which have been-
(i) designated as requiring protection from unrestricted commerce by any foreign nation, or pursuant to any international agreement; or
(ii) identified as in danger of extinction, or likely to become so within the foreseeable future, by any State agency or by any agency of a foreign nation that is responsible for the conservation of fish or wildlife or plants.

(2) The Secretary shall designate critical habitat, and make revisions thereto, under subsection (a) (3) of this section on the basis of the best scientific data available and after taking into consideration the economic impact, the impact on national security, and any other relevant impact, of specifying any particular area as critical habitat. The Secretary may exclude any area from critical habitat if he determines that the benefits of such exclusion outweigh the benefits of specifying such area as part of the critical habitat, unless he determines, based on the best scientific and commercial data available, that the failure to designate such area as critical habitat will result in the extinction of the species concerned.

(3)   (A) To the maximum extent practicable, within 90 days after receiving the petition of an interested person under section 553(e) of Title 5, to add a species to, or to remove a species from, either of the lists published under subsection (c) of this section, the Secretary shall make a finding as to whether the petition presents substantial scientific or commercial information indicating that the petitioned action may be warranted. If such a petition is found to present such information, the Secretary shall promptly commence a review of the status of the species concerned. The Secretary shall promptly publish each finding made under this subparagraph in the Federal Register.

(B) Within 12 months after receiving a petition that is found under subparagraph (A) to present substantial information indicating that the petitioned action may be warranted, the Secretary shall make one of the following findings:
(i) The petitioned action is not warranted, in which case the Secretary shall promptly publish such finding in the Federal Register.
(ii) The petitioned action is warranted, in which case the Secretary shall promptly publish in the Federal Register a general notice and the complete text of a proposed regulation to implement such action in accordance with paragraph (5).

(iii) The petitioned action is warranted, but that--

(I) the immediate proposal and timely promulgation of a final regulation implementing the petitioned action in accordance with paragraphs (5) and (6) is precluded by pending proposals to determine whether any species is an endangered species or a threatened species, and

(II) expeditious progress is being made to add qualified species to either of the lists published under subsection (c) of this section and to remove from such lists species for which the protections of this chapter are no longer necessary,in which case the Secretary shall promptly publish such finding in the Federal Register, together with a description and evaluation of the reasons and data on which the finding is based.

(C)   (i) A petition with respect to which a finding is made under subparagraph (B)(iii) shall be treated as a petition that is resubmitted to the Secretary under subparagraph (A) on the date of such finding and that presents substantial scientific or commercial information that the petitioned action may be warranted.

(ii) Any negative finding described in subparagraph (A) and any finding described in subparagraph (B) (i) or (iii) shall be subject to judicial review.

(iii) The Secretary shall implement a system to monitor effectively the status of all species with respect to which a finding is made under subparagraph (B)(iii) and shall make prompt use of the authority under paragraph 7[1]to prevent a significant risk to the well being of any such species.

(D)   (i) To the maximum extent practicable, within 90 days after receiving the petition of an interested person under section 553(e) of Title 5, to revise a critical habitat designation, the Secretary shall make a finding as to whether the petition presents substantial scientific information indicating that the revision may be warranted. The Secretary shall promptly publish such finding in the Federal Register.

(ii) Within 12 months after receiving a petition that is found under clause (i) to present substantial information indicating that the requested revision may be warranted, the Secretary shall determine how he intends to proceed with the requested revision, and shall promptly publish notice of such intention in the Federal Register.

...

(c) Lists

(1) The Secretary of the Interior shall publish in the Federal Register a list of all species determined by him or the Secretary of Commerce to be endangered species and a list of all species determined by him or the Secretary of Commerce to be threatened species. Each list shall refer to the species contained therein by scientific and common name or names, if any, specify with respect to each such species over what portion of its range it is endangered or threatened, and specify any critical habitat within such range. The Secretary shall from time to time revise each list published under the authority of this subsection to reflect recent determinations, designations, and revisions made in accordance with subsections (a) and (b) of this section.

(2) The Secretary shall—

(A) conduct, at least once every five years, a review of all species included in a list which is published pursuant to paragraph (1) and which is in effect at the time of such review; and

(B) determine on the basis of such review whether any such species should--

(i) be removed from such list;

(ii) be changed in status from an endangered species to a threatened species; or

(iii) be changed in status from a threatened species to an endangered species.

Each determination under subparagraph (B) shall be made in accordance with the provisions of subsections (a) and (b) of this section.

(d) Protective regulations [omitted]

(f) Recovery plans

(1) The Secretary shall develop and implement plans (hereinafter in this subsection referred to as "recovery plans") for the conservation and survival of endangered species and threatened species listed pursuant to this section, unless he finds that such a plan will not promote the conservation of the species. The Secretary, in developing and implementing recovery plans, shall, to the maximum extent practicable--

(A) give priority to those endangered species or threatened species, without regard to taxonomic classification, that are most likely to benefit from such plans, particularly those species that are, or may be, in conflict with construction or other development projects or other forms of economic activity;

(B) incorporate in each plan--

(i) a description of such site-specific management actions as may be necessary to achieve the plan's goal for the conservation and survival of the species;

(ii) objective, measurable criteria which, when met, would result in a determination, in accordance with the provisions of this section, that the species be removed from the list; and

(iii) estimates of the time required and the cost to carry out those measures needed to achieve the plan's goal and to achieve intermediate steps toward that goal.

(2) The Secretary, in developing and implementing recovery plans, may procure the services of appropriate public and private agencies and institutions, and other qualified persons. Recovery teams appointed pursuant to this subsection shall not be subject to the Federal Advisory Committee Act.

...

(5) Each Federal agency shall, prior to implementation of a new or revised recovery plan, consider all information presented during the public comment period under paragraph (4). ...

QUESTIONS

1. What is the process for "listing" a species as "endangered" under Section 4?
2. Same, for "threatened." Same, for "critical habitat."
3. What is the role of costs in listing species as T&E? How about for identifying "critical habitat?"
4. Who decides whether to list a species? Based upon what evidence?
5. What is a "recovery plan? How is it established and implemented?

B. LISTING SPECIES AND HABITAT IN CONTEXT

As you can appreciate, the process for identifying T&E species and their critical habitat is scientifically and administratively complex. Now let's have a look at a case in which a court struggled and muddled through the issues regarding the Alabama Sturgeon. As you shall soon see, the court took the time to unpack the purposes, language and legislative history of the ESA in reaching a result. (The judge who wrote the decision is also obviously very well read, and a bit of a show-off. ☺ Enjoy.). Questions follow.

ALABAMA-TOMBIGBEE RIVERS COALITION V. KEMPTHORNE
477 F.3d 1250 (2007)

CARNES, Circuit Judge:

Two fish, or not two fish? That is the question. More specifically, are the Alabama sturgeon and the shovelnose sturgeon separate species? The answer lies primarily in the field of taxonomy, which one observer has noted "is described sometimes as a science and sometimes as an art, but really it's a battleground." Bill Bryson, *A Short History of Nearly Everything* 437 (2003). The battle over the Alabama sturgeon has been more like the Thirty Years War. A scientist first classified this small freshwater fish found in the Mobile River Basin of Alabama as endangered in 1976. Three decades and three trips to this Court later the fight over whether the Alabama sturgeon is an endangered species continues. On one side are various business interests, including the Alabama-Tombigbee Rivers Coalition, and on the other are the Fish and Wildlife Service and several federal officials involved with it.

I.

The background facts of this litigation are set out in our 2003 opinion. *See Alabama-Tombigbee Rivers Coal. v. Norton (Alabama-Tombigbee II)*, 338 F.3d 1244 (11th Cir.2003). We won't wade back through all of the facts but will instead focus on those essential to the issues raised in this appeal.

The Alabama sturgeon was once so plentiful that it was captured commercially. At the end of the nineteenth century, an estimated 20,000 of the fish were caught commercially, but its numbers have declined drastically and it is now thought to reside only in small portions of the Alabama River channel in south Alabama and downstream to the mouth of the Tombigbee River. The historic decline of the species-if it is a species-is due to a combination of over-fishing, dam construction for power production, dredging and channeling to improve navigation in the Mobile River Basin, and declines in water and habitat quality resulting from river and land management practices. The Service began to study the decline of the Alabama sturgeon in 1980, four years after a scientist first classified it as endangered.

In June 1993, the Fish and Wildlife Service first proposed listing the fish as an endangered species under the Endangered Species Act of 1973. That proposed listing led to these litigants' first visit to our Court, when the Alabama-Tombigbee River Coalition, a group of industries and associations opposed to the listing, obtained an order from the United States District Court for the Northern District of Alabama granting a permanent injunction against the Service's use of a scientific report prepared in violation of the Federal Advisory Committee Act in making its listing determination. The Service appealed, and we affirmed. Several months later, the Service withdrew the proposed listing "on the basis of insufficient information that the Alabama sturgeon continued to exist."

Over the next few years, the capture of several Alabama sturgeon confirmed that the fish was still around, although barely-despite diligent efforts to locate the fish, there were only eight confirmed catches in the 1990s-and in 1999 the Service again proposed listing the Alabama sturgeon as endangered. On May 5, 2000, it issued a final rule listing the fish as an endangered species. Although the Service is responsible for designating the "critical habitat" of land animals and freshwater fish, it did not do so at the time it issued the Final Rule. And it still has not done so.

The Coalition brought suit under the citizen-suit provision of the ESA, 16 U.S.C. § 1540(g)(1), and under the judicial review provisions of the Administrative Procedure Act, 5 U.S.C. §§ 701-06, alleging several defects in the listing process. The district court dismissed the Coalition's lawsuit for lack of standing, but on appeal we reversed after concluding that the Coalition did have standing to challenge the listing decision.

On remand, the district court granted the Service's motion for summary judgment but ordered it to issue both a proposed and a final rule designating critical habitat for the Alabama sturgeon by May 14, 2006 and November 14, 2006, respectively. The Coalition appealed the judgment, which the district court stayed pending review by this Court.

We review the district court's grant of summary judgment *de novo*, viewing the facts and drawing all reasonable inferences in favor of the nonmoving party. However, "even in the context of summary judgment, an agency action is entitled to great deference." Under the Administrative Procedure Act, we must set aside any agency action that is arbitrary, capricious, or an abuse of discretion, 5 U.S.C. § 706(2)(A), but we cannot substitute our judgment for that of the agency. We look at "whether an agency's decision was based on a consideration of the relevant factors and whether there has been a clear error of judgment."

II.

The Coalition first contends that we must vacate the Final Rule because the Fish and Wildlife Service failed to consider the relevant factors in reaching its listing decision. Section 4(b)(1)(A) of the ESA requires the Service to make listing determinations "solely on the basis of the best scientific and commercial data available." 16 U.S.C. § 1533(b)(1)(A) (codifying Section 4(b)(1)(A)). The Coalition argues that the Service failed to rely on the best scientific data available in three ways: First, it discounted genetic typing in favor of morphological taxonomy. Second, the agency did not examine the best available taxonomic data. Third, it allegedly interfered with the research of one of its employees, Dr. Steven Fain.

The Administrative Procedure Act instructs reviewing courts to "hold unlawful and set aside agency action, findings, and conclusions" that are "arbitrary, capricious, an abuse of discretion, or otherwise not in accordance with law." 5 U.S.C. § 706(2)(A). We "may not set aside an agency rule that is rational, based on consideration of the relevant factors, and within the scope of the authority delegated to the agency by the statute." *Motor Vehicle Mfrs. Ass'n of U.S., Inc. v. State Farm Mut. Auto. Ins. Co.*, 463 U.S. 29, 42, 103 (1983). Under this "narrow" form of review, we may find a rule arbitrary and capricious where "the agency has relied on factors which Congress has not intended it to consider, entirely failed to consider an important aspect of the problem, offered an explanation for its decision that runs counter to the evidence before the agency, or is so implausible that it could not be ascribed to a difference in view or the product of agency expertise." The reviewing court may not make up for these deficiencies, which is to say that "we may not supply a reasoned basis for the agency's action that the agency itself has not given."

A.

The Coalition's first argument in support of its contention that the Service failed to consider the best scientific data is that it used "the older, subjective method of morphological taxonomy" instead of "the modern, objective science of genetics," to classify the Alabama sturgeon as a separate species. Genetics is the superior science, according to the Coalition, and in its view "[a]ll reliable genetic evidence" confirms that the Alabama sturgeon and the more-abundant shovelnose sturgeon are "genetically identical."

The Service responds by arguing that the Coalition is creating a false dichotomy between "taxonomy" and "genetics." "Taxonomy" is "the science or technique of classification" or the "science dealing with the description, identification, naming, and classification of organisms." *Random House Unabridged Dictionary* 1947 (2d ed.1993). "Genetics," which is "the science of heredity, dealing with resemblances and differences of related organisms resulting from the interaction of their genes and the environment," is one tool-but not the only tool-used to resolve taxonomic questions.

The Service believes that instead of relying on genetics alone, "[t]he most scientifically credible approach to making taxonomic determinations is to consider all available data involving as many different classes of characters as possible." The class of relevant characters "includes morphological, karyological (chromosomal), biochemical (including DNA analysis and other molecular genetic techniques), physiological, behavioral, ecological, and biogeographic characters." The Service argues that it did consider genetics, and simply concluded that the available genetic studies could not definitively resolve the taxonomic status of the Alabama sturgeon, and that the balance of the relevant data supported classifying the fish as its own species.

1.

The Coalition overstates its case when it asserts that "[a]ll reliable genetic evidence" confirms that the Alabama sturgeon and the shovelnose sturgeon are "identical." The two types of fish are not "genetically identical." If two complete samples of animal genetic material truly are identical, then they did not just come from the same species, they came from the same animal (or perhaps from a pair of twins). What the evidence tendered by the Coalition actually reveals is that when scientists have examined particular segments of the mitochondrial cytochrome *b* gene, a gene that scientists often test to help them distinguish between vertebrate species, they have found that the cytochrome *b* samples taken from those particular genetic segments of the Alabama sturgeon are very similar-not identical, but very similar-to those taken from shovelnose sturgeon.

At several points in the Final Rule, the agency addressed the significance of genetic testing. It found that the genetic evidence was much less lopsided-and much more consistent with other taxonomic indicators-than the Coalition suggests. The Service distinguished between three types of genetic studies. First were the studies of the mitochondrial cytochrome *b* gene which we have already mentioned. The agency agrees with the Coalition that one study by Schill and Walker "found no sequence divergence in a cytochrome *b* mtDNA sequence between a single specimen of the Alabama sturgeon and shovelnose sturgeon." A subsequent study by Fain *et al.* using a larger sample size found small but consistent differences between Alabama and shovelnose sturgeon, though the study concluded that these differences were too insignificant to support the use of cytochrome *b* testing in criminal prosecutions.

The second type of genetic study discussed in the Final Rule examined the "d-loop" or "control region" of the sturgeons' mitochondrial DNA. In 1995, Campton *et al.* found that a unique haplotype (a single insertion point on a genetic chain) distinguished the Alabama sturgeon from pallid and shovelnose sturgeon. However, the Campton report cautioned that this level of divergence was small, and suggested adding sturgeon from the lower Mississippi River to the study. In 1999, the Campton group completed phase II of that study, which included sturgeon from the lower Mississippi River. The phase II results were consistent with those of phase I, leading the scientists to conclude that "[t]hese mtDNA results provide the first genetic evidence that the three species of [sturgeon] are indeed distinct evolutionarily and thus support current conservation efforts to protect pallid and Alabama sturgeon as endangered *species* under the ESA." A study by Mayden *et al.* found the differences in the d-loop to be significant even after factoring in the similarity of the sturgeons' cytochrome *b* genes. It concluded that "the Alabama sturgeon and the shovelnose sturgeon were found to exhibit significant genetic heterogeneity based on both the control region sequences and the control region and cytochrome *b* combined data sets."

The third type of study discussed in the Final Rule examined nuclear DNA. A 1994 study by Genetic Analyses, Inc. found that "when the total available nuclear DNA markers are assessed, considerable genetic differences between the Alabama and both shovelnose and pallid sturgeon individuals are observed," but noted that "this result is based upon only one individual" Alabama sturgeon specimen. In 1995, Genetic Analyses tested two additional Alabama sturgeon specimens. This further examination "supports previous results indicating substantial genetic divergence of Alabama sturgeons from the other two recognized [sturgeon] species," leading Genetic Analyses to conclude that "the data presented here suggest strongly that Alabama sturgeons are more genetically divergent from pallid and shovelnose sturgeons than the latter taxa are from each other."

After addressing individually each type of genetic study in the administrative record, the Service expressed its general doubt that examination of genetic data could definitively resolve the Alabama sturgeon's taxonomic status. The Service explained in the Final Rule:

Genetic data have their greatest utility in making species-level taxonomic determinations when the putative species are sympatric (occur together) and the degree of natural genetic interaction can be evaluated. When the putative species are allopatric, as with Alabama and shovelnose sturgeons, genetic data provide a measure of divergence that must be evaluated along with all other available measures of divergence in making a determination whether species-level differences exist. When sample sizes are small, either in terms of number of individuals or number of genetic regions or loci tested, the taxonomic value of genetic data is diminished.

The Service specifically questioned the value of cytochrome *b* studies:
Cytochrome *b* is not the best choice of a genetic region for resolving the closely related species in the genus *Scaphirhynchus*. In such cases it is appropriate to examine a gene region known to have a faster rate of evolution that might be reflected in a difference between species. The study of Campton *et al.* (in press) employed the more rapidly evolving control region of mtDNA with the results described under Issue 59. Campton *et al.* (in press) also discuss other cases where speciation has occurred in fishes with very little genetic divergence in cytochrome b, and Fain *et al.* (2000) identifies lack of divergence between pairs of other sturgeon species. Interpreted in light of the minimal gene regions studied, the small sample sizes of Alabama sturgeon, and evidence from other species that species formation can occur with minimal detectable genetic differentiation in DNA regions commonly studied, the genetic data are consistent with and do not demand the rejection of taxonomic conclusions based on morphological and biogeographical data that the Alabama sturgeon qualifies for recognition as a valid species.

The Coalition emphasizes the fact that the cytochrome *b* genes of the Alabama sturgeon and the shovelnose sturgeon are very similar. As it points out, the Service uses cytochrome *b* testing to criminally prosecute defendants for violating federal species protection laws. According to the Fain report, examination of the cytochrome *b* gene can be used to positively identify fifteen of the world's twenty-seven sturgeon and paddlefish species. The implication the Coalition wishes us to draw is that if the Service considers cytochrome *b* testing to be conclusive enough for criminal prosecutions, it ought to be conclusive enough for rule making as well.

This argument misapprehends both the conclusions of the Fain study and the role of cytochrome *b* testing in criminal trials. The Fain study did not conclude that the Alabama sturgeon is not a distinct species. The report of that study states that the 5' end of the cytochrome *b* gene exhibits significant interspecific variation in sturgeon, which is to say that some species of sturgeon have very different cytochrome *b* genes than other species of sturgeon. When the cytochrome *b* genes of two species of sturgeon vary significantly from one another, but their intraspecific variation, or variance among individual members of each species, is low, the gene provides a useful marker to distinguish between the two types of sturgeon. Under these conditions, scientists can use cytochrome *b* testing to debunk a criminal defendant's false claim that caviar taken from an endangered species of sturgeon came from another non-endangered species.

The Fain report also states that cytochrome *b* testing cannot be used to distinguish between caviar from Alabama sturgeon and caviar from shovelnose sturgeon with sufficient reliability to be useful for forensic identification. The Coalition argues that because cytochrome *b* testing cannot reliably prove that the Alabama sturgeon is a distinct species, it must not be. Holding a position of centrality in that argument is the idea that inconclusive results of difference are conclusive proof of sameness. The reasoning is a species of *argumentum ad ignorantiam,* a fancier, and hence less denigrating, way of describing "an argument from ignorance." An argument from ignorance is "the mistake that is committed whenever it is argued that a proposition is true simply on the basis that it has not been proved false, or that it is false because it has not been proved true." Irving M. Copi & Carl Cohen, *Introduction to Logic* 93 (8th ed.1990). Our point is that difficulty in proving a proposition (particularly by only one method) does not prove its opposite.

Of course, an argument from ignorance is not always a fallacy. Under some circumstances, such as where a scientific inquiry produces a complete knowledge base, or where an experiment is certain to reveal a fact if that fact exists and it fails to do so, the lack of positive evidence can prove a negative-the absence of evidence can be conclusive evidence. But not here. Examining one mitochondrial DNA gene hardly provides scientists with a total picture of the entire Alabama sturgeon genome, which would be necessary for a complete knowledge base. There are a multitude of mitochondrial and nuclear genes in every species of animal. That one particular gene does not demonstrably vary between two species is not, by itself, exceptional. Humans and chimpanzees, in genetic terms, are nearly 99% identical, yet we generally have little difficulty distinguishing between the two species. Michael D. Lemonick et al., *What Makes Us Different?,* Time, Oct. 9, 2006, at 44.

Differences in the cytochrome *b* gene often correlate with speciation in vertebrates, but the Service had a reasonable basis for believing that gene would not serve as an effective, species-differentiating genetic marker in this case. Biogeographic evidence indicates that the Alabama and shovelnose sturgeon diverged only within the past 10,000 years, an eyeblink in evolutionary terms, and speciation can outpace differentiation of the cytochrome *b* marker which would explain the absence of a detectable difference. The rule making record included evidence of other separate species of fish with very little genetic divergence in the cytochrome *b* gene.

The decreased utility of the cytochrome *b* marker in younger species, combined with some evidence of divergence at other genetic markers, creates substantial doubt about whether genetic typing can conclusively resolve the proper taxonomic classification of the Alabama sturgeon. At a minimum, it justifies the Service's decision to examine the entirety of the taxonomic record, rather than ending its analysis with the DNA results. We now turn to the taxonomic evidence.

2.

The Service began its examination of the taxonomic evidence by reviewing the existing literature, which revealed that:

[t]he Alabama sturgeon is nationally and internationally considered a valid species. The Alabama sturgeon was initially described as a distinct species in a peer-reviewed, widely distributed museum periodical. The species was considered valid in a catalog of fishes of Alabama and in a catalog of fishes of North America. Species status was reassessed, reaffirmed, and published in the ichthyological journal *Copeia.* The Alabama sturgeon is listed as a separate species in State fish books for Alabama and Mississippi. The Alabama sturgeon is listed as a valid species in a

catalog of fishes of the world. Birstein *et al.* included the Alabama sturgeon in a list of all sturgeon species of the world. The Alabama sturgeon is considered a distinct and valid species by the American Society of Ichthyologists and Herpetologists, and by the Southern Fishes Council Technical Advisory Committee. Thus, the Alabama sturgeon is currently recognized as a valid taxonomic species and will continue to be so recognized unless overturned at some future date by the scientific community through the formal publication and peer review process.

The Service acknowledged that some scientists have questioned the taxonomy of the Alabama sturgeon, but noted that the only thorough taxonomic treatment of the species since the fish was first described, which was done by Mayden and Kuhajda, concluded that the sturgeon was a distinct species. Only one peer-reviewed paper-the Bartolucci *et al.* study-questions the taxonomy of the Alabama sturgeon. The Service found that study to be less probative than the Mayden and Kuhajda study, and also against the weight of the remainder of the taxonomic record.

The Service then supplemented the existing literature by requesting that five academicians who possessed expertise on Alabama sturgeon and shovelnose sturgeon taxonomy review the proposed rule. Of the four who responded to the Service's request, all expressed their belief that the data supported protecting the sturgeon under the Endangered Species Act. Three peer reviewers "strongly supported the taxonomic status of the Alabama sturgeon." The remaining reviewer "expressed some personal doubt regarding the taxonomic status of the Alabama sturgeon," but concluded that the fish represented at least a subspecies or unique population eligible for protection under the Act. That reviewer also described the Mayden and Kuhajda article, which had come down on the separate species side of the question, as convincing. The fifth proposed reviewer did not respond to the Service's request to engage in peer review, but provided comments opposing the listing at the public hearing.

Only after reviewing the existing literature and the additional expert opinions did the Service conclude that the available genetic evidence did not compel the conclusion that the Alabama sturgeon was not a separate species. The agency considered every available genetic study, but found that none were decisive on the issue. Two types of studies-the control region and nuclear DNA studies-supported the Service's ultimate conclusion. While the cytochrome *b* genes of the Alabama sturgeon and the shovelnose sturgeon are nearly identical, this fact is consistent with the theory that the two species began to diverge only recently (in evolutionary terms) when the Alabama sturgeon became isolated in the Mobile River Basin approximately 10,000 years ago. It does not rule out the two types of fish being separate species. The Service's decision to read the mixed genetic data in conformity with the remainder of the taxonomic record, which supported classifying the Alabama sturgeon as a distinct species, was not arbitrary and capricious.

B.

The Coalition's second argument in support of its contention that the Service failed to consider the best scientific data is that the taxonomic evidence in the administrative record demonstrates that the Alabama and shovelnose sturgeons are the same species. We have just discussed the reasoning behind the Service's conclusion that the Alabama sturgeon is a distinct species and the studies underlying that reasoning. The Coalition contends, however, that the Service "blatantly cherry-picked" a few taxonomic studies to support its position. It argues that "the Final Rule references, but erroneously discounts" studies that oppose classifying the Alabama sturgeon as a unique species.

The Coalition characterizes the Service as dismissing Bartolucci's study "primarily because it was published in a 'statistically oriented journal and not in a zoological, ichthyological, or systematics journal.'" Putting aside whether that reason alone would justify discounting Bartolucci's findings, the Final Rule deals with that study more thoroughly than the Coalition lets on:

Only a single peer-reviewed paper has been published that questions the taxonomy of the Alabama sturgeon (Bartolucci *et al.*1998). However, that publication was a methods paper concerning a statistical approach to compare the significance of morphological characters. It was published in a statistically oriented journal and not in a zoological, ichthyological, or systematics journal, and it made no attempt to formally revise the taxonomy of the Alabama sturgeon. We received letters from ichthyologists during the comment period pointing out shortcomings of Bartolucci *et al.* (1998) for taxonomic purposes. In a review of the systematics and taxonomy of the Alabama sturgeon, Mayden and Kuhajda (1996) presented new data, addressed many of the criticisms of the original description, and substantiated species status for the Alabama sturgeon ... The [Bartolucci study] did not identify the measurement data that were analyzed, nor was the source of their data cited. Dr. Bartolucci later clarified in submissions at the June 1999 public hearing on the proposed rule that data provided by Williams and Clemmer (1991) were used. In addition, Bartolucci *et al.* (1998) did not review, criticize, or even reference the Mayden and Kuhajda (1996) evaluation of the taxonomy and systematics of the Alabama sturgeon, and additional mensural (based on measurements) and meristic (based on counts) data, as well as new diagnostic characters presented by Mayden and Kuhajda (1996) were not addressed.

The Coalition points to two other studies that the Service addressed only summarily in its Final Rule, but as the Service points out, those studies were not made available for review by the ichthyological community through peer review and publication.

Given the nature of taxonomy, it would be surprising if there were not some disagreement about the proper classification of the Alabama sturgeon, but disagreement in the field does not preclude agency decision making. "When specialists express conflicting views, an agency must have discretion to rely on the reasonable opinions of its own qualified experts even if, as an original matter, a court might find contrary views more persuasive." *Marsh v. Or. Natural Res. Council,* 490 U.S. 360, 378 (1989). This principle does not mean that the agency has wholesale latitude to arbitrarily dismiss relevant scientific data, 16 U.S.C. § 1533(b)(1)(A), but that is not what happened. The Service's finding that the Alabama sturgeon is a separate species is consistent with the position of the American Society of Ichthyologists and Herpetologists on the question and is supported by the conclusion of the only peer-reviewed article published in an ichthyological journal addressing the issue, by the opinion of the Service's own experts, and by the views of most of the academicians asked to comment on the question. Given all of that support for the view taken in the Final Rule, we will not find that the Service failed to consider the best scientific evidence simply because it decided not to credit the contrary view, which is contained in one article published in a statistical journal and in several unpublished reports.

C.

The third argument behind the Coalition's contention that the Service failed to consider the best scientific data is that it wrongfully interfered with the research of Dr. Steven Fain. Before the Service issued the Final Rule, Mike Howell, a scientist working for the Coalition, sent an e-mail seeking to discuss with Fain the genetic similarity between the Alabama sturgeon and the shovelnose sturgeon. Fain initially appeared receptive to discussing the issue, but later quit communicating with Howell. He did so after speaking with Paul Hartsfield, a Service biologist.

Apparently, Hartsfield began to inquire into what Fain was doing-and with whom he was doing it-after the Coalition told the Service that it had requested samples of an Alabama sturgeon specimen from the Alabama Department of Conservation and Natural Resources so that the

Coalition could conduct its own DNA work. Service officials asked the Department to whom it had sent the samples, and were told that they had been sent to Fain. Hartsfield was understandably surprised to learn that one of the Service's own scientists was conducting studies for an interested party in an agency rule making. He e-mailed his supervisor, asking if Fain comprehends "the taxonomic problems and implications" of the work he was doing and inquiring, "can we afford to call him off?" Another e-mail refers to the value of Hartsfield having a "frank talk" with Fain.

After a little investigation, the Service determined that Fain was unaware that Howell was passing his work on to the Coalition. Hartsfield spoke with Fain over the telephone, explained Howell's affiliation with the Coalition, and the two men "had a very good discussion about taxonomy and cytochrome *b*." Hartsfield followed up the phone call by sending Fain copies of all of the relevant research in his possession.

The facts in the administrative record do not demonstrate that the Service sought to squelch Fain's research or control his opinion. They show that the Service initially inquired into whether one of its scientists was moonlighting for an interested party in a pending rule making. Once the Service determined that Fain was simply sharing research that he was conducting in the course of his employment, Hartsfield told Fain a key fact that Howell had failed to disclose: Howell was not a disinterested scientist but was instead affiliated with the Coalition. Hartsfield also offered to send Fain copies of prior research in the area. There was nothing improper about that.

Even if we assume that Service officials engaged in improper conduct towards Fain, the Coalition's argument still fails for two reasons. First, it has presented no evidence that Fain altered his study as a result of the Service's conduct. The Coalition highlights the fact that Fain uses more cautious language in his final report than he did in his initial e-mail to Howell. Fain's "quick note" to Howell stated that "[w]e've sequenced only one sample ... and its sequence is identical to pallid and shovelnose sturgeon ... [w]e are currently canvassing all 250 of the Scaphirhynchus samples we have .... I agree with your proposal to consider all three as conspecific." His final report is arguably more equivocal than that statement, but Fain wrote the e-mail to Howell after he had sequenced only a single sample, before he had reviewed the Mayden and Kuhajda study, and six months before completing his final report. That final report, which Fain co-authored with two other scientists, examined ninety-nine sturgeon specimen and referred to twenty-five prior publications on genetic testing and sturgeon taxonomy. Scientists may spend months or years painstakingly producing and checking findings before publication, even though they, like everyone else, may fire off in a matter of minutes a "quick note" containing an initial inclination or beginning hypothesis. It is not at all surprising that a scientific paper about a completed study would use different language, or even reach a different conclusion, than a six-sentence e-mail sent at the very beginning of the study.

Second, even if Fain did temper his language as a result of some higher-up's meddling, that fact would not establish that the Service violated the Endangered Species Act's mandate to consider the "best scientific and commercial data available." 16 U.S.C. § 1533(b)(1)(A). The Coalition agrees that the final report of Fain's study is "entirely consistent" with the tentative views reflected in his e-mail to Howell in 1999. Its criticism is that the final report did not state his views as explicitly as the e-mail did. Fain's views are clear enough to have been properly considered, as they were, by the Service. The Endangered Species Act requires the Service to make its listing determination on the basis of the best scientific data available; it does not require scientists who produce reports relevant to the listing decision to achieve a particular level of clarity in stating their views.

If Fain had stated in the most unequivocal terms that the Alabama and shovelnose sturgeon have the same cytochrome *b* gene, which is what the Coalition says he should have done, it would not have altered the analysis in the Final Rule. The Service properly characterized Fain's report as showing an "absence of detectable differences" between the sturgeons' cytochrome *b* genes, but reasonably concluded that this similarity "only attests to the very close evolutionary relationship" between the species. The Service's decision is not based on the Alabama sturgeon and the shovelnose sturgeon having dissimilar cytochrome *b* genes, and would be the same no matter how definitively the Fain report had stated that they do not.

The Coalition, which acquired the e-mails relating to this issue that we have quoted through a public records request, contends that the district court abused its discretion by refusing to allow additional discovery on the subject. "The focal point for judicial review of an administrative agency's action should be the administrative record." *PEACH,* 87 F.3d at 1246. Though certain circumstances may justify the district court going beyond the administrative record, it is not generally empowered to do so. It should do so only where there is initially "a strong showing of bad faith or improper behavior" by the agency. *Overton Park,* 401 U.S. at 420. Here, because the Coalition failed to make such a showing, we conclude that the district court did not abuse its discretion in disallowing the discovery the Coalition sought. *See PEACH,* 87 F.3d at 1246.

III.
The Coalition's second contention is that even if the Fish and Wildlife Service did consider all the relevant factors and make the listing decision on the basis of the best scientific data available, the Final Rule containing that decision still must be vacated because the Service violated Section 4 of the Endangered Species Act. That section requires the Service to designate the critical habitat of a species concurrently with its decision to list the species as endangered. Section 4 twice mentions a concurrence requirement.

The relevant provisions read:
The Secretary, by regulation promulgated in accordance with subsection (b) of this section and *to the maximum extent prudent and determinable-*
(i) *shall, concurrently with making a determination ... that a species is an endangered species* or a threatened species, *designate any habitat* of such species which is then considered to be critical habitat; and
(ii) may, from time-to-time thereafter as appropriate, revise such designation.
16 U.S.C. § 1533(a)(3)(A) (emphasis added). Later, the section provides:
A final regulation designating critical habitat of an endangered species or a threatened species shall be published concurrently with the final regulation implementing the determination that such species is endangered or threatened, unless the Secretary deems that-
(i) it is essential to the conservation of such species that the regulation implementing such determination be promptly published; or
(ii) critical habitat of such species is not then determinable, in which case the Secretary, with respect to the proposed regulation to designate such habitat, may extend the one-year period specified in subparagraph (A) by not more than one additional year, but not later than the close of such additional year the Secretary must publish a final regulation, based on such data as may be available at that time, designating, to the maximum extent prudent, such habitat.

16 U.S.C. § 1533(b)(6)(C) (emphasis added). The Service did not designate critical habitat of the Alabama sturgeon when it issued the Final Rule on May 5, 2000 listing the fish as endangered, and it has not done so in the six-and-a-half years since then.

In the proposed rule, which was issued in 1999, the Service determined that it would not be "prudent" to designate critical habitat at that time. ("Proposed Rule"). As a result of feedback received during the public comment period, however, the Service was persuaded that designation would be prudent. It nonetheless declined to designate critical habitat in the Final Rule, instead finding that the Alabama sturgeon's habitat was not then "determinable." Under Section 4(b)(6)(A) of the Act, the Service must normally issue a final rule designating critical habitat within one year of issuing a proposed habitat designation. *See* 16 U.S.C. § 1533(b)(6)(A) (Section 4(b)(6)(A)). However, Section 4(b)(6)(C) allows the Service to extend this one-year period by an additional year if critical habitat is not determinable at the time of the listing decision, provided that it designates habitat to the maximum extent prudent by the end of that additional year. The Service exercised this option, which means that it had a maximum of two years from the date the Final Rule was published to issue a final rule designating critical habitat. *See* 16 U.S.C. § 1533(b)(6)(C) (Section 4(b)(6)(C)).

The Coalition asked the district court to vacate the Final Rule containing the listing decision because of the Service's failure to designate critical habitat concurrently with the publication of the Final Rule. The Service conceded that it had violated the Act by failing to designate critical habitat for the Alabama sturgeon by the end of the two-year period following the publication of the Final Rule. The district court, however, refused to order what it described as "the extraordinary and unprecedented remedy of vacating the listing decision in its entirety thus causing the Service to begin the listing process of the Alabama Sturgeon anew." Instead, the court ordered the Service to complete the habitat decision within two years of the conclusion of this appeal. The effect is to give the Service more time to designate critical habitat than the Act allows.

A.

The district court's remedy is improper, according to the Coalition, because the failure to propose and designate critical habitat at the same time that the endangered species listing is being proposed and decided undermines the accuracy of the listing decision itself. Providing notice of critical habitat designation may encourage some who would not otherwise do so to participate in the public comment process for the listing decision. The more people who know they will be affected, the more who may participate. The additional participation could conceivably affect the Service's analysis and modify the decision contained in the Final Rule. The law, after all, provides notice and an opportunity to be heard because it may make a difference. Not only that, the Coalition argues, but the literal language of the Endangered Species Act can be satisfied only by starting the listing process anew, because no other result will allow the listing decision and the habitat designation decision to be issued "concurrently."

The Coalition's standing to raise this challenge does not flow from any harm that it suffers from the Service's failure to actually designate critical habitat, because the Coalition is not injured by that. Indeed, it would prefer that critical habitat never be designated. The harm the Coalition claims is that the failure to propose critical habitat may have reduced participation in the rule making process resulting in a flawed decision to list the Alabama sturgeon as an endangered species, and we have held that the listing decision does threaten the Coalition with harm.

In *Sierra Club,* we held that "a plaintiff has established procedural injury standing if he has established that the claimed violation of the procedural right caused a concrete injury in fact to an interest of the plaintiff that the statute was designed to protect." 436 F.3d at 1278. In that case, we vacated an order by the Environmental Protection Agency that failed to object to issuance of a Clean Air Act permit by a state that had not implemented a required mailing list to notify the public of the proposed action and of the comment period. We reasoned that use of the mailing list would have led to additional public input, which in turn could have improved the permitting process. Applying the logic of *Sierra Club* to this case, we agree with the Coalition that it has standing to litigate whether there is a procedural right in the Endangered Species Act to public notice, during the comment period on a listing decision, of the area that may be designated as critical habitat.

Standing to raise a claim is one thing, the merits of the claim is another. If there is a procedural right to notice during the comment period of what the critical habitat may be, that right cannot be found in the text of the Act or in its history. Neither indicates that notice of proposed habitat designation is meant to be a participation booster for the listing decision. The language of the Act does not require the Service to publish a proposed habitat designation simultaneously with the proposed listing, nor does it require that the Service publish its proposed habitat designation prior to the close of the comment period on the proposed listing. *See* 16 U.S.C. § 1533(a)(3)(A)(i) (requiring that the Service make a final habitat determination concurrently with the listing decision); (allowing the Service to publish its proposed habitat designation "not less than 90 days before the effective date" of the final habitat designation). Instead, the Service may delay habitat designation by up to two years when it finds that designation is not "determinable."

Nor is there anything in the history of the Act to support the Coalition's position. As originally enacted in 1973, the Act did not even use the term "critical habitat." Endangered Species Act of 1973, Pub. L. No. 93-205, 87 Stat. 884. However, the Act did require all federal agencies to take "such action necessary to insure that actions authorized, funded, or carried out by them do not ... result in the destruction or modification of habitat of such species which is determined by the Secretary ... to be critical." The Act required the Service to give general notice of listing decisions, but provided no guidance on how or when it should determine a species' critical habitat.

Congress became aware of the significance of designating a species' critical habitat when the Supreme Court issued its decision in *Tennessee Valley Authority v. Hill,* 437 U.S. 153, 98 S.Ct. 2279, 57 L.Ed.2d 117 (1978). In that case the Supreme Court upheld the Service's decision to protect the critical habitat of a small number of snail darters, a three-inch fish, which "would require the permanent halting of a virtually completed dam for which Congress has expended more than $100 million." Within five months after the *Hill* decision, Congress amended the Act to provide a narrow definition of the term "critical habitat" and to establish a new set of public notice requirements for the designation of habitat. Endangered Species Act Amendments of 1978, Pub. L. No. 95-632, 92 Stat. 3751. Those 1978 amendments applied the general notice requirement for listing decisions to critical habitat determinations, and they required that notice of the proposed habitat be given in an area newspaper of general circulation and in appropriate scientific journals, and that actual notice be given to local governments. The amendments also added the requirement that "[a]t the time [a listing] *is proposed,* the Secretary shall also by regulation, to the maximum extent prudent, specify any habitat of such species which is then considered to be critical habitat."

It did not take long for Congress to have second thoughts about the 1978 amendments. In the three years following those amendments, only one new species proposed for listing successfully navigated both the listing and habitat designation processes. S. Rep. No. 97-418, at 4 (1982) ("Senate Report"). In the view of the Senate committee with jurisdiction over the subject, "[t]he listing process under section 4 of the current law ha[d] been seriously hampered since the 1978 amendments to the Act." The requirement that the Secretary propose critical habitat "at the time a species is proposed" had "indirectly introduced economic considerations into the listing process by requiring the Secretary to consider the economic impact of specifying the habitat." "[A]s a result of numerous procedural requirements and the absence of meaningful time limits, the listing process ha[d] come to a virtual standstill." The Senate committee's proposed amendments replaced the language from the 1978 Amendments that the Service designate tentative critical habitat at the time it issues the proposed listing with the modern "concurrently" requirement. H.R. Conf. Rep. No. 97-835, at 19-20 (1982), *reprinted in* 1982 U.S.C.C.A.N. 2860 ("Conference Report"). It also shortened the time line for acting on listing decisions and streamlined the notice process.

The relevant House committee had similar concerns. In recommending reauthorization of the Act, it issued a report stating that "[o]ne of the principal problems noted was the decline in the pace of listing species." H.R. Rep. No. 97-567, at 11 (1982), *reprinted in* 1982 U.S.C.C.A.N. 2807 ("House Report"). The House committee believed that tentatively designating critical habitat in the proposed listing "adds some confusion to the listing phase." The need to take into account "the economic impacts of listing such habitat as critical" had slowed the listing process to a crawl. The House bill included the Senate's requirement that the critical habitat be listed "concurrently," and also specified that listing decisions must be based "solely" on the basis of the best scientific and commercial data available. Conference Report at 20.

The Senate and House bills went to conference. The Conference Committee adopted the amendment included by both chambers of Congress to strike the language that had been added in 1978 requiring that critical habitat be designated in the proposed listing. It instead added the "concurrently" requirement and specified that the Service must "designate critical habitat *at the time a species is listed.*" The Conference Committee then adopted the Senate's proposed time provisions and the House's limitation on economic analysis in listing decisions. After those amendments, which were enacted into law in 1982, Pub. L. No. 97-304, no part of the Act-including Section 4(a)(3)(A) and Section 4(b)(6)(C)-required the Service to propose critical habitat at the time of the *proposed* listing of the species as endangered. 16 U.S.C. § 1533(a)(3)(A). The only requirement was that the Service designate critical habitat concurrently with its final listing decision, if doing so then would be prudent and if the habitat would be determinable at that time.

The requirement that the Secretary designate habitat concurrently with the final listing decision, which is the current version of the law, could not have been intended to increase public participation in the listing process. It could not have been because under that provision the Service need not (indeed, if "concurrently" is read strictly, it *must* not) designate critical habitat until the moment it reaches a final listing decision. By then the public comment period on the listing decision will have closed. Of course, the Service could propose critical habitat before the close of the comment period for the final listing decision, but nowhere in the Act is the Service obligated to do so. There is nothing in the Act to prevent the Service from proposing the listing, receiving comments about it and then, after that comment period has closed, proposing critical habitat and receiving comments about it. For that reason, we cannot say that the concurrence requirement was designed to spur greater public participation in the listing decision process.

We do not think that this lack of synchronization is the result of a Congressional oversight. One of the primary purposes of the 1982 amendments was to divorce from the listing decision the economic analysis that comes with critical habitat designation. *See* Senate Report at 11; House Report at 11-12; Conference Report at 19. The amendments added the word "solely" before the phrase "on the basis of the best scientific and commercial data available" to insulate the listing decision from the influence of economic factors. 16 U.S.C. § 1533(b)(1)(A); Senate Report at 4, 11; House Report at 20; Conference Report at 19. While "economic analysis" is meant to "offer[ ] some counter-point to the listing of species without due consideration for the effects on land use and other development interests," Congress wanted "to *prevent* [habitat] designation from influencing the decision on the listing of a species," and for that reason intended that the "balancing between science and economics should occur *subsequent to listing* through the exemption process." House

Report at 12 (emphasis added); *cf.* Senate Report at 4. The Coalition's position runs counter to Congressional intent.

That Congress did not intend the word "concurrently" to spur participation in the listing process does not mean that it was blind to the value of public input into agency action. The Act requires the Service to publish notice both of proposed listing decisions and of proposed critical habitat designations, 16 U.S.C. § 1533(b)(5), but it does not require that notice of the proposals be published concurrently. The language of the concurrence requirement applies only to the final decisions: "concurrently with making a determination," and "[a] final regulation designating critical habitat ... shall be published concurrently with the final regulation [listing the species]," and even then, there are escape valves that permit the habitat designation decision to come as long as two years after the final listing decision.

The problem that the 1982 amendments were aimed at was that difficulties in designating critical habitat were slowing to a virtual standstill the listing process. Congress uncoupled the two to some extent by removing the requirement, which had been added during the 1978 amendments, that habitat designation be proposed at the same time the listing was. Although Congress did not want delays in designating critical habitat to hamper listings decisions, if it had simply removed the time limits it imposed in 1978 the Service would have had free range to indefinitely postpone habitat designation. By adding the concurrence requirement Congress provided a deadline which requires, with the escape clauses considered, that within two years of the proposed listing of the species as endangered, the Service "must designate to the maximum extent prudent, on the basis of such data as may be available at that time, critical habitat of such species." Conference Report at 24. The term creates a "mandatory, nondiscretionary duty" that the Secretary designate critical habitat within the time specified. Senate Report at 13; *see also* Conference Report at 20.

For this reason, we are unpersuaded by the Coalition's assertion that if we do not read "concurrently" to require concurrent proposals that term will serve no purpose. The purpose it serves is to prevent the Service from putting off indefinitely-more than two years after the final listing decision-the designation of critical habitat for a listed species. 16 U.S.C. § 1533(b)(6)(C).

The only other provisions governing the timing of critical habitat designation are reflexive: Section 4(b)(5) requires the Service to provide general notice of a habitat designation "not less than 90 days" before its final decision on habitat designation, and Section 4(b)(6)(A) requires the Service to make a final decision "within the one-year period beginning on the date on which general notice is published," subject to the one-year extension under Section 4(b)(6)(C). 16 U.S.C. §§ 1533(b)(5), (b)(6)(A)-(C). It is the requirement that the regulation designating critical habitat "be published concurrently with" the listing decision that forces the Service to start those other clocks ticking. The Service's failure to designate habitat concurrently with (or within two years of) its decision to list the Alabama sturgeon as endangered places it behind on its statutory responsibilities, but it does not necessarily mean that the Service has violated any procedural notice rule in the Act.

If this case were being decided under the Endangered Species Act as it existed between the time of the 1978 and the 1982 amendments, the Coalition would have a much stronger case. During that interval, the Act provided that: "At the time [a listing] *is proposed,* the Secretary shall also by regulation, to the maximum extent prudent, specify any habitat of such species which is then considered to be critical habitat." Endangered Species Act Amendments of 1978, Pub. L. No. 95-632, 92 Stat. 3751 (emphasis added). Congress modified the critical language, uncoupling the species listing and habitat designation, or at least moving the coupling forward to the final rule stage, leaving the Service free to make the proposals at different times with comment periods that do not overlap. Endangered Species Act Amendments of 1982, Pub. L. No. 97-304, 96 Stat. 1411. The use of the word "concurrently" refers to the final decisions, not to the initial proposals. For these reasons we do not believe that the Endangered Species Act provides a procedural right to have the critical habitat proposal issued at the same time as the listing proposal, or to have the habitat proposed before time runs out for commenting about the listing.

B.

That said, this too should be said. We are troubled by the Service's apparent practice of routinely delaying critical habitat designation until forced to act by court order. *See Ctr. for Biological Diversity v. Norton,* 240 F.Supp.2d 1090, 1103 (D.Ariz.2003). The Congressional Research Service reports that, as of 1999, the Service had designated critical habitat "for only about 10% of listed domestic species; in every case brought against the agency for failure to designate [critical habitat], the agency has lost." The Senate Committee on Environment and Public Works after examining the Service's practices, concluded that "[p]roblems with critical habitat have been chronic over the life of the ESA." S. Rep. 106-126, at 2 (1999).

The Service's motives for delaying designation of critical habitat may have changed over the years. Before enactment of the 1982 amendments, critics accused the executive branch of stalling on habitat designation to derail protection for species entirely. Other critics have charged that during the late 1990s the Department of the Interior may have simply viewed the Service's failure to designate critical habitat as an acceptable budgetary policy. Most of the protections afforded endangered species attach as soon as the species is listed, and it would be reasonable to believe that the resources required to collect and analyze critical habitat data could better be spent on listing additional species.

At oral argument in this case counsel for the government, explaining the Service's failure to comply with the statutory deadlines for designating habitat for the Alabama sturgeon, characterized the Service as "chronically underfunded to meet its obligations under [the] statute." The Service, like all agencies, undoubtedly would be better able to carry out all of its statutory duties if it could appropriate funds for itself, but under our separation of powers that is the prerogative of the legislative branch. As a result, the same legislature that has enacted standards for an executive agency's performance can through the appropriations process effectively prevent the agency from meeting those standards. The problem of "unfunded mandates" is not limited to federal-state relations. We do not know and have no occasion to decide whether that is what is at work here.

Regardless of the cause, it is clear that the Service chronically fails to meet its statutory duty of designating critical habitat of endangered species within the time the Endangered Species Act requires. The Coalition argues that a stronger remedy is needed than the order the district court issued, which requires the Service to designate the Alabama sturgeon's critical habitat within two years of the conclusion of this case (apparently meaning two years after the end of this appeal). Of course, the Coalition is not interested in any remedy that would force the Service to designate the fish's habitat sooner instead of later. Instead, the Coalition's proposed remedy, which coincides perfectly with its interest, would not only delay the designation of habitat for many more years but would also strip the Alabama sturgeon of the protection that being listed provides. What we ought to do, the Coalition argues, is overturn the listing decision as a sanction for the Service's failure to designate habitat on time. That would teach the Service not to disregard Congressional requirements, the Coalition assures us.

It would also make a bad situation worse, and defeat the Congressional intent behind the Endangered Species Act. As the Supreme Court stated in *Hill,* "[t]he dominant theme pervading all Congressional discussion of the proposed [Endangered Species Act of 1973] was the overriding need to devote whatever effort and resources were necessary to avoid further diminution of national and worldwide wildlife resources." Congress intended to protect endangered species, not to strip them of protection in order to motivate an administrative agency to protect them.

The Alabama sturgeon is a fish so near extinction that the Service withdrew its first attempt to list it as endangered because there was then no evidence that the species still existed. Four thousand man hours of fishing effort on the rivers produced a total of five Alabama sturgeon. That result probably would not bring tears to the collective eyes of the Coalition, but it is not one to which the group is entitled. The Endangered Species Act does not require that a species be destroyed in order to preserve a part of the process meant to save it.

The legislative history of the Act contains repeated statements indicating that Congress meant for species to be protected by listing decisions even if determination of their critical habitats were delayed. The Conference Report for the 1982 amendments states:

If at the end of the one-year period (or 18 month period) provided for in new Section 4(b)(6) the scientific and commercial information indicates that the species should be listed but the analysis necessary to determine and designate critical habitat has not been completed, the Secretary *must comply* with the new Section 4(b)(6) time requirement and promulgate the proposal to list as a final regulation.

Conference Report at 24 (emphasis added). Likewise, the Senate Report states:

At the end of such 12 month period (or 18 month period, if an extension occurs), the Secretary *must make a final determination* with respect to the listing proposal. He *must* determine, on the basis of the information then available, either that the species should be listed or delisted, or that the proposal for listing or delisting should not be promulgated as a final regulation.

Senate Report at 14. Nothing in the language of either report suggests an exception to the listing requirement even if a court concludes that the Service intentionally delayed designation of critical habitat, which is not surprising because one of the principal purposes of the 1982 amendments was to prevent delays in habitat designation from holding up a listing decision.

The House Report accompanying the 1982 amendments is even more emphatic. It repeatedly states that a delay in habitat designation should never be used to delay the listing of a species. First, the Report states:

The Committee feels strongly, however, that where the biology relating to the status of the species is clear, it should not be denied the protection of the Act because of the inability of the Secretary to complete the work necessary to designate critical habitat.

House Report at 19. Then it states:

The Committee expects the agencies to make the strongest attempt possible to determine critical habitat within the time period designated for listing, but stresses that the listing of a species is not to be delayed in any instance past the time period allocated for such listing if the biological data is clear but the habitat designation process is not complete.

And then a third time:

At the end of the one year period, if the scientific evidence indicates that the species should be listed, the Secretary must do so regardless of whether the analysis necessary to designate critical habitat has been completed.

And then a fourth time:

The Committee intends that this [six month extension to the listing period] apply only to those instances where the biological status of the species is being questioned by scientists knowledgeable about the species and not to allow additional time for the economic or other analyses related to the designation of critical habitat.

And finally, in case anyone missed the import of its first four statements, the House Committee states in its report that under the Act:

If, for whatever reason, a critical habitat is not designated at the end of the required period, the original listing of the species is not withdrawn.

To throw out a congressionally mandated listing decision because of the Service's failure to comply with time limits for making a habitat decision would defeat, not further, congressional intent.

It may be that in an appropriate case a court should use its contempt powers or fashion some creative remedy to spur the Fish and Wildlife Service on with habitat designation. But delisting is not creative, it is destructive. A species in free fall needs all the protection it can get. We would not cut the cords of a skydiver's main parachute to punish the jump master for failing to pack the fellow a reserve chute. Any beneficial effect that sanction might have on the jump master's future performance would come at too high a cost to the poor soul hurtling toward the earth at terminal velocity. And so it is here. We will not order that the Alabama sturgeon be stripped of the protection that the listing decision provides as a remedy for the failure of the Service to extend to the creature the additional benefit that comes from designation of critical habitat. Removing one protection is not a fit remedy for the lack of another.

QUESTIONS

1. What happened in *ATRC v. Kempthorne?*
2. What were the issues?
3. How did the court decide the question as to whether the Alabama Sturgeon was properly listed, and why? Do you agree or disagree?
4. How did the court decide the question as to whether the Secretary had unlawfully failed to identify critical habitat? Do you agree or disagree?
5. What role did legislative history play? Give examples.
6. What role did science play? Give examples.
7. What role did experts play? Give examples.
8. What role did the public play? Give examples.
9. This is one of my more favorite judicial opinions, and not necessarily because I agree with it or not. It has a fair amount of 'quotables.' What's your favorite?
10. What do you think about the process for listing T&E species and critical habitat? Any surprises?

IV.   CONSULTATION

Section 7 requires that federal agencies 'consult' prior to authorizing, funding or carrying out activities that may affect the continued existence of any listed T&E species. Section 7 is primarily procedural, and in this regard is analogous to NEPA. The following two sections detail and contextualize Section 7.

A. STATUTORY LANGUAGE

16 U.S.C.A. § 1536: Interagency cooperation

(a) Federal agency actions and consultations

(1) The Secretary shall review other programs administered by him and utilize such programs in furtherance of the purposes of this chapter. All other Federal agencies shall, in consultation with and with the assistance of the Secretary, utilize their authorities in furtherance of the purposes of this chapter by carrying out programs for the conservation of endangered species and threatened species listed pursuant to section 1533 of this title.

(2) Each Federal agency shall, in consultation with and with the assistance of the Secretary, insure that any action authorized, funded, or carried out by such agency (hereinafter in this section referred to as an "agency action") is not likely to jeopardize the continued existence of any endangered species or threatened species or result in the destruction or adverse modification of habitat of such species which is determined by the Secretary, after consultation as appropriate with affected States, to be critical, unless such agency has been granted an exemption for such action by the Committee pursuant to subsection (h) of this section. In fulfilling the requirements of this paragraph each agency shall use the best scientific and commercial data available.

(3) Subject to such guidelines as the Secretary may establish, a Federal agency shall consult with the Secretary on any prospective agency action at the request of, and in cooperation with, the prospective permit or license applicant if the applicant has reason to believe that an endangered species or a threatened species may be present in the area affected by his project and that implementation of such action will likely affect such species.

(4) Each Federal agency shall confer with the Secretary on any agency action which is likely to jeopardize the continued existence of any species proposed to be listed under section 1533 of this title or result in the destruction or adverse modification of critical habitat proposed to be designated for such species. This paragraph does not require a limitation on the commitment of resources as described in subsection (d) of this section.

(b) Opinion of Secretary

(1)(A) Consultation under subsection (a) (2) of this section with respect to any agency action shall be concluded within the 90-day period beginning on the date on which initiated or, subject to subparagraph (B), within such other period of time as is mutually agreeable to the Secretary and the Federal agency.

(B) In the case of an agency action involving a permit or license applicant, the Secretary and the Federal agency may not mutually agree to conclude consultation within a period exceeding 90 days unless the Secretary, before the close of the 90th day referred to in subparagraph (A)--
(i) if the consultation period proposed to be agreed to will end before the 150th day after the date on which consultation was initiated, submits to the applicant a written statement setting forth--
(I) the reasons why a longer period is required,
(II) the information that is required to complete the consultation, and
(III) the estimated date on which consultation will be completed; or

(ii) if the consultation period proposed to be agreed to will end 150 or more days after the date on which consultation was initiated, obtains the consent of the applicant to such period.
The Secretary and the Federal agency may mutually agree to extend a consultation period established under the preceding sentence if the Secretary, before the close of such period, obtains the consent of the applicant to the extension.

(2) Consultation under subsection (a) (3) of this section shall be concluded within such period as is agreeable to the Secretary, the Federal agency, and the applicant concerned.

(3)(A) Promptly after conclusion of consultation under paragraph (2) or (3) of subsection (a) of this section, the Secretary shall provide to the Federal agency and the applicant, if any, a written statement setting forth the Secretary's opinion, and a summary of the information on which the opinion is based, detailing how the agency action affects the species or its critical habitat. If jeopardy or adverse modification is found, the Secretary shall suggest those reasonable and prudent alternatives which he believes would not violate subsection (a) (2) of this section and can be taken by the Federal agency or applicant in implementing the agency action.

(B) Consultation under subsection (a) (3) of this section, and an opinion issued by the Secretary incident to such consultation, regarding an agency action shall be treated respectively as a consultation under subsection (a) (2) of this section, and as an opinion issued after consultation under such subsection, regarding that action if the Secretary reviews the action before it is commenced by the Federal agency and finds, and notifies such agency, that no significant changes have been made with respect to the action and that no significant change has occurred regarding the information used during the initial consultation.

(4) If after consultation under subsection (a)(2) of this section, the Secretary concludes that-

(A) the agency action will not violate such subsection, or offers reasonable and prudent alternatives which the Secretary believes would not violate such subsection;

(B) the taking of an endangered species or a threatened species incidental to the agency action will not violate such subsection; and

(C) if an endangered species or threatened species of a marine mammal is involved, the taking is authorized pursuant to section 1371(a)(5) of this title;

the Secretary shall provide the Federal agency and the applicant concerned, if any, with a written statement that--
(i) specifies the impact of such incidental taking on the species,
(ii) specifies those reasonable and prudent measures that the Secretary considers necessary or appropriate to minimize such impact,
(iii) in the case of marine mammals, specifies those measures that are necessary to comply with section 1371(a)(5) of this title with regard to such taking, and
(iv) sets forth the terms and conditions (including, but not limited to, reporting requirements) that must be complied with by the Federal agency or applicant (if any), or both, to implement the measures specified under clauses (ii) and (iii).

(c) Biological assessment

(1) To facilitate compliance with the requirements of subsection (a) (2) of this section, each Federal agency shall, with respect to any agency action of such agency for which no contract for

construction has been entered into and for which no construction has begun on November 10, 1978, request of the Secretary information whether any species which is listed or proposed to be listed may be present in the area of such proposed action. If the Secretary advises, based on the best scientific and commercial data available, that such species may be present, such agency shall conduct a biological assessment for the purpose of identifying any endangered species or threatened species which is likely to be affected by such action. Such assessment shall be completed within 180 days after the date on which initiated (or within such other period as is mutually agreed to by the Secretary and such agency, except that if a permit or license applicant is involved, the 180-day period may not be extended unless such agency provides the applicant, before the close of such period, with a written statement setting forth the estimated length of the proposed extension and the reasons therefor) and, before any contract for construction is entered into and before construction is begun with respect to such action. Such assessment may be undertaken as part of a Federal agency's compliance with the requirements of section 102 of the National Environmental Policy Act of 1969 (42 U.S.C. 4332).

(2) Any person who may wish to apply for an exemption under subsection (g) of this section for that action may conduct a biological assessment to identify any endangered species or threatened species which is likely to be affected by such action. Any such biological assessment must, however, be conducted in cooperation with the Secretary and under the supervision of the appropriate Federal agency.

(d) Limitation on commitment of resources

After initiation of consultation required under subsection (a) (2) of this section, the Federal agency and the permit or license applicant shall not make any irreversible or irretrievable commitment of resources with respect to the agency action which has the effect of foreclosing the formulation or implementation of any reasonable and prudent alternative measures which would not violate subsection (a) (2) of this section.

(e) Endangered Species Committee

(1) There is established a committee to be known as the Endangered Species Committee (hereinafter in this section referred to as the "Committee").

(2) The Committee shall review any application submitted to it pursuant to this section and determine in accordance with subsection (h) of this section whether or not to grant an exemption from the requirements of subsection (a) (2) of this section for the action set forth in such application.

(3) The Committee shall be composed of seven members as follows:
(A) The Secretary of Agriculture.
(B) The Secretary of the Army.
(C) The Chairman of the Council of Economic Advisors.
(D) The Administrator of the Environmental Protection Agency.
(E) The Secretary of the Interior.
(F) The Administrator of the National Oceanic and Atmospheric Administration.
(G) The President, after consideration of any recommendations received pursuant to subsection (g) (2) (B) of this section shall appoint one individual from each affected State, as determined by the Secretary, to be a member of the Committee for the consideration of the application for exemption for an agency action with respect to which such recommendations are made, not later than 30 days after an application is submitted pursuant to this section.

[Author's note: (f) – (i) describe the intricate process for granting or denying petitions, and are omitted].

(j) Exemption for national security reasons

Notwithstanding any other provision of this chapter, the Committee shall grant an exemption for any agency action if the Secretary of Defense finds that such exemption is necessary for reasons of national security.

(k) Exemption decision not considered major Federal action; environmental impact statement

An exemption decision by the Committee under this section shall not be a major Federal action for purposes of the National Environmental Policy Act of 1969 [42 U.S.C.A. § 4321 et seq.]: *Provided*, That an environmental impact statement which discusses the impacts upon endangered species or threatened species or their critical habitats shall have been previously prepared with respect to any agency action exempted by such order.

[Author's note: (l) – (p) omitted]

(p) Exemptions in Presidentially declared disaster areas

In any area which has been declared by the President to be a major disaster area under the Disaster Relief and Emergency Assistance Act [42 U.S.C.A. § 5121 et seq.], the President is authorized to make the determinations required by subsections (g) and (h) of this section for any project for the repair or replacement of a public facility substantially as it existed prior to the disaster under section 405 or 406 of the Disaster Relief and Emergency Assistance Act [42 U.S.C.A. §§ 5171 or 5172], and which the President determines (1) is necessary to prevent the recurrence of such a natural disaster and to reduce the potential loss of human life, and (2) to involve an emergency situation which does not allow the ordinary procedures of this section to be followed. Notwithstanding any other provision of this section, the Committee shall accept the determinations of the President under this subsection.

QUESTIONS

1. What is the purpose of the consultation process?
2. What triggers the consultation process under Section 7?
3. What is the process for consultation?
4. What is the purpose of a "biological assessment," who performs it, and what are its consequences?
5. What is the purpose of a "biological opinion," who performs it, and what are its consequences?
6. What is the purpose of the "limitation on commitment of resources?"
7. What is the purpose of the "Endangered Species Committee," and what are its consequences? Are its decisions judicially reviewable, and if so, how and where?
8. Under what circumstances is consultation excused?

B. CONSULTATION IN CONTEXT

If you recall, an allegation of a failure to consult is central to *TVA v. Hill*. In the first case that follows, the SCOTUS had to determine whether the plaintiffs possessed standing to challenge an agency's failure to follow Section 7. So, while the case turns on standing, along the way, the court does a good deal to contextualize consultation. In the second case, the SCOTUS engages Section 7's biological assessment and opinion components, again in the context of standing.

DEFENDERS OF WILDLIFE V. LUJAN
504 U.S. 555 (1992)

Justice SCALIA delivered the opinion of the Court with respect to Parts I, II, III-A, and IV, and an opinion with respect to Part III-B, in which THE CHIEF JUSTICE, Justice WHITE, and Justice THOMAS join.

[Note to Reader: This means that Part III-B represents a plurality, and not a majority, of the court. In short, plurality opinions of the SCOTUS are persuasive but not controlling.]

This case involves a challenge to a rule promulgated by the Secretary of the Interior interpreting § 7 of the Endangered Species Act of 1973 (ESA), 16 U.S.C. § 1536, in such fashion as to render it applicable only to actions within the United States or on the high seas. The preliminary issue, and the only one we reach, is whether respondents here, plaintiffs below, have standing to seek judicial review of the rule.

I

The ESA, 16 U.S.C. § 1531 *et seq.*, seeks to protect species of animals against threats to their continuing existence caused by man. See generally *TVA v. Hill,* 437 U.S. 153 (1978). The ESA instructs the Secretary of the Interior to promulgate by regulation a list of those species which are either endangered or threatened under enumerated criteria, and to define the critical habitat of these species. 16 U.S.C. §§ 1533, 1536. Section 7(a)(2) of the Act then provides, in pertinent part:

"Each Federal agency shall, in consultation with and with the assistance of the Secretary [of the Interior], insure that any action authorized, funded, or carried out by such agency ... is not likely to jeopardize the continued existence of any endangered species or threatened species or result in the destruction or adverse modification of habitat of such species which is determined by the Secretary, after consultation as appropriate with affected States, to be critical." 16 U.S.C. § 1536(a)(2).

In 1978, the Fish and Wildlife Service (FWS) and the National Marine Fisheries Service (NMFS), on behalf of the Secretary of the Interior and the Secretary of Commerce respectively, promulgated a joint regulation stating that the obligations imposed by § 7(a)(2) extend to actions taken in foreign nations. 43 Fed.Reg. 874 (1978). The next year, however, the Interior Department began to reexamine its position. Letter from Leo Kuliz, Solicitor, Department of the Interior, to Assistant Secretary, Fish and Wildlife and Parks, Aug. 8, 1979. A revised joint regulation, reinterpreting § 7(a)(2) to require consultation only for actions taken in the United States or on the high seas, was proposed in 1983.

Shortly thereafter, respondents, organizations dedicated to wildlife conservation and other environmental causes, filed this action against the Secretary of the Interior, seeking a declaratory judgment that the new regulation is in error as to the geographic scope of § 7(a)(2) and an injunction requiring the Secretary to promulgate a new regulation restoring the initial interpretation. The District Court granted the Secretary's motion to dismiss for lack of standing. *Defenders of Wildlife v. Hodel,* 658 F.Supp. 43, 47-48 (Minn.1987). The Court of Appeals for the Eighth Circuit reversed by a divided vote. *Defenders of Wildlife v. Hodel,* 851 F.2d 1035 (1988). On remand, the Secretary moved for summary judgment on the standing issue, and respondents moved for summary judgment on the merits. The District Court denied the Secretary's motion, on the ground that the Eighth Circuit had already determined the standing question in this case;

it granted respondents' merits motion, and ordered the Secretary to publish a revised regulation. *Defenders of Wildlife v. Hodel,* 707 F.Supp. 1082 (Minn.1989). The Eighth Circuit affirmed. 911 F.2d 117 (1990). We granted certiorari.

II

While the Constitution of the United States divides all power conferred upon the Federal Government into "legislative Powers," Art. I, § 1, "[t]he executive Power," Art. II, § 1, and "[t]he judicial Power," Art. III, § 1, it does not attempt to define those terms. To be sure, it limits the jurisdiction of federal courts to "Cases" and "Controversies," but an executive inquiry can bear the name "case" (the Hoffa case) and a legislative dispute can bear the name "controversy" (the Smoot-Hawley controversy). Obviously, then, the Constitution's central mechanism of separation of powers depends largely upon common understanding of what activities are appropriate to legislatures, to executives, and to courts. In The Federalist No. 48, Madison expressed the view that "[i]t is not infrequently a question of real nicety in legislative bodies whether the operation of a particular measure will, or will not, extend beyond the legislative sphere," whereas "the executive power [is] restrained within a narrower compass and ... more simple in its nature," and "the judiciary [is] described by landmarks still less uncertain." The Federalist No. 48, p. 256 (Carey and McClellan eds. 1990). One of those landmarks, setting apart the "Cases" and "Controversies" that are of the justiciable sort referred to in Article III - "serv[ing] to identify those disputes which are appropriately resolved through the judicial process," is the doctrine of standing. Though some of its elements express merely prudential considerations that are part of judicial self-government, the core component of standing is an essential and unchanging part of the case-or-controversy requirement of Article III. See, *e.g., Allen v. Wright,* 468 U.S. 737, 751 (1984).

Over the years, our cases have established that the irreducible constitutional minimum of standing contains three elements. First, the plaintiff must have suffered an "injury in fact"-an invasion of a legally protected interest which is (a) concrete and particularized, and (b) "actual or imminent, not 'conjectural' or 'hypothetical,' " Second, there must be a causal connection between the injury and the conduct complained of-the injury has to be "fairly ... trace[able] to the challenged action of the defendant, and not ... th[e] result [of] the independent action of some third party not before the court." *Simon v. Eastern Ky. Welfare Rights Organization,* 426 U.S. 26 (1976). Third, it must be "likely," as opposed to merely "speculative," that the injury will be "redressed by a favorable decision."

The party invoking federal jurisdiction bears the burden of establishing these elements. ... Since they are not mere pleading requirements but rather an indispensable part of the plaintiff's case, each element must be supported in the same way as any other matter on which the plaintiff bears the burden of proof, *i.e.,* with the manner and degree of evidence required at the successive stages of the litigation. See *Lujan v. National Wildlife Federation,* 497 U.S. 871, 883-889 (1990). ... At the pleading stage, general factual allegations of injury resulting from the defendant's conduct may suffice, for on a motion to dismiss we "presum[e] that general allegations embrace those specific facts that are necessary to support the claim." *National Wildlife Federation.* In response to a summary judgment motion, however, the plaintiff can no longer rest on such "mere allegations," but must "set forth" by affidavit or other evidence "specific facts," Fed. Rule Civ. Proc. 56(e), which for purposes of the summary judgment motion will be taken to be true. And at the final stage, those facts (if controverted) must be "supported adequately by the evidence adduced at trial."

When the suit is one challenging the legality of government action or inaction, the nature and extent of facts that must be averred (at the summary judgment stage) or proved (at the trial stage) in order to establish standing depends considerably upon whether the plaintiff is himself an object of the action (or forgone action) at issue. If he is, there is ordinarily little question that the action or inaction has caused him injury, and that a judgment preventing or requiring the action will redress it. When, however, as in this case, a plaintiff's asserted injury arises from the government's allegedly unlawful regulation (or lack of regulation) of *someone else,* much more is needed. In that circumstance, causation and redressability ordinarily hinge on the response of the regulated (or regulable) third party to the government action or inaction-and perhaps on the response of others as well. The existence of one or more of the essential elements of standing "depends on the unfettered choices made by independent actors not before the courts and whose exercise of broad and legitimate discretion the courts cannot presume either to control or to predict," ... and it becomes the burden of the plaintiff to adduce facts showing that those choices have been or will be made in such manner as to produce causation and permit redressability of injury. Thus, when the plaintiff is not himself the object of the government action or inaction he challenges, standing is not precluded, but it is ordinarily "substantially more difficult" to establish.

III

We think the Court of Appeals failed to apply the foregoing principles in denying the Secretary's motion for summary judgment. Respondents had not made the requisite demonstration of (at least) injury and redressability.

A

Respondents' claim to injury is that the lack of consultation with respect to certain funded activities abroad "increas[es] the rate of extinction of endangered and threatened species." Of course, the desire to use or observe an animal species, even for purely esthetic purposes, is undeniably a cognizable interest for purpose of standing. See, *e.g., Sierra Club v. Morton,* 405 U.S., at 734. "But the 'injury in fact' test requires more than an injury to a cognizable interest. It requires that the party seeking review be himself among the injured." *Id.,* at 734-735. To survive the Secretary's summary judgment motion, respondents had to submit affidavits or other evidence showing, through specific facts, not only that listed species were in fact being threatened by funded activities abroad, but also that one or more of respondents' members would thereby be "directly" affected apart from their "'special interest' in th[e] subject." See generally *Hunt v. Washington State Apple Advertising Comm'n,* 432 U.S. 333, 343 (1977).

With respect to this aspect of the case, the Court of Appeals focused on the affidavits of two Defenders' members-Joyce Kelly and Amy Skilbred. Ms. Kelly stated that she traveled to Egypt in 1986 and "observed the traditional habitat of the endangered Nile crocodile there and intend[s] to do so again, and hope[s] to observe the crocodile directly," and that she "will suffer harm in fact as the result of [the] American ... role ... in overseeing the rehabilitation of the Aswan High Dam on the Nile ... and [in] develop [ing] ... Egypt's ... Master Water Plan." Ms. Skilbred averred that she traveled to Sri Lanka in 1981 and "observed th[e] habitat" of "endangered species such as the Asian elephant and the leopard" at what is now the site of the Mahaweli project funded by the Agency for International Development (AID), although she "was unable to see any of the endangered species"; "this development project," she continued, "will seriously reduce endangered, threatened, and endemic species habitat including areas that I visited ... [, which] may severely shorten the future of these species"; that threat, she concluded, harmed her because she "intend[s] to return to Sri Lanka in the future and hope[s] to be more fortunate in spotting at least the endangered elephant and leopard." When Ms. Skilbred was asked at a subsequent deposition if and when she had any plans to return to Sri Lanka, she reiterated that "I intend to go back to Sri Lanka," but confessed that she had no current plans: "I don't know [when]. There is a civil war going on right now. I don't know. Not next year, I will say. In the future."

We shall assume for the sake of argument that these affidavits contain facts showing that certain agency-funded projects threaten listed species-though that is questionable. They plainly contain no facts, however, showing how damage to the species will produce "imminent" injury to Mses. Kelly and Skilbred. That the women "had visited" the areas of the projects before the projects commenced proves nothing. As we have said in a related context, 'Past exposure to illegal conduct does not in itself show a present case or controversy regarding injunctive relief ... if unaccompanied by any continuing, present adverse effects." And the affiants' profession of an "inten[t]" to return to the places they had visited before-where they will presumably, this time, be deprived of the opportunity to observe animals of the endangered species-is simply not enough. Such "some day" intentions-without any description of concrete plans, or indeed even any specification of *when* the some day will be-do not support a finding of the "actual or imminent" injury that our cases require.

There is no substance to the dissent's suggestion that imminence is demanded only when the alleged harm depends upon "the affirmative actions of third parties beyond a plaintiff's control." Our cases *mention* third-party-caused contingency, naturally enough; but they also mention the plaintiff's failure to show that he will soon expose *himself* to the injury. And there is certainly no reason in principle to demand evidence that third persons will take the action exposing the plaintiff to harm, while *presuming* that the plaintiff himself will do so.

Our insistence upon these established requirements of standing does not mean that we would, as the dissent contends, "demand ... detailed descriptions" of damages, such as a "nightly schedule of attempted activities" from plaintiffs alleging loss of consortium. That case and the others posited by the dissent all involve *actual* harm; the existence of standing is clear, though the precise extent of harm remains to be determined at trial. Where there is no actual harm, however, its imminence (though not its precise extent) must be established.

Besides relying upon the Kelly and Skilbred affidavits, respondents propose a series of novel standing theories. The first, inelegantly styled "ecosystem nexus," proposes that any person who uses *any part* of a "contiguous ecosystem" adversely affected by a funded activity has standing even if the activity is located a great distance away. This approach, as the Court of Appeals correctly observed, is inconsistent with our opinion in *National Wildlife Federation*, which held that a plaintiff claiming injury from environmental damage must use the area affected by the challenged activity and not an area roughly "in the vicinity" of it. It makes no difference that the general-purpose section of the ESA states that the Act was intended in part "to provide a means whereby the ecosystems upon which endangered species and threatened species depend may be conserved." To say that the Act protects ecosystems is not to say that the Act creates (if it were possible) rights of action in persons who have not been injured in fact, that is, persons who use portions of an ecosystem not perceptibly affected by the unlawful action in question.

Respondents' other theories are called, alas, the "animal nexus" approach, whereby anyone who has an interest in studying or seeing the endangered animals anywhere on the globe has standing; and the "vocational nexus" approach, under which anyone with a professional interest in such animals can sue. Under these theories, anyone who goes to see Asian elephants in the Bronx Zoo, and anyone who is a keeper of Asian elephants in the Bronx Zoo, has standing to sue because the Director of the Agency for International Development (AID) did not consult with the Secretary regarding the AID-funded project in Sri Lanka. This is beyond all reason. Standing is not "an ingenious academic exercise in the conceivable," *United States v. Students Challenging Regulatory Agency Procedures (SCRAP)*, 412 U.S. 669, (1973), but as we have said requires, at the summary judgment stage, a factual showing of perceptible harm. It is clear that the person who observes or works with a particular animal threatened by a federal decision is facing perceptible harm, since the very subject of his interest will no longer exist. It is even plausible-though it goes to the outermost limit of plausibility-to think that a person who observes or works with animals of a particular species in the very area of the world where that species is threatened by a federal decision is facing such harm, since some animals that might have been the subject of his interest will no longer exist, see *Japan Whaling Assn. v. American Cetacean Society,* 478 U.S. 221, 231, n. 4 (1986). It goes beyond the limit, however, and into pure speculation and fantasy, to say that anyone who observes or works with an endangered species, anywhere in the world, is appreciably harmed by a single project affecting some portion of that species with which he has no more specific connection.

Justice STEVENS, by contrast, would allow standing on an apparent "animal nexus" theory to all plaintiffs whose interest in the animals is "genuine." Such plaintiffs, we are told, do not have to visit the animals because the animals are analogous to family members. We decline to join Justice STEVENS in this Linnaean leap. It is unclear to us what constitutes a "genuine" interest; how it differs from a "nongenuine" interest (which nonetheless prompted a plaintiff to file suit); and why such an interest in animals should be different from such an interest in anything else that is the subject of a lawsuit.

B

Besides failing to show injury, respondents failed to demonstrate redressability. Instead of attacking the separate decisions to fund particular projects allegedly causing them harm, respondents chose to challenge a more generalized level of Government action (rules regarding consultation), the invalidation of which would affect all overseas projects. This programmatic approach has obvious practical advantages, but also obvious difficulties insofar as proof of causation or redressability is concerned. As we have said in another context, "suits challenging, not specifically identifiable Government violations of law, but the particular programs agencies establish to carry out their legal obligations ... [are], even when premised on allegations of several instances of violations of law, ... rarely if ever appropriate for federal-court adjudication." *Allen,* 468 U.S., at 759-760.

The most obvious problem in the present case is redressability. Since the agencies funding the projects were not parties to the case, the District Court could accord relief only against the Secretary: He could be ordered to revise his regulation to require consultation for foreign projects. But this would not remedy respondents' alleged injury unless the funding agencies were bound by the Secretary's regulation, which is very much an open question. Whereas in other contexts the ESA is quite explicit as to the Secretary's controlling authority, see, *e.g.,* 16 U.S.C. § 1533(a)(1) ("The Secretary shall" promulgate regulations determining endangered species); § 1535(d)(1) ("The Secretary is authorized to provide financial assistance to any State"), with respect to consultation the initiative, and hence arguably the initial responsibility for determining statutory necessity, lies with the agencies, see § 1536(a)(2) (*"Each Federal agency shall,* in consultation with and with the assistance of the Secretary, insure that any" funded action is not likely to jeopardize endangered or threatened species) (emphasis added). When the Secretary promulgated the regulation at issue here, he thought it was binding on the agencies, see 51 Fed.Reg. 19928 (1986). The Solicitor General, however, has repudiated that position here, and the agencies themselves apparently deny the Secretary's authority. (During the period when the Secretary took the view that § 7(a)(2) did apply abroad, AID and FWS engaged in a running controversy over whether consultation was required with respect to the Mahaweli project, AID insisting that consultation applied only to domestic actions.)

Respondents assert that this legal uncertainty did not affect redressability (and hence standing) because the District Court itself could resolve the issue of the Secretary's authority as a necessary part of its standing inquiry. Assuming that it is appropriate to resolve an issue of law such as this in connection with a threshold standing inquiry, resolution by the District Court would not have remedied respondents' alleged injury anyway, because it would not have been binding upon the agencies. They were not parties to the suit, and there is no reason they should be obliged to honor an incidental legal determination the suit produced. The Court of Appeals tried to finesse this problem by simply proclaiming that "[w]e are satisfied that an injunction requiring the Secretary to publish [respondents' desired] regulatio[n] ... would result in consultation." *Defenders of Wildlife*, 851 F.2d, at 1042, 1043-1044. We do not know what would justify that confidence, particularly when the Justice Department (presumably after consultation with the agencies) has taken the position that the regulation is not binding. The short of the matter is that redress of the only injury in fact respondents complain of requires action (termination of funding until consultation) by the individual funding agencies; and any relief the District Court could have provided in this suit against the Secretary was not likely to produce that action.

The dissent's rejoinder that redressability *was* clear at the outset because the *Secretary* thought the regulation binding on the agencies, continues to miss the point: The *agencies* did not *agree* with the Secretary, nor would they be bound by a district court holding (as to this issue) in the Secretary's favor. There is no support for the dissent's novel contention, that Rule 19 of the Federal Rules of Civil Procedure, governing joinder of indispensable parties, somehow alters our longstanding rule that jurisdiction is to be assessed under the facts existing when the complaint is filed. The redressability element of the Article III standing requirement and the *"complete relief"* referred to by Rule 19 are not identical. Finally, we reach the dissent's contention, that by refusing to waive our settled rule for purposes of this case we have made "federal subject-matter jurisdiction ... a one-way street running the Executive Branch's way." That is so, we are told, because the Executive can dispel jurisdiction where it previously existed (by either conceding the merits or by pointing out that nonparty agencies would not be bound by a ruling), whereas a plaintiff cannot retroactively create jurisdiction based on postcomplaint litigation conduct. But *any* defendant, not just the Government, can dispel jurisdiction by conceding the merits (and presumably thereby suffering a judgment) or by demonstrating standing defects. And permitting a defendant to point out a pre-existing standing defect late in the day is not remotely comparable to permitting a plaintiff to *establish* standing on the basis of the defendant's litigation conduct occurring after standing is erroneously determined.

A further impediment to redressability is the fact that the agencies generally supply only a fraction of the funding for a foreign project. AID, for example, has provided less than 10% of the funding for the Mahaweli project. Respondents have produced nothing to indicate that the projects they have named will either be suspended, or do less harm to listed species, if that fraction is eliminated. [I]t is entirely conjectural whether the nonagency activity that affects respondents will be altered or affected by the agency activity they seek to achieve. There is no standing.

....

Justice BLACKMUN, with whom Justice O'CONNOR joins, dissenting.

I part company with the Court in this case in two respects. First, I believe that respondents have raised genuine issues of fact-sufficient to survive summary judgment-both as to injury and as to redressability. Second, I question the Court's breadth of language in rejecting standing for "procedural" injuries. I fear the Court seeks to impose fresh limitations on the constitutional authority of Congress to allow citizen suits in the federal courts for injuries deemed "procedural" in nature. I dissent.

***

QUESTIONS

1. What happened in *Defenders of Wildlife?*
2. What was the agency action or inaction at issue?
3. How was "consultation" at issue?
4. What components of constitutional standing did the SCOTUS identify, and upon what basis(es)?
5. How did the plaintiffs attempt to demonstrate standing?
6. How did the court rule on each standing component, and why?
7. Do you agree with the majority's standing analysis? Why or why not?
8. Why did Justice Kennedy write separately?
9. Why did Justices Blackmun and O'Connor dissent?
10. What does this case suggest about what at least Justice Scalia might think about the value of consultation?

C. CONSULTATION CONSEQUENCES: BIOLOGICAL OPINIONS

BENNETT V. SPEAR
520 U.S. 154 (1997)

Justice SCALIA delivered the opinion of the Court.

This is a challenge to a biological opinion issued by the Fish and Wildlife Service in accordance with the Endangered Species Act of 1973 (ESA), 16 U.S.C. § 1531 *et seq.*, concerning the operation of the Klamath Irrigation Project by the Bureau of Reclamation, and the project's impact on two varieties of endangered fish. The question for decision is whether the petitioners, who have competing economic and other interests in Klamath Project water, have standing to seek judicial review of the biological opinion under the citizen-suit provision of the ESA, § 1540(g)(1), and the Administrative Procedure Act (APA), 5 U.S.C. § 701 *et seq.*

I

The ESA requires the Secretary of the Interior to promulgate regulations listing those species of animals that are "threatened" or "endangered" under specified criteria, and to designate their "critical habitat." 16 U.S.C. § 1533. The ESA further requires each federal agency to "insure that any action authorized, funded, or carried out by such agency ... is not likely to jeopardize the continued existence of any endangered species or threatened species or result in the destruction or adverse modification of habitat of such species which is determined by the Secretary ... to be critical." § 1536(a)(2). If an agency determines that action it proposes to take may adversely affect a listed species, it must engage in formal consultation with the Fish and Wildlife Service, as delegate of the Secretary, after which the Service must provide the agency with a written statement (the Biological Opinion) explaining how the proposed action will affect the species or its habitat, 16 U.S.C. § 1536(b)(3)(A). If the Service concludes that the proposed action will "jeopardize the continued existence of any [listed] species or threatened species or result in the destruction or adverse modification of [critical habitat]," § 1536(a)(2), the Biological Opinion must outline any "reasonable and prudent alternatives" that the Service believes will avoid that consequence, § 1536(b)(3)(A). Additionally, if the Biological Opinion concludes that the agency action will not result in jeopardy or adverse habitat modification, or if it offers reasonable and prudent alternatives to avoid that consequence, the Service must provide the agency with a written statement (known as the Incidental Take Statement) specifying the "impact of such incidental taking on the species," any "reasonable and prudent measures that the [Service] considers necessary or appropriate to minimize such impact," and setting forth "the terms and conditions ... that must be complied with by the Federal agency ... to implement [those measures]." § 1536(b)(4).

The Klamath Project, one of the oldest federal reclamation schemes, is a series of lakes, rivers, dams, and irrigation canals in northern California and southern Oregon. The project was undertaken by the Secretary of the Interior pursuant to the Reclamation Act of 1902, 32 Stat. 388, as amended, 43 U.S.C. § 371 *et seq.,* and the Act of Feb. 9, 1905, 33 Stat. 714, and is administered by the Bureau of Reclamation, which is under the Secretary's jurisdiction. In 1992, the Bureau notified the Service that operation of the project might affect the Lost River Sucker *(Deltistes luxatus)* and Shortnose Sucker *(Chasmistes brevirostris),* species of fish that were listed as endangered in 1988. After formal consultation with the Bureau in accordance with, the Service issued a Biological Opinion which concluded that the " 'long-term operation of the Klamath Project was likely to jeopardize the continued existence of the Lost River and shortnose suckers.' " The Biological Opinion identified "reasonable and prudent alternatives" the Service believed would avoid jeopardy, which included the maintenance of minimum water levels on Clear Lake and Gerber reservoirs. The Bureau later notified the Service that it intended to operate the project in compliance with the Biological Opinion.

Petitioners, two Oregon irrigation districts that receive Klamath Project water and the operators of two ranches within those districts, filed the present action against the director and regional director of the Service and the Secretary of the Interior. Neither the Bureau nor any of its officials is named as defendant. The complaint asserts that the Bureau "has been following essentially the same procedures for storing and releasing water from Clear Lake and Gerber reservoirs throughout the twentieth century;" that "[t]here is no scientifically or commercially available evidence indicating that the populations of endangered suckers in Clear Lake and Gerber reservoirs have declined, are declining, or will decline as a result" of the Bureau's operation of the Klamath Project; that "[t]here is no commercially or scientifically available evidence indicating that the restrictions on lake levels imposed in the Biological Opinion will have any beneficial effect on the ... populations of suckers in Clear Lake and Gerber reservoirs;" and that the Bureau nonetheless "will abide by the restrictions imposed by the Biological Opinion."

Petitioners' complaint included three claims for relief that are relevant here. The first and second claims allege that the Service's jeopardy determination with respect to Clear Lake and Gerber reservoirs, and the ensuing imposition of minimum water levels, violated § 7 of the ESA, 16 U.S.C. § 1536. The third claim is that the imposition of minimum water elevations constituted an implicit determination of critical habitat for the suckers, which violated § 4 of the ESA, 16 U.S.C. § 1533(b)(2), because it failed to take into consideration the designation's economic impact. Each of the claims also states that the relevant action violated the APA's prohibition of agency action that is "arbitrary, capricious, an abuse of discretion, or otherwise not in accordance with law." 5 U.S.C. § 706(2)(A).

The complaint asserts that petitioners' use of the reservoirs and related waterways for "recreational, aesthetic and commercial purposes, as well as for their primary sources of irrigation water," will be "irreparably damaged" by the actions complained of, and that the restrictions on water delivery "recommended" by the Biological Opinion "adversely affect plaintiffs by substantially reducing the quantity of available irrigation water." In essence, petitioners claim a competing interest in the water the Biological Opinion declares necessary for the preservation of the suckers.

[]

In this Court, petitioners raise two questions: first, whether the prudential standing rule known as the "zone of interests" test applies to claims brought under the citizen-suit provision of the ESA; and second, if so, whether petitioners have standing under that test notwithstanding that the interests they seek to vindicate are economic rather than environmental. In this Court, the Government has made no effort to defend the reasoning of the Court of Appeals. Instead, it advances three alternative grounds for affirmance: (1) that petitioners fail to meet the standing requirements imposed by Article III of the Constitution; (2) that the ESA's citizen-suit provision does not authorize judicial review of the types of claims advanced by petitioners; and (3) that judicial review is unavailable under the APA because the Biological Opinion does not constitute final agency action.

II
[]

The Service itself is, to put it mildly, keenly aware of the virtually determinative effect of its biological opinions. The Incidental Take Statement at issue in the present case begins by instructing the reader that any taking of a listed species is prohibited unless "such taking is in compliance with this incidental take statement," and warning that "[t]he measures described below are nondiscretionary, and must be taken by [the Bureau]." Given all of this, and given petitioners' allegation that the Bureau had, until issuance of the Biological Opinion, operated the Klamath Project in the same manner throughout the 20th century, it is not difficult to conclude that petitioners have met their burden—which is relatively modest at this stage of the litigation—of alleging that their injury is "fairly traceable" to the Service's Biological Opinion and that it will "likely" be redressed—*i.e.,* the Bureau will not impose such water level restrictions—if the Biological Opinion is set aside.

* * *

The Court of Appeals erred in affirming the District Court's dismissal of petitioners' claims for lack of jurisdiction. Petitioners' complaint alleges facts sufficient to meet the requirements of Article III standing, and none of their ESA claims is precluded by the zone-of-interests test. Petitioners' § 1533 claim is reviewable under the ESA's citizen-suit provision, and petitioners' remaining claims are reviewable under the APA.

The judgment of the Court of Appeals is reversed, and the case is remanded for further proceedings consistent with this opinion.

It is so ordered.

QUESTIONS

1. What is a "biological opinion"?
2. How does it fit into the scheme of Section 7?
3. What happened in *Bennett v. Spear?*

4. What were the species and the agency action or inaction at issue?
5. Who issued the "biological opinion," and what were the "reasonable and prudent measures" it included?
6. What components of constitutional standing did the SCOTUS identify, and upon what basis(es)?
7. How did the plaintiffs attempt to demonstrate standing?
8. How did the court rule on each standing component, and why?
9. Do you agree with the plurality's standing analysis? Why or why not?
10. What do you think the opinion suggests about how at least Justice Scalia regards the issuance of a "biological opinion?"

V.   PROHIBITIONS

Section 9 prohibits the "taking" of T&E species, unless it is an activity that enjoys a federally-permitted "incidental take" under Section 10. The next two sections both textualize and contextualize the "pit bull" portion of the ESA.

A. LANGUAGE

1. Takings: 16 U.S.C.A. § 1538: Prohibited acts (Section 9)

(a) Generally

(1) Except as provided in sections 1535(g)(2) and 1539 of this title, with respect to any endangered species of fish or wildlife listed pursuant to section 1533 of this title it is unlawful for any person subject to the jurisdiction of the United States to--
(A) import any such species into, or export any such species from the United States;
(B) take any such species within the United States or the territorial sea of the United States;
(C) take any such species upon the high seas;
(D) possess, sell, deliver, carry, transport, or ship, by any means whatsoever, any such species taken in violation of subparagraphs (B) and (C);
(E) deliver, receive, carry, transport, or ship in interstate or foreign commerce, by any means whatsoever and in the course of a commercial activity, any such species;
(F) sell or offer for sale in interstate or foreign commerce any such species; or
(G) violate any regulation pertaining to such species or to any threatened species of fish or wildlife listed pursuant to section 1533 of this title and promulgated by the Secretary pursuant to authority provided by this chapter.

(2) Except as provided in sections 1535(g)(2) and 1539 of this title, with respect to any endangered species of plants listed pursuant to section 1533 of this title, it is unlawful for any person subject to the jurisdiction of the United States to--
(A) import any such species into, or export any such species from, the United States;
(B) remove and reduce to possession any such species from areas under Federal jurisdiction; maliciously damage or destroy any such species on any such area; or remove, cut, dig up, or damage or destroy any such species on any other area in knowing violation of any law or regulation of any State or in the course of any violation of a State criminal trespass law;
(C) deliver, receive, carry, transport, or ship in interstate or foreign commerce, by any means whatsoever and in the course of a commercial activity, any such species;
(D) sell or offer for sale in interstate or foreign commerce any such species; or

(E) violate any regulation pertaining to such species or to any threatened species of plants listed pursuant to section 1533 of this title and promulgated by the Secretary pursuant to authority provided by this chapter.

(b) Species held in captivity or controlled environment

(1) The provisions of subsections (a)(1)(A) and (a)(1)(G) of this section shall not apply to any fish or wildlife which was held in captivity or in a controlled environment on (A) December 28, 1973, or (B) the date of the publication in the Federal Register of a final regulation adding such fish or wildlife species to any list published pursuant to subsection (c) of section 1533 of this title: *Provided*, That such holding and any subsequent holding or use of the fish or wildlife was not in the course of a commercial activity. With respect to any act prohibited by subsections (a)(1)(A) and (a)(1)(G) of this section which occurs after a period of 180 days from (i) December 28, 1973, or (ii) the date of publication in the Federal Register of a final regulation adding such fish or wildlife species to any list published pursuant to subsection (c) of section 1533 of this title, there shall be a rebuttable presumption that the fish or wildlife involved in such act is not entitled to the exemption contained in this subsection.

(2)(A) The provisions of subsection (a) (1) of this section shall not apply to--

(i) any raptor legally held in captivity or in a controlled environment on November 10, 1978; or

(ii) any progeny of any raptor described in clause (i); until such time as any such raptor or progeny is intentionally returned to a wild state.

(B) Any person holding any raptor or progeny described in subparagraph (A) must be able to demonstrate that the raptor or progeny does, in fact, qualify under the provisions of this paragraph, and shall maintain and submit to the Secretary, on request, such inventories, documentation, and records as the Secretary may by regulation require as being reasonably appropriate to carry out the purposes of this paragraph. Such requirements shall not unnecessarily duplicate the requirements of other rules and regulations promulgated by the Secretary.

2. Incidental Take Permits: 16 U.S.C.A. § 1539 (Section 10)

(a) Permits

(1) The Secretary may permit, under such terms and conditions as he shall prescribe--

(A) any act otherwise prohibited by section 1538 of this title for scientific purposes or to enhance the propagation or survival of the affected species, including, but not limited to, acts necessary for the establishment and maintenance of experimental populations pursuant to subsection (j) of this section; or

(B) any taking otherwise prohibited by section 1538(a)(1)(B) of this title if such taking is incidental to, and not the purpose of, the carrying out of an otherwise lawful activity.

(2)(A) No permit may be issued by the Secretary authorizing any taking referred to in paragraph (1)(B) unless the applicant therefor submits to the Secretary a conservation plan that specifies--

(i) the impact which will likely result from such taking;

(ii) what steps the applicant will take to minimize and mitigate such impacts, and the funding that will be available to implement such steps;

(iii) what alternative actions to such taking the applicant considered and the reasons why such alternatives are not being utilized; and

(iv) such other measures that the Secretary may require as being necessary or appropriate for purposes of the plan.

(B) If the Secretary finds, after opportunity for public comment, with respect to a permit application and the related conservation plan that--

(i) the taking will be incidental;

(ii) the applicant will, to the maximum extent practicable, minimize and mitigate the impacts of such taking;

(iii) the applicant will ensure that adequate funding for the plan will be provided;

(iv) the taking will not appreciably reduce the likelihood of the survival and recovery of the species in the wild; and

(v) the measures, if any, required under subparagraph (A)(iv) will be met;

and he has received such other assurances as he may require that the plan will be implemented, the Secretary shall issue the permit. The permit shall contain such terms and conditions as the Secretary deems necessary or appropriate to carry out the purposes of this paragraph, including, but not limited to, such reporting requirements as the Secretary deems necessary for determining whether such terms and conditions are being complied with.

(C) The Secretary shall revoke a permit issued under this paragraph if he finds that the permittee is not complying with the terms and conditions of the permit.

QUESTIONS

1. What actions does Section 9 make unlawful as pertains to wildlife?
2. Ditto, for plants?
3. Ditto, for captive species? (What are these?)
4. Ditto, for imported species?
5. Ditto, for exported species?
6. What is an "incidental take" and why does it matter?
7. Under what circumstances is an incidental "taking" not unlawful? What is an "ITP"?
8. What is a "conservation plan," what does it have to do with Section 10, and what must it entail?

B. UNLAWFUL ACTIONS (TAKE) IN CONTEXT

BABBITT V. SWEET HOME CHAPTER OF COMMUNITIES FOR A GREAT OREGON
515 U.S. 687 (1995)

Justice STEVENS delivered the opinion of the Court.

The Endangered Species Act of 1973 (ESA or Act), contains a variety of protections designed to save from extinction species that the Secretary of the Interior designates as endangered or threatened. Section 9 of the Act makes it unlawful for any person to "take" any endangered or threatened species. The Secretary has promulgated a regulation that defines the statute's prohibition on takings to include "significant habitat modification or degradation where it actually kills or injures wildlife." This case presents the question whether the Secretary exceeded his authority under the Act by promulgating that regulation.

I

Section 9(a)(1) of the Act provides the following protection for endangered species:

> "Except as provided in sections 1535(g)(2) and 1539 of this title, with respect to any endangered species of fish or wildlife listed pursuant to section 1533 of this title it is unlawful for any person subject to the jurisdiction of the United States to—....

"(B) take any such species within the United States or the territorial sea of the United States." 16 U.S.C. § 1538(a)(1).

Section 3(19) of the Act defines the statutory term "take":

> "The term 'take' means to harass, harm, pursue, hunt, shoot, wound, kill, trap, capture, or collect, or to attempt to engage in any such conduct." 16 U.S.C. § 1532(19).
> The Act does not further define the terms it uses to define "take." The Interior Department regulations that implement the statute, however, define the statutory term "harm":
> *Harm* in the definition of 'take' in the Act means an act which actually kills or injures wildlife. Such act may include significant habitat modification or degradation where it actually kills or injures wildlife by significantly impairing essential behavioral patterns, including breeding, feeding, or sheltering." 50 CFR § 17.3 (1994).

This regulation has been in place since 1975.

A limitation on the § 9 "take" prohibition appears in § 10(a)(1)(B) of the Act, which Congress added by amendment in 1982. That section authorizes the Secretary to grant a permit for any taking otherwise prohibited by § 9(a)(1)(B) "if such taking is incidental to, and not the purpose of, the carrying out of an otherwise lawful activity." 16 U.S.C. § 1539(a)(1)(B).

In addition to the prohibition on takings, the Act provides several other protections for endangered species. Section 4, 16 U.S.C. § 1533, commands the Secretary to identify species of fish or wildlife that are in danger of extinction and to publish from time to time lists of all species he determines to be endangered or threatened. Section 5, 16 U.S.C. § 1534, authorizes the Secretary, in cooperation with the States, see § 1535, to acquire land to aid in preserving such species. Section 7 requires federal agencies to ensure that none of their activities, including the granting of licenses and permits, will jeopardize the continued existence of endangered species "or result in the destruction or adverse modification of habitat of such species which is determined by the Secretary ... to be critical." 16 U.S.C. § 1536(a)(2).

Respondents in this action are small landowners, logging companies, and families dependent on the forest products industries in the Pacific Northwest and in the Southeast, and organizations that represent their interests. They brought this declaratory judgment action against petitioners, the Secretary of the Interior and the Director of the Fish and Wildlife Service, in the United States District Court for the District of Columbia to challenge the statutory validity of the Secretary's regulation defining "harm," particularly the inclusion of habitat modification and degradation in the definition. Respondents challenged the regulation on its face. Their complaint alleged that application of the "harm" regulation to the red-cockaded woodpecker, an endangered species, and the northern spotted owl, a threatened species, had injured them economically.

Respondents advanced three arguments to support their submission that Congress did not intend the word "take" in § 9 to include habitat modification, as the Secretary's "harm" regulation provides. First, they correctly noted that language in the Senate's original version of the ESA would have defined "take" to include "destruction, modification, or curtailment of [the] habitat or range" of fish or wildlife, but the Senate deleted that language from the bill before enacting it. Second, respondents argued that Congress intended the Act's express authorization for the Federal Government to buy private land in order to prevent habitat degradation in § 5 to be the exclusive check against habitat modification on private property. Third, because the Senate added the term "harm" to the definition of "take" in a floor amendment without debate, respondents argued that the court should not interpret the term so expansively as to include habitat modification.

The District Court considered and rejected each of respondents' arguments, finding "that Congress intended an expansive interpretation of the word 'take,' an interpretation that encompasses habitat modification." The court noted that in 1982, when Congress was aware of a judicial decision that had applied the Secretary's regulation, it amended the Act without using the opportunity to change the definition of "take." The court stated that, even had it found the ESA " 'silent or ambiguous' " as to the authority for the Secretary's definition of "harm," it would nevertheless have upheld the regulation as a reasonable interpretation of the statute. The District Court therefore entered summary judgment for petitioners and dismissed respondents' complaint.

A divided panel of the Court of Appeals initially affirmed the judgment of the District Court. After granting a petition for rehearing, however, the panel reversed. Although acknowledging that "[t]he potential breadth of the word 'harm' is indisputable," the majority concluded that the immediate statutory context in which "harm" appeared counseled against a broad reading; like the other words in the definition of "take," the word "harm" should be read as applying only to "the perpetrator's direct application of force against the animal taken.... The forbidden acts fit, in ordinary language, the basic model 'A hit B.' " The majority based its reasoning on a canon of statutory construction called *noscitur a sociis*, which holds that a word is known by the company it keeps.

The majority claimed support for its construction from a decision of the Ninth Circuit that narrowly construed the word "harass" in the Marine Mammal Protection Act of 1972; from the legislative history of the ESA; from its view that Congress must not have intended the purportedly broad curtailment of private property rights that the Secretary's interpretation permitted; and from the ESA's land acquisition provision in § 5 and restriction on federal agencies' activities regarding habitat in § 7, both of which the court saw as evidence that Congress had not intended the § 9 "take" prohibition to reach habitat modification. Most prominently, the court performed a lengthy analysis of the 1982 amendment to § 10 that provided for "incidental take permits" and concluded that the amendment did not change the meaning of the term "take" as defined in the 1973 statute.

Chief Judge Mikva, who had announced the panel's original decision, dissented. In his view, a proper application of *Chevron* indicated that the Secretary had reasonably defined "harm," because respondents had failed to show that Congress unambiguously manifested its intent to exclude habitat modification from the ambit of "take." Chief Judge Mikva found the majority's reliance on *noscitur a sociis* inappropriate in light of the statutory language and unnecessary in light of the strong support in the legislative history for the Secretary's interpretation. He did not find the 1982 "incidental take permit" amendment alone sufficient to vindicate the Secretary's definition of "harm," but he believed the amendment provided additional support for that definition because it reflected Congress' view in 1982 that the definition was reasonable.

The Court of Appeals' decision created a square conflict with a 1988 decision of the Ninth Circuit that had upheld the Secretary's definition of "harm." We granted certiorari to resolve the conflict. Our consideration of the text and structure of the Act, its legislative history, and the significance of the 1982 amendment persuades us that the Court of Appeals' judgment should be reversed.

II

Conserving Endangered and Threatened Species

Because this case was decided on motions for summary judgment, we may appropriately make certain factual assumptions in order to frame the legal issue. First, we assume respondents have no desire to harm either the red-cockaded woodpecker or the spotted owl; they merely wish to continue logging activities that would be entirely proper if not prohibited by the ESA. On the other hand, we must assume, *arguendo,* that those activities will have the effect, even though unintended, of detrimentally changing the natural habitat of both listed species and that, as a consequence, members of those species will be killed or injured. Under respondents' view of the law, the Secretary's only means of forestalling that grave result—even when the actor knows it is certain to occur[9]—is to use his § 5 authority to purchase the lands on which the survival of the species depends. The Secretary, on the other hand, submits that the § 9 prohibition on takings, which Congress defined to include "harm," places on respondents a duty to avoid harm that habitat alteration will cause the birds unless respondents first obtain a permit pursuant to § 10.

The text of the Act provides three reasons for concluding that the Secretary's interpretation is reasonable. First, an ordinary understanding of the word "harm" supports it. The dictionary definition of the verb form of "harm" is "to cause hurt or damage to: injure." Webster's Third New International Dictionary 1034 (1966). In the context of the ESA, that definition naturally encompasses habitat modification that results in actual injury or death to members of an endangered or threatened species.

Respondents argue that the Secretary should have limited the purview of "harm" to direct applications of force against protected species, but the dictionary definition does not include the word "directly" or suggest in any way that only direct or willful action that leads to injury constitutes "harm." Moreover, unless the statutory term "harm" encompasses indirect as well as direct injuries, the word has no meaning that does not duplicate the meaning of other words that § 3 uses to define "take." A reluctance to treat statutory terms as surplusage supports the reasonableness of the Secretary's interpretation.

Second, the broad purpose of the ESA supports the Secretary's decision to extend protection against activities that cause the precise harms Congress enacted the statute to avoid. In *TVA v. Hill,* 437 U.S. 153 (1978), we described the Act as "the most comprehensive legislation for the preservation of endangered species ever enacted by any nation." Whereas predecessor statutes enacted in 1966 and 1969 had not contained any sweeping prohibition against the taking of endangered species except on federal lands. As stated in § 2 of the Act, among its central purposes is "to provide a means whereby the ecosystems upon which endangered species and threatened species depend may be conserved...." 16 U.S.C. § 1531(b).

In *Hill,* we construed § 7 as precluding the completion of the Tellico Dam because of its predicted impact on the survival of the snail darter. Both our holding and the language in our opinion stressed the importance of the statutory policy. "The plain intent of Congress in enacting this statute," we recognized, "was to halt and reverse the trend toward species extinction, whatever the cost. This is reflected not only in the stated policies of the Act, but in literally every section of the statute." Although the § 9 "take" prohibition was not at issue in *Hill,* we took note of that prohibition, placing particular emphasis on the Secretary's inclusion of habitat modification in his definition of "harm." In light of that provision for habitat protection, we could "not understand how TVA intends to operate Tellico Dam without 'harming' the snail darter. Congress' intent to provide comprehensive protection for endangered and threatened species supports the permissibility of the Secretary's "harm" regulation.

Respondents advance strong arguments that activities that cause minimal or unforeseeable harm will not violate the Act as construed in the "harm" regulation. Respondents, however, present a facial challenge to the regulation. Thus, they ask us to invalidate the Secretary's understanding of "harm" in every circumstance, even when an actor knows that an activity, such as draining a pond, would actually result in the extinction of a listed species by destroying its habitat. Given Congress' clear expression of the ESA's broad purpose to protect endangered and threatened wildlife, the Secretary's definition of "harm" is reasonable.

Third, the fact that Congress in 1982 authorized the Secretary to issue permits for takings that § 9(a)(1)(B) would otherwise prohibit, "if such taking is incidental to, and not the purpose of, the carrying out of an otherwise lawful activity," 16 U.S.C. § 1539(a)(1)(B), strongly suggests that Congress understood § 9(a)(1)(B) to prohibit indirect as well as deliberate takings. The permit process requires the applicant to prepare a "conservation plan" that specifies how he intends to "minimize and mitigate" the "impact" of his activity on endangered and threatened species, 16 U.S.C. § 1539(a)(2)(A), making clear that Congress had in mind foreseeable rather than merely accidental effects on listed species. No one could seriously request an "incidental" take permit to avert § 9 liability for direct, deliberate action against a member of an endangered or threatened species, but respondents would read "harm" so narrowly that the permit procedure would have little more than that absurd purpose. "When Congress acts to amend a statute, we presume it intends its amendment to have real and substantial effect." Congress' addition of the § 10 permit provision supports the Secretary's conclusion that activities not intended to harm an endangered species, such as habitat modification, may constitute unlawful takings under the ESA unless the Secretary permits them.

The Court of Appeals made three errors in asserting that "harm" must refer to a direct application of force because the words around it do. First, the court's premise was flawed. Several of the words that accompany "harm" in the § 3 definition of "take," especially "harass," "pursue," "wound," and "kill," refer to actions or effects that do not require direct applications of force. Second, to the extent the court read a requirement of intent or purpose into the words used to define "take," it ignored § 11's express provision that a "knowin[g]" action is enough to violate the Act. Third, the court employed *noscitur a sociis* to give "harm" essentially the same function as other words in the definition, thereby denying it independent meaning. The canon, to the contrary, counsels that a word "gathers meaning from the words around it." The statutory context of "harm" suggests that Congress meant that term to serve a particular function in the ESA, consistent with, but distinct from, the functions of the other verbs used to define "take." The Secretary's interpretation of "harm" to include indirectly injuring endangered animals through habitat modification permissibly interprets "harm" to have "a character of its own not to be submerged by its association."

Nor does the Act's inclusion of the § 5 land acquisition authority and the § 7 directive to federal agencies to avoid destruction or adverse modification of critical habitat alter our conclusion. Respondents' argument that the Government lacks any incentive to purchase land under § 5 when it can simply prohibit takings under § 9 ignores the practical considerations that attend enforcement of the ESA. Purchasing habitat lands may well cost the Government less in many circumstances than pursuing civil or criminal penalties. In addition, the § 5 procedure allows for protection of habitat before the seller's activity has harmed any endangered animal, whereas the Government cannot enforce the § 9 prohibition until an animal has actually been killed or injured. The Secretary may also find the § 5 authority useful for preventing modification of land that is not yet but may in the future become habitat for an endangered or threatened species. The § 7 directive applies only to the Federal Government, whereas the § 9 prohibition applies to "any person." Section 7 imposes a broad, affirmative duty to avoid adverse habitat modifications that § 9 does not replicate, and § 7 does not limit its admonition to habitat modification that "actually kills or injures wildlife." Conversely, § 7 contains limitations that § 9 does not, applying only to actions "likely to jeopardize the continued existence of any endangered species or threatened species," 16 U.S.C. § 1536(a)(2), and to modifications of habitat that has been designated "critical" pursuant to § 4, 16 U.S.C. § 1533(b)(2). Any overlap that § 5 or § 7 may have with § 9 in particular cases is unexceptional, and simply reflects the broad purpose of the Act set out in § 2 and acknowledged in *TVA v. Hill*.

We need not decide whether the statutory definition of "take" compels the Secretary's interpretation of "harm," because our conclusions that Congress did not unambiguously manifest its intent to adopt respondents' view and that the Secretary's interpretation is reasonable suffice to decide this case. See generally *Chevron U.S.A. Inc. v. Natural Resources Defense Council, Inc.*, 467 U.S. 837. The latitude the ESA gives the Secretary in enforcing the statute, together with the degree of regulatory expertise necessary to its enforcement, establishes that we owe some degree of deference to the Secretary's reasonable interpretation. See Breyer, Judicial Review of Questions of Law and Policy, 38 Admin.L.Rev. 363, 373 (1986).

III

Our conclusion that the Secretary's definition of "harm" rests on a permissible construction of the ESA gains further support from the legislative history of the statute. The Committee Reports accompanying the bills that became the ESA do not specifically discuss the meaning of "harm," but they make clear that Congress intended "take" to apply broadly to cover indirect as well as purposeful actions. The Senate Report stressed that " '[t]ake' is defined ... in the broadest possible manner to include every conceivable way in which a person can 'take' or attempt to 'take' any fish or wildlife." The House Report stated that "the broadest possible terms" were used to define restrictions on takings. The House Report underscored the breadth of the "take" definition by noting that it included "harassment, *whether intentional or not.*" The Report explained that the definition "would allow, for example, the Secretary to regulate or prohibit the activities of birdwatchers where the effect of those activities might disturb the birds and make it difficult for them to hatch or raise their young." These comments, ignored in the dissent's welcome but selective foray into legislative history, support the Secretary's interpretation that the term "take" in § 9 reached far more than the deliberate actions of hunters and trappers.

Two endangered species bills, S. 1592 and S. 1983, were introduced in the Senate and referred to the Commerce Committee. Neither bill included the word "harm" in its definition of "take," although the definitions otherwise closely resembled the one that appeared in the bill as ultimately enacted. Senator Tunney, the floor manager of the bill in the Senate, subsequently introduced a floor amendment that added "harm" to the definition, noting that this and accompanying amendments would "help to achieve the purposes of the bill." Respondents argue that the lack of debate about the amendment that added "harm" counsels in favor of a narrow interpretation. We disagree. An obviously broad word that the Senate went out of its way to add to an important statutory definition is precisely the sort of provision that deserves a respectful reading.

The definition of "take" that originally appeared in S. 1983 differed from the definition as ultimately enacted in one other significant respect: It included "the destruction, modification, or curtailment of [the] habitat or range" of fish and wildlife. Respondents make much of the fact that the Commerce Committee removed this phrase from the "take" definition before S. 1983 went to the floor. We do not find that fact especially significant. The legislative materials contain no indication why the habitat protection provision was deleted. That provision differed greatly from the regulation at issue today. Most notably, the habitat protection provision in S. 1983 would have applied far more broadly than the regulation does because it made adverse habitat modification a categorical violation of the "take" prohibition, unbounded by the regulation's limitation to habitat modifications that actually kill or injure wildlife. The S. 1983 language also failed to qualify "modification" with the regulation's limiting adjective "significant." We do not believe the Senate's unelaborated disavowal of the provision in S. 1983 undermines the reasonableness of the more moderate habitat protection in the Secretary's "harm" regulation.

The history of the 1982 amendment that gave the Secretary authority to grant permits for "incidental" takings provides further support for his reading of the Act. The House Report expressly states that "[b]y use of the word 'incidental' the Committee intends to cover situations in which it is known that a taking will occur if the other activity is engaged in but such taking is incidental to, and not the purpose of, the activity."This reference to the foreseeability of incidental takings undermines respondents' argument that the 1982 amendment covered only accidental killings of endangered and threatened animals that might occur in the course of hunting or trapping other animals. Indeed, Congress had habitat modification directly in mind: Both the Senate Report and the House Conference Report identified as the model for the permit process a cooperative state-federal response to a case in California where a development project threatened incidental harm to a species of endangered butterfly by modification of its habitat. Thus, Congress in 1982 focused squarely on the aspect of the "harm" regulation at issue in this litigation. Congress' implementation of a permit program is consistent with the Secretary's interpretation of the term "harm."

IV

When it enacted the ESA, Congress delegated broad administrative and interpretive power to the Secretary. See 16 U.S.C. §§ 1533, 1540(f). The task of defining and listing endangered and threatened species requires an expertise and attention to detail that exceeds the normal province of Congress. Fashioning appropriate standards for issuing permits under § 10 for takings that would otherwise violate § 9 necessarily requires the exercise of broad discretion. The proper interpretation of a term such as "harm" involves a complex policy choice. When Congress has entrusted the Secretary with broad discretion, we are especially reluctant to substitute our views of wise policy for his. In this case, that reluctance accords with our conclusion, based on the text, structure, and legislative history of the ESA, that the Secretary reasonably construed the intent of Congress when he defined "harm" to include "significant habitat modification or degradation that actually kills or injures wildlife."

In the elaboration and enforcement of the ESA, the Secretary and all persons who must comply with the law will confront difficult questions of proximity and degree; for, as all recognize, the Act encompasses a vast range of economic and social enterprises and endeavors. These questions must be addressed in the usual course of the law, through case-by-case resolution and adjudication.

The judgment of the Court of Appeals is reversed.

It is so ordered.

Justice O'CONNOR, concurring.

My agreement with the Court is founded on two understandings. First, the challenged regulation is limited to significant habitat modification that causes actual, as opposed to hypothetical or speculative, death or injury to identifiable protected animals. Second, even setting aside difficult questions of scienter, the regulation's application is limited by ordinary principles of proximate causation, which introduce notions of foreseeability. These limitations, in my view, call into question and with it, many of the applications derided by the dissent. Because there is no need to strike a regulation on a facial challenge out of concern that it is susceptible of erroneous application, however, and because there are many habitat-related circumstances in which the regulation might validly apply, I join the opinion of the Court.

In my view, the regulation is limited by its terms to actions that actually kill or injure individual animals. Justice SCALIA disagrees, arguing that the harm regulation "encompasses injury inflicted, not only upon individual animals, but upon populations of the protected species." At one level, I could not reasonably quarrel with this observation; death to an individual animal always reduces the size of the population in which it lives, and in that sense, "injures" that population. But by its insight, the dissent means something else. Building upon the regulation's use of the word "breeding," Justice SCALIA suggests that the regulation facially bars significant habitat modification that actually kills or injures *hypothetical* animals (or, perhaps more aptly, causes potential additions to the population not to come into being). Because "[i]mpairment of breeding does not 'injure' living creatures," Justice SCALIA reasons, the regulation *must* contemplate application to "*a population* of animals which would otherwise have maintained or increased its numbers."

I disagree. As an initial matter, I do not find it as easy as Justice SCALIA does to dismiss the notion that significant impairment of breeding injures living creatures. To raze the last remaining ground on which the piping plover currently breeds, thereby making it impossible for any piping plovers to reproduce, would obviously injure the population (causing the species' extinction in a generation). But by completely preventing breeding, it would also injure the individual living bird, in the same way that sterilizing the creature injures the individual living bird. To "injure" is, among other things, "to impair." Webster's Ninth New Collegiate Dictionary 623 (1983). One need not subscribe to theories of "psychic harm," to recognize that to make it impossible for an animal to reproduce is to impair its most essential physical functions and to render that animal, and its genetic material, biologically obsolete. This, in my view, is actual injury.

In any event, even if impairing an animal's ability to breed were not, *in and of itself,* an injury to that animal, interference with breeding can cause an animal to suffer other, perhaps more obvious, kinds of injury. The regulation has clear application, for example, to significant habitat modification that kills or physically injures animals which, because they are in a vulnerable breeding state, do not or cannot flee or defend themselves, or to environmental pollutants that cause an animal to suffer physical complications during gestation. Breeding, feeding, and sheltering are what animals do. If significant habitat modification, by interfering with these essential behaviors, actually kills or injures an animal protected by the Act, it causes "harm" within the meaning of the regulation. In contrast to Justice SCALIA, I do not read the regulation's "breeding" reference to vitiate or somehow to qualify the clear actual death or injury requirement, or to suggest that the regulation contemplates extension to nonexistent animals.

[Author's note: Remainder of Justice O'Connor's concurrence analogizing to proximate causation in tort law omitted]

In my view, then, the "harm" regulation applies where significant habitat modification, by impairing essential behaviors, proximately (foreseeably) causes actual death or injury to identifiable animals that are protected under the Endangered Species Act. Pursuant to my interpretation, *Palila II*—under which the Court of Appeals held that a state agency committed a "taking" by permitting mouflon sheep to eat mamane-naio seedlings that, when full grown, might have fed and sheltered endangered palila—was wrongly decided according to the regulation's own terms. Destruction of the seedlings did not proximately cause actual death or injury to identifiable birds; it merely prevented the regeneration of forest land not currently sustaining actual birds.

This case, of course, comes to us as a facial challenge. We are charged with deciding whether the regulation on its face exceeds the agency's statutory mandate. I have identified at least one application of the regulation (*Palila II*) that is, in my view, inconsistent with the regulation's *own* limitations. That misapplication does not, however, call into question the validity of the regulation itself. One can doubtless imagine questionable applications of the regulation that test the limits of the agency's authority. However, it seems to me clear that the regulation does not on its terms exceed the agency's mandate, and that the regulation has innumerable valid habitat-related applications. Congress may, of course, see fit to revisit this issue. And nothing the Court says today prevents the agency itself from narrowing the scope of its regulation at a later date.

With this understanding, I join the Court's opinion.

SCALIA, Justice, with whom THE CHIEF JUSTICE and Justice THOMAS join, dissenting.

I think it unmistakably clear that the legislation at issue here (1) forbade the hunting and killing of endangered animals, and (2) provided federal lands and federal funds *for the acquisition of private lands,* to preserve the habitat of endangered animals. The Court's holding that the hunting and killing prohibition incidentally preserves habitat on private lands imposes unfairness to the point of financial ruin—not just upon the rich, but upon the simplest farmer who finds his land conscripted to national zoological use. I respectfully dissent.

The Endangered Species Act is a carefully considered piece of legislation that forbids all persons to hunt or harm endangered animals, but places upon the public at large, rather than upon fortuitously accountable individual landowners, the cost of preserving the habitat of endangered species. There is neither textual support for, nor even evidence of congressional consideration of, the radically different disposition contained in the regulation that the Court sustains. For these reasons, I respectfully dissent.

[Remainder of Justice Scalia's dissent omitted.]

QUESTIONS

1. What happened in *Sweet Home Chapter*?
2. What was being "taken"?
3. What was the legal issue? What is the role of "habitat"?
4. How did the majority resolve it, and why?
5. What is the relevance to tort causation?
6. Why did Justice O'Connor concur?
7. Why did Justices Scalia, Rehnquist, and Thomas dissent? What did they think the majority got wrong?
8. Which argument do you think is better?

VI. ENFORCEMENT

The ESA possesses a rather intricate architecture of penalties and enforcement, recounted in the ESA provisions that follow.

§ 1540. Penalties and enforcement (Section 11)

(a) Civil penalties

(1) Any person who knowingly violates, and any person engaged in business as an importer or exporter of fish, wildlife, or plants who violates, any provision of this chapter, or any provision of any permit or certificate issued hereunder, or of any regulation issued in order to implement subsection (a)(1)(A), (B), (C), (D), (E), or (F), (a)(2)(A), (B), (C), or (D), (c), (d) (other than regulation relating to recordkeeping or filing of reports), (f) or (g) of section 1538 of this title, may be assessed a civil penalty by the Secretary of not more than $25,000 for each violation. Any person who knowingly violates, and any person engaged in business as an importer or exporter of fish, wildlife, or plants who violates, any provision of any other regulation issued under this chapter may be assessed a civil penalty by the Secretary of not more than $12,000 for each such violation. Any person who otherwise violates any provision of this chapter, or any regulation, permit, or certificate issued hereunder, may be assessed a civil penalty by the Secretary of not more than $500 for each such violation. No penalty may be assessed under this subsection unless such person is given notice and opportunity for a hearing with respect to such violation. Each violation shall be a separate offense. Any such civil penalty may be remitted or mitigated by the Secretary. Upon any failure to pay a penalty assessed under this subsection, the Secretary may request the Attorney General to institute a civil action in a district court of the United States for any district in which such person is found, resides, or transacts business to collect the penalty and such court shall have jurisdiction to hear and decide any such action. The court shall hear such action on the record made before the Secretary and shall sustain his action if it is supported by substantial evidence on the record considered as a whole.

(2) Hearings held during proceedings for the assessment of civil penalties authorized by paragraph (1) of this subsection shall be conducted in accordance with section 554 of Title 5. The Secretary may issue subpenas for the attendance and testimony of witnesses and the production of relevant papers, books, and documents, and administer oaths. Witnesses summoned shall be paid the same fees and mileage that are paid to witnesses in the courts of the United States. In case of contumacy or refusal to obey a subpena served upon any person pursuant to this paragraph, the district court of the United States for any district in which such person is found or resides or transacts business, upon application by the United States and after notice to such person, shall have jurisdiction to issue an order requiring such person to appear and give testimony before the Secretary or to appear and produce documents before the Secretary, or both, and any failure to obey such order of the court may be punished by such court as a contempt thereof.

(3) Notwithstanding any other provision of this chapter, no civil penalty shall be imposed if it can be shown by a preponderance of the evidence that the defendant committed an act based on a good faith belief that he was acting to protect himself or herself, a member of his or her family, or any other individual from bodily harm, from any endangered or threatened species.

(b) Criminal violations

(1) Any person who knowingly violates any provision of this chapter, of any permit or certificate issued hereunder, or of any regulation issued in order to implement subsection (a)(1)(A), (B), (C), (D), (E), or (F); (a)(2)(A), (B), (C), or (D), (c), (d) (other than a regulation relating to recordkeeping, or filing of reports), (f), or (g) of section 1538 of this title shall, upon conviction, be fined not more than $50,000 or imprisoned for not more than one year, or both. Any person who knowingly violates any provision of any other regulation issued under this chapter shall, upon conviction, be fined not more than $25,000 or imprisoned for not more than six months, or both.

(2) The head of any Federal agency which has issued a lease, license, permit, or other agreement authorizing a person to import or export fish, wildlife, or plants, or to operate a quarantine station for imported wildlife, or authorizing the use of Federal lands, including grazing of domestic livestock, to any person who is convicted of a criminal violation of this chapter or any regulation, permit, or certificate issued hereunder may immediately modify, suspend, or revoke each lease, license, permit or other agreement. The Secretary shall also suspend for a period of up to one year, or cancel, any Federal hunting or fishing permits or stamps issued to any person who is convicted of a criminal violation of any provision of this chapter or any regulation, permit, or certificate issued hereunder. The United States shall not be liable for the payments of any compensation, reimbursement, or damages in connection with the modification, suspension, or revocation of any leases, licenses, permits, stamps, or other agreements pursuant to this section.

(3) Notwithstanding any other provision of this chapter, it shall be a defense to prosecution under this subsection if the defendant committed the offense based on a good faith belief that he was acting to protect himself or herself, a member of his or her family, or any other individual, from bodily harm from any endangered or threatened species.

(c) District court jurisdiction

The several district courts of the United States, including the courts enumerated in <u>section 460 of Title 28</u>, shall have jurisdiction over any actions arising under this chapter. For the purpose of this chapter, American Samoa shall be included within the judicial district of the District Court of the United States for the District of Hawaii.

...

(e) Enforcement

(1) The provisions of this chapter and any regulations or permits issued pursuant thereto shall be enforced by the Secretary, the Secretary of the Treasury, or the Secretary of the Department in which the Coast Guard is operating, or all such Secretaries. Each such Secretary may utilize by agreement, with or without reimbursement, the personnel, services, and facilities of any other Federal agency or any State agency for purposes of enforcing this chapter.

[Remainder omitted]
(f) Regulations [omitted]

(g) Citizen suits

(1) Except as provided in paragraph (2) of this subsection any person may commence a civil suit on his own behalf--
(A) to enjoin any person, including the United States and any other governmental instrumentality or agency (to the extent permitted by the eleventh amendment to the Constitution), who is alleged to be in violation of any provision of this chapter or regulation issued under the authority thereof; or
(B) to compel the Secretary to apply, pursuant to section 1535(g)(2)(B)(ii) of this title, the prohibitions set forth in or authorized pursuant to section 1533(d) or 1538(a)(1)(B) of this title with respect to the taking of any resident endangered species or threatened species within any State; or
(C) <u>against the Secretary where there is alleged a failure of the Secretary to perform any act or duty undersection 1533 of this title which is not discretionary with the Secretary.</u>

The district courts shall have jurisdiction, without regard to the amount in controversy or the citizenship of the parties, to enforce any such provision or regulation, or to order the Secretary to perform such act or duty, as the case may be. In any civil suit commenced under subparagraph (B) the district court shall compel the Secretary to apply the prohibition sought if the court finds that the allegation that an emergency exists is supported by substantial evidence.

(2)(A) No action may be commenced under subparagraph (1)(A) of this section--
(i) prior to sixty days after written notice of the violation has been given to the Secretary, and to any alleged violator of any such provision or regulation;
(ii) if the Secretary has commenced action to impose a penalty pursuant to subsection (a) of this section; or
(iii) if the United States has commenced and is diligently prosecuting a criminal action in a court of the United States or a State to redress a violation of any such provision or regulation.
(B) No action may be commenced under subparagraph (1)(B) of this section--
(i) prior to sixty days after written notice has been given to the Secretary setting forth the reasons why an emergency is thought to exist with respect to an endangered species or a threatened species in the State concerned; or
(ii) if the Secretary has commenced and is diligently prosecuting action under section 1535(g)(2)(B)(ii) of this title to determine whether any such emergency exists.
(C) No action may be commenced under subparagraph (1) (C) of this section prior to sixty days after written notice has been given to the Secretary; except that such action may be brought immediately after such notification in the case of an action under this section respecting an emergency posing a significant risk to the well-being of any species of fish or wildlife or plants.

(3)(A) Any suit under this subsection may be brought in the judicial district in which the violation occurs.
(B) In any such suit under this subsection in which the United States is not a party, the Attorney General, at the request of the Secretary, may intervene on behalf of the United States as a matter of right.
(4) The court, in issuing any final order in any suit brought pursuant to paragraph (1) of this subsection, may award costs of litigation (including reasonable attorney and expert witness fees) to any party, whenever the court determines such award is appropriate.
(5) The injunctive relief provided by this subsection shall not restrict any right which any person (or class of persons) may have under any statute or common law to seek enforcement of any standard or limitation or to seek any other relief (including relief against the Secretary or a State agency).

(h) Coordination with other laws [omitted]

NOTE

In a case that both pits two of the nation's more venerated environmental statutes crosswise, the Court decided by a 5-4 majority that EPA's delegation to a State of an environmental permitting program under the Clean Water Act does not trigger "consultation" under the Endangered Species Act ("ESA"). In *National Ass'n of Home Builders v. Defenders of Wildlife,* 551 U.S. 664 (2007), an environmental organization challenged EPA's decision that it is not authorized to conduct "consultation" with federal wildlife agencies to "insure" conservation of threatened and endangered species before delegating Clean Water Act permit authority to a State. Section 402(b) of the Clean Water Act lists criteria that if satisfied dictate that EPA "shall approve" the State's authority to issue permits under the Act. These criteria do not include effects on threatened and endangered species. On the other hand the ESA impels that federal agencies "shall" "consult" with federal wildlife agencies prior to conducting any "agency action" "authorized, funded or carried out" by the agency.

Writing for the majority, Justice Samuel Alito upheld EPA's "expert interpretation" (and one it changed from an earlier interpretation) that the ESA must yield to the CWA's permitting authority: "the transfer of permitting authority to state authorities—who will exercise that authority under continuing federal oversight to ensure compliance with relevant mandates of the Endangered Species Act and other federal environmental protection statutes—was proper." Curiously, the Court held that Section 7 of the Endangered Species Act only applies to agency actions that are "discretionary." Because Section 402(b) is nondiscretionary, Section 7 does not apply.

In so doing, the Court rejected the U.S. Court of Appeals for the Ninth Circuit's conclusions (1) that the ESA, as an independent source of legal authority, trumps the CWA, (2) applying *Dep't of Transportation v. Public Citizen*, in concluding that EPA's approval of Arizona's NPDES permitting program was the legally relevant cause of impacts to threatened and endangered species resulting from future private land-use activities, and (3) EPA's application of the act is arbitrary and capricious.

Stevens, writing for himself and Justices David Souter, Ruth Bader Ginsburg, and Stephen Breyer dissented. For that conclusion, the dissenters relied principally on ESA Section 7's express application to "all federal agencies" for all "actions authorized, funded or carried out by them," and the broad reading of the statute dating back to *Tennessee Valley Auth. v. Hill*).

QUESTIONS

1. What options are available to enforce the ESA, and what is the difference between them?
2. What are the potential fines for a civil violation? Criminal? Administrative? What are the burdens of proof for each, and under what circumstances would a federal prosecutor use each?
3. Think back to Administrative Law (perish the thought, eh?). What is the role of the APA in ESA Section 11? What kind of actions constitute formal adjudications, for example?
4. What are environmental citizen suits?
5. What is the role citizen suits play in enforcing the ESA?
6. What must citizens do prior to filing a citizen suit?
7. How can the government preclude a citizen suit?
8. What are the potential remedies resulting from a citizen suit?
9. What happened in *NAHB*?
10. What were the issues in *NAHB*, and what did the SCOTUS decide?

VII. ENDANGERED SPECIES CRIME

Global trafficking of plants and animals, including rare ones, presents enormous geopolitical and conservation challenges. Humans use animals for all sorts of purposes, including for food, pets, clothing, medicines, knick-knacks, scrimshaws, and in the case of plants, ornamentals. Much of associated activity is regulated and/or otherwise not illegal. Some of it, however, is prohibited, which often has the perverse effect of fueling a multibillion-dollar black market. Still other activity is subject to multilateral efforts to promote free trade.

This part addresses what is largely considered the world's leading collective effort to combat illegal trade in rare species, the International Convention on Trade in Endangered Species, known as "CITES." Section A provides a background to the inquiry. Section B examines the text of CITES. Section C takes a peek at implementing CITES, primarily in regard to President Obama's executive order concerning illegal trafficking in rare species, and a recent Fatwa out of Indonesia. Questions follow each part.

A. INTRODUCTION TO INTERNATIONAL TRADE IN RARE SPECIES

Wildlife trafficking and trade is complicated and controversial. Cultural, historical, religious, and societal norms and modalities differ from continent to continent, nation to nation, region to region, state to state, locality to locality, and generation to generation. Below, Ruth Braun describes the scope of illegal trafficking in rare species.

EXCERPT: RUTH A. BRAUN, LIONS, TIGERS AND BEARS [OH MY]: HOW TO STOP ENDANGERED SPECIES CRIME
Fordham Envtl. L. Jrnl (2000)

I. THE IMPORTANCE OF PROTECTING ENDANGERED SPECIES AND THE FORMATION OF CITES

Endangered species are an integral part of our environment and their benefits would be irretrievably lost by extinction. Many factors in the twentieth century have led to the endangerment and extinction of species worldwide. In order to develop the best methods to protect endangered species, it is first necessary to explore the reasons that endangered species have become extinct.

A. *Why Endangered Species Have Become Extinct*

The leading cause of the decline of endangered species is loss of critical habitat. In 1978, the United States Supreme Court noted that loss of critical habitat is among the greatest threats to endangered species. The critical habitats of species, as defined by the Endangered Species Act ("ESA"), are specific areas within the geographical domain of the species that include the physical or biological features essential to the conservation of the species. Changes in habitat may lead to the depletion of species unable to live in their new surroundings. As a result of environmental changes, "half of the recorded extinction of mammals over the past 2000 years occurred in the most recent 50 years."

Another significant factor causing endangerment of species is poaching. Poaching is the unlawful hunting of wildlife and poses a threat to many protected animals. For example, poaching of tigers over the past century has led to a 95% reduction of the species. Researchers estimate that at this rate, tigers will become extinct within the next 20 years. The rhinoceros population faces a similar fate, due to the illegal trade of rhinoceros horn. It is estimated that poaching of both the tiger and rhinoceros populations have decreased each species by 90% in the past two decades.

Illegal trade of wildlife is another leading cause of endangered species extinction. In fact, the illegal trade of endangered species is the third largest illegal trade worldwide, after illegal trade of drugs and weapons. The high profits procured from the illegal trade of endangered species provide incentive for commission of illegal wildlife crime, which generates more than $5 billion in profits annually.

B. *The Importance of Protecting Endangered Species*

Endangered species should be protected because they are irreplaceable. Although all of the potential benefits of every species may not be fully realized, endangered species provide valuable resources for our future. "Humans benefit economically and biologically, both directly and indirectly, from a diversity of species. The more biological diversity on Earth, the larger the potential for human benefit." The loss of endangered species may not be realized until long after their extinction, at this point, the damage will be irreversible.

Another reason to protect endangered species is that endangered species may hold the key to new discoveries for medicine. The continued existence of certain endangered species may enable scientists to discover new cures for illnesses. For example, a new, highly effective painkiller was developed from the poison skin of a frog. The scientists discovered that the toxic sweat of the *Epibpedobates Tricolor* frog was more powerful than morphine and did not have the same serious side effects. If this species had become extinct prior to the scientific finding, the painkiller would never have been discovered. Due to the loss of endangered species, countless medicines and vaccines may never be discovered.

In addition to health benefits species, the environment also benefits from protection of endangered species. Although it is natural for species to come in and out of existence, the current rate of species extinction has increased to an unnatural level. There are several possible benefits to the environment that may result from the protection of endangered species. First, since some species are dependent on others for survival; protection of endangered species may prevent disruption in the natural food chain. Second, protection of endangered species preserves our normal supply of oxygen and food. Finally, if we do not protect endangered species, we may "trigger a downward spiral of extinction that could eventually swallow us."

One solution to protect endangered species may be to relocate them. Another possible solution is to breed them. The argument against removing wildlife from their natural surroundings is that this would be a "failure to see the necessary relationship between the species and its ecosystem." For example, in *Tennessee Valley Authority v. Hill*, the United States Supreme Court interpreted the ESA as protecting the snail darter against removal from its critical habitat. Similarly, it would be unfair for humans to remove wildlife from its natural habitat for the purposes of breeding simply because humans are unable to protect species from harm — the harm that humans caused. Since people have caused the problem of endangered species, humans should stop it. CITES was created to take appropriate measures for the protection of endangered species.

***

II. ENDANGERED SPECIES TRAFFICKING

Endangered species crimes are committed worldwide. A variety of individuals and organizations trade illegally in endangered species for many different reasons. This Section examines the crimes associated with endangered species committed by various countries and evaluates the ineffectiveness of CITES to prevent these crimes.

A. *Endangered Species Crimes*

1. Crimes Committed in Various Countries

Thousands of animals are needlessly killed each year. For example, in Africa, hundreds of elephants are killed []for their ivory tusks. It is estimated that between 1979 and 1989, the African elephant population was reduced by half. In 1989, CITES implemented a worldwide ban on the trade of ivory in an effort to save the elephants. During the ensuing ten years, poaching rates of elephants decreased and the elephant populations began to recover. In 1999, the members of CITES agreed to limited trade of raw ivory, resulting in the rise of elephant poaching again. Some African countries argue that the ban on ivory trade should be lifted to give locals an economic stake in preservation and thus an incentive to conserve elephants.

Endangered species crime is committed in impoverished countries as a means of income. For example, in Latin America, illegal animal smuggling is one of the largest illegal exports, second only to drugs. Indigents in the local communities hunt and capture highly sought after animals and sell them to smugglers for a relatively nominal price. The sale of endangered species to smugglers has become a livelihood for impoverished citizens. Large drug cartels take advantage of impoverished locals by purchasing endangered species from them and then smuggling drugs and animals at a large profit.

In contrast to the poverty that contributes to endangered species crime in developing countries, citizens in the United States may commit endangered species crimes because of their wealth. For example, the United States has the largest market for endangered reptiles. In September 1998, the United States Fish and Wildlife Service completed a three-year investigation of a large Asian reptile ring. A businessman from Malaysia was arrested along with two Americans for smuggling more than 39 species, totaling over 300 animals, worth $500,000 into the United States.

Although the United States has taken an aggressive approach to punishing illegal endangered species traders, not every CITES member country has taken a similar approach. For example, in Mexico, animal traffickers have only been minimally punished for illegal endangered species trade. Without the threat of arrest, traffickers may have more freedom to capture and kill endangered species. Since many countries do not have the economic reserves to prevent import and export of endangered species, smuggling has become increasingly easy. One of the results of the lack of punishment is that organized crime has now formed an intricate web of animal traffickers.

2. Extinction of Endangered Species Caused by Organized Crime

Organized crime significantly contributes to the extinction of endangered species worldwide. The reason for this is that organized crime under CITES entails few risks and high profit. Even more compelling than the lucrative profits generated by endangered species crime is the relationship between endangered species and drugs. Many organized crime rings that trade in wildlife also trade in drugs and weapons. They use the same methods of transport and the same trafficking routes to conduct both illegal businesses. Endangered species are also used within drug rings to smuggle drugs. For example, boa constrictors and alligators are used to smuggle drugs from Mexico into the United States because of their large stomach cavities. In fact, more than one-third of all cocaine seized in the United States was found in shipments of animals. It is not only profitable for drug traffickers to use the same channels of distribution for drugs and endangered species, but the subterfuge of animals to transport drugs may reduce the risk of getting caught for drug smuggling.

3. Endangerment of Species Caused by Animal Advocates

Illegal trade of endangered species may even be committed by animal advocates. For example, in *United States v. Silva*, the defendant was a recognized advocate for the protection of endangered parrots. Nonetheless, the defendant admitted that he combined shipments of illegal birds with shipments of legal birds. This case was part of an investigation that resulted in over thirty arrests and convictions. The smuggling conspiracy, which took place from 1986 to 1991, yielded over $1 million in illegal trade of endangered species.

The illegal trafficking of endangered species has many causes. The problem is finding a solution that addresses the various causes. Although CITES attempts to provide a solution, whether CITES effectively achieves this is doubtful: "compliance with the treaty remains problematic and various states have achieved divergent levels of success in implementing the treaty."

***

6. Organizational Efforts

The World Wildlife Fund ("WWF") is the largest independent organization created to protect wildlife from exploitation. The organization has five million supporters and a global network of offices in over fifty countries. In the 1970's, the WWF became involved in preventing the extinction of endangered species. In 1976, the WWF joined forces with The World Conservation Union ("IUCN") to create TRAFFIC. TRAFFIC was established to monitor and help prevent the illegal trade of endangered species. TRAFFIC analyzes trade statistics and develops recommendations for the conservation of endangered species. The organization works closely with CITES to control endangered species crimes and assist in the investigations of such crimes. However, while identifying the problem is the first step, it is not the solution. CITES needs to be consistently applied and universally adopted.

***

QUESTIONS

1. What is the importance of species protection globally?
2. If at all, how does the ESA address the import and export of T & E species? (Refer to Module 6 if need be).
3. What are the shortcomings, if any, of the ESA's approach to global loss of species?
4. What is/are causing the loss or diminution of so many species?
5. What is the role of state actors?
6. Ditto, of organized crime?
7. Ditto, of environmentalists?

VIII. INTERNATIONAL TRADE IN SPECIES

As Ruth Braun describes, implementing the International Convention on Trade in Endangered Species in the U.S. has been a mixed bag, culminated with the establishment of an Executive Order by President Obama, recapped below.

EXCERPT: RUTH A. BRAUN, LIONS, TIGERS AND BEARS [OH MY]: HOW TO STOP ENDANGERED SPECIES CRIME
Fordham Envtl. L. Jrnl (2000)

1. The United States' Endangered Species Policy

The evolution of endangered species protection in the United States provides a good basis upon which to evaluate the effectiveness of CITES. The first statute protecting wildlife in the United States, the Lacey Act, was enacted in 1900. Originally, the legislation was drafted primarily to protect birds and regulate the international trade of birds. The Lacey Act was amended in 1981 to prohibit trafficking in endangered wildlife in violation of any law, treaty or regulation of the United States. The Lacey Act helps control illegal trade of endangered species by imposing monetary and penal sanctions on violators.

The ESA was enacted in 1973 to enforce the various international endangered species agreements to which the United States is a party. The purpose of the ESA is to conserve endangered species. The ESA prohibits importing, exporting, taking, or trading endangered species. The term "taking" means to "harass, harm, pursue, hunt, shoot, wound, kill, trap, capture or collect." Species become protected under the ESA when either the Secretary of the Interior or the Secretary of Commerce of the United States determines that a particular species is in danger of extinction. The ESA, like the Lacey Act, also provides for monetary and penal sanctions to be imposed on violators. Violators may be prosecuted under both the Lacey Act and the ESA. For example, in *United States v. Bernal*, the defendant was convicted of attempting to export endangered species from the United States under both statutes. Where CITES fails to provide monetary sanctions, the United States succeeds, at least theoretically.

The ESA provides for sanctions action against violators in order to achieve its purpose. Congress has recognized that the need to protect endangered species is based on the "aesthetic, ecological, educational, historical, recreational and scientific value" of various species to the United States. However, while Congress has a commitment to protect endangered species, it needs to increase its financial commitment.

Enforcement of the ESA and the Lacey Act is very difficult due to a lack of resources. For example, in 1995, there were only seventy-four federal wildlife inspectors for over three hundred ports of entry into the United States, making it virtually impossible for law enforcement officials to oversee every entryway. It is therefore inevitable that thousands of illegally traded species are entering the United States each year.

The ESA may also be difficult to enforce because endangered species may be difficult to identify. For example, in *United States v. One Handbag of Crocodilius Species*, identification difficulty associated with crocodile hides interfered with enforcement of the ESA. Similarly, in *United States v. 3210 Crusted Sides of Caiman Crocodilius Yacare*, the government had to first identify the correct crocodile species before it could demonstrate probable cause for a forfeiture action. In order to prevent endangered species trafficking, the United States should devote more resources to hire and train more inspectors.

An example of an effective allocation of resources is found at the United States Fish and Wildlife Service. In 1989, the USFWS opened the first and only wildlife forensics lab. The lab analyzes an endangered species crime scene and makes the "crucial link between victim, criminal and crime scene." The lab has become a useful tool to combat wildlife crime.

Ironically, in spite of the United States' extensive regulations to prohibit endangered species trafficking, the United States leads the world in importation of illegal wildlife and wildlife parts. The failure to commit sufficient resources to properly police endangered species traffickers could only increase the problem. Unfortunately, even though the United States has stringent laws against endangered species trafficking, it may not be enough to preserve endangered species. For CITES to be effective, the United States as well as other member countries, have to measure up to the goal of CITES.

EXECUTIVE ACTION

Implementation of CITES in the U.S. and elsewhere leaves a lot to be desired. Accordingly, the Obama Administration issued an executive order to combat illegal trafficking in rare species.

EXECUTIVE ORDER NO. 13648
78 Fed. Reg. 40621 (July 1, 2013)

COMBATING WILDLIFE TRAFFICKING

By the authority vested in me as President by the Constitution and the laws of the United States of America, and in order to address the significant effects of wildlife trafficking on the national interests of the United States, I hereby order as follows:

Section 1. Policy. The poaching of protected species and the illegal trade in wildlife and their derivative parts and products (together known as "wildlife trafficking") represent an international crisis that continues to escalate. Poaching operations have expanded beyond small-scale, opportunistic actions to coordinated slaughter commissioned by armed and organized criminal syndicates. The survival of protected wildlife species such as elephants, rhinos, great apes, tigers, sharks, tuna, and turtles has beneficial economic, social, and environmental impacts that are important to all nations. Wildlife trafficking reduces those benefits while generating billions of dollars in illicit revenues each year, contributing to the illegal economy, fueling instability, and undermining security. Also, the prevention of trafficking of live animals helps us control the spread of emerging infectious diseases. For these reasons, it is in the national interest of the United States to combat wildlife trafficking.

In order to enhance domestic efforts to combat wildlife trafficking, to assist foreign nations in building capacity to combat wildlife trafficking, and to assist in combating transnational organized crime, executive departments and agencies (agencies) shall take all appropriate actions within their authority, including the promulgation of rules and regulations and the provision of technical and financial assistance, to combat wildlife trafficking in accordance with the following objectives:

(a) in appropriate cases, the United States shall seek to assist those governments in anti-wildlife trafficking activities when requested by foreign nations experiencing trafficking of protected wildlife;

(b) the United States shall promote and encourage the development and enforcement by foreign nations of effective laws to prohibit the illegal taking of, and trade in, these species and to prosecute those who engage in wildlife trafficking, including by building capacity;

(c) in concert with the international community and partner organizations, the United States shall seek to combat wildlife trafficking; and

(d) the United States shall seek to reduce the demand for illegally traded wildlife, both at home and abroad, while allowing legal and legitimate commerce involving wildlife.

Sec. 2. Establishment. There is established a Presidential Task Force on Wildlife Trafficking (Task Force), to be co-chaired by the Secretary of State, Secretary of the Interior, and the Attorney General (Co-Chairs), or their designees, who shall report to the President through the National

Security Advisor. The Task Force shall develop and implement a National Strategy for Combating Wildlife Trafficking in accordance with the objectives outlined in section 1 of this order, consistent with section 4 of this order.

Sec. 3. Membership. (a) In addition to the Co-Chairs, the Task Force shall include designated senior-level representatives from:

(i) the Department of the Treasury;
(ii) the Department of Defense;
(iii) the Department of Agriculture;
(iv) the Department of Commerce;
(v) the Department of Transportation;
(vi) the Department of Homeland Security;
(vii) the United States Agency for International Development;
(viii) the Office of the Director of National Intelligence;
(ix) the National Security Staff;
(x) the Domestic Policy Council;
(xi) the Council on Environmental Quality;
(xii) the Office of Science and Technology Policy;
(xiii) the Office of Management and Budget;
(xiv) the Office of the United States Trade Representative; and
(xv) such agencies and offices as the Co-Chairs may, from time to time, designate.

(b) The Task Force shall meet not later than 60 days from the date of this order and periodically thereafter.

Sec. 4. Functions. Consistent with the authorities and responsibilities of member agencies, the Task Force shall perform the following functions:

(a) not later than 180 days after the date of this order, produce a National Strategy for Combating Wildlife Trafficking that shall include consideration of issues relating to combating trafficking and curbing consumer demand, including:

(i) effective support for anti-poaching activities;
(ii) coordinating regional law enforcement efforts;
(iii) developing and supporting effective legal enforcement mechanisms; and
(iv) developing strategies to reduce illicit trade and reduce consumer demand for trade in protected species;

(b) not later than 90 days from the date of this order, review the Strategy to Combat Transnational Organized Crime of July 19, 2011, and, if appropriate, make recommendations regarding the inclusion of crime related to wildlife trafficking as an implementation element for the Federal Government's transnational organized crime strategy;

(c) coordinate efforts among and consult with agencies, as appropriate and consistent with the Department of State's foreign affairs role, regarding work with foreign nations and international bodies that monitor and aid in enforcement against crime related to wildlife trafficking; and

(d) carry out other functions necessary to implement this order.

S/B Barak Obama.

QUESTIONS

1. What is "CITES"? How does it reflect international efforts to address trade in endangered species?
2. What motivates illegal trade in rare species?
3. What is an "executive order"? To whom and what does it apply?
4. What does President Obama's Executive Order aim to do, and how?

CHAPTER 4: THE CLEAN WATER ACT

Chapter 4 pivots to pollution control, and with it, the Clean Water Act (CWA). The CWA is or was perhaps the nation's greatest public works success story, helping to protect rivers, streams, and wetlands across the United States in ways common law cannot, as Part I details. The linchpin of regulation under the CWA is deceptively simple: You need a permit to discharge, the subject of Part II. The Permit must require technology-based controls that EPA has set for the type of discharger involved (Part III), plus any water-quality based controls based on water quality standards established by each state (Part IV). As you'll see, there is unfinished business here.

I.   INTRODUCTION TO THE CLEAN WATER ACT

Prior to about 100 years ago, human waste was commonly discarded into open ditches, sinks and gutters. This, of course, diminished the quality of urban life, and helped to spread disease, particularly in urban areas.

Thus, cities began to design sewer and other sanitary systems to transport human waste for discharge into nearby water bodies, often used for drinking. This led to further spread of disease, including typhoid due to discharge of raw sewage into these sources of drinking water.

Scientific advancements and the discovery of germ theory changed this practice. This led in turn to discharge of raw sewage into surface waters, including ocean waters, estuaries, lakes, rivers and streams not directly used for drinking. This once again led to concerns about the spread of disease from urban centers elsewhere, including those from scientists' that human waste from New York City caused or contributed to the spread of disease in New Jersey, or Chicago's wastes causing sickness and death in St. Louis and elsewhere. See, e.g., New York v. New Jersey, 256 U.S. 296 (1921); Missouri v. Illinois, 200 U.S. 496 (1906).

Clean, safe, fresh water is important to the nation's environment, economy, and security. If all of the water in the world were represented as 100 gallons, 97 would be undrinkable saltwater. Two gallons would be trapped in glaciers and icecaps. Two quarts would be groundwater. Less than one-half pint (size of elementary school milk) would be freshwater. Of that one-half pint, roughly one teaspoon exists within a half day's drive of Delaware Law School. 60 million people live within a two-hour drive. 50 million more people visit the region, making 250 million trips annually, and spending $20 billion on services, $5 billion on tourism, $75 billion on food and fiber, and enjoying 3 billion pounds of fish and shellfish. Manufacturers and cattle and crop farmers need clean water too. The ones in this region alone use more than 15 billion gallons of water a year, producing products worth more than $25 billion.

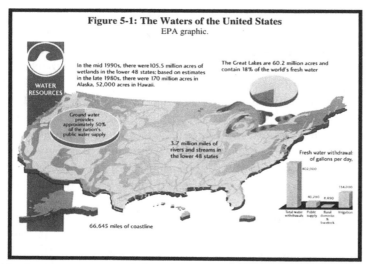

Figure 5-1: The Waters of the United States
EPA graphic.

The nation's great commercial and social traditions depend on ready access to clean, dependable water. A century ago, DuPont depended on the fast, clean-flowing Brandywine River to fuel his first powder mills and usher in the petrochemical revolution. Today, clean water is no less important than it was then. It goes without saying that clean water is important for fish and wildlife and their habitat. What we often forget is that clean water is essential to the nation's great petrochemical, pharmaceutical, agricultural and animal farming, mining, automotive, port, fishing, crabbing, housing, shopping, motel, restaurant and tourism industries. The nation's manufacturing sector depends on clean water to run efficiently. By maintaining property values, clean water is good for homeowners and developers. It helps keep health care, taxes and insurance costs down. In short, clean water is essential to the success of the nation's economy, sustains our values and quality of life, and is good for business.

Following the Great Depression and World War II, Congress sought to apply broad federal regulatory programs to address national challenges, from commerce to clean water. During this time, federal approaches to water pollution evolved away from focusing on local water conditions through the use of common law (e.g., nuisance, trespass, etc.) to establishing national, technology-based standards based upon feasible an engineering practices.

It took a while to submit to a technology-based approach. Congress enacted the Water Pollution Control Act of 1948 (Pub. L. 845, 80th Congress), which established a kind of quasi state and federal cooperative to provide means for resolving disputes about interstate water quality. The Federal Water Pollution Control Act (Pub. L. 660, 84th Congress) of 1956 continued this approach. Neither law did much if anything to improve water quality.

With the Water Quality Act of 1965 Congress had states set water quality standards, for example, maintaining 5 parts per million of oxygen in interstate freshwater used for trout fishing. The federal role was minimal, however, largely consigned to helping to resolve interstate disputes. Again, the 1965 Act resulted in little activity, and water quality continued to decline dramatically.

Indeed, at this time most people in the country lived near water too polluted to use. One could not fish, swim or even boat in large parts of the Delaware and Schuylkill Rivers, suppressing commerce, home values and health. The Anacostia River was dying. Baltimore Harbor and the Port of Wilmington closed to all but tanker traffic, and major rivers like the Delaware and the Susquehanna were open sewers, dashing hopes of urban revitalization.

Congress considered how to improve water throughout the late 1960's and early 1970's. At core were two schools of thought about how to make the nation's waters "fishable and swimmable." The first, largely based in the Senate, would dispatch with water quality standards-based approaches in favor of a command and control, technology-based approach led by the newly established EPA. The second, largely from the House of Representatives, would use a more muscular ambient-based approach than contained in the 1965 Act. It had EPA set water quality criteria for certain "designated" uses, such as swimming, fishing, drinking or recreation. It then had the states – as had the 1965 Act – develop and implement water quality standards to meet designated uses. The compromise legislation largely embraced the Senate's technology-based approach, with consideration of local water quality conditions in those instances where installation of innovative technologies alone was not sufficient to achieve water quality standards.

While water quality has improved, according to EPA, approximately 60 percent of assessed waters nationally are safe enough for fishing and swimming. Wetland losses have slowed to one-quarter the rate of 30 years ago. These efforts have helped clean up pollutant discharges throughout the nation, from waters of the Delaware Basin and the Inland Bays, to the Baltimore Harbor and the Chesapeake Bay, to the Susquehanna and the Three Rivers system, to Lake Erie, to the Potomac and the Anacostia, to the Blackwater, to name a few.

Notwithstanding what's been done, to borrow from David Frost, it seems we still have far to go before we sleep. Pollutant discharges from factories are on the upswing. Polluted runoff from farm fields, city streets and parking lots is virtually uncontrolled, choking half the nation's waters. Wetlands continue to be destroyed at an alarming rate, nearly 250,000 acres (one-half the size of Delaware) each year. Thousands of lakes, streams, and miles of rivers used by 3 in 4 in the mid-Atlantic fail to meet some basic water quality standard.

From 1998 to 2000, the percentage of polluted rivers rose from 35 to 40 percent, shorelines from 12 to 15 percent, and polluted estuaries – the best measure of ecosystem health -- from 44 to 51. The latest statistics reveal there were more than 400 beach closings because of health advisories, 2,500 waters with fish consumption advisories or bans, 37 "water outbreaks" in 17 states assessed by the CDC, including red tide and algae outbreaks in Delaware, Pfiesteria in Maryland and Delaware, and shellfish contamination in the Chesapeake.

These statistics obscure that the vast majority of the nation's waters are not even assessed. This suggests water quality is worse now than 30 years ago, but due to the lack of data, concluded no trends could be forecasted.

A. Goals and Purposes

Congress determined that there is not sufficient scientific certainty to measure the "tolerable effects" of discharges. EPA v. California State Water Resources Control Board, 426 U.S. 200, 202 (1976). Thus Congress opted for an innovative approach based on national, uniform technology based standards for categories and classes of point sources. The Clean Water Act of 1972, 33 U.S.C. §§ 1251–1387, is largely a response to earlier failed approaches rooted in common law that linked compliance responses to the ability of the water body to withstand the polluting activity.

Congress identified the goals and policies in enacting the CWA:

§ 101 [33 USC 1251] Declaration of Goals and Policy

(a) The objective of this Act is to restore and maintain the chemical, physical, and biological integrity of the Nation's waters. In order to achieve this objective it is hereby declared that, consistent with the provisions of this Act—

(1) it is the national goal that the discharge of pollutants into the navigable waters be eliminated by 1985;

(2) it is the national goal that wherever attainable, an interim goal of water quality which provides for the protection and propagation of fish, shellfish, and wildlife and provides for recreation in and on the water be achieved by July 1, 1983;

(3) it is the national policy that the discharge of toxic pollutants in toxic amounts be prohibited;

(4) it is the national policy that Federal financial assistance be provided to construct publicly owned waste treatment works;

(5) it is the national policy that areawide waste treatment management planning processes be developed and implemented to assure adequate control of sources of pollutants in each State;

(6) it is the national policy that a major research and demonstration effort be made to develop technology necessary to eliminate the discharge of pollutants into the navigable waters, waters of the contiguous zone, and the oceans; and

(7) it is the national policy that programs for the control of nonpoint sources of pollution be developed and implemented in an expeditious manner so as to enable the goals of this Act to be met through the control of both point and nonpoint sources of pollution.

***

For our purposes you can think of the CWA as having three main features. The first is the prohibition against the "discharge of a pollutant" without a permit. The second is the establishment of technology-based "effluent limitations" for categories and classes of dischargers. The third is a backstop, that is, assuring achievement of water quality standards. These are taken in turn below.

II.   PERMIT REQUIREMENT

The Clean Water Act provides:

"(a) Except as in compliance with this section and sections 302, 306, 307, 318, 402, and 404 of this Act [that is, obtaining a permit], the discharge of any pollutant by any person shall be unlawful." § 301 [33 USC 1311].

The CWA then defines "discharge of any pollutant" to be "any addition of any pollutant to navigable waters from any point source." § 502(14). In other words, a permit is required if these five pieces exist:

(1) "Any addition"
(2) "Of any pollutant"
(3) "From any point source"
(4) "To Navigable Waters"

(5) By a "Person," meaning "an individual, corporation, partnership, association, State, municipality, commission, or political subdivision of a State, or any interstate body." §502(5)

Permits serve "to transform generally applicable effluent limitations and other standards—including those based on water quality—into the obligations (including a timetable for compliance) of the individual discharger." EPA v. California ex rel. State Water Resources Control Board, 126 U.S. 200, 204-205 (1976). The 1899 Rivers and Harbors Act offered a "rudimentary permitting system" that was the precursor to the modern-day Clean Water Act. In subsequent legislation, the federal government attempted to devolve water regulatory efforts to state governments, with federal authorities taking more of an oversight role.

Under the Clean Water Act the federal government established nationwide system of limiting water pollution. This permit process, known as the National Pollutant Discharge Elimination System (NPDES), is primarily enforced by state governments, although regional Environmental Protection Agency offices administer the process when state agencies lack the relevant authorization. While water pollution occurs in a variety of forms, the NPDES system focuses primarily on industrial and municipal facilities that release pollutants into surface waters.

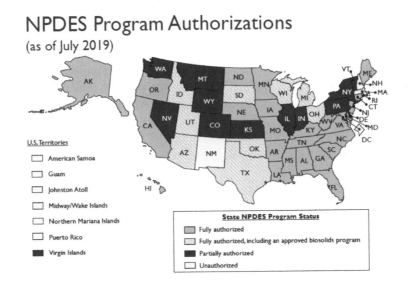

A. ADDITION OF A POLLUTANT

The CWA does not define "addition." Case law has established that it means introduced "from the outside world." See e.g., National Wildlife Federation v. Gorsuch, 693 F.2d 156 (D.C. Cir. 1982).

The CWA defines "pollutant" as "dredged spoil, solid waste, incinerator residue, sewage, garbage, sewage sludge, munitions, chemical wastes, biological materials, radioactive materials, heat, wrecked or discarded equipment, rock, sand, cellar dirt and industrial, municipal, and agricultural waste discharged into water." § 502(6). If the "pollutant" is so called "dredge and fill" material, then a permit is needed from the U.S. Corps of Engineers. Section 404. All other permits are issued by the U.S. Environmental Protection Agency or a state with delegated authority to do so.

B. POINT SOURCE

The CWA defines "point source: as "any discernible, confined and discrete conveyance, including but not limited to any pipe, ditch, channel, tunnel, conduit, well, discrete fissure, container, rolling stock, concentrated animal feeding operation, or vessel or other floating craft, from which pollutants are or may be discharged. This term does not include agricultural stormwater discharges and return flows from irrigated agriculture. § 502(14). The following case addresses whether point sources can discharge into groundwater.

COUNTY OF MAUI, HAWAII V. HAWAII WILDLIFE FUND
590 U.S. ___ (2020)

Breyer, J., delivered the opinion of the Court.

The Clean Water Act forbids the "addition" of any pollutant from a "point source" to "navigable waters" without the appropriate permit from the Environmental Protection Agency (EPA). Federal Water Pollution Control Act, §§ 301(a), 502(12)(A), as amended by the Federal Water Pollution Control Act Amendments of 1972 (Clean Water Act) § 2, 86 Stat. 844, 886, 33 U.S.C. §§ 1311(a), 1362(12)(A). The question presented here is whether the Act "requires a permit when pollutants originate from a point source but are conveyed to navigable waters by a nonpoint source," here, "groundwater." Suppose, for example, that a sewage treatment plant discharges polluted water into the ground where it mixes with groundwater, which, in turn, flows into a navigable river, or perhaps the ocean. Must the plant's owner seek an EPA permit before emitting the pollutant? We conclude that the statutory provisions at issue require a permit if the addition of the pollutants through groundwater is the functional equivalent of a direct discharge from the point source into navigable waters.

I

A

Congress' purpose as reflected in the language of the Clean Water Act is to "'restore and maintain the ... integrity of the Nation's waters,'" § 101(a), 86 Stat. 816. Prior to the Act, Federal and State Governments regulated water pollution in large part by setting water quality standards. The Act restructures federal regulation by insisting that a person wishing to discharge any pollution into navigable waters first obtain EPA's permission to do so.

The Act's provisions use specific definitional language to achieve this result. First, the Act defines "pollutant" broadly, including in its definition, for example, any solid waste, incinerator residue, "'heat,'" " 'discarded equipment,' " or sand (among many other things). § 502(6). Second, the Act defines a "point source" as " 'any discernible, confined and discrete conveyance ... from which pollutants are or may be discharged,' " including, for example, any " 'container,' " " 'pipe, ditch, channel, tunnel, conduit,' " or " 'well.' " § 502(14). Third, it defines the term "discharge of a pollutant" as " 'any addition of any pollutant to navigable waters [including navigable streams, rivers, the ocean, or coastal waters] from any point source.' " § 502(12).

The Act then sets forth a statutory provision that, using these terms, broadly states that (with certain exceptions) " 'the discharge of any pollutant by any person' " without an appropriate permit " 'shall be unlawful.' " § 301. The question here, as we have said, is whether, or how, this statutory language applies to a pollutant that reaches navigable waters only after it leaves a "point source" and then travels through groundwater before reaching navigable waters. In such an instance, has there been a "discharge of a pollutant," that is, has there been "any addition of any pollutant to navigable waters from any point source?"

B

The petitioner, the County of Maui, operates a wastewater reclamation facility on the island of Maui, Hawaii. The facility collects sewage from the surrounding area, partially treats it, and pumps the treated water through four wells hundreds of feet underground. This effluent, amounting to about 4 million gallons each day, then travels a further half mile or so, through groundwater, to the ocean.

In 2012, several environmental groups, the respondents here, brought this citizens' Clean Water Act lawsuit against Maui. See § 505(a), id., at 888. They claimed that Maui was "discharg[ing]" a "pollutant" to "navigable waters," namely, the Pacific Ocean, without the permit required by the Clean Water Act. The District Court, relying in part upon a detailed study of the discharges, found that a considerable amount of effluent from the wells ended up in the ocean (a navigable water). It wrote that, because the "path to the ocean is clearly ascertainable," the discharge from Maui's wells into the nearby groundwater was "functionally one into navigable water." And it granted summary judgment in favor of the environmental groups.

The Ninth Circuit affirmed the District Court, but it described the relevant statutory standard somewhat differently. The appeals court wrote that a permit is required when "the pollutants are fairly traceable from the point source to a navigable water such that the discharge is the functional equivalent of a discharge into the navigable water." The court left "for another day the task of determining when, if ever, the connection between a point source and a navigable water is too tenuous to support liability ...."

Maui petitioned for certiorari. In light of the differences in the standards adopted by the different Courts of Appeals, we granted the petition.

II

The linguistic question here concerns the statutory word "from." Is pollution that reaches navigable waters only through groundwater pollution that is "from" a point source, as the statute uses the word? The word "from" is broad in scope, but context often imposes limitations. "Finland," for example, is often not the right kind of answer to the question, "Where have you come from?" even if long ago you were born there.

* * *

We agree that statutory context limits the reach of the statutory phrase "from any point source" to a range of circumstances narrower than that which the Ninth Circuit's interpretation suggests. At the same time, it is significantly broader than the total exclusion of all discharges through groundwater described by Maui and the Solicitor General.

III

Virtually all water, polluted or not, eventually makes its way to navigable water. This is just as true for groundwater. See generally 2 VAN NOSTRAND'S SCIENTIFIC ENCYCLOPEDIA 2600 (10th ed. 2008) (defining "Hydrology"). Given the power of modern science, the Ninth Circuit's limitation, "fairly traceable," may well allow EPA to assert permitting authority over the release of pollutants that reach navigable waters many years after their release (say, from a well or pipe or compost heap) and in highly diluted forms.

The respondents suggest that the standard can be narrowed by adding a "proximate cause" requirement. That is, to fall within the permitting provision, the discharge from a point source must "proximately cause" the pollutants' eventual addition to navigable waters. But the term "proximate cause" derives from general tort law, and it takes on its specific content based primarily on "policy" considerations. In the context of water pollution, we do not see how it significantly narrows the statute beyond the words "fairly traceable" themselves.

Our view is that Congress did not intend the point source-permitting requirement to provide EPA with such broad authority as the Ninth Circuit's narrow focus on traceability would allow. First, to interpret the word "from" in this literal way would require a permit in surprising, even bizarre, circumstances, such as for pollutants carried to navigable waters on a bird's feathers, or, to mention more mundane instances, the 100-year migration of pollutants through 250 miles of groundwater to a river.

Second, and perhaps most important, the structure of the statute indicates that, as to groundwater pollution and nonpoint source pollution, Congress intended to leave substantial responsibility and autonomy to the States. See, e.g., § 101(b), 86 Stat. 816 (stating Congress' purpose in this regard). Much water pollution does not come from a readily identifiable source. See 3 VAN NOSTRAND'S SCIENTIFIC ENCYCLOPEDIA, at 5801 (defining "Water Pollution"). Rainwater, for example, can carry pollutants (say, as might otherwise collect on a roadway); it can pollute groundwater, and pollution collected by unchanneled rainwater runoff is not ordinarily considered point source pollution. Over many decades, and with federal encouragement, the States have developed methods of regulating nonpoint source pollution through water quality standards, and otherwise.

The Act envisions EPA's role in managing nonpoint source pollution and groundwater pollution as limited to studying the issue, sharing information with and collecting information from the States, and issuing monetary grants. Although the Act grants EPA specific authority to regulate certain point source pollution (it can also delegate some of this authority to the States acting under EPA supervision, see § 402(b), 86 Stat. 880), these permitting provisions refer to "point sources" and "navigable waters," and say nothing at all about nonpoint source regulation or groundwater regulation. We must doubt that Congress intended to give EPA the authority to apply the word "from" in a way that could interfere as seriously with States' traditional regulatory authority—authority the Act preserves and promotes—as the Ninth Circuit's "fairly traceable" test would.

Third, those who look to legislative history to help interpret a statute will find that this Act's history strongly supports our conclusion that the permitting provision does not extend so far. Fifty years ago, when Congress was considering the bills that became the Clean Water Act, William Ruckelshaus, the first EPA Administrator, asked Congress to grant EPA authority over "ground waters" to "assure that we have control over the water table ... so we can ... maintai[n] a control over all the sources of pollution, be they discharged directly into any stream or through the ground water table." Water Pollution Control Legislation–1971 (Proposed Amendments to Existing Legislation): Hearings before the House Committee on Public Works, 92d Cong., 1st Sess., 230 (1971). Representative Les Aspin similarly pointed out that there were "conspicuou[s]" references to groundwater in all sections of the bill except the permitting section at issue here. ... The Senate Committee on Public Works "recognize[d] the essential link between ground and surface waters."

But Congress did not accept these requests for general EPA authority over groundwater. It rejected Representative Aspin's amendment that would have extended the permitting provision to groundwater. Instead, Congress provided a set of more specific groundwater-related measures such as those requiring States to maintain "affirmative controls over the injection or placement in wells" of "any pollutants that may affect ground water." Ibid. These specific state-related programs were, in the words of the Senate Public Works Committee, "designed to protect ground waters and eliminate the use of deep well disposal as an uncontrolled alternative to toxic and pollution control." The upshot is that Congress was fully aware of the need to address groundwater pollution, but it satisfied that need through a variety of state-specific controls. Congress left general groundwater regulatory authority to the States; its failure to include groundwater in the general EPA permitting provision was deliberate.

Finally, longstanding regulatory practice undermines the Ninth Circuit's broad interpretation of the statute. EPA itself for many years has applied the permitting provision to pollution discharges from point sources that reached navigable waters only after traveling through groundwater. But, in doing so, EPA followed a narrower interpretation than that of the Ninth Circuit. EPA has opposed applying the Act's permitting requirements to discharges that reach groundwater only after lengthy periods. Indeed, in this very case (prior to its recent Interpretive Statement), EPA asked the Ninth Circuit to apply a more limited "direct hydrological connection" test. The Ninth Circuit did not accept this suggestion.

We do not defer here to EPA's interpretation of the statute embodied in this practice. Indeed, EPA itself has changed its mind about the meaning of the statutory provision. But this history, by showing that a comparatively narrow view of the statute is administratively workable, offers some additional support for the view that Congress did not intend as broad a delegation of regulatory authority as the Ninth Circuit test would allow.

As we have said, the specific meaning of the word "from" necessarily draws its meaning from context. The apparent breadth of the Ninth Circuit's "fairly traceable" approach is inconsistent with the context we have just described.

IV

A

Maui and the Solicitor General argue that the statute's permitting requirement does not apply if a pollutant, having emerged from a "point source," must travel through any amount of groundwater before reaching navigable waters. That interpretation is too narrow, for it would risk serious interference with EPA's ability to regulate ordinary point source discharges.

Consider a pipe that spews pollution directly into coastal waters. There is an "addition of" a "pollutant to navigable waters from [a] point source." Hence, a permit is required. But Maui and the Government read the permitting requirement not to apply if there is any amount of groundwater between the end of the pipe and the edge of the navigable water. If that is the correct interpretation of the statute, then why could not the pipe's owner, seeking to avoid the permit requirement, simply move the pipe back, perhaps only a few yards, so that the pollution must travel through at least some groundwater before reaching the sea? We do not see how Congress could have intended to create such a large and obvious loophole in one of the key regulatory innovations of the Clean Water Act.

B

Maui argues that the statute's language requires its reading. That language requires a permit for a "discharge." A "discharge" is "any addition" of a pollutant to navigable waters "from any point source." And a "point source" is "any discernible, confined and discrete conveyance" (such as a pipe, ditch, well, etc.). Reading "from" and "conveyance" together, Maui argues that the statutory meaning of "from any point source" is not about where the pollution originated, but about how it got there. Under what Maui calls the means-of-delivery test, a permit is required only if a point source itself ultimately delivers the pollutant to navigable waters. Under this view, if the pollutant must travel through groundwater to reach navigable waters, then it is the groundwater, not the pipe, that is the conveyance.

Congress sometimes adopts less common meanings of common words, but this esoteric definition of "from," as connoting a means, does not remotely fit in this context. The statute couples the word "from" with the word "to"—strong evidence that Congress was referring to a destination ("navigable waters") and an origin ("any point source"). Further underscoring that

Congress intended this every day meaning is that the object of "from" is a "point source"—a source, again, connoting an origin. That Maui's proffered interpretation would also create a serious loophole in the permitting regime also indicates it is an unreasonable one.

C

The Solicitor General agrees that, as a general matter, the permitting requirement applies to at least some additions of pollutants to navigable waters that come indirectly from point sources. But the Solicitor General argues that the proper interpretation of the statute is the one reflected in EPA's recent Interpretive Statement. After receiving more than 50,000 comments from the public, and after the Ninth Circuit released its opinion in this case, EPA wrote that "the best, if not the only, reading" of the statutory provisions is that "all releases of pollutants to groundwater" are excluded from the scope of the permitting program, "even where pollutants are conveyed to jurisdictional surface waters via groundwater."

Neither the Solicitor General nor any party has asked us to give what the Court has referred to as Chevron deference to EPA's interpretation of the statute. See Chevron U.S.A. Inc. v. Natural Resources Defense Council, Inc., 467 U.S. 837, 844 (1984). Even so, we often pay particular attention to an agency's views in light of the agency's expertise in a given area, its knowledge gained through practical experience, and its familiarity with the interpretive demands of administrative need. See United States v. Mead Corp., 533 U.S. 218, 234–235 (2001); Skidmore v. Swift & Co., 323 U.S. 134, 139–140 (1944). But here, as we have explained, to follow EPA's reading would open a loophole allowing easy evasion of the statutory provision's basic purposes. Such an interpretation is neither persuasive nor reasonable.

EPA correctly points out that Congress did not require a permit for all discharges to groundwater; rather, Congress authorized study and funding related to groundwater pollution. But there is quite a gap between "not all" and "none." The statutory text itself alludes to no exception for discharges through groundwater. These separate provisions for study and funding that EPA points to would be a "surprisingly indirect route" to convey "an important and easily expressed message"—that the permit requirement simply does not apply if the pollutants travel through groundwater. In truth, the most these provisions show is that Congress thought that the problem of groundwater pollution, as distinct from navigable water pollution, would primarily be addressed by the States or perhaps by other federal statutes.

EPA's new interpretation is also difficult to reconcile with the statute's reference to "any addition" of a pollutant to navigable waters. It is difficult to reconcile EPA's interpretation with the statute's inclusion of "wells" in the definition of "point source," for wells most ordinarily would discharge pollutants through groundwater. And it is difficult to reconcile EPA's interpretation with the statutory provisions that allow EPA to delegate its permitting authority to a State only if the State (among other things) provides "'adequate authority'" to "'control the disposal of pollutants into wells.'" § 402(b). What need would there be for such a proviso if the federal permitting program the State replaces did not include such discharges (from wells through groundwater) in the first place?

In short, EPA's oblique argument about the statute's references to groundwater cannot overcome the statute's structure, its purposes, or the text of the provisions that actually govern.

* * *

E

For the reasons set forth in Part III and in this Part, we conclude that, in light of the statute's language, structure, and purposes, the interpretations offered by the parties, the Government, and the dissents are too extreme.

V

Over the years, courts and EPA have tried to find general language that will reflect a middle ground between these extremes. The statute's words reflect Congress' basic aim to provide federal regulation of identifiable sources of pollutants entering navigable waters without undermining the States' longstanding regulatory authority over land and groundwater. We hold that the statute requires a permit when there is a direct discharge from a point source into navigable waters or when there is the functional equivalent of a direct discharge. We think this phrase best captures, in broad terms, those circumstances in which Congress intended to require a federal permit. That is, an addition falls within the statutory requirement that it be "from any point source" when a point source directly deposits pollutants into navigable waters, or when the discharge reaches the same result through roughly similar means.

Time and distance are obviously important. Where a pipe ends a few feet from navigable waters and the pipe emits pollutants that travel those few feet through groundwater (or over the beach), the permitting requirement clearly applies. If the pipe ends 50 miles from navigable waters and the pipe emits pollutants that travel with groundwater, mix with much other material, and end up in navigable waters only many years later, the permitting requirements likely do not apply.

The object in a given scenario will be to advance, in a manner consistent with the statute's language, the statutory purposes that Congress sought to achieve. As we have said (repeatedly), the word "from" seeks a "point source" origin, and context imposes natural limits as to when a point source can properly be considered the origin of pollution that travels through groundwater. That context includes the need, reflected in the statute, to preserve state regulation of groundwater and other nonpoint sources of pollution. Whether pollutants that arrive at navigable waters after traveling through groundwater are "from" a point source depends upon how similar to (or different from) the particular discharge is to a direct discharge.

The difficulty with this approach, we recognize, is that it does not, on its own, clearly explain how to deal with middle instances. But there are too many potentially relevant factors applicable to factually different cases for this Court now to use more specific language. Consider, for example, just some of the factors that may prove relevant (depending upon the circumstances of a particular case): (1) transit time, (2) distance traveled, (3) the nature of the material through which the pollutant travels, (4) the extent to which the pollutant is diluted or chemically changed as it travels, (5) the amount of pollutant entering the navigable waters relative to the amount of the pollutant that leaves the point source, (6) the manner by or area in which the pollutant enters the navigable waters, (7) the degree to which the pollution (at that point) has maintained its specific identity. Time and distance will be the most important factors in most cases, but not necessarily every case.

At the same time, courts can provide guidance through decisions in individual cases. The Circuits have tried to do so, often using general language somewhat similar to the language we have used. And the traditional common-law method, making decisions that provide examples that in turn lead to ever more refined principles, is sometimes useful, even in an era of statutes.

The underlying statutory objectives also provide guidance. Decisions should not create serious risks either of undermining state regulation of groundwater or of creating loopholes that undermine the statute's basic federal regulatory objectives.

EPA, too, can provide administrative guidance (within statutory boundaries) in numerous ways, including through, for example, grants of individual permits, promulgation of general permits, or the development of general rules. Indeed, over the years, EPA and the States have often considered the Act's application to discharges through groundwater.

Both Maui and the Government object that to subject discharges to navigable waters through groundwater to the statute's permitting requirements, as our interpretation will sometimes do, would vastly expand the scope of the statute, perhaps requiring permits for each of the 650,000 wells like petitioner's or for each of the over 20 million septic systems used in many Americans' homes.

But EPA has applied the permitting provision to some (but not to all) discharges through groundwater for over 30 years. In that time we have seen no evidence of unmanageable expansion. EPA and the States also have tools to mitigate those harms, should they arise, by (for example) developing general permits for recurring situations or by issuing permits based on best practices where appropriate. Judges, too, can mitigate any hardship or injustice when they apply the statute's penalty provision. That provision vests courts with broad discretion to set a penalty that takes account of many factors, including "any good-faith efforts to comply" with the Act, the "seriousness of the violation," the "economic impact of the penalty on the violator," and "such other matters as justice may require." See 33 U.S.C. § 1319(d). We expect that district judges will exercise their discretion mindful, as we are, of the complexities inherent to the context of indirect discharges through groundwater, so as to calibrate the Act's penalties when, for example, a party could reasonably have thought that a permit was not required.

In sum, we recognize that a more absolute position, such as the means-of-delivery test or that of the Government or that of the Ninth Circuit, may be easier to administer. But, as we have said, those positions have consequences that are inconsistent with major congressional objectives, as revealed by the statute's language, structure, and purposes. We consequently understand the permitting requirement, § 301, as applicable to a discharge (from a point source) of pollutants that reach navigable waters after traveling through groundwater if that discharge is the functional equivalent of a direct discharge from the point source into navigable waters.

VI

Because the Ninth Circuit applied a different standard, we vacate its judgment and remand the case for further proceedings consistent with this opinion.

It is so ordered.

QUESTIONS

1. What happened in this case?
2. What was/were the issue/issues?
3. How did the Court resolve it/them, and why?
4. What are the strengths and weaknesses in the Court's reasoning?

C. NAVIGABLE WATERS

The CWA defines "navigable waters" as "the waters of the United States, including the territorial seas." § 502(7). Congress didn't define "waters of the United States," however, leaving it to EPA and the Corps to do so as:

"waters of the United States" include:

(a) All waters which are currently used, were used in the past, or may be susceptible to use in interstate or foreign commerce, including all waters which are subject to the ebb and flow of the tide;

(b) All interstate waters, including interstate "wetlands;"

(c) All other waters such as intrastate lakes, rivers, streams (including intermittent streams), mudflats, sandflats, "wetlands," sloughs, prairie potholes, wet meadows, playa lakes, or natural lakes the use, degradation, or destruction of which would affect or could affect interstate or foreign commerce including any such waters:

>   (1) Which are or could be used by interstate or foreign travelers for recreation or other purposes;

>   (2) From which fish or shellfish are or could be taken and sold in interstate or foreign commerce; or

>   (3) Which are or could be used for industrial purposes by industries in interstate commerce;

(d) All impoundments of waters otherwise defined as waters of the United States under this definition;

(e) Tributaries of waters identified in paragraphs (a) through (d) of this definition;

(f) The territorial sea; and

(g) "Wetlands" adjacent to waters (other than waters that are themselves wetlands) identified in paragraphs (a) through (f) of this definition.

40 C.F.R. § 122.2 (EPA, for 402 program); 33 C.F.R. § 328.3(a) (Army Corps, for 404 program)(joint definition).

EPA's and the Corps' definition of WOUS has been subject to numerous challenges that have reached the SCOTUS, and most recently in the case that follows.

SACKETT V. ENVIRONMENTAL PROTECTION AGENCY
598 U.S. ___ (2023)

Justice Alito delivered the opinion of the Court.

This case concerns a nagging question about the outer reaches of the Clean Water Act (CWA), the principal federal law regulating water pollution in the United States. By all accounts, the Act has been a great success. Before its enactment in 1972, many of the Nation's rivers, lakes, and streams were severely polluted, and existing federal legislation had proved to be inadequate. Today, many formerly fetid bodies of water are safe for the use and enjoyment of the people of this country.

There is, however, an unfortunate footnote to this success story: the outer boundaries of the Act's geographical reach have been uncertain from the start. The Act applies to "the waters of the United States," but what does that phrase mean? Does the term encompass any backyard that is soggy enough for some minimum period of time? Does it reach "mudflats, sandflats, wetlands, sloughs, prairie potholes, wet meadows, [or] playa lakes?" How about ditches, swimming pools, and puddles?

For more than a half century, the agencies responsible for enforcing the Act have wrestled with the problem and adopted varying interpretations. On three prior occasions, this Court has tried to clarify the meaning of "the waters of the United States." But the problem persists. When we last addressed the question 17 years ago, we were unable to agree on an opinion of the Court. Today, we return to the problem and attempt to identify with greater clarity what the Act means by "the waters of the United States."

I

A

For most of this Nation's history, the regulation of water pollution was left almost entirely to the States and their subdivisions. The common law permitted aggrieved parties to bring nuisance suits against polluters. But as industrial production and population growth increased the quantity and toxicity of pollution, States gradually shifted to enforcement by regulatory agencies.

Conversely, federal regulation was largely limited to ensuring that "traditional navigable waters"—that is, interstate waters that were either navigable in fact and used in commerce or readily susceptible of being used in this way—remained free of impediments. See, e.g., Rivers and Harbors Act of 1899, 30Stat. 1151; see also United States v. Appalachian Elec. Power Co., <u>311 U.S. 377</u>, 406–407 (1940); The Daniel Ball, 10 Wall. 557, 563 (1871).

Congress's early efforts at directly regulating water pollution were tepid. Although the Federal Water Pollution Control Act of 1948 allowed federal officials to seek judicial abatement of pollution in interstate waters, it imposed high hurdles, such as requiring the consent of the State where the pollution originated. Despite repeated amendments over the next two decades, few actions were brought under this framework.

Congress eventually replaced this scheme in 1972 with the CWA. The Act prohibits "the discharge of any pollutant" into "navigable waters." 33 U. S. C. §§1311(a), 1362(12)(A). It broadly defines the term " 'pollutant' " to include not only contaminants like "chemical wastes," but also more mundane materials like "rock, sand," and "cellar dirt." §1362(6).

The CWA is a potent weapon. It imposes what have been described as "crushing" consequences "even for inadvertent violations." Army Corps of Engineers v. Hawkes Co., 578 U.S. 590, 602 (2016) (Kennedy, J., concurring). Property owners who negligently discharge "pollutants" into covered waters may face severe criminal penalties including imprisonment. §1319(c). These penalties increase for knowing violations. On the civil side, the CWA imposes over $60,000 in fines per day for each violation. And due to the Act's 5-year statute of limitations, and expansive interpretations of the term "violation," these civil penalties can be nearly as crushing as their criminal counterparts, see, e.g., Borden Ranch Partnership v. United States Army Corps of Engineers, <u>261 F.3d 810</u>, 813, 818 (CA9 2001) (upholding Agency decision to count each of 348 passes of a plow by a farmer through "jurisdictional" soil on his farm as a separate violation), aff'd by an equally divided Court, <u>537 U.S. 99</u> (2002) (per curiam).

The Environmental Protection Agency (EPA) and the Army Corps of Engineers (Corps) jointly enforce the CWA. The EPA is tasked with policing violations after the fact, either by issuing orders demanding compliance or by bringing civil actions. §1319(a). The Act also authorizes private plaintiffs to sue to enforce its requirements. §1365(a). On the front end, both agencies are empowered to issue permits exempting activity that would otherwise be unlawful under the Act. Relevant here, the Corps controls permits for the discharge of dredged or fill material into covered waters. See §1344(a). The costs of obtaining such a permit are "significant," and both agencies have admitted that "the permitting process can be arduous, expensive, and long." Success is also far from guaranteed, as the Corps has asserted discretion to grant or deny permits based on a long, nonexclusive list of factors that ends with a catchall mandate to consider "in general, the needs and welfare of the people."

Due to the CWA's capacious definition of "pollutant," its low mens rea, and its severe penalties, regulated parties have focused particular attention on the Act's geographic scope. While its predecessor encompassed "interstate or navigable waters," 33 U. S. C. §1160(a) (1970 ed.), the CWA prohibits the discharge of pollutants into only "navigable waters," which it defines as "the waters of the United States, including the territorial seas," 33 U. S. C. §§1311(a), 1362(7), (12)(A) (2018 ed.). The meaning of this definition is the persistent problem that we must address.

B

Michael and Chantell Sackett have spent well over a decade navigating the CWA, and their voyage has been bumpy and costly. In 2004, they purchased a small lot near Priest Lake, in

Bonner County, Idaho. In preparation for building a modest home, they began backfilling their property with dirt and rocks. A few months later, the EPA sent the Sacketts a compliance order informing them that their backfilling violated the CWA because their property contained protected wetlands. The EPA demanded that the Sacketts immediately " 'undertake activities to restore the Site' " pursuant to a " 'Restoration Work Plan' " that it provided. Sackett v. EPA, <u>566 U.S. 120</u>, 125 (2012). The order threatened the Sacketts with penalties of over $40,000 per day if they did not comply.

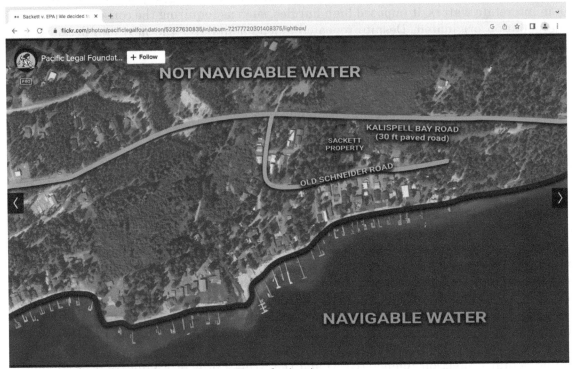

(Image courtesy of the Pacific Legal Foundation.)

At the time, the EPA interpreted "the waters of the United States" to include "[a]ll . . . waters" that "could affect interstate or foreign commerce," as well as "[w]etlands adjacent" to those waters. 40 CFR §§230.3(s)(3), (7) (2008). "[A]djacent" was defined to mean not just "bordering" or "contiguous," but also "neighboring." §230.3(b). Agency guidance instructed officials to assert jurisdiction over wetlands "adjacent" to non-navigable tributaries when those wetlands had "a significant nexus to a traditional navigable water."[6] A "significant nexus" was said to exist when " 'wetlands, either alone or in combination with similarly situated lands in the region, significantly affect the chemical, physical, and biological integrity' " of those waters. 2007 Guidance 8 (emphasis added). In looking for evidence of a "significant nexus," field agents were told to consider a wide range of open-ended hydrological and ecological factors.

According to the EPA, the "wetlands" on the Sacketts' lot are "adjacent to" (in the sense that they are in the same neighborhood as) what it described as an "unnamed tributary" on the other side of a 30-foot road. That tributary feeds into a non-navigable creek, which, in turn, feeds into Priest Lake, an intrastate body of water that the EPA designated as traditionally navigable. To establish a significant nexus, the EPA lumped the Sacketts' lot together with the Kalispell Bay Fen, a large nearby wetland complex that the Agency regarded as "similarly situated." According to the EPA, these properties, taken together, "significantly affect" the ecology of Priest Lake. Therefore, the

EPA concluded, the Sacketts had illegally dumped soil and gravel onto "the waters of the United States."

The Sacketts filed suit under the Administrative Procedure Act, 5 U. S. C. §702 et seq., alleging that the EPA lacked jurisdiction because any wetlands on their property were not "waters of the United States." The District Court initially dismissed the suit, reasoning that the compliance order was not a final agency action, but this Court ultimately held that the Sacketts could bring their suit under the APA. See Sackett, 566 U. S., at 131. After seven years of additional proceedings on remand, the District Court entered summary judgment for the EPA. The Ninth Circuit affirmed, holding that the CWA covers adjacent wetlands with a significant nexus to traditional navigable waters and that the Sacketts' lot satisfied that standard.

We granted certiorari to decide the proper test for determining whether wetlands are "waters of the United States." 595 U. S. ___ (2022).

II

A

In defining the meaning of "the waters of the United States," we revisit what has been "a contentious and difficult task." The phrase has sparked decades of agency action and litigation. In order to resolve the CWA's applicability to wetlands, we begin by reviewing this history.

The EPA and the Corps initially promulgated different interpretations of "the waters of the United States." The EPA defined its jurisdiction broadly to include, for example, intrastate lakes used by interstate travelers. Conversely, the Corps, consistent with its historical authority to regulate obstructions to navigation, asserted jurisdiction over only traditional navigable waters. But the Corps' narrow definition did not last. It soon promulgated new, much broader definitions designed to reach the outer limits of Congress's commerce power.

Eventually the EPA and Corps settled on materially identical definitions. See 45 Fed. Reg. 33424 (1980); 47 Fed. Reg. 31810–31811 (1982). These broad definitions encompassed "[a]ll . . . waters" that "could affect interstate or foreign commerce." 40 CFR §230.3(s)(3) (2008). So long as the potential for an interstate effect was present, the regulation extended the CWA to, for example, "intrastate lakes, rivers, streams (including intermittent streams), mudflats, sandflats, wetlands, sloughs, prairie potholes, wet meadows, playa lakes, or natural ponds." The agencies likewise took an expansive view of the CWA's coverage of wetlands "adjacent" to covered waters. §230.3(s)(7). As noted, they defined "adjacent" to mean "bordering, contiguous, or neighboring" and clarified that "adjacent" wetlands include those that are separated from covered waters "by man-made dikes or barriers, natural river berms, beach dunes and the like." §230.3(b). They also specified that "wetlands" is a technical term encompassing "those areas that are inundated or saturated by surface or ground water at a frequency and duration sufficient to support, and that under normal conditions do support, a prevalence of vegetation typically adapted for life in saturated soil conditions." §230.3(t). The Corps released what would become a 143-page manual to guide officers when they determine whether property meets this definition.

This Court first construed the meaning of "the waters of the United States" in United States v. Riverside Bayview Homes, Inc., 474 U.S. 121 (1985). There, we were confronted with the Corps' assertion of authority under the CWA over wetlands that "actually abut[ted] on a navigable waterway." Id., at 135. Although we expressed concern that wetlands seemed to fall outside "traditional notions of 'waters,'" we nonetheless deferred to the Corps, reasoning that "the transition from water to solid ground is not necessarily or even typically an abrupt one."

The agencies responded to Riverside Bayview by expanding their interpretations even further. Most notably, they issued the "migratory bird rule," which extended jurisdiction to any waters or wetlands that "are or would be used as [a] habitat" by migratory birds or endangered species. As the Corps would later admit, "nearly all waters were jurisdictional under the migratory bird rule."

In Solid Waste Agency of Northern Cook Cty. v. Army Corps of Engineers, 531 U.S. 159 (2001) (SWANCC), this Court rejected the migratory bird rule, which the Corps had used to assert jurisdiction over several isolated ponds located wholly within the State of Illinois. Disagreeing with the Corps' argument that ecological interests supported its jurisdiction, we instead held that the CWA does not "exten[d] to ponds that are not adjacent to open water."

Days after our decision, the agencies issued guidance that sought to minimize SWANCC's impact. They took the view that this Court's holding was "strictly limited to waters that are 'nonnavigable, isolated, and intrastate' " and that "field staff should continue to exercise CWA jurisdiction to the full extent of their authority" for "any waters that fall outside of that category." The agencies never defined exactly what they regarded as the "full extent of their authority." They instead encouraged local field agents to make decisions on a case-by-case basis.

What emerged was a system of "vague" rules that depended on "locally developed practices." GAO Report 26. Deferring to the agencies' localized decisions, lower courts blessed an array of expansive interpretations of the CWA's reach. See, e.g., United States v. Deaton, 332 F.3d 698, 702 (CA4 2003) (holding that a property owner violated the CWA by piling soil near a ditch 32 miles from navigable waters). Within a few years, the agencies had "interpreted their jurisdiction over 'the waters of the United States' to cover 270-to-300 million acres" of wetlands and "virtually any parcel of land containing a channel or conduit . . . through which rainwater or drainage may occasionally or intermittently flow." Rapanos v. United States, 547 U.S. 715, 722 (2006) (plurality opinion).

It was against this backdrop that we granted review in Rapanos v. United States. The lower court in the principal case before us had held that the CWA covered wetlands near ditches and drains that eventually emptied into navigable waters at least 11 miles away, a theory that had supported the petitioner's conviction in a related prosecution. Although we vacated that decision, no position commanded a majority of the Court. Four Justices concluded that the CWA's coverage did not extend beyond two categories: first, certain relatively permanent bodies of water connected to traditional interstate navigable waters and, second, wetlands with such a close physical connection to those waters that they were "as a practical matter indistinguishable from waters of the United States." Four Justices would have deferred to the Government's determination that the wetlands at issue were covered under the CWA. Finally, one Justice concluded that jurisdiction under the CWA requires a "significant nexus" between wetlands and navigable waters and that such a nexus exists where "the wetlands, either alone or in combination with similarly situated lands in the region, significantly affect the chemical, physical, and biological integrity" of those waters. Id., at 779–780 (Kennedy, J., concurring in judgment).

In the decade following Rapanos, the EPA and the Corps issued guidance documents that "recognized larger grey areas and called for more fact-intensive individualized determinations in those grey areas." As discussed, they instructed agency officials to assert jurisdiction over wetlands "adjacent" to non-navigable tributaries based on fact-specific determinations regarding the presence of a significant nexus. 2008 Guidance 8. The guidance further advised officials to make this determination by considering a lengthy list of hydrological and ecological factors. Ibid. Echoing what they had said about the migratory bird rule, the agencies later admitted that "almost all waters and wetlands across the country theoretically could be subject to a case-specific jurisdictional determination" under this guidance. 80 Fed. Reg. 37056 (2015); see, e.g., Hawkes Co., 578 U. S., at 596 (explaining that the Corps found a significant nexus between wetlands and a river "some 120 miles away").

More recently, the agencies have engaged in a flurry of rulemaking defining "the waters of the United States." In a 2015 rule, they offered a muscular approach that would subject "the vast majority of the nation's water features" to a case-by-case jurisdictional analysis.[11] Although the rule listed a few examples of "waters" that were excluded from regulation like "[p]uddles" and "swimming pools," it categorically covered other waters and wetlands, including any within 1,500 feet of interstate or traditional navigable waters. And it subjected a wider range of other waters, including any within 4,000 feet of indirect tributaries of interstate or traditional navigable waters, to a case-specific determination for significant nexus.

The agencies repealed this sweeping rule in 2019. Shortly afterwards, they replaced it with a narrower definition that limited jurisdiction to traditional navigable waters and their tributaries, lakes, and "adjacent" wetlands. 85 Fed. Reg. 22340 (2020). They also narrowed the definition of "[a]djacent," limiting it to wetlands that "[a]but" covered waters, are flooded by those waters, or are separated from those waters by features like berms or barriers.This rule too did not last. After granting the EPA's voluntary motion to remand, a District Court vacated the rule.

The agencies recently promulgated yet another rule attempting to define waters of the United States. 88 Fed. Reg. 3004 (2023) (to be codified in 40 CFR §120.2). Under that broader rule, traditional navigable waters, interstate waters, and the territorial seas, as well as their tributaries and adjacent wetlands, are waters of the United States. 88 Fed. Reg. 3143. So are any "[i]ntrastate lakes and ponds, streams, or wetlands" that either have a continuous surface connection to categorically included waters or have a significant nexus to interstate or traditional navigable waters. . Like the post-Rapanos guidance, the rule states that a significant nexus requires consideration of a list of open-ended factors. 88 Fed. Reg. 3006, 3144. Finally, the rule returns to the broad pre-2020 definition of "adjacent." Acknowledging that "[f]ield work is often necessary to confirm the presence of a wetland" under these definitions, the rule instructs local agents to continue using the Corps' Wetlands Delineation Manual. 88 Fed. Reg. 3117.

B

With the benefit of a half century of practice under the CWA, it is worth taking stock of where things stand. The agencies maintain that the significant-nexus test has been and remains sufficient to establish jurisdiction over "adjacent" wetlands. And by the EPA's own admission, "almost all waters and wetlands" are potentially susceptible to regulation under that test. 80 Fed. Reg. 37056. This puts many property owners in a precarious position because it is "often difficult to determine whether a particular piece of property contains waters of the United States." Hawkes Co., 578 U. S., at 594; see 40 CFR §230.3(t) (2008). Even if a property appears dry, application of the guidance in a complicated manual ultimately decides whether it contains wetlands. See 88 Fed. Reg. 3117; Wetlands Delineation Manual 84–85 (describing "not . . . atypical" examples of wetlands that periodically lack wetlands indicators); see also Hawkes Co. v. United States Army Corps of Engineers, 782 F.3d 994, 1003 (CA8 2015) (Kelly, J., concurring) ("This is a unique aspect of the CWA; most laws do not require the hiring of expert consultants to determine if they even apply to you or your property"). And because the CWA can sweep broadly enough to criminalize mundane activities like moving dirt, this unchecked definition of "the waters of the United States" means that a staggering array of landowners are at risk of criminal prosecution or onerous civil penalties.

What are landowners to do if they want to build on their property? The EPA recommends asking the Corps for a jurisdictional determination, which is a written decision on whether a particular site contains covered waters. But the Corps maintains that it has no obligation to provide jurisdictional determinations, and it has already begun announcing exceptions to the legal effect of some previous determinations. Even if the Corps is willing to provide a jurisdictional determination, a property owner may find it necessary to retain an expensive expert consultant who is capable of putting together a presentation that stands a chance of persuading the Corps. And even then, a landowner's chances of success are low, as the EPA admits that the Corps finds jurisdiction approximately 75% of the time.

If the landowner is among the vast majority who receive adverse jurisdictional determinations, what then? It would be foolish to go ahead and build since the jurisdictional determination might form evidence of culpability in a prosecution or civil action. The jurisdictional determination could be challenged in court, but only after the delay and expense required to exhaust the administrative appeals process. And once in court, the landowner would face an uphill battle under the deferential standards of review that the agencies enjoy. See 5 U. S. C. §706. Another alternative would be simply to acquiesce and seek a permit from the Corps. But that process can take years and cost an exorbitant amount of money. Many landowners faced with this unappetizing menu of options would simply choose to build nothing.

III

With this history in mind, we now consider the extent of the CWA's geographical reach.

A

We start, as we always do, with the text of the CWA. As noted, the Act applies to "navigable waters," which had a well-established meaning at the time of the CWA's enactment. But the CWA complicates matters by proceeding to define "navigable waters" as "the waters of the United States," §1362(7), which was decidedly not a well-known term of art. This frustrating drafting choice has led to decades of litigation, but we must try to make sense of the terms Congress chose to adopt. And for the reasons explained below, we conclude that the Rapanos plurality was correct: the CWA's use of "waters" encompasses "only those relatively permanent, standing or continuously flowing bodies of water 'forming geographic[al] features' that are described in ordinary parlance as 'streams, oceans, rivers, and lakes.'" 547 U. S., at 739 (quoting Webster's New International Dictionary 2882 (2d ed. 1954) (Webster's Second); original alterations omitted).

This reading follows from the CWA's deliberate use of the plural term "waters." See 547 U. S., at 732–733. That term typically refers to bodies of water like those listed above. See, e.g., Webster's Second 2882; Black's Law Dictionary 1426 (5th ed. 1979) ("especially in the plural, [water] may designate a body of water, such as a river, a lake, or an ocean, or an aggregate of such bodies of water, as in the phrases 'foreign waters,' 'waters of the United States,' and the like" (emphasis added)); Random House Dictionary of the English Language 2146 (2d ed. 1987) (Random House Dictionary) (defining "waters" as "a. flowing water, or water moving in waves: The river's mighty waters. b. the sea or seas bordering a particular country or continent or located in a particular part of the world" (emphasis deleted)). This meaning is hard to reconcile with classifying "'lands,' wet or otherwise, as 'waters.'" Rapanos, 547 U. S., at 740 (plurality opinion) (quoting Riverside Bayview, 474 U. S., at 132).

This reading also helps to align the meaning of "the waters of the United States" with the term it is defining: "navigable waters." See Bond v. United States, 572 U.S. 844, 861 (2014) ("In settling on a fair reading of a statute, it is not unusual to consider the ordinary meaning of a defined term, particularly when there is dissonance between that ordinary meaning and the reach of the definition"). Although we have acknowledged that the CWA extends to more than traditional navigable waters, we have refused to read "navigable" out of the statute, holding that it at least shows that Congress was focused on "its traditional jurisdiction over waters that were or had been navigable in fact or which could reasonably be so made." SWANCC, 531 U. S., at 172; see also Appalachian Electric, 311 U. S., at 406–407; The Daniel Ball, 10 Wall., at 563. At a minimum, then, the use of "navigable" signals that the definition principally refers to bodies of navigable water like rivers, lakes, and oceans. See Rapanos, 547 U. S., at 734 (plurality opinion).

More broadly, this reading accords with how Congress has employed the term "waters" elsewhere in the CWA and in other laws. The CWA repeatedly uses "waters" in contexts that confirm the term refers to bodies of open water. See 33 U. S. C. §1267(i)(2)(D) ("the waters of the Chesapeake Bay"); §1268(a)(3)(I) ("the open waters of each of the Great Lakes"); §1324(d)(4)(B)(ii) ("lakes and other surface waters"); §1330(g)(4)(C)(vii) ("estuarine waters"); §1343(c)(1) ("the waters of the territorial seas, the contiguous zone, and the oceans"); §§1346(a)(1), 1375a(a) ("coastal recreation waters"); §1370 (state "boundary waters"). The use of "waters" elsewhere in the U. S. Code likewise correlates to rivers, lakes, and oceans.

Statutory history points in the same direction. The CWA's predecessor statute covered "interstate or navigable waters" and defined "interstate waters" as "all rivers, lakes, and other waters that flow across or form a part of State boundaries." 33 U. S. C. §§1160(a), 1173(e) (1970 ed.) (emphasis added); see also Rivers and Harbors Act of 1899, 30Stat. 1151 (codified, as amended, at 33 U. S. C. §403) (prohibiting unauthorized obstructions "to the navigable capacity of any of the waters of the United States").

This Court has understood the CWA's use of "waters" in the same way. Even as Riverside Bayview grappled with whether adjacent wetlands could fall within the CWA's coverage, it acknowledged that wetlands are not included in "traditional notions of 'waters.'" 474 U. S., at 133. It explained that the term conventionally refers to "hydrographic features" like "rivers" and "streams." SWANCC went even further, repeatedly describing the "waters" covered by the Act as "open water" and suggesting that "the waters of the United States" principally refers to traditional navigable waters. 531 U. S., at 168–169, 172. That our CWA decisions operated under this assumption is unsurprising. Ever since Gibbons v. Ogden, 9 Wheat. 1 (1824), this Court has used "waters of the United States" to refer to similar bodies of water, almost always in relation to ships. Id., at 218 (discussing a vessel's "conduct in the waters of the United States").

The EPA argues that "waters" is "naturally read to encompass wetlands" because the "presence of water is 'universally regarded as the most basic feature of wetlands.'" Brief for Respondents 19. But that reading proves too much. Consider puddles, which are also defined by the ordinary presence of water even though few would describe them as "waters." This argument is also tough to square with SWANCC, which held that the Act does not cover isolated ponds, or Riverside Bayview, which would have had no need to focus so extensively on the adjacency of wetlands to covered waters if the EPA's reading were correct. Finally, it is also instructive that the CWA expressly "protect[s] the primary responsibilities and rights of States to prevent, reduce, and eliminate pollution" and "to plan the development and use . . . of land and water resources." §1251(b). It is hard to see how the States' role in regulating water resources would remain "primary" if the EPA had jurisdiction over anything defined by the presence of water. See County of Maui v. Hawaii Wildlife Fund, 590 U. S. ___, ___ (2020) (slip op., at 7); Rapanos, 547 U. S., at 737 (plurality opinion).

B

Although the ordinary meaning of "waters" in §1362(7) might seem to exclude all wetlands, we do not view that provision in isolation. The meaning of a word "may only become evident when placed in context," FDA v. Brown & Williamson Tobacco Corp., 529 U.S. 120, 132 (2000), and statutory context shows that some wetlands qualify as "waters of the United States."

In 1977, Congress amended the CWA and added §1344(g)(1), which authorizes States to apply to the EPA for permission to administer programs to issue permits for the discharge of dredged or fill material into some bodies of water. In simplified terms, the provision specifies that state permitting programs may regulate discharges into (1) any waters of the United States, (2) except for traditional navigable waters, (3) "including wetlands adjacent thereto."

When this convoluted formulation is parsed, it tells us that at least some wetlands must qualify as "waters of the United States." The provision begins with a broad category, "the waters of the United States," which we may call category A. The provision provides that States may permit discharges into these waters, but it then qualifies that States cannot permit discharges into a subcategory of A: traditional navigable waters (category B). Finally, it states that a third category (category C), consisting of wetlands "adjacent" to traditional navigable waters, is "includ[ed]" within B. Thus, States may permit discharges into A minus B, which includes C. If C (adjacent wetlands) were not part of A ("the waters of the United States") and therefore subject to regulation under the CWA, there would be no point in excluding them from that category. See Riverside Bayview, 474 U. S., at 138, n. 11 (recognizing that §1344(g) "at least suggest[s] strongly that the term 'waters' as used in the Act does not necessarily exclude 'wetlands' "); Rapanos, 547 U. S., at 768 (opinion of Kennedy, J.). Thus, §1344(g)(1) presumes that certain wetlands constitute "waters of the United States."

But what wetlands does the CWA regulate? Section 1344(g)(1) cannot answer that question alone because it is not the operative provision that defines the Act's reach. See Riverside Bayview, 474 U. S., at 138, n. 11. Instead, we must harmonize the reference to adjacent wetlands in §1344(g)(1) with "the waters of the United States," §1362(7), which is the actual term we are tasked with interpreting. The formulation discussed above tells us how: because the adjacent wetlands in §1344(g)(1) are "includ[ed]" within "the waters of the United States," these wetlands must qualify as "waters of the United States" in their own right. In other words, they must be indistinguishably part of a body of water that itself constitutes "waters" under the CWA.

This understanding is consistent with §1344(g)(1)'s use of "adjacent." Dictionaries tell us that the term "adjacent" may mean either "contiguous" or "near." Random House Dictionary 25; see Webster's Third New International Dictionary 26 (1976); see also Oxford American Dictionary & Thesaurus 16 (2d ed. 2009) (listing "adjoining" and "neighboring" as synonyms of "adjacent"). But "construing statutory language is not merely an exercise in ascertaining 'the outer limits of a word's definitional possibilities,' " FCC v. AT&T Inc., 562 U.S. 397, 407 (2011) (alterations omitted), and here, "only one . . . meanin[g] produces a substantive effect that is compatible with the rest of the law," United Sav. Assn. of Tex. v. Timbers of Inwood Forest Associates, Ltd., 484 U.S. 365, 371 (1988). Wetlands that are separate from traditional navigable waters cannot be considered part of those waters, even if they are located nearby.

In addition, it would be odd indeed if Congress had tucked an important expansion to the reach of the CWA into convoluted language in a relatively obscure provision concerning state permitting programs. We have often remarked that Congress does not "hide elephants in mouseholes" by "alter[ing] the fundamental details of a regulatory scheme in vague terms or ancillary provisions." Whitman v. American Trucking Assns., Inc., 531 U.S. 457, 468 (2001). We cannot agree with such an implausible interpretation here.

If §1344(g)(1) were read to mean that the CWA applies to wetlands that are not indistinguishably part of otherwise covered "waters of the United States," it would effectively amend and substantially broaden §1362(7) to define "navigable waters" as "waters of the United States and adjacent wetlands." But §1344(g)(1)'s use of the term "including" makes clear that it does not purport to do—and in fact, does not do—any such thing. See National Assn. of Home Builders v. Defenders of Wildlife, 551 U.S. 644, 662–664, and n. 8 (2007) (recognizing that implied amendments require " 'clear and manifest' " evidence of congressional intent). It merely reflects Congress's assumption that certain "adjacent" wetlands are part of "waters of the United States."

This is the thrust of observations in decisions going all the way back to Riverside Bayview. In that case, we deferred to the Corps' decision to regulate wetlands actually abutting a navigable waterway, but we recognized "the inherent difficulties of defining precise bounds to regulable waters." 474 U. S., at 134; see also id., at 132 (noting that "the transition from water to solid ground is not necessarily or even typically an abrupt one" due to semi-aquatic features like shallows and swamps). In such a situation, we concluded, the Corps could reasonably determine that wetlands "adjoining bodies of water" were part of those waters. Id., at 135, and n. 9; see also SWANCC, 531 U. S., at 167 (recognizing that Riverside Bayview "held that the Corps had . . . jurisdiction over wetlands that actually abutted on a navigable waterway").

In Rapanos, the plurality spelled out clearly when adjacent wetlands are part of covered waters. It explained that "waters" may fairly be read to include only those wetlands that are "as a practical matter indistinguishable from waters of the United States," such that it is "difficult to determine where the 'water' ends and the 'wetland' begins." 547 U. S., at 742, 755 (emphasis deleted). That occurs when wetlands have "a continuous surface connection to bodies that are 'waters of the United States' in their own right, so that there is no clear demarcation between 'waters' and wetlands." Id., at 742; cf. 33 U. S. C. §2802(5) (defining "coastal waters" to include wetlands "having unimpaired connection with the open sea up to the head of tidal influence"). We agree with this formulation of when wetlands are part of "the waters of the United States." We also acknowledge that temporary interruptions in surface connection may sometimes occur because of phenomena like low tides or dry spells.

In sum, we hold that the CWA extends to only those wetlands that are "as a practical matter indistinguishable from waters of the United States." Rapanos, 547 U. S., at 755 (plurality opinion) (emphasis deleted). This requires the party asserting jurisdiction over adjacent wetlands to establish "first, that the adjacent [body of water constitutes] . . . 'water[s] of the United States,' (i.e., a relatively permanent body of water connected to traditional interstate navigable waters); and second, that the wetland has a continuous surface connection with that water, making it difficult to determine where the 'water' ends and the 'wetland' begins."

IV

The EPA resists this reading of §1362(7) and instead asks us to defer to its understanding of the CWA's jurisdictional reach, as set out in its most recent rule defining "the waters of the United States." See 88 Fed. Reg. 3004. This rule, as noted, provides that "adjacent wetlands are covered by the Act if they 'possess a "significant nexus" to' traditional navigable waters." Brief for Respondents 32 (quoting Rapanos, 547 U. S., at 759 (opinion of Kennedy, J.)); see 88 Fed. Reg. 3143. And according to the EPA, wetlands are "adjacent" when they are "neighboring" to covered waters, even if they are separated from those waters by dry land. Brief for Respondents 20; 88 Fed. Reg. 3144.

A

For reasons already explained, this interpretation is inconsistent with the text and structure of the CWA. Beyond that, it clashes with "background principles of construction" that apply to the interpretation of the relevant statutory provisions. Bond, 572 U. S., at 857. Under those presumptions, the EPA must provide clear evidence that it is authorized to regulate in the manner it proposes.

1

First, this Court "require[s] Congress to enact exceedingly clear language if it wishes to significantly alter the balance between federal and state power and the power of the Government over private property." United States Forest Service v. Cowpasture River Preservation Assn., 590 U. S. ___, ___–___ (2020) (slip op., at 15–16); see also Bond, 572 U. S., at 858. Regulation of land and water use lies at the core of traditional state authority. See, e.g., SWANCC, 531 U. S., at 174 (citing Hess v. Port Authority Trans-Hudson Corporation, 513 U.S. 30, 44 (1994)); Tarrant Regional Water Dist. v. Herrmann, 569 U.S. 614, 631 (2013). An overly broad interpretation of the CWA's reach would impinge on this authority. The area covered by wetlands alone is vast—greater than the combined surface area of California and Texas. And the scope of the EPA's conception of "the waters of the United States" is truly staggering when this vast territory is supplemented by all the additional area, some of which is generally dry, over which the Agency asserts jurisdiction. Particularly given the CWA's express policy to "preserve" the States' "primary" authority over land and water use, §1251(b), this Court has required a clear statement from Congress when determining the scope of "the waters of the United States." SWANCC, 531 U. S., at 174; accord, Rapanos, 547 U. S., at 738 (plurality opinion).

The EPA, however, offers only a passing attempt to square its interpretation with the text of §1362(7), and its "significant nexus" theory is particularly implausible. It suggests that the meaning of "the waters of the United States" is so "broad and unqualified" that, if viewed in isolation, it would extend to all water in the United States. Brief for Respondents 32. The EPA thus turns to the "significant nexus" test in order to reduce the clash between its understanding of "the waters of the United States" and the term defined by that phrase, i.e., "navigable waters." As discussed, however, the meaning of "waters" is more limited than the EPA believes. See supra, at 14. And, in any event, the CWA never mentions the "significant nexus" test, so the EPA has no statutory basis to impose it. See Rapanos, 547 U. S., at 755–756 (plurality opinion).

2

Second, the EPA's interpretation gives rise to serious vagueness concerns in light of the CWA's criminal penalties. Due process requires Congress to define penal statutes " 'with sufficient definiteness that ordinary people can understand what conduct is prohibited' " and " 'in a manner that does not encourage arbitrary and discriminatory enforcement.' "

The EPA contends that the only thing preventing it from interpreting "waters of the United States" to "conceivably cover literally every body of water in the country" is the significant-nexus test. But the boundary between a "significant" and an insignificant nexus is far from clear. And to add to the uncertainty, the test introduces another vague concept—"similarly situated" waters—and then assesses the aggregate effect of that group based on a variety of open-ended factors that evolve as scientific understandings change. This freewheeling inquiry provides little notice to landowners of their obligations under the CWA. Facing severe criminal sanctions for even negligent violations, property owners are "left 'to feel their way on a case-by-case basis.' " Sackett, 566 U. S., at 124 (quoting Rapanos, 547 U. S., at 758 (Roberts, C. J., concurring)). Where a penal statute could sweep so broadly as to render criminal a host of what might otherwise be considered ordinary activities, we have been wary about going beyond what "Congress certainly intended the statute to cover." Skilling, 561 U. S., at 404.

Under these two background principles, the judicial task when interpreting "the waters of the United States" is to ascertain whether clear congressional authorization exists for the EPA's claimed power. The EPA's interpretation falls far short of that standard.

B

While mustering only a weak textual argument, the EPA justifies its position on two other grounds. It primarily claims that Congress implicitly ratified its interpretation of "adjacent" wetlands when it adopted §1344(g)(1). Thus, it argues that "waters of the United States" covers any wetlands that are "bordering, contiguous, or neighboring" to covered waters. 88 Fed. Reg. 3143. The principal opinion concurring in the judgment adopts the same position. See post, at 10–12 (Kavanaugh, J., concurring in judgment). The EPA notes that the Corps had promulgated regulations adopting that interpretation before Congress amended the CWA in 1977 to include the reference to "adjacent" wetlands in §1344(g)(1). This term, the EPA contends, was " ' "obviously transplanted from" ' " the Corps' regulations and thus incorporates the same definition.

This argument fails for at least three reasons. First, as we have explained, the text of §§1362(7) and 1344(g)(1) shows that "adjacent" cannot include wetlands that are not part of covered "waters."

Second, this ratification theory cannot be reconciled with our cases. We have repeatedly recognized that §1344(g)(1) " 'does not conclusively determine the construction to be placed on . . . the relevant definition of "navigable waters." ' " SWANCC, 531 U. S., at 171 (quoting Riverside Bayview, 474 U. S., at 138, n. 11); accord, Rapanos, 547 U. S., at 747–748, n. 12 (plurality opinion). Additionally, SWANCC rejected the closely analogous argument that Congress ratified the Corps' definition of "waters of the United States" by including " 'other . . . waters' " in §1344(g)(1). 531 U. S., at 168–171. And yet, the EPA's argument would require us to hold that §1344(g)(1) actually did amend the definition of "navigable waters" precisely for the reasons we rejected in SWANCC.

Third, the EPA cannot provide the sort of "overwhelming evidence of acquiescence" necessary to support its argument in the face of Congress's failure to amend §1362(7). Id., at 169–170, n. 5. We will infer that a term was " 'transplanted from another legal source' . . . only when a term's meaning was 'well-settled' before the transplantation." Kemp v. United States, 596 U. S. ___, ___– ___ (2022) (slip op., at 9–10). Far from being well settled, the Corps' definition was promulgated mere months before the CWA became law, and when the Corps adopted that definition, it candidly acknowledged the "rapidly changing nature of [its] regulatory programs." 42 Fed. Reg. 37122. Tellingly, even the EPA would not adopt that definition for several more years. See 45 Fed. Reg. 85345 (1980). This situation is a far cry from any in which we have found ratification. See, e.g., George v. McDonough, 596 U. S. ___, ___ (2022) (slip op., at 5) (finding ratification when "Congress used an unusual term that had a long regulatory history in [the] very regulatory context" at issue).

The EPA also advances various policy arguments about the ecological consequences of a narrower definition of adjacent. But the CWA does not define the EPA's jurisdiction based on ecological importance, and we cannot redraw the Act's allocation of authority. See Rapanos, 547 U. S., at 756 (plurality opinion). "The Clean Water Act anticipates a partnership between the States and the Federal Government." Arkansas v. Oklahoma, 503 U.S. 91, 101 (1992). States can and will continue to exercise their primary authority to combat water pollution by regulating land and water use.

V

Nothing in the separate opinions filed by Justice Kavanaugh and Justice Kagan undermines our analysis. Justice Kavanaugh claims that we have "rewrit[ten]" the CWA (opinion concurring in judgment), and Justice Kagan levels similar charges (opinion concurring in judgment). These arguments are more than unfounded. We have analyzed the statutory language in detail, but the separate opinions pay no attention whatsoever to §1362(7), the key statutory provision that limits the CWA's geographic reach to "the waters of the United States." Thus, neither separate opinion even attempts to explain how the wetlands included in their interpretation fall within a fair reading of "waters." Textualist arguments that ignore the operative text cannot be taken seriously.

VI

In sum, we hold that the CWA extends to only those "wetlands with a continuous surface connection to bodies that are 'waters of the United States' in their own right," so that they are "indistinguishable" from those waters. Rapanos, 547 U. S., at 742, 755 (plurality opinion) (emphasis deleted). This holding compels reversal here. The wetlands on the Sacketts' property are distinguishable from any possibly covered waters.

* * *

We reverse the judgment of the United States Court of Appeals for the Ninth Circuit and remand the case for further proceedings consistent with this opinion.
It is so ordered.

QUESTIONS

1. What happened in this case?
2. What was/were the issue/issues?
3. How did the Court resolve it/them, and why?
4. What are the strengths and weaknesses in the Court's reasoning?

III. TECHNOLOGY-BASED STANDARDS

The Clean Water Act requires EPA to set technology-based standards for categories and classes of point source dischargers, such as pulp and paper mills, breweries, and steam-electric fossil-fuel burning steam electric generating stations (powerplants). When calculating these standards, regulators "aim to set effluent limits at feasible levels while still encouraging innovation."

* * *

EXCERPT: JAMES R. MAY & PATRICK CLARY, THE ROLE OF SCIENCE AND ENGINEERING IN WATER POLLUTION CONTROL DURING THE PAST 100 YEARS
100 American Inst. Chem. Engr. (2008)

* * *

1. The Use of Technology Based Standards

Most federal environmental laws contain provisions that require EPA to set national technology-based standards on the regulated community, rejecting quasi-common law regulatory approaches that link the regulatory response to local conditions. For example, the first such statute to do so in 1970 – The Clean Air Act – requires EPA to develop and implement technology-based standards for "stationary" and "mobile" of air pollution. Clean Air Act of 1970. Pub. L. No. 91-604, 84 Stat. 1676 (codified as amended at 42 U.S.C. §§ 7401-7671g (1994)). Since 1972, the Clean Water Act has required EPA to set and implement technology-based standards for "point sources" of water pollution. Clean Water Act of 1972, Pub. L. No. 92-500, 86 Stat. 816 (codified as amended at 33 U.S.C. §§ 1251-1385 (1994)). The Safe Drinking Water Act requires EPA to set technology-based standards drinking water from "public drinking water systems." Safe Drinking Water Act, 33 U.S.C. § 300g-1(b)(4). The Resource Conservation and Recovery Act requires EPA to set technology-based standards for facilities that dispose hazardous wastes. Resource Conservation and Recovery Act, Pub. L. No. 94-580, 90 Stat. 2795 (codified as amended at 42 U.S.C. §§ 6901-6992K). See e.g., Patricia McCubbin, The Risk in Technology Based Standards, 16 Duke Envtl. L. & Pol'y F. 1, 7-8 (2005).

Congress has turned to technology-based standards because they are fair, predictable, efficient, adaptable, and enforceable. First, they are even-handed. Rather than allowing inefficiently disparate, site-specific standards, national technology-based standards level the playing field by treating those who engage in regulated activity to meet a certain threshold standard. Second, they are predictable. Rather than being subjected to agency decisionmaking on an ad hoc basis, national technology-based standards allow the regulated community to forecast regulatory requirements. Third, they are socially efficient. Regulatory rulemaking – even that taking many years as in the case at hand – is still generally a more efficient regulatory mechanism than case-by-case determinations. Fourth, they are adaptable. Technology based standards can be adjusted to fit innovation and feedback. Last, they are readily enforceable. Technology based standards are usually embodied by a particular technological requirement or a performance standard, either which are readily discernable by governmental enforcement agencies and by courts. Wendy Wagner, The Triumph of Technology Based Standards, 2000 U. Ill. L. Rev. 83, 87-105 (2000).

2)   Water Pollution Control is Primarily Technology-based

Technology-based standards are the central regulatory tool adopted in the Clean Water Act for achieving the "national goal that wherever attainable, an interim goal of water quality which provides for the protection and propagation of fish, shellfish, and wildlife and ... for recreation in and on the water." 33 U.S.C. § 1311. Under this approach, Congress instructed industry to reduce environmental harms as much as technology allows. In so doing, Congress made a sharp break with the failed regulatory approach that had governed until 1972, which sought to meet water quality standards by trying to determine how much pollution the water could assimilate and still be clean enough for human and aquatic uses. Congress found this pre-1972 approach to be "inadequate in every vital respect." See Milwaukee v. Illinois, 451 U.S. 304, 310 (1980), quoting S. Rep. No. 92-414, 7 (1971), 2 Legislative History of the Water Pollution Control Act Amendments of 1972, 1425 (Committee Print compiled for the Senate Committee on Public Works by the Library of Congress), Ser. No. 93-1 (1973). Instead, technology-based standards "facilitate enforcement by making it unnecessary to work backward from an overpolluted body of water to determine which point sources are responsible and which must be abated." EPA v. California ex rel. State Water Resources Control Board, 126 U.S. 200, 204 (1976).

Technology based standards apply to existing and new point sources. The level of performance for existing facilities is a function of pollutant and becomes more stringent over time. Initially, existing point sources were to meet "best practicable control technology currently available" (BPT) for all regulated pollutants. 33 U.S.C. 301(b)(1)(A). Thereafter, they were to meet more stringent technology-based standards, as a function of whether the regulated pollutant is "conventional" (such as oil & grease, pH, nitrogen, phosphorus and dissolved oxygen) or non-conventional (such as toxics and metals). Conventional pollutants discharges were to comply with "best conventional pollutant control technology," (BCT). 33 U.S.C. 301(b)(2)(E). Non-conventional pollutant discharges were to comply with "best available control technology economically achievable ... which will result in reasonable further progress toward the national goal of eliminating the discharge of all pollutants," (BAT). 33 U.S.C. 301(b)(2)(A). New sources were to meet "best available demonstrated control technology" (BADT). EPA, or a state with delegated permitting authority, would then implement the applicable technology-based standards when issuing National Pollutant Discharge Elimination System (NPDES) permits. The CWA prohibits the discharge of a "pollutant" from a point source in the absence of a permit. 33 U.S.C. §1311. EPA must set technology-based standards for point source discharges of pollutants, 33 U.S.C. §§ 1311 (existing sources) & 1316 (new sources), including for discharges of "heat." 33 U.S.C. 1362(6).

3.) Examples of Technology Based Standards Under the Clean Water Act
a.) Best Practicable Technology

The Clean Water Act has a broad range of technology-based standards. Best Practicable Technology (BPT) is the least restrictive techonology-based standard. Instead of setting forth a standard not widely available in an industry, BPT surveys existing technologies and selects those operating at the most efficient levels. Facilities may adopt the specific technology used by the top-performing facilities, or develop an alternative that performs at the same level. Compliance may therefore take the form of further innovation. As companies seek to lower the costs of modifying their facilities to meet the BPT standard, engineers and other scientific professionals assume a very important role.

With water regulation, these technology-based standards describe the desirable characteristics of water when it is released from some municipal or commercial facility. This type of regulation is called "effluent limitations," because the concern is the integrity of the water as it enters the nation's streams, lakes, and rivers. A selected few "effluent limitations" will be discussed to highlight how regulators create and enforce technology-based standards.

Water regulation touches many subjects, and in 1976 the EPA codified effluent limitations on the photography process. This regulation is a Best Practicable Technology standard. These regulations describe a permissible daily discharge of certain contaminants (silver and carbon nitrate, as well as parameters for pH levels) that are used in the photography process. The regulation places an additional limitation on the average daily discharge for a 30 day period. These limitations are:

Effluent characteristic	Effluent limitations	
	Maximum for any 1 day	Average of daily values for 30 consecutive days shall not exceed—
	Metric units (kilograms per 1,000 m^2 of product)	
Ag	0.14	0.07
CN	0.18	0.09
pH	6.0-9.0	6.0-9.0

The regulation educates on how these numbers were calculated. Because of a lack of industry-wide information regarding photography and its manufacturing process, a Best Practicable Technology standard was advisable Regulators were also unable to effectively sub-categorize the manufacturing process because of this lack of information. It is thus more advisable to use a less stringent standard (BPT) and to allow more discretion in the permit process when comprehensive data is unattainable. To mandate stricter requirements without an understanding on its economic impact would offend the overarching purpose of technology-based standards, which seeks to balance the interests of the environment with the economic interests of the regulated industry.

b.) Best Available Technology

Best Available Technology Economically Achievable (BAT) mandates "the maximum feasible pollution reduction for an industry." A more stringent standard than BPT, this approach designs regulation on "the optimally operating plant," seeking to maximize pollution reduction without causing large-scale facility closures, even if the technology is not widely used in the industry. The role for innovation is even more relevant in this circumstance. While this standard only requires what is theoretically achievable by the industry, there is always pressure to find a more cost-efficient means of compliance. Scientists and engineers undoubtedly play a major part in the research and development of these cleaner technologies. Similarly, when determining BAT, regulators must consult with those developing technology in a specific industry and determine the outer limits of pollution reduction.

As stated above, Best Available Technology Economically Achievable (BAT) is most applicable in a circumstance where the regulated contaminants are especially harmful, or when the costs of a "heightened" technology can be reasonably borne by the industry. In 1976, EPA codified regulations regarding the manufacturing process of oil-based paints. These regulations apply a BAT standard by simply declaring that "there shall be no discharge of process waste water pollutants to navigable waters." Regulators determined that the state of technology permitted a wholesale ban on the release of oil-based paint into the nation's water. Correlatively, such an approach reflects the danger that oil-based paint poses to the nation's water supply. Also, from the perspective of a layperson, it follows logic to place the most restrictive regulation on something like paint. In other words, it would be unsettling to think that manufacturers could lawfully release paint into our water supply.

IV.   WATER QUALITY STANDARDS

Congress enacted the CWA to "restore and maintain the chemical, physical and biological integrity of the nation's waters." 33 U.S.C. § 1251(a). The goal of the CWA is to eliminate "the discharge of pollutants into the navigable waters," and in the interim, to attain "water quality which provides for the protection and propagation of fish, shellfish, and wildlife and provides for recreation in and on the water." 33 U.S.C. § 1251(a)(1) and (2). The passage of the CWA "marked the ascendancy of water-quality control to the status of a major national priority." Monongahela Power Co. v. Marsh, 809 F.2d 41, 45-46 (D.C. Cir. 1987).

A. ACHIEVING WATER QUALITY STANDARDS

What about waters for which technology-based standards alone are not sufficient to protect water quality and ensure that otherwise allowable pollutant loadings do not exceed the assimilative capacity of the water receiving the discharge? In modern times, this is largely accomplished by developing and implementing "water quality standards" under the Clean Water Act. The Clean Water Act is intended to ensure protection of our nation's waters by requiring states to take certain measures to ensure both that safe and healthy waters would not become more polluted and that impaired waters would be restored. To meet these objectives, the CWA requires EPA to set water quality "criteria" to protect uses, such as fishing, swimming, drinking and recreation. The CWA then has states identify impaired waters, establish pollutant load limitations for such impaired waters to ensure that they meet water quality standards, and develop an implementation plan to see to it that such standards are met for all waters in a state.

To achieve these ends, section 303 of the CWA requires the establishment and implementation of water quality standards. 33 U.S.C. § 1313. States are required to establish water quality standards subject to review and approval by EPA. 33 U.S.C. § 1313(a). The Supreme Court has described the achievement of water quality standards as one of the CWA's "central objectives." Arkansas v. Oklahoma, 503 U.S. 91, 105 (1992).

The linchpin to achieving water quality standards is the "Total Maximum Daily Load" ("TMDL") program of Section 303(d) of the Clean Water Act. 33 U.S.C. § 1313(d). This provision establishes a detailed interrelated process. First, section 303(d)(1) of the CWA requires every state in the mid-Atlantic to identify every segment of the waters within its boundaries that does not meet or is not expected to meet applicable water standards even after the imposition of best-practicable technology-based effluent limitations, secondary treatment standards for publicly owned treatment works, and controls on thermal discharges. 33 U.S.C. §§ 1313(d)(1)(A) and (B). EPA refers to these impaired waters as "Water Quality Limited Segments" ("WQLSs"). 40 C.F.R. § 130.7(b)(1) and (2).

Following its identification of impaired waters, states must determine the maximum tolerable pollution so that pollutant loading in an impaired water body does not, taking into account seasonal variations and allowing an ample margin of safety, exceed the standards established for the water body. Section 303(d)(1)(C) requires states to develop the limits or load. 33 U.S.C. § 1313(b)(1)(C). In its simplest term, a total maximum daily load is a calculation of the maximum amount of a pollutant that a waterbody can receive and still meet water quality standards, and an allocation of that amount to the point and nonpoint sources of that pollutant.

Once states complete the above steps, they are to submit the list of standards and allowable loadings to the United States Environmental Protection Agency ("EPA") for review. Section 303(d)(2) states: "Each State shall submit to the Administrator ... for his approval the waters identified and the loads established under paragraphs (1)(A), (1)(B), (1)(C), and (1)(D) of this subsection." 33 U.S.C. § 1313(d)(2). EPA either must approve or disapprove the list of impaired waters and allowable loadings. If EPA disapproves, EPA must promulgate a new list of standards or allowable loadings within 30 days.

Thus, the CWA establishes a dual approach to achieving water quality goals, with national technology-based standards as the primary tool, and local, ambient-based standards as a safety net for waters for which technology-based standards alone are not sufficient to achieve water quality standards. See James R. May, The Rise and Repose of Assimilation-Based Water Quality, Part I: TMDL Litigation, 34 Envt'l L. Rep. 10247 (Env. L. Inst. 2004). Scientists in turn play an important role at every stage of this process. They help develop criteria, set standards, identify impaired waters, develop assimilative loading capacities, and determine allowable discharges. They also help to design and enforce permits that incorporate technology-based and water quality-based standards.

ARKANSAS V. OKLAHOMA
503 U.S. 91 (1992)

Pursuant to the Clean Water Act, 86 Stat. 816, as amended, 33 U.S.C. § 1251 et seq., the Environmental Protection Agency (EPA or agency) issued a discharge permit to a new point source in Arkansas, about 39 miles upstream from the Oklahoma state line. The question presented in this litigation is whether the EPA's finding that discharges from the new source would not cause a detectable violation of Oklahoma's water quality standards satisfied the EPA's duty to protect the interests of the downstream State. Disagreeing with the Court of Appeals, we hold that the Agency's action was authorized by the statute.

I

In 1985, the city of Fayetteville, Arkansas, applied to the EPA, seeking a permit for the city's new sewage treatment plant under the National Pollution Discharge Elimination System (NPDES). After the appropriate procedures, the EPA, pursuant to § 402(a)(1) of the Act, 33 U.S.C. § 1342(a)(1), issued a permit authorizing the plant to discharge up to half of its effluent (to a limit of 6.1 million gallons per day) into an unnamed stream in northwestern Arkansas. That flow passes through a series of three creeks for about 17 miles, and then enters the Illinois River at a point 22 miles upstream from the Arkansas–Oklahoma border.

The permit imposed specific limitations on the quantity, content, and character of the discharge and also included a number of special conditions, including a provision that if a study then underway indicated that more stringent limitations were necessary to ensure compliance with Oklahoma's water quality standards, the permit would be modified to incorporate those limits.

Respondents challenged this permit before the EPA, alleging, inter alia, that the discharge violated the Oklahoma water quality standards. Those standards provide that "no degradation [of water quality] shall be allowed" in the upper Illinois River, including the portion of the river immediately downstream from the state line.

Following a hearing, the Administrative Law Judge (ALJ) concluded that the Oklahoma standards would not be implicated unless the contested discharge had "something more than a mere de minimis impact" on the State's waters. He found that the discharge would not have an "undue impact" on Oklahoma's waters and, accordingly, affirmed the issuance of the permit.

On a petition for review, the EPA's Chief Judicial Officer first ruled that § 301(b)(1)(C) of the Clean Water Act "requires an NPDES permit to impose any effluent limitations necessary to comply with applicable state water quality standards." He then held that the Act and EPA regulations offered greater protection for the downstream State than the ALJ's "undue impact" standard suggested. He explained the proper standard as follows:

"[A] mere theoretical impairment of Oklahoma's water quality standards—i.e., an infinitesimal impairment predicted through modeling but not expected to be actually detectable or measurable—should not by itself block the issuance of the permit. In this case, the permit should be upheld if the record shows by a preponderance of the evidence that the authorized discharges would not cause an actual detectable violation of Oklahoma's water quality standards."

On remand, the ALJ made detailed findings of fact and concluded that the city had satisfied the standard set forth by the Chief Judicial Officer. Specifically, the ALJ found that there would be no detectable violation of any of the components of Oklahoma's water quality standards. The Chief Judicial Officer sustained the issuance of the permit.

Both the petitioners * * * (collectively Arkansas) and the respondents in this litigation sought judicial review. Arkansas argued that the Clean Water Act did not require an Arkansas point source to comply with Oklahoma's water quality standards. Oklahoma challenged the EPA's determination that the Fayetteville discharge would not produce a detectable violation of the Oklahoma standards.

The Court of Appeals did not accept either of these arguments. The court agreed with the EPA that the statute required compliance with Oklahoma's water quality standards, and did not disagree with the Agency's determination that the discharges from the Fayetteville plant would not produce a detectable violation of those standards. Nevertheless, relying on a theory that neither party had advanced, the Court of Appeals reversed the Agency's issuance of the Fayetteville permit. The court first ruled that the statute requires that "where a proposed source would discharge effluents that would contribute to conditions currently constituting a violation of applicable water quality standards, such [a] proposed source may not be permitted." Then the court found that the Illinois River in Oklahoma was "already degraded," that the Fayetteville effluent would reach the Illinois River in Oklahoma, and that that effluent could "be expected to contribute to the ongoing deterioration of the scenic river" in Oklahoma even though it would not detectably affect the river's water quality.

The importance and the novelty of the Court of Appeals' decision persuaded us to grant certiorari. We now reverse.

II

Interstate waters have been a font of controversy since the founding of the Nation. This Court has frequently resolved disputes between States that are separated by a common river, that border the same body of water, or that are fed by the same river basin.

Among these cases are controversies between a State that introduces pollutants to a waterway and a downstream State that objects. See, e.g., Missouri v. Illinois, 200 U.S. 496 (1906). In such cases, this Court has applied principles of common law tempered by a respect for the sovereignty of the States. Compare id., at 521, with Georgia v. Tennessee Copper Co., 206 U.S. 230, 237 (1907). In forging what "may not improperly be called interstate common law," Illinois v. Milwaukee, 406 U.S. 91, 105–106 (1972) (Milwaukee I), however, we remained aware "that new federal laws and new federal regulations may in time pre-empt the field of federal common law of nuisance." Id. at 107.

In Milwaukee v. Illinois, 451 U.S. 304 (1981) (Milwaukee II), we held that the Federal Water Pollution Control Act Amendments of 1972 did just that. In addressing Illinois' claim that Milwaukee's discharges into Lake Michigan constituted a nuisance, we held that the comprehensive regulatory regime created by the 1972 amendments pre-empted Illinois' federal common law remedy. * * *

In Milwaukee II, the Court did not address whether the 1972 amendments had supplanted state common law remedies as well as the federal common law remedy. ... This Court subsequently endorsed that [remedy] in International Paper Co. v. Ouellette, 479 U.S. 481 (1987), in which Vermont property owners claimed that the pollution discharged into Lake Champlain by a paper company located in New York constituted a nuisance under Vermont law. The Court held the Clean Water Act taken "as a whole, its purposes and its history" pre-empted an action based on the law of the affected State and that the only state law applicable to an interstate discharge is "the law of the State in which the point source is located." Id., at 493, 487. * * *

Unlike the foregoing cases, this litigation involves not a state-issued permit, but a federally issued permit. To explain the significance of this distinction, we comment further on the statutory scheme before addressing the specific issues raised by the parties.

III

The Clean Water Act anticipates a partnership between the States and the Federal Government, animated by a shared objective: "to restore and maintain the chemical, physical, and biological integrity of the Nation's waters." 33 U.S.C. § 1251(a). Toward this end, the Act provides for two sets of water quality measures. "Effluent limitations" are promulgated by the EPA and restrict the quantities, rates, and concentrations of specified substances which are discharged from point sources. See §§ 1311, 1314. "[W]ater quality standards" are, in general, promulgated by the States and establish the desired condition of a waterway. See § 1313. These standards supplement effluent limitations "so that numerous point sources, despite individual compliance with effluent limitations, may be further regulated to prevent water quality from falling below acceptable levels." EPA v. California ex rel. State Water Resources Control Bd., 426 U.S. 200, 205 n.12 (1976).

The EPA provides States with substantial guidance in the drafting of water quality standards. See generally 40 CFR pt. 131 (1991) (setting forth model water quality standards). Moreover, § 303 of the Act requires, inter alia, that state authorities periodically review water quality standards and secure the EPA's approval of any revisions in the standards. If the EPA recommends changes to the standards and the State fails to comply with that recommendation, the Act authorizes the EPA to promulgate water quality standards for the State. 33 U.S.C. § 1313(c).

The primary means for enforcing these limitations and standards is the NPDES, enacted in 1972 as a critical part of Congress' "complete rewriting" of federal water pollution law. Milwaukee II, 451 U.S., at 317. Section 301(a) of the Act, 33 U.S.C. § 1311(a), generally prohibits the discharge of any effluent into a navigable body of water unless the point source has obtained an NPDES permit. Section 402 establishes the NPDES permitting regime, and describes two types of permitting systems: state permit programs that must satisfy federal requirements and be approved by the EPA, and a federal program administered by the EPA.

Section 402(b) authorizes each State to establish "its own permit program for discharges into navigable waters within its jurisdiction." 33 U.S.C. § 1342(b). Among the requirements the state program must satisfy are the procedural protections for downstream States discussed in Ouellette and Milwaukee II. See §§ 1342(b)(3), (5). Although these provisions do not authorize the downstream State to veto the issuance of a permit for a new point source in another State, the Administrator retains authority to block the issuance of any state-issued permit that is outside the guidelines and requirements of the Act. § 1342(d)(2).

In the absence of an approved state program, the EPA may issue an NPDES permit under § 402(a) of the Act. (In these cases, for example, because Arkansas had not been authorized to issue NPDES permits when the Fayetteville plant was completed, the permit was issued by the EPA itself.) The EPA's permit program is subject to the "same terms, conditions, and requirements" as a state permit program. 33 U.S.C. § 1342(a)(3). Notwithstanding this general symmetry, the EPA has construed the Act as requiring that EPA-issued NPDES permits also comply with § 401(a). That section, which predates § 402 and the NPDES, applies to a broad category of federal licenses, and sets forth requirements for "[a]ny applicant for a Federal license or permit to conduct any activity including, but not limited to, the construction or operation of facilities, which may result in any discharge into the navigable waters." 33 U.S.C. § 1341(a). Section 401(a)(2) appears to prohibit the issuance of any federal license or permit over the objection of an affected State unless compliance with the affected State's water quality requirements can be ensured.

IV

The parties have argued three analytically distinct questions concerning the interpretation of the Clean Water Act. First, does the Act require the EPA, in crafting and issuing a permit to a point source in one State, to apply the water quality standards of downstream States? Second, even if the Act does not require as much, does the Agency have the statutory authority to mandate such compliance? Third, does the Act provide, as the Court of Appeals held, that once a body of water fails to meet water quality standards no discharge that yields effluent that reach the degraded waters will be permitted?

In these cases, it is neither necessary nor prudent for us to resolve the first of these questions. In issuing the Fayetteville permit, the EPA assumed it was obligated by both the Act and its own regulations to ensure that the Fayetteville discharge would not violate Oklahoma's standards. As we discuss below, this assumption was permissible and reasonable and therefore there is no need for us to address whether the Act requires as much. * * *

Our decision not to determine at this time the scope of the Agency's statutory obligations does not affect our resolution of the second question, which concerns the Agency's statutory authority. Even if the Clean Water Act itself does not require the Fayetteville discharge to comply with Oklahoma's water quality standards, the statute clearly does not limit the EPA's authority to mandate such compliance.

Since 1973, EPA regulations have provided that an NPDES permit shall not be issued "[w]hen the imposition of conditions cannot ensure compliance with the applicable water quality requirements of all affected States." Those regulations—relied upon by the EPA in the issuance of the Fayetteville permit—constitute a reasonable exercise of the Agency's statutory authority.

Congress has vested in the Administrator broad discretion to establish conditions for NPDES permits. Section 402(a)(2) provides that for EPA-issued permits "[t]he Administrator shall prescribe conditions . . . to assure compliance with the requirements of [§ 402(a)(1)] and such other requirements as he deems appropriate." 33 U.S.C. § 1342(a)(2) (emphasis added). Similarly, Congress preserved for the Administrator broad authority to oversee state permit programs * * *.

The regulations relied on by the EPA were a perfectly reasonable exercise of the Agency's statutory discretion. The application of state water quality standards in the interstate context is wholly consistent with the Act's broad purpose "to restore and maintain the chemical, physical, and biological integrity of the Nation's waters." 33 U.S.C. § 1251(a). Moreover, as noted above, § 301(b)(1)(C) expressly identifies the achievement of state water quality standards as one of the Act's central objectives. The Agency's regulations conditioning NPDES permits are a well-tailored means of achieving this goal.

* * * Arkansas argues that regulations requiring compliance with downstream standards are at odds with the legislative history of the Act and with the statutory scheme established by the Act. Although we agree with Arkansas that the Act's legislative history indicates that Congress intended to grant the Administrator discretion in his oversight of the issuance of NPDES permits, we find nothing in that history to indicate that Congress intended to preclude the EPA from establishing a general requirement that such permits be conditioned to ensure compliance with downstream water quality standards.

Similarly, we agree with Arkansas that in the Clean Water Act Congress struck a careful balance among competing policies and interests, but do not find the EPA regulations concerning the application of downstream water quality standards at all incompatible with that balance. Congress, in crafting the Act, protected certain sovereign interests of the States; for example, § 510 allows States to adopt more demanding pollution-control standards than those established under the Act. Arkansas emphasizes that § 510 preserves such state authority only as it is applied to the waters of the regulating State. Even assuming Arkansas' construction of § 510 is correct,

* * * that section only concerns state authority and does not constrain the EPA's authority to promulgate reasonable regulations requiring point sources in one State to comply with water quality standards in downstream States.

For these reasons, we find the EPA's requirement that the Fayetteville discharge comply with Oklahoma's water quality standards to be a reasonable exercise of the Agency's substantial statutory discretion. Cf. Chevron U.S.A. Inc. v. Natural Resources Defense Council, Inc., 467 U.S. 837, 842–845 (1984).

V

The Court of Appeals construed the Clean Water Act to prohibit any discharge of effluent that would reach waters already in violation of existing water quality standards. We find nothing in the Act to support this reading.

The interpretation of the statute adopted by the court had not been advanced by any party during the Agency or court proceedings. * * * Although the Act contains several provisions directing compliance with state water quality standards, see, e.g., § 1311(b)(1)(C), the parties have pointed to nothing that mandates a complete ban on discharges into a waterway that is in violation of those standards. The statute does, however, contain provisions designed to remedy existing water quality violations and to allocate the burden of reducing undesirable discharges between existing sources and new sources. See, e.g., § 1313(d). Thus, rather than establishing the categorical ban announced by the Court of Appeals—which might frustrate the construction of new plants that would improve existing conditions—the Clean Water Act vests in the EPA and the States broad authority to develop long-range, area-wide programs to alleviate and eliminate existing pollution. See, e.g., § 1288(b)(2).

To the extent that the Court of Appeals relied on its interpretation of the Act to reverse the EPA's permitting decision, that reliance was misplaced.

[EPA's] interpretation of the Oklahoma standards is certainly reasonable and consistent with the purposes and principles of the Clean Water Act. * * * Moreover, this interpretation of the Oklahoma standards makes eminent sense in the interstate context: If every discharge that had some theoretical impact on a downstream State were interpreted as "degrading" the downstream waters, downstream States might wield an effective veto over upstream discharges.

The EPA's application of those standards in these cases was also sound. On remand, the ALJ scrutinized the record and made explicit factual findings regarding four primary measures of water quality under the Oklahoma standards: eutrophication, esthetics, dissolved oxygen, and metals. In each case, the ALJ found that the Fayetteville discharge would not lead to a detectable change in water quality. He therefore concluded that the Fayetteville discharge would not violate the Oklahoma water quality standards. Because we agree with the Agency's Chief Judicial Officer that these findings are supported by substantial evidence, we conclude that the Court of Appeals should have affirmed both the EPA's construction of the regulations and the issuance of the Fayetteville permit.

* * * [End.]

The CWA also allows EPA and states to set more stringent requirements wherever technology-based standards alone are not sufficient to protect water quality for a particular water body. The CWA in this way seeks to protect our nation's waters by requiring states to take certain measures to ensure both that safe and healthy waters not become more polluted and that impaired waters are restored. To meet these objectives, Congress requires the listing and assignment of priorities to impaired waters, the establishment of pollutant load limitations for such impaired waters to ensure that they meet water quality standards, and the development of a plan to comply with such standards for all waters now and in the future. These requirements are examined in the following passages.

QUESTIONS

1. What happened in this case?
2. What was/were the issue/issues?
3. How did the Court resolve it/them, and why?
4. What are the strengths and weaknesses in the Court's reasoning?

EXCERPT: JAMES R. MAY, UNFINISHED BUSINESS RESTORING WATER QUALITY IN DELAWARE

Del. Lawyer 14 (1998)

The great commercial and social traditions of Delaware revolve around ready access to clean, dependable water. A century ago, DuPont depended on the fast, clean-flowing Brandy-wine to fuel its first powder mills and usher in the petrochemical revolution. Today, clean water is no less important. It goes without saying that clean water is important for fish and wildlife and their habitat in the State. But what we often forget is that clean water is essential to Delaware's great petrochemical, pharmaceutical, agricultural and animal farming, automotive, port, fishing, crabbing, housing, shopping, motel, restaurant, and tourism industries. The State's manufacturing sector depends on clean water to run efficiently. By maintaining property values, clean water is good for homeowners and developers. It helps keep health care, taxes, and insurance costs down. In short, clean water is essential to the success of our State's economy, sustains our values and quality of life, and is good for business.

There is no shortage of water bodies in Delaware. Delaware contains approximately: 3,160 miles of rivers and streams; 4,500 acres of lakes, reservoirs, and ponds; 132,000 acres of freshwaters wetlands; 89,760 acres of coastal and tidal wetlands; 866 square miles of estuaries and bays; and, 25 ocean coastal miles. Until a quarter century ago, we treated much of these waters with contempt. Our most important and historic rivers, the Delaware, the Christina, the Brandywine, the Indian, the Nanticoke and others were virtually devoid of life. Devoid of fish. Devoid of people enjoying these waters. Devoid of residential and commercial developments. Devoid of fishers earning a living from these affected waters. So twenty-five years ago, the Governor of Delaware and each of our federally elected officials enthusiastically supported the Clean Water Act (hereafter "CWA"), which was a bipartisan effort to clean up the nation's--and Delaware's--waters. With the CWA, Congress declared war on pollution. The authors of CWA aspired to making all waters safe and healthy and to eliminating all discharges of pollution. Water quality in Delaware has correspondingly improved. The stench is gone from the Delaware and Christina Rivers and people and fish are returning to these living resources. Delaware's coastal tourism has never been more robust.

Unfortunately, however, most of Delaware's waters still do not meet the water quality standards established to protect human health and aquatic life. Astoundingly, a full ninety percent of inspected rivers and streams and three-quarters of lakes do not comply with water quality standards. Fish advisories plague scores of our waters, including the Christina and the Brandywine. Health advisories still plague many of our coastal waters, many in coastal communities. Blue crab populations are in imminent peril. A toxic organism, pfeisteria piscieida, continually threatens our health and fishing industries. Sea lettuce grows with abandon in artificially nutrient-rich waters to the detriment of aquatic life. A myriad of pollutants or other stressors and sources are responsible, including bacteria, nutrients like nitrogen and phosphorous, dissolved oxygen, PCBs, zinc, chlorinated benzenes, chlorinated pesticides, metals and temperature. These are discharged by point sources (such as a plant or factory), and non-point sources (such as farms, parking lots, lawns, roadways and Superfund sites, contaminated groundwater discharges to surface water, and atmospheric deposition) with little or no prospect of enforcement by governmental agencies.

Worse still, we do not understand the extent of the State's water quality problems because most of Delaware's waters have yet to be inspected to see if they meet "water quality standards" ("WQSs"). Surprisingly, in the CWA's twenty-five year history, only about 3 percent of estuarine waters, 15 percent of river and stream miles and 60 percent of lakes have been assessed, and wetlands and coastal waters have not been assessed for compliance with water quality standards.

By now, EPA and the State of Delaware were supposed to have worked together to restore the State's most polluted waters.

They were to have identified and assigned priorities to all of the "water quality limited segments" or "WQLSs" in the State, which are waters that are not safe and healthy for fish and people. They were to have set "total maximum daily loads," or "TMDLs," and "total maximum daily thermal loads," or "TMDTLs," which is the amount of pollution that can be absorbed before a body of water ceases to meet WQLs. They were to have developed a "continuing planning process" or "CPP," for the State, which is a continually upgraded plan for ensuring that State waters meet WQSs at all times. They were to have set WQSs for all waters, including wetlands.

Unfortunately, these requirements have largely gone unmet in Delaware. Most of the State's waters have not been surveyed. Many impaired waters have not been identified. There are 159 known waters needing TMDLs or TMDTLs, but not a single one has yet been developed. The State has never developed a CPP. There are no water quality standards for wetlands. By and large, EPA has stood by, watching quietly, unwilling to intervene until and unless ordered to do so by a federal court.

In August of 1996, the inevitable happened. The Widener University School of Law Environmental Law Clinic brought suit on behalf of the Sierra Club, the American Littoral Society and the Delaware Riverkeeper Network to restore Delaware's waters. American Littoral Society and Sierra Club v. EPA, (D. Del., 1996) Civ. Action No. 591 - SLR. The CWA requirements the lawsuit sought to vindicate, and how EPA agreed to settle the action, are described below.

I. REQUIREMENTS OF THE CWA

B. Water Quality Standards and Implementation Plans: Section 303.

Entitled "Water Quality Standards and Implementation Plans," section 303 of the CWA specifies the efforts that states must make to maintain water quality and eliminate pollution. The section requires states to adopt state WQSs, which must subsequently be approved by the EPA. States are then required to review, and when necessary, revise these standards at least once every three years. In accord, EPA and Delaware have spent the better part of the last quarter century developing WQSs to protect the people and wildlife who use Delaware's waters. Delaware's most recent WQSs set numerical, narrative, and anti-degradation requirements to protect swimming, fishing, recreation, drinking, aquatic life support, and other uses.

But setting standards is an exercise in futility unless the standards are actually met. Fortunately, as the United States Supreme Court has noted, section 303 "contain[s] provisions designed to remedy existing water quality violations and to allocate the burden of reducing undesirable discharges between existing sources and new sources."

1. Identification of Water Quality Limited Segments

A WQLS is any water that does not meet or is not expected to meet an applicable WQS even after the application of technology-based effluent limitations (required by sections 301(b) or 306), and for which controls on thermal discharges are not stringent enough to assure protection and propagation of indigenous shellfish, fish, and wildlife. All WQLSs within each state must be identified every two years in a "section 303(d) submission." The section 303(d) submission must comprise all state waters that are exceeding standards because of point, nonpoint, or natural sources of pollution. The section 303(d) submission must then assign priorities to the targeted waters in the order of use and severity of nonattainment. The underlying scientific rationale for its establishment must accompany the submission. It must also "assemble and evaluate all existing and readily available water quality-related data and information" used to develop the WQLS list. Further, it must provide documentation to support any determinations to identify or not to identify any waters as required by either section 303(d)(1) or its implementing regulation. This documentation must include, at a minimum:
(i) a description of the methodology used to develop the list;

(ii) a description of the data and information used to identify waters;

(iii) a rationale for any decision not to use existing and readily available water quality-related data and information as required by 40 C.F.R. 130.7(b)(5); and

(iv) any other reasonable information requested by EPA.

The section 303(d) submission's priority ranking must "specifically include the identification of waters targeted for TMDL development in the next two years." To ensure that the 303(d) submission "identifies" all impaired waters, as required, the state must monitor and assess all state waters. If the state fails to comply with any of these requirements, then EPA must do so.

2. Total Maximum Daily Loads (TMDLs) and Total Maximum Daily Thermal Loads (TMDTLs).

To ensure that WQSs are met, either the state or EPA must develop TMDLS or TMDTLs for each WQLS. TMDLS and TMDTLs are the maximum amount of pollution (including heat) an impaired water can withstand before it no longer attains water quality standards. TMDLs are the sum of individual "wasteload allocations" for point source and "load allocations" for nonpoint and natural sources of pollution. TMDTLs are an estimation of the maximum heat input that a WQLS may tolerate to ensure protection and propagation of a balanced, indigenous population of shellfish, fish and wildlife. Once initially approved, TMDL and TMDTL submissions must then be updated with each 303(d) submission. Once again, if a state fails to develop adequate load reductions, then EPA must do so.

Once TMDLs and TMDTLs are established, they must be incorporated into NPDES permits. CWA and its regulations prohibit the issuance of an NPDES permit if it will cause or contribute to non-compliance of WQSs. Moreover, EPA regulations prohibit the issuance of any permit if the terms and conditions it contains would fail to ensure compliance with any applicable water quality requirements. Further, new NPDES permits must include conditions meeting effluent limitations and standards under section 303. An existing permit may be modified if information received by

EPA indicate that its cumulative effects on the environment are unacceptable. The process for implementing TMDL and TMDTLs must be described in the State water quality management plan.

3. Implementing Water Quality Standards: The Continuous Planning Process.

To integrate all of the activities required by section 303, section 303(e) of the CWA requires a continuous planning process (CPP) to ensure that water quality standards are met. This plan must be submitted to EPA for its approval. The CPP must, inter alia, describe the process for establishing TMDLs and TMDTLs and incorporate the approved TMDLs and TMDTLs to ensure that water quality management is coordinated. After initial approval of the CPP, EPA must "from time to time review each state's approved planning process for the purpose of insuring that the planning process is at all times consistent with the CWA." The CWA and its accompanying regulations prohibit EPA *21 from approving any CWA permit program for any state which does not have an approved CPP.

III. REQUIREMENTS OF CONSENT ORDER AND AGREEMENT

Following initiation of the above discussed lawsuit in the U.S. District Court of Delaware, the plaintiffs, EPA and the State worked quickly to negotiate an agreement to comply with these requirements. With the assistance of mediator Edwin Naythons--a retired United States Magistrate Judge with a quarter of a century's experience with complex litigation on the federal bench in Philadelphia--the parties reached agreement by May, 1997. They then submitted a proposed Consent Order and Settlement Agreement ("Agreement") to the court for approval. Judge Sue L. Robinson approved and entered the Agreement on August 4, 1997.

The Agreement requires EPA and the State to identify all impaired waters, including waters subjected to habitat degradation from agricultural and urban activities. The Delaware Department of Natural Resources and Environmental Control ("DNREC") (with EPA oversight) will soon be evaluating a river, stream, lake pond or coastal water where you live, swim, fish, or work. EPA must then ensure that the next State's submission of impaired waters, which is due by April 1, 1998, completely considers existing and readily available information.

The Agreement requires that EPA and the State establish TMDLs and TMDTLs for all of the State's WQLSs within nine years. Some TMDLs and TMDTLs will be established sooner and others later. For example, EPA has already proposed a TMDL for the Appoquinimink River. TMDLs for the Nanticoke, Indian, Lower Broad and the Choptank and other waters must be established in 1998. All other TMDLs and TMDTLs for the WQLSs in each of Delaware's five basins (Piedmont, Delaware Estuary, Delaware Bay, Inland Bays and Chesapeake) must be established in accordance with the times specified in the Agreement. EPA and the State must work together to apply TMDLs and TMDTLs to those point and nonpoint sources responsible for contributing the type of pollutant or stressor causing impairment. It also requires that the State develop, and EPA review, a CPP.

Other provisions require EPA to evaluate the State's water quality and its water quality programs, address wetlands, and coordinate its activities with federal wildlife agencies. TMDLs and TMDTLs must then be allocated to point and nonpoint sources, and incorporated into the State's CPP.

The Agreement aims to be flexible. Its requirements will be integrated with the programs that already have good potential to work well in the State. For example, the Agreement provides for its integration with the State's commendable and forward-looking whole-basin management approach.

The Agreement has specific deadlines that may be enforced in federal court if needs be. Thus far EPA and the State have met the Agreement's deadlines. Besides establishing a TMDL for the Appoquinimink, EPA has conducted its comprehensive assessment of the State's water quality program. It has developed guidance regarding the use of data and information including biological and habitat indicators.

DNREC is contributing to EPA's compliance efforts. It has entered into a Memorandum of Understanding with EPA to effectuate compliance. It has published its own TMDL Implementation Program. It has developed an approach to have the Agreement coordinated with the State's much vaunted Whole Basin Management Plan. It has provided technical assistance to EPA's efforts to develop a TMDL for the Appoquinimink. It is developing its inaugural CPP.

Despite the marginal successes of the CWA, water quality in Delaware remains in jeopardy, but the Agreement provides the needed tools to restore the State's polluted waters. Within a decade the State's impaired waters should be cleaner. Federally protected species should be better conserved. Our tax dollars should be put to more effective use. People and aquatic life who use the State's waters should be better protected. Both the State's environment and its economy should be better sustained.

CHAPTER 5: THE CLEAN AIR ACT

This chapter turns to the CWA's messier but more ambitious cousin, the Clean Air Act (CAA). The CAA is sort of a box of chocolates, you never know what you're going to get in word or decision. That said, as Part I explains, it's been another widely successful federal law in improving public health throughout the nation. The CAA's primary objective is to achieve national "ambient air quality standards" designed to ensure that the air is safe to breathe for everyone, everywhere, as Part II explores. Like the CWA, the CAA has a permit requirement, although not for all emissions. Like the CWA, those who need a permit must also comply with technology-based controls that EPA establishes and states implement (Part III), including for hazardous air pollutants (Part IV). One of the CAA's innovations is a market-based scheme to address acid deposition (Part V).

I.   INTRODUCTION TO THE CLEAN AIR ACT

Just about everything we do creates air pollution. The largest sources of air pollution are energy and transportation. The majority of electricity in the United States still comes from burning fossil fuels such as coal and natural gas. As much as 25 percent of all air pollution comes from getting around: driving internal-combustion fueled automobiles; flying an airliner to wherever you're going; even public transportation (buses) and diesel-driven trains (most of them). And, these days, giant forest fires in Canada like humanity has never seen are polluting the air hundreds if not thousands of miles away, including where I sit as I write this.

Air pollution causes different kinds of problems. Small particles created by burning fossil fuels and forests contribute to asthma and exacerbate lung disease. Tropospheric ozone is a heavy oxygen molecule caused by the marriage of what are known as "volatile organic compounds" (also known as hydrocarbons), nitrogen (NOx) and sunlight (think summer in Los Angeles or any major city) that causes a host of human health problems. Other pollutants resulting from burning fossil fuels diminish immunological protection, such as Sulphur Dioxide (SO_2) and Nitrogen Oxides (NOx). Hazardous air pollutants ("HAPs") like mercury (Hg). Chlorinated hydrocarbons – used, for example as conducting fluid in refrigerators, freezers and air conditioners – wreak havoc on the stratospheric ozone layer, a shield that makes life possible by protecting Earth from ultraviolet radiation. And then of course there is climate change, the result of human burning of fossil fuels, and the topic of a different chapter (although we'll touch upon it here to the extent EPA can regulate emissions of greenhouse gases).

The Clean Air Act, codified as 42 U.S.C. 7401 et seq., seeks to protect human health and the environment from emissions that pollute ambient, or outdoor, air. It requires EPA to establish minimum national standards for air quality and assigns primary responsibility to the states to assure compliance with the standards. Areas not meeting the standards, referred to as "nonattainment areas," are required to implement specified air pollution control measures. The Act establishes federal standards for mobile sources of air pollution and their fuels and for sources of 187 hazardous air pollutants, and it establishes a cap-and-trade program for the emissions that cause acid rain. It also establishes a comprehensive permit system for all major sources of air pollution. Further, it addresses the prevention of pollution in areas with clean air and protection of the stratospheric ozone layer.

II.   NATIONAL AMBIENT AIR QUALITY STANDARDS

EXCERPT: CLEAN AIR ACT: A SUMMARY OF THE ACT AND ITS MAJOR REQUIREMENTS
Congressional Research Service (Updated September 13, 2022), available at: (file:///Users/jamesmay/Desktop/RL30853.pdf

In Section 109, the act requires EPA to establish National Ambient Air Quality Standards (NAAQS) for air pollutants that endanger public health or welfare, in the administrator's judgment, and whose presence in ambient air results from numerous or diverse sources. The NAAQS must be designed to protect public health with an adequate margin of safety and to protect public welfare from any known or anticipated adverse effects. Using this authority, EPA has promulgated NAAQS for six air pollutants or groups of pollutants: sulfur dioxide (SO_2), particulate matter ($PM_{2.5}$ and PM_{10}), nitrogen dioxide (NO_2), carbon monoxide (CO), ozone, and lead. The act requires EPA to review the scientific data upon which the standards are based every five years, and revise the standards, if necessary. More often than not, EPA has taken more than five years in reviewing the standards, but the establishment of a deadline has allowed interested parties to force review of the standards by filing suit.
Originally, the act required that the NAAQS be attained by 1977 at the latest, but the states experienced widespread difficulty in complying with this deadline. As a result, the deadlines for achieving NAAQS have been extended several times. Under the 1990 amendments, most areas not in attainment with NAAQS must meet special compliance schedules, staggered according to the severity of an area's air pollution problem. The amendments also established specific requirements for each nonattainment category, as described below.

While the act authorizes EPA to set NAAQS, the states are responsible for establishing procedures to attain and maintain the standards. Under Section 110 of the act, the states adopt plans, known as State Implementation Plans (SIPs), and submit them to EPA to ensure that they are adequate to meet statutory requirements.

SIPs are based on emission inventories and computer models to determine whether air quality violations will occur. If these data show that standards would be exceeded, the state must impose additional controls on existing sources to ensure that emissions do not cause "exceedances" of the standards. Proposed new and modified sources must obtain state construction permits in which the applicant shows how the anticipated emissions will not exceed allowable limits. In nonattainment areas, emissions from new or modified sources must also be offset by reductions in emissions from existing sources.

The 1990 amendments require EPA to impose sanctions in areas which fail to submit a SIP, fail to submit an adequate SIP, or fail to implement a SIP: unless the state corrects such failures, a 2-to-1 emissions offset for the construction of new polluting sources is imposed 18 months after notification to the state, and a ban on most new federal highway grants is imposed 6 months later. An additional ban on air quality grants is discretionary. Ultimately, a Federal Implementation Plan may be imposed if the state fails to submit or implement an adequate SIP. The amendments also require that, in nonattainment areas, no federal permits or financial assistance may be granted for activities that do not "conform" to a SIP. This requirement can cause a temporary suspension in funding for most new highway and transit projects if an area fails to demonstrate that the emissions caused by such projects are consistent with attainment and maintenance of ambient air quality standards. Demonstrating conformity of transportation plans and SIPs is required in nonattainment areas whenever new plans are submitted.

The non-delegation doctrine bubbled up under the Clean Air Act in American Trucking Ass'n v. EPA. At issue in that case was Congress' instruction to EPA to establish ambient air quality standards that "are requisite to protect the public health." Despite ample supposition that the case raised the prospect of a resurgence of the doctrine, Justice Scalia writing for a unanimous Court found that the provision "falls comfortably within the scope of the discretion permitted by our precedent," as set forth in the case that follows.

WHITMAN V. AMERICAN TRUCKING ASSOCIATIONS
531 U.S. 464 (2000)

Justice Scalia delivered the [unanimous] opinion of the Court.

These cases present the following questions: (1) Whether § 109(b)(1) of the Clean Air Act (CAA) delegates legislative power to the Administrator of the Environmental Protection Agency (EPA). (2) Whether the Administrator may consider the costs of implementation in setting national ambient air quality standards (NAAQS) under § 109(b)(1). (3) Whether the Court of Appeals had jurisdiction to review the EPA's interpretation of Part D of Title I of the CAA, 42 U. S. C. §§ 7501–7515, with respect to implementing the revised ozone NAAQS. (4) If so, whether the EPA's interpretation of that part was permissible.

[The excerpts below are limited to the SCOTUS's treatment of the non-delegation issue. Internal references omitted.]

I.
Section 109(a) of the CAA requires the Administrator of the EPA to promulgate NAAQS for each air pollutant for which "air quality criteria" have been issued under § 108. Once a NAAQS has been promulgated, the Administrator must review the standard (and the criteria on which it is based) "at five-year intervals" and make "such revisions . . . as may be appropriate." CAA § 109(d)(1). These cases arose when, on July 18, 1997, the Administrator revised the NAAQS for particulate matter and ozone. American Trucking Associations, Inc., and other private companies, [and] the States of Michigan, Ohio, and West Virginia—challenged the new standards in the Court of Appeals for the District of Columbia Circuit [].

The District of Columbia Circuit accepted some of the challenges and rejected others. It agreed with the respondents that § 109(b)(1) delegated legislative power to the Administrator in contravention of the United States Constitution, Art. I, § 1, because it found that the EPA had interpreted the statute to provide no "intelligible principle" to guide the agency's exercise of authority. American Trucking Assns., Inc. v. EPA, 175 F. 3d 1027, 1034 (1999). The court thought, however, that the EPA could perhaps avoid the unconstitutional delegation by adopting a restrictive construction of § 109(b)(1), so instead of declaring the section unconstitutional the court remanded the NAAQS to the agency. (On this delegation point, Judge Tatel dissented, finding the statute constitutional as written. [] On the EPA's petition for rehearing, the panel adhered to its position on these points, and unanimously rejected the EPA's new argument that the court lacked jurisdiction to reach the implementation question because there had been no "final" implementation action. American Trucking Assns., Inc. v. EPA, 195 F. 3d 4 (CADC 1999).

The Court of Appeals denied the EPA's suggestion for rehearing en banc, with five judges dissenting.

The Administrator and the EPA petitioned this Court for review .... We granted certiorari on both petitions, 529 U. S. 1129 (2000); 530 U. S. 1202 (2000), and scheduled the cases for argument in tandem. We have now consolidated the cases for purposes of decision.

[In Part II of its opinion, the Court rejected the Petitioners' argument that EPA is required to consider costs in setting national ambient air quality standards].

III.
Section 109(b)(1) of the CAA instructs the EPA to set "ambient air quality standards the attainment and maintenance of which in the judgment of the Administrator, based on [the] criteria [documents of § 108] and allowing an adequate margin of safety, are requisite to protect the public health." The Court of Appeals held that this section as interpreted by the Administrator did not provide an "intelligible principle" to guide the EPA's exercise of authority in setting NAAQS. "[The] EPA," it said, "lack[ed] any determinate criteria for drawing lines. It has failed to state intelligibly how much is too much." 175 F. 3d, at 1034. The court hence found that the EPA's interpretation (but not the statute itself) violated the nondelegation doctrine. Id., at 1038. We disagree.

In a delegation challenge, the constitutional question is whether the statute has delegated legislative power to the agency. Article I, § 1, of the Constitution vests "[a]ll legislative Powers herein granted . . . in a Congress of the United States." This text permits no delegation of those powers, Loving v. United States, 517 U. S. 748, 771 (1996); see id., at 776–777 (Scalia, J., concurring in part and concurring in judgment), and so we repeatedly have said that when Congress confers decisionmaking authority upon agencies Congress must "lay down by legislative act an intelligible principle to which the person or body authorized to [act] is directed to conform." J. W. Hampton, Jr., & Co. v. United States, 276 U. S. 394, 409 (1928). We have never suggested that an agency can cure an unlawful delegation of legislative power by adopting in its discretion a limiting construction of the statute. Both Fahey v. Mallonee, 332 U. S. 245, 252–253 (1947), and Lichter v. United States, 334 U. S. 742, 783 (1948), mention agency regulations in the course of their nondelegation discussions, but Lichter did so because a subsequent Congress had incorporated the regulations into a revised version of the statute, ibid., and Fahey because the customary practices in the area, implicitly incorporated into the statute, were reflected in the regulations, 332 U. S., at 250.

The idea that an agency can cure an unconstitutionally standardless delegation of power by declining to exercise some of that power seems to us internally contradictory. The very choice of which portion of the power to exercise—that is to say, the prescription of the standard that Congress had omitted— would itself be an exercise of the forbidden legislative authority. Whether the statute delegates legislative power is a question for the courts, and an agency's voluntary selfdenial has no bearing upon the answer.

We agree with the Solicitor General that the text of § 109(b)(1) of the CAA at a minimum requires that "[f]or a discrete set of pollutants and based on published air quality criteria that reflect the latest scientific knowledge, [the] EPA must establish uniform national standards at a level that is requisite to protect public health from the adverse effects of the pollutant in the ambient air." Tr. of Oral Arg. In No. 99–1257, p. 5. Requisite, in turn, "mean[s] sufficient, but not more than necessary." Id., at 7. These limits on the EPA's discretion are strikingly similar to the ones we approved in Touby v. United States, 500 U. S. 160 (1991), which permitted the Attorney General to designate a drug as a controlled substance for purposes of criminal drug enforcement if doing so was " 'necessary to avoid an imminent hazard to the public safety.' " Id., at 163. They also resemble the Occupational Safety and Health Act of 1970 provision requiring the agency to " 'set the standard which most adequately assures, to the extent feasible, on the basis of the best available evidence, that no employee will suffer any impairment of health' "—which the Court upheld in Industrial Union Dept., AFL–CIO v. American Petroleum Institute, 448 U. S. 607, 646 (1980), and which even then-Justice Rehnquist, who alone in that case thought the statute violated the nondelegation doctrine, see id., at 671 (opinion concurring in judgment), would have upheld if, like the statute here, it did not permit economic costs to be considered. See American Textile Mfrs. Institute, Inc. v. Donovan, 452 U. S. 490, 545 (1981) (Rehnquist, J., dissenting).

The scope of discretion § 109(b)(1) allows is in fact well within the outer limits of our nondelegation precedents. In the history of the Court we have found the requisite "intelligible principle" lacking in only two statutes, one of which provided literally no guidance for the exercise of discretion, and the other of which conferred authority to regulate the entire economy on the basis of no more precise a standard than stimulating the economy by assuring "fair competition." See Panama Refining Co. v. Ryan, 293 U. S. 388 (1935); A. L. A. Schechter Poultry Corp. v. United States, 295 U. S. 495 (1935). We have, on the other hand, upheld the validity of § 11(b)(2) of the Public Utility Holding Company Act of 1935, 49 Stat. 821, which gave the Securities and Exchange Commission authority to modify the structure of holding company systems so as to ensure that they are not "unduly or unnecessarily complicate[d]" and do not "unfairly or inequitably distribute voting power among security holders." American Power & Light Co. v. SEC, 329 U. S. 90, 104 (1946). We have approved the wartime conferral of agency power to fix the prices of commodities at a level that " 'will be generally fair and equitable and will effectuate the [in some respects conflicting] purposes of th[e] Act.' " Yakus v. United States, 321 U. S. 414, 420, 423–426 (1944). And we have found an "intelligible principle" in various statutes authorizing regulation in the "public interest." See, e. g., National Broadcasting Co. v. United States, 319 U. S. 190, 225–226 (1943) (Federal Communications Commission's power to regulate airwaves); New York Central Securities Corp. v. United States, 287 U. S. 12, 24–25 (1932) (Interstate Commerce Commission's power to approve railroad consolidations). In short, we have "almost never felt qualified to second-guess Congress regarding the permissible degree of policy judgment that can be left to those executing or applying the law." Mistretta v. United States, 488 U. S. 361, 416 (1989) (Scalia, J., dissenting); see id., at 373 (majority opinion).

It is true enough that the degree of agency discretion that is acceptable varies according to the scope of the power congressionally conferred. See Loving v. United States, 517 U. S., at 772–773; United States v. Mazurie, 419 U. S. 544, 556–557 (1975). While Congress need not provide any direction to the EPA regarding the manner in which it is to define "country elevators," which are to be exempt from new stationary- source regulations governing grain elevators, see 42 U. S. C. § 7411(i), it must provide substantial guidance on setting air standards that affect the entire national economy. But even in sweeping regulatory schemes we have never demanded, as the Court of Appeals did here, that statutes provide a "determinate criterion" for saying "how much [of the regulated harm] is too much." 175 F. 3d, at 1034. In Touby, for example, we did not require the statute to decree how "imminent" was too imminent, or how "necessary" was necessary enough, or even—most relevant here—how "hazardous" was too hazardous. 500 U. S., at 165–167. Similarly, the statute at issue in Lichter authorized agencies to recoup "excess profits" paid under wartime Government contracts, yet we did not insist that Congress specify how much profit was too much. 334 U. S., at 783–786. It is therefore not conclusive for delegation purposes that, as respondents argue, ozone and particulate matter are "nonthreshold" pollutants that inflict a continuum of adverse health effects at any airborne concentration greater than zero, and hence require the EPA to make judgments of degree. "[A] certain degree of discretion, and thus of lawmaking, inheres in most executive or judicial action." Mistretta v. United States, supra, at 417 (Scalia, J., dissenting) (emphasis deleted); see 488 U. S., at 378–379 (majority opinion). Section 109(b)(1) of the CAA, which to repeat we interpret as requiring the EPA to set air quality standards at the level that is "requisite"—that is, not lower or higher than is necessary—to protect the public health with an adequate margin of safety, fits comfortably within the scope of discretion permitted by our precedent.

We therefore reverse the judgment of the Court of Appeals remanding for reinterpretation that would avoid a supposed delegation of legislative power. It will remain for the Court of Appeals—on the remand that we direct for other reasons—to dispose of any other preserved challenge to the NAAQS under the judicial-review provisions contained in 42 U. S. C. § 7607(d)(9).

QUESTIONS

1. In light of American Trucking, what would you now say constitutes an "intelligible principle?" Do you agree that asking an agency to set a standard that is "requisite to protect human health" is sufficient?
2. Why do you think Chief Justice Rehnquist joined the unanimous majority? Why was it Justice Scalia who wrote the opinion and not the Chief Justice?
3. The SCOTUS has not confronted the doctrine squarely since 2000. Can you surmise why this might be?

A. REGULATED POLLUTANTS

The next case covers the extent to which EPA has authority to regulate pollutants other than those covered by the NAAQS (SO2, NOx, CO, PB, VOCs and PM2.5), namely, greenhouse gas emissions.

MASSACHUSETTS V. ENVIRONMENTAL PROTECTION AGENCY
549 U.S. 497 (2007)

STEVENS, J., delivered the opinion of the Court, in which KENNEDY, SOUTER, GINSBURG, and BREYER, JJ., joined.

A well-documented rise in global temperatures has coincided with a significant increase in the concentration of carbon dioxide in the atmosphere. Respected scientists believe the two trends are related. For when carbon dioxide is released into the atmosphere, it acts like the ceiling of a greenhouse, trapping solar energy and retarding the escape of reflected heat. It is therefore a species—the most important species—of a "greenhouse gas."

Calling global warming "the most pressing environmental challenge of our time," a group of States, local governments, and private organizations, alleged in a petition for certiorari that the Environmental Protection Agency (EPA) has abdicated its responsibility under the Clean Air Act to regulate the emissions of four greenhouse gases, including carbon dioxide. Specifically, petitioners asked us to answer two questions concerning the meaning of § 202(a)(1) of the Act: whether EPA has the statutory authority to regulate greenhouse gas emissions from new motor vehicles; and if so, whether its stated reasons for refusing to do so are consistent with the statute.

* * *

I

Section 202(a)(1) of the Clean Air Act . . . provides:

"The [EPA] Administrator shall by regulation prescribe (and from time to time revise) in accordance with the provisions of this section, standards applicable to the emission of any air pollutant from any class or classes of new motor vehicles or new motor vehicle engines, which in his judgment cause, or contribute to, air pollution which may reasonably be anticipated to endanger public health or welfare. . . ."

The Act defines "air pollutant" to include "any air pollution agent or combination of such agents, including any physical, chemical, biological, radioactive . . . substance or matter which is emitted into or otherwise enters the ambient air." § 7602(g). "Welfare" is also defined broadly: among other things, it includes "effects on . . . weather . . . and climate." § 7602(h).

When Congress enacted these provisions, the study of climate change was in its infancy. In 1959, shortly after the U.S. Weather Bureau began monitoring atmospheric carbon dioxide levels, an observatory in Mauna Loa, Hawaii, recorded a mean level of 316 parts per million. * * * By the time Congress drafted § 202(a)(1) in 1970, carbon dioxide levels had reached 325 parts per million.

In the late 1970's, the Federal Government began devoting serious attention to the possibility that carbon dioxide emissions associated with human activity could provoke climate change. In 1978, Congress enacted the National Climate Program Act, 92 Stat. 601, which required the President to establish a program to "assist the Nation and the world to understand and respond to natural and man-induced climate processes and their implications." President Carter, in turn, asked the National Research Council, the working arm of the National Academy of Sciences, to investigate the subject. The Council's response was unequivocal: "If carbon dioxide continues to increase, the study group finds no reason to doubt that climate changes will result and no reason to believe that these changes will be negligible. . . . A wait-and-see policy may mean waiting until it is too late."

Congress next addressed the issue in 1987, when it enacted the Global Climate Protection Act, Title XI of Pub. L. 100–204, 101 Stat. 1407, note following 15 U.S.C. § 2901. * * *

Meanwhile, the scientific understanding of climate change progressed. In 1990, the Intergovernmental Panel on Climate Change (IPCC), a multinational scientific body organized under the auspices of the United Nations, published its first comprehensive report on the topic. Drawing on expert opinions from across the globe, the IPCC concluded that "emissions resulting from human activities are substantially increasing the atmospheric concentrations of . . . greenhouse gases [which] will enhance the greenhouse effect, resulting on average in an additional warming of the Earth's surface."

* * * Some five years later—after the IPCC issued a second comprehensive report in 1995 concluding that "[t]he balance of evidence suggests there is a discernible human influence on global climate"—the UNFCCC signatories met in Kyoto, Japan, and adopted a protocol that assigned mandatory targets for industrialized nations to reduce greenhouse gas emissions. Because those targets did not apply to developing and heavily polluting nations such as China and India, the Senate unanimously passed a resolution expressing its sense that the United States should not enter into the Kyoto Protocol. President Clinton did not submit the protocol to the Senate for ratification.

II

On October 20, 1999, a group of 19 private organizations filed a rulemaking petition asking EPA to regulate "greenhouse gas emissions from new motor vehicles under § 202 of the Clean Air Act." * * * Fifteen months after the petition' submission, EPA requested public comment on "all the issues raised in [the] petition," adding a "particular" request for comments on "any scientific, technical, legal, economic or other aspect of these issues that may be relevant to EPA's consideration of this petition." 66 Fed. Reg. 7486, 7487 (2001). EPA received more than 50,000 comments over the next five months. See 68 Fed. Reg. 52924 (2003).

Before the close of the comment period, the White House sought "assistance in identifying the areas in the science of climate change where there are the greatest certainties and uncertainties" from the National Research Council, asking for a response "as soon as possible." The result was a 2001 report titled *Climate Change: An Analysis of Some Key Questions* (NRC Report), which, drawing heavily on the 1995 IPCC report, concluded that "[g]reenhouse gases are accumulating in Earth's atmosphere as a result of human activities, causing surface air temperatures and subsurface ocean temperatures to rise. Temperatures are, in fact, rising." *NRC Report* 1.

On September 8, 2003, EPA entered an order denying the rulemaking petition. 68 Fed. Reg. 52922. The agency gave two reasons for its decision: (1) that contrary to the opinions of its former general counsels, the Clean Air Act does not authorize EPA to issue mandatory regulations to address global climate change, see *id.*, at 52925–52929; and (2) that even if the agency had the authority to set greenhouse gas emission standards, it would be unwise to do so at this time, *id.*, at 52929–52931.

In concluding that it lacked statutory authority over greenhouse gases, EPA observed that Congress "was well aware of the global climate change issue when it last comprehensively amended the [Clean Air Act] in 1990," yet it declined to adopt a proposed amendment establishing binding emissions limitations. *Id.*, at 52926. Congress instead chose to authorize further investigation into climate change. *Ibid.* (citing §§ 103(g) and 602(e) of the Clean Air Act Amendments of 1990, 104 Stat. 2652, 2703, 42 U.S.C. §§ 7403(g)(1) and 7671a(e)). * * *

EPA stated that it was "urged on in this view" by this Court's decision in *FDA v. Brown & Williamson Tobacco Corp.*, 529 U.S. 120 (2000). In that case, relying on "tobacco['s] unique political history," *id.*, at 159, we invalidated the Food and Drug Administration's reliance on its general authority to regulate drugs as a basis for asserting jurisdiction over an "industry constituting a significant portion of the American economy," *ibid.*

EPA reasoned that climate change had its own "political history": Congress designed the original Clean Air Act to address *local* air pollutants rather than a substance that "is fairly consistent in its concentration throughout the *world's* atmosphere," 68 Fed. Reg. 52927 (emphasis added); declined in 1990 to enact proposed amendments to force EPA to set carbon dioxide emission standards for motor vehicles, *ibid.* (citing H.R. 5966, 101st Cong., 2d Sess. (1990)); and addressed global climate change in other legislation, 68 Fed. Reg. 52927. Because of this political history, and because imposing emission limitations on greenhouse gases would have even greater economic and political repercussions than regulating tobacco, EPA was persuaded that it lacked the power to do so. In essence, EPA concluded that climate change was so important that unless Congress spoke with exacting specificity, it could not have meant the agency to address it.

Having reached that conclusion, EPA believed it followed that greenhouse gases cannot be "air pollutants" within the meaning of the Act. * * *

Even assuming that it had authority over greenhouse gases, EPA explained in detail why it would refuse to exercise that authority. The agency began by recognizing that the concentration of greenhouse gases has dramatically increased as a result of human activities, and acknowledged the attendant increase in global surface air temperatures. EPA nevertheless gave controlling importance to the NRC Report's statement that a causal link between the two " 'cannot be unequivocally established.' " Given that residual uncertainty, EPA concluded that regulating greenhouse gas emissions would be unwise.

The agency furthermore characterized any EPA regulation of motor-vehicle emissions as a "piecemeal approach" to climate change, and stated that such regulation would conflict with the

President's "comprehensive approach" to the problem. That approach involves additional support for technological innovation, the creation of nonregulatory programs to encourage voluntary private-sector reductions in greenhouse gas emissions, and further research on climate change—not actual regulation. According to EPA, unilateral EPA regulation of motor-vehicle greenhouse gas emissions might also hamper the President's ability to persuade key developing countries to reduce greenhouse gas emissions.

III

Petitioners, now joined by intervenor States and local governments, sought review of EPA's order in the United States Court of Appeals for the District of Columbia Circuit. Although each of the three judges on the panel wrote a separate opinion, two judges agreed "that the EPA Administrator properly exercised his discretion under § 202(a)(1) in denying the petition for rule making." The court therefore denied the petition for review.

* * *

IV

[The majority found that Massachusetts had standing to bring this lawsuit.]

V

The scope of our review of the merits of the statutory issues is narrow. As we have repeated time and again, an agency has broad discretion to choose how best to marshal its limited resources and personnel to carry out its delegated responsibilities. See *Chevron U.S.A. Inc. v. Natural Resources Defense Council, Inc.,* 467 U.S. 837, 842–845 (1984). That discretion is at its height when the agency decides not to bring an enforcement action. * * *

* * * EPA concluded in its denial of the petition for rulemaking that it lacked authority under 42 U.S.C. § 7521(a)(1) to regulate new vehicle emissions because carbon dioxide is not an "air pollutant" as that term is defined in § 7602. In the alternative, it concluded that even if it possessed authority, it would decline to do so because regulation would conflict with other administration priorities. As discussed earlier, the Clean Air Act expressly permits review of such an action. § 7607(b)(1). We therefore "may reverse any such action found to be . . . arbitrary, capricious, an abuse of discretion, or otherwise not in accordance with law." § 7607(d)(9).

VI

On the merits, the first question is whether § 202(a)(1) of the Clean Air Act authorizes EPA to regulate greenhouse gas emissions from new motor vehicles in the event that it forms a "judgment" that such emissions contribute to climate change. We have little trouble concluding that it does. In relevant part, § 202(a)(1) provides that EPA "shall by regulation prescribe . . . standards applicable to the emission of any air pollutant from any class or classes of new motor vehicles or new motor vehicle engines, which in [the Administrator's] judgment cause, or contribute to, air pollution which may reasonably be anticipated to endanger public health or welfare." 42 U.S.C. § 7521(a)(1). Because EPA believes that Congress did not intend it to regulate substances that contribute to climate change, the agency maintains that carbon dioxide is not an "air pollutant" within the meaning of the provision.

The statutory text forecloses EPA's reading. The Clean Air Act's sweeping definition of "air pollutant" includes "*any* air pollution agent or combination of such agents, including *any* physical, chemical . . . substance or matter which is emitted into or otherwise enters the ambient air. . . ." § 7602(g) (emphasis added). On its face, the definition embraces all airborne compounds of whatever stripe, and underscores that intent through the repeated use of the word "any." Carbon dioxide, methane, nitrous oxide, and hydrofluorocarbons are without a doubt "physical [and] chemical ... substance [s] which [are] emitted into ... the ambient air." The statute is unambiguous.

Rather than relying on statutory text, EPA invokes postenactment congressional actions and deliberations it views as tantamount to a congressional command to refrain from regulating greenhouse gas emissions. Even if such postenactment legislative history could shed light on the meaning of an otherwise-unambiguous statute, EPA never identifies any action remotely suggesting that Congress meant to curtail its power to treat greenhouse gases as air pollutants.

* * *

EPA's reliance on *Brown & Williamson Tobacco Corp.*, 529 U.S. 120, is similarly misplaced. In holding that tobacco products are not "drugs" or "devices" subject to Food and Drug Administration (FDA) regulation pursuant to the Food, Drug and Cosmetic Act (FDCA), see 529 U.S., at 133, we found critical at least two considerations that have no counterpart in this case.

First, we thought it unlikely that Congress meant to ban tobacco products, which the FDCA would have required had such products been classified as "drugs" or "devices." *Id.*, at 135–137. Here, in contrast, EPA jurisdiction would lead to no such extreme measures. EPA would only *regulate* emissions, and even then, it would have to delay any action "to permit the development and application of the requisite technology, giving appropriate consideration to the cost of compliance," § 7521(a)(2). However much a ban on tobacco products clashed with the "common sense" intuition that Congress never meant to remove those products from circulation, *Brown & Williamson*, 529 U.S., at 133, there is nothing counterintuitive to the notion that EPA can curtail the emission of substances that are putting the global climate out of kilter.

Second, in *Brown & Williamson* we pointed to an unbroken series of congressional enactments that made sense only if adopted "against the backdrop of the FDA's consistent and repeated statements that it lacked authority under the FDCA to regulate tobacco." *Id.*, at 144. We can point to no such enactments here: EPA has not identified any congressional action that conflicts in any way with the regulation of greenhouse gases from new motor vehicles. * * *

EPA finally argues that it cannot regulate carbon dioxide emissions from motor vehicles because doing so would require it to tighten mileage standards, a job (according to EPA) that Congress has assigned to DOT. See 68 Fed. Reg. 52929. But that DOT sets mileage standards in no way licenses EPA to shirk its environmental responsibilities. * * *

While the Congresses that drafted § 202(a)(1) might not have appreciated the possibility that burning fossil fuels could lead to global warming, they did understand that without regulatory flexibility, changing circumstances and scientific developments would soon render the Clean Air Act obsolete. The broad language of § 202(a)(1) reflects an intentional effort to confer the flexibility necessary to forestall such obsolescence. Because greenhouse gases fit well within the Clean Air Act's capacious definition of "air pollutant," we hold that EPA has the statutory authority to regulate the emission of such gases from new motor vehicles.

VII

The alternative basis for EPA's decision—that even if it does have statutory authority to regulate greenhouse gases, it would be unwise to do so at this time—rests on reasoning divorced from the statutory text. While the statute does condition the exercise of EPA's authority on its formation of a "judgment," 42 U.S.C. § 7521(a)(1), that judgment must relate to whether an air pollutant "cause[s], or contribute[s] to, air pollution which may reasonably be anticipated to endanger public health or welfare," *ibid.* Put another way, the use of the word "judgment" is not a roving license to ignore the statutory text. It is but a direction to exercise discretion within defined statutory limits.

* * * Under the clear terms of the Clean Air Act, EPA can avoid taking further action only if it determines that greenhouse gases do not contribute to climate change or if it provides some reasonable explanation as to why it cannot or will not exercise its discretion to determine whether they do. To the extent that this constrains agency discretion to pursue other priorities of the Administrator or the President, this is the congressional design.

EPA has refused to comply with this clear statutory command. Instead, it has offered a laundry list of reasons not to regulate. * * * Although we have neither the expertise nor the authority to evaluate these policy judgments, it is evident they have nothing to do with whether greenhouse gas emissions contribute to climate change. Still less do they amount to a reasoned justification for declining to form a scientific judgment. In particular, while the President has broad authority in foreign affairs, that authority does not extend to the refusal to execute domestic laws. * * *

Nor can EPA avoid its statutory obligation by noting the uncertainty surrounding various features of climate change and concluding that it would therefore be better not to regulate at this time. See 68 Fed. Reg. 52930–52931. If the scientific uncertainty is so profound that it precludes EPA from making a reasoned judgment as to whether greenhouse gases contribute to global warming, EPA must say so. That EPA would prefer not to regulate greenhouse gases because of some residual uncertainty—which, contrary to Justice SCALIA's apparent belief, is in fact all that it said, see 68 Fed. Reg. 52929 ("We do not believe . . . that it would be either effective or appropriate for EPA *to establish [greenhouse gas] standards for motor vehicles* at this time" (emphasis added))—is irrelevant. The statutory question is whether sufficient information exists to make an endangerment finding.

In short, EPA has offered no reasoned explanation for its refusal to decide whether greenhouse gases cause or contribute to climate change. Its action was therefore "arbitrary, capricious, . . . or otherwise not in accordance with law." 42 U.S.C. § 7607(d)(9)(A). We need not and do not reach the question whether on remand EPA must make an endangerment finding, or whether policy concerns can inform EPA's actions in the event that it makes such a finding. We hold only that EPA must ground its reasons for action or inaction in the statute.

VIII

The judgment of the Court of Appeals is reversed, and the case is remanded for further proceedings consistent with this opinion.

It is so ordered.

QUESTIONS

5. What happened in this case?
6. What was/were the issue/issues?
7. How did the Court resolve it/them, and why?
8. What are the strengths and weaknesses in the Court's reasoning?

B. NONATTAINMENT REQUIREMENTS

In a major departure from the prior law, the 1990 Clean Air Act Amendments grouped most nonattainment areas into classifications based on the extent to which the NAAQS is exceeded, and established specific pollution controls and attainment dates for each classification.

Nonattainment areas are classified on the basis of a "design value," which is derived from the pollutant concentration (in parts per million or micrograms per cubic meter) recorded by air quality monitoring devices. The design value for the one-hour ozone standard was the fourth highest hourly reading measured during the most recent three-year period. Using these design values, the act created five classes of ozone nonattainment. Initially, only Los Angeles fell into the "extreme" class, but 97 other areas were classified in one of the other four ozone categories. (The classification system and design values have since been adapted twice as the ozone standard has been revised. Under the 2015 standard, there are 49 nonattainment areas as of July 2022, all but 10 of which are classified as "marginal" or "moderate"). A simpler classification system established moderate and serious nonattainment areas for carbon monoxide and particulate matter with correspondingly more stringent control requirements for the more polluted class.

Requirements for nonattainment areas depend on the severity with which an area is out of attainment. For Ozone, it is, in ascending order: marginal, moderate, serious, severe and extreme (there are comparable divisions for CO2). The worse the nonattainment, the more requirements there are. For example, for areas that are severely out of attainment, the requirements are:

Serious Areas
- Meet all requirements for moderate areas.
- Reduce definition of a major source of VOCs from emissions of 100 tons per year to 50 tons per year for the purpose of imposing RACT.
- Reduce VOCs 3% annually for years 7 to 9 after the 15% reduction already required by year 6.
- Improve monitoring, in order to obtain more comprehensive and representative data on ozone pollution.
- Adopt an enhanced vehicle inspection and maintenance program.
- Require fleet vehicles to use clean alternative fuels.
- Adopt transportation control measures if the number of vehicle miles traveled in the area is greater than expected.
- Require 1.2 to 1 offsets.
- Adopt contingency measures if the area does not meet required VOC reductions.

Severe Areas
- Meet all requirements for serious areas.
- Reduce definition of a major source of VOCs from emissions of 50 tons per year to 25 tons per year for the purpose of imposing RACT.
- Adopt specified transportation control measures.
- Implement a reformulated gasoline program.
- Require 1.3 to 1 offsets.
- Impose $5,000 per ton penalties on major sources if the area does not meet required reductions.

III. PERMITTING AND TECHNOLOGY-BASED STANDARDS

EXCERPT: CLEAN AIR ACT: A SUMMARY OF THE ACT AND ITS MAJOR REQUIREMENTS
Congressional Research Service (Updated September 13, 2022), available at:
(file:///Users/jamesmay/Desktop/RL30853.pdf

Permits

The Clean Air Act Amendments of 1990 added a Title V to the act which requires states to administer a comprehensive permit program for the operation of sources emitting air pollutants. These requirements are modeled after similar provisions in the Clean Water Act. Previously, the Clean Air Act contained limited provision for permits, requiring only new or modified major stationary sources to obtain construction permits (under Section 165 of the act).

Sources subject to the permit requirements generally include major sources that emit or have the potential to emit 100 tons per year of any regulated pollutant, plus stationary and area sources that emit or have potential to emit lesser specified amounts of hazardous air pollutants. However, in nonattainment areas, the permit requirements also include sources which emit as little as 50, 25, or 10 tons per year of VOCs, depending on the severity of the region's ozone nonattainment status (serious, severe, or extreme).

States were required to develop permit programs and to submit those programs for EPA approval by November 15, 1993. EPA had one year to approve or disapprove a state's submission in whole or in part. After the effective date of a state plan, sources had 12 months to submit an actual permit application.

States are to collect annual fees from sources sufficient to cover the "reasonable costs" of administering the permit program, with revenues to be used to support the agency's air pollution control program. The fee must be at least $25 per ton of regulated pollutants (excluding carbon monoxide). Permitting authorities have discretion not to collect fees on emissions in excess of 4,000 tons per year and may collect other fee amounts, if appropriate.

The permit states how much of which air pollutants a source is allowed to emit. As a part of the permit process, a source must prepare a compliance plan and certify compliance. The term of permits is limited to no more than five years; sources are required to renew permits at that time. State permit authorities must notify contiguous states of permit applications that may affect them; the application and any comments of contiguous states must be forwarded to EPA for review. EPA can veto a permit; however, this authority is essentially limited to major permit changes. EPA review need not include permits which simply codify elements of a state's overall clean air plan, and EPA has discretion to not review permits for small sources. Holding a permit to some extent shields a source from enforcement actions: the act provides that a source cannot be held in violation if it is complying with explicit requirements addressed in a permit, or if the state finds that certain provisions do not apply to that source.

***

Section 111 of the act requires EPA to establish nationally uniform, technology-based standards (called New Source Performance Standards, or NSPS) for categories of new industrial facilities. These standards accomplish two goals: first, they establish a consistent baseline for pollution control that competing firms must meet, and thereby remove any incentive for states or communities to weaken air pollution standards in order to attract polluting industry; and second, they preserve clean air to accommodate future growth, as well as for its own benefits.

NSPS establish maximum emission levels for new major stationary sources—power plants, steel mills, and smelters, for example—with the emission levels determined by the best system of emission reduction (BSER) "adequately demonstrated," taking costs into account. At least every eight years, EPA must review and, if appropriate, revise NSPS applicable to designated sources, since the goal is to prevent new pollution problems from developing and to force the installation of new control technology.

The standards also apply to modifications of existing facilities, through a process called New Source Review (NSR). The law's ambiguity regarding what constitutes a modification (subject to NSR) as opposed to routine maintenance of a facility has led to litigation, with EPA proposing in recent years to modify its interpretation of the requirements of this section.

Section 111 can also be used to set standards for existing stationary sources of pollution. Under Section 111(d), EPA is to require the states to submit plans establishing standards of performance for existing sources that would be subject to NSPS if they were new, unless the sources or the pollutants regulated by the NSPS are already subject to standards under other sections of the act. This authority has rarely been used, because most pollutants and sources are subject to regulation under other sections of the act; but it served as the basis of a rulemaking intended to limit carbon dioxide emissions from existing fossil-fueled power plants, methane emissions from existing crude oil and natural gas production, transmission, and storage equipment, and methane emissions from existing municipal solid waste landfills.

***

WEST VIRGINIA V. EPA
142 S. Ct. 2587 (2022)

Chief Justice Roberts delivered the opinion of the Court.

The Clean Air Act authorizes the Environmental Protection Agency to regulate power plants by setting a "standard of performance" for their emission of certain pollutants into the air. That standard may be different for new and existing plants, but in each case it must reflect the "best system of emission reduction" that the Agency has determined to be "adequately demonstrated" for the particular category. For existing plants, the States then implement that requirement by issuing rules restricting emissions from sources within their borders.

Since passage of the Act 50 years ago, EPA has exercised this authority by setting performance standards based on measures that would reduce pollution by causing plants to operate more cleanly. In 2015, however, EPA issued a new rule concluding that the "best system of emission reduction" for existing coal-fired power plants included a requirement that such facilities reduce their own production of electricity, or subsidize increased generation by natural gas, wind, or solar sources.

The question before us is whether this broader conception of EPA's authority is within the power granted to it by the Clean Air Act.

I

A

The Clean Air Act establishes three main regulatory programs to control air pollution from stationary sources such as power plants. One program is the New Source Performance Standards program of Section 111, at issue here. The other two are the National Ambient Air Quality Standards (NAAQS) program, set out in Sections 108 through 110 of the Act, 42 U. S. C. §§7408-7410, and the Hazardous Air Pollutants (HAP) program, set out in Section 112, §7412. To understand the place and function of Section 111 in the statutory scheme, some background on the other two programs is in order.

The NAAQS program addresses air pollutants that "may reasonably be anticipated to endanger public health or welfare," and "the presence of which in the ambient air results from numerous or diverse mobile or stationary sources." §7408(a)(1). After identifying such pollutants, EPA establishes a NAAQS for each. The NAAQS represents "the maximum airborne concentration of [the] pollutant that the public health can tolerate." EPA, though, does not choose which sources must reduce their pollution and by how much to meet the ambient pollution target. Instead, Section 110 of the Act leaves that task in the first instance to the States, requiring each "to submit to [EPA] a plan designed to implement and maintain such standards within its boundaries."

The second major program governing stationary sources is the HAP program. The HAP program primarily targets pollutants, other than those already covered by a NAAQS, that present "a threat of adverse human health effects," including substances known or anticipated to be "carcinogenic, mutagenic, teratogenic, neurotoxic," or otherwise "acutely or chronically toxic."

EPA's regulatory role with respect to these toxic pollutants is different in kind from its role in administering the NAAQS program. There, EPA is generally limited to determining the maximum safe amount of covered pollutants in the air. As to each hazardous pollutant, by contrast, the Agency must promulgate emissions standards for both new and existing major sources. Those standards must "require the maximum degree of reduction in emissions . . . that the [EPA] Administrator, taking into consideration the cost of achieving such emission reduction, and any non-air quality health and environmental impacts and energy requirements, determines is achievable . . . through application of measures, processes, methods, systems or techniques" of emission reduction. In other words, EPA must directly require all covered sources to reduce their emissions to a certain level. And it chooses that level by determining the "maximum degree of reduction" it considers "achievable" in practice by using the best existing technologies and methods.

Thus, in the parlance of environmental law, Section 112 directs the Agency to impose "technology-based standard[s] for hazardous emissions. This sort of "'technology-based' approach focuses upon the control technologies that are available to industrial entities and requires the agency to . . . ensur[e] that regulated firms adopt the appropriate cleanup technology." T. McGarity, Media-Quality, Technology, and Cost-Benefit Balancing Strategies for Health and Environmental Regulation, 46 Law & Contemp. Prob. 159, 160 (Summer 1983) (McGarity). (Such "technologies" are not limited to literal technology, such as scrubbers; "changes in the design and operation" of the facility, or "in the way that employees perform their tasks," are also available options.

The third air pollution control scheme is the New Source Performance Standards program of Section 111. §7411. That section directs EPA to list "categories of stationary sources" that it determines "cause[ ], or contribute[ ] significantly to, air pollution which may reasonably be anticipated to endanger public health or welfare." Under Section 111(b), the Agency must then promulgate for each category "Federal standards of performance for new sources," §7411(b)(1)(B). A "standard of performance" is one that

> "reflects the degree of emission limitation achievable through the application of the best system of emission reduction which (taking into account the cost of achieving such

reduction and any nonair quality health and environmental impact and energy requirements) the [EPA] Administrator determines has been adequately demonstrated."

Thus, the statute directs EPA to (1) "determine[ ]," taking into account various factors, the "best system of emission reduction which . . . has been adequately demonstrated," (2) ascertain the "degree of emission limitation achievable through the application" of that system, and (3) impose an emissions limit on new stationary sources that "reflects" that amount. Generally speaking, a source may achieve that emissions cap any way it chooses; the key is that its pollution be no more than the amount "achievable through the application of the best system of emission reduction . . . adequately demonstrated," or the BSER. EPA undertakes this analysis on a pollutant-by-pollutant basis, establishing different standards of performance with respect to different pollutants emitted from the same source category.

Although the thrust of Section 111 focuses on emissions limits for new and modified sources—as its title indicates—the statute also authorizes regulation of certain pollutants from existing sources. Under Section 111(d), once EPA "has set new source standards addressing emissions of a particular pollutant under . . . section 111(b)," 80 Fed. Reg. 64711, it must then address emissions of that same pollutant by existing sources—but only if they are not already regulated under the NAAQS or HAP programs. §7411(d)(1). Existing power plants, for example, emit many pollutants covered by a NAAQS or HAP standard. Section 111(d) thus "operates as a gap-filler," empowering EPA to regulate harmful emissions not already controlled under the Agency's other authorities.

Although the States set the actual rules governing existing power plants, EPA itself still retains the primary regulatory role in Section 111(d). The Agency, not the States, decides the amount of pollution reduction that must ultimately be achieved. It does so by again determining, as when setting the new source rules, "the best system of emission reduction . . . that has been adequately demonstrated for [existing covered] facilities." The States then submit plans containing the emissions restrictions that they intend to adopt and enforce in order not to exceed the permissible level of pollution established by EPA.

Reflecting the ancillary nature of Section 111(d), EPA has used it only a handful of times since the enactment of the statute in 1970. See 80 Fed. Reg. 64703, and n. 275 (past regulations pertained to "four pollutants from five source categories"). For instance, the Agency has established emissions limits on acid mist from sulfuric acid production, 41 Fed. Reg. 48706 (1976) (identifying "fiber mist eliminator" technology as BSER); sulfide gases released by kraft pulp mills, 44 Fed. Reg. 29829 (1979) (determining BSER to be a combination of scrubbers, incineration, filtration systems, and temperature control); and emissions of various harmful gases from municipal landfills, 61 Fed. Reg. 9907 (1996) (setting BSER as use of a flare to combust the gases). It was thus only a slight overstatement for one of the architects of the 1990 amendments to the Clean Air Act to refer to Section 111(d) as an "obscure, never-used section of the law." Hearings on S. 300 et al. before the Subcommittee on Environmental Protection of the Senate Committee on Environment and Public Works, 100th Cong., 1st Sess., 13 (1987) (remarks of Sen. Durenberger).

B

Things changed in October 2015, when EPA promulgated two rules addressing carbon dioxide pollution from power plants—one for new plants under Section 111(b), the other for existing plants under Section 111(d). Both were premised on the Agency's earlier finding that carbon dioxide is an "air pollutant" that "may reasonably be anticipated to endanger public health or welfare" by causing climate change. 80 Fed. Reg. 64530. Carbon dioxide is not subject to a NAAQS and has not been listed as a hazardous pollutant.

The first rule announced by EPA established federal carbon emissions limits for new power plants of two varieties: fossil-fuel-fired electric steam generating units (mostly coal fired) and natural-gas-fired stationary combustion turbines. Id., at 64512. Following the statutory process set out above, the Agency determined the BSER for the two categories of sources. For steam generating units, for instance, EPA determined that the BSER was a combination of high-efficiency production processes and carbon capture technology. EPA then set the emissions limit based on the amount of carbon dioxide that a plant would emit with these technologies in place.

The second rule was triggered by the first: Because EPA was now regulating carbon dioxide from new coal and gas plants, Section 111(d) required EPA to also address carbon emissions from existing coal and gas plants. See §7411(d)(1). It did so through what it called the Clean Power Plan rule.

In that rule, EPA established "final emission guidelines for states to follow in developing plans" to regulate existing power plants within their borders. Id., at 64662. To arrive at the guideline limits, EPA did the same thing it does when imposing federal regulations on new sources: It identified the BSER.

The BSER that the Agency selected for existing coal-fired power plants, however, was quite different from the BSER it had chosen for new sources. The BSER for existing plants included three types of measures, which the Agency called "building blocks." The first building block was "heat rate improvements" at coal-fired plants—essentially practices such plants could undertake to burn coal more efficiently. But such improvements, EPA stated, would "lead to only small emission reductions," because coal-fired power plants were already operating near optimum efficiency. On the Agency's view, "much larger emission reductions [were] needed from [coal-fired plants] to address climate change."

So the Agency included two additional building blocks in its BSER, both of which involve what it called "generation shifting from higher-emitting to lower-emitting" producers of electricity. Building block two was a shift in electricity production from existing coal-fired power plants to natural-gas-fired plants. Because natural gas plants produce "typically less than half as much" carbon dioxide per unit of electricity created as coal-fired plants, the Agency explained, "this generation shift [would] reduce[] CO2 emissions." Building block three worked the same way, except that the shift was from both coal- and gas-fired plants to "new low- or zero-carbon generating capacity," mainly wind and solar. "Most of the CO2 controls" in the rule came from the application of building blocks two and three.

The Agency identified three ways in which a regulated plant operator could implement a shift in generation to cleaner sources. First, an operator could simply reduce the regulated plant's own production of electricity. Second, it could build a new natural gas plant, wind farm, or solar installation, or invest in someone else's existing facility and then increase generation there. Ibid. Finally, operators could purchase emission allowances or credits as part of a cap-and-trade regime. Under such a scheme, sources that achieve a reduction in their emissions can sell a credit representing the value of that reduction to others, who are able to count it toward their own applicable emissions caps.

EPA explained that taking any of these steps would implement a sector-wide shift in electricity production from coal to natural gas and renewables. Given the integrated nature of the power grid, "adding electricity to the grid from one generator will result in the instantaneous reduction in generation from other generators," and "reductions in generation from one generator lead to the instantaneous increase in generation" by others. So coal plants, whether by reducing their own production, subsidizing an increase in production by cleaner sources, or both, would cause a shift toward wind, solar, and natural gas.

Having decided that the "best system of emission reduction . . . adequately demonstrated" was one that would reduce carbon pollution mostly by moving production to cleaner sources, EPA then set about determining "the degree of emission limitation achievable through the application" of that system. The Agency recognized that—given the nature of generation shifting—it could choose from "a wide range of potential stringencies for the BSER." Put differently, in translating the BSER into an operational emissions limit, EPA could choose whether to require anything from a little generation shifting to a great deal. The Agency settled on what it regarded as a "reasonable" amount of shift, which it based on modeling of how much more electricity both natural gas and renewable sources could supply without causing undue cost increases or reducing the overall power supply. Based on these changes, EPA projected that by 2030, it would be feasible to have coal provide 27% of national electricity generation, down from 38% in 2014.

From these significant projected reductions in generation, EPA developed a series of complex equations to "determine the emission performance rates" that States would be required to implement. The calculations resulted in numerical emissions ceilings so strict that no existing coal plant would have been able to achieve them without engaging in one of the three means of shifting generation described above. Indeed, the emissions limit the Clean Power Plan established for existing power plants was actually stricter than the cap imposed by the simultaneously published standards for new plants.

The point, after all, was to compel the transfer of power generating capacity from existing sources to wind and solar. The White House stated that the Clean Power Plan would "drive a[n] . . . aggressive transformation in the domestic energy industry." EPA's own modeling concluded that the rule would entail billions of dollars in compliance costs (to be paid in the form of higher energy prices), require the retirement of dozens of coal-fired plants, and eliminate tens of thousands of jobs across various sectors. The Energy Information Administration reached similar conclusions, projecting that the rule would cause retail electricity prices to remain persistently 10% higher in many States, and would reduce GDP by at least a trillion 2009 dollars by 2040.

C

These projections were never tested, because the Clean Power Plan never went into effect. The same day that EPA promulgated the rule, dozens of parties (including 27 States) petitioned for review in the D. C. Circuit. After that court declined to enter a stay of the rule, the challengers sought the same relief from this Court. We granted a stay, preventing the rule from taking effect. West Virginia v. EPA, 577 U. S. 1126 (2016). The Court of Appeals later heard argument on the merits en banc. But before it could issue a decision, there was a change in Presidential administrations. The new administration requested that the litigation be held in abeyance so that EPA could reconsider the Clean Power Plan. The D. C. Circuit obliged, and later dismissed the petitions for review as moot.

EPA eventually repealed the rule in 2019, concluding that the Clean Power Plan had been "in excess of its statutory authority" under Section 111(d). Specifically, the Agency concluded that generation shifting should not have been considered as part of the BSER. The Agency interpreted Section 111 as "limit[ing] the BSER to those systems that can be put into operation at a building, structure, facility, or installation," such as "add-on controls" and "inherently lower-emitting processes/practices/designs." It then explained that the Clean Power Plan, rather than setting the standard "based on the application of equipment and practices at the level of an ndividual facility," had instead based it on "a shift in the energy generation mix at the grid level," not the sort of measure that has "a potential for application to an individual source."

The Agency determined that "the interpretative question raised" by the Clean Power Plan—"i.e., whether a 'system of emission reduction' can consist of generation-shifting measures"—fell under the "major question doctrine." Under that doctrine, EPA explained, courts "expect Congress to speak clearly if it wishes to assign to an agency decisions of vast economic and political significance." Ibid. The Agency concluded that the Clean Power Plan was such a decision, for a number of reasons. Its "generation-shifting scheme was projected to have billions of dollars of impact." "[N]o section 111 rule of the scores issued ha[d] ever been based on generation shifting." Ibid. And that novel reading of the statute would empower EPA "to order the wholesale restructuring of any industrial sector" based only on its discretionary assessment of "such factors as 'cost' and 'feasibility.'"

EPA argued that under the major questions doctrine, a clear statement was necessary to conclude that Congress intended to delegate authority "of this breadth to regulate a fundamental sector of the economy." It found none. "Indeed," it concluded, given the text and structure of the statute, "Congress has directly spoken to this precise question and precluded" the use of measures such as generation shifting. Ibid.

In the same rulemaking, the Agency replaced the Clean Power Plan by promulgating a different Section 111(d) regulation, known as the Affordable Clean Energy (ACE) Rule. Id., at 32532. Based on its view of what measures may permissibly make up the BSER, EPA determined that the best system would be akin to building block one of the Clean Power Plan: a combination of equipment upgrades and operating practices that would improve facilities' heat rates. Id., at 32522, 32537. The ACE Rule determined that the application of its BSER measures would result in only small reductions in carbon dioxide emissions.

D

A number of States and private parties immediately filed petitions for review in the D. C. Circuit, challenging EPA's repeal of the Clean Power Plan and its enactment of the replacement ACE Rule. Other States and private entities—including petitioners here West Virginia, North Dakota, Westmoreland Mining Holdings LLC, and The North American Coal Corporation (NACC)—intervened to defend both actions.

The Court of Appeals consolidated all 12 petitions for review into one case. It then held that EPA's "repeal of the Clean Power Plan rested critically on a mistaken reading of the Clean Air Act"—namely, that generation shifting cannot be a "system of emission reduction" under Section 111. To the contrary, the court concluded, the statute could reasonably be read to encompass generation shifting. As part of that analysis, the Court of Appeals concluded that the major questions doctrine did not apply, and thus rejected the need for a clear statement of congressional intent to delegate such power to EPA. Having found that EPA misunderstood the scope of its authority under the Clean Air Act, the Court vacated the Agency's repeal of the Clean Power Plan and remanded to the Agency for further consideration. It also vacated and remanded the replacement rule, the ACE Rule, for the same reason.

The court's decision, handed down on January 19, 2021, was quickly followed by another change in Presidential administrations. One month later, EPA moved the Court of Appeals to partially stay the issuance of its mandate as it pertained to the Clean Power Plan. The Agency did so to ensure that the Clean Power Plan would not immediately go back into effect. Respondents' Motion for a Partial Stay of Issuance of the Mandate in American Lung Assn. v. EPA, No. 19-1140 etc.

(CADC), p. 4. EPA believed that such a result would not make sense while it was in the process of considering whether to promulgate a new Section 111(d) rule. Ibid. No party opposed the motion, and the court accordingly stayed its vacatur of the Agency's repeal of the Clean Power Plan.

Westmoreland, NACC, and the States defending the repeal of the Clean Power Plan all filed petitions for certiorari. We granted the petitions and consolidated the cases. 595 U. S. ___ (2021).

II

We first consider the Government's contention that no petitioner has Article III standing to seek our review.

Although most disputes over standing concern whether a plaintiff has satisfied the requirement when filing suit, "Article III demands that an actual controversy persist throughout all stages of litigation." The requirement of standing "must be met by persons seeking appellate review, just as it must be met by persons appearing in courts of first instance." In considering a litigant's standing to appeal, the question is whether it has experienced an injury "fairly traceable to the judgment below." If so, and a "favorable ruling" from the appellate court "would redress [that] injury," then the appellant has a cognizable Article III stake.

Here, it is apparent that at least one group of petitioners—the state petitioners—are injured by the Court of Appeals' judgment. That judgment vacated "the ACE rule and its embedded repeal of the Clean Power Plan," and accordingly purports to bring the Clean Power Plan back into legal effect. Thus, to the extent the Clean Power Plan harms the States, the D. C. Circuit's judgment inflicts the same injury. And there can be "little question" that the rule does injure the States, since they are "the object of" its requirement that they more stringently regulate power plant emissions within their borders. Lujan v. Defenders of Wildlife, 504 U. S. 555, 561-562 (1992).

The Government counters that "agency and judicial actions" subsequent to the court's entry of judgment have "eliminated any . . . possibility" of injury. Brief for Federal Respondents 16. First, after the decision, EPA informed the Court of Appeals that it does not intend to enforce the Clean Power Plan because it has decided to promulgate a new Section 111(d) rule. Second, on EPA's request, the lower court stayed the part of its judgment that vacated the repeal, pending that new rulemaking. "These circumstances," says the Government, "have mooted the prior dispute as to the CPP Repeal Rule's legality."

That Freudian slip, however, reveals the basic flaw in the Government's argument: It is the doctrine of mootness, not standing, that addresses whether "an intervening circumstance [has] deprive[d] the plaintiff of a personal stake in the outcome of the lawsuit." The distinction matters because the Government, not petitioners, bears the burden to establish that a once-live case has become moot.

That burden is "heavy" where, as here, "[t]he only conceivable basis for a finding of mootness in th[e] case is [the respondent's] voluntary conduct." Friends of the Earth, 528 U. S., at 189. Although the Government briefly argues that the lower court's stay of its mandate extinguished the controversy, it cites no authority for that proposition, and it does not make sense: Lower courts frequently stay their mandates when notified that the losing party intends to seek our certiorari review. So the Government's mootness argument boils down to its representation that EPA has no intention of enforcing the Clean Power Plan prior to promulgating a new Section 111(d) rule.

But "voluntary cessation does not moot a case" unless it is "absolutely clear that the allegedly wrongful behavior could not reasonably be expected to recur." Here the Government "nowhere suggests that if this litigation is resolved in its favor it will not" reimpose emissions limits predicated on generation shifting; indeed, it "vigorously defends" the legality of such an approach. We do not dismiss a case as moot in such circumstances. The case thus remains justiciable, and we may turn to the merits.

III

A

In devising emissions limits for power plants, EPA first "determines" the "best system of emission reduction" that—taking into account cost, health, and other factors—it finds "has been adequately demonstrated." The Agency then quantifies "the degree of emission limitation achievable" if that best system were applied to the covered source. The BSER, therefore, "is the central determination that the EPA must make in formulating [its emission] guidelines" under Section 111. The issue here is whether restructuring the Nation's overall mix of electricity generation, to transition from 38% coal to 27% coal by 2030, can be the "best system of emission reduction" within the meaning of Section 111.

"It is a fundamental canon of statutory construction that the words of a statute must be read in their context and with a view to their place in the overall statutory scheme." Where the statute at issue is one that confers authority upon an administrative agency, that inquiry must be "shaped, at least in some measure, by the nature of the question presented"—whether Congress in fact meant to confer the power the agency has asserted. In the ordinary case, that context has no great effect on the appropriate analysis. Nonetheless, our precedent teaches that there are "extraordinary cases" that call for a different approach—cases in which the "history and the breadth of the authority that [the agency] has asserted," and the "economic and political significance" of that assertion, provide a "reason to hesitate before concluding that Congress" meant to confer such authority.

Such cases have arisen from all corners of the administrative state. In Brown & Williamson, for instance, the Food and Drug Administration claimed that its authority over "drugs" and "devices" included the power to regulate, and even ban, tobacco products. We rejected that "expansive construction of the statute," concluding that "Congress could not have intended to delegate" such a sweeping and consequential authority "in so cryptic a fashion." In Alabama Assn. of Realtors v. Department of Health and Human Servs. we concluded that the Centers for Disease Control and Prevention could not, under its authority to adopt measures "necessary to prevent the . . . spread of " disease, institute a nationwide eviction moratorium in response to the COVID-19 pandemic. We found the statute's language a "wafer-thin reed" on which to rest such a measure, given "the sheer scope of the CDC's claimed authority," its "unprecedented" nature, and the fact that Congress had failed to extend the moratorium after previously having done so.

Our decision in Utility Air addressed another question regarding EPA's authority—namely, whether EPA could construe the term "air pollutant," in a specific provision of the Clean Air Act, to cover greenhouse gases. Despite its textual plausibility, we noted that the Agency's interpretation would have given it permitting authority over millions of small sources, such as hotels and office buildings, that had never before been subject to such requirements. We declined to uphold EPA's claim of "unheralded" regulatory power over "a significant portion of the American economy." In Gonzales v. Oregon, 546 U. S. 243 (2006), we confronted the Attorney General's assertion that he could rescind the license of any physician who prescribed a controlled substance for assisted suicide, even in a State where such action was legal. The

Attorney General argued that this came within his statutory power to revoke licenses where he found them "inconsistent with the public interest." We considered the "idea that Congress gave [him] such broad and unusual authority through an implicit delegation . . . not sustainable." Similar considerations informed our recent decision invalidating the Occupational Safety and Health Administration's mandate that "84 million Americans . . . either obtain a COVID-19 vaccine or undergo weekly medical testing at their own expense." National Federation of Independent Business v. Occupational Safety and Health Administration We found it "telling that OSHA, in its half century of existence," had never relied on its authority to regulate occupational hazards to impose such a remarkable measure.

All of these regulatory assertions had a colorable textual basis. And yet, in each case, given the various circumstances, "common sense as to the manner in which Congress [would have been] likely to delegate" such power to the agency at issue, Brown & Williamson, 529 U. S., at 133, made it very unlikely that Congress had actually done so. Extraordinary grants of regulatory authority are rarely accomplished through "modest words," "vague terms," or "subtle device[s]." Nor does Congress typically use oblique or elliptical language to empower an agency to make a "radical or fundamental change" to a statutory scheme. Agencies have only those powers given to them by Congress, and "enabling legislation" is generally not an "open book to which the agency [may] add pages and change the plot line." We presume that "Congress intends to make major policy decisions itself, not leave those decisions to agencies."

Thus, in certain extraordinary cases, both separation of powers principles and a practical understanding of legislative intent make us "reluctant to read into ambiguous statutory text" the delegation claimed to be lurking there. To convince us otherwise, something more than a merely plausible textual basis for the agency action is necessary. The agency instead must point to "clear congressional authorization" for the power it claims.

The dissent criticizes us for "announc[ing] the arrival" of this major questions doctrine, and argues that each of the decisions just cited simply followed our "ordinary method" of "normal statutory interpretation." But in what the dissent calls the "key case" in this area, Brown & Williamson, the Court could not have been clearer: "In extraordinary cases . . . there may be reason to hesitate" before accepting a reading of a statute that would, under more "ordinary" circumstances, be upheld. Or, as we put it more recently, we "typically greet" assertions of "extravagant statutory power over the national economy" with "skepticism." The dissent attempts to fit the analysis in these cases within routine statutory interpretation, but the bottom line—a requirement of "clear congressional authorization," ibid.—confirms that the approach under the major questions doctrine is distinct.

As for the major questions doctrine "label[ ]," it took hold because it refers to an identifiable body of law that has developed over a series of significant cases all addressing a particular and recurring problem: agencies asserting highly consequential power beyond what Congress could reasonably be understood to have granted. Scholars and jurists have recognized the common threads between those decisions. So have we.

B

Under our precedents, this is a major questions case. In arguing that Section 111(d) empowers it to substantially restructure the American energy market, EPA "claim[ed] to discover in a long-extant statute an unheralded power" representing a "transformative expansion in [its] regulatory authority." It located that newfound power in the vague language of an "ancillary provision[ ]" of the Act, Whitman, 531 U. S., at 468, one that was designed to function as a gap filler and had rarely been used in the preceding decades. And the Agency's discovery allowed it to adopt a regulatory program that Congress had conspicuously and repeatedly declined to enact itself. Given these circumstances, there is every reason to "hesitate before concluding that Congress" meant to confer on EPA the authority it claims under Section 111(d).

Prior to 2015, EPA had always set emissions limits under Section 111 based on the application of measures that would reduce pollution by causing the regulated source to operate more cleanly. See, e.g., 41 Fed. Reg. 48706 (requiring "degree of control achievable through the application of fiber mist eliminators"). It had never devised a cap by looking to a "system" that would reduce pollution simply by "shifting" polluting activity "from dirtier to cleaner sources." 80 Fed. Reg. 64726; see id., at 64738 ("[O]ur traditional interpretation . . . has allowed regulated entities to produce as much of a particular good as they desire provided that they do so through an appropriately clean (or low-emitting) process."). And as Justice Frankfurter has noted, "just as established practice may shed light on the extent of power conveyed by general statutory language, so the want of assertion of power by those who presumably would be alert to exercise it, is equally significant in determining whether such power was actually conferred."

The Government quibbles with this description of the history of Section 111(d), pointing to one rule that it says relied upon a cap-and-trade mechanism to reduce emissions. See 70 Fed. Reg. 28616 (2005) (Mercury Rule). The legality of that choice was controversial at the time and was never addressed by a court. Even assuming the Rule was valid, though, it still does not help the Government. In that regulation, EPA set the actual "emission cap"—i.e., the limit on emissions that sources would be required to meet—"based on the level of [mercury] emissions reductions that w[ould] be achievable by" the use of "technologies [that could be] installed and operational on a nationwide basis" in the relevant timeframe—namely, wet scrubbers. In other words, EPA set the cap based on the application of particular controls, and regulated sources could have complied by installing them. By contrast, and by design, there is no control a coal plant operator can deploy to attain the emissions limits established by the Clean Power Plan. The Mercury Rule, therefore, is no precedent for the Clean Power Plan. To the contrary, it was one more entry in an unbroken list of prior Section 111 rules that devised the enforceable emissions limit by determining the best control mechanisms available for the source.

This consistent understanding of "system[s] of emission reduction" tracked the seemingly universal view, as stated by EPA in its inaugural Section 111(d) rulemaking, that "Congress intended a technology-based approach" to regulation in that Section. 40 Fed. Reg. 53343 (1975); see id., at 53341 ("degree of control to be reflected in EPA's emission guidelines" will be based on "application of best adequately demonstrated control technology"). A technology-based standard, recall, is one that focuses on improving the emissions performance of individual sources. EPA "commonly referred to" the "level of control" required as a "best demonstrated technology (BDT)" standard, 73 Fed. Reg. 34073, and consistently applied it as such. E.g., 61 Fed. Reg. 9907 (declaring "BDT" to be "a well-designed and well-operated gas collection system and . . . a control device capable of reducing [harmful gases] in the collected gas by 98 weight-percent.").

Indeed, EPA nodded to this history in the Clean Power Plan itself, describing the sort of "systems of emission reduction" it had always before selected—"efficiency improvements, fuel-switching," and "add-on controls"—as "more traditional air pollution control measures." The Agency noted that it had "considered" such measures as potential systems of emission reduction for carbon dioxide, ibid., including a measure it ultimately adopted as a "component" of the BSER, namely, heat rate improvements.

But, the Agency explained, in order to "control[ ] CO2 from affected [plants] at levels . . . necessary to mitigate the dangers presented by climate change," it could not base the emissions limit on "measures that improve efficiency at the power plants." "The quantity of emissions reductions resulting from the application of these measures" would have been "too small." Instead, to attain the necessary "critical CO2 reductions," EPA adopted what it called a "broader, forward-thinking approach to the design" of Section 111 regulations. Rather than focus on improving the performance of individual sources, it would "improve the overall power system by lowering the carbon intensity of power generation." And it would do that by forcing a shift throughout the power grid from one type of energy source to another. In the words of the then-EPA Administrator, the rule was "not about pollution control" so much as it was "an investment opportunity" for States, especially "investments in renewables and clean energy." Oversight Hearing on EPA's Proposed Carbon Pollution Standards for Existing Power Plants before the Senate Committee on Environment and Public Works, 113th Cong., 2d Sess., p. 33 (2014).

This view of EPA's authority was not only unprecedented; it also effected a "fundamental revision of the statute, changing it from [one sort of] scheme of . . . regulation" into an entirely different kind. Under the Agency's prior view of Section 111, its role was limited to ensuring the efficient pollution performance of each individual regulated source. Under that paradigm, if a source was already operating at that level, there was nothing more for EPA to do. Under its newly "discover[ed]" authority, however, EPA can demand much greater reductions in emissions based on a very different kind of policy judgment: that it would be "best" if coal made up a much smaller share of national electricity generation. And on this view of EPA's authority, it could go further, perhaps forcing coal plants to "shift" away virtually all of their generation—i.e., to cease making power altogether.

The Government attempts to downplay the magnitude of this "unprecedented power over American industry." The amount of generation shifting ordered, it argues, must be "adequately demonstrated" and "best" in light of the statutory factors of "cost," "nonair quality health and environmental impact," and "energy requirements." 42 U. S. C. §7411(a)(1)EPA therefore must limit the magnitude of generation shift it demands to a level that will not be "exorbitantly costly" or "threaten the reliability of the grid."

But this argument does not so much limit the breadth of the Government's claimed authority as reveal it. On EPA's view of Section 111(d), Congress implicitly tasked it, and it alone, with balancing the many vital considerations of national policy implicated in deciding how Americans will get their energy. EPA decides, for instance, how much of a switch from coal to natural gas is practically feasible by 2020, 2025, and 2030 before the grid collapses, and how high energy prices can go as a result before they become unreasonably "exorbitant."

There is little reason to think Congress assigned such decisions to the Agency. For one thing, as EPA itself admitted when requesting special funding, "Understand[ing] and project[ing] system-wide . . . trends in areas such as electricity transmission, distribution, and storage" requires "technical and policy expertise not traditionally needed in EPA regulatory development." EPA, Fiscal Year 2016: Justification of Appropriation Estimates for the Committee on Appropriations 213 (2015). "When [an] agency has no comparative expertise" in making certain policy judgments, we have said, "Congress presumably would not" task it with doing so.

We also find it "highly unlikely that Congress would leave" to "agency discretion" the decision of how much coal- based generation there should be over the coming decades. MCI, 512 U. S., at 231; see also Brown & Williamson, 529 U. S., at 160 ("We are confident that Congress could not have intended to delegate a decision of such economic and political significance to an agency in so cryptic a fashion."). The basic and consequential tradeoffs involved in such a choice are ones that Congress would likely have intended for itself. See W. Eskridge, Interpreting Law: A Primer on

How To Read Statutes and the Constitution 288 (2016) ("Even if Congress has delegated an agency general rulemaking or adjudicatory power, judges presume that Congress does not delegate its authority to settle or amend major social and economic policy decisions."). Congress certainly has not conferred a like authority upon EPA anywhere else in the Clean Air Act. The last place one would expect to find it is in the previously little-used backwater of Section 111(d).

The dissent contends that there is nothing surprising about EPA dictating the optimal mix of energy sources nationwide, since that sort of mandate will reduce air pollution from power plants, which is EPA's bread and butter. But that does not follow. Forbidding evictions may slow the spread of disease, but the CDC's ordering such a measure certainly "raise[s] an eyebrow." We would not expect the Department of Homeland Security to make trade or foreign policy even though doing so could decrease illegal immigration. And no one would consider generation shifting a "tool" in OSHA's "toolbox," even though reducing generation at coal plants would reduce workplace illness and injury from coal dust.

The dissent also cites our decision in American Elec. Power Co. v. Connecticut, 564 U. S. 410 (2011). The question there, however, was whether Congress wanted district court judges to decide, under unwritten federal nuisance law, "whether and how to regulate carbon dioxide emissions from powerplants." We answered no, given the existence of Section 111(d). But we said nothing about the ways in which Congress intended EPA to exercise its power under that provision. And it is doubtful we had in mind that it would claim the authority to require a large shift from coal to natural gas, wind, and solar. After all, EPA had never regulated in that manner, despite having issued many prior rules governing power plants under Section 111.

Finally, we cannot ignore that the regulatory writ EPA newly uncovered conveniently enabled it to enact a program that, long after the dangers posed by greenhouse gas emissions "had become well known, Congress considered and rejected" multiple times. Brown & Williamson, 529 U. S., at 144 (lack of authority not previously exercised "reinforced by [agency's] unsuccessful attempt . . . to secure from Congress an express grant of [the challenged] authority"). At bottom, the Clean Power Plan essentially adopted a cap-and-trade scheme, or set of state cap-and-trade schemes, for carbon. See 80 Fed. Reg. 64734 ("Emissions trading is . . . an integral part of our BSER analysis."). Congress, however, has consistently rejected proposals to amend the Clean Air Act to create such a program. It has also declined to enact similar measures, such as a carbon tax. "The importance of the issue," along with the fact that the same basic scheme EPA adopted "has been the subject of an earnest and profound debate across the country, . . . makes the oblique form of the claimed delegation all the more suspect."

C

Given these circumstances, our precedent counsels skepticism toward EPA's claim that Section 111 empowers it to devise carbon emissions caps based on a generation shifting approach. To overcome that skepticism, the Government must—under the major questions doctrine—point to "clear congressional authorization" to regulate in that manner.

All the Government can offer, however, is the Agency's authority to establish emissions caps at a level reflecting "the application of the best system of emission reduction . . . adequately demonstrated." 42 U. S. C. §7411(a)(1). As a matter of "definitional possibilities," FCC v. AT&T Inc., 562 U. S. 397, 407 (2011), generation shifting can be described as a "system"—"an aggregation or assemblage of objects united by some form of regular interaction," capable of reducing emissions. But of course almost anything could constitute such a "system"; shorn of all context, the word is an empty vessel. Such a vague statutory grant is not close to the sort of clear authorization required by our precedents.

The Government, echoed by the other respondents, looks to other provisions of the Clean Air Act for support. It points out that the Act elsewhere uses the word "system" or "similar words" to describe cap-and-trade schemes or other sector-wide mechanisms for reducing pollution. The Acid Rain program set out in Title IV of the Act establishes a cap-and-trade scheme for reducing sulfur dioxide emissions, which the statute refers to as an "emission allocation and transfer system." And Section 110 of the NAAQS program specifies that "marketable permits" and "auctions of emissions rights" qualify as "control measures, means, or techniques" that States may adopt in their state implementation plans in order "to meet the applicable requirements of " a NAAQS. §7410(a)(2)(A). If the word "system" or similar words like "technique" or "means" can encompass cap-and-trade, the Government maintains, why not in Section 111?

But just because a cap-and-trade "system" can be used to reduce emissions does not mean that it is the kind of "system of emission reduction" referred to in Section 111. Indeed, the Government's examples demonstrate why it is not.

First, unlike Section 111, the Acid Rain and NAAQS programs contemplate trading systems as a means of complying with an already established emissions limit, set either directly by Congress (as with Acid Rain, see 42 U. S. C. §7651c) or by reference to the safe concentration of the pollutant in the ambient air (as with the NAAQS). In Section 111, by contrast, it is EPA's job to come up with the cap itself: the "numerical limit on emissions" that States must apply to each source. We doubt that Congress directed the Agency to set an emissions cap at the level "which reflects the degree of emission limitation achievable through the application of [a cap-and-trade] system," for that degree is indeterminate. It is one thing for Congress to authorize regulated sources to use trading to comply with a preset cap, or a cap that must be based on some scientific, objective criterion, such as the NAAQS. It is quite another to simply authorize EPA to set the cap itself wherever the Agency sees fit.

Second, Congress added the above authorizations for the use of emissions trading programs in 1990, simultaneous with amending Section 111 to its present form. At the time, cap-and-trade was a novel and highly touted concept. The Acid Rain program was "the nation's first-ever emissions trading program." And Congress went out of its way to amend the NAAQS statute to make absolutely clear that the "measures, means, [and] techniques" States could use to meet the NAAQS included cap-and-trade. §7410(a)(2)(A). Yet "not a peep was heard from Congress about the possibility that a trading regime could be installed under §111."

Finally, the Government notes that other parts of the Clean Air Act, past and present, have "explicitly limited the permissible components of a particular 'system'" of emission reduction in some regard. For instance, a separate section of the statute empowers EPA to require the "degree of reduction achievable through the retrofit application of the best system of continuous emission reduction." §7651f(b)(2). The comparatively unadorned use of the phrase "best system of emission reduction" in Section 111, the Government urges, "suggest[s] a conscious congressional" choice not to limit the measures that may constitute the BSER to those applicable at or to an individual source.

These arguments, however, concern an interpretive question that is not at issue. We have no occasion to decide whether the statutory phrase "system of emission reduction" refers exclusively to measures that improve the pollution performance of individual sources, such that all other actions are ineligible to qualify as the BSER. To be sure, it is pertinent to our analysis that EPA has acted consistent with such a limitation for the first four decades of the statute's existence. But the only interpretive question before us, and the only one we answer, is more narrow: whether the "best system of emission reduction" identified by EPA in the Clean Power Plan was within the authority granted to the Agency in Section 111(d) of the Clean Air Act. For the reasons given, the answer is no.

***

Capping carbon dioxide emissions at a level that will force a nationwide transition away from the use of coal to generate electricity may be a sensible "solution to the crisis of the day." New York v. United States, 505 U. S. 144, 187 (1992). But it is not plausible that Congress gave EPA the authority to adopt on its own such a regulatory scheme in Section 111(d). A decision of such magnitude and consequence rests with Congress itself, or an agency acting pursuant to a clear delegation from that representative body. The judgment of the Court of Appeals for the District of Columbia Circuit is reversed, and the cases are remanded for further proceedings consistent with this opinion.

It is so ordered.

[Concurring and dissenting opinions omitted.]

QUESTIONS

1. What is a "major question," and what does it mean to be one?
2. What was this case about?
3. What was the "major question" in this case?
4. What is the "clear statement" rule, and what did/does it have to do with the outcome here?
5. What are the consequences of something being a 'major question'?

Prevention of Significant Deterioration of Areas in Attainment

Sections 160-169 of the act establish requirements for the Prevention of Significant Deterioration (PSD) of air quality. The PSD program reflects the principle that areas where air quality is better than that required by NAAQS should be protected from significant new air pollution even if NAAQS would not be violated.

The act divides clean air areas into three classes, and specifies the increments of sulfur dioxide (SO_2) and particulate pollution allowed in each. Class I areas include international and national parks, wilderness and other pristine areas; allowable increments of new pollution are very small. Class II areas include all attainment and not classifiable areas, not designated as Class I; allowable increments of new pollution are modest. Class III represents selected areas that states may designate for development; allowable increments of new pollution are large (but not so large that the area would exceed NAAQS). Through an elaborate hearing and review process, a state can have regions redesignated from Class II to Class III (although no Class III areas have yet been designated).

While the 1977 amendments only stipulated PSD standards for two pollutants, SO_2 and particulates, EPA is supposed to establish standards for other criteria pollutants. Thus far, only one of the other four (NO_2) has been addressed: the agency promulgated standards for NO_2 in 1988.

Newly constructed polluting sources in PSD areas must install best available control technology (BACT) that may be more strict than that required by NSPS. The justifications of the policy are that it protects air quality, provides an added margin of health protection, preserves clean air for future development, and prevents firms from gaining a competitive edge by "shopping" for clean air to pollute.

In Sections 169A and B, the act also sets a national goal of preventing and remedying impairment of visibility in national parks and wilderness areas, and requires EPA to promulgate regulations to assure reasonable progress toward that goal. In the 1990 Amendments, Congress strengthened these provisions, which had not been implemented.

The next case involves an EPA interpretation of the term "stationary source" under the federal Clean Air Act that regulated all pollution-emitting devices within the same industrial grouping as though they were encased within a single "bubble." (As a practical matter, this usually means more air pollution.) The Court of Appeals rejected EPA's interpretation, and adopted NRDC's, which applied the definition of "stationary source" to individual industrial stacks (which usually results in tighter standards and less pollution). The SCOTUS then issued the landmark case that follows, in a highly redacted and edited form.

CHEVRON V. NATURAL RESOURCES DEFENSE COUNCIL
467 U.S. 837 (1984)

Justice STEVENS delivered the opinion of the Court.

In the Clean Air Act Amendments of 1977, Congress enacted certain requirements applicable to States that had not achieved the national air quality standards established by the Environmental Protection Agency (EPA) pursuant to earlier legislation. The amended Clean Air Act required these "nonattainment" States to establish a permit program regulating "new or modified major stationary sources" of air pollution. Generally, a permit may not be issued for a new or modified major stationary source unless several stringent conditions are met. The EPA regulation promulgated to implement this permit requirement allows a State to adopt a plantwide definition of the term "stationary source." Under this definition, an existing plant that contains several pollution-emitting devices may install or modify one piece of equipment without meeting the permit conditions if the alteration will not increase the total emissions from the plant. The question presented by these cases is whether EPA's decision to allow States to treat all of the pollution-emitting devices within the same industrial grouping as though they were encased within a single "bubble" is based on a reasonable construction of the statutory term "stationary source."

I

***

The court observed that the relevant part of the amended Clean Air Act "does not explicitly define what Congress envisioned as a 'stationary source, to which the permit program ... should apply," and further stated that the precise issue was not "squarely addressed in the legislative history." Id., at 273, 685 F.2d, at 723. In light of its conclusion that the legislative history bearing on the question was "at best contradictory," it reasoned that "the purposes of the nonattainment program should guide our decision here." Id., at 276, n. 39, 685 F.2d, at 726, n. 39. Based on two of its precedents concerning the applicability of the bubble concept to certain Clean Air Act programs, the court stated that the bubble concept was "mandatory" in programs designed merely to maintain existing air quality, but held that it was "inappropriate" in programs enacted to improve air quality. Id., at 276, 685 F.2d, at 726. Since the purpose of the permit program—its "raison d'être," in the court's view—was to improve air quality, the court held that the bubble concept was inapplicable in these cases under its prior precedents. It therefore set aside the regulations embodying the bubble concept as contrary to law. We granted certiorari to review that judgment, and we now reverse.

The basic legal error of the Court of Appeals was to adopt a static judicial definition of the term "stationary source" when it had decided that Congress itself had not commanded that definition. Respondents do not defend the legal reasoning of the Court of Appeals. Nevertheless, since this Court reviews judgments, not opinions, we must determine whether the Court of Appeals' legal error resulted in an erroneous judgment on the validity of the regulations.

II

When a court reviews an agency's construction of the statute which it administers, it is confronted with two questions. First, always, is the question whether Congress has directly spoken to the precise question at issue. If the intent of Congress is clear, that is the end of the matter; for the court, as well as the agency, must give effect to the unambiguously expressed intent of Congress. If, however, the court determines Congress has not directly addressed the precise question at issue, the court does not simply impose its own construction on the statute, as would be necessary in the absence of an administrative interpretation. Rather, if the statute is silent or ambiguous with respect to the specific issue, the question for the court is whether the agency's answer is based on a permissible construction of the statute ... [A] court may not substitute its own construction of a statutory provision for a reasonable interpretation made by the administrator of an agency.

We have long recognized that considerable weight should be accorded to an executive department's construction of a statutory scheme it is entrusted to administer, and the principle of deference to administrative interpretations. [It] "has been consistently followed by this Court whenever decision as to the meaning or reach of a statute has involved reconciling conflicting policies, and a full understanding of the force of the statutory policy in the given situation has depended upon more than ordinary knowledge respecting the matters subjected to agency regulations."

"*** If this choice represents a reasonable accommodation of conflicting policies that were committed to the agency's care by the statute, we should not disturb it unless it appears from the statute or its legislative history that the accommodation is not one that Congress would have sanctioned."

In light of these well-settled principles it is clear that the Court of Appeals misconceived the nature of its role in reviewing the regulations at issue. Once it determined, after its own examination of the legislation, that Congress did not actually have an intent regarding the applicability of the bubble concept to the permit program, the question before it was not whether in its view the concept is "inappropriate" in the general context of a program designed to improve air quality, but whether the Administrator's view that it is appropriate in the context of this particular program is a reasonable one. Based on the examination of the legislation and its history which follows, we agree with the Court of Appeals that Congress did not have a specific intention on the applicability of the bubble concept in these cases, and conclude that the EPA's use of that concept here is a reasonable policy choice for the agency to make.

***

*** EPA adopted a regulation that, in essence, applied the basic reasoning of the Court of Appeals in these cases. The EPA took particular note of the two then-recent Court of Appeals decisions, which had created the bright-line rule that the "bubble concept" should be employed in a program designed to maintain air quality but not in one designed to enhance air quality. Relying heavily on those cases, EPA adopted a dual definition of "source" for nonattainment areas that required a permit whenever a change in either the entire plant, or one of its components, would result in a significant increase in emissions even if the increase was completely offset by reductions elsewhere in the plant. The EPA expressed the opinion that this interpretation was "more consistent with congressional intent" than the plantwide definition because it "would bring in more sources or modifications for review," but its primary legal analysis was predicated on the two Court of Appeals decisions.

In 1981 a new administration took office and initiated a "Government-wide reexamination of regulatory burdens and complexities." In the context of that review, the EPA reevaluated the various arguments that had been advanced in connection with the proper definition of the term "source" and concluded that the term should be given the same definition in both nonattainment areas and PSD areas.

In explaining its conclusion, the EPA first noted that the definitional issue was not squarely addressed in either the statute or its legislative history and therefore that the issue involved an agency "judgment as how to best carry out the Act." It then set forth several reasons for concluding that the plantwide definition was more appropriate. It pointed out that the dual definition "can act as a disincentive to new investment and modernization by discouraging modifications to existing facilities" and "can actually retard progress in air pollution control by discouraging replacement of older, dirtier processes or pieces of equipment with new, cleaner ones." Moreover, the new definition "would simplify EPA's rules by using the same definition of 'source' for PSD, nonattainment new source review and the construction moratorium. This reduces confusion and inconsistency." Finally, the agency explained that additional requirements that remained in place would accomplish the fundamental purposes of achieving attainment with NAAQS's as expeditiously as possible. These conclusions were expressed in a proposed rulemaking in August 1981 that was formally promulgated in October.

VII

In this Court respondents expressly reject the basic rationale of the Court of Appeals' decision. That court viewed the statutory definition of the term "source" as sufficiently flexible to cover either a plantwide definition, a narrower definition covering each unit within a plant, or a dual definition that could apply to both the entire "bubble" and its components. It interpreted the policies of the statute, however, to mandate the plantwide definition in programs designed to maintain clean air and to forbid it in programs designed to improve air quality. Respondents place a fundamentally different construction on the statute. They contend that the text of the Act requires the EPA to use a dual definition—if either a component of a plant, or the plant as a whole, emits over 100 tons of pollutant, it is a major stationary source. They thus contend that the EPA rules adopted in 1980, insofar as they apply to the maintenance of the quality of clean air, as well as the 1981 rules which apply to nonattainment areas, violate the statute.

Statutory Language

The definition of the term "stationary source" in § 111(a)(3) refers to "any building, structure, facility, or installation" which emits air pollution. See supra, at 2784. This definition is applicable only to the NSPS program by the express terms of the statute; the text of the statute does not make this definition applicable to the permit program. Petitioners therefore maintain that there is no statutory language even relevant to ascertaining the meaning of stationary source in the permit program aside from § 302(j), which defines the term "major stationary source." We disagree with petitioners on this point.

The definition in § 302(j) tells us what the word "major" means—a source must emit at least 100 tons of pollution to qualify—but it sheds virtually no light on the meaning of the term "stationary source." It does equate a source with a facility—a "major emitting facility" and a "major stationary source" are synonymous under § 302(j). The ordinary meaning of the term "facility" is some collection of integrated elements which has been designed and constructed to achieve some purpose. Moreover, it is certainly no affront to common English usage to take a reference to a major facility or a major source to connote an entire plant as opposed to its constituent parts. Basically, however, the language of § 302(j) simply does not compel any given interpretation of the term "source."

Respondents recognize that, and hence point to § 111(a)(3). Although the definition in that section is not literally applicable to the permit program, it sheds as much light on the meaning of the word "source" as anything in the statute. As respondents point out, use of the words "building, structure, facility, or installation," as the definition of source, could be read to impose the permit conditions on an individual building that is a part of a plant. A "word may have a character of its own not to be submerged by its association." On the other hand, the meaning of a word must be ascertained in the context of achieving particular objectives, and the words associated with it may indicate that the true meaning of the series is to convey a common idea. The language may reasonably be interpreted to impose the requirement on any discrete, but integrated, operation which pollutes. This gives meaning to all of the terms—a single building, not part of a larger operation, would be covered if it emits more than 100 tons of pollution, as would any facility, structure, or installation. Indeed, the language itself implies a "bubble concept" of sorts: each enumerated item would seem to be treated as if it were encased in a bubble. While respondents insist that each of these terms must be given a discrete meaning, they also argue that § 111(a)(3) defines "source" as that term is used in § 302(j). The latter section, however, equates a source with a facility, whereas the former defines "source" as a facility, among other items.

We are not persuaded that parsing of general terms in the text of the statute will reveal an actual intent of Congress. We know full well that this language is not dispositive; the terms are overlapping and the language is not precisely directed to the question of the applicability of a given term in the context of a larger operation. To the extent any congressional "intent" can be discerned from this language, it would appear that the listing of overlapping, illustrative terms was intended to enlarge, rather than to confine, the scope of the agency's power to regulate particular sources in order to effectuate the policies of the Act.

Legislative History
In addition, respondents argue that the legislative history and policies of the Act foreclose the plantwide definition, and that the EPA's interpretation is not entitled to deference because it represents a sharp break with prior interpretations of the Act.
Based on our examination of the legislative history, we agree with the Court of Appeals that it is unilluminating.

***

Our review of the EPA's varying interpretations of the word "source"—both before and after the 1977 Amendments—convinces us that the agency primarily responsible for administering this important legislation has consistently interpreted it flexibly—not in a sterile textual vacuum, but in the context of implementing policy decisions in a technical and complex arena. The fact that the agency has from time to time changed its interpretation of the term "source" does not, as respondents argue, lead us to conclude that no deference should be accorded the agency's interpretation of the statute. An initial agency interpretation is not instantly carved in stone. On the contrary, the agency, to engage in informed rulemaking, must consider varying interpretations and the wisdom of its policy on a continuing basis. Moreover, the fact that the agency has adopted different definitions in different contexts adds force to the argument that the definition itself is flexible, particularly since Congress has never indicated any disapproval of a flexible reading of the statute.

Significantly, it was not the agency in 1980, but rather the Court of Appeals that read the statute inflexibly to command a plantwide definition for programs designed to maintain clean air and to forbid such a definition for programs designed to improve air quality. The distinction the court drew may well be a sensible one, but our labored review of the problem has surely disclosed that it is not a distinction that Congress ever articulated itself, or one that the EPA found in the statute before the courts began to review the legislative work product. We conclude that it was the Court of Appeals, rather than Congress or any of the decisionmakers who are authorized by Congress to administer this legislation that was primarily responsible for the 1980 position taken by the agency.

Policy

The arguments over policy that are advanced in the parties' briefs create the impression that respondents are now waging in a judicial forum a specific policy battle which they ultimately lost in the agency and in the 32 jurisdictions opting for the "bubble concept," but one which was never waged in the Congress. Such policy arguments are more properly addressed to legislators or administrators, not to judges.

In these cases, the Administrator's interpretation represents a reasonable accommodation of manifestly competing interests and is entitled to deference: the regulatory scheme is technical and complex, the agency considered the matter in a detailed and reasoned fashion, and the decision involves reconciling conflicting policies. Congress intended to accommodate both interests, but did not do so itself on the level of specificity presented by these cases. Perhaps that body consciously desired the Administrator to strike the balance at this level, thinking that those with great expertise and charged with responsibility for administering the provision would be in a better position to do so; perhaps it simply did not consider the question at this level; and perhaps Congress was unable to forge a coalition on either side of the question, and those on each side decided to take their chances with the scheme devised by the agency. For judicial purposes, it matters not which of these things occurred.

Judges are not experts in the field, and are not part of either political branch of the Government. Courts must, in some cases, reconcile competing political interests, but not on the basis of the judges' personal policy preferences. In contrast, an agency to which Congress has delegated policy-making responsibilities may, within the limits of that delegation, properly rely upon the incumbent administration's views of wise policy to inform its judgments. While agencies are not directly accountable to the people, the Chief Executive is, and it is entirely appropriate for this political branch of the Government to make such policy choices—resolving the competing interests which Congress itself either inadvertently did not resolve, or intentionally left to be resolved by the agency charged with the administration of the statute in light of everyday realities.

When a challenge to an agency construction of a statutory provision, fairly conceptualized, really centers on the wisdom of the agency's policy, rather than whether it is a reasonable choice within a gap left open by Congress, the challenge must fail. In such a case, federal judges—who have no constituency—have a duty to respect legitimate policy choices made by those who do. The responsibilities for assessing the wisdom of such policy choices and resolving the struggle between competing views of the public interest are not judicial ones: "Our Constitution vests such responsibilities in the political branches." TVA v. Hill, 437 U.S. 153, 195 (1978).

We hold that the EPA's definition of the term "source" is a permissible construction of the statute which seeks to accommodate progress in reducing air pollution with economic growth. "The Regulations which the Administrator has adopted provide what the agency could allowably view as ... [an] effective reconciliation of these twofold ends...."

The judgment of the Court of Appeals is reversed.

It is so ordered.

QUESTIONS

1. What is the "Chevron Two-Step"?
2. When does it apply?
3. What happened in Chevron?
4. Was the agency's interpretation consistent? Why might it have changed?
5. What was the statutory interpretation at issue in Chevron?
6. What standard of review did the SCOTUS apply?
7. Is this standard more or less favorable to government? To the regulated?
8. Did the SCOTUS uphold the agency's interpretation? Why or why not?
9. Where does this standard appear in the CAA? In the Constitution?
10. Does the Chevron test raise separation of powers issues? Why or why not?

IV. HAZARDOUS AIR POLLUTANTS

EXCERPT: CLEAN AIR ACT: A SUMMARY OF THE ACT AND ITS MAJOR REQUIREMENTS
Congressional Research Service (Updated September 13, 2022), available at:
(file:///Users/jamesmay/Desktop/RL30853.pdf

Section 112 of the act establishes programs for protecting public health and the environment from exposure to toxic air pollutants. As revised by the 1990 amendments, the section contains four major provisions: Maximum Achievable Control Technology (MACT) requirements; health-based standards; Generally Available Control Technology (GACT) standards for stationary "area sources" (small, but numerous sources, such as gas stations or dry cleaners, that collectively emit significant quantities of hazardous pollutants); and requirements for the prevention of catastrophic releases.

First, EPA is to establish technology-based emission standards, called MACT standards, for sources of 187 pollutants listed in the legislation, and to specify categories of sources subject to the emission standards.12 EPA is to revise the standards periodically (at least every eight years). EPA can, on its own initiative or in response to a petition, add or delete substances or source categories from the lists.

Section 112 establishes a presumption in favor of regulation for the designated chemicals; it requires regulation of a designated pollutant unless EPA or a petitioner is able to show "that there is adequate data on the health and environmental effects of the substance to determine that emissions, ambient concentrations, bioaccumulation or deposition of the substance may not reasonably be anticipated to cause any adverse effects to human health or adverse environmental effects" (Clean Air Act Section 112(b)(3)).

EPA is required to set standards for sources of the listed pollutants that achieve "the maximum degree of reduction in emissions" taking into account cost and other non-air-quality factors. These MACT standards for new sources "shall not be less stringent than the most stringent emissions level that is achieved in practice by the best controlled similar source" (Clean Air Act Section 112(d)(3)). The standards for existing sources may be less stringent than those for new sources, but must be no less stringent than the emission limitations achieved by either the best performing 12% of existing sources (if there are more than 30 such sources in the category or subcategory) or the best performing 5 similar sources (if there are fewer than 30). Existing sources are given three years following promulgation of standards to achieve compliance, with a possible one-year extension; additional extensions may be available for special circumstances or for certain categories of sources. Existing sources that achieve voluntary early emissions reductions received a six-year extension for compliance with MACT.

The second major provision of Section 112 directs EPA to set health-based standards to address situations in which a significant residual risk of adverse health effects or a threat of adverse environmental effects remains after installation of MACT. This provision requires that EPA, after consultation with the Surgeon General of the United States, submit a report to Congress on the public health.

MICHIGAN V. EPA
576 U.S. ___ (2015)

Justice Scalia delivered the opinion of the Court.

The Clean Air Act directs the Environmental Protection Agency to regulate emissions of hazardous air pollutants from power plants if the Agency finds regulation "appropriate and necessary." We must decide whether it was reasonable for EPA to refuse to consider cost when making this finding.

I

The Clean Air Act establishes a series of regulatory programs to control air pollution from stationary sources (such as refineries and factories) and moving sources (such as cars and airplanes). One of these is the National Emissions Standards for Hazardous Air Pollutants Program--the hazardous-air-pollutants program, for short. Established in its current form by the Clean Air Act Amendments of 1990, this program targets for regulation stationary-source emissions of more than 180 specified "hazardous air pollutants."

For stationary sources in general, the applicability of the program depends in part on how much pollution the source emits. A source that emits more than 10 tons of a single pollutant or more than 25 tons of a combination of pollutants per year is called a major source. EPA is required to regulate all major sources under the program. A source whose emissions do not cross the just-mentioned thresholds is called an area source. The Agency is required to regulate an area source under the program if it "presents a threat of adverse effects to human health or the environment . . . warranting regulation."

At the same time, Congress established a unique procedure to determine the applicability of the program to fossil-fuel-fired power plants. The Act refers to these plants as electric utility steam generating units, but we will simply call them power plants. Quite apart from the hazardous-air-pollutants program, the Clean Air Act Amendments of 1990 subjected power plants to various regulatory requirements. The parties agree that these requirements were expected to have the collateral effect of reducing power plants' emissions of hazardous air pollutants, although the extent of the reduction was unclear. Congress directed the Agency to "perform a study of the hazards to public health reasonably anticipated to occur as a result of emissions by [power plants] of [hazardous air pollutants] after imposition of the requirements of this chapter." If the Agency "finds . . . regulation is appropriate and necessary after considering the results of the study," it "shall regulate [power plants] under [§7412]." EPA has interpreted the Act to mean that power plants become subject to regulation on the same terms as ordinary major and area sources, and we assume without deciding that it was correct to do so.

And what are those terms? EPA must first divide sources covered by the program into categories and subcategories in accordance with statutory criteria. For each category or subcategory, the Agency must promulgate certain minimum emission regulations, known as floor standards. The statute generally calibrates the floor standards to reflect the emissions limitations already achieved by the best-performing 12% of sources within the category or subcategory. In some circumstances, the Agency may also impose more stringent emission regulations, known as beyond-the-floor standards. The statute expressly requires the Agency to consider cost (alongside other specified factors) when imposing beyond-the-floor standards.

EPA completed the study required by §7412(n)(1)(A) in 1998, , and concluded that regulation of coal- and oil-fired power plants was "appropriate and necessary" in 2000. In 2012, it reaffirmed the appropriate-and-necessary finding, divided power plants into subcategories, and promulgated floor standards. The Agency found regulation "appropriate" because (1) power plants' emissions of mercury and other hazardous air pollutants posed risks to human health and the environment and (2) controls were available to reduce these emissions. It found regulation "necessary" because the imposition of the Act's other requirements did not eliminate these risks. Ibid. EPA concluded that "costs should not be considered" when deciding whether power plants should be regulated under §7412.

In accordance with Executive Order, the Agency issued a "Regulatory Impact Analysis" alongside its regulation. This analysis estimated that the regulation would force power plants to bear costs of $9.6 billion per year. The Agency could not fully quantify the benefits of reducing power plants' emissions of hazardous air pollutants; to the extent it could, it estimated that these benefits were worth $4 to $6 million per year. The costs to power plants were thus between 1,600 and 2,400 times as great as the quantifiable benefits from reduced emissions of hazardous air pollutants. The Agency continued that its regulations would have ancillary benefits--including cutting power plants' emissions of particulate matter and sulfur dioxide, substances that are not covered by the hazardous-air-pollutants program. Although the Agency's appropriate-and-necessary finding did not rest on these ancillary effects, the regulatory impact analysis took them into account, increasing the Agency's estimate of the quantifiable benefits of its regulation to $37 to $90 billion per year, id., at 9306. EPA concedes that the regulatory impact analysis "played no role" in its appropriate-and-necessary finding.

Petitioners (who include 23 States) sought review of EPA's rule in the Court of Appeals for the D. C. Circuit. As relevant here, they challenged the Agency's refusal to consider cost when deciding whether to regulate power plants. The Court of Appeals upheld the Agency's decision not to consider cost, with Judge Kavanaugh concurring in part and dissenting in part. We granted certiorari. 574 U. S. ___ (2014).

II

Federal administrative agencies are required to engage in "reasoned decisionmaking." "Not only must an agency's decreed result be within the scope of its lawful authority, but the process by which it reaches that result must be logical and rational." It follows that agency action is lawful only if it rests "on a consideration of the relevant factors." Motor Vehicle Mfrs. Assn. of United States, Inc. v. State Farm Mut. Automobile Ins. Co., 463 U. S. 29, 43 (1983).

EPA's decision to regulate power plants under §7412 allowed the Agency to reduce power plants' emissions of hazardous air pollutants and thus to improve public health and the environment. But the decision also ultimately cost power plants, according to the Agency's own estimate, nearly $10 billion a year. EPA refused to consider whether the costs of its decision outweighed the benefits. The Agency gave cost no thought at all, because it considered cost irrelevant to its initial decision to regulate.

EPA's disregard of cost rested on its interpretation of §7412(n)(1)(A), which, to repeat, directs the Agency to regulate power plants if it "finds such regulation is appropriate and necessary." The Agency accepts that it could have interpreted this provision to mean that cost is relevant to the decision to add power plants to the program. But it chose to read the statute to mean that cost makes no difference to the initial decision to regulate. See 76 Fed. Reg. 24988 (2011) ("We further interpret the term 'appropriate' to not allow for the consideration of costs"); 77 Fed. Reg. 9327 ("Cost does not have to be read into the definition of 'appropriate' ").

We review this interpretation under the standard set out in Chevron U. S. A. Inc. v. Natural Resources Defense Council, Inc., 467 U. S. 837 (1984). Chevron directs courts to accept an agency's reasonable resolution of an ambiguity in a statute that the agency administers. Even under this deferential standard, however, "agencies must operate within the bounds of reasonable interpretation. " EPA strayed far beyond those bounds when it read §7412(n)(1) to mean that it could ignore cost when deciding whether to regulate power plants.

A

The Clean Air Act treats power plants differently from other sources for purposes of the hazardous-air-pollutants program. Elsewhere in §7412, Congress established cabined criteria for EPA to apply when deciding whether to include sources in the program. It required the Agency to regulate sources whose emissions exceed specified numerical thresholds (major sources). It also required the Agency to regulate sources whose emissions fall short of these thresholds (area sources) if they "presen[t] a threat of adverse effects to human health or the environment . . . warranting regulation." In stark contrast, Congress instructed EPA to add power plants to the program if (but only if) the Agency finds regulation "appropriate and necessary." One does not need to open up a dictionary in order to realize the capaciousness of this phrase. In particular, "appropriate" is "the classic broad and all-encompassing term that naturally and traditionally includes consideration of all the relevant factors." 748 F. 3d, at 1266 (opinion of Kavanaugh, J.). Although this term leaves agencies with flexibility, an agency may not "entirely fai[l] to consider an important aspect of the problem" when deciding whether regulation is appropriate.

Read naturally in the present context, the phrase "appropriate and necessary" requires at least some attention to cost. One would not say that it is even rational, never mind "appropriate," to impose billions of dollars in economic costs in return for a few dollars in health or environmental benefits. In addition, "cost" includes more than the expense of complying with regulations; any disadvantage could be termed a cost. EPA's interpretation precludes the Agency from considering any type of cost--including, for instance, harms that regulation might do to human health or the environment. The Government concedes that if the Agency were to find that emissions from power plants do damage to human health, but that the technologies needed to eliminate these emissions do even more damage to human health, it would still deem regulation appropriate. No regulation is "appropriate" if it does significantly more harm than good.

There are undoubtedly settings in which the phrase "appropriate and necessary" does not encompass cost. But this is not one of them. Section 7412(n)(1)(A) directs EPA to determine whether "regulation is appropriate and necessary." (Emphasis added.) Agencies have long treated cost as a centrally relevant factor when deciding whether to regulate. Consideration of cost reflects the understanding that reasonable regulation ordinarily requires paying attention to the advantages and the disadvantages of agency decisions. It also reflects the reality that "too much wasteful expenditure devoted to one problem may well mean considerably fewer resources available to deal effectively with other (perhaps more serious) problems." Entergy Corp. v. Riverkeeper, Inc., 556 U. S. 208, 233 (2009) (BREYER, J., concurring in part and dissenting in part). Against the backdrop of this established administrative practice, it is unreasonable to read an instruction to an administrative agency to determine whether "regulation is appropriate and necessary" as an invitation to ignore cost.

Statutory context reinforces the relevance of cost. The procedures governing power plants that we consider today appear in §7412(n)(1), which bears the caption "Electric utility steam generating units." In subparagraph (A), the part of the law that has occupied our attention so far, Congress required EPA to study the hazards to public health posed by power plants and to determine whether regulation is appropriate and necessary. But in subparagraphs (B) and (C), Congress called for two additional studies. One of them, a study into mercury emissions from power plants and other sources, must consider "the health and environmental effects of such emissions, technologies which are available to control such emissions, and the costs of such technologies." This directive to EPA to study cost is a further indication of the relevance of cost to the decision to regulate.

In an effort to minimize this express reference to cost, EPA now argues that §7412(n)(1)(A) requires it to consider only the study mandated by that provision, not the separate mercury study, before deciding whether to regulate power plants. But when adopting the regulations before us, the Agency insisted that the provisions concerning all three studies "provide a framework for [EPA's] determination of whether to regulate [power plants]." It therefore decided "to interpret the scope of the appropriate and necessary finding in the context of all three studies." For example:

- EPA considered environmental effects relevant to the appropriate-and-necessary finding. It deemed the mercury study's reference to this factor "direct evidence that Congress was concerned with environmental effects." 76 Fed. Reg. 24987.
- EPA considered availability of controls relevant to the appropriate-and-necessary finding. It thought that doing so was "consistent with" the mercury study's reference to availability of controls. Id., at 24989.
- EPA concluded that regulation of power plants would be appropriate and necessary even if a single pollutant emitted by them posed a hazard to health or the environment. It believed that "Congress' focus" on a single pollutant in the mercury study "support[ed]" this interpretation. Ibid.
- EPA has not explained why §7412(n)(1)(B)'s reference to "environmental effects . . . and

... costs" provides "direct evidence that Congress was concerned with environmental effects," but not "direct evidence" that it was concerned with cost. Chevron allows agencies to choose among competing reasonable interpretations of a statute; it does not license interpretive gerrymanders under which an agency keeps parts of statutory context it likes while throwing away parts it does not.

B

EPA identifies a handful of reasons to interpret §7412(n)(1)(A) to mean that cost is irrelevant to the initial decision to regulate. We find those reasons unpersuasive.

EPA points out that other parts of the Clean Air Act expressly mention cost, while §7412(n)(1)(A) does not. But this observation shows only that §7412(n)(1)(A)'s broad reference to appropriateness encompasses multiple relevant factors (which include but are not limited to cost); other provisions' specific references to cost encompass just cost. It is unreasonable to infer that, by expressly making cost relevant to other decisions, the Act implicitly makes cost irrelevant to the appropriateness of regulating power plants. (By way of analogy, the Fourth Amendment's Reasonableness Clause requires searches to be "[r]easonable," while its Warrant Clause requires warrants to be supported by "probable cause." Nobody would argue that, by expressly making level of suspicion relevant to the validity of a warrant, the Fourth Amendment implicitly makes level of suspicion categorically irrelevant to the reasonableness of a search. To the contrary, all would agree that the expansive word "reasonable" encompasses degree of suspicion alongside other relevant circumstances.) Other parts of the Clean Air Act also expressly mention environmental effects, while §7412(n)(1)(A) does not. Yet that did not stop EPA from deeming environmental effects relevant to the appropriateness of regulating power plants.

Along similar lines, EPA seeks support in this Court's decision in Whitman v. American Trucking Assns., Inc., 531 U. S. 457 (2001). There, the Court addressed a provision of the Clean Air Act requiring EPA to set ambient air quality standards at levels "requisite to protect the public health" with an "adequate margin of safety." 42 U. S. C. §7409(b). Read naturally, that discrete criterion does not encompass cost; it encompasses health and safety. The Court refused to read that provision as carrying with it an implicit authorization to consider cost, in part because authority to consider cost had "elsewhere, and so often, been expressly granted." 531 U. S., at 467. American Trucking thus establishes the modest principle that where the Clean Air Act expressly directs EPA to regulate on the basis of a factor that on its face does not include cost, the Act normally should not be read as implicitly allowing the Agency to consider cost anyway. That principle has no application here. "Appropriate and necessary" is a far more comprehensive criterion than "requisite to protect the public health"; read fairly and in context, as we have explained, the term plainly subsumes consideration of cost.

Turning to the mechanics of the hazardous-air-pollutants program, EPA argues that it need not consider cost when first deciding whether to regulate power plants because it can consider cost later when deciding how much to regulate them. The question before us, however, is the meaning of the "appropriate and necessary" standard that governs the initial decision to regulate. And as we have discussed, context establishes that this expansive standard encompasses cost. Cost may become relevant again at a later stage of the regulatory process, but that possibility does not establish its irrelevance at this stage. In addition, once the Agency decides to regulate power plants, it must promulgate certain minimum or floor standards no matter the cost (here, nearly $10 billion a year); the Agency may consider cost only when imposing regulations beyond these minimum standards. By EPA's logic, someone could decide whether it is "appropriate" to buy a Ferrari without thinking about cost, because he plans to think about cost later when deciding whether to upgrade the sound system.

EPA argues that the Clean Air Act makes cost irrelevant to the initial decision to regulate sources other than power plants. The Agency claims that it is reasonable to interpret §7412(n)(1)(A) in a way that "harmonizes" the program's treatment of power plants with its treatment of other sources. This line of reasoning overlooks the whole point of having a separate provision about power plants: treating power plants differently from other stationary sources. Congress crafted narrow standards for EPA to apply when deciding whether to regulate other sources; in general, these standards concern the volume of pollution emitted by the source, §7412(c)(1), and the threat posed by the source "to human health or the environment," §7412(c)(3). But Congress wrote the provision before us more expansively, directing the Agency to regulate power plants if "appropriate and necessary." "That congressional election settles this case. [The Agency's] preference for symmetry cannot trump an asymmetrical statute."

EPA persists that Congress treated power plants differently from other sources because of uncertainty about whether regulation of power plants would still be needed after the application of the rest of the Act's requirements. That is undoubtedly one of the reasons Congress treated power plants differently; hence §7412(n)(1)(A)'s requirement to study hazards posed by power plants' emissions "after imposition of the requirements of [the rest of the Act]." But if uncertainty about the need for regulation were the only reason to treat power plants differently, Congress would have required the Agency to decide only whether regulation remains "necessary," not whether regulation is "appropriate and necessary." In any event, EPA stated when it adopted the rule that "Congress did not limit [the] appropriate and necessary inquiry to [the study mentioned in §7412(n)(1)(A)]." 77 Fed. Reg. 9325. The Agency instead decided that the appropriate-and-necessary finding should be understood in light of all three studies required by §7412(n)(1), and as we have discussed, one of those three studies reflects concern about cost.*****

D

Our reasoning so far establishes that it was unreasonable for EPA to read §7412(n)(1)(A) to mean that cost is irrelevant to the initial decision to regulate power plants. The Agency must consider cost--including, most importantly, cost of compliance--before deciding whether regulation is appropriate and necessary. We need not and do not hold that the law unambiguously required the Agency, when making this preliminary estimate, to conduct a formal cost-benefit analysis in which each advantage and disadvantage is assigned a monetary value. It will be up to the Agency to decide (as always, within the limits of reasonable interpretation) how to account for cost.

***

We hold that EPA interpreted §7412(n)(1)(A) unreasonably when it deemed cost irrelevant to the decision to regulate power plants. We reverse the judgment of the Court of Appeals for the D. C. Circuit and remand the cases for further proceedings consistent with this opinion.
It is so ordered.

QUESTIONS

1. What happened in this case?
2. What was/were the issue/issues?
3. How did the Court resolve it/them, and why?
4. What are the strengths and weaknesses in the Court's reasoning?
5.

V.   ACID DEPOSITION CONTROL

The Clean Air Act Amendments of 1990 added an acid deposition control program (Title IV) to the act. It set goals for the year 2000 of reducing annual SO_2 emissions by 10 million tons from 1980 levels and reducing annual NO_x emissions by 2 million tons, also from 1980 levels.
The SO_2 reductions were imposed in two steps. Under Phase 1, owners/operators of 110 high emitting electric generating facilities listed in the law had to meet tonnage emission limitations by January 1, 1995. This would reduce SO_2 emissions by about 3.5 million tons. Phase 2 included facilities with a nameplate capacity greater than or equal to 75 megawatts, with a deadline of January 1, 2000. Compliance was 100%.

To introduce some flexibility in the distribution and timing of reductions, the act created a comprehensive permit and emissions allowance system. An allowance is a limited authorization to emit a ton of SO_2. Issued by EPA, the allowances would be allocated to Phase 1 and Phase 2 units in accordance with baseline emissions estimates. Power plants which commenced operation after November 15, 1990 would not receive any allowances. These new units would have to obtain allowances (offsets) from holders of existing allowances. Allowances were allowed to be traded nationally during either phase. The law also permitted industrial sources and power plants to sell allowances to utility systems under regulations developed by EPA. Allowances were allowed to be banked by a utility for future use or sale.

The act provided for two types of sales to improve the liquidity of the allowance system and to ensure the availability of allowances for utilities and independent power producers who need them. First, a special reserve fund consisting of 2.8% of Phase 1 and Phase 2 allowance allocations was set aside for sale. Allowances from this fund (25,000 annually from 1993 to 1999 and 50,000 thereafter) were sold at a fixed price of $1,500 an allowance. Independent power producers had guaranteed rights to these allowances under certain conditions. Second, an annual, open auction sold allowances (150,000 from 1993 to 1995, and 250,000 from 1996 to 1999) with no minimum price. Utilities with excess allowances could have them auctioned off at this auction, and any person could buy allowances.

The act essentially capped SO_2 emissions at individual existing sources through a tonnage limitation, and at future plants through the allowance system. First, emissions from most existing sources were capped at a specified emission rate times an historic baseline level. Second, for plants commencing operation after November 15, 1990, emissions had to be completely offset with additional reductions at existing facilities beginning after Phase 2 compliance. However, as noted above, the law provided some allowances to future power plants which met certain criteria. The utility SO_2 emission cap was set at 8.9 million tons, with some exceptions.

The act provided that if an affected unit did not have sufficient allowances to cover its emissions, it would be subject to an excess emission penalty of $2,000 per ton of SO_2 and required to reduce an additional ton of SO_2 the next year for each ton of excess pollutant emitted.

The act also required EPA to inventory industrial emissions of SO_2 and to report every five years, beginning in 1995. If the inventory showed that industrial emissions may reach levels above 5.60 million tons per year, then EPA was to take action under the act to ensure that the 5.60 million ton cap would not be exceeded.

The act required EPA to set specific NO_x emission rate limitations—0.45 lb. per million Btu for tangentially-fired boilers and 0.50 lb. per million Btu for wall-fired boilers—unless those rates cannot be achieved by low-NO_x burner technology. Tangentially and wall-fired boilers affected by Phase 1 SO_2 controls must also meet NO_x requirements. EPA was to set emission limitations for other types of boilers by 1997 based on low-NO_x burner costs, which EPA did. In addition, EPA was to propose and promulgate a revised new source performance standard for NO_x from fossil fuel steam generating units, which EPA also did, in 1998.

In 2005, 2011, and 2016, EPA used the authority described in the section on "Transported Air Pollution" to further lower the caps on SO_2 and NO_x emissions in the eastern half of the country. As a result, SO_2 and NO_x emissions have been reduced by at least a further 50% since 2005.

In conclusion, the CAA has been another widely successful federal law in improving public health and welfare. The CAA's primary objective is to achieve national "ambient air quality standards" designed to ensure that the air is safe to breathe for everyone, everywhere. Like the CWA, the CAA has a permit requirement, although not for all emissions. Like the CWA, those who need a permit must also comply with technology-based controls that EPA establishes and states implement, including for hazardous air pollutants. One of the CAA's innovations is a market-based scheme to address acid deposition. All of this said, recent decisions from the SCOTUS have had the effect of diminishing the CAA's reach and effectiveness.

CHAPTER 6: CLIMATE CHANGE AND THE ANTHROPOCENE

Chapter 6 extends our involvement with air pollution, this time specifically about climate change, or what is known as the "Anthropocene." Part I explores international and global regulation of climate change, and in particular the inroads of constitutionalizing climate change. Part II then examines the role of courts and constitutional law in addressing the subject, which is to say not in a good way, although we'll learn about a novel federal case and legal theory that look to provide a legal foothold.

I.   INTRODUCTION TO CLIMATE CHANGE

The evolution of the human species has made a mess of things. We hunt, burn, eat, kill, cut, capture, fight, control and reproduce as if there were 'no tomorrow'—an idiom now laced with irony. Human activity releases carbon that blankets the planet, resulting in much more than 'normal' planetary warming, as well as melting polar icecaps, swelling seas, and what-used-to-be unusual storm events. To make an extremely complex scientific debate simple and sobering, there is evidence that modern human activity is currently causing geologically significant changes to the biosphere alongside mass extinction—a shift known as the 'Anthropocene'.

Climate change is perhaps the most evident result of the Anthropocene, and is at least somewhat attributable to anthropogenic greenhouse gas (GHG) emissions from the use and combustion of fossil fuels. Extracted from underground sources derived from the decomposition of plants and animals that lived and died millions of years ago, fossil fuels (e.g., petroleum, natural gas) have become an indispensable component of life in the modern world. Burning fossil fuels in turn produces copious amounts of GHGs, contributing to global climate change.

The evidence of climate change is exhibited by ice sheet disintegration, regional climate disruptions, changes in precipitation patterns, increasing storm intensity in the Americas, southern Africa, the Mediterranean and southern Asia, warming polar regions, significant species loss of isotherm displacement that is outpacing adaptation and migration, and more extreme weather events including droughts, floods, and fires. As the United States Supreme Court recently observed, "[t]he harms associated with climate change are serious and well recognized," potentially including "a precipitate rise in sea levels by the end of the century, . . . 'irreversible changes to natural ecosystems,' a 'significant reduction in water storage in winter snowpack in mountainous regions . . ,' and an increase in the spread of disease." Coastal states in the United States, for example, have reported rising sea levels, flooding, snowfall reductions, and coastal erosion. And the situation is worsening. GHG emissions are expected to increase at about 2 percent per annum, resulting in a global increase of at least two to three degrees Celsius by 2100, burdening generations to come.

Understanding climate change and the Anthropocene invites a basic primer on the geologic origins of life, the evolution of human beings, and species extinction. As far as we can tell life did not take hold on Earth for at least half a billion years, when Prokaryotes (think bacteria) entered the scene, single-celled micro-organisms lacking even so much as a nucleus or membrane or much of anything at all. Nearly 2 billion more years elapsed before multi-cellular organisms known as Eukaryotes joined the scene.

Most of life has happened over the last one billion years. Land fungi came along about 1.3 billion years ago. Life over the last one-half billion years has become increasingly more complex, first slowly and then insistently and ubiquitously. Arthropods — invertebrates with hard exoskeletons well suited for a planet still angry, roiling and boiling with a carbonated atmosphere — are considered by some to be the planet's first real animals. Flora and fauna galore in geologic terms then followed and flourished, including the first fish, forests, amphibians, reptiles, dinosaurs, mammals, birds, flowering plants and bees.

Humans have been around a mere 0.004 percent of Earth existence. Great apes — our evolutionary ancestors — did not appear until about 15 million years ago. The first human ancestors appeared between 5 and 7 million years ago. The tool-making Genus Homo (on the road to being human) emerged in what is now the Great Rift Valley in Kenya about 2.5 million years ago. Diaspora by Homo Erectus (nearly human but not there yet) from Africa to modern Asia and Europe started about 2 million years ago. One population of Homo Erectus remained behind in Africa but then jumped ahead by evolving large brains about 130,000 years or so ago, leading to Homo Sapiens, sub nom 'humans'. Humans started controlling fire about 100,000 years ago, and with it, the urge to burn began. The last Ice Age ended 10,000 years ago, concurrent with the dawn of civilization, and with it, the seeds of the Anthropocene.

Geologists organize the history of the Earth into periods (longer) and epochs (shorter). Periods are separated by major geological or palaeontological events, such as mass extinctions. The Earth has experienced five great extinctions, that is, evolutionary episodes during which at least 75 percent of all species disappear from the face of the planet. These are described as the End Ordovician (444 million years ago, 86 percent of species lost), Late Devonian (375, 75), End Permian (251, 96), End Triassic (200, 80), and End Cretaceous-Tertiary ('K-T') (66, 76), which wiped out the dinosaurs. Geologists generally agree that we are amid the sixth mass extinction, known as the 'Holocene' extinction, or the Anthropocene extinction, largely caused by human population growth and consumption. The other five mass extinctions had other precursors, including volcanoes, asteroid strikes and climate change.

The Anthropocene is the next mass extinction and is caused by human activity. At present, the rate of extinction of species is estimated to be at least 100 to 1,000 times higher than what is called the natural 'background extinction rate', and at least 10 to 100 times faster than the fastest extinction rate at any point, ever.

Much about the Anthropocene is contested, including when it began. Some believe it started at the end of the last Ice Age. Others contend it began when humans hit the scene between 100,000 and 200,000 years ago, evinced by mass megafaunal extinction following human colonization of the planet. Others claim it is a much more recent phenomenon induced by the industrial revolution or even by post World War II population and consumptive growth and exponential growth in the production of greenhouse gases. Most agree that ever-increasing human-induced greenhouse gas emissions are a central feature of the Anthropocene.

Emission of greenhouse gases has increased by nearly 100 percent in only the last 50 years. The concentration of carbon dioxide in the atmosphere has increased by 75 percent in 100 years, from 290 to 425 or so parts per million, far higher than any amount of the known geologic record (about 800,000 years) of atmospheric CO_2 loadings. Over this time, mean global temperatures have increased to 15 degrees C, from 13.7, a rate of warming far exceeding anything seen in the geologic record. Indeed, the 18 warmest years in human experience have occurred over the last 19 years, with almost every succeeding year warmer than the one preceding it. And, the Earth has experienced its two warmest days in recorded history as I write this (July 2023).

Meanwhile, the limitations of international and regional responses to climate change in the age of the Anthropocene are also well documented. The international order has found climate change nearly impossible to fix thus far. For example, while engaging climate change in general, existing treaties — including the *United Nations Framework Convention on Climate Change* (UNFCCC), the *Kyoto Protocol*, and the *Paris Agreement* — remain woefully under-enforced and far from effective.

The lack of international response coupled with tepid local action invites consideration of the role of environmental constitutionalism, if any, in addressing climate change. International initiatives have not managed to take hold for the most part, while domestic responses have been uneven, inconsistent and unreliable. A quarter of a century ago, James Hansen and others alerted the planet about the impending perils of climate change. By 1992, most of the planet joined the U.N. Framework Convention on Global Climate Change (UNFCC). By 1997, a majority of the world's major GHG emitters signed the Kyoto Protocol on Global Climate Change, agreeing to reduce emissions before the onset of the new century. Many countries, however, neglected to ratify the Protocol, and GHG reductions never happened, except in desultory and piecemeal fashions. Since then, the international community has said much and done relatively little to reduce GHG emissions or address climate change.

Domestic responses to climate change have not fared much better. Just by way of example, political and policy responses to climate change in the U.S. have lacked coordination and cohesion. While most federal representatives lend their name to pending climate legislation, as of 2013 Congress has yet to enact any of it. With Australia's late ratification of the Kyoto Protocol in 2007, the U.S. has the dubious distinction of being the only major industrialized country in the world that has not done so. Moreover, the U.S. Congress has not allocated or appropriated funds to pay for the direct effects of climate change, including loss of shoreline, property damage, crop diminution, and personal health and welfare injuries. While the Obama and Biden administrations have taken strides to reduce emissions, domestic responses have overall been sporadic and have made little dent in national emissions. Other political and social responses have yet to stem and reverse emissions and are unlikely to do so anytime soon, even if binding and enforceable international accords are placed into effect. Realized reductions are largely due to recessionary economics, not policy. While hardly a model, domestic responses in the U.S. are representative of those exhibited by much of the industrialized and developing world. Nonetheless, Europe is developing a climate change model, though based more on its structure of regional governance than on environmental constitutionalism.

In addition to those mentioned, environmental constitutionalism offers at least two additional avenues for legal responses to the Anthropocene. The first is by the express incorporation of climate change into constitutional text. Indeed, several countries have recently incorporated climate change into their domestic constitutions. Venezuela (1999) may have been the first to make a constitutional commitment to address climate change, followed by the Dominican Republic (2006), Ecuador (2008), Viet Nam (2013), Tunisia (2014), Cote D'Avoire (2016), Zambia (2016) and Thailand (2017). In the absence of that, the second is to infer a right to a stable climate from other express constitutional rights, including to life, dignity, due process, or a healthy environment.

Shortcomings in international and domestic responses to climate change create opportunities for tactical deployment of environmental constitutionalism. Thus far, however, very few countries have seen fit to address climate change constitutionally. Only the Dominican Republic's constitution is explicit on the point, with a provision under "The Organization of the Territory" that provides for a "plan of territorial ordering that assures the efficient and sustainable use of the natural resources of the Nation, in accordance with the need of adaptation to climate change . . ." Other nations, like Scotland, are also considering referencing climate change in their constitutions. Without effective international treaty and domestic legislative responses to climate change, one might expect to see more countries elect to entrench express constitutional measures.

A. CLIMATE CHANGE REGULATION AROUND THE GLOBE

The causes and consequences of climate change make it a rough fit for domestic constitutional response. Climate change is, of course, a global issue requiring concerted and coordinated global efforts adjunct to mitigation, adaptation, and compensation. Its effects, however, are absorbed locally by nations in response to sea level rise, loss of shoreline, drought, severe weather, and other consequences often attributed to climate change. These local effects are where environmental constitutionalism might play an important, if limited, role. Constitutions can, for one, direct governments to enact and implement policies to address the effects of climate change in ways not accomplished through existing international and national laws. And once absorbed into constitutional texts, courts can impel action by enforcing these provisions even through progressive realization.

EXCERPT: JAMES R. MAY & ERIN DALY, GLOBAL CLIMATE CONSTITUTIONALISM AND JUSTICE IN THE COURTS

Research Handbook on Global Climate Constitutionalism (Jordi Jaria-Manzano Susana Borràs, Eds. 2019).

I. INTRODUCTION

This chapter explores developments at the boundary between environmental constitutionalism and climate justice. There are two trends. First, a growing group of countries now expressly address climate change in their constitutions. Second, courts from diverse parts of the world are recognizing that governmental inaction in the face of climate change can abridge a right to a healthy climate as implied by an express constitutional right to life, dignity or due process, or the right to a healthy environment. These trends are likely reflective of an emerging worldwide phase in constitutional litigation.

Part II conceptualizes and contextualizes what has come to called 'climate justice,' that is, the social and economic consequences of the disproportionate effect of climate change. Part III details the extent to which countries have adopted express constitutional means to address governmental inaction about climate change. Part IV then reports on how courts have engaged these and associated provisions. We conclude that climate constitutionalism has significant potential for shaping how the rule of law can contribute to climate justice, especially at the domestic level.

II. CLIMATE JUSTICE AND CONSTITUTIONALISM

Climate justice promotes policies, practices and jurisprudence that advance the rights and dignity of the world's most vulnerable people. Climate justice falls at the vertex of international, regional, national and the common law, basic notions of human and environmental rights, and human dignity. The anticipated impacts of climate change are well known, which the United Nations Human Rights Council (UNHRC) recounts as follows:

> [T]he adverse effects of climate change have a range of implications, both direct and indirect, for the effective enjoyment of human rights, including, inter alia, the right to life, the right to adequate food, the right to the enjoyment of the highest attainable standard of physical and mental health, the right to adequate housing, the right to self-determination, the right to safe drinking water and sanitation and the right to development.

These conditions are mostly likely to have direct adverse impacts on community cohesiveness, access to education, and family bonds that imperil human dignity and especially the healthy development of the next generation, and the ones yet to come. The Intergovernmental Panel on Climate Change (IPCC) has detailed the impacts, adaptation, vulnerabilities and mitigation associated with climate change. These effects, however, are not experienced equally everywhere by all global citizens. Suffice to say that most effects of climate change are more acutely experienced by women and by those living in coastal communities, mega-cities, areas of conflict, drought or flood-prone areas, and by experiencing disease, political or social strife, or poverty.

There are complementary and sometimes conflicting perspectives on how to advance climate justice. The international order has found it challenging enough to ensure social and environmental justice, not to mention climate justice. While engaging climate change in general, existing treaties —including the United Nations Framework Convention on Climate Change (UNFCC) the Kyoto Protocol, and the Paris Agreement— require implementation by ratifying nations to go into effect. Perhaps the Preamble to Paris Agreement comes closest to engaging climate justice:

> Climate change is a common concern of humankind, Parties should, when taking action to address climate change, respect, promote and consider their respective obligations on human rights, the right to health, the rights of indigenous peoples, local communities, migrants, children, persons with disabilities and people in vulnerable situations and the right to development, as well as gender equality, empowerment of women and intergenerational equity.

But this provision too is unenforceable. Thus, international law mechanisms remain largely out of reach and irrelevant to most human beings seeking climate justice. Moreover, UN Resolutions are not binding. The recently proposed Global Pact and the Third International Covenant on the Environment are inspirational and aspirational, but again, unenforceable. Moreover, there is, of course, no Global Treaty on Climate Justice or similar accord.

Climate justice has fared hardly any better in law at the domestic level. As noted, only a handful of the world's constitutions address climate change in explicit terms, and legislatures have been slow to provide private causes of action to address or advance climate justice. Moreover, subnational efforts to reduce greenhouse gas emissions and advance climate justice have largely failed. For instance, many efforts by subnational governmental agencies in the United States to impose carbon taxes, fuel efficiency requirements, or restrict greenhouse gas emissions have been found to be preempted by federal law, or otherwise to run afoul of the Commerce Clause of the U.S. Constitution.

Attempts to advance climate justice in the courts are replete with false starts and failures. In particular, common law notions of public and private nuisance, trespass, negligence and strict liability for abnormally dangerous activity have shown little capacity for advancing climate justice. A leading example comes from the United States in the case of *Native Village of Kivalina v. ExxonMobil Corp.*, in which an Inuit community living on an island that was likely to be submerged by rising sea levels induced by climate change filed a federal lawsuit against the world's largest producers of petroleum and natural gas, seeking $40 million in damages to relocate to higher ground. But the lawsuit failed when a federal court found that a federal statute (the Clean Air Act) has 'displaced' the federal common law tort system, even though the statute did not provide the necessary protection. The result in *Kivalina* followed the U.S. Supreme Court's earlier dismissal of a similar action for injunctive relief against fossil-fuel burning electric utilities in *American Electric Power (AEP) v. Connecticut*. In *AEP*, the U.S. Supreme Court held that because the Clean Air Act regulates air pollutants through U.S. Environmental Protection Agency (EPA) action, federal law 'displaced' federal common law, leaving no margin for a parallel track for imposition of injunctive relief by federal courts under federal common law. The appellate court in *Kivalina* extended this reasoning to preclude federal common law claims seeking monetary damages. Together, these cases suggest that federal common law in the U.S. does not provide a basis for tort actions regarding climate change.

American courts have also found that federal law preempts common law claims to advance climate justice under subnational law. For example, in *Comer v. Murphy Oil*, the plaintiffs alleged that that the world's largest oil and natural gas-producing companies are jointly and severally liable for the effects of climate change (which had contributed to the 2010 hurricane that had devastated New Orleans). Yet a federal appellate court upheld a lower court's dismissal of the claims as 'preempted' by federal law. Moreover, climate justice cases can also be thwarted by myriad constitutional defenses, including lack of justiciability, the standing doctrine, and (in the U.S.) procedural and substantive due process, which can limit both access to courts and the availability of damages to prevailing parties.

With few exceptions, courts have not been receptive to claims seeking to advance climate justice. But, as the following sections explain, constitutionalism —either by express constitutional incorporation of climate change, or by inferring causes of action from other recognized constitutional rights— affords new theories that have the potential to take better account of climate justice.

III. EXPRESS CONSTITUTIONAL PROVISIONS ADDRESSING CLIMATE CHANGE

Express constitutional incorporation of provisions addressing climate change provides new avenues for advancing climate justice. These developments reflect the broader and steady accretion of global environmental constitutionalism, which explores the constitutional incorporation, implementation, and jurisprudence of environmental rights, duties, procedures, policies and other provisions to promote environmental protection. Indeed, about one-half of the nations on the planet have seen fit to incorporate an express environmental right into their constitution. It has also inspired considerations of constitutional reform at the subnational level.

Environmental constitutionalism has provided new causes of action and stretched existing environmental rights into new forms. It has also served to promote human and environmental rights, procedural guarantees, remedies, and judicial engagement. Environmental constitutionalism has also animated international considerations about inherent rights to a healthy planet, including the United Nations mandate on human rights and the environment and the appointment of a special rapporteur, culminating in Framework Principles on Human Rights and the Environment and calls for the United Nations to recognize the human right to a healthy environment.

Environmental constitutionalism also has normative spillover effects, and has been correlated with lower greenhouse gas emissions and with other environmental benefits. Yet environmental constitutionalism is still young in constitutional timeframes, and implementation has been inconsistent. Thus it has so far come up short in addressing "pervasive global environmental problems," such as climate justice.

Climate constitutionalism, however, offers at least two additional avenues for advancing climate justice. The first is by the express incorporation of climate change into constitutional text. In the absence of that, the second trend is to infer that other express constitutional rights to life, dignity, due process, or a healthy environment, impliedly incorporate obligations to respond to climate change.

At least seven countries have so far incorporated responses to climate change into their domestic constitutions. The Dominican Republic may have been the first to make a constitutional commitment to do so in 1998, followed by Venezuela the following year. The last decade has seen further related developments. For example, the new constitution of Ecuador in 2008 included comprehensive climate mitigation measures, limit greenhouse gas emissions and deforestation, and promote the use of renewable energy. In 2013, Viet Nam amended its constitution to ensure that the government "takes initiative in prevention and resistance against natural calamities and response to climate change." Tunisia —which stands to lose up to one-third of its land to climate change— entered the canon of climate constitutionalism in 2014, guaranteeing the "right to participate in the protection of the climate." The Preamble to Cote d'Ivoire's 2016 constitution now provides for the government's express "commitment to [...] contributing to climate protection." And in 2017, Thailand amended its constitution to provide for protection of water resources under threat from climate change.

These provisions have helped to spur national action on climate change. For example, the Dominican Republic has developed a National Development Strategy that aims to reduce emissions of greenhouse gases by 25 percent by 2030. Ecuador engaged in a national campaign to convert to hydroelectric, wind and solar energy. And Tunisia was one of the first countries to adopt a climate action plan in advance of the Paris climate talks in 2015. These developments provide bases for considering climate justice in the national conversation about climate change.

IV. CLIMATE CONSTITUTIONALISM AND JUSTICE IN THE COURTS

There is a growing body of jurisprudence from international and regional courts and tribunals surrounding climate change worldwide, including a recent decision that recognizes climate change's disproportionate impact from the Inter-American Court on Human Rights. Yet almost none of it yet involves express provisions about climate change; an advisory opinion from Ecuador upholding the constitutionality of a bilateral agreement between Ecuador and Peru seems to be an outlier. Yet an increasing number of courts have turned to other constitutional rights — including environmental rights, as well as the right to life, health or dignity— to advance climate justice.

A leading example stems from the Constitutional Court of Colombia, which in 2018 issued a landmark decision involving the need to protect the Amazon rainforest as a palliative against climate change. In that case, 25 plaintiffs between the ages of 7 and 26 sought individualized constitutional protection against the government's failure to protect against deforestation in the Colombian Amazon (an area roughly the size of Germany and the U.K. combined), which was increasing at the alarming rate of 44% between 2015 and 2016. The nation's most senior judge, following a 2016 judgment which had recognized the juridical personality of the Atrato River reasoned that because the Amazonian ecosystem is vital for the future of the globe, that the Colombian Amazon, too, enjoys legal rights to protection, conservation, maintenance, and restauration from the State. Following the Rio Atrato case, the Court based its ruling on "many clauses" of the Colombian Constitution which, collectively, make it an "Ecological Constitution" or a "Green Constitution."

With respect to the particular problem of climate change, the Court recognized the imperative necessity to adopt corrective and palliative measures regarding "i) the excessive expansion of illicit agriculture and illegal mining that are irrationally destroying the Amazon forest; ii) to fill the void left by FARC and paramilitary groups when they had an active presence in the State in favor of the conservation of the Amazon territories which, in the context of the armed conflict, were controlled by insurgent groups, merciless predators, irrational colonizers and in general persons and organizations at the margins of the law; iii) impede and mitigate the increasing fires, deforestation, and the irrational expansion of the agricultural frontier, iv) the failure of prevention of the inherent consequences of the building of roads, and issuance of property rights and mineral concessions; v) the expansion of large scale agro-industrial cultivation; vi) the preservation of this ecosystem for its importance in regulating the global climate; vii) the absence of scientific studies and the liberal increase in the release of tons of carbon burned and loss of biomass from vegetation; and viii) to confront climate change, given the destruction of the amazon forest in the national territory." The court recognized the standing of the young people to sue in their individual capacities because of the direct effects of climate change on their enjoyment of their constitutional rights.

In countries where the text of the constitution is not as green, courts has looked elsewhere to advance climate justice, often in the rights of life and dignity, exemplified by three recent cases. First, in 2018's *Ashgar Leghari v. Federation of Pakistan*, the Lahore High Court invoked continuing mandamus jurisdiction to assess the work of the Climate Change Commission it had established pursuant to a ruling in 2015 to implement climate change mitigation and adaptation plans to fulfill constitutional rights to life and dignity. In the 2018 decision, the Court reviewed at some length the threats of climate change in Pakistan, considering its effects on water resources as well as forestry and agriculture, among other things but found that the Commission had been the driving force in sensitizing the Governments and other stakeholders regarding the gravity and importance of climate change and had accomplished 66 percent of the goals assigned to it. The Court then dissolved the CCC and established a Standing Committee to act, on an ongoing basis, as a link between the Court and the Executive and to render assistance to the government to further implementation.

Second, in a 2017 case of "losing the battle but winning the war," an Irish environmental organization challenged a permit issued by the Fingal County Council authorizing an expansion of the Dublin Airport. The plaintiffs argued that the permit violated statutory and regulatory requirements, as well as Ireland's obligations relating to climate change. The Irish High Court, finding no standing, nonetheless issued an opinion of nearly 300 pages in which found that "an unenumerated personal constitutional right to an environment that is consistent with the human dignity and well-being of citizens at large" exists in the Irish Constitution, whose Article 40.3.1, "guarantees in its laws to respect, and, as far as practicable, by its laws to defend and vindicate the personal rights of the citizen."

Last, the court in *Gbemre v. Shell Petroleum Development Company Nigeria*, sounded a claim by farmers to address natural gas flaring and climate change in a constitutional right to dignity. It held that the petroleum developers' flaring of 'waste' natural gas in the Niger Delta without the preparation of an environmental impact statement abridged the community plaintiffs' constitutionally guaranteed right to dignity. In observing that flaring activities contributes to climate change, the court held: "the inherent jurisdiction to grant leave to the applicants to apply for the enforcement of their fundamental rights to life and dignity of the human person as guaranteed by sections 33(1) and 34(1) of the Constitution of the Federal Republic of Nigeria, 1999 and moreover, that these constitutionally guaranteed rights inevitably include the right to a clean, poison-free, pollution-free healthy environment."

Constitutional rights to health and welfare can also be used to advance climate justice. The leading case so far is *Urgenda Foundation v. Kingdom of the Netherlands*, where a trial court ordered the federal government to reduce greenhouse gas emissions and to mitigate the effects of climate change as a means of fulfilling constitutionally recognized rights to health and welfare.

Oblique notions of 'due process' may form the basis for a constitutional claim to address climate change. Deprivation of due process can have substantive or procedural dimensions. On the substantive side, the leading case is *Juliana v. United States,* in which a federal trial court held that the plaintiffs had a legally cognizable cause of action in to assert that the U.S. government's collective actions and inactions concerning greenhouse gas emissions deprived them of a "right to a stable climate" under the Due Process Clause of the 5th Amendment. In a case of first impression, the court agreed that plaintiffs pled a plausible cause of action, concluding: "Exercising my 'reasoned judgment,' I have no doubt that the right to a climate system capable of sustaining human life is fundamental to a free and ordered society." In finding that Plaintiffs had alleged an infringement of a fundamental right sufficient to withstand a motion to dismiss, the court noted:

> where a complaint alleges governmental action is affirmatively and substantially damaging the climate system in a way that will cause human deaths, shorten human lifespans, result in widespread damage to property, threaten human food sources, and dramatically alter the planet's ecosystem, it states a claim for a due process violation. To hold otherwise would be to say that the Constitution affords no protection against a government's knowing decision to poison the air its citizens breathe or the water its citizens drink.

Although the United States government took the extraordinary step of asking the 9th Circuit Court of Appeals to intercept the case from the lower court and dismiss it without further proceedings, the motion was denied and trial is set for October 2018.

On the procedural side, the leading case is *In Re Application of Maui Electric Company*, in which the Supreme Court of Hawai'i held that the Hawai'i constitution's explicit right to a healthy environment is a protectable property interest under the Due Process Clause of the Hawai'i constitution. Accordingly, the Court held that Petitioner-Sierra Club is entitled to a due process hearing to challenge the Public Utility Commission's grant of a Power Purchase Agreement to continue to combust fossil fuels that it claims does not comport with the state's statutory goal to convert to 100 percent renewable energy by 2045. The Court also held that Sierra Club possesses constitutional standing to challenge the permit because the injury of its members is fairly traceable to greenhouse gas emissions.

Some courts have turned to constitutionally-entrenched environmental rights provisions to resolve climate justice-based claims. For example, in *Earthlife Africa Johannesburg v Minister of Environmental Affairs* (2017), an ENGO appealed the issuance of a permit to build a large coal-fired power station without having considered the climate change impacts. The Court considered the regulations and the environmental management act in light of South Africa's constitutional environmental rights provision and under international law. The Court held that even in the absence of an express obligation to consider climate change, the ministry is nonetheless required to consider all the relevant issues and this includes climate change and to do so before, and not after, the permit is issued.

Lastly, *Teitiota v Ministry of Business Innovation and Employment* (2015) involved an application for refugee status for natives of Kiribati displaced by climate change. However, the Court found that the applicant did not face "serious harm" and that there was no evidence that the Government of Kiribati is failing to take steps to protect its citizens from the effects of environmental degradation to the extent that it can. The chief obstacle to relief was rooted not in environmental or climate change law, but in refugee law: although the climatic conditions threatened the applicant's life, they did not create a well-founded fear of persecution, as required to establish a claim of asylum.

V. CONCLUSION

This paper has conceptualized and contextualized the role of constitutionalism in advancing responses to climate change. It has detailed how at least seven national constitutions expressly embrace climate change. More importantly, it has demonstrated how courts are vindicating climate-based claims sounding in other constitutional rights, including to life, dignity, and to a healthy environment. For example, the High Court in South Africa has found protection against climate change in environmental rights provisions of the South African constitution that do not expressly mention climate change but are broad enough to cover it. Courts elsewhere have found protection against climate change in, for example, constitutional rights to life, dignity, or welfare, including courts in Pakistan, Nigeria and the Netherlands, and the United States. These developments show that climate constitutionalism has significant potential for shaping how the rule of law can contribute to climate justice, especially at the domestic level.

B. CLIMATE CHANGE IN THE U.S. SUPREME COURT

In the Court's initial foray into the global climate change imbroglio, the Court decided in *Massachusetts v. EPA*, that Title II of the Clean Air Act authorizes EPA to regulate greenhouse gas emissions from new motor vehicles that "endanger" public health or welfare, thereby promoting sustainable air emissions and energy policy. In this case, the Commonwealth of Massachusetts and a litany of mostly downwind "blue" states and environmental organizations contended that EPA improperly exercised its discretion in denying petition by several states calling for rulemaking to regulate carbon dioxide and three other greenhouse gas emissions—methane, nitrous oxide, and hydrofluorocarbons—from new motor vehicles under Title II of the Clean Air Act. Section 202(a)(1) of the Act directs EPA to regulate tailpipe emissions that (1) "in his judgment" (2) "may reasonably be anticipated to endanger public health or welfare." Massachusetts et al. maintained both prongs had been met. EPA argued that the Clean Air Act does not authorize it to regulate emissions to address global climate change and that it has discretion not to regulate based on policy considerations, including foreign policy.

The Court decided three issues. First, that petitioners (namely, Massachusetts) demonstrated standing under Article III of the U.S. Constitution to challenge EPA's inaction. The Court held that states enjoy "special solicitude" in demonstrating standing. Second, the Court held that greenhouse gas emissions constituted an "air pollutant" under the Clean Air Act's "capacious definition of air pollutant." Last, it held that EPA "offered no reasoned explanation" and that it was arbitrary and capricious for the agency to refuse to decide whether these emissions "endanger public health and welfare" due to policy considerations not listed in the Clean Air Act, mainly foreign policy.

In dissent, Roberts questioned Stevens' "state solicitude" standard as an "implicit concession that petitioners cannot establish standing on traditional terms." Scalia thought the Court should have deferred to EPA in what he says is a "straightforward administrative-law case," and that it had "...no business substituting its own desired outcome for the reasoned judgment of the [EPA]."

EXCERPT: KATY KUH AND JAMES R. MAY, CONSTITUTIONAL CLIMATE CHANGE, IN DEMOCRACY IN A HOTTER TIME
Can the Constitution Save the Planet? (David Orr, Ed., forthcoming).

Fossil fuels were the toast of the town. For its centennial in 1959 the American Petroleum Institute threw itself a party at Columbia University in New York City called "Energy and Man." All the Big Oil big wigs were there, representing most worldwide fossil fuel production. The celebration culminated with a not-to-be-missed keynote speech by Edward Teller, a political conservative largely credited with being the "father of the hydrogen bomb." A celebrated scientist, Time Magazine named Teller a "Man of the Year" in 1960. It was a standing room only event.

But to everyone's astonishment, Teller wasn't in a cheering mood. After clearing his throat, he said:

> *Ladies and gentlemen, I am to talk to you about energy in the future. [T]his, strangely, is the question of contaminating the atmosphere. Whenever you burn conventional fuel, you create carbon dioxide. The carbon dioxide is invisible, it is transparent, you can't smell it, it is not dangerous to health, so why should one worry about it?*

Teller was worried in 1959 when human-caused atmospheric CO_2 loadings were about 9 billion metric tons per year, less than one-quarter of what they now are. Moreover, since 1959, the concentration of CO_2 in the atmosphere has increased from 315 to more than 420 parts per million, and the Earth's average temperature has risen to 57 from 51 degrees Fahrenheit. As explained elsewhere in this volume, the causes and effects are unprecedented.

Teller continued:

Carbon dioxide has a strange property. It transmits visible light but it absorbs the infrared radiation which is emitted from the earth. Its presence in the atmosphere causes a greenhouse effect. It has been calculated that a temperature rise corresponding to a 10 per cent increase in carbon dioxide will be sufficient to melt the icecap and submerge New York. All the coastal cities would be covered, and since a considerable percentage of the human race lives in coastal regions, I think that this chemical contamination is more serious than most people tend to believe.

The underlying processes were not hard to grasp; in 1958, a popular children's science program directed by Frank Capra, who studied chemical engineering at Cal Tech before becoming a movie director, explained the relevant physical and chemical mechanisms. And Teller's "more serious chemical contamination" was no surprise to the Federal Government. Within a decade, policymakers like Senator Daniel Patrick Moynihan sounded alarms. The summer of 1988 was dominated by congressional hearings about climate change. Big Oil knew, too. After a 5-year investigation the Philippines Human Rights Commission recently determined that that Big Oil suppressed climate science for a half-century, and then lied about it, repeatedly. Avoidable Apocalypse awaits, even the 9th Circuit agrees.

Yet here we are: No national, economy-wide emission limits. Increasing emissions (again). Not a single case that's yet reached the merits of the causes of climate change, who knew what and when, who is responsible, and what to do. No one has gone to jail. No executive has been fined. No oil lawyer has been disciplined.

Even a healthy American democracy would struggle mightily to respond effectively to the "wicked" problem of climate change. As humans, we would have to overcome innate cognitive limitations to accept the connection between everyday actions like driving and attenuated effects on climate. As voters, we would have to appreciate the importance of addressing a problem with limited immediate salience primarily for the benefit of future generations. Politicians would need the courage to fight for policies that would yield no visible benefits for voters in their political lifetimes. Change would have to occur over the tooth-and-nail opposition of the fossil fuel companies, among the most powerful corporate special interests in the history of our country. And we would need to be open to transformative change and a rethinking of values and priorities to develop a shared vision for a future radically different from settled expectations, all while reckoning with how historical injustice, most notably colonialism and racism, produced and remain embedded in the systems that brought us to this precipice.

And our democracy is decidedly not healthy. Corporations pour money into elections virtually unrestrained and face no consequences for flagrantly lying to the public—most notably for present purposes about whether climate change is real and dangerous and what causes it—to maximize their profits. The right to vote is now more theoretical than real, with federal protections dismantled and many state and local governments adopting measures that make it harder (especially for disfavored people) to vote. The votes of those who make it into the voting booth are counted–our electoral system is sound. But it is not perceived as such; ideological fantasies of voting fraud cause wide swaths of the public to reject legitimate electoral outcomes. And myriad pathologies in the information environment, from social media algorithms to purposeful disinformation efforts, have fractured our ability to talk to and reason with one another.

Nor is our climate system healthy or stable. We already limp from unprecedented crisis to unprecedented crisis—the Pacific Northwest heatwave, deadly fires, a hurricane that makes landfall in Louisiana and drowns eleven people in New York City basement apartments— with hardly a chance to catch our breath in between. This rapidly changing physical reality adds further stress to our ailing democracy. We face the daunting task of attempting to transform our society, law, and economy to cease emissions and sequester carbon while also transforming our society, law, and economy to adapt to ongoing and worsening dislocations from climate change. In short, our democracy must somehow martial focus, purpose, and resources to address climate change's long-term challenges to life and justice while enduring increasingly frequent and extreme climate-related events that take lives, exacerbate injustice, and put unprecedented strain on democracy and governance.

Sections 1 and 2 detail how and why the Constitution is hostile to climate policy. Section 3 explains why courts are reluctant to engage climate change. Section 4 explores what it means for our brand of democracy.

How the Constitution Obstructs Climate Policy

How and why does the constitutional status quo fail to meet the climate crisis? It begins with constitutional design. The Constitution grants the SCOTUS and such lower courts as Congress establishes "judicial authority." The SCOTUS was thought to be the "least dangerous branch," and a less prestigious appointment than to, say, supreme courts in Virginia or New York, among the reasons the first appointed justices Jay and Rutledge Supreme Court quit the bench. But the import of judicial review transformed in *Marbury v. Madison* when Chief Justice John Marshall famously declared that it is "emphatically the duty of the Judicial Department to say what the law is," as it has in more than 20,000 decisions since its inception in 1789.

The U.S. Supreme Court has nine members, which it did during the 1959-60 term when Teller gave his remarks. Twenty-eight more people have been appointed since then. It has had 115 members in all. Yet very few have acknowledged that catastrophic climate change is both happening and caused by humans. And even those that acknowledge climate change don't believe there is anything courts can do about it.

The U.S. Constitution's 7,369 words all but ignore environmental concerns. It was crafted to address separation of powers, federalism, and civil liberties. Here we provide a taxonomy of the sources of and limits to federal and state authority to reach climate change. Virtually nothing is uncontested, giving rich context to Chief Justice John Marshall's maxim that, "we must never forget that it is *a constitution* we are expounding." But, forget it or not, the Constitution has failed the climate. To understand how and why, we explain that myriad constitutional provisions relate to climate change and, in many cases constrain, climate action. Taken together these provisions contribute to an often unacknowledged yet critically important shared understanding of the power to make and the permissible content of climate policies within our constitutional framework. These are the constitutional shoals to navigate to answer, for example, Daniel Lindvall's query about whether democracy can safeguard the rights of future generations, as well as to achieve the climate-effective, bottom-up, all-hands-on-deck Earth systems governance endorsed by Ann Florini, Gordon LaForge and Anne-Marie Slaughter elsewhere in this volume.

A. Sources of and Limits to Federal Regulation of Climate Change

Sources

The <u>Commerce Clause</u> provides that "Congress shall have the power . . . [t]o regulate Commerce . . . among the several states." The Court has held that the Commerce Clause permits Congress to regulate in three areas: channels of interstate commerce (such as navigable waters), instrumentalities of interstate commerce, and activities that "substantially affect" interstate commerce. The Court then described the substantially affects test as a function of whether (1) the underlying activity is "inherently economic," (2) Congress has made specific findings as to effect, (3) the law contains a jurisdictional element, and (4) the overall effects of the activity are actually substantial. Seldom in applying this vigorous analysis have courts found Congress lacks constitutional authority to protect fish, flies, spiders, 'hapless toads,' waters or wolves that exist solely within a single state. Moreover, the Court has upheld congressional authority when Congress could have a 'rational basis' for concluding that "activities, taken in the aggregate, substantially affect interstate commerce." Yet, despite this wide authority, there are those who question whether Congress has authority to address climate change because climate change is not an inherently economic activity (selling oil is, but not changing the climate).

The <u>Treaty Clause</u> provides that the executive branch "shall have power, by and with the advice and consent of the Senate, to make Treaties, provided two thirds of the Senators present concur." After a treaty is approved, Congress has the power under the Necessary and Proper Clause "to make all laws which shall be necessary and proper for carrying into execution . . . all . . . powers vested by this Constitution in the Government of the United States." Because of the Supremacy Clause, these laws effectively preempt any conflicting laws enacted by states, although states are inclined to argue that the Tenth Amendment's reservation of power "to the states . . . or to the people" limits the federal reach of statutes on matters traditionally left to the states. While the Senate ratified the UN Global Climate Change Convention in 1992, Congress neglected to enact implementing legislation. While the U.S. State Department under the Clinton Administration signed the emission-reducing 1997 Kyoto Protocol, the U.S. Senate tabled it. The Senate ignored the 2015 Paris Agreement altogether.

The Spending and General Welfare Clauses permit Congress to tax and spend to "provide for the common defense and General Welfare of the United States," by attaching conditions to the receipt of federal funds, provided the conditions are not coercive, authority that has been used to implement various federal environmental laws. Such "cooperative federalism" is the bulwark of most of the nation's health and welfare legislation, including environmental protection, but again, not about climate change.

The Property Clause authorizes Congress to make all "needful" rules concerning federal land, which constitutes about 28 percent of the country. The Court has interpreted the scope of this authority to be "virtually without limitation." With this authority, Congress has enacted numerous laws allowing for development, use, and exploitation of natural resources on federal lands. Other provisions of the Constitution have allowed Congress to exercise relatively unquestioned authority to protect natural resources on federal enclaves under the Enclave Clause. Congress also has authority to "acquiesce" to presidential power to "reserve" natural resources on federal land. Yet again these constitutional authorities are generally used to develop and not diminish fossil fuel production, as the Biden Administration's responses to the Russian Oil Embargo demonstrate.

Limits

The Tenth Amendment provides that "the powers not delegated to the United States by the Constitution, nor prohibited by it to the States, are reserved to the States." Tenth Amendment jurisprudence has curtailed environmental programs that upset political accountability and diminish state dignity. The Court has held that Congress may not "commandeer" state political or personnel resources by requiring a state to "take title" of its own low-level radioactive waste even if it fails to arrange for proper disposal under federal law. In the climate context, this jurisprudence has all but foreclosed using state resources to implement climate policies.

The Eleventh Amendment provides that "[t]he Judicial power of the United States shall not be construed to extend to any suit in law or equity, commenced or prosecuted against one of the United States by Citizens of another State." Absent express consent, states are immune from accountability under federal law, in federal court, in state court, or before federal agencies. This again ties Congress' hands in holding states to account for climate change. State officials are still subject to federal causes of action for prospective injunctive relief, a tack left available under *Ex parte Young*. Yet no jurisprudence yet exists to hold state officials to account for climate change.

The Fifth Amendment forbids the government from "taking private property for public use without just compensation." "Taking" includes so-called "regulatory" takings that arise when regulation goes "too far." This involves a balancing approach that turns on how closely the impact of the challenged regulation resembles a physical occupation of the regulated property. In so doing, courts weigh three factors to determine whether a government regulation triggers the obligation to compensate the property owners: (1) "the economic impact of the regulation on the claimant," (2) "the extent to which the regulation has interfered with distinct investment-backed expectations," and (3) the "character of the governmental action," that is, whether it amounts to a physical invasion or merely affects property interests through "some public program adjusting the benefits and burdens of economic life to promote the common good." The Court has held as too far depriving a landowner of all economically viable use of property, requiring the owner to maintain a public pathway to the beach, or set aside land for a greenway along a nearby creek goes too far, unless such use constitutes a nuisance under the state's traditional common law. Moreover, even preexisting state laws can constitute a compensable taking. The prospects of extensive compensation make governments shy about progressive climate programs.

The <u>Due Process Clause</u> of the 5th & 14th Amendments prevents the government from "depriv[ing] any person of life, liberty, or property, without due process of law." Substantive Due Process secures "fundamental rights," which the Court has never interpreted to include anything about the environment. Almost without exception, however, courts have declined to find that individuals have a substantive right to a stable climate. The procedural prong of the Due Process Clause also requires sufficient process associated with individualized decisionmaking associated with deprivation of a constitutionally protected interest, and that any punitive damages be proportional to compensatory damages, both of which tap the brakes on progressive climate regulation.

The <u>Equal Protection Clause</u> of the 14th Amendment provides "nor shall any state deny to any person within its jurisdiction the equal protection of the laws." The Supreme Court has interpreted this to require evidence of "invidious" express or intentional racial discrimination to warrant heightened scrutiny to discriminatory governmental action. Thus far, no court has held that climate policies contravene equal protection.

The <u>Privileges and Immunities Clauses</u> provide that the government "shall make or enforce any law which shall abridge the privileges or immunities of the citizens ..." While several current SCOTUS members have expressed an interest in reviving it, the U.S. Supreme Court has largely read the clause out of the constitution for modern applications, making it unavailable for addressing climate change. Likewise, the Court has never construed the <u>9th Amendment</u>'s text that "The enumeration in the Constitution, of certain rights, shall not be construed to deny or disparage others retained by the people," as affording a right to a healthy environment or stable climate.

The "<u>Nondelegation Doctrine</u>" stems from Article I of the Constitution, which vests "all legislative" authority in Congress, and presumably not in agencies charged with implementing national policies. Nonetheless, while Congress may not "delegate" legislative authority to agencies that administer federal law, legislation that provides an "intelligible principle" to guide the exercise of agency discretion will be upheld. The Court declined to use the doctrine to strike a provision of the CAA that charges EPA with the duty to set national ambient air quality standards as "requisite" to protect public health and welfare. Yet echoes of the doctrine can be seen in rulings that are skeptical of whether the Clean Air Act's definition of "air pollutants" includes greenhouse gases.

The <u>Political Question Doctrine</u> holds that matters demonstrably committed to a coordinate branch of government, or that lack ascertainable standards, or that could otherwise result in judicial embarrassment are nonjusticiable. The Court has recognized that executive powers over foreign affairs, impeachment, and treaty abrogation are political questions into which courts "ought not . . . enter [the] political thicket." The Court has declined to engage arguments inviting analysis under the political question doctrine in holding that the federal CAA provides EPA with authority to regulate emissions of GHGs from new motor vehicles. Nonetheless, several federal courts have turned recently to the political question doctrine in deciding that cases involving climate change are nonjusticiable.

The <u>Displacement Doctrine</u> is grounded in separation of powers. It stands for the proposition that federal law enacted by Congress or implemented by the Executive can displace the role that federal courts have to hear (at least) federal common law causes of action. The Court has held that the discretionary authority that the Clean Air Act provides to EPA to regulate greenhouse gases coupled with the corresponding regulatory actions EPA has taken, displaces the federal common law for public nuisance actions brought under federal common law concerning climate change.

The <u>Standing Doctrine</u> has had a pervasive and deeply imbedded influence on environmental law. Article III extends "judicial authority" to "Cases . . . and Controversies." In general, the Supreme Court has construed this provision to require that a plaintiff show a personal injury that can be traced to the defendant's conduct and redressed by a judicial remedy. The Court recognized noneconomic, aesthetic, and environmental interests as legally cognizable "injuries" that can serve as a sufficient basis for constitutional standing under Article III, and made clear that it is injury to a person, and not the environment, that matters, thus obviating any need to show environmental degradation to support constitutional injury. States are entitled to "special solicitude" in standing analysis in cases involving state efforts to protect natural resources. There, the Court recognized Massachusetts's potential shoreline loss as a legally cognizable injury in allowing it to challenge EPA's failure to regulate GHG emissions. Individuals, on the other hand, must still show a tight "geographic nexus" between the claimed injury and the federal action. Thus, standing remains a tough obstacle to plaintiffs in climate cases.

Sources of and Limits to State Regulation of Climate Change

Sources

The <u>Tenth Amendment</u> "reserves" state authority in areas neither reserved for Congress nor withheld from the states. Many states have adopted extensive laws governing the environment, especially when federal regulation has left gaps. Yet states generally have avoided enacting laws that limit GHG emissions, largely owing to limitations on state authority discussed below.

The <u>Compact Clause</u> of the U.S. Constitution provides that "no state shall, without the consent of Congress . . . enter into any agreement or compact with another state." Historically, water resource allocation has been the area where regional issues warranted an appreciation of the Compact Clause. The Regional Greenhouse Gas Initiative is a cooperative, market-based effort among 11 states to reduce GHG emissions. Yet Congress hasn't approved the compact, and it isn't enforceable.

Limits

The <u>Dormant Commerce Clause</u> is most often used to describe limits on a state's authority to adopt laws or policies that discriminate against interstate commerce because they favor one state or impose an excessive burden on outsiders. For example, the Court has struck down a ban on the importation of dangerous out-of-state waste, higher tipping fees or surcharges for wastes generated out of state, and waste flow control ordinances prohibiting landfill operators from accepting out-of-state waste or requiring all county waste be processed at the county's facility, and a state statute that restricted withdrawal of groundwater from any well in the state for use in an adjoining state, a state law that prohibited the export of energy generated within the state, and other state initiatives awarding tax credits for in-state ethanol production and requiring that in-state power plants burn in-state-mined coal. The body of caselaw here suggests obstacles for states aiming to reduce GHG emissions by promoting in-state renewables, for example.

Public facilities that regulate the environment for public benefit may enjoy wider latitude under the Dormant Commerce Clause, such as a flow control ordinance that required that all solid waste generated within the county be delivered to the county's publicly owned solid waste processing facility does not violate the dormant Commerce Clause. Yet energy companies are privately owned, even if pervasively regulated.

The <u>Supremacy Clause</u> provides that "[t]he Constitution and the Laws of the United States which shall be made in Pursuance thereof . . . shall be the Supreme Law of the Land." Absent specific intent to preempt, the modern Court has held that Congress may preempt state law implicitly by "field" preemption, when Congress occupies a field of interest so pervasively that preemption is assumed, or when state law "conflicts" with federal law. The Court has held that a comprehensive regulatory scheme involving environmental protection may occupy the field and thus implicitly preempt state common law. Thus, preemption limits the availability of private causes of action (e.g., public or private nuisance) to address climate change.

Constitutional Omission

The Constitution presumes the existence of an environment capable of supporting a flourishing society but does not explicitly recognize or protect the environment. Indeed, it was historically uncertain whether the Constitution empowered the federal government to act to protect the environment at all. The textual silence of the Constitution with respect to the environment is mirrored by judicial silence about how the environment supports other rights explicitly recognized in the Constitution. Despite the obvious fact that there can be no life or liberty without functioning ecosystems, courts in the United States do not recognize any federal constitutional environmental rights, even to the extent an environmental right might be deemed appurtenant to explicitly enshrined constitutional rights. The constitutions of many countries explicitly protect the environment and in many others courts have interpreted non-environmental constitutional provisions to necessarily include environmental rights. That is not the case in the United States. The Constitution does not explicitly protect the environment nor is protection of the environment recognized as required to protect other constitutional rights.

The absence of clear and broad constitutional authority to protect the environment—explicit in the text of the constitution or understood by courts to reside within other enumerated powers— limits the scope of federal environmental law. One aspect of this limit is foundational. It required judicial willingness and a stretching of doctrine to find constitutional authority upon which to adopt our core federal environmental laws. What might the laws coming out of our great public awakening to modern environmental problems in the 1970s—the National Environmental Policy Act, the Clean Air Act, the Clean Water Act, the Endangered Species Act—look like had they been adopted against a backdrop of clear and broad constitutional authority?

The dearth of constitutional authority limits not just the structure of our core federal environmental statutes, but also the way that they are interpreted and applied. Internalized understandings of the limits of what is constitutionally possible constrain our policymaking imagination when it is imperative that we effect systemic, transformational change to respond effectively to today's environmental challenges.

And the absence of clear and broad authority to protect the environment is merely one side of the coin. In addition to failing to give the federal government clear power to *protect* the environment, the Constitution also fails to impose clear limits on the federal government's power to *harm* the environment, let alone impose a duty on the government to prevent harm to the environment. The Constitution's failure to identify limits on government harm to the environment compounds the lack of express power to act to protect the environment. The Constitution is (at least as a matter of express text) silent when it comes to protecting individuals from government destruction of the ecological necessities for healthful life. And, unlike in the case of constitutional power to legislate on environmental matters, courts have been largely unwilling to read such limits into the Constitution.

To appreciate how constitutional silence on the environment contributes to constitutional hostility to environmental protection, it is important to recall that the Constitution affords other values—private property, speech, states' rights—explicit recognition and protection. The constitutional omission of the environment thus diminishes the constitutional importance of environmental interests when considered relative to other interests explicitly protected by the Constitution. One-sided constitutional protection for private property, for example, hobbles adaptation policy by dissuading governments from restricting new development in climate-vulnerable locations out of fear of triggering an obligation to compensate private landowners.

The textual constitutional omission of the environment could be overcome by judicial interpretation. For example, during the Progressive Era, scientists, attorneys, and politicians succeeded in persuading courts to interpret the Commerce Clause to give the federal government significant constitutional environmental authority. And there are many powerful arguments that, despite the lack of explicit text and a historical doctrinal focus on the Commerce Clause, the Constitution can and should be understood to afford broader environmental powers to and impose environmental limits and duties on the government. To date, however, courts have largely abdicated their institutional role in the development of climate policy.

Judicial Abdication

Advocates, alarmed at the closing window to mitigate to avoid catastrophic warming, have repeatedly beseeched the courts to use their constitutional authority to compel or prompt more meaningful mitigation policy. Courts decline, insisting that our constitutional structure (the separation of powers between the legislative, executive, and judicial branches of government) renders climate change policy exclusively a matter for the elected branches. In doing so, the courts hold up the need to respect democracy, positing that climate change policy is so complex and central to the polity that decisions about it should not and cannot be made by unelected judges. But this view abdicates the essential role of courts in our constitutional democracy to protect rights, correct for pathologies that subvert the political process, and engage in conversation with the other branches.

Courts have declined to even consider whether the federal government has a constitutional duty to its citizens to prevent (or at least not inflict) climate harms; blocked those harmed by climate change from seeking relief directly from emitters and fossil fuel producers under the federal common law; and rejected interpretations of the Clean Air Act that would allow for meaningful federal mitigation under existing law. Although the decisions technically reside within distinct legal doctrines (standing, displacement, statutory interpretation), substantively the decisions all reflect the judiciary's conviction that it would offend the constitutional structure for courts to engage on climate change policy because in so doing courts would overstep their constitutional role in our system of separated powers.

For example, a federal appellate court held that the children did not have standing to challenge federal climate policies because:

> It is beyond the power of an Article III court to order, design, supervise, or implement the plaintiffs' requested remedial plan. As the opinions of their experts make plain, any effective plan would necessarily require a host of complex policy decisions entrusted, for better or worse, to the wisdom and discretion of the executive and legislative branches.

This is especially evident in the climate context. In holding that federal common law-based claims are displaced by federal law, the Court reasoned:

> It is altogether fitting that Congress designated an expert agency, here, EPA, as best suited to serve as primary regulator of greenhouse gas emissions. The expert agency is surely better equipped to do the job than individual district judges issuing ad hoc, case-by-case injunctions. Federal judges lack the scientific, economic, and technological resources an agency can utilize in coping with issues of this order.

Yet, when asked to allow agencies to interpret the Clean Air Act to require significant reductions in emissions form those same power companies, the courts hesitate, fretting that robust regulation of the emissions from existing power plants would have significant societal impacts and therefore requires additional and clear congressional authorization:

> Capping carbon dioxide emissions at a level that will force a nationwide transition away from the use of coal to generate electricity may be a sensible "solution to the crisis of the day." . . . But it is not plausible that Congress gave EPA the authority to adopt on its own such a regulatory scheme in Section 111(d). A decision of such magnitude and consequence rests with Congress itself, or an agency acting pursuant to a clear delegation from that representative body.

Additionally consequential is the current Court's interest in curtailing unenumerated rights, such as to abortion: "The Constitution makes no reference to abortion, and no such right is implicitly protected by any constitutional provision [as] any such right must be 'deeply rooted in this Nation's history and tradition' and 'implicit in the concept of ordered liberty.' The right to abortion does not fall within this category. Until the latter part of the 20th century, such a right was entirely unknown in American law." The logical extension of this reasoning would seem to call into question implicit constitutional recognition of a healthy environment or a stable climate.

When invited to speak to climate change policy, courts thus decline with blushing modesty, insisting that they must defer to the elected branches because it would be undemocratic for unelected judges to weigh in. Courts fail, however, to acknowledge the democratic *harms* of judicial disengagement on climate change policy. The courts' insistence that they have no role in climate change policy perpetuates special interest-fueled federal climate gridlock that is at odds with popular will and is produced in part by democratic pathologies created or exacerbated by the judiciary itself.

Democratic Pathologies

Clear public majorities support federal mitigation policy in the U.S., yet climate change policy gridlock persists. This is due in part because the constitutional structure of our representative democracy gives outsized political power to less populated states both in the Senate and in the

Electoral College. On key questions—Is global warming caused most by human activities? Should global warming be a high priority for the President and Congress?—a majority of the public agrees at the national level, but public support falls well below fifty percent in states with a low population but an outsized political voice. The impact of the opposition of low-population, overrepresented states on climate policy is clear. On numerous occasions, the U.S. House has passed significant climate change legislation, only to see it blocked in the Senate.

The impact of the overrepresentation of minority climate change policy views through the Electoral College is also clear. President George W. Bush lost the popular vote when first elected and assumed the presidency over climate advocate Al Gore. Despite promising during his campaign to cut emissions from power plants, President Bush proceeded, in office, to fight tooth and nail against the adoption of federal climate legislation and the use of existing authority under the Clean Air Act to limit emissions. President Donald J. Trump likewise lost the popular vote and then used the full scope of his executive authority to push against federal mitigation policy, including withdrawing the U.S. from the Paris Agreement. The way that the Electoral College privileges minority climate change policy preferences is also visible in the courts. Of nine Justices on the Supreme Court, three (Justices Barrett, Gorsuch, and Kavanaugh) were appointed by a President who lost the popular vote, Donald J. Trump, and two (Justices Roberts and Alito) were appointed by a President who lost the popular when first elected, George W. Bush. And it is those five justices, along with Justice Thomas, who, focusing on concerns about economic impacts on the coal industry and the political controversy surrounding climate change, struck down EPA's effort to use authority under the Clean Air Act to compel a shift away from the coal-fired plants that continue to spew high volumes of carbon dioxide into the atmosphere.

The constitutional structure of our representative democracy thus creates an obstacle to mitigation. While courts withdraw from engaging on climate change policy, reasoning that it would be countermajoritarian for judges to weigh in, the reality is that the political process that produces climate change process is not, by design or in practice, majoritarian. And in the context of climate change, the Senate and Electoral College resolutely skew against climate change mitigation, allowing a public and political minority to obstruct the adoption and implementation of robust mitigation law.

Moreover, it is not simply that courts decline to exercise their constitutional authority to engage with climate policy out of a mistaken belief that it would be "undemocratic." Courts affirmatively exacerbate the obstacle that our constitutional structure poses to the adoption of mitigation law through interpretations of the Constitution that limit voting rights (thereby decreasing majority voice) and elevate the rights of corporations (thereby increasing corporate voice). Judicial interpretations of the Constitution help to produce, sustain, and afford veto power to the minority public and political block obstructing federal mitigation policy. Fossil fuel interests, gifted a First Amendment right by the Supreme Court to make effectively unlimited donations to political campaigns in *Citizens United v. Federal Election Commission*, orchestrated a well-documented and effective campaign to convince a relevant swath of the American public and their representatives—the group with a smaller population but greater representation through the Electoral College and Senate— that climate change is not real, not human caused, not dangerous, and or/not imminent. And now, in lawsuits brought by plaintiffs against fossil fuel companies seeking to held them accountable for their lies, the companies, without shame, respond essentially that they have a right to lie under the First Amendment, especially if they are lying to influence public policy. And the constitutional status quo, defined by a series of judicial interpretations and decisions, fails on climate because it fails more broadly on democracy, neglecting to protect fundamental rights like the right to vote while enshrining new rights for corporate interests.

Conclusion

The Constitution as presently worded, interpreted, and applied is obstructing the development of a robust societal response to climate change, in part by failing adequately to protect healthy democratic processes and advance real social justice. We could, of course, amend the Constitution to explicitly support protection of the environment and/or better protect democratic processes and advance social justice. We could also encourage new understandings of existing Constitutional text that cognize the fundamental value of and right to a healthful environment, more effectively support healthy democratic processes, and go further to advance social justice. Any approach will require an open-eyed reckoning with how and why the constitutional status quo is failing to meet the climate moment.

We previously read the trial court's decision in *Juliana v. U.S.*, which the 9th Circuit reversed on standing grounds, as explained next.

JULIANA V. UNITED STATES
947 F.3d 1159 (2021)

HURWITZ, Circuit Judge:

In the mid-1960s, a popular song warned that we were "on the eve of destruction." The plaintiffs in this case have presented compelling evidence that climate change has brought that eve nearer. A substantial evidentiary record documents that the federal government has long promoted fossil fuel use despite knowing that it can cause catastrophic climate change, and that failure to change existing policy may hasten an environmental apocalypse.

The plaintiffs claim that the government has violated their constitutional rights, including a claimed right under the Due Process Clause of the Fifth Amendment to a "climate system capable of sustaining human life." The central issue before us is whether, even assuming such a broad constitutional right exists, an Article III court can provide the plaintiffs the redress they seek—an order requiring the government to develop a plan to "phase out fossil fuel emissions and draw down excess atmospheric CO2." Reluctantly, we conclude that such relief is beyond our constitutional power. Rather, the plaintiffs' impressive case for redress must be presented to the political branches of government.

I.

The plaintiffs are twenty-one young citizens, an environmental organization, and a "representative of future generations." Their original complaint named as defendants the President, the United States, and federal agencies (collectively, "the government"). The operative complaint accuses the government of continuing to "permit, authorize, and subsidize" fossil fuel use despite long being aware of its risks, thereby causing various climate-change related injuries to the plaintiffs. Some plaintiffs claim psychological harm, others impairment to recreational interests, others exacerbated medical conditions, and others damage to property. The complaint asserts violations of: (1) the plaintiffs' substantive rights under the Due Process Clause of the Fifth Amendment; (2) the plaintiffs' rights under the Fifth Amendment to equal protection of the law; (3) the plaintiffs' rights under the Ninth Amendment; and (4) the public trust doctrine. The plaintiffs seek declaratory relief and an injunction ordering the government to implement a plan to "phase out fossil fuel emissions and draw down excess atmospheric [carbon dioxide]."

The district court denied the government's motion to dismiss, concluding that the plaintiffs had standing to sue, raised justiciable questions, and stated a claim for infringement of a Fifth

<u>Amendment</u> due process right to a "climate system capable of sustaining human life." The court defined that right as one to be free from catastrophic climate change that "will cause human deaths, shorten human lifespans, result in widespread damage to property, threaten human food sources, and dramatically alter the planet's ecosystem." The court also concluded that the plaintiffs had stated a viable "danger-creation due process claim" arising from the government's failure to regulate third-party emissions. Finally, the court held that the plaintiffs had stated a public trust claim grounded in the Fifth and the <u>Ninth Amendments</u>.

The government unsuccessfully sought a writ of mandamus. Shortly thereafter, the Supreme Court denied the government's motion for a stay of proceedings. United States v. U.S. Dist. Court for Dist. of Or., 139 S. Ct. 1 (2018). Although finding the stay request "premature," the Court noted that the "breadth of respondents' claims is striking . . . and the justiciability of those claims presents substantial grounds for difference of opinion." Id.

The government then moved for summary judgment and judgment on the pleadings. The district court granted summary judgment on the <u>Ninth Amendment</u> claim, dismissed the President as a defendant, and dismissed the equal protection claim in part. But the court otherwise denied the government's motions, again holding that the plaintiffs had standing to sue and finding that they had presented sufficient evidence to survive summary judgment. The court also rejected the government's argument that the plaintiffs' exclusive remedy was under the <u>Administrative Procedure Act ("APA"), 5 U.S.C. § 702 et seq.</u>

The district court initially declined the government's request to certify those orders for interlocutory appeal. But, while considering a second mandamus petition from the government, we invited the district court to revisit certification, noting the Supreme Court's justiciability concerns. The district court then reluctantly certified the orders denying the motions for interlocutory appeal under <u>28 U.S.C. § 1292(b)</u> and stayed the proceedings, while "stand[ing] by its prior rulings . . . as well as its belief that this case would be better served by further factual development at trial." We granted the government's petition for permission to appeal.

II.

The plaintiffs have compiled an extensive record, which at this stage in the litigation we take in the light most favorable to their claims. The record leaves little basis for denying that climate change is occurring at an increasingly rapid pace. It documents that since the dawn of the Industrial Age, atmospheric carbon dioxide has skyrocketed to levels not seen for almost three million years. For hundreds of thousands of years, average carbon concentration fluctuated between 180 and 280 parts per million. Today, it is over 410 parts per million and climbing. Although carbon levels rose gradually after the last Ice Age, the most recent surge has occurred more than 100 times faster; half of that increase has come in the last forty years.

Copious expert evidence establishes that this unprecedented rise stems from fossil fuel combustion and will wreak havoc on the Earth's climate if unchecked. Temperatures have already risen 0.9 degrees Celsius above pre-industrial levels and may rise more than 6 degrees Celsius by the end of the century. The hottest years on record all fall within this decade, and each year since 1997 has been hotter than the previous average. This extreme heat is melting polar ice caps and may cause sea levels to rise 15 to 30 feet by 2100. The problem is approaching "the point of no return." Absent some action, the destabilizing climate will bury cities, spawn life-threatening natural disasters, and jeopardize critical food and water supplies.

The record also conclusively establishes that the federal government has long understood the risks of fossil fuel use and increasing carbon dioxide emissions. As early as 1965, the Johnson

Administration cautioned that fossil fuel emissions threatened significant changes to climate, global temperatures, sea levels, and other stratospheric properties. In 1983, an Environmental Protection Agency ("EPA") report projected an increase of 2 degrees Celsius by 2040, warning that a "wait and see" carbon emissions policy was extremely risky. And, in the 1990s, the EPA implored the government to act before it was too late. Nonetheless, by 2014, U.S. fossil fuel emissions had climbed to 5.4 billion metric tons, up substantially from 1965. This growth shows no signs of abating. From 2008 to 2017, domestic petroleum and natural gas production increased by nearly 60%, and the country is now expanding oil and gas extraction four times faster than any other nation.

The record also establishes that the government's contribution to climate change is not simply a result of inaction. The government affirmatively promotes fossil fuel use in a host of ways, including beneficial tax provisions, permits for imports and exports, subsidies for domestic and overseas projects, and leases for fuel extraction on federal land.

The government also argues that the plaintiffs lack Article III standing to pursue their constitutional claims. To have standing under Article III, a plaintiff must have (1) a concrete and particularized injury that (2) is caused by the challenged conduct and (3) is likely redressable by a favorable judicial decision. A plaintiff need only establish a genuine dispute as to these requirements to survive summary judgment.

The district court correctly found the injury requirement met. At least some plaintiffs claim concrete and particularized injuries. Jaime B., for example, claims that she was forced to leave her home because of water scarcity, separating her from relatives on the Navajo Reservation. These injuries are not simply "'conjectural' or 'hypothetical;'" at least some of the plaintiffs have presented evidence that climate change is affecting them now in concrete ways and will continue to do so unless checked.

The government argues that the plaintiffs' alleged injuries are not particularized because climate change affects everyone. But, "it does not matter how many persons have been injured" if the plaintiffs' injuries are "concrete and personal." And, the Article III injury requirement is met if only one plaintiff has suffered concrete harm.

2.

The district court also correctly found the Article III causation requirement satisfied for purposes of summary judgment. Causation can be established "even if there are multiple links in the chain," as long as the chain is not "hypothetical or tenuous." The causal chain here is sufficiently established. The plaintiffs' alleged injuries are caused by carbon emissions from fossil fuel production, extraction, and transportation. A significant portion of those emissions occur in this country; the United States accounted for over 25% of worldwide emissions from 1850 to 2012, and currently accounts for about 15%. See Massachusetts, 549 U.S. at 524-25 (finding that emissions amounting to about 6% of the worldwide total showed cause of alleged injury "by any standard"). And, the plaintiffs' evidence shows that federal subsidies and leases have increased those emissions. About 25% of fossil fuels extracted in the United States come from federal waters and lands, an activity that requires authorization from the federal government.

Relying on Washington Environmental Council v. Bellon, 732 F.3d 1131, 1141-46 (9th Cir. 2013), the government argues that the causal chain is too attenuated because it depends in part on the independent actions of third parties. Bellon held that the causal chain between local agencies' failure to regulate five oil refineries and the plaintiffs' climate-change related injuries was "too tenuous to support standing" because the refineries had a "scientifically indiscernible" impact on climate change. But the plaintiffs here do not contend that their injuries were caused by a few isolated agency decisions. Rather, they blame a host of federal policies, from subsidies to drilling permits, spanning "over 50 years," and direct actions by the government. There is at least a genuine factual dispute as to whether those policies were a "substantial factor" in causing the plaintiffs' injuries

3.

The more difficult question is whether the plaintiffs' claimed injuries are redressable by an Article III court. In analyzing that question, we start by stressing what the plaintiffs do and do not assert. They do not claim that the government has violated a statute or a regulation. They do not assert the denial of a procedural right. Nor do they seek damages under the Federal Tort Claims Act, 28 U.S.C. § 2671 et seq. Rather, their sole claim is that the government has deprived them of a substantive constitutional right to a "climate system capable of sustaining human life," and they seek remedial declaratory and injunctive relief.

Reasonable jurists can disagree about whether the asserted constitutional right exists. Compare Clean Air Council v. United States, 362 F. Supp. 3d 237, 250-53 (E.D. Pa. 2019) (finding no constitutional right), with Juliana, 217 F. Supp. 3d at 1248-50; see also In re United States, 139 S. Ct. at 453 (reiterating "that the 'striking' breadth of plaintiffs' below claims 'presents substantial grounds for difference of opinion'"). In analyzing redressability, however, we assume its existence. But that merely begins our analysis, because "not all meritorious legal claims are redressable in federal court." Id. To establish Article III redressability, the plaintiffs must show that the relief they seek is both (1) substantially likely to redress their injuries; and (2) within the district court's power to award. Id. Redress need not be guaranteed, but it must be more than "merely speculative."

The plaintiffs first seek a declaration that the government is violating the Constitution. But that relief alone is not substantially likely to mitigate the plaintiffs' asserted concrete injuries. A declaration, although undoubtedly likely to benefit the plaintiffs psychologically, is unlikely by itself to remediate their alleged injuries absent further court action.

The crux of the plaintiffs' requested remedy is an injunction requiring the government not only to cease permitting, authorizing, and subsidizing fossil fuel use, but also to prepare a plan subject to judicial approval to draw down harmful emissions. The plaintiffs thus seek not only to enjoin the Executive from exercising discretionary authority expressly granted by Congress, but also to enjoin Congress from exercising power expressly granted by the Constitution over public lands.

As an initial matter, we note that although the plaintiffs contended at oral argument that they challenge only affirmative activities by the government, an order simply enjoining those activities will not, according to their own experts' opinions, suffice to stop catastrophic climate change or even ameliorate their injuries. The plaintiffs' experts opine that the federal government's leases and subsidies have contributed to global carbon emissions. But they do not show that even the total elimination of the challenged programs would halt the growth of carbon dioxide levels in the atmosphere, let alone decrease that growth. Nor does any expert contend that elimination of the challenged pro-carbon fuels programs would by itself prevent further injury to the plaintiffs. Rather, the record shows that many of the emissions causing climate change happened decades ago or come from foreign and non-governmental sources.

Indeed, the plaintiffs' experts make plain that reducing the global consequences of climate change demands much more than cessation of the government's promotion of fossil fuels. Rather, these experts opine that such a result calls for no less than a fundamental transformation of this country's energy system, if not that of the industrialized world. One expert opines that atmospheric carbon reductions must come "largely via reforestation," and include rapid and immediate decreases in emissions from many sources. "[L]eisurely reductions of one of two percent per year," he explains, "will not suffice." Another expert has opined that although the required emissions reductions are "technically feasible," they can be achieved only through a comprehensive plan for "nearly complete decarbonization" that includes both an "unprecedently rapid build out" of renewable energy and a "sustained commitment to infrastructure transformation over decades." And, that commitment, another expert emphasizes, must include everything from energy efficient lighting to improved public transportation to hydrogen-powered aircraft.

The plaintiffs concede that their requested relief will not alone solve global climate change, but they assert that their "injuries would be to some extent ameliorated." Relying on Massachusetts v. EPA, the district court apparently found the redressability requirement satisfied because the requested relief would likely slow or reduce emissions. That case, however, involved a procedural right that the State of Massachusetts was allowed to assert "without meeting all the normal standards for redressability;" in that context, the Court found redressability because "there [was] some possibility that the requested relief [would] prompt the injury-causing party to reconsider the decision that allegedly harmed the litigant." The plaintiffs here do not assert a procedural right, but rather a substantive due process claim.

We are therefore skeptical that the first redressability prong is satisfied. But even assuming that it is, the plaintiffs do not surmount the remaining hurdle—establishing that the specific relief they seek is within the power of an Article III court. There is much to recommend the adoption of a comprehensive scheme to decrease fossil fuel emissions and combat climate change, both as a policy matter in general and a matter of national survival in particular. But it is beyond the power of an Article III court to order, design, supervise, or implement the plaintiffs' requested remedial plan. As the opinions of their experts make plain, any effective plan would necessarily require a host of complex policy decisions entrusted, for better or worse, to the wisdom and discretion of the executive and legislative branches. These decisions range, for example, from determining how much to invest in public transit to how quickly to transition to renewable energy, and plainly require consideration of "competing social, political, and economic forces," which must be made by the People's "elected representatives, rather than by federal judges interpreting the basic charter of Government for the entire country."

The plaintiffs argue that the district court need not itself make policy decisions, because if their general request for a remedial plan is granted, the political branches can decide what policies will best "phase out fossil fuel emissions and draw down excess atmospheric CO2." To be sure, in some circumstances, courts may order broad injunctive relief while leaving the "details of implementation" to the government's discretion. But, even under such a scenario, the plaintiffs' request for a remedial plan would subsequently require the judiciary to pass judgment on the sufficiency of the government's response to the order, which necessarily would entail a broad range of policymaking. And inevitably, this kind of plan will demand action not only by the Executive, but also by Congress. Absent court intervention, the political branches might conclude—however inappropriately in the plaintiffs' view—that economic or defense considerations called for continuation of the very programs challenged in this suit, or a less robust approach to addressing climate change than the plaintiffs believe is necessary. "But we cannot substitute our own assessment for the Executive's [or Legislature's] predictive judgments on such matters, all of which 'are delicate, complex, and involve large elements of prophecy.'" And, given the complexity and long-lasting nature of global climate change, the court would be required to supervise the government's compliance with any suggested plan for many decades.

As the Supreme Court recently explained, "a constitutional directive or legal standards" must guide the courts' exercise of equitable power. Rucho found partisan gerrymandering claims presented political questions beyond the reach of Article III courts. The Court did not deny extreme partisan gerrymandering can violate the Constitution. But, it concluded that there was no "limited and precise" standard discernible in the Constitution for redressing the asserted violation. The Court rejected the plaintiffs' proposed standard because unlike the one-person, one-vote rule in vote dilution cases, it was not "relatively easy to administer as a matter of math."

Rucho reaffirmed that redressability questions implicate the separation of powers, noting that federal courts "have no commission to allocate political power and influence" without standards to guide in the exercise of such authority. Absent those standards, federal judicial power could be "unlimited in scope and duration," and would inject "the unelected and politically unaccountable branch of the Federal Government [into] assuming such an extraordinary and unprecedented roleBecause "it is axiomatic that 'the Constitution contemplates that democracy is the appropriate process for change,'" some questions—even those existential in nature—are the province of the political branches. The Court found in Rucho that a proposed standard involving a mathematical comparison to a baseline election map is too difficult for the judiciary to manage. It is impossible to reach a different conclusion here.

The plaintiffs' experts opine that atmospheric carbon levels of 350 parts per million are necessary to stabilize the global climate. But, even accepting those opinions as valid, they do not suggest how an order from this Court can achieve that level, other than by ordering the government to develop a plan. Although the plaintiffs' invitation to get the ball rolling by simply ordering the promulgation of a plan is beguiling, it ignores that an Article III court will thereafter be required to determine whether the plan is sufficient to remediate the claimed constitutional violation of the plaintiffs' right to a "climate system capable of sustaining human life." We doubt that any such plan can be supervised or enforced by an Article III court. And, in the end, any plan is only as good as the court's power to enforce it.

C.

Our dissenting colleague quite correctly notes the gravity of the plaintiffs' evidence; we differ only as to whether an Article III court can provide their requested redress. In suggesting that we can, the dissent reframes the plaintiffs' claimed constitutional right variously as an entitlement to "the country's perpetuity," Diss. at 35-37, 39, or as one to freedom from "the amount of fossil-fuel emissions that will irreparably devastate our Nation," id. at 57. But if such broad constitutional rights exist, we doubt that the plaintiffs would have Article III standing to enforce them. Their alleged individual injuries do not flow from a violation of these claimed rights. Indeed, any injury from the dissolution of the Republic would be felt by all citizens equally, and thus would not constitute the kind of discrete and particularized injury necessary for Article III standing. A suit for a violation of these reframed rights, like one for a violation of the Guarantee Clause, would also plainly be nonjusticiable.

More importantly, the dissent offers no metrics for judicial determination of the level of climate change that would cause "the willful dissolution of the Republic," nor for measuring a constitutionally acceptable "perceptible reduction in the advance of climate change." Contrary to the dissent, we cannot find Article III redressability requirements satisfied simply because a court order might "postpone[] the day when remedial measures become insufficiently effective." Indeed, as the dissent recognizes, a guarantee against government conduct that might threaten the Union—whether from political gerrymandering, nuclear proliferation, Executive misconduct, or climate change—has traditionally been viewed by Article III courts as "not separately enforceable." Nor has the Supreme Court recognized "the perpetuity principle" as a basis for interjecting the judicial branch into the policy-making purview of the political branches.

Contrary to the dissent, we do not "throw up [our] hands" by concluding that the plaintiffs' claims are nonjusticiable. Rather, we recognize that "Article III protects liberty not only through its role in implementing the separation of powers, but also by specifying the defining characteristics of Article III judges." Not every problem posing a threat—even a clear and present danger—to the American Experiment can be solved by federal judges. As Judge Cardozo once aptly warned, a judicial commission does not confer the power of "a knight-errant, roaming at will in pursuit of his own ideal of beauty or of goodness;" rather, we are bound "to exercise a discretion informed by tradition, methodized by analogy, disciplined by system.'" Benjamin N. Cardozo, The Nature of the Judicial Process 141 (1921).

The dissent correctly notes that the political branches of government have to date been largely deaf to the pleas of the plaintiffs and other similarly situated individuals. But, although inaction by the Executive and Congress may affect the form of judicial relief ordered when there is Article III standing, it cannot bring otherwise nonjusticiable claims within the province of federal courts. See Rucho, 139 S. Ct. at 2507-08; Gill, 138 S. Ct. at 1929 ("'Failure of political will does not justify unconstitutional remedies.' . . . Our power as judges . . . rests not on the default of politically accountable officers, but is instead grounded in and limited by the necessity of resolving, according to legal principles, a plaintiff's particular claim of legal right."); Brown, 902 F.3d at 1087 ("The absence of a law, however, has never been held to constitute a 'substantive result' subject to judicial review[.]").

The plaintiffs have made a compelling case that action is needed; it will be increasingly difficult in light of that record for the political branches to deny that climate change is occurring, that the government has had a role in causing it, and that our elected officials have a moral responsibility to seek solutions. We do not dispute that the broad judicial relief the plaintiffs seek could well goad the political branches into action. Diss. at 45-46, 49-50, 57-61. We reluctantly conclude, however, that the plaintiffs' case must be made to the political branches or to the electorate at large, the latter of which can change the composition of the political branches through the ballot box. That the other branches may have abdicated their responsibility to remediate the problem does not confer on Article III courts, no matter how well-intentioned, the ability to step into their shoes.

III.

For the reasons above, we reverse the certified orders of the district court and remand this case to the district court with instructions to dismiss for lack of Article III standing.

Reversed.

STATON, DISTRICT JUDGE, dissenting:

In these proceedings, the government accepts as fact that the United States has reached a tipping point crying out for a concerted response—yet presses ahead toward calamity. It is as if an asteroid were barreling toward Earth and the government decided to shut down our only defenses. Seeking to quash this suit, the government bluntly insists that it has the absolute and unreviewable power to destroy the Nation.

My colleagues throw up their hands, concluding that this case presents nothing fit for the Judiciary. On a fundamental point, we agree: No case can singlehandedly prevent the catastrophic effects of climate change predicted by the government and scientists. But a federal court need not manage all of the delicate foreign relations and regulatory minutiae implicated by climate change to offer real relief, and the mere fact that this suit cannot alone halt climate change does not mean that it presents no claim suitable for judicial resolution.

Plaintiffs bring suit to enforce the most basic structural principle embedded in our system of ordered liberty: that the Constitution does not condone the Nation's willful destruction. So viewed, plaintiffs' claims adhere to a judicially administrable standard. And considering plaintiffs seek no less than to forestall the Nation's demise, even a partial and temporary reprieve would constitute meaningful redress. Such relief, much like the desegregation orders and statewide prison injunctions the Supreme Court has sanctioned, would vindicate plaintiffs' constitutional rights without exceeding the Judiciary's province. For these reasons, I respectfully dissent.

QUESTIONS

1. What happened in Juliana v. U.S.?
2. What was the agency action or inaction at issue?
3. What components of constitutional standing did the court subject to scrutiny?
4. How did the plaintiffs attempt to demonstrate standing?
5. How did the court rule on each standing component, and why?
6. Do you agree with the court's standing analysis? Why or why not?

EXCERPT: JAMES R. MAY & ERIN DALY, CAN THE U.S. CONSTITUTION ENCOMPASS A RIGHT TO A STABLE CLIMATE (YES, IT CAN)
39 UCLA Envtl. L. Rev. 39 (2021)

Introduction

Much scholarship about the climate crisis commences with the Four Horsemen of the Apocalypse entering stage right, making the case for action (and causes of action) in the face of catastrophe. Climate change is raising global temperatures, heating oceans, melting glaciers and ice caps, and wreaking havoc on weather patterns. Suffice it to say that an unstable climate disrupts most aspects of day-to-day life, including family, food, water, employment, education, and shelter, and the pursuit of equality, dignity, justice, peace and happiness. Climate change in general presents new challenges to the human rights regime as it increases human vulnerability to poverty and disease, which in turn creates opportunities for political oppression and myriad other forms of human rights abuses – all of which disproportionately threaten the lives and, health and dignity of future generations. Climate change may well turn entire populations into refugees, raising human rights issues to a new level.

Increasingly, courts are hearing claims alleging infringement of a right akin to a stable climate, including in the Netherlands, Ireland, Pakistan, Colombia and elsewhere. But not so much in the United States, owing to a conservative tradition of judicial deference if not diffidence on issues thought to be best left to the political branches. Yet this is slowly changing. One example is *Juliana v. U.S.*, in which children argue that action and inaction by the U.S. Government's actions and inactions have caused or contributed to the climate crisis in violation of a fundamental constitutional right to a stable climate.

Growing up in the shadow of this environmental apocalypse, the *Juliana* plaintiffs — 21 youths who have been fighting this fight since most were in high school — asked a federal court to do three things. First, to recognize that constitutional liberty includes a right to climate capable of sustaining human life — a claim that the district court upheld and the Ninth Circuit assumed to be legitimate. Second, to declare that the federal government has violated this right by decades of administrative policies and programs including subsidies, taxes, and other favorable economic advantages that have promoted the use of fossil fuels to the detriment of the climate. And third, to require the government to cease violating the plaintiffs' rights by developing and implementing a plan that would reduce the threats to the planet's climate. This may sound complex but, as pleaded, it was in fact an ordinary case: plaintiffs ask the court to define the contours of a constitutional right, to find a violation, and then to issue a remedy to redress the violation. This is what courts do.

In the five years since it was launched, *Juliana* has spawned abundant spools of scholarship and conference proceedings, similar and copycat cases, and tributes and critiques. But it has not, so far, yielded an affirmative response to this question on the merits. In response, however, the U.S. Government argues no such right exists, and even if it does that federal courts can't do anything about it. We are of the view, however, that the Constitution can accommodate, and that federal courts have authority to engage, such a claim.

Two caveats should be recognized from the outset. First, the point here *is not* that the Constitution *necessarily* protects people from climate change, but that courts should be open to deciding whether it does. Second, and relatedly, the point here *is not* that bringing such constitutional claims in federal court is the best or only way to address climate change. Of course, legislative action at the international, regional, national and subnational levels is preferable, with enforceable emission limits and/or workable market-based mechanisms, and mitigation and reparation available to those most affected. But, as noted, that has not happened.

Rather, the important points are threefold. First, the Constitution is relevant to the protection of people's lives and liberties – a position that should be beyond cavil after more than 230 years of our constitutional experiment. Second, the Constitution's protection is not abrogated simply because the threat to life and liberty comes from decades of governmental action contributing to climate change. The Constitution does not have a climate change, or even an environmental, exception. And, third, the federal judiciary is the body that, in our constitutional system, is best suited to hold accountable government actors when they imperil the constitutional rights of the people.

We focus on the United States because it is unusual in two relevant regards. First, the political branches have not been as responsive to the needs of climate as either the situation requires or as the population would want. Second, the United States Constitution is and has been interpreted by federal courts to be particularly restrictive in allowing the political branches to act. These two facts -- combined with America's seemingly insatiable appetite for fossil fuels -- have made the country an outlier in its failure to address the threats of climate change.

Hence, we inquire as to whether the United States Constitution accommodate a claim based on a right to a stable climate? We believe it can (and should), for three reasons addressed in the sections that follow. First, federal courts should not shirk their constitutional obligations when presented with novel or controversial claims. Second, a right to a stable climate can be a constitutionally cognizable cause of action under the Due Process Clause because such a right is both deeply rooted in American legal history and essential to ordered liberty. Third, climate claims are justiciable because the political question doctrine does not apply to individual constitutional rights, and even if it does, well-established judicially discoverable and manageable constitutional standards exist to evaluate such claims. As a case in point, we then turn to *Juliana v. U.S.* in concluding that the U.S. Constitution can accommodate a claim based on a right to a healthy climate and that the federal judiciary should be available to hear it.

I. Federal Courts have the Authority to Engage Such a Claim

A claim based on a due process right to a stable climate is within judicial cognizance. To determine the constitutional merits of such claims through trial is the core function of the federal judiciary. Federal courts should be permitted to perform their constitutional functions to manage a case "preservative of [other] rights," including developing a record, issuing rulings, and reaching a decision, as they would in any other constitutional case, The Supreme Court has held that jurisdiction in cases like this is mandatory. The Court said that "where the complaint . . . is so drawn as to seek recovery directly under the Constitution . . . the federal court . . . *must* entertain the suit . . . " and that "the court *must* assume jurisdiction to decide whether the allegations state a cause of action on which the court can grant relief, as well as to determine issues of fact arising in the controversy." This follows from the mandatory language of Article III which establishes that the federal judicial power *shall* extend to all cases or controversies arising under the federal Constitution (among other things). Moreover, a judicial audience is especially necessary where the plaintiffs *have no alternative for redress* for reasons both factual (the government has proven unwilling to curb its appetite for fossil fuels) and legal (plaintiffs are denied the right to vote due to their age).

There is little question that federal courts can handle the constitutional claims presented to it under the Due Process clauses. For more than 230 years, they have been deciding constitutional claims. Some of these claims were novel; some asked the courts to extend the understanding of an established constitutional principle; some asked the courts to apply constitutional rights to new situations, or to recognize for the first time values which, though not express, have always undergirded our constitutional system; and some asked the courts to harmonize U.S. law with the law in other democratic countries. Courts have resolved even the most contentious and profound questions, including the constitutionality of slavery, the scope of executive authority, and the constitutionality of discrimination and affirmative action in a series of cases spanning more than 50 years. Some cases in which lower courts were asked to decide difficult questions of first impression were reversed when they reached the Supreme Court and some were not. Any student of constitutional law would likely have their own list of examples and cases to add to these.

In all of these cases, regardless of the novelty of the claims, the complexity of the issues, the importance of the case, or the social or political implications of the judicial determination, lower courts were able to make an independent judgment of the claims, and any errors were corrected in appellate courts or the Supreme Court. Regardless of the final outcome, litigants had their day in court.

That a right to a stable climate is novel or controversial makes it all the more amenable to judicial resolution. The constitution protects what is of fundamental importance and what cannot be relegated to protection in the political branches alone. A stable climate system satisfies both of these and does so, arguably more than anything else in history. Protection against the degradation of the environment is precisely the kind of problem that the political branches are *least* likely to be able to protect: it requires long-term thinking for the benefit of those who have no political voice (because they are young, or not yet born).

Resistance to judicial engagement rests on two fundamental errors. First, it makes the profoundly misplaced argument that it is clearly erroneous for federal courts to consider tough cases involving the government. Second, it ignores the core federal judicial function of holding a trial to determine the meaning of a constitutionally protected fundamental right. Simply, disappointed parties too have at their disposal the same rights, defenses and ability for appeal as they would in other constitutional cases.

Separation of powers considerations should not be a bar to judicial engagement of cases alleging a constitutional right to a stable climate just because these are cases of first impression. Every case involves a controversy, and many of them tough. That is what makes it a *case*. Every federal case involving the federal government implicates separation of powers. That is why *powers are separated*. The district court should be permitted to perform its constitutional functions under our tripartite system to manage the case, develop a record, issue rulings, and reach a decision.

Now no less than ever before, courts must be available to hear all constitutional claims, even those that raise factual issues the framers might not even have dimly foreseen. Changing circumstances must be provided for as they occur. As the Supreme Court recently noted:

> The nature of injustice is that we may not always see it in our own times. The generations that wrote and ratified the Bill of Rights and the Fourteenth Amendment did not presume to know the extent of freedom in all of its dimensions, and so they entrusted to future generations a charter protecting the right of all persons to enjoy liberty as we learn its meaning. When new insight reveals discord between the Constitution's central protections and a received legal stricture, a claim to liberty must be addressed.

Nor is it a jurisdictional bar that the claim concerns important questions that are essential to our system of ordered liberty – that is, to the various crises of human affairs. Rather, to determine the constitutional merits of such claims is the core function of the federal judiciary. Through the ages, federal courts have been the locus for resolving even the most contentious and profound questions: slavery in *Pennsylvania v. Prigg*, presidential authority in *Youngstown Sheet & Tube Co. v. Sawyer*, segregation in *Cooper v. Aaron*, affirmative action in *Grutter v. Bollinger*, immigration in *Department of Homeland Security v. Regents of California*, health care in *Sebelius v. NFIB*, and elections in *Bush v. Gore*. In the due process context as well, the federal courts have not demurred from deciding cases that raise profound and complex questions of policy: nationalism in *Meyer v. Nebraska*, reproductive rights in *Griswold v. Connecticut*, the nature of family in *Moore v. City of East Cleveland*, marriage equality in *Obergefell v. Hodges,* and even the war on terror in *Boumediene v. Bush*. While one may agree or disagree with the holdings in these cases, there is no doubt whatsoever that the federal judiciary had jurisdiction to hear them. Whether these partake of global phenomena or implicate sensitive political matters is irrelevant to a federal court's authority to hear a well-pleaded claim.

The climate context of this case makes it all the more amenable to judicial resolution. Government action can and does impact the stability of the climate system and the ability of American citizens to own property along the shoreline for fishing and farming, to exercise all their other rights, and indeed to live full and free lives. Federal courts can apply well-entrenched constitutional principles to determine the limits of governmental power to infringe on these liberty interests.

Rather than violating separation of powers, the federal judicial department's assertion of jurisdiction over this Fifth Amendment claim implicates the core function of the federal courts in our system of separation of powers: to determine the meaning and scope of constitutionally protected fundamental rights. This is, essentially, the power to say what the law is, a power that has been allocated to the federal judicial department since *Marbury v. Madison* and repeated ever since Chief Justice John Marshall's determination that it is "emphatically the province and duty of the judicial department to say what the law is." such as in *Cooper v. Aaron,* in which the Court "declared the basic principle that the federal judiciary is supreme in the exposition of the law of the Constitution, and that principle has ever since been respected by this Court and the Country as a permanent and indispensable feature of our constitutional system."

To place the question before the federal courts is not to remove it from the political sphere. As the *Obergefell* court reminded us in the context of marriage, "changed understandings of marriage are characteristic of a Nation where new dimensions of freedom become apparent to new generations, often through perspectives that begin in pleas or protests and then are considered in the political sphere and the judicial process." In our constitutional democracy, policies are shaped within the limits of the Constitution. The question before federal courts concerns not the wisdom of the polices but their compliance with constitutional rights. That is fundamentally a judicial question, a "claim to liberty [that] must be addressed."

Indeed, it would be an unprecedented arrogation of *executive* power for the Court to concede to the executive the power to say what the law is and to hold itself immune from judicial scrutiny where due process rights are at stake. The Supreme Court has said as much in a series of cases on another unprecedented, and global phenomenon: the war on terror. Indeed, the Supreme Court recently rejected a similar claim of political branch authority "to govern without legal constraint" in a brief but firm paragraph in *Boumediene v. Bush*: "Even when the United States acts outside its borders, its powers are not 'absolute and unlimited' but are subject 'to such restrictions as are expressed in the Constitution' . . . [t]o hold the political branches have the power to switch the Constitution on or off at will . . . would permit a striking anomaly in our tripartite system of government, leading to a regime in which Congress and the President, not this Court, say 'what the law is.'" Indeed, it would be an unprecedented abdication of the role of the Court to cede its role of interpreting the law to a coordinate branch. Such an abdication of the role of the court to say what the law is would undermine the separation of powers on which the rule of law depends and breach the duty of the court to fulfill its constitutional role. It would allow the executive to hold itself immune from judicial scrutiny despite violating due process rights of its citizens—a result profoundly inconsistent with the constitutional design. Climate change does not justify departing from these principles.

II. The Due Process Clause Can Accommodate a Right to a Stable Climate

The Due Process Clause(s) of the United States Constitution can accommodate a right to a stable climate. As applied to federal action, it provides: "No person shall be ... deprived of life, liberty or property, without due process of law," and as to state action, "nor shall any State deprive any person of life, liberty or property, without due process of law." How can this seemingly rather simply phrasing reach something as stark as the climate crisis?

Landmark decisions exist from almost every decade of the last one hundred years establishing and reaffirming that, in addition to incorporating most of the enumerated rights, the liberty clauses of the Fifth and Fourteenth Amendments protects unenumerated rights. These include rights to direct the education and upbringing of one's children, procreation, bodily integrity, contraception, abortion, sexual intimacy, family, and marriage, possession of weapons, and against grossly excessive punitive damages. Moreover, many of the Court's liberty cases have shown special concern for the interests of children, acutely menaced by the climate crisis now, and later. Denying this would amount to constitutional interpretation frozen in time, either at the time of the nation's founding or at a time long before and a place far away. We believe, on the other hand, that there are fair arguments that the government's obligation not to destabilize the climate is deeply rooted in our nation's history and tradition and implicit in the concept of ordered liberty.

A. The Government's Obligation to Not to Destabilize the Climate is Deeply Rooted in the Nation's History

History is relevant to constitutional interpretation, but not in the way the government surmises. Rather, the Supreme Court has always understood that history and traditions are relevant to how it interprets the Due Process Clause. For decades, it has recognized fundamental rights under the Due Process Clause as those that are (1) deeply rooted in American history and tradition or (2) essential to ordered liberty. We turn next to the consideration of climate stability as inherent in our history, traditions, and system of ordered liberty. While it is not a conventional value, it is no less essential to our constitutional democracy than privacy, family, child protection, and other recognized fundamental rights.

First, the *Juliana* plaintiffs rely on the government's obligation to hold the air in public trust for present and future generations. This obligation, the plaintiffs argue, creates a due process right to a stable climate. To support the claim, the plaintiffs point to the longstanding recognition of the public trust doctrine both as a matter of common law and as a constitutional imperative.

Protection of environmental conditions is deeply rooted in Anglo-Saxon law and legal traditions. The public trust doctrine derives from a historical notion that the sovereign holds certain natural resources and objects of nature in trust for the benefit of current and future generations. In 533, the Romans codified the right of public ownership of important natural resources: "The things which are naturally everybody's are: air, flowing water, the sea, and the sea-shore."

The *Magna Carta Libertatum*, where the due process clause finds its earliest roots, drew a direct link between the environment and individual liberties. In particular, it resulted in the Carta de Foresta (Forest Charter) in 1217. This guaranteed the "liberties of the forest and free customs traditionally had, both within and without the royal forests" and obliged all "to observe the liberties and customs granted in the Forest Charter."

English common law continued the public trust tradition: "There are some few things which, notwithstanding the general introduction and continuance of property, must still unavoidably remain in common . . . Such (among others) are the elements of light, air, and water . . . ." The doctrine was since incorporated into common and statutory laws throughout the United States, amply "rooted in the precept that some resources are so central to the well-being of the community that they must be protected by distinctive, judge-made principles." The principle was then incorporated into American constitutional law in the Supreme Court's 1892 decision in Illinois Central Railroad Company v Illinois.

The outer boundaries of the due process clauses – no more than any other aspect of the Constitution – are not frozen in time. As Justice Frankfurter explained, "[t]o believe that this judicial exercise of judgment could be avoided by freezing 'due process of law' at some fixed stage of time or thought is to suggest that the most important aspect of constitutional adjudication is a function for inanimate machines and not for judges." Rather, for nearly 200 years, the Constitution has been understood to be adaptive: it was, Chief Justice John Marshall said,

> [I]ntended to endure for ages to come, and consequently to be adapted to the various crises of human affairs. To have prescribed the means by which Government should, in all future time, execute its powers would have been to change entirely the character of the instrument . . . It would have been an unwise attempt to provide by immutable rules for exigencies which, if foreseen at all, must have been seen dimly, and which can be best provided for as they occur.

And, as Justice Harlan said, and as others have often repeated:

> Due process has not been reduced to any formula; its content cannot be determined by reference to any code. The best that can be said is that through the course of this Court's decisions it has represented the balance which our Nation, built upon postulates of respect for the liberty of the individual, has struck between that liberty and the demands of organized society.... The balance of which I speak is the balance struck by this country, having regard to what history teaches are the traditions from which it developed as well as the traditions from which it broke. That tradition is a living thing.

The Supreme Court has long treated the Due Process Clause as a living thing. For example, in elucidating "[t]he identification and protection of fundamental rights," *Obergefell* emphasized that courts must "exercise reasoned judgment in identifying interests of the person so fundamental that the State must accord them its respect." In exercising such "reasoned judgment," courts should keep in mind that "[h]istory and tradition guide and discipline this inquiry but do not set its outer boundaries." This approach allows "future generations [to] protect . . . the right of all persons to enjoy liberty as we learn its meaning."

Indeed, the Court has shown a capacity to adapt the Constitution to contemporary conditions. It has coupled a willingness to protect modern day interests with the true meaning of the Constitution, even if the eighteenth-century framers could not have foreseen modern social, technological, or environmental conditions.

Just as the Court can stretch the language of the First Amendment to address speech on the internet and the Fourth Amendment to address surveillance, the Fifth Amendment can accommodate rights beyond the framers' imaginations, a such as that to a stable climate.

By contrast, the U.S. Government has argued that the unenumerated rights stemming from the Due Process Clause are limited to what rights were recognized at the time of the Court of Westminster. This would freeze rights only to those afforded by the British Empire in the 17th Century, that is, before women's suffrage, the Civil War, abolishment of slavery in the United Kingdom, the ratification of the Constitution and even the American Revolution. This sweep of this argument is astonishing. There is no basis for freezing federal court jurisdiction to a time before the existence of federal courts, not to mention what was in the court at Westminster. Simply, it is hard to see how the judicial power of the courts at Westminster should hold any sway as a matter of *American constitutional* law, given that (1) those courts decided cases under *common* law, (2) England lacked (and still lacks) a constitutional document, and (3) its decisions were not final insofar as they could be overturned by the Parliament. All three factors show the Westminster courts to be an irrelevant baseline.

***

B. A Stable Climate is Essential to Ordered Liberty

The other factor indicating a fundamental interest is whether recognizing the right as fundamental is essential to ordered liberty such that "neither liberty nor justice would exist if they were sacrificed." The district court in *Juliana* correctly reasoned, "a stable climate system is quite literally the foundation 'of society, without which there would be neither civilization nor progress.'" Interests essential to ordered liberty are undoubtedly at stake in this case. Ordered liberty means more than freedom from bodily restraint. As the Court wrote nearly 100 years ago:

While this Court has not attempted to define with exactness the liberty thus guaranteed, the term has received much consideration and some of the included things have been definitely stated. Without doubt, it denotes not merely freedom from bodily restraint, but also the right of the individual to contract, to engage in any of the common occupations of life, to acquire useful knowledge, to marry, establish a home and bring up children, to worship God according to the dictates of his own conscience, and generally to enjoy those privileges long recognized at common law as essential to the orderly pursuit of happiness by free men.

Constitutional 'liberty' is not fixed in time but is instead a rational continuum requiring close examination of governmental justification of deprivation:

[T]he full scope of the liberty guaranteed by the Due Process Clause cannot be found in or limited by the precise terms of the specific guarantees elsewhere provided in the Constitution. This 'liberty' is not a series of isolated points .... It is a rational continuum which, broadly speaking, includes a freedom from all substantial arbitrary impositions and purposeless restraints ... and which also recognizes, what a reasonable and sensitive judgment must, that certain interests require particularly careful scrutiny of the state needs asserted to justify their abridgment.

Supreme Court jurisprudence insists that the right to liberty requires close examination of governmental justification of deprivation in a wide range of areas. Thus, the district court in *Juliana* was correct to find that a stable climate is essential to ordered liberty: "I have no doubt that the right to a climate system capable of sustaining human life is fundamental to a free and ordered society." Ordered liberty cannot exist in an unstable climate, where increasingly severe storms, fires, and floods threaten every American's home, family, and community. An unstable climate system can also adversely affect many profound extensions of liberty, including occupation, education, family, food, shelter, travel, drinking water, residence, and relationships.

III. The Right to a Stable Climate is Justiciable

In addition to being within judicial authority and constitutionally cognizable, the right to a stable climate is justiciable. The Due Process Clauses of the United States Constitution can accommodate a fundamental right to a climate capable of sustaining human life. However, the federal judiciary has, over time, established a number of doctrines that would limit their availability to hear their claim. The most significant of these conflates the doctrine of standing with the political question doctrine to preclude judicial review. Acceptance of this argument is not a judgment on the merits that plaintiffs have not established a right or a violation; rather, it would prevent their claims from even being heard. What is at stake at this stage is whether these youth —seeking to use the constitutional right of due process of law to fight for their lives and for a sustainable planet—are even entitled to have a judge hear their claim.

The political question doctrine, by definition, does not apply: if the right exists under the Constitution, it is a legal right, not a political question. The Court has been making this distinction since *Marbury v. Madison*. Second, if the right exists under the Constitution, then the Court can discern and manage the standards by which a violation is to be identified and a remedy to be assessed.

A. Constitutional Rights are Not Political Questions

While the Constitution does not identify a field of 'political questions' beyond the reach of the federal judiciary, the Supreme Court has concluded that matters that are textually committed to an elected branch of government, or otherwise imprudent for judicial evaluation, are not justiciable. The doctrine's political philosophy is "essentially a function of the separation of powers" rooted in Jeffersonian notions of constitutional theory that democracy is best served by having coordinate elected branches resolve political questions rather than politically unaccountable federal judges. The doctrine applies to disable federal courts from reviewing matters when they "ought not enter [the] political thicket." Yet the political question doctrine never applies to individual rights, including to a stable climate.

***

B. Constitutional Standards Are Judicially Discoverable and Manageable

The political question doctrine precludes jurisdiction not when the question is novel, but when it is governed by *no standard at all*. For example, in *Vieth*, the plurality held that political gerrymandering claims are non-justiciable, not because they require courts to apply a broad standard like reasonableness, but because courts could not articulate any meaningful standard whatsoever.

The applicable standards are a function of the right or interest at issue, whether strict scrutiny, rational basis, or any other standard the Court has devised in its voluminous rights jurisprudence. Balancing individual liberties against governmental interests, as due process analysis requires courts to do, is a task presumptively appropriate for federal courts. Indeed, in *Baker*, the Court held reapportionment claims to be justiciable because "[j]udicial standards under the Equal Protection Clause are well developed and familiar." This is exactly what courts do in all cases involving fundamental individual rights.

Here, a legal framework of judicially discoverable and manageable standards exists for evaluating these youth plaintiffs' claims. Under the law of the Ninth Circuit, for instance, "the crux of this inquiry is . . . not whether the case is unmanageable in the sense of being large, complicated, or otherwise difficult to tackle from a logistical standpoint," but rather whether "a legal framework exists by which courts can evaluate . . . claims in a reasoned manner."

The standards requested by the youth plaintiffs are judicially discoverable. Courts regularly engage with complex scientific issues and have established standards for resolving them. As Justice Breyer has observed:

The Supreme Court has . . . decided basic questions of human liberty, the resolution of which demanded an understanding of scientific matters . . . Scientific issues permeate the law . . . [W]e must search for law that reflects an understanding of the relevant underlying science, not for law that frees [defendants] to cause serious harm.

To remedy systemic constitutional violations, courts have overseen remedial plans of much greater complexity, touching on difficult issues of social science, when compared with the hard science involved in climate change.

***

It is fair to say that *all* five federal judges involved since the outset of the case —the three judges on the appellate panel, the district court judge, and the magistrate judge initially assigned to the case with the district court— agree about most everything the plaintiffs sought to establish judicially:

☐ Climate change is real "and occurring at an increasingly rapid pace";
☐ We are in the midst of a human-induced ecological "apocalypse";
☐ The Government knowingly caused and facilitated emissions of massive amounts of greenhouse gases for decades ("substantial evidentiary record documents that the federal government has long promoted fossil fuel use despite knowing that it can cause catastrophic climate change, and that failure to change existing policy may hasten an environmental apocalypse.");
☐ The Government's administrative policies and programs promote the use of fossil fuels, threatening the climate ("A significant portion of those emissions occur in this country; the United States accounted for over 25% of worldwide emissions from 1850 to 2012, and currently accounts for about 15%.");
☐ The Government *knew* their actions could contribute to "catastrophic climate change, and that failure to change existing policy may hasten an environmental apocalypse";
☐ The youth plaintiffs have pled a constitutionally valid fundamental right to be free from actions of the Defendants that destroys the capability of the climate system to sustain human life;
☐ The youth plaintiffs have suffered imminent, ongoing, concrete, and particularized injuries ("The plaintiffs' alleged injuries are caused by carbon emissions from fossil fuel production, extraction, and transportation");
☐ The actions and inactions of Defendants caused these injuries;
☐ There is a judicial role in administering justice ("We do not dispute that the . . . relief the plaintiffs seek could well goad the political branches into action");
☐ Action is needed ("Absent some action, the destabilizing climate will bury cities, spawn life-threatening natural disasters, and jeopardize critical food and water supplies"); and
☐ The youth plaintiffs have pled meritorious claims ("The plaintiffs have made a compelling case that action is needed; it will be increasingly difficult in light of that record for the political branches to deny that climate change is occurring, [and] that the government has had a role in causing it . . . .").

The most recent decision is from the Ninth Circuit, which, 2-1, dismissed the case for lack of standing. Most of the opinion reads as though the plaintiffs prevail at every turn. The full panel assumed that the government had violated plaintiffs' constitutionally protected liberty interest to live in a climate system capable of sustaining human life. It found that a "substantial evidentiary record documents that the federal government has long promoted fossil fuel use despite knowing that it can cause catastrophic climate change, and that failure to change existing policy may hasten an environmental apocalypse." It held that plaintiffs met their *prima facie* burden of proof that climate change is real, "apocalyptic," and caused in part by actions and inactions of the U.S. Government, noting: "The plaintiffs have made a compelling case that action is needed; it will be increasingly difficult in light of that record for the political branches to deny that climate change is occurring, that the government has had a role in causing it, and that our elected officials have a moral responsibility to seek solutions. We do not dispute that the broad judicial relief the plaintiffs seek could well goad the political branches into action."

Nonetheless, two judges voted to dismiss the case on the ground that Ninth Circuit plaintiffs lacked Article III standing to sue the federal government; more particularly, they had, prior to trial, failed to prove that a court could redress their actual and particular injuries. The court was skeptical that the relief sought would reduce plaintiffs' injuries and thought any remedy would require judicial action in areas entrusted to the other two branches of the government. The case made headlines worldwide, in part because it went against the tenor the times, as courts are increasingly finding judicial power to act in the face of climate change.

The Ninth Circuit, agreed with plaintiffs about the importance of the rights at stake. The Court also agreed that plaintiffs have been specifically and personally injured by the government's conduct over decades, and agreed that such conduct has contributed to a worsening of the planet's climate to the point where it may not longer be capable of sustaining human life. Nonetheless, it held that plaintiffs' injuries were not "redressable" by the Court because there lacked judicially discoverable and manageable standards."

The Ninth Circuit, however, found that the plaintiffs lacked standing because (sliding into political question territory) there are no judicially discoverable and manageable standards by which the injury could be redressed. The Court here not only conflates standing and political question doctrines, but abdicates responsibility to remedy the violation of a constitutional right because it is confused about climate change.

***

In a spirited dissent in a case even the majority described as a last ditch effort to avoid apocalypse, Judge Josephine L. Staton put it this way: "My colleagues throw up their hands, concluding that this case presents nothing fit for the Judiciary. On a fundamental point, we agree: No case can singlehandedly prevent the catastrophic effects of climate change predicted by the government and scientists. But a federal court need not manage all of the delicate foreign relations and regulatory minutiae implicated by climate change to offer real relief, and the mere fact that this suit cannot alone halt climate change does not mean that it presents no claim suitable for judicial resolution."

As the dissent in *Juliana* correctly observes, however, the majority's Article III analysis misperceives the role of federal courts in protecting youth plaintiffs' individual constitutional rights. While the majority may be correct in saying "it is beyond the power of an Article III court to ... design [] ... or implement the plaintiffs' requested remedial plan," the youth plaintiffs have not asked the courts to make a plan or implement an action otherwise committed to an elected branch of government. Instead, they seek *declaratory* relief and, if appropriate, following a bifurcated trial's remedial phase, an injunction ordering *the Government* to develop and implement a plan to reduce fossil fuel emissions and atmospheric carbon dioxide. These youth plaintiffs simply request that federal courts recognize contravention of a constitutional right and, if necessary, use reasoned judgment to dispense a remedy for the Defendants to implement.

***

The court was also wrong for an even more profound and disturbing reason: assuming the United States government is continuing to take actions that are violating the plaintiffs' constitutional rights to a climate system capable of sustaining human life and hastening a global environmental apocalypse, how can courts avoid their responsibility to the young plaintiffs and to the world? The

Ninth Circuit's answer is not reassuring. Saying that it was dismissing the case "reluctantly," the court reassured the plaintiffs by saying that their "impressive case for redress must be presented to the political branches of government." In ordinary times, this is often the refrain of a reticent court.

The extraordinariness of this litigation is patent on both the plaintiff side and on the defense side. On the plaintiff side, the case serves as a stress test underlying the relationship between the climate crisis and the U.S. Constitution, with the underlying question being whether the Constitution can accommodate a right to a stable climate. In *Juliana*, the Ninth Circuit *accepted* the opinion of the youth plaintiffs' experts that a stable climate—safe for the youth plaintiffs and capable of sustaining human life—requires atmospheric CO_2 levels of no more than 350 parts per million. Regardless, the majority pretermitted a trial that would help it utilize the scientific testimony and evidence to decide whether the defendant's knowing causation of catastrophic climate destabilization, and resulting endangerment of youth plaintiffs, violates their individual constitutional rights. Because executive officials presumptively "abide by an authoritative interpretation of the Constitution," declaratory relief would prompt the Defendants to reduce their contributions to the climate crisis—an outcome that would be sufficient for redressability. Bifurcating proceedings into two steps would have helped. Step one would have been to determine whether it is necessary to order the Defendants to prepare and implement a remedial plan. Step two would have been to assess, utilizing the best available science and the aid of special masters, whether the cumulative emissions reductions effectuated would put the Government on a path consistent with stabilizing the climate at 350 ppm by 2100.

On the defense side, the case serves as a stress test for something almost as important as climate change: the rule of law. The government's position that its actions are judicially unreviewable does not contain a limiting principle. But in our constitutional system, judicial review of governmental authority has been, at least since 1803, the single thing that ensures that ours is "a government of laws, and not of men," and it is the *only* form of accountability that exists at all, other than biennial elections -- which, again, have no resonance for youths disallowed from voting.

***We make three points. First, that courts should not shirk their constitutional function to review constitutional claims concerning climate change. Second is that the Constitution can accommodate a right to a stable climate. And third, that constitutional claims are justiciable. The fact that this case challenges government action that promoted climate change is no reason to depart from well-settled principles of separation of powers and rule of law.

In the final analysis, can the U.S. Constitution accommodate a claim pursuing a right to a stable climate? Yes, it can.

QUESTIONS

1. Does the U.S. Constitution provide aa right to a healthy environment?
2. How about to a stable climate?
3. Are you convinced it does? That it should?
4. If not, is/are there other ways to have the law recognize such rights?

CHAPTER 7: ENVIRONMENTAL RIGHTS

Chapter 7 explains the role of environmental rights in environmental law. 'Rights' typically derive expressly or implicitly from constitutional text. As Parts I and II explain, many nations and some states afford or recognize a judicially-cognizable right to a healthy environment. We'll then explore questions as to whether Nature (Part III) and other Animals (Part IV) have rights. Part V finishes by considering how constitutions can and do protect the right to participate in environmental policymaking.

I. INTRODUCTION TO ENVIRONMENTAL RIGHTS

EXCERPT: JAMES R. MAY, THE CASE FOR ENVIRONMENTAL HUMAN RIGHTS: RECOGNITION, IMPLEMENTATION AND OUTCOMES
42 Cardozo L. Rev. 983 (2021).

The idea that every human being has a right to a clean and healthy environment has caught the imagination of people across religious, cultural, constitutional, national, and continental divides. What, though, is the case for environmental human rights? This question incorporates many others, including whether there is or ought to be a human right to a healthy environment; where and how it should be recognized; how to implement it; and the extent to which it causes or correlates to improvements in outcomes. Simply, the case for environmental human rights is complicated and complex. There are normative, ethical, and moral justifications that both the planet and people living on it are better off in a world that recognizes a right to a healthy environment. Reflecting this, a majority of nations already do so, and the effort for international recognition is gaining momentum. Ultimately, however, while it is compelling, the case for environmental human rights has shortcomings that warrant consideration and further analytical interrogation.

The query begins with orienting environmental rights in the vast wilderness of human rights. The field of human rights engages rights that are thought to inhere to humanness, commonly categorized as either civil and political, or social, economic, and cultural. Civil and political rights include the rights to vote, assemble, and participate, as well as the rights to free speech, religion, and legal processes. Socioeconomic and cultural rights include those to dignity, education, health, food, water, sick leave, family leave, and employment, to name a few. A right to a healthy environment straddles the liminality between and among other rights.

Yet most human rights instruments all but ignore the existence of anything akin to a human right to a healthy environment. The Charter of the United Nations (1945), the Universal Declaration of Human Rights (1948), and the twin covenants on human rights, the International Covenant on Civil and Political Rights (ICCPR) and the International Covenant on Economic, Social, and Cultural Rights (ICESCR) (both adopted in 1966 and entered into force in 1977), mention not at all whether being human includes such a right. And, until fairly recently, the human rights oeuvre largely avoided the question as to whether humans are entitled to a healthy environment.

But that is changing. A human right to a healthy environment has taken hold in constitutions and courts and is of increasing cognizance under international governance regimes. As of this writing, around 136 nations grant something akin to a potentially enforceable right to a healthy environment, including about 84 expressly and at least 6 more impliedly through some other express right, such as to life, dignity, or health. Also, there is an increasing effort for global recognition of a right to a healthy environment, in part fueled by domestic developments. Courts often lead these domestic efforts. As discussed below, judges in Argentina have ordered the clean-up of a major urban river; judges in the Philippines and Chile have ordered protection of old growth forests from clear-cutting; judges in Pakistan have ordered the creation of a climate change agency; judges in the American state of Pennsylvania have protected residents from the environmental ravages of hydrofracking and directed revenues from oil and gas leases toward the public good, while judges in Nigeria ordered the cessation of gas flaring; and in Ecuador, Colombia, and India, judges have recognized personhood for nature, for its own sake. Courts have also been willing to bend socioeconomic rights to address climate change, as recently evidenced by major decisions issued by the Constitutional Court of Germany and the Supreme Court of Pakistan.

Thus, there are decisions by thoughtful judges hewing closely to the words of their constitutions and choosing not to skirt engagement of provisions guaranteeing a right to a clean and healthy environment.

Recognition of a right to a healthy environment is now the subject of considerable effort and within humanity's reach, if only we can grasp it. But what is less clear is whether and the extent to which all of this is worth the coin, yet, and if so, why it is a better use of time and energy than by, say, protecting *other* established rights, working to enact and enforce environmental laws, or by implementing other regimes, such as the United Nations' Sustainable Development Goals, discussed below. It is complicated and hard to know. Ultimately, however, while the case is solid, it has shortcomings that warrant consideration and further analytical interrogation. In the end, the outcome and objective converge: the world is better off for recognizing everyone's right to a healthy environment.

Thus, this Article examines three aspects of the case for environmental human rights, and includes an associated Appendix. Part I considers the extent to which environmental human rights have been recognized in law, such as by international instrument, constitution, or court decision. Part II then examines the extent to which courts are reaching results because of an environmental right. Part III then contemplates the extent to which recognizing environmental human rights in law improves environmental outcomes. Last, the Appendix lists countries that currently recognize a right to a healthy environment constitutionally.

This Article concludes that although environmental human rights have found footholds about half the world over, judicial recognition has been slow in coming and mixed in results. There remain few cases issued from apex courts (that is, courts that issue controlling opinions) engaging environmental rights, leaving much opportunity for the development of legal principles. There is also spare demonstrable evidence that legal recognition of a right to a healthy environment improves environmental outcomes, suggesting a need for further interrogation.

I.   Recognition of a Right to a Healthy Environment

Conceptually, the human right to environmental rights is deeply rooted in Anglo-Saxon law and legal traditions. The *Magna Carta Libertatum* (Medieval Latin for "the Great Charter of the Liberties"), adopted at Runnymede in 1215 ("[t]o no one will we sell, to no one deny or delay right or justice[]") drew a direct link between the environment and individual liberties. The Magna Carta produced the *Carta de Foresta*, or "Forest Charter," in 1217, which guaranteed the "liberties of the forest and free customs traditionally had, both within and without the Royal Forests," and obliged all "to observe the liberties and customs granted in the Forest Charter." The Magna Carta remains influential today, for example, informing interpretation of the U.S. Constitution: "The American colonists . . . widely adopted Magna [Carta's] 'law of the land' guarantee . . . ."

Yet recognition of a legal right to a healthy environment was a long time coming. If anything, its recognition is defined by evolution of outright denial of such a right, to hesitating acceptance in constitutions over the course of fifty years, to the present-day enthusiasm to recognize such a right in international law. The following sections track the development of recognition of a right to a healthy environment domestically, internationally, and regionally.

A.   Recognition in Domestic Constitutional Law

There are myriad arguments in support of constitutionalizing rights in the first place, including that doing so embodies "aspirational goals" and "relations between citizens," and "enable[s] citizens to counter constitutional challenges to their rights to sue with a constitutional right of their own, forcing federal courts to accommodate co-equal rights and principles . . . ." In particular, constitutions can promote human and environmental rights, procedural guarantees, remedies, and judicial engagement. Such constitutionalization advances the environmental human rights of everyday people to enforce the law.

The recognition of a right to a healthy environment has grown symbiotically with "Global Environmental Constitutionalism," which explores the constitutional engagement, incorporation, adjudication and implementation of environmental rights, duties, responsibilities, procedures, policies, and other measures that promote the twin aims of environmental protection and a right to a healthy environment around the globe. Environmental human rights are reflected by other constitutional means, including by granting rights to water, sustainable development, and a safe climate; by recognizing the rights of children, current and future generations, indigenous peoples, and nature; by imposing (sometimes reciprocal) duties to protect the environment and the climate; and by guaranteeing access to information, participation, and justice in environmental matters and/or ensuring environmental impact assessment. The world has turned slowly if inexorably toward recognizing a right to a healthy environment, most significantly at the constitutional level by recognizing an express or implied substantive right to a healthy environment, discussed below.

1.   Express Constitutional Recognition of a Substantive Right

The first efforts to enshrine a substantive right to a healthy environment came from what now seems an unlikely source—the United States, where constitutional recognition first found its voice in the early 1960s. In 1962, none other than Rachel Carson—renowned author, marine biologist, and future Presidential Medal of Freedom awardee—called for a federal constitutional amendment to protect people from chemical poisons. Then, in 1968, a junior congressman from New York State—Richard Ottinger—took up the charge for constitutional recognition for a right to a healthy environment (or "decent," the nomenclature of the day), reasoning that "'only an amendment to the Constitution, guaranteeing to each citizen a wholesome and unimpaired environment, can overcome' the ease with which current conservation efforts may be evaded." A similar bill was introduced in the United States Senate to "guarantee every person . . . an inalienable right to a decent environment." These are, evidently, the first efforts at constitutional recognition of something resembling a right to a healthy environment.

Both support for and opposition to these bills was bipartisan. After these bills stalled, Congress enacted—and the President signed—the National Environmental Policy Act (NEPA), which is the closest the United States has ever come to recognizing a right to a healthy environment, if only with the hortatory to "encourage productive and enjoyable harmony between man and his environment." NEPA in turn became one of Congress's most influential legislative exports throughout the world.

Lacking an express constitutional provision, litigants tried to insinuate environmental rights within the U.S. Constitution under various theories, including the Due Process and Equal Protection Clauses and the Ninth Amendment. Nothing stuck.

There were coincident efforts to recognize the right constitutionally at the subnational level, beginning in 1968 with Franklin Kury, a state representative from Pennsylvania. These efforts hit paydirt in a handful of states, becoming the first places anywhere to constitutionalize rights to a healthy environment. In 1970, the State of Illinois got there first with a provision reading: "Each person has the right to a healthful environment." Other states soon followed, led by Pennsylvania in 1971, Massachusetts and Montana in 1972, and Hawai'i in 1978. No two provisions are the same. While most of these five provide a "right" to the "environment," the adjectival objective—"clean" or "healthful" or "quality"—differs from state to state. For example, Hawai'i's and Montana's constitutions aim to afford a "clean and healthful environment," Illinois's "the right to a healthful environment," and Massachusetts's a "right to clean air and water, freedom from excessive and unnecessary noise, and the natural, scenic, historic, and esthetic qualities of their environment." Pennsylvania's provision is the most progressive of the lot, providing twin attributes of rights and public trust:

> The people have a right to clean air, pure water, and to the preservation of the natural, scenic, historic and esthetic values of the environment. Pennsylvania's public natural resources are the common property of all the people, including generations yet to come. As trustee of these resources, the Commonwealth shall conserve and maintain them for the benefit of all the people.

The most elaborate of the bunch, this provision stayed largely dormant for forty years, until the Pennsylvania Supreme Court resuscitated it beginning in 2013. In addition, some states in the United States have adopted legislation advancing other rights, including a right to water. Subsequently, a right to a healthy environment has been recognized at the subnational constitutional level in Brazil, Germany, Iraq, and Bosnia and Herzegovina.

The network of countries recognizing a constitutional right to a healthy environment has grown from none to nearly half the world. In 1976, Portugal was thought to be the first country to embed a constitutional right to a healthy environment. Other countries followed suit. In the mid-1990s, Edith Brown Weiss identified about fifty constitutional provisions globally that explicitly recognized a fundamental right to a quality environment. I reported that this number had grown to around sixty by 2004, sixty-five by 2009, and seventy-six by 2014.

As of this writing in mid-2021, I count 84 of 193 United Nations (U.N.) member states as recognizing an express substantive constitutional right to a healthy environment.

What circumstances make constitutional recognition of a right to a healthy environment more likely? A decade ago, [we] concluded that countries are more likely to add a substantive right to a healthy environment if they have already recognized multiple other economic, social, and cultural rights in their constitutions. In a pioneering 2012 report, the Toronto Initiative for Economic and Social Rights (TIESR) dataset measured the presence, absence, and justiciability of seventeen economic and social rights (ESRs), including a right to a healthy environment, among constitutions worldwide. The TIESR study determined that countries with multiple ESRs are more likely to enshrine a right to a healthy environment.

Josh Gellers suggests that three factors contribute to constitutional instantiation of environmental rights. First, that "the likelihood that a country will adopt a constitutional environmental right is directly associated with its domestic political conditions and structures, and indirectly associated with the international normative context in which its constitution is written." Second, that countries with poor human rights records are more likely to adopt constitutional environmental rights: "[I]n accordance with expectations, I found that the worse a country's human rights record in terms of its protection of civil liberties, the more likely it is to promulgate an environmental right in its constitution." And third, that proximity to other countries that have enshrined environmental rights has nothing to do with it: "[G]lobally speaking, the enactment of environmental rights does not appear to be influenced by the extent to which such rights have been constitutionalized elsewhere in a given region."

Gellers concludes that there is not a paradigmatic legal system for accommodating individual rights to a healthy environment. To be sure, the list of those nations who have is hardly discriminating. It includes developing and developed nations, north and south, east and west. It contains nations from the four corners: Africa, the Middle East, Western Europe, the former Soviet Bloc, Latin America, and Oceania and archipelago, as well as those with civil, common law, Islamic, Native American, and other traditions. Moreover, the constitutions of many more contain "directive principles" and reciprocal "duties" to guide national policy and individual action for matters affecting the environment. The United Nations Environment Programme (UNEP) concludes that at least 150 countries recognize a right to a healthy environment in some fashion, including by regional agreement and domestic legislation. This does not begin to count constitutional provisions addressing a wide range of environmental matters, including rights to water. Furthermore, nearly twenty countries expressly recognize a constitutional goal of "sustainability" or "sustainable development," although most of these are in sections of the constitutions or written in language that suggests non-enforceability.

Nonetheless, as Gellers and Jeffords acknowledge, constitutionalizing environmental rights is not always commendable: "'The results, however, do not support unqualified constitutionalization of environmental rights without careful deliberation.'" For example, it can involve trade-offs that may be detrimental to other valued rights, such as to employment, water, fishing, farming, family, travel, and property.

2. Implied Constitutional Recognition of a Substantive Right

Constitutional environmental rights can be derived from other rights as well. Courts in several countries have held that other socioeconomic rights, including rights to life, health, and dignity, implicitly incorporate environmental rights, although only a handful with a controlling and durable legal presence. In his annual Thematic Report from 2020, the UN Special Rapporteur on a Right to a Healthy Environment lists eighteen countries that recognize an "implied" right to a healthy environment: Bangladesh, Cyprus, El Salvador, Estonia, Ghana, Guatemala, India, Ireland, Italy, Liberia, Lithuania, Malaysia, Namibia, Nigeria, Pakistan, Panama, Sri Lanka, and Tanzania.

But upon closer examination of the summaries provided by the Special Rapporteur, the list of countries to imply environmental human rights appears to be closer to six than eighteen, as a vast majority of the cases cited have been reversed, ignored, or fallen into desuetude. In *Friends of the Irish Environment CLG v. Fingal County Council*, the Supreme Court of Ireland rejected and reversed the plaintiffs' claim that the Constitution of Ireland's right to life and dignity provision incorporates an implied right to a healthy environment. The case listed in support of recognition of an implied right to a healthy environment in Nigeria—*Gbemre v. Shell Petroleum*

Development—was decided fifteen years ago by a lower court, did not serve as precedent, and was not enforced. The case from Malaysia—*Tan Teck Seng v. Suruhanjaya Perkhidmatan Pendidikan*—is from a lower court twenty-five years ago, and admittedly relies on "obiter dicta," that is, a superfluous remark from the court. The case relied upon for Cyprus—*Republic v. Pyrgon Community*—was again decided twenty-five years ago does not seem to have lasting purchase. The cases from Italy—including *Decision No. 5172/1989* (Corte di Gassazione Sezioni Unite)— are even older, although there are more of them. Then there are cases that do not seem to be based on a determination that there is an implied right to a healthy environment. The cases relied upon for El Salvador do not appear to determine that other socioeconomic rights confer an implied right to a healthy environment and in any event were decided a quarter of a century ago and have not served as precedent. While the case relied upon for Ghana—*Centre for Public Interest Law v. Environmental Protection Agency*—appears to comment on the governmental duties to protect the environment, it does not recognize an implied substantive right to a healthy environment. The case from Estonia——Case No. 3-3-1-101-09—is dated and revolves around procedural rights, and in any event seems to lack precedential moment. Liberia lacks either express or implied environmental rights from other socioeconomic rights and seems to be listed solely due to membership in the African Charter on Human and Peoples' Rights.

Of the nine countries remaining, courts in Bangladesh, India, Pakistan, and Sri Lanka regularly recognize an implied right to a healthy environment. In addition, Guatemala and Panama appear to possess relatively strong jurisprudence in support of an implied right to a healthy environment as well. Yet Lithuania, Namibia, and Tanzania do not have sufficient (or much of any) track record to support legal recognition of an implied right. In any event, Namibia is evidently mentioned because its constitution incorporates international agreements, arguably including Article 24 of the African Charter on Human and Peoples' Rights, which includes a right to live in a healthy environment, which is not implied recognition.

Thus, at this point only courts in Bangladesh, Guatemala, India, Pakistan, Panama, and Sri Lanka can confidently be said to recognize an implied right to a healthy environment regularly. What this suggests is not that there are eighteen countries that imply a right to a healthy environment from other socioeconomic rights, but that in eighteen countries, there is jurisprudence that could conceivably support such a claim, and that in all but six of these countries, the claim to an implied right has not been established.

B.   Recognition in Domestic Legislation

Some countries have granted a right to a healthy environment under domestic legislation, but not under that country's constitution. The Special Rapporteur reports that an additional twenty-three countries recognize a right to a healthy environment under domestic legislation that do not do so constitutionally. Further research is needed to ascertain the extent to which this legislation is impactful.

C.   Recognition in International Law

The international community has taken notice of environmental human rights, initially at Stockholm in 1972, and more recently by the United Nations Human Rights Council (UNHRC), the UNEP, various regional bodies, and elsewhere.

Shortly after the initial incorporation of environmental rights at the subnational level in the United States, in June 1972, the U.N. General Assembly convened the first United Nations Conference on the Human Environment (Conference) in Stockholm, Sweden. The meeting's principal purpose was to negotiate a legal document about the environment. In the days leading up to that watershed meeting, a group of "dissidents" led by Jacques Cousteau, concerned about the meeting's lack of emphasis on a human right to a healthy environment, called a "counter-summit" across the street to encourage nations to recognize environmental rights in their constitutions if the resulting declaration did not. Marathon negotiations ensued.

Then, on June 16, the Conference issued the Declaration of the United Nations Conference on the Human Environment, or Stockholm Declaration, which says: "Man has the fundamental right to freedom, equality and adequate conditions of life, in an environment of a quality that permits a life of dignity and well-being, and he bears a solemn responsibility to protect and improve the environment for present and future generations." The Stockholm Declaration was the first international document to recognize what has become known as a right to a healthy environment. This "most innocuous" language has changed the world.

While initially resistant, human rights-based thinking about the environment emerged nonetheless, and has enjoyed increasing prominence at the table of human rights.

Nonetheless, international law and especially multilateral environmental agreements do not say much about human rights to a healthy environment. There are some exceptions, including the 1989 Hague Declaration (recognizing "the right to live in dignity in a viable global environment"), and Principle 1 of the 1992 Rio Declaration ("Human beings are at the centre of concerns for sustainable development. They are entitled to a healthy and productive life in harmony with nature."). The Paris Climate Agreement also has preambulatory recognition of human rights ("Parties should, when taking action to address climate change, respect, promote and consider their respective obligations on human rights . . . .").

There are efforts for international recognition of a right to a healthy environment. A quarter-century ago, the United Nations commissioned the influential Ksentini Report, published in 1994, which concluded that "[e]nvironmental damage has direct effects on the enjoyment of a series of human rights, such as the right to life, to health, [and] to a satisfactory standard of living." More recently, the UNHRC appointed an Independent Expert, and then a Special Rapporteur on Human Rights and the Environment, who, among many other things, has agitated for international recognition of such rights, issued "Framework Principles on Human Rights and the Environment," supported a "Global Pact for the Environment," joined judicial workshops on a right to a healthy environment, written amicus briefs advocating for recognition of such rights, and appealed to the United Nations General Assembly and the UNHRC to adopt a resolution recognizing a right to a healthy environment.

International recognition of a right seems to be gaining traction in other ways, too. The United Nations Human Rights Committee (a treaty body overseeing the International Covenant on Civil and Political Rights) recently issued a Comment and several important decisions connecting human rights to environmental outcomes, including the climate crisis. The UNEP—which in part administers multilateral environmental agreements—recently launched an "Environmental Rights Initiative" to conduce constitutional rights to a healthy environment. Environmental human rights can also help operationalize the U.N.'s Sustainable Development Goals.

Yet, the world still lacks an overarching legal treaty recognizing the right to a healthy environment. The Global Pact for the Environment hit headwinds from several directions (political, geographic, socioeconomic). Whether a right to a healthy environment is a matter of customary international law is a difficult case to make. Perhaps additional headway can be made as the fiftieth anniversary of the Stockholm Conference draws near, including efforts to have the U.N. General Assembly or the UNHRC issue a resolution or declaration in support of it. Time will tell.

D.   Recognition in Regional Law

The story at the regional level is very different. Since the 1992 Rio Declaration on Environment and Development, about 130 nations have endorsed regional agreements that mention a right to a healthy environment, including the Additional Protocol to the American Convention on Human Rights in the Area of Economic, Social, and Cultural Rights ("Everyone shall have the right to live in a healthy environment . . . ."); the African (Banjul) Charter on Human and Peoples' Rights ("All peoples shall have the right to a general satisfactory environment favorable to their development."); the Arab Charter on Human Rights ("Every person has the right to an adequate standard of living for himself and his family, which ensures their well-being and a decent life, including food, clothing, housing, services and the right to a healthy environment."); and the Association of Southeast Asian Nations Human Rights Declaration ("Every person has . . . the right to a safe, clean and sustainable environment."). Neither the European Convention on Human Rights nor the European Social Charter includes an express right to a healthy environment.

Mentioning a right to a healthy environment is not the same thing as conferring one, of course. Among the regional agreements doing so, "the African Charter on Human and Peoples' Rights is the only human rights treaty, albeit a regional one, to include a justiciable right to a healthy environment." As of this writing, fifty-four out of fifty-five countries of the African Union Member States have ratified the African Charter. Of these ratifying countries, thirty-one already recognize a right to a healthy environment.

Thus, the African Charter provides legal basis for recognition in an additional twenty-three countries (54−31=23). Yet courts in some of these countries have held that the African Charter is not enforceable there, such as Nigeria. Thus, it is a leap of faith to conclude that twenty-three additional countries are subject to the African Charter, but lacking an express right to a healthy environment, nonetheless recognize such a right.

Recognition of something akin to a right to a healthy environment does not make it legally enforceable. For instance, the Preamble to the 1998 United Nations Economic Commission for Europe (UNECE) Convention on Access to Information, Public Participation in Decision-Making, and Access to Justice in Environmental Matters (commonly known as the Aarhus Convention) recognizes also that "every person has the right to live in an environment adequate to his or her health and well-being, and the duty, both individually and in association with others, to protect and improve the environment for the benefit of present and future generations." Moreover, Article 1 provides:

> In order to contribute to the protection of the right of every person of present and future generations to live in an environment adequate to his or her health and well-being, each Party shall guarantee the rights of access to information, public participation in decision-making, and access to justice in environmental matters in accordance with the provisions of this Convention.

Yet neither the Preamble nor Article I are enforceable. For example, reading the Aarhus Convention's preambulatory mention of a "right to live in an environment" among twenty-four other such provisions as legal recognition would likely come as a surprise to those countries that have long joined international conventions that commonly contain preambulatory provisions, meaning all of them. Indeed, the United Kingdom and Ireland emphasized in signing statements their view that the seventh clause is aspirational but not enforceable. Moreover, the Aarhus Convention's "Compliance Mechanism" applies to procedural rights to information, participation, and access to justice, but does not grant substantive rights. In this vein, the former Special Rapporteur on Human Rights and the Environment, John Knox, has observed:

> The rapid growth of the right to a healthy environment might suggest that it is well on its way to joining the list of generic rights. . . . However, not all recognitions are equal. . . . Becoming a party to the Aarhus Convention, for example, evidences less commitment to the right than adding it to a constitution.

Next, as with the Aarhus Convention, the United Nations Regional Agreement on Access to Information, Public Participation and Justice in Environmental Matters in Latin America and the Caribbean (also known as the Escazú Agreement)—which entered into force on April 22, 2021—mentions a right to a healthy environment among a long list of preambulatory provisions. Again, these are not legally enforceable.

Neither the Aarhus Convention nor the Escazú Agreement provides a basis for enforcing a right to a healthy environment. Moreover, only a minority of signatory states have seen fit to constitutionalize such a right, including only twenty of forty-seven countries that have ratified the Aarhus Convention, and just four of those that have ratified the Escazú Agreement, which would further seem to suggest that joining these important conventions does not signify legal recognition of such rights.

Mentioning a right to a healthy environment in a legal instrument is not the same thing as legal recognition of an enforceable right. As mentioned, the Stockholm Declaration recognized "the fundamental right to . . . an environment of a quality that permits a life of dignity and well-being." Yet it would misapprehend international law to contend that such mention amounts to "legal recognition" of such a fundamental right, but if so, why constitutional incorporation was necessary in the first place or took the twisted route detailed above. But assuming mention amounts to legal recognition, then it would be fair to contend that the member states that supported the Stockholm Declaration—including the United States—and the 112 countries of the U.N. General Assembly that supported the resolution adopting it therefore legally recognize a right to a healthy environment. But that clearly was not and is not the case.

E. Extent to Which Environmental Human Rights Are Recognized

Thus, the number of countries legally subject to a right to a healthy environment would seem to be 136 as follows: 84 (express substantive right) + 6 (implied substantive right) + 23 (subject to the African Charter but lacking an express or implied right) + 23 (recognized legislatively but lacking an express or implied right (84+6+23+23=136). More research is needed to ascertain whether and the extent to which this recognition improves environmental outcomes.

II.   Implementing Environmental Human Rights

Recognizing a right to a clean and healthy environment without judicial, legislative, regulatory, and other means to implement them is tantamount to Pyrrhic victory. Examining the extent to which recognition amounts to implementation is complex. Predictors of effective implementation include clear constitutional text, a commitment to the rule of law, respect for separation of powers, participation, democracy, and an active civil society. For example, the French system's two forms of constitutional review (procedural and substantive), may be "a model in the field of environmental constitutionalism." And combining procedural and substantive provisions can help. Political disruption can, perhaps unexpectedly, also foster development and implementation. And a recent report identifies laws from 110 countries that it says expressly grant a right to a healthy environment.

Yet the most consequential implementation thus far is judicial engagement and enforcement. Even if courts in many countries continue to be reluctant to engage environmental rights provisions,

> [T]he trend is positive and powerful. Those courts that have embraced these provisions have transformed a notion writ large—environmental human rights—into a multitude of national narratives writ small. . . . In many cases constitutionally enshrined environmental rights provided the last clear chance at vindicating a human right to an adequate environment.

There is a small but growing body of case law engaging express environmental rights, including in the climate context. The *Arctic Oil* case—construing Article 112 of the Constitution of Norway—was a leading example, until it was dismissed by the Supreme Court of Norway. Moreover, in 2018 the Constitutional Court of Colombia held that the Colombian Amazon enjoys legal rights to protection, and in 2017 the High Court of South Africa required the preparation of a climate impact assessment prior to the issuance of a permit to build a large coal-fired power station as a means to meet constitutional demands.

In countries where the text of the constitution is not as green, courts have looked elsewhere to advance climate justice—often in the rights of life and dignity. For example, a 2005 case from an intermediate court in Nigeria derived environmental values from that country's constitutional right to dignity. The court held that the petroleum developers' flaring of "waste" natural gas in the Niger Delta abridged the community plaintiffs' constitutionally guaranteed right to dignity. The court granted "leave to the [a]pplicants . . . to apply for . . . the enforcement of their fundamental rights to life and dignity of [the] human person as provided by . . . the Constitution of the Federal Republic of Nigeria." Moreover, these constitutionally guaranteed rights inevitably include the right to a clean, poison-free, pollution-free, healthy environment. Accordingly, the court issued an injunction, which was not enforced. Notice the courage of the judge who found a constitutional, actionable right to a quality environment based on the dignity of people in the situation of the petitioner.

While *Gbmere* did not stop or even alter gas-flaring practices in Nigeria, it was among the first decisions to find that environmental degradation diminishes constitutionally-protected human dignity:

> Gbemre stands as an important decision despite not ultimately diminishing the extent of flaring in Nigeria. . . . First, dignity rights provide a vocabulary for foregrounding the damage to people from environmental and climate injustices. Second, they draw attention to how environmental injustice affect all the essential aspects of a person's life: where food security, access to clean water, and breathable air are threatened; a person's ability to design her own life plan is weakened, and her ability to live in material comfort is impossible. Third, Gbemre shows how attention to the equal worth of all those involved in environmental outcomes evidences a respect for the human dignity of each person. Perhaps most importantly, Gbemre signals a growing appreciation in jurisprudence of the connection between dignity and environmental conditions.

Ensuring human dignity can be the basis for addressing climate change, even in the absence of other legal means. For example, while the Constitution of Pakistan lacks a specific right to a healthy environment, Article 14 provides: "The dignity of man and, subject to law, the privacy of home, shall be inviolable." In a series of groundbreaking cases, the Lahore High Court turned to Article 14 to address climate change. First in 2015, the court established a "Climate Change Commission" (CCC) to review the threats of climate change in Pakistan, considering its effects on water resources, forestry, agriculture, and environmental, climate, and water justice. And then, in 2018, the Lahore High Court dissolved the CCC, finding it had accomplished two-thirds of its goals, and established a "Standing Committee" to help the government implement greenhouse reduction strategies.

There also seems to be a growing recognition of the link between human dignity and the environment. For example, the U.N. Special Rapporteur on Human Rights and the Environment determined that: "Human rights are grounded in respect for fundamental human attributes such as dignity, equality and liberty. The realization of these attributes depends on an environment that allows them to flourish. . . . Human rights and environmental protection are inherently interdependent." These developments suggest the inexorable relationship between human dignity and a healthy environment.

Recognizing environmental rights informs related environmental considerations, such as environmental justice. Environmental justice recognizes that every person has equal dignity and equal rights to a clean and healthy environment and access to information, participation, justice, and remedies in environmental matters. It aims to address and redress the disproportionate effects of environmental policies and practices on the politically underrepresented, vulnerable, and disempowered, including low-income, indigenous, minority, and other vulnerable communities.

Courts remain essential to the implementation of environmental human rights. Nearly a decade ago Daly and I observed that "courts and international tribunals are enforcing constitutionally enshrined environmental rights with growing frequency, recognising basic human rights to clean water, air, and land, and environmental opportunity," and that "courts are increasingly taking seriously the challenge of enforcing both substantive and procedural constitutional environmental rights, to the benefit of constitutional law generally and environmental rights in particular." In addition, "[t]here is also a "growing body of judicial decisions concerning constitutional rights to participate in environmental matters[,]" including in 2015 by the Constitutional Court of Colombia, in 2000 by the Ecuador Constitutional Tribunal, and in 1999 by the Supreme Court of South Africa.

Some courts have been receptive to "harmonious construction," that is, construing fundamental rights to life and dignity to incorporate a right to a healthy environment, as easing judicial roadblocks to public interest litigation. For example, observing that "it cannot be imagined to live with dignity in a polluted environment," in 2015 the Supreme Court of Nepal enjoined marble mining in a UNESCO-protected site. Then in 2017, the High Court of Ireland construed the constitutional "right to dignity" as incorporating a right to a healthy environment.

Environmental human rights are finding footholds under regional treaties, too, led by the Inter-American Court of Human Rights, which in 2017 issued an advisory opinion recognizing a right to a healthy environment in the context of climate change's disproportionate impact on vulnerable persons, and in 2020 applying a right to a healthy environment in a contested (as-applied) case. The European Union is contemplating legislation to recognize biodiversity as a basic human right. And the Supreme Court of the Netherlands relied on rights conferred by the European Convention on Human Rights to life and family to order the government to reduce greenhouse gas emissions by twenty-five percent.

The rights of nature have been subject to increased judicial cognizance as well. For example, the Constitutional Court of Ecuador has engaged that country's first-ever recognition of the rights of nature. In 2016, the Colombian Constitutional Court issued a landmark decision recognizing the Rio Atrato's legal ability to assert its rights in court under that country's "Ecological Constitution." In 2017, the High Court of Uttarakhand in India found that the Rivers Ganges and Yamuna, along with their tributaries, are juristic persons, and declared that "Rivers, Forests, Lakes, Water Bodies, Air, Glaciers, and Springs have a right to exist, persist, maintain, sustain and regenerate their own vital ecology system" and have "the status of legal persons," with all corresponding rights. However, the Supreme Court of India subsequently reversed and dismissed this decision. Other courts followed this example, including the Supreme Court of Justice of Colombia, which, in 2018, held that the Colombian Amazon enjoys legal rights. And in 2020, the Islamabad High Court recognized the legal personhood of an elephant, ruling that it possesses a constitutional protection to dignity.

However, courts still have yet to engage express environmental rights as often as might be expected. As Daly and I noted in 2009, "[t]here are surprisingly few judicial decisions implementing constitutionally enshrined environmental rights provisions. Assuming the existence of litigants and lawyers and commencement of an action, there remain trenchant obstacles to judicial vindication of environmental rights, including text, meaning, judicial receptivity, and political will." More than a decade on, we identified fifty leading cases in a 2019 UNEP report, few of which are based on an express constitutional environmental right. Moreover, many constitutional provisions have not been the subject of judicial examination. Of those that have, few have yielded judicial orders. Judicial orders are then often not implemented or monitored, or are ignored or neglected altogether. Few have resulted in the relief requested and ultimate transformation of environmental conditions.

There are multiple inhibitors to implementation. One is the lack of standards, which are few and far between. Another is enforceability. For example, while the constitutions of at least eight countries address climate change, there is of yet no caselaw engaging these provisions, suggesting that they are not enforceable. Implementation challenges persist, including in Brazil, owing to a host of geographic and political reasons, and in Colombia, where an extraction-based, business-friendly, and corrupt system, coupled with recovery from long-running armed conflict, provide steep challenges to implementation.

A 2013 case in Pennsylvania shows how much difference an enforceable provision can make, finding a right to be "on par with, and enforceable to the same extent as, any other right reserved to the people in Article I," and invalidating major aspects of a state oil and gas law designed to facilitate the development of "shale gas." The same provision was enforced in 2017 to hold that the government was (1) (mis)using proceeds generated from the sale of its public natural resources, and (2) (wrongfully) transferring significant parts of a public park to a real estate developer.

In the aggregate, these adjudicative developments show "that collectively the judiciary will continue to play a necessary, if not sufficient, role in the vindication of fundamental environmental rights worldwide." Caution about conclusions is warranted here, too. "No judicial order can resolve the problems of environmental degradation or climate change; in many cases, the most that a court can do is galvanise the political process to take environmental protection seriously. But this, in and of itself, is worth the effort to vindicate constitutional environmental rights." Thus "it is essential that new cases be brought to courts, building on the constitutional principles and the laws that make them effective. Only when jurisprudence improves can a conclusion be made on whether constitutional environmental rights [bring] real change."

III.   Outcomes in Environmental Rights

Given the evolution and implementation of environmental human rights, what difference does legal recognition make? The above tracks the recognition and implementation of environmental human rights across the globe. What is less clear is whether and the extent to which all of that effort is worth the coin, or if anything a better use of time and energy than working to recognize and implement *other* established rights, enacting and enforcing environmental laws, or implementing existing international schema, such as the U.N. Sustainable Development Goals. The results are mixed, despite a surfeit of good intentions and practices.

Evidence of implementation has various disputed inputs. The current Special Rapporteur on Human Rights and the Environment has previously concluded that constitutionalizing environmental rights contributes to an assortment of causal and correlative outcomes, including a decrease in pollution (including emissions of greenhouse gases), and an increase in both the enactment and enforcement of environmental laws. Others (including me) have posited that constitutionalizing environmental rights can also serve to promote human and environmental rights, procedural guarantees, remedies, and judicial engagement.

But perhaps a fair assessment is that the most common global attribute in environmental constitutionalism is under-recognition and under-enforcement. Simply, outcomes lag the feel-good narrative. Standards designed to implement environmental rights have been few and far between. And while consistent with them, environmental rights constructs do not easily fit into existing international environmental frameworks, such as the U.N. Sustainable Development Goals. Environmental rights approaches have yet to do much to address environmental injustice. And while more and more courts are issuing opinions that engage claims or devise remedies in the service of environmental rights, courts worldwide have generally been reluctant to recognize or effectuate remedies to implement constitutionally-instantiated environmental rights, including in the context of climate change. Perhaps unexpectedly, much of the advancement of the idea of a human right to a healthy environment has been achieved through the enforcement of classic "first generation rights," such as a right to life, health, or dignity.

This result is partially explained by the limits of language. The right to a healthy environment engenders a welter of questions, including those steeped in epistemology (understanding desired ends), etymology (what words mean, including "environment," "healthy," etc.), and implementation (the extent to which constitutional rights are operationalized and enforced). Outcomes are also complex and fraught with interpretive challenges that are the result of a collection of actions taken over time by various actors public and private: the decision to constitutionalize environmental rights and/or values, the enactment of legislative and regulatory rules to support the constitutional right, the allocation of national resources to create judicial systems that respect the rule of law, the decision to provide broad standing to plaintiffs to sue in courts of competent jurisdiction, and the private resources that enable individuals to take advantage of all these things.

Indeed, relying on judicial decisions as indicia of outcomes is itself fraught. Adjudicative and legal tradition, engagement, activism, and interpretation vary wildly, even within a single country. Legal comparativism is fraught with misinterpretation, mistranslation, cultural and class bias, and the vestiges of colonialism. Moreover, the subject field is also intrinsically unreliable, as only a fraction of constitutionally-incorporated environmental rights have been the subject of judicial examination by apex courts, Of these, few have yielded judicial orders, and fewer yet of these have resulted in the relief requested. Simply, the causative evidence that environmental rights improve environmental outcomes is lacking.

Moreover, even judicial decrees granting relief do not secure improvements in environmental conditions. Just by way of example, nearly three decades after the celebrated *Minors Oposa* case, the government continues to permit timber harvesting largely unaffected by the case; a decade after issuance of a remarkably ambitious judicial order in the *Manila Bay Case*, it remains heavily polluted; the Matanza-Riachuelo River is still heavily polluted notwithstanding the issuance of another ambitious judicial decree in the *Beatriz Mendoza* case from Argentina; and the flaring of natural gas remains virtually unabated in the Niger Delta despite a court issuing a restraining order in another pioneering case, *Gbemre v. Shell*.

Furthermore, while embedding a right to a healthy environment in a constitution may *correlate* (or be "positively associated") with better environmental performance (and the results here are mixed), evidence demonstrating that doing so necessarily *causes* improvement is lacking. Jeffords and Gellers observe:

> Yet much work remains in order to firm up these claims. Future research should consider a meaningful way to control for existing statutory laws and policies associated with environmental outcomes and related human rights outcomes and environmental justice concerns. . . . Going forward, it is important to consider the role of existing statutory laws and regulations as either a complement or a supplement to constitutional frameworks.

In fact, as they note:

> [S]ome countries without constitutional environmental rights often have better environmental performance records. Failing to control for existing environmental policy thus likely biases the estimated association between constitutional environmental rights provisions and environmental outcomes, human rights outcomes, and environmental justice concerns. This is a serious problem of omitted variables that has the potential effect of "making something from nothing."

Suffice to say that much more replicated and analytically sophisticated research is needed to support claims that constitutional entrenchment results in better environmental performance: "Future research, including case studies and quantitative cross-sectional, panel, and time-series analyses, should attempt to address the various limitations and qualifications of the existing empirical research in an effort to maximize the effectiveness of such rights while acknowledging the realities and constraints inherent to different legal and political contexts."

Recognizing environmental human rights can contribute to qualitative improvements, such as participation in governance. Indeed, one study found that embedding both substantive and procedural rights is "positively associated" with access to water sources and sanitation facilities. Yet others argue that proceduralizing environmental rights diminishes their import: "It is becoming increasingly clear that substantive environmental rights without complementary procedural components usually fail to protect human interests (often due to a lack of justiciability) and that procedural environmental rights (by themselves) guarantee nothing more than that ecologically disastrous decisions will be made after due process."

Analytical frameworks could help to improve outcomes. In his role as Special Rapporteur, John H. Knox issued "Framework Principles" on a right to "a safe, clean, healthy and sustainable environment." More recently, the World Resources Institute recently released a comprehensive "toolkit" for advancing environmental rights through information and participation in decision-making.

Environmental rights can improve environmental outcomes by the institution of certain "good practices." In his prior role as the Independent Expert on Human Rights Obligations Relating to the Enjoyment of a Safe, Clean, Healthy and Sustainable environment, Knox issued a report that

> [D]escribes good practices of Governments, international organizations, civil society organizations, corporations and others in the use of human rights obligations relating to the environment, including (a) procedural obligations to make environmental information public, to facilitate public participation in environmental decision-making, to protect rights of expression and association, and to provide access to legal remedies; (b) substantive obligations, including obligations relating to non-State actors; (c) obligations relating to transboundary harm; and (d) obligations relating to those in vulnerable situations.

Additional good practices include having an objective, clear text, self-execution, scaffolding with other rights, access to information, participation and justice, and, most importantly, judicial and legislative engagement.

In sum, while some studies show an association between environmental rights and environmental performance, and good practices and structures can help improve outcomes, more studies replicating these outcomes are warranted before statistically confident causal connections can be drawn.

Conclusion

The case for environmental human rights is complicated and complex. There are normative, ethical, and moral justifications that both the planet and people living on it are better off in a world that recognizes a right to a healthy environment. Reflecting this, a majority of nations already recognize a right to a healthy environment, and the effort for international recognition is gaining momentum. But what is less clear is whether and the extent to which all of this is worth the coin, yet, and if so, why it is a better use of time and energy than by, say, protecting *other* established rights, working to enact and enforce environmental laws, or by implementing other regimes, such as the U.N. Sustainable Development Goals. Ultimately, however, while the case for environmental human rights is solid, it has shortcomings that warrant consideration and further analytical interrogation.

Human rights enthusiasts were slow to realize a right to a healthy environment. Environmental constitutionalism picked up the slack and has provided a consequential means for legal recognition, which now propels efforts for international recognition. Still, implementation remains challenging in ways great and small, and, most especially, judicially.

There is also no question that environmental human rights possess normative and moral suasion. On balance, however, questions about outcomes remain. Yet in the end, recognizing a right to a healthy environment cannot hurt, and if anything, is likely to shape positive stories if not outcomes. In the end, the outcome and objective converge: the world is better off for recognizing everyone's right to a healthy environment.

II.   STATE ENVIRONMENTAL RIGHTS

States accomplish most environmental regulation through legislation and regulatory means. Some states, including Pennsylvania, have constitutions that contain provisions designed to address environmental considerations, as a recent case from the Supreme Court of Pennsylvania demonstrates.

Here we return to *Robinson Township v. Commonwealth of Pennsylvania*, a remarkable tour de force in subnational constitutionalism. If you recall, in *Robinson Township*, a team of municipalities and individuals challenged the constitutionality of "Act 13," Act 13: Act No. 13 of Feb. 14, 2012, P.L. 87, *eff.* immediately (in part) and Apr. 16, 2012 (in part), 58 Pa.C.S. §§ 2301–3504, a Pennsylvania state law that promotes hydraulic fracking by preempting local regulation and providing power of eminent domain to natural gas corporations. The Commonwealth Court, en banc, No. 284 MD 2012, 52 A.3d 463 (2012), found that the act was unconstitutional in part and enjoined application of certain provisions. The Supreme Court affirmed in part and reversed in part. Earlier we learned of how the court addressed the public trust portions of the court's opinion. Below we turn to the "rights" based portion.

ROBINSON TWP. V. COMMONWEALTH OF PENNSYLVANIA
83 A.3d 901 (2013)

Chief Justice CASTILLE.

In this matter, multiple issues of constitutional import arise in cross-appeals taken from the decision of the Commonwealth Court ruling upon expedited challenges to Act 13 of 2012, a statute amending the Pennsylvania Oil and Gas Act ("Act 13"). Act 13 comprises sweeping legislation affecting Pennsylvania's environment and, in particular, the exploitation and recovery of natural gas in a geological formation known as the Marcellus Shale. The litigation proceeded below in an accelerated fashion, in part because the legislation itself was designed to take effect quickly and imposed obligations which required the challengers to formulate their legal positions swiftly; and in part in recognition of the obvious economic importance of the legislation to the Commonwealth and its citizens.

The litigation implicates, among many other sources of law, a provision of this Commonwealth's organic charter, specifically Section 27 of the Declaration of Rights in the Pennsylvania Constitution, which states:

> The people have a right to clean air, pure water, and to the preservation of the natural, scenic, historic and esthetic values of the environment. Pennsylvania's public natural resources are the common property of all the people, including generations yet to come. As trustee of these resources, the Commonwealth shall conserve and maintain them for the benefit of all the people.

PA. CONST. art. I, § 27 (the "Environmental Rights Amendment").

* * *

I. Background

* * *

The Marcellus Shale Formation has been a known natural gas reservoir (containing primarily methane) for more than 75 years. Particularly in northeastern Pennsylvania, the shale rock is organic-rich and thick. Early drilling efforts revealed that the gas occurred in "pockets" within the rock formations, and that the flow of natural gas from wells was not continuous. Nonetheless, geological surveys in the 1970s showed that the Marcellus Shale Formation had "excellent potential to fill the needs of users" if expected technological development continued and natural gas prices increased. Those developments materialized and they permitted shale drilling in the Marcellus Formation to start in 2003; production began in 2005.

In shale formations, organic matter in the soil generates gas molecules that absorb onto the matrix of the rock. Over time, tectonic and hydraulic stresses fracture the rock and natural gas (*e.g.*, methane) migrates to fill the fractures or pockets. In the Marcellus Shale Formation, fractures in the rock and naturally-occurring gas pockets are insufficient in size and number to sustain consistent industrial production of natural gas. The industry uses two techniques that enhance recovery of natural gas from these "unconventional" gas wells: hydraulic fracturing or "fracking" (usually slick-water fracking) and horizontal drilling. Both techniques inevitably do violence to the landscape. Slick-water fracking involves pumping at high pressure into the rock formation a mixture of sand and freshwater treated with a gel friction reducer, until the rock cracks, resulting in greater gas mobility. Horizontal drilling requires the drilling of a vertical hole to 5,500 to 6,500 feet—several hundred feet above the target natural gas pocket or reservoir— and then directing the drill bit through an arc until the drilling proceeds sideways or horizontally. One unconventional gas well in the Marcellus Shale uses several million gallons of water. The development of the natural gas industry in the Marcellus Shale Formation prompted enactment of Act 13.

In February 2012, the Governor of Pennsylvania, Thomas W. Corbett, signed Act 13 into law. Act 13 repealed parts of the existing Pennsylvania Oil and Gas Act and added provisions re-codified into six new chapters in Title 58 of the Pennsylvania Consolidated Statutes. The new chapters of the Oil and Gas Act are:

— Chapter 23, which establishes a fee schedule for the unconventional gas well industry, and provides for the collection and distribution of these fees;

— Chapter 25, which provides for appropriation and allocation of funds from the Oil and Gas Lease Fund;

— Chapter 27, which creates a natural gas energy development program to fund public or private projects for converting vehicles to utilize natural gas fuel;

— Chapter 32, which describes the well permitting process and defines statewide limitations on oil and gas development;

— Chapter 33, which prohibits any local regulation of oil and gas operations, including via environmental legislation, and requires statewide uniformity among local zoning ordinances with respect to the development of oil and gas resources;

— Chapter 35, which provides that producers, rather than landowners, are responsible for payment of the unconventional gas well fees authorized under Chapter 23.

See 58 Pa.C.S. §§ 2301–3504. Chapter 23's fee schedule became effective immediately upon Act 13 being signed into law, on February 14, 2012, while the remaining chapters were to take effect sixty days later, on April 16, 2012.

II. Justiciability: Standing, Ripeness, Political Question

Author's note: Omitted. The court held that the plaintiffs possessed standing, that the case was ripe, and that the political question doctrine did not preclude review. With regard to the last of these, the Court noted:

"Litigation polemics aside, Act 13 is a legislative act subject to the strictures of the Pennsylvania Constitution and the U.S. Constitution. The Commonwealth offers no persuasive argument that the citizens' varied challenges raise only questions essentially political in nature regarding the validity of Act 13. The parties' dispute implicates questions of whether Act 13 was adopted pursuant to constitutional procedures, and of whether Act 13 impinges upon the rights reserved to citizens and guaranteed by the Pennsylvania Constitution and the U.S. Constitution. The evident investment of the parties to this dispute in the policies articulated in and the politics behind Act 13 do not serve to alter the nature as "questions of law" of the specific legal issues before us. The nature of the citizens' claims requires nothing more than the exercise of powers within the courts' core province: the vindication of a constitutional right. Accordingly, we conclude that the citizens' claims are justiciable and, as a result, the Commonwealth Court's decision on this point is affirmed."

III. The Constitutionality of Act 13

As noted, on the merits, the Commonwealth Court held that certain specific provisions of Act 13 were unconstitutional. The *en banc* panel enjoined enforcement of Sections 3215(b)(4) and 3304 of Act 13, and of those provisions of Chapter 33 which enforce Section 3304. The effect of the injunction was to prohibit the Department of Environmental Protection from granting waivers of mandatory setbacks from certain types of waters of the Commonwealth, and to permit local government to enforce existing zoning ordinances, and adopt new ordinances, that diverge from the Act 13 legal regime, without concern for the legal or financial consequences that would otherwise attend non-compliance with Act 13.

The Commonwealth Court rejected the citizens' remaining claims. Specifically, the panel sustained the Commonwealth's preliminary objections to claims: (1) that provisions of Act 13 violate the Environmental Rights Amendment, Article I, Section 27 of the Pennsylvania Constitution ...

A. Article I, Section 27 of the Pennsylvania Constitution (Environmental Rights) Article I, Section 1 of the Pennsylvania Constitution and the Fourteenth Amendment to the U.S. Constitution (Due Process);

***

Article I is the Commonwealth's Declaration of Rights, which delineates the terms of the social contract between government and the people that are of such "general, great and essential" quality as to be ensconced as "inviolate." PA. CONST. art. I, Preamble & § 25; *see also* PA. CONST. art. I, § 2 ("All power is inherent in the people, and all free governments are founded on their authority and instituted for their peace, safety and happiness."); *accord Edmunds*, 586 A.2d at 896 (since 1776, Declaration of Rights has been "organic part" of Constitution, and "appear[s] (not coincidentally) first in that document"). The Declaration of Rights assumes that the rights of the people articulated in Article I of our Constitution—vis-à-vis the government created by the people—are inherent in man's nature and preserved rather than created by the Pennsylvania Constitution. ... *accord Edmunds*, 586 A.2d at 896 (Pennsylvania's original constitution of 1776 "reduce[d] to writing a deep history of unwritten legal and moral codes which had guided the colonists from the beginning of William Penn's charter in 1681."). This concept is illustrated in the basic two-part scheme of our Constitution, which has persisted since the original post-colonial document: one part establishes a government and another part limits that government's powers. ... The Declaration of Rights is that general part of the Pennsylvania Constitution which limits the power of state government; additionally, "particular sections of the Declaration of Rights represent specific limits on governmental power."

The first section of Article I "affirms, among other things, that all citizens 'have certain inherent and indefeasible rights.' " ... Among the inherent rights of the people of Pennsylvania are those enumerated in Section 27, the Environmental Rights Amendment:

> The people have a right to clean air, pure water, and to the preservation of the natural, scenic, historic and esthetic values of the environment. Pennsylvania's public natural resources are the common property of all the people, including generations yet to come. As trustee of these resources, the Commonwealth shall conserve and maintain them for the benefit of all the people.

PA. CONST. art. I, § 27 (Natural resources and the public estate).

Before examining the application of Section 27 to the controversy before us, it is necessary to identify and appreciate the rights protected by this provision of the Constitution. ... Much as is the case with other Declaration of Rights provisions, Article I, Section 27 articulates principles of relatively broad application, whose development in practice often is left primarily to the judicial and legislative branches. ... Articulating judicial standards in the realm of constitutional rights may be a difficult task, as our developing jurisprudence vis-à-vis rights affirmed in the Pennsylvania Constitution well before environmental rights amply shows. ...

The actions brought under Section 27 since its ratification, which we will describe further below, have provided this Court with little opportunity to develop a comprehensive analytical scheme based on the constitutional provision. Moreover, it would appear that the jurisprudential development in this area in the lower courts has weakened the clear import of the plain language of the constitutional provision in unexpected ways. As a jurisprudential matter (and, as we explain below, as a matter of substantive law), these precedents do not preclude recognition and enforcement of the plain and original understanding of the Environmental Rights Amendment. ... The matter now before us offers appropriate circumstances to undertake the necessary explication of the Environmental Rights Amendment, including foundational matters. ...

4. Plain language

Initially, we note that the Environmental Rights Amendment accomplishes two primary goals, via prohibitory and non-prohibitory clauses: (1) the provision identifies protected rights, to prevent the state from acting in certain ways, and (2) the provision establishes a nascent framework for the Commonwealth to participate affirmatively in the development and enforcement of these rights. Section 27 is structured into three mandatory clauses that define rights and obligations to accomplish these twin purposes; and each clause mentions "the people."

A legal challenge pursuant to Section 27 may proceed upon alternate theories that either the government has infringed upon citizens' rights or the government has failed in its trustee obligations, or upon both theories, given that the two paradigms, while serving different purposes in the amendatory scheme, are also related and overlap to a significant degree. *Accord* 1970 Pa. Legislative Journal–House 2269, 2272 (April 14, 1970) (Section 27 "can be viewed almost as two separate bills—albeit there is considerable interaction between them, and the legal doctrines invoked by each should tend mutually to support and reinforce the other because of their inclusion in a single amendment."). Facing a claim premised upon Section 27 rights and obligations, the courts must conduct a principled analysis of whether the Environmental Rights Amendment has been violated. *See Payne,* 361 A.2d at 273.

To determine the merits of a claim that the General Assembly's exercise of its police power is unconstitutional, we inquire into more than the intent of the legislative body and focus upon the effect of the law on the right allegedly violated. The General Assembly's declaration of policy does not control the judicial inquiry into constitutionality. Indeed, "for this Court to accept the notion that legislative pronouncements of benign intent can control a constitutional inquiry ... would be tantamount to ceding our constitutional duty, and our independence, to the legislative branch."

I. *First Clause of Section 27—Individual Environmental Rights*

According to the plain language of Section 27, the provision establishes two separate rights in the people of the Commonwealth. The first—in the initial, prohibitory clause of Section 27—is the declared "right" of citizens to clean air and pure water, and to the preservation of natural, scenic, historic and esthetic values of the environment.[39] This clause affirms a limitation on the state's power to act contrary to this right. While the subject of the right certainly may be regulated by the Commonwealth, any regulation is "subordinate to the enjoyment of the right ... [and] must be regulation purely, not destruction"; laws of the Commonwealth that unreasonably impair the right are unconstitutional.

The terms "clean air" and "pure water" leave no doubt as to the importance of these specific qualities of the environment for the proponents of the constitutional amendment and for the ratifying voters. Moreover, the constitutional provision directs the "preservation" of broadly defined values of the environment, a construct that necessarily emphasizes the importance of each value separately, but also implicates a holistic analytical approach to ensure both the protection from harm or damage and to ensure the maintenance and perpetuation of an environment of quality for the benefit of future generations.

Although the first clause of Section 27 does not impose express duties on the political branches to enact specific affirmative measures to promote clean air, pure water, and the preservation of the different values of our environment, the right articulated is neither meaningless nor merely aspirational. The corollary of the people's Section 27 reservation of right to an environment of quality is an obligation on the government's behalf to refrain from unduly infringing upon or violating the right, including by legislative enactment or executive action. Clause one of Section 27 requires each branch of government to consider in advance of proceeding the environmental effect of any proposed action on the constitutionally protected features. The failure to obtain information regarding environmental effects does not excuse the constitutional obligation because the obligation exists *a priori* to any statute purporting to create a cause of action.

Moreover, as the citizens argue, the constitutional obligation binds all government, state or local, concurrently.

Also apparent from the language of the constitutional provision are the substantive standards by which we decide a claim for violation of a right protected by the first clause of Section 27. The right to "clean air" and "pure water" sets plain conditions by which government must abide. We recognize that, as a practical matter, air and water quality have relative rather than absolute attributes. Furthermore, state and federal laws and regulations both govern "clean air" and "pure water" standards and, as with any other technical standards, the courts generally defer to agency expertise in making a factual determination whether the benchmarks were met. *Accord* 35 P.S. § 6026.102(4) (recognizing that General Assembly "has a duty" to implement Section 27 and devise environmental remediation standards). That is not to say, however, that courts can play no role in enforcing the substantive requirements articulated by the Environmental Rights Amendment in the context of an appropriate challenge. Courts are equipped and obliged to weigh parties' competing evidence and arguments, and to issue reasoned decisions regarding constitutional compliance by the other branches of government. The benchmark for decision is the express purpose of the Environmental Rights Amendment to be a bulwark against actual or likely degradation of, *inter alia,* our air and water quality. *Accord Montana Env'l Info. Ctr. v. Dep't of Env'l Quality,* 296 Mont. 207, 988 P.2d 1236, 1249 (1999) (constitutional "inalienable ... right to a clean and healthful environment" did not protect merely against type of environmental degradation "conclusively linked" to ill health or physical endangerment and animal death, but could be invoked to provide anticipatory and preventative protection against unreasonable degradation of natural resources).

Section 27 also separately requires the preservation of "natural, scenic, historic and esthetic values of the environment." PA. CONST. art. I, § 27. By calling for the "preservation" of these broad environmental values, the Constitution again protects the people from governmental action that unreasonably causes actual or likely deterioration of these features. The Environmental Rights Amendment does not call for a stagnant landscape; nor, as we explain below, for the derailment of economic or social development; nor for a sacrifice of other fundamental values. But, when government acts, the action must, on balance, reasonably account for the environmental features of the affected locale, as further explained in this decision, if it is to pass constitutional muster. *Accord* John C. Dernbach, *Taking the Pennsylvania Constitution Seriously When It Protects the Environment: Part II—Environmental Rights and Public Trust,* 104 Dickinson L. Rev. 97, 17–20 (1999).

The right delineated in the first clause of Section 27 presumptively is on par with, and enforceable to the same extent as, any other right reserved to the people in Article I. *See* PA. CONST. art. I, § 25 ("everything" in Article I is excepted from government's general powers and is to remain inviolate); *accord* 1970 Pa. Legislative Journal–House at 2272 ("If we are to save our natural environment we must therefore give it the same Constitutional protection we give to our political environment."); Kury, app. C (Questions and answers). This parity between constitutional provisions may serve to limit the extent to which constitutional environmental rights may be asserted against the government if such rights are perceived as potentially competing with, for example, property rights as guaranteed in Sections 1, 9, and 10. PA. CONST. art. I, §§ 1, 9, 10, 27.

Relatedly, while economic interests of the people are not a specific subject of the Pennsylvania Declaration of Rights, we recognize that development promoting the economic well-being of the citizenry obviously is a legitimate state interest. In this respect, and relevant here, it is important to note that we do not perceive Section 27 as expressing the intent of either the unanimous legislative sponsors or the ratifying voters to deprive persons of the use of their property or to derail development leading to an increase in the general welfare, convenience, and prosperity of the people. But, to achieve recognition of the environmental rights enumerated in the first clause of Section 27 as "inviolate" necessarily implies that economic development cannot take place at the expense of an unreasonable degradation of the environment. As respects the environment, the state's plenary police power, which serves to promote said welfare, convenience, and prosperity, must be exercised in a manner that promotes sustainable property use and economic development. *See* John C. Dernbach, *Taking the Pennsylvania Constitution Seriously When It Protects the Environment: Part I—An Interpretive Framework for Article I, Section 27,* 103 Dickinson L. Rev. 693, 718–20 (1999); *accord* 1970 Pa. Legislative Journal–House at 2270 ("the measure of our progress is not just what we have but how we live, that it is not man who must adapt himself to technology but technology which must be adapted to man").

[Remainder of case found elsewhere.]

QUESTIONS

1. What is the history of natural gas exploration in Pennsylvania?
2. What is the significance of the 'Marcellus Shale Play?'' including its development?
3. What state law(s) were at issue in *Robinson Township?*
4. How did these laws come about?
5. What aspects of Act 13 were at issue in *RT?*
6. Ditto, for the Environmental Rights Amendment?

III.   RIGHTS OF NATURE

Recognizing the rights of Nature is part of a growing global movement highlighting the importance of the natural environment for its own sake and as a whole, rather than as an aggregation of resources to be harnessed by humans for various purposes. Moral philosophers have long proposed that nature should have a legally protected right to self-protection. The United Nations has affirmed the importance of such rights in the "Universal Declaration of the Rights of Nature." The rights of nature have also been considered by constitutional and other apex courts, including by one former member of the U.S. Supreme Court who a half-century ago promoted the idea that trees and rivers possess constitutional standing that can be vindicated by interested parties.

Some nations have recognized that Nature itself, or natural elements, have rights that are legally cognizable, and sometimes permitting rights-based claims brought *on behalf of* Nature. In 2008 Ecuador became the first country to do so under its constitution. Other States are considering such measures, including The Republic of Turkey. In 2010, Bolivia recognized the rights of Nature. In 2017, the New Zealand Parliament enacted the *Te Awa Tupua Act,* which recognized the legal status of the Whanganui River.

Nature has found additional legal recognition sub-nationally. In 2006, Tamaqua Borough, Schuylkill County, Pennsylvania (US), became the first community to recognize the Rights of Nature under law. In 2010, the City of Pittsburgh, Pennsylvania (US), followed suit. In 2017, Mexico City "recognize[d] the broader protection of the rights of nature." In 2019, the Municipality of Florianopolis (Brazil) recognized the rights of Nature, and Toledo, Ohio (US) adopted a Lake Erie Bill of Rights. In 2020, Curridabat, Costa Rica granted citizenship to pollinators, trees and native plants, and the Nez Perce Tribe General Council granted rights to the Snake River. In 2021, the Muteshekau-shipu (Magpie River) in Canada was recognized as possessing legal rights by joint resolution of local and municipal councils. And this is only a partial list.

Courts play a key role in recognizing the rights of Nature: "On a jurisprudential plane, a judge today must be conscious and alive to the beauty and magnificence of nature, the interconnectedness of life systems on this planet and the interdependence of ecosystems." In 2018, the Colombian Supreme Court of Justice held that the Colombian Amazon enjoys legal rights. And in 2016 the Colombian Constitutional Court recognized the rights of the Atrato River. Another court ordered mining operations despoiling the Santiago, Bogotá, Ónzole, and Cayapas Rivers to cease immediately "for the protection of the rights of nature and of the people." Courts elsewhere have recognized the rights of Nature. In 2011, a court in Ecuador invoked the constitutional right to Nature to protect the Vilcabamba River." In 2017, a court in India held that the Rivers Ganges and Yamuna, along with their tributaries, are juristic persons, and that "Rivers, Forests, Lakes, Water Bodies, Air, Glaciers, and Springs have a right to exist."

Rights of Nature are being tested in courts in the United States as well. At this writing, a case brought by the White Earth Nation of Ojibwe against the Minnesota Department of Natural Resources alleging violations against wild rice is winding its way through the courts. And in Florida, lawyers have recently filed suit on behalf of Mary Jane Lake which claims rights to exist, against the threats caused by new development.

A. NATURE AS A CONSTITUTIONAL FEATURE

Rights of Nature appear as either governmental duties or substantive rights of nature. First, the constitutions of some countries require all branches of government to protect nature. Germany's constitution, for instance, requires the government to protect "the natural bases of life and the animals within the framework of the constitutional order by legislation, and in accordance with law and justice, by executive and judicial power." Sudan's forbids the government from pursuing "any policy, or take or permit any action, which may adversely affect the existence of any species of animal or vegetative life, their natural or adopted habitat." Kuwait's requires that the government ensure the "preservation and proper exploitation" of natural resources.

Lithuania's constitution is particularly descriptive, requiring the government to "concern itself with the protection of the natural environment, its fauna and flora, separate objects of nature and particularly valuable districts, and shall supervise the moderate utilization of natural resources as well as their restoration and augmentation," and prohibits the "exhaustion of land and entrails of the earth, the pollution of waters and air, the production of radioactive impact, as well as the impoverishment of fauna and flora shall be prohibited by law." These are unlikely to be viewed as self-executing and are in any event unlikely to be judicially enforceable.

Second, the *right of nature*—has been pushed most emphatically so far by a couple of countries in South America. In 2008, Ecuador amended its constitution to recognize the right of nature, providing that: "Nature, or Pachamama, where life is reproduced and created, has the right to integral respect for her existence, her maintenance, and for the regeneration of her vital cycles, structure, functions, and evolutionary processes." In a nine-paragraph chapter devoted exclusively to the rights of nature, the Ecuadorian constitution invites implementation of the provision by empowering each "person, community, people, or nationality" to exercise public authority to enforce the right, according to normal constitutional processes. Bolivia has a framework law recognizing the rights of nature, and discussions of constitutional reforms to recognize them have taken place in Turkey.

B. JUDICIAL RECEPTIVITY

Constitutional and other apex courts have begun to address these rights of nature provisions. One court put it this way:

> On a jurisprudential plane, a judge today must be conscious and alive to the beauty and magnificence of nature, the interconnectedness of life systems on this planet and the interdependence of ecosystems.

In *República del Ecuador Asamblea Nacional, Comisión de la Biodivesidad y Recursos Naturales, Acta de Sesión*, the Ecuadorian government invoked the constitutional rights of nature to stop illegal gold mining operations. The Interior Minister argued that the illegal mining that was polluting the Santiago, Bogotá, Ónzole, and Cayapas Rivers violated the rights of nature. The Second Court of Criminal Guarantees of Pichincha issued an injunction ordering the mining operations to cease immediately "for the protection of the rights of nature and of the people." Remarkably, to enforce the prohibition, the court ordered that the "armed forces of Ecuador and the national police should collaborate to control the illegal mining [in the area], including by destroying all of the items, tools, and other utensils [used in the mining activities] that constitute a grave danger to nature and that are found in the site where there is serious harm to the environment." A few days after the order, military forces dropped explosives from helicopters to destroy between 70 and 120 backhoes and other machinery by the miners.

But this decision was not without controversy: even some supporters of the enforcement of rights of nature questioned whether the judge should have subordinated the miners' property rights to the rights of nature. Importantly, however, following the dramatic events in this case, the government held hearings in which representatives from the region supported the military operation due to the "the dramatic and unhealthy situation that exists because of the mining contamination."

The other Ecuadorian case vindicating the rights of nature to date —known as the *Wheeler* case — is much more typical of constitutional environmental rights. The issue in *Wheeler* was whether the provincial government's construction and expansion of a highway in the mountains of southern Ecuador violated the constitutional rights of nature. Here, the provincial authorities commenced road construction without first completing an environmental impact assessment, securing planning permits for the construction, or planning for the proper disposal of rocks, sand, gravel, trees, and other excavation and construction debris. The debris was then discharged illegally along the banks of the Rio Vilcabamba, narrowing its width, quadrupling its rate of flow, and causing significant erosion and flooding in downriver areas, particularly during vernal rains. Affected landowners brought suit, invoking the constitutional rights of nature.

In a ruling unprecedented "in the history of humanity," the provincial court agreed with the affected landowners, explaining: "[W]e cannot forget that injuries to Nature are 'generational injuries' which are such that, in their magnitude have repercussions not only in the present generation but whose effects will also impact future generations." In support of this strong commitment to protecting the environment, the court quoted Alberto Acosta, who had been the President of the Constituent Assembly and largely responsible for the rights of nature provisions: "The human being is a part of nature, and ▯we▯must prohibit human beings from bringing about the extinction of other species or destroying the functioning of natural ecosystems." Remarkably, the court went so far as to say that rights of nature trump other constitutional rights because in its view a "healthy" environment is more important, and more pervasive, than any other constitutional right. In other words, and consistently with the illegal mining case, the court emphasized the need to protect Nature in Ecuador, where oil extraction in the Amazon has caused profound environmental degradation and where what would be the world's second largest metals mine is currently under development in the Condor region.

Elsewhere

Rights of Nature have been subject to increased judicial cognizance elsewhere. In 2016, the Colombian Constitutional Court issued a landmark decision recognizing the Rio Atrato's legal ability to assert its rights in court under that country's "Ecological Constitution." In 2017, the High Court at Uttarakhand in India found that the Rivers Ganges and Yamuna, along with their tributaries, are juristic persons, and declared that "Rivers, Forests, Lakes, Water Bodies, Air, Glaciers, and Springs have a right to exist, persist, maintain, sustain and regenerate their own vital ecology system" and have "the status of legal persons," with all corresponding rights. However, the Supreme Court subsequently reversed and dismissed this decision. Other courts followed this example, including the Colombian Supreme Court of Justice, which, in 2018, held that the Colombian Amazon enjoys legal rights. Moreover, rights of nature have recently found traction at the super-subnational level, including in various municipalities in the United States.

Some courts are recognizing the rights of animals as exponents of nature. In 2020, the Islamabad High Court recognized the legal personhood of an elephant, ruling that it possesses a constitutional protection to dignity. The Supreme Court of Colombia has written:

> "[T]he protection of nature should not only be done in order to protect to the human person. The environment should not be conceived only from an anthropocentric perspective, understanding that the sole purpose of preservation is that in the future nature has some use for the human person and is encouraged in the progress of humanity, but rather that the approach must be one of respect and care. Taking into account that there must be a harmonious development where the actions of human beings in relation to the environment must reflect a vision where all members of the environment have dignity and are not simply subject to the absolute and unlimited use of people. In this way, it must be seen and understood under the assumption that the human being is one element of nature and not a superior one that has the environment at his disposal."

QUESTIONS

1. What are "rights of Nature" and where do they come from?
2. Does Nature have "rights"? Why or why not?
3. What are the implications of recognizing rights of Nature?
4. To what extent do cultural biases affect answers to these questions?

IV.   ANIMAL RIGHTS

Managing species triggers just about every conceivable facet of law, from local land use restrictions to international treaties, from civil to criminal to customary law, and everything in between.

A. ANIMAL RIGHTS

EXCERPT: MAUREEN L. ROWLANDA, LEGAL STANDING OF ANIMALS TODAY
40 Md. Bar. Jrnl, 10 (2007)

In France, 1266, a pig was tried for murder. The Ecclesiastical court conducted the trial and many others in which animals were accused of crimes. In fact, throughout the thirteenth to eighteenth centuries, European Ecclesiastical courts tried many animals accused of crimes. The Church denied they had souls, but did not deny them their "day in court." Even though the judges usually convicted them, the animals did have full legal process— including a lawyer. One well-respected attorney secured an acquittal for a donkey tried for bestiality, arguing that the donkey was not a willing participant.

For obvious reasons, animals do not have the physical ability to bring an action to court. There are, however, numerous examples throughout history of legal proceedings involving animals. The law says animals are property yet recognizes that they are different from property in many ways. Most humans believe that Man is a superior being and animals exist for the benefit of Man. Yet humans also attribute human characteristics to animals and very often react as if an animal were engaging in conscious thought—such as accusing them of crimes.

Clearly, animals do have some significance in our legal system. Not quite human, but not quite property either. While the animal may not bring an action to court, the court may render judgment that impacts the animal. The question is not whether the animals themselves have standing to bring a matter to court, but who has standing to bring actions on the animals' behalf and under what circumstances.

There are two well-recognized avenues for litigating on behalf of an animal or group of animals. First, there are federal statutes, such as the Endangered Species Act, Animal Welfare Act and Marine Mammal Protection Act that protect animals by prohibiting conduct detrimental to their welfare or by mandating certain actions to assure their well-being. Individual advocates and animal advocacy organizations may file actions pursuant to these statutes in federal court seeking to prevent some harm to an animal or group of animals or to force an agency to take a particular action that will benefit the animal or group of animals. The authority for bringing these actions is vested in either the statutes themselves, by providing for citizen suits, or in the Administrative Procedures Act, 5 U.S.C. § 702, which permits a person suffering a legal wrong by agency action to seek judicial review.

The second avenue consists of state anti-cruelty statutes and state laws requiring proper care and treatment of domestic and farm animals. This, of course, depends upon the local prosecutor's willingness to prosecute the cases. However, clearly the fact that these laws exist—and have existed for a long time—gives animals a status that no other form of "property" enjoys. Criminal statutes place a duty on all persons to treat animals, at least some of them, humanely. If you have an animal in your care, you assume an obligation to provide proper care and treatment for that animal. In this respect, animals have a status similar to children and incompetent persons.

A. Traditional Requirements for Standing. [omitted.]

B. State Anti-Cruelty and Proper Care Laws
Our society clearly accepts the notion that animals are entitled to protection and that the government has the authority to enforce the laws that protect them. Use of the courts for the benefit of animals is hardly a new concept. In 1641, in its first set of laws, "The Body of Liberties," the Massachusetts Bay Colony provided for the welfare of animals and made it a crime to abuse or treat a domestic animal inhumanely. Note: this is the same society that burned women as witches.

These laws have become progressively stronger with more severe penalties. According to the Animal Legal Defense Fund, since 1994, forty-two states have enacted felony anti-cruelty statutes.

The problem is uniform enforcement. At least one state has attempted to improve enforcement of these statutes by enacting legislation permitting citizens to enforce the law. North Carolina law authorizes citizen standing for the enforcement of anti-cruelty laws, thus supplementing criminal prosecution through means not authorized in any other state. Citizens, cities, counties, and animal welfare organizations can enforce animal cruelty laws through a civil injunction. Many other states, including Maryland, authorize either general humane organizations or a specifically named humane society to enforce the states criminal anti-cruelty statute by arresting violators, performing investigations, or participating in the prosecution. Maryland's statute, Md. Ann. Code, Criminal Law § 10-609, provides: "... if an officer of a humane society sees a person committing a misdemeanor that involves cruelty to an animal, the officer shall arrest and bring before the District Court the person committing the misdemeanor."

Other states with similar language include Arkansas (Ark. Code Ann. § 5-62-113), California (Cal. Corp. Code Ann. § 10404), Delaware (Del. Code Ann. tit. 3, § 7901), District of Columbia (D.C. Code Ann. § 22-1006), Florida (Fla. Stat. Ann. § 828.03), Kentucky (Ky. Rev. Stat. Ann. § 436.605), Louisiana (La. Rev. Stat. Ann. § 3:2391), Maine (17 Me. Rev. Stat. Ann. § 1023), Minnesota (Minn. Stat. Ann. § 343.01), New Hampshire (N.H. Rev. Stat. Ann. § 105:18), New Jersey (N.J. Stat. Ann. § 4:22-3(d)), New York (N.Y. Agric. & Mkts. Law § 371), Ohio (Ohio Rev. Code Ann. §§ 1717.04, 1717.06), Tennessee (Tenn. Code Ann. § 39-14-210), Vermont (Vt. Stat. Ann. tit. 13, § 354), and Washington (Wash. Rev. Code Ann. § 16.52.015).

Unfortunately, these statutes still depend on a local prosecutor to actually move forward with the case. Prosecutors enjoy virtually unchecked discretion in deciding whom to prosecute. Hot media topics are at the top of their list. Currently, anything with the word "gang" has priority. In Baltimore City, firearms remain a high priority due to federal funding. Despite the volume of data regarding the connection between abuse of animals and more serious, violent behavior, animals will never enjoy this sort of media attention.

The unusual approach that North Carolina has taken to animal cruelty may prove to be the most effective.

C. Expanding Availability of Judicial Redress to Animals

1. Torts

If any area of law is ripe for expansion to include animals it is Torts. There are many people for whom their pets are their children. No one denies that the loss of a pet is a devastating, traumatic and emotional event for the pet's owner. If the purpose of tort law is to compensate the injured by making the tortfeasor pay, then including pain and suffering, and other non-economic damages, is long overdue. In 2000, the Tennessee legislature recognized this and enacted a statute allowing non-economic damages in negligence actions where a pet has been injured or killed. Damages are capped at $5,000. However, this is a move in the right direction.

Lawyers have not been shy in seeking appropriate damages for the death or injury of a pet. The problem in collecting the damages is not the jury but the judiciary. Few judges are known for their courage to "go where no man has gone before." Thus, in terms of damages, pets remain considered as property. However, there have been some success stories.

In Florida, the Florida Supreme Court held that a dog owner was entitled to recover for mental suffering as an element of damages for the malicious killing of her dog by the employee of a trash removal service. The court also upheld an award of punitive damages in the amount of $1000. In a second Florida case, the appellate court upheld a jury award of $13,000 for the mental pain and suffering of the family of a dog that had suffered severe burns and disfigurement caused by their veterinarian. In Hawaii, the Hawaii Supreme Court upheld an award of damages to a family for the emotional distress suffered when their pet Boxer died while being transported by a state agency. The award was upheld despite the fact that the family was not present when the dog died and had not witnessed the wrongful conduct.

These are but a small sample. The cases are out there. Valiant lawyers continue to seek judgments for loss of companionship and pain and suffering. Juries have demonstrated a willingness to recognize these injuries and award damages. Historically, the fear of a high civil judgment has been very effective in controlling human behavior. (Better than the threat of criminal prosecution.) In light of the recent pet food scare, animal advocates remain hopeful that the volume of cases they anticipate will be filed may lead to a more thoughtful discussion over the value of companion animals.

2. Pet Trusts

Owners of companion animals have been seeking ways to provide for their pets' future in the event of their own death for many years. We are all familiar with stories of people leaving multimillion dollar estates to their pets. The creation of "Pet Trusts" is a recent trend in Estate and Trust law. The Uniform Trust Code adopted a pet trust provision in 2000. By recognizing an animal as the beneficiary of an enforceable trust, the law again expands the notion of "standing." Personal property generally does not enjoy this kind of protection in the courts.

Maryland came close to enacting a pet trust provision in 2006. Despite being passed in the Senate, it was held up in the House and failed to move forward. Senate Bill 235 (2005 Session). To date thirty-two states have adopted some variation of a pet trust.

3. Custody Disputes

It comes as no surprise that companion animals have been the subject of custody battles for quite some time. Unfortunately, courts have been slow to recognize the emotional stake that owners have in the family pet. When there are no children, the "custody" of a pet can become a monumental issue. Rather than treating the pet as a child instead of a toaster, solutions to the "custody" and "visitation" issues that arise in divorce have been left largely in the hands of the warring parties.

Custody is not limited to divorce and separation. Who can forget the victims of Hurricane Katrina who had to fight to regain the custody of pets they lost during the storm. The new "parents" were not keen to relinquish custody of the pet they had rescued and had grown attached to.

Americans love their pets. Couples with pets that head for divorce court are unable to treat them as property. Pets, like children, can be used by one spouse against the other, can complicate an otherwise equitable separation agreement, and can cause emotions to spin out of control. The courts need to adopt better methods to deal with the custody and visitation of pets if for no other reason than to maintain equity in the judicial process. In addition, the law has an interest in protecting pets from abuse and from suffering unnecessary mental stress. Like children, pets suffer when their circumstances change.

Conclusion

Standing for animals continues to evolve. Animal welfare has been a legitimate goal of our legal system longer than the right to vote, civil rights, and women's rights. The federal Animal Welfare Act, as well as numerous other federal regulatory statutes, provides a broad range of legal remedies to animals. Animals are the direct beneficiaries of federal and state statutes enacted for their protection. This presents an opportunity for lawyers to blaze new legal trails and, to once again, be the guardians of those who cannot speak for themselves.

QUESTIONS

5. What are "animal rights" and where do they come from?
6. Do (other) animals have "rights"? Why or why not?

7. What are the implications of recognizing animal rights?

8. To what extent do cultural biases affect answers to these questions?

V.   PROCEDURAL RIGHTS

EXCERPT: JAMES R. MAY, CONSTITUTIONAL DIRECTIONS IN PROCEDURAL ENVIRONMENTAL RIGHTS
28 J. Envtl. L. & Lit. 101 (2013)

Nearly three-quarters of the nations on the planet have chosen to adopt constitutions with environmental provisions that aim to advance an end. These provisions take various forms. Some confer a substantive right to a quality environment or impose a duty to protect it. Some impose duties on governmental decisions affecting the environment, such as sustainability or the public trust. Still others address specific concerns, such as water rights or climate change. The constitutions of some countries reflect several varieties of these provisions. Some constitutional provisions, however, focus more on the means of making decisions in environmental matters than on the ends to be achieved. Over the last two decades, nearly three-dozen countries have chosen to have their constitutions embed procedural rights in environmental matters. This article concludes that these provisions have untapped potential for advancing environmental protection worldwide.

Environmental issues are best handled with the participation of all concerned citizens, at the relevant level. At the national level, each individual shall have appropriate access to information concerning the environment that is held by public authorities . . . and the opportunity to participate in decision-making processes. States shall facilitate and encourage public awareness and participation by making information widely available. Effective access to judicial and administrative proceedings, including redress and remedy, shall be provided.

1992 United Nations Conference on Environment
and Development, Principle 10

Introduction

Participatory rights are an essential ingredient for securing substantive constitutional rights, such as rights to liberty, property, dignity, education, and the environment. In the absence of the means to participate meaningfully, constitutional rights can wither on the vine. Rights to information, participation, and access to justice embody evolving international human and international rights norms, coupled with a dash of the advancing democratization of the planet. Such procedural rights can provide means to an end or ends in themselves. Procedural rights can be a means for achieving human rights, including those to life, property, water, welfare, education, and the environment. Procedural rights are also their own reward, promoting discourse and democratization and concomitant rights to assemble, speak, and participate in governance.

Countries can enforce international protocols reflecting procedural rights or provide procedural rights on their own. Countries can also develop procedural rights to advance specific normative values, such as a quality environment. This article describes the emerging trend of constitutional instantiation of procedural environmental rights ...

Procedural rights can be provided internationally and domestically in various ways. Various international human rights regimes advance ready access to information, participation in decision making, and means to resolve disputes. Moreover, the constitutions of most nations also afford some degree of civil and political rights to speak, assemble, petition, or vote. Most countries also afford some degree of process under governing statutes or administrative regulations. But these provisions standing alone can fall short in advancing environmental protection norms. Thus, there is an emerging conversation about the importance of recognizing procedural rights in environmental matters, which I refer to as 'procedural environmental rights.'

Underlying procedural environmental rights is a growing appreciation that human and environmental rights are inextricably intertwined. Many argue that there is a basic human right to a quality environment. Accordingly, constitutional rights to a quality environment are now guaranteed by about one-half of the nations on Earth. Corresponding rights to information, participation, and justice provide ineluctable means for achieving these substantive ends. Indeed, substantive environmental rights can "include a procedural element aimed at enhancing their positive effect on democratic practice." Without adequate ability to participate meaningfully, substantive environmental rights are less effective.

Besides supporting substantive environmental rights, procedural environmental rights are also ends unto themselves: raising awareness and autonomy; fostering public participation and empowerment; and contributing to the legitimacy of governmental action. Criticisms of procedural rights include that they can result in an inefficient allocation of scarce government resources, hindering problem solving; can be ineffective in producing desired results for an under or ill-informed public, leading to lowest common denominator decision making; foster decisional paralysis by requiring abject compliance with multivariate administrative demands; and, paradoxically produce outcomes most favored by a few special interest groups and the ruling classes.

The advantages of providing special rights to information, participation, and justice in environmental matters, however, outweigh the disadvantages. Simply, well-informed stakeholders are in a better position to allay concerns, mitigate impacts, and make decisions regarding matters affecting the environment. Local communities whose drinking water is at risk, whose forests will be harvested, whose biodiversity will be lost, for example, should have a seat at the table and a ballot to cast when it comes time to decide what to do. Informed stakeholders are also more likely to be able to weigh the environmental costs and benefits that a particular project may have upon future generations.

Underscoring the gravity of process in environmental matters, some nations have adopted corresponding constitutional guarantees to information, participation, and justice. This development has the potential to have a profound impact on the possibilities of constitutional reformation, intergenerational equity, legislative responses to environmental challenges, and the preference for policy decisions in environmental matters to be made through open and inclusive processes.

Constitutional enshrinement of procedural rights in environmental matters is an extension of a polymorphic approach first exhibited by the Aarhus Convention. Dr. Kravchenko and others exhorted the importance of the Aarhus Convention in advancing procedural rights in environmental matters. But what may be underappreciated is the Aarhus Convention's normative effect, that is, how it has contributed to the domestic constitutionalization of procedural environmental rights around the globe. Prior to the Aarhus Convention, few nations provided constitutional rights to due process in environmental matters. Yet the majority of constitutions amended or adopted since Aarhus guarantee some degree of constitutional procedural rights in environmental matters. As listed in the Appendix, about three-dozen nations have adopted constitutional procedural environmental rights, including rights to information, participation, and access to justice. Many of these constitutional components were enacted after the Aarhus Convention, suggesting that it played a key prefiguring role. These provisions have the potential to advance environmental human rights worldwide in profound ways.

While constitutional procedural environmental rights have significant potential, they are nonetheless hamstrung in two important ways in expression and enforcement. Part I examines how it is that procedural environmental rights are underrepresented in the canon of constitutionalism and constitutional law around the globe. As listed in the Appendix, only about three-dozen countries guarantee either a right to information, participation, or access to justice, and just a handful guarantee all three rights. Part II explores the inroads constitutional procedural environmental rights have already made in domestic courts around the globe, providing a glimpse of their potential to advance environmental protection interests. The article concludes that constitutional procedural environmental rights have untapped potential for advancing access to information, participation, and justice in matters affecting the environment.

Emergence of Constitutional Procedural Environmental Rights

The following sections examine the origins of procedural rights in environmental matters, constitutional codification of such rights, and why so few countries have yet to guarantee procedural environmental rights constitutionally.

A. Origins of Procedural Environmental Rights

One need only review a variety of international human rights conventions to see how procedural rights have evolved. These include the 1948 Universal Declaration of Human Rights, the 1966 International Covenant on Civil and Political Rights (which reiterated the importance of procedural rights in governance), the 1950 European Convention for the Protection of Human Rights and Fundamental Freedoms, the 1969 American Convention on Human Rights, and the 1981 African Charter on Human and Peoples' Rights. Indeed, some constitutional systems incorporate and make enforceable international or regional human rights that grant procedural rights, making them domestically enforceable, and thereby decreasing the utility of an express provision granting procedural rights in environmental matters.

In addition, international environmental agreements have extolled the virtues of public involvement for decades. The landmark 1972 Stockholm Declaration promotes public involvement to "defend and improve the human environment." The 1992 Rio Declaration on Environment and Development (known as the "Earth Summit") recognized the paramount importance of procedural rights in environmental matters. More specifically, as described above, the Aarhus Convention sets procedural rights and imposes duties on member states concerning decisions that affect the environment. The Aarhus Convention's most innovative feature is its "compliance mechanism," which permits individuals and non-governmental organizations to petition for enforcement of its provisions against member states. Dozens of countries have signed the Aarhus Convention.

Moreover, many substantive international environmental agreements advance access to information and participation, if not provide actual remedies. For example, the 1992 United Nations Framework Convention on Climate Change maintains that its parties "[p]romote and facilitate at the national and, as appropriate, subregional and regional levels, and in accordance with national laws and regulations, and within their respective capacities: [p]ublic access to information . . . [and p]ublic participation."

B. Constitutional Manifestation of Procedural Environmental Rights

What should be the constitutional manifestation of procedural environmental rights? Classic procedural rights consist of three pillars: rights to information, participation, and access to justice. These same features are displayed in the constitutional embodiment of procedural environmental rights.

How have procedural environmental rights come to be entrenched constitutionally? International developments, such as enactment of the Aarhus Convention, along with mounting pressure from non-governmental organizations to advance public involvement in environmental decision making, hastened the constitutional development of procedural environmental rights. Ukraine appears to be the first country to have implemented procedural environmental rights. Almost three-dozen countries have done so in some fashion since then. Following the pattern of the Aarhus Convention, most focus on three pillars of procedural rights: access to information, participation in decision making, and access to justice. Brazil's constitution, for instance, protects the substantive right "to an ecologically balanced environment" but also imposes obligations on the government to "ensure the effectiveness of this right," including the obligation to demand and make public environmental impact studies. The French constitutional block incorporates the 2004 Charter for the Environment which guarantees that "[e]veryone has the right, in the conditions and to the extent provided for by law, to have access to information pertaining to the environment in the possession of public bodies and to participate in the public decision-making process likely to affect the environment." The gold standard of a nation that commits each of these rights to constitutional protection is found in Iceland's new constitution, which provides:

> The public authorities shall inform the public on the state of the environment and nature and the impact of construction thereon. The public authorities and others shall provide information on an imminent danger to nature, such as environmental pollution. The law shall secure the right of the public to have the opportunity to participate in the preparation of decisions that have an impact on the environment and nature as well as the possibility to seek independent verdicts thereon. In taking decisions regarding Iceland's nature and environment, the public authorities shall base their decisions on the main principles of environmental law.

In addition, many countries' judicial systems include environmental tribunals, chambers, or courts that have special procedures designed to facilitate legal actions to promote vindication of environmental rights.

Of the constitutions that implement procedural environmental rights, only Austria's does not contain a corresponding substantive right to a quality environment. Thus, substantive and procedural environmental rights appear to use similar means—individually vindicable constitutional rights—in pursuit of the same end of environmental protection. And insofar as they entail similar language, they confront courts with similar challenges.

To the extent they reflect procedural rights in environmental matters, constitutions tend to do so in the classical sense, that is, by granting rights to information, participation, or access to justice, discussed in the subsections below. The most common procedural environmental rights pertain to the first pillar, access to timely information about activities that affect the environment. The ability of the public to receive information from the government in a timely fashion is a cornerstone of good governance, especially in democratic societies. Access to information about environmental matters "ensures that members of the public can understand what is happening in the environment around them . . . [and] participate in an informed manner." Such transparency "means that the public can clearly follow the path of environmental information, understanding its origin, the criteria that govern its collection, holding and dissemination, and how it can be obtained."

Procedural rights to information internalize a variety of multi- and bi-lateral international treaties expressly promoting rights to information held by governmental authorities. An example of the former includes the 1948 Universal Declaration of Human Rights, which promotes the freedom "to seek, receive and impart information and ideas through any media and regardless of frontiers." The International Covenant on Civil and Political Rights reiterated the importance of procedural rights in governance. Exemplar of the latter includes the 1950 European Convention for the Protection of Human Rights and Fundamental Freedoms, and the American Convention on Human Rights, both of which provide similar language – that "[e]veryone has the right to freedom of expression. This right shall include freedom . . . to receive and impart information and ideas without interference by public authority and regardless of frontiers."

Likewise, the 1981 African Charter on Human and Peoples' Rights declares that "every individual shall have the right to receive information . . . [and] to express and disseminate his opinions within the law."

International environmental treaties also promote informational rights. For example, Principle 10 of the Rio Declaration on Environment and Development ("Agenda 21") promotes free access to information about environmental matters stating:

> [Individuals] shall have appropriate access to information concerning the environment that is held by public authorities, including information on hazardous materials and activities in their communities, and the opportunity to participate in decision-making processes. States shall facilitate and encourage public awareness and participation by making information widely available. Effective access to judicial and administrative proceedings, including redress and remedy, shall be provided.

The 1992 United Nations Framework Convention on Climate Change mandates that parties "[p]romote and facilitate . . . public access to information on climate change and its effects."

The Aarhus Convention requires parties, "in response to a request for environmental information," to "make such information available to the public, within the framework of national legislation," subject to certain conditions. Environmental information includes the "state of the elements of the environment, factors that affect the environment, decision-making processes, and the state of human health and safety."

The right of access to official information is now protected by the constitutions of some sixty countries. At least fifty-two, and arguably fifty-nine, of these countries expressly guarantee a "right" to "information" or "documents," or else impose an obligation on the government to make information available to the public. The top courts of five of these countries have interpreted their constitution to recognize the right implicitly. According to a recent survey:

> [T]he constitutions of the following 60 countries guarantee a right to information: 12 countries in the Americas (Argentina, Brazil, Chile, Colombia, Costa Rica, Ecuador, Mexico, Nicaragua, Panama, Paraguay, Peru, and Venezuela); 18 in Europe clearly grant a right to information (Albania, Bulgaria, Czech Republic, Estonia, Finland, Greece, Hungary, Lithuania, Moldova, Montenegro, Norway, Poland, Portugal, Romania, Serbia, Slovakia, Slovenia, Sweden); 7 in Europe arguably guarantee a right to information (Austria, Azerbaijan, Belgium, Georgia, Macedonia, Russia, Ukraine); 6 in Asia and the Pacific (Nepal, New Zealand, Pakistan, Papua New Guinea, Philippines, Thailand); and 17 in Africa (Burkina Faso, Cameroon, Democratic Republic of Congo, Egypt, Eritrea,

Ghana, Guinea Bissau, Kenya, Madagascar, Malawi, Morocco, Mozambique, Senegal, Seychelles, South Africa, Tanzania, and Uganda).

These include most recently written constitutions from countries in transition, including most in Latin America, central and eastern Europe, and central and east Asia. One of the most expansive provisions stems from South Africa, which gives individuals the right to demand information "that is held by another person and that is required for the exercise or protection of any rights." In the aftermath of the secrecy surrounding the disaster at the Chernobyl nuclear power plant in the Ukraine, the then newly independent country adopted—as one of its first laws—a constitutional right to information. It provides a "guaranteed [] right of free access to information about the environmental situation," and that "[n]o one shall make such information secret." Moreover, the highest courts in a number of countries have held that informational rights are implicit in first-order political rights, including freedom of expression and the press.

Moreover, many countries have enacted legislation that gives the public some degree of access to information held by governing bodies. Among the more comprehensive measures include India's Right to Information Act. It establishes a commission that can order disclosure and impose financial penalties and attorney fees for noncompliance. And in the United States, the federal Freedom of Information Act has permitted citizens to request federal agencies to disclose governmental records since 1967. Furthermore, all fifty states in the United States have enacted laws that permit access to governmental records.

Some legislative freedom of information laws enjoy explicit constitutional protection. Sweden's Freedom of Press Act is incorporated into the Swedish Constitution. Freedom of information laws in some countries are viewed as "quasi-constitutional," including those of Canada and New Zealand. Such provisions can be used to promote more effective public participation in environmental governance.

However, these international treaties and general domestic constitutional measures can come up short in providing access to information in environmental matters. With the exception of the Aarhus Convention, provisions promoting access to information found in international agreements are hortatory. And even the Aarhus Convention has limitations. It applies only to member states. It is not enforceable domestically even in member states, for the most part. Also, filing a petition to the Commission can be expensive and time-consuming. Enforcing domestic constitutional provisions respecting access to information can be limited by standing and justiciability doctrines.

Access to information under national freedom of information laws can also be severely curtailed by multifarious exemptions, for example, for national security, internal agency rules, information protected by other statutes, business information, inter and intra-agency memoranda, personal privacy, law enforcement records, financial data, business records, records that would reveal trade secrets, and records about such environmentally destructive activities as oil and gas wells data.

To compensate for these shortcomings, a handful of countries specifically provide for procedural rights to information in environmental matters, as listed in the Appendix. For example, Article 50 of Ukraine's constitution declares: "Everyone is guaranteed the right of free access to information about the environmental situation . . . and also the right to disseminate such information." Other countries that have constituted rights to information about environmental matters include Albania, Argentina, Azerbaijan Republic, Chechnya, Eritrea,

France, Georgia, Moldova, Montenegro, Norway, Poland, the Russian Federation, Serbia, and Zambia.

The second pillar of procedural rights provides for participation in environmental matters. Participatory rights allow the public to shape environmental decision making through comments and other means. As listed in the Appendix, countries with constitutions that embed rights to participate in environmental governance include Brazil, Colombia, Ecuador, Eritrea, Ethiopia, Finland, France, Kosovo, Poland, and Zambia. Most of these provisions are of very recent vintage.

The third pillar of procedural rights, access to justice, involves standing and remedies. First, some constitutions expressly provide for expansive or open standing to the judicial process to pursue environmental rights. A leading example is Brazil, whose constitution declares that: "[A]ny citizen has standing to bring a popular action to annul an act injurious to the public patrimony or the patrimony of an entity in which the State participates . . . to the environment . . . ." Other countries that expressly recognize standing in environmental matters include Bolivia, Burkina Faso, Mozambique, and Portugal. The constitutions of several countries provide an express right to file lawsuits to vindicate substantive environmental rights. A leading example is Angola's, which provides: "Every citizen, either individually or through associations representing specific interests, shall have the right to take legal action in the cases and under the terms established by law, with the aim of annulling acts which are harmful to . . . the environment . . . ." Other countries to recognize such rights include Chile, Costa Rica, Kazakhstan, Kenya, and Madagascar. Some countries expressly provide for constitutional remedies in the face of violations of substantive environmental rights. An exemplar is Chechnya, whose constitution states that "[e]veryone has the right to a decent environment . . . and compensation for damage caused to their health or property as a result of violation of ecological violations of the law." Other countries that do so include the Azerbaijan Republic and the Russian Federation.

Some constitutions at the subnational level in the United States provide similar rights to enforcement remedies, including Hawai'i ("Each person has the right to a clean and healthful environment, as defined by laws relating to environmental quality . . . . Any person may enforce this right against any party, public or private, through appropriate legal proceedings, subject to reasonable limitations and regulation as provided by law.") and Illinois ("Each person has the right to a healthful environment. Each person may enforce this right against any party . . . through appropriate legal proceedings subject to reasonable limitation and regulation as the General Assembly may provide by law.").

***

Judicial Engagement of Constitutional Procedural Environmental Rights

The jurisprudence surrounding procedural environmental rights is sparce but growing, most commonly around informational rights. Constitutional and other "apex" courts in some countries have upheld express constitutional rights to information in environmental matters. For example, in *Van Huyssteen v. Minister of Environmental Affairs and Tourism*, the High Court of Africa held that the South African Constitution grants citizens a constitutional right to information held by governmental agencies respecting the environmental effects of constructing a new steel mill near the West Coast National Park. In *Sociedad Peruana de Derecho Ambiental contra Ministerio de Energia y Minas*, the Peru Constitutional Division held that the Peruvian Constitution protected an environmental law society's access to information about the environmental effects of mining. In the *Forest Survey Inspection Request Case*, the Constitutional Court of South Korea upheld a constitutional right to inspect and copy forest title records, private forest use surveys, land surveys, and land tax ledgers kept by governmental authorities: "a person who is denied information could rely on the constitutional provision and sue in Constitutional Court without following procedures required by the country's access to information legislation."

Courts in other countries have found informational rights in environmental matters as an extension of a long line of judicial recognition of constitutional rights to information in general. The Supreme Court of India recognized constitutional rights to information thirty years ago. In *S.P. Gupta v. President of India*, the Supreme Court of India found that the public has a constitutional right to correspondence regarding judicial appointments between the Law Minister, the Chief Justice of Delhi, and the Chief Justice of India: "open government is the direct emanation from the right to know which seems to be implicit in the right of free speech and expression guaranteed under Article 19(1)(a)."

The Indian Supreme Court has extended this reasoning to recognize constitutional entitlement to information in cases that happen to involve the environment. For example, in *Reliance Petrochemicals v. Proprietors of Indian Express Newspapers, Bombay*, in ordering the disclosure of information regarding development of oil reserves, the Court observed that "the right to know is a basic right which citizens of a free country aspire the broader horizon of the right to live in this age in our land under Article 21 of our Constitution." And in *Bombay Environmental Action Group v. Pune Cantonment Board*, the Court held that the Indian Constitution required a governmental land use planning agency to disclose applications for building permits, stating that "[p]eople's participation in the movement for the protection of the environment cannot be over-emphasized. It is wrong to think that by trying to protect the environment they are opposing the various development projects."

Next, there is a growing body of judicial decisions concerning constitutional rights to participate in environmental matters. Some courts have enforced specific constitutional provisions that grant a right to participate in environmental matters. For example, in *Federación Independiente del Pueblo Shuar del Ecuador (FIPSE) c. Arco Oriente s/ Amparo*, the Ecuador Constitutional Tribunal found that government license to permit hydrocarbon exploration violated citizens' constitutional right to be "consulted and . . . participate in the design, implementation and evaluation of national and regional development plans and programs potentially affecting them directly." In *The Director: Mineral Development v. Save the Vaal Environment*, the Supreme Court of Appeal of South Africa decided that a decision to allow mining operations had violated constitutional rights of notification and participation: "Our Constitution, by including environmental rights as fundamental, justiciable human rights, by necessary implication, requires that environmental considerations be accorded appropriate recognition and respect in the administrative processes in our country. Together with the change in the ideological climate must also come a change in our legal and administrative approach to environmental concerns." And in *Decision U-I-416/98-38*, the Constitutional Court of Slovenia upheld villagers' constitutional rights to participate in decision making in environmental matters.

Constitutional rights to access to justice include issues of standing, enforceability, and remedy, and serve as a capstone to enforce rights to information and participation, as the European Court of Human Rights has remarked:

> Where a State must determine complex issues of environmental and economic policy, the decision-making process must firstly involve appropriate investigations and studies in order to allow them to predict and evaluate in advance the effects of those activities which might damage the environment and infringe individuals' rights and to enable them to strike a fair balance between the various conflicting interests at stake . . . . The importance of public access to the conclusions of such studies and to information which

would enable members of the public to assess the danger to which they are exposed is beyond question . . . . Lastly, the individuals concerned must also be able to appeal to the courts against any decision, act or omission where they consider that their interests or their comments have not been given sufficient weight in the decision-making process . . . .

In some constitutional systems, courts assume that a grant of a substantive right to a healthy environment implicitly provides parties with standing, including the Constitutional Court of Slovenia. Likewise, in *Christopher Mtikila v. Attorney General*, the High Court in Tanzania ruled that parties have standing to vindicate constitutional rights:

A person who sues because he desires to be an independent parliamentary candidate where the system does not so allow necessarily shoulders the burden for the public. It is also important to note that under this provision action lies where a person's right has been, is being or is likely to be contravened. Standing is therefore available under the Constitution even where contravention of a basic right is reasonably apprehended.

These decisions show a glimpse of the potential for constitutionally instantiated procedural environmental rights in achieving human rights and environmental protection goals.

QUESTIONS

1. What are the different types of "procedural rights"
2. Where do they come from?
3. What is the relationship between procedural and substantive rights?
4. What is the relationship between procedural rights and democracy?
5. Do you agree that the environment warrants procedural rights? Why or why not?

CHAPTER 8: WATER RIGHTS

"Water is life. Without it, nothing organic grows. Human beings need water to drink, to cook, to wash and to grow our food. Without it, we will die. It is not surprising then that our Constitution entrenches the right of access to water."

--Mazibuko et al. v City of Johannesburg
Case CCT 39/09, [2009] ZACC 28, Constitutional Court of South Africa

Chapter 8 considers the related but different subject of water rights, which for the most part is about who has 'rights' to use or own it. It's another complicated area of law. Part I turns outward, surveying how constitutions the world over recognize a right to water. Part II chains inward with water rights in the United States, featuring the First State.

I.   INTRODUCTION TO WATER RIGHTS

The constitutions of nearly three-quarters of the world's countries address environmental matters in some way, either by guaranteeing substantive or procedural environmental rights, by imposing duties and responsibilities, by promoting specific policy objectives such as sustainable development, or by addressing competing demands over specific resources. This chapter addresses the most prominent of the last listed variant—rights to water.

EXCERPT: JAMES R. MAY & ERIN DALY, WATER RIGHTS
Global Environmental Constitutionalism (Cambridge University Press 2015).

Water is becoming a critical issue for nations in every part of the world. At any given moment in the early twenty-first century, somewhere in the world water is the subject of protests, theft, litigation, warfare, and increasingly, constitutional reform and adjudication. Water's significance is recognized by all those who need it or who would exploit it, including individuals, industry, state governments, and non-state actors with good, as well as nefarious, intents. One recent assessment from the United States intelligence community concluded that stresses on the supply of clean water in many countries "will risk instability and state failure" and will "hinder the ability of key countries to produce food and generate energy, posing a risk to global food markets and hobbling economic growth." There is, as a result, growing concern that water can be used as a justification for war, as a weapon of war by states against neighboring states, and for terrorist purposes by non-state actors. Indeed, what have come to be called "water wars" have already broken out in Bolivia and elsewhere, spurred by the failure of the state to provide adequate, affordable, and clean water.

Population growth is increasing the demand for clean water, while climate change, pollution, and the impact of floods are decreasing its supply. The combination is threatening access to clean water for billions of people worldwide. Some nations have responded by recognizing some type of right to water in their constitutions. For example, Somalia's interim constitution, which was adopted by a parliamentary majority in 2012, includes the human right to water. Zimbabwe's 2013 constitution includes the right to safe and potable drinking water. In the drought-prone countries of eastern Africa, including Tanzania and Sudan, where persistent and bloody conflicts erupt between herders and farmers over the allocation of scarce water resources on disputed lands, constitutional reformation is emerging as a preferable construct for resolving competing claims to water.

Accordingly, as more constitutions recognize the importance of water, domestic courts are increasingly being called upon to adjudicate water issues arising under constitutional law. For instance, in Malaysia, citizens have turned to the courts to apply constitutional provisions concerning a private water company's threat to ration water in response to governmental failure to approve a rate hike. In South Africa, people who have little or no access to drinking water have asserted constitutional rights to water to force government action to protect water resources from mining pollution. In India, questions about which level of government should manage water resources—the states, as is stipulated by the Constitution, the central government, or local communities—are continually simmering, as groundwater levels decline in the service of development and industrialization. In all of these situations, the discourse of complaint and remedy adopts constitutional language: whether the government has the constitutional responsibility or the constitutional authority to manage the distribution of water, its price, and its use and availability now and for future generations.

Constitutional water rights raise issues of both quantity and quality. Some constitutional provisions guarantee a right to a quantity of water for drinking or irrigation, for example. Generally, these provisions can be thought of as providing a human right to water. Other provisions are qualitative, for instance guaranteeing rights to unpolluted water. These types of provisions can be thought of as guaranteeing rights akin to the environmental rights discussed elsewhere in this book.

Constitutional courts do not tend to distinguish between claims relating to human and environmental rights. Nor do they treat water-based claims any differently than any other human or environmental claims. In water-related human rights cases, the courts proceed as they ordinarily would, considering whether the plaintiffs have standing, whether the remedy is immediately or progressively realizable, and so on. And when the cases concern environmental rights, courts routinely apply general principles of environmental law, such as the public trust doctrine and the polluter pays principle. Where courts are inclined to grant open standing or shift the burden of proof from the claimant to the party in the best position to assert the evidence, they will do so without regard to whether the cases concern land or water.

But water is different in both contexts. It is more likely than other rights considered here to straddle the environmental right-human right divide. And rights to water are more likely in the coming years to be the subject of contestation in almost all nations of the world—contests that will be resolved through violence, if not as a matter of constitutional law. And while a constitutional right to water will not always prevent violence, it may galvanize and inform public debate, shape legal rights and responsibilities, and put the onus on government to ensure adequate access to clean water for all.

This chapter proceeds in four parts. First, it discusses water's unique features that warrant constitutional recognition. Second, it assesses the various ways in which constitutions recognize the importance of water, either as a marker of jurisdiction and authority or as an enforceable human or environmental right. Third, it surveys the cases that have vindicated water rights either as a human or environmental right, or both. Fourth, it considers the challenges of fashioning and enforcing remedies in cases involving water.

A. THE UNIQUENESS OF WATER

Although all elements of the environment may impact the human right to health or in some circumstances even life, the human rights dimensions of water are far more pronounced. Water is essential for life in a way that healthy forests or pristine mountains are not. Water must be accessible in certain amounts and at certain levels of quality for consumption and sanitation, as well as for other uses. As a result, clean water must be made available to people to ensure that neither quantity nor quality fall below a certain minimum level.

Because it is necessary not only to maintain clean water but also to provide it, water requires management in a way that air and soil do not. It is not enough to leave water alone it its natural state; those in control of water resources must take affirmative steps to ensure its protection, its equitable distribution, and its appropriate use for personal, communal, and industrial purposes. This is just as true in drought-prone countries like South Africa and Mozambique as in water-rich environments like Brazil; water must be managed everywhere. As a result, the regulation of water, more than of other parts of the environment, is interlaced in regulatory, statutory, and constitutional arenas.

The need to manage water resources imposes a positive obligation on states, which means that governments can be sued for failure to act much more readily in this area of law than in others. And this obligation, whether voluntarily undertaken or judicially imposed, usually requires ongoing administration and coordination with multiple parts of government—including legislative and executive authorities at both the central and subnational levels—and often with the private sector as well. This contrasts with the constitutional mandate to protect the environment, which may often be satisfied by the negative responsibility to avoid endangerment. And this difference impacts the role that courts play in vindicating these constitutional rights: imposing a positive obligation to manage water resources effectively and equitably can be far more challenging for courts than ordering the cancelation of a timber license or even overseeing the remedial clean up of a bay.

The need to manage water resources also differs from most environmental regulation because it requires significant infrastructure. To satisfy these capital and operational demands, governments often find themselves turning to non-governmental actors, increasingly including multi-national enterprises and international financing organizations that have more fiscal resources than over-extended or debt-ridden nations; in fact, tax, licensing, and other revenues derived from the privatization of water can be a significant source of income for nations. Moreover, the global financing system often prefers privatization, both because it produces a better return on investment and because it meshes with western concepts of marketization.

And yet, water privatization is enormously controversial politically. Privatization also raises important constitutional questions, particularly insofar as the state retains a constitutional obligation to manage water or to hold it in the public trust. For some, the privatization of water raises conceptual questions of a political nature because it may be seen to commoditize a public or social good, often to the detriment of those who lack the resources to enter the market. Indeed, in many countries, the poor pay substantially more for water than those who are well-to-do. As Malgosia Fitzmaurice writes, "Poor people living in slums often pay 5-10 times more per litre of water than wealthy people in the same place, since water passes through intermediaries and each adds transport and marketing fees." This is so even though most people recognize that water has positive externalities in that safe and adequate water for drinking and sanitation improves health, enables education (particularly for girls, which has still other follow-on benefits), increases productivity, and is indispensable to human dignity.

But the concern about privatization may be overstated. The worst form of privatization, from the standpoint of constitutional accountability, is foreign and global investment, but "about 90% of investment comes from domestic sources." Moreover, there is no clear consensus on whether public or private distribution of water is better in terms of cost and availability: there are shining examples, as well as disasters, in both columns. But the critical point is that "the crucial factor of successful privatization is good governance and the right institutional framework (i.e. an effective regulation)." And if governance is effective enough adequately to regulate the private water distribution system, it may be effective enough to provide the water in the first place—and with greater public input, public oversight, and compliance with constitutional norms.

Part of the reason that water management is so costly is that it requires a comprehensive and integrated approach. Managing water at its source may not take into account the complexities of transport or result in appropriate distribution to all those who need it; managing its distribution may not take into account the limits of the source. Unlike other parts of the environment, water management must be integrated across an entire ecosystem, and throughout a social system. Water flows, changes form, and changes functions as it moves from glacier to river and groundwater to ocean. It moves through space and time, in a way that is unique in the natural world. One Indian case, for example, examines how pumping groundwater near the Arabian Sea could produce seepage of the ocean water, which would contaminate the residents' drinking water.

This difference between water cases and other environmental cases may be more of degree than of character. Water cases involving boreholes or rights of dumping in a local bay can be localized, while climate change poses global environmental challenges to all environments. But the difference is noticeable in the run of cases. Water cases pose significant new challenges to judicial tribunals seeking to adjudicate and remedy rights relating to water in all its forms. In fact, in the majority of cases, water must be regarded not only as part of an ecosystem, but as an ecosystem in and of itself, because the changes that water undergoes in one place will affect it in other places: melting glaciers will affect the river flow of water for miles, just as pollution in a water catchment area can diminish the availability of clean drinking water for scores of communities near and far.

Water also provides different kinds of value to those who interact with it. In many cultures throughout the world—both indigenous and not—it has enormous and unique religious and spiritual significance. It has economic value to those who would use the resources it harbors, from marine life to natural gas, and to those who would use it as a means of transportation, a basis for tourism, a source of energy production or for other industrial purposes. And it has value to a nation's sovereignty, as a marker of its boundaries and a defining value of its patrimony.

But perhaps the most significant difference between water and other parts of the environment is that water is fast becoming scarce, both economically and in fact. Indeed, as water becomes scarce, environmental harms almost invariably devolve into human rights harms because pollution or other forms of degradation in the quality of water reduce the quantity of water to which people have access, resulting in deprivations that threaten health and life. Because people *need* water to survive, the severe degradation in the quality of water will implicate basic human rights, including first generation human rights. This can happen as well in particular cases involving other environmental elements, such as where a forest is cut down resulting in loss of home or diminution in access to food for local inhabitants; the difference with water is that scarcity on a global scale is inevitable, life-threatening, and invariably affects far more people than those living adjacent to the locality of the problem. And distribution and use of water is more likely than other environmental issues to adversely affect vulnerable populations, including those displaced by war or natural calamities, women, the poor, small-scale farmers, and others who depend on an effective infrastructure to ensure water security. In many countries, where the most vulnerable populations are racial or ethnic minorities, there is an additional overlay of injustice. These problems exist in some form whether the government controls the allocation of water or whether it relegates it to private hands. As a result, the constitutional dimensions of water quality and access are unavoidable.

B. CONSTITUTIONAL RECOGNITION OF RIGHTS TO WATER

The term "water" or "waters" appears in the constitutions of almost half the countries of the world, cumulatively more than 300 times.While most of these references are concerned with governmental authority to control and allocate water resources, about 30 constitutions provide for a human right to water or an environmental right to clean water. *See* Appendix I. We focus on these rights provisions first because they are more likely to support constitutional claims for vindication.

1.   Human and Environmental Rights to Water

The constitutions from at least 14 countries instantiate a human right to a fair distribution of clean, safe, or potable water. For example, South Africa's constitution makes a strong commitment to acknowledging water as a fundamental human right by asserting an enforceable individual right to drinking water. Kenya's 2010 constitution follows this course with a provision that gives "[e]very person []the right— ... to clean and safe water in adequate quantities." But in most other countries, the right to water must be inferred from other rights – such as the right to life, to dignity, or to health – if it is to be recognized at all.

Other constitutions reflect the environmental-rights perspective to protection of water. In Andorra, for instance, "The State has the task of ensuring the rational use of the soil and of all the natural resources, so as to guarantee a befitting quality of life for all and, for the sake of the coming generations, to restore and maintain a reasonable ecological balance in the atmosphere, water and land, as well as to protect the autochthonous flora and fauna." In Guyana, the environment, including water, is protected "In the interests of the present and future generations" and, likewise, in Tajikistan, the constitutional provisions strongly imply fundamental environmental law principles like the public trust doctrine, guaranteeing that the state will guarantee the "effective utilization" of "the earth, its resources, water, the atmosphere, flora, fauna, and other natural resources ... in the interests of the people." By contrast, the constitution of Laos imposes on the people the duty to protect the environment: "All organisations and citizens must protect the environment and natural resources: land, underground, forests, fauna, water sources and atmosphere."

In general, these provisions track the twin paths for managing water resources at the international level. As an international human right, water is recognized as a basic necessity for life to be allocated for adequate access to maximum numbers of people. In 2002, the Committee on Economic, Social and Cultural Rights issued General Comment 15, which confirmed a "human right to water" as "indispensable for leading a life in human dignity" and a "prerequisite for the realization of other human rights." This is probably the strongest statement to date at the international level of the human right to water and has been reinforced by a 2009 Human Rights Council Resolution (adopted by the General Assembly in 2010) on access to safe drinking water and sanitation. This Resolution calls on states to, among other things, "develop appropriate tools and mechanisms, which may encompass legislation, comprehensive plans and strategies for the sector, including financial ones, to achieve progressively the full realization of human rights obligations related to access to safe drinking water and sanitation, including in currently unserved and underserved areas" and to "ensure effective remedies for human rights violations by putting in place accessible accountability mechanisms at the appropriate level." The United Nations Development Programme's Millennium Development Goals also include the need to improve access to drinking water and sanitation although, like many constitutions and cases, they conflate the importance of water as a human right and as an environmental right, by including this target into the goal on environmental sustainability.

As a purely environmental issue, water has been recognized at the international level as a natural resource to be used in accordance with environmental values for the preservation for future generations at, for instance, the 2002 World Summit on Sustainable Development in South Africa. Regional international law has also recognized the importance of water: it is the subject of a 2000 European Framework Directive under which the European Commission can bring a state to the European Court of Justice for violation or failure of implementation. The European approach depends on management by geographic, rather than according to administrative or political boundaries; since many river basins straddle national boundaries, this may implicate how nations interpret and implement their obligations under their national constitutions. At the same time, Latin America has gone one step further by establishing a "Water Court" to hear both interstate and intrastate disputes. This tribunal "follows a model of exigent ethics and alternative justice" and, according to the OECD, it "is indeed an autonomous, independent and international organization of environmental justice created to contribute in the solution of water related conflicts in Latin America. It is not only an ethical institution committed to preserving the water and to guaranteeing its access as a human right or current and future generations, but also a justice setting for searching solutions to the water conflicts, in addition to those efforts made by Latin-American citizens before other judicial and administrative institutions for the preservation of the environment and the water protection."

The principles developed through these regional and international systems to protect water resources as both a human and environmental right are often seamlessly and implicitly integrated into domestic constitutional law. Still, constitutional water cases tend to rely less on international law than other constitutional environmental cases simply because the international body of law relating to the human and environmental rights to water is less developed than it is for environmental rights generally.

Through these various constitutional provisions, we can begin to see the complexity of protecting water at a constitutional level. One aspect of that complexity is that water *is* so many different things and its value changes with its form, whether in the ground, as freshwater or saltwater, and whether it is to be used for personal, industrial, political or ecological purposes. Nonetheless, environmental constitutionalism is commonly used to address how water is or should be used to advance human rights, and/or protect the environment.

C. GOVERNMENTAL CONTROL OVER WATER RESOURCES

Because water is inherently valuable, and because it is, in and of itself, a natural resource capable of being managed, exploited, used or abused by anyone who can assert control over it, it has political significance as well as personal value. Nations recognize the need to protect waterways from harms both internal and external and have vested interests in asserting control over water within their territory.

Accordingly, the vast majority of constitutional water provisions relate to the control and use of a nation's waters. Sometimes, waters are included in general environmental provisions, such as when the Indian Constitution protects " . . . forests, lakes, rivers, wild life . . . ," but more often, constitutions contain separate provisions relating to how water should be classified and how its exploitation should be managed. Typically, they refer to some specific form of water: oceans, rivers, and reservoirs, including underground aquifers, ice, glaciers, ports, and so on.

The most common reference to water in constitutions is as a limit on the nation's territory. The Mexican constitution, for instance, defines "the national territory" as comprising, among other things, "The continental shelf and the submarine shelf of the islands' keys, and reefs; [and] The waters of the territorial seas."

Beyond establishing the sovereign territory, many constitutions also assert the right to control and govern the waters within the territories. For example, the Slovak constitution asserts that "Natural wealth, caves, underground water, natural medicinal springs, and waterways are in the ownership of the Slovak Republic." Likewise, "In Mongolia the land, its subsoil, forests, water, fauna and flora and other natural resources shall be subject to people's power and State protection." Some constitutions assert public control over waters and their associated resources subject to private ownership ("Land, water and natural resources below and above the surface of the land and in the continental shelf and within the territorial waters and the exclusive economic zone of Namibia shall belong to the State if they are not otherwise lawfully owned"), while others, such as Haiti, limit private ownership over waters ("The right to own property does not extend to the coasts, springs, rivers, water courses, mines and quarries. They are part of the State's public domain"). Still others seek to develop a cooperative model of public-private control.

These simple assertions of control often mask deeply contentious tensions in the allocation of power over important and often scarce water resources. In particular, constitutional language reflects a balance of power as between the public and private sectors, and within the government itself as between the central authority and the subnational or regional authorities. Both of these aspects of the allocation of control can be fractious and highly politicized. With respect to the first —the allocation of control between public and private authorities—many constitutions assert public control over water, and yet, scarce economic resources, as well as pressure from international banks and donor nations have especially since the end of the Cold War, resulted in the ceding of that control to private national and foreign concerns. This leaves open important political and constitutional questions about the degree of control that the government needs to assert to comply with its constitutional obligations to control water and in what forms that control needs to be asserted. For instance, must the government regulate the cost of water to consumers and the level of subsidy for those who can't pay, even if the private enterprise controls the distribution of water? Questions like these are significant in many countries, particularly where the government is not able to exert exclusive control over water resources. In Chile, for instance, what has been called "extreme privatization" resulted in foreign companies owning rivers for purposes of developing hydro-electric dams, especially in Patagonia. In Indonesia, the treatment and distribution of piped water in Jakarta "has been run by two foreign companies since the final years of then-President Suharto regime" although efforts continue to try to ensure that at least the price of water is regulated by the government. There is an inevitable tension between public and private control over water and there are good and bad examples of each, although the IUCN insists that, at a minimum, "the stewardship function of water management cannot be privatized." The inextricability of the tension between public and private authority in the management of water is one reason constitutional water cases can sometimes be more complex than cases involving other elements of the environment.

With respect to the second aspect of control—as between the central government and the subnational entities—there is also a range across the globe. In many countries, control over water resources is a matter of exclusive federal or national control (whether as an incident of sovereignty or otherwise), though in some countries it is listed as a concurrent power shared between the center and the states, while a very few countries allocate water management to local authorities. In Paraguay, for instance, "A departmental government will have jurisdiction: To coordinate activities among the various municipalities within the department, to organize joint departmental services such as public works, power supply, potable water, and others that would serve more than one municipality; as well as to promote associations to promote cooperation among them." In several countries, the question of the allocation of control over waters is a recurring sources of tension. Collectively, these provisions evince a paradoxical attitude toward water-related resources. Their ubiquity in constitutions throughout the world indicates the critical importance of water in its various forms to national sovereignty and governance. On the other hand, the fact that most of these provisions simply assert authority over water, without indicating *how* it will be managed or how the competing claims on water will be negotiated and resolved, indicates a reluctance to make difficult decisions about water management and a willingness to leave the details to others in the near or distant future. While the failure to resolve water management issues in the constitutional text makes sense in that constitutions are not appropriate vehicles for specifying the details of a water management plan, excessive vagueness can thwart the aims of protecting water resources if they are left to vagaries of economic and political jockeying; these provisions all but guarantee that questions about the quality of and access to water will be resolved, if at all, in the political and judicial realms and offer little or no guidance about how the decisions should be made in the context of a particular nation's needs and resources.

In the aggregate, constitutions contain virtually no indication of how political and judicial actors ought to balance competing claims on water—whether using water for agricultural, industrial, or personal purposes should be privileged over other uses, or over leaving water in its pristine state—nor do these mere assertions of jurisdictional authority identify the appropriate institutional actors who should be making the decisions, nor the institutional or individual competences that these actors should have. Malaysia's constitution presents an extreme example of this. While it refers to water 31 times, all references are associated with jurisdiction and none with the substance or values associated with the management of water. This suggests that water, in this peninsular and island nation, is viewed as an economic and political resource whose control must be rigorously managed, rather than as an integral part of an ecosystem, or an essential element of life. Many other constitutions protect the interest as a directive of social policy rather than as a judicially enforceable right. While some of these provisions recognize water as a basic human need, they more often value it as a lucrative economic asset. In Cambodia, for example, water is protected solely for its economic value. Under the Constitution's section on "The Economy," the state is required to "protect the environment and balance of abundant natural resources and establish a precise plan of management of land, water, air, wind, geology, ecological systems, mines, energy, petrol and gas, rocks and sand, gems, forests and forestrial products, wildlife, fish and aquatic resources." Likewise, Eritrea's strong protection for the environment is nonetheless found in a section on social and economic development: "The State shall have the responsibility to regulate all land, water and natural resources and to ensure their management in a balanced and sustainable manner and in the interest of the present and future generations; and to create the right conditions for securing the participation of the people to safeguard the environment."

The Philippine Constitution also integrates economic and environmental protection: "The State shall protect the nation's marine wealth in its archipelagic waters, territorial sea, and exclusive economic zone, and reserve its use and enjoyment exclusively to Filipino citizens." In Korea, the commodification of water is explicit: "Licenses to exploit, develop, or utilize minerals and all other important underground resources, marine resources, water power, and natural powers are available for economic use," although in the next paragraph, the Constitution affirms that "The land and natural resources are protected by the State and the State establishes a plan necessary for their balanced development and utilization." Some constitutions recognize the importance of water both as a right and as a social policy priority. The December 2013 draft constitution of Egypt protects the environment, the Nile, and the Suez Canal as elements of the "economic component" of society (as opposed to the social or cultural components). The Nile, which features prominently if symbolically throughout the Constitution; in Article 44, the state commits to protecting it but also recognizes the human right that every citizen has to "enjoy the Nile River" as well as the need to protect "the river environment" itself by prohibiting encroachments upon it. In addition, the draft requires the state to commit to "protecting its seas, beaches, lakes, waterways, mineral water, and natural reserves" and prohibits encroachments upon or pollution or use of them "in a manner that contradicts their nature." The state also "commits to the protection and development of green space in urban areas; the protection of plants, livestock, and fishers; the protection of endangered species; and the prevention of cruelty to animals.... as regulated by law." Textual provisions like these go beyond merely asserting sovereignty or control and begin to suggest the values that should undergird decisions about water management.

D. ADJUDICATING RIGHTS TO WATER

As a result of water's unique but critically important attributes and the growing competition over limited resources, domestic constitutional and apex courts are increasingly being called upon to settle disputes over who has rights to water and who has responsibility to ensure that it is available in adequate quantities and in clean condition to all those who need it. This trend is likely to accelerate in the coming years because these courts are uniquely situated to help mediate these complex and controversial disputes.

Relying on constitutional rights and principles, courts can help to limit the influence that money and politics play in the distribution of water; they can help protect unrepresented interests—including those of poor people, of women, of minority populations, of children, and even of future generations, as well as the rights of nature itself—because they are less beholden to majoritarian politics; they can help to ensure that equitable water distribution remains atop the nation's political agenda; they can help to ensure the availability of public information and the participation of the public in policy decisions affecting the management of water resources; and they can make justice more accessible than is possible under international and regional regimes. Indeed, many of the purported benefits of international law—among them, in the words of Rose Francis, to translate the right to water into specific legal obligations and responsibilities, to renew national governments' efforts to meet the basic water needs of their populations, and to financially prioritize meeting basic human water requirements over other investment and management decisions—are more likely to be more effective at the domestic constitutional level because the pressure on national governments may be far more direct. At the same time, constitutional courts often have more political and moral authority than local courts and may, as a result, be more effective.

Overall, constitutional and other apex courts have been responsive to claims based on access to and quality of water and have recognized the need for comprehensive and sensible water management plans to protect both environmental and human rights. But they have not effectively provided guidance as to when water should be treated as an environmental right, when it should be treated as a human right, and when it should be treated as presenting a unique set of problems warranting a unique jurisprudential approach, as the following sections explain.

E. VINDICATING HUMAN RIGHTS TO WATER

Many constitutional and other apex domestic courts have vindicated the constitutional human right to water by following principles similar to those that have developed in the context of other environmental human rights. Principles of justiciability, including those relating to standing, apply identically whether the case involves water or some other part of the environment. For instance, when the environmental activist M.C. Mehta sought enforcement of environmental laws protecting the River Ganges from excessive pollution, the Indian Supreme Court recognized that "The petitioner in the case before us is no doubt not a riparian owner. He is a person interested in protecting the lives of the people who make use of the water flowing in the river Ganga and his right to maintain the petition cannot be disputed. The nuisance caused by the pollution of the river Ganga is a public nuisance, which is wide spread in range and indiscriminate in its effect and it would not be reasonable to expect any particular person to take proceedings to stop it as distinct from the community at large." Given these facts, the court said, the plaintiff had standing to pursue the action as public interest litigation.

The Colombian Constitutional Court has given content to the right to water by defining it as involving "availability, quality, access, and non-discrimination in distribution, consistent with the obligation to use maximum available resources to effectuate the right to water for all." Three of these requirements are necessarily and exclusively for the benefit of humans; the requirement of quality may be to ensure that the access people have is to water of a certain quality so that it is in fact potable and available for use for washing and other purposes, but ensuring the quality of water may also promote the environmental interest in protecting the quality of an ecosystem. And indeed while Colombia has recognized the interests of nature *per se,* the emphasis in the water cases is on a human right to water. In fact, the constitutional court has recognized that it is a human right on its own merit, as well as being implicit in other fundamental human rights. As a result, the Constitutional Court has recognized that it can be enforced by any person through the informal mechanisms of the *tutela* action or, when the right is collective, through an *acción de inconstitucionalidad.* In a 2010 case, for instance, the court ordered a water company to supply water to an apartment building, inferring the right to water from the well-recognized rights to life, health, and dignity. The court attempted to encapsulate the various values of the right to water: "to define the content of the fundamental right to water it is necessary to consider that it is an essential prerequisite for the enjoyment of other fundamental rights, such as the right to education, since it is necessary to have functioning water and sewage services in any educational establishment; the right to a healthy environment; and rights to ethnic and cultural diversity, taking into account that some indigenous and afrocolombian communities believe that water has special cosmological significance."

Most constitutional water cases from around the world concern one or more of the four elements of the right to water identified by the Colombian court—availability, quality, access, and non-discrimination—and treat the rights as deriving either from an explicit right to water or from other fundamental human rights typically protected in constitutions. The South African Constitutional Court decided its first right to water case in *Mazibuko* in 2009, recognizing that the claims of the residents of a township to adequate water were based on section 27 of that country's constitution, which, as the Court explained, "provides that everyone has the right to have access to sufficient water. Cultures in all parts of the world acknowledge the importance of water. Water is life. Without it, nothing organic grows. Human beings need water to drink, to cook, to wash and to grow our food. Without it, we will die. It is not surprising then that our Constitution entrenches the right of access to water." Notwithstanding water's obvious indispensability to each and every individual, the court ruled that this provision guaranteed not an individual right of each person to sufficient potable water but a social right that the state was obligated to progressively realize. As such, the court upheld Johannesburg's water policy of providing for free only 6 kiloliters per household per month because it was "reasonable," even though it did not consider the number of people in the household; the court also upheld as reasonable the policy of installing pre-paid water meters, which would result in intermittent cessations in water service.

Where there is no explicit right to water, courts have been no less willing to recognize the need for water as a mandate impelled by some other constitutional right, such as a right to dignity or life. For example, in a 2011 case from Israel, neither party disputed that the rights of Bedouins to water was part of their basic right to live in dignity and that this imposed on the state an affirmative obligation to provide them with some amount of water in some way; the application of that principle in the facts of the case, however, raised a socially and politically complex question of the extent of water rights of Bedouins who lived illegally in an unrecognized community in the Negev desert. In India, the Supreme Court has held repeatedly that water is part of the right to life. "Water is the basic need for the survival of human beings and is part of the right of life and human rights as enshrined in Article 21 of the Constitution of India . . . "The court has explained that "The right to live is a fundamental right under Art. 21 of the Constitution and it includes the right of enjoyment of pollution free water and air for full enjoyment of life. If anything endangers or impairs that quality of life in derogation of laws, a citizen has the right to have recourse to Art. 32 of the Constitution for removing the pollution of water or air which may be determined to the quality of life." In Colombia, the Constitutional Court has read the right to water "for human consumption" into the rights to life, to health, and to dignity, which it understands as "the possibility of enjoying the material conditions of existence (of life) that will permit a person to develop an active role in society." Another example comes from Chile, where the Supreme Court in 2009 used a property rights analysis to vindicate the water resources claim of an indigenous community. Over the objections of a private company that sought to bottle and sell the water from the springs, the court recognized the property rights of the Aymara to the land where the springs lay. Although the Aymara's property rights had not been formalized, the court found they were nonetheless ancient and consistent with common and customary law and therefore were valid prior to the company's ownership claims. Whoever controlled the land would control access to the water. But not all human-rights based claims present such critical concerns: some courts have recognized the right of the public to enjoyment of the beaches.

In one notable case from Botswana, a group of Basawra from the Central Kalahari region sought access to boreholes that had originally been installed for mining purposes but were then closed when the mining operations ceased and the Basawra were evicted from the lands to make way for a game reserve. When the eviction was found to be illegal, the Basawra moved back to the area but then had to sue again to gain access to water. Deriving the right to access to water from the constitution's prohibition against inhuman or degrading punishment or treatment, and interpreting the constitution in light of international law, the court ordered the boreholes re-opened, though at the Basawra's own expense, and upon conditions including limiting access to personal uses. Since the decision in early 2011, the Gem Diamonds Company was granted mining rights on the game reserve and it has been reported that private capital has contributed to the opening up of the boreholes for drinking water.

The South African *Mazibuko* case and the Botswanan case concerning the Basawra people illustrate the challenges that poor and marginalized people face in gaining access to sufficient amounts of water necessary for their survival. Anticipating that the relevant governments would simply ignore judicial orders to comply with the international recommendations of 50 liters per person per day, the South African court held that a significantly lesser amount is constitutionally permissible, so long as the government's efforts are reasonable and there is indication that the right to more appropriate amounts of water may be progressively realized; with no greater sympathy to Botswana's most vulnerable people, the Botswanan court ordered that while water must be made available, the people themselves must pay for it. In both cases, the value of the right to water though partially vindicated, was significantly diminished for the impoverished communities.

As a matter of legal analysis, the two African cases also reflect the melting away of legal boundaries in this area: while both cases referred to both domestic and international law, the Botswana case converted a civil and political right (against inhuman treatment) into a right of access to water, while the South African court did the opposite in treating a constitutionally explicit individual right of access to sufficient water into social right, whose minimum core may be vindicated over time. The conflation of different types of human rights claims is characteristic of the judicial treatment of water-related constitutional claims, where practical and economic limitations on political authority often override human needs or the principled vindication of a human right. Where significant political and economic interests are at play, a textual guarantee to water may be less effective.

The cases also reflect the porous boundaries between public and private actors in the provision water for basic drinking and sanitation needs. In most countries, though public authority alone is responsible for satisfying the constitutional obligations, it lacks the capacity on its own to secure even basic water needs for drinking and sanitation. In South Africa, the water was provided by a municipal corporation, whereas in Botswana, the government was responsible for providing the water, but this obligation could only be fulfilled when a large multinational mining corporation stepped in and, for its own economic reasons, reopened the boreholes. Should the company decide in the future not to maintain the water supply for the members of the local Baswara community, it will be difficult for the government to hold anyone accountable, since the company is under no constitutional obligation to supply water for them, and the government is unable or unwilling to do so.

The disconnect between private control and government responsibility, which is replicated throughout the world, has prompted plaintiffs' groups, particularly in Latin America, to seek to vindicate water rights against both corporate and governmental entities. This happened in the Mendoza case from Argentina discussed in the previous chapter, where plaintiffs sought to hold more than 40 public and private entities responsible for the disastrous condition of the river.

In India, however, the success of constitutional litigation against private actors has been less evident. In the most prominent effort to hold corporations accountable, it has taken not only litigation but coordinated and sophisticated public protests lasting years, as well as efforts in administrative, legislative, and judicial arenas in all levels of government to protect access to clean drinking water from over-exploitation by Coca-Cola. These cases evidence the complex interplay between public and private authorities that is inherent in all the constitutional litigation but especially pronounced in cases involving the right to water.

Even cases that nominally challenge jurisdictional authority to control water or to assert property rights over land that has water can become human rights cases, particularly as water claims become ever more dire with water's increasing scarcity. For example, the High Court of South Africa ordered a municipality to restore a discontinued flow of free potable water as necessary for survival. More recently, litigation in South Africa challenged the failure of the government to provide drinking water to residents of Mpumalunga where, after heavy rains, the water became unsafe for drinking and even for washing due to the pollution of the main water supply by acid mine water caused by environmentally irresponsible mining nearby. The national government, who was thought to be responsible both for ensuring compliance with environmental mining laws and for supplying drinking water to all South Africans, quickly argued that it was the responsibility of the local municipalities to provide drinking water for their residents, while the municipalities took the position that they lacked the resources to provide the essential water.

The flood planning controversy in Bangladesh illustrates how flawed water management can have adverse impacts on all aspects of human life. The Supreme Court in *Farooque v. Bangladesh* granted standing to an environmental organization to challenge the implementation of a flood action plan that had been years in development and heavily supported by the international community. The plan would have increased the area of arable land by reducing the likelihood of flooding; while this would have benefited those in a position to own land, it would have destroyed the livelihood of those fishers who depend on the waters for their income and for their nutritional needs, including, in particular, women and Hindus who have turned to fishing because they have traditionally been barred from owning land. The Court found that the constitutional right of "any person aggrieved" to bring a claim included an organization whose principal purpose was environmental protection even though the claims were largely framed in terms of human rights.

The question of standing can be particularly important in water rights cases because there is often little opportunity for participation in the decisionmaking. Although "'public participation' has become the new watchword in national water policies," Jona Razzaque concludes that "people rarely participate in decisionmaking," particularly, she notes, in projects involving dams. Indeed, because water management tends to require comprehensive, rather than discrete or limited, solutions and because it often involves a complex relationship between government and private (often international) enterprises, procedural water rights can be hard to secure and exercise. And yet, public participation (as discussed in Chapter 8) is as important in preserving rights to water as other environmental rights and in some ways more so because of its indispensability to human life and the likelihood that poor decisionmaking will adversely affect vulnerable populations.

Throughout these cases, the focus of the court's attention tends to be on fixing the immediate problem of ensuring access to healthful water in adequate quantities to the individual or community plaintiffs. This is as it should be because the plaintiffs are often in desperate need and the courts are their only recourse. But courts should also consider the environmental aspects of these cases: they should understand the environmental causes of the claimed injuries as well as the environmental implications of alternative remedial courses. In order to protect the rights of future generations, courts must keep in mind both human and environmental factors.

Vindicating Environmental Rights to Water

Because water is also an essential element of the broader ecosystem, pollution and misuse or overuse can degrade the *quality* of water as well, giving rise to claims typically thought of as environmental claims asserting the right to clean water.

Most environmental water rights cases arise due to pollution, which impairs the local ecology but does not necessarily threaten the health or lives of people living in the local communities. Treating water cases like other environmental rights cases, courts tend to incorporate general substantive principles of environmental law, including polluter pays, the public trust doctrine, precautionary principle, and principles of sustainable development (including especially the need to balance development and ecology), without making special reference to the water-specific aspects of the case, if any. For instance, the balancing that is required in sustainable development cases is the same whether the places to be developed are terrain or waterways. As the Indian Supreme Court wrote in the context of coastal areas where land development affects the quality of the water,

"Both development and environment must go hand in hand, in other words, there should not be development at the cost of environment and vice versa, but there should be development while taking due care and ensuring the protection of environment."

In a landmark decision from Chile, the Supreme Court enjoined a copper mining company from continuing to dump waste onto the beaches of Chile, as it had done for 50 years. The court explained: "Never will it be said that a person or authority has the right to pollute the environment, in which a community of people live and grow, by a voluntary act of its own, as is occurring in this case. Moreover, said act, by affecting nature itself, is violating all civilized norms of cohabitation of man with his environment. The preservation of nature and conservation of the environmental heritage is an obligation of the State, according to our Fundamental Constitution..." The claims were asserted in purely environmental terms, and the evidence relied on related to the color of the ocean water, the adverse impact on marine life, the creation of artificial beaches, and other evidence of environmental degradation. Nonetheless, the Court found that the harm to nature and to humans was inextricably linked and, however it was categorized, the conduct of the copper company violated the rights of Chileans to live in an environment free of pollution. And nowhere in the case was particular mention made of the fact that the harm was to water rather than to land.

Likewise, the judicial recognition of the importance of environmental protection for future generations applies equally in water and non-water environmental cases. As the Philippine court has said, "Even assuming the absence of a categorical legal provision specifically prodding petitioners to clean up the bay, they and the men and women representing them cannot escape their obligation to future generations of Filipinos to keep the waters of the Manila Bay clean and clear as humanly as possible. Anything less would be a betrayal of the trust reposed in them." Moreover, the adjustments that many courts have made to procedural rules in constitutional environmental cases apply with equal vigor to cases involving water rights. For instance, the tenet that the burden of persuasion is not on the party making the claim as it would ordinarily be, but on the party seeking to prove that *no* damage has been done, applies equally in water and non-water environmental cases.

The two lower court cases vindicating the Ecuadorian rights of nature both involved damage to rivers, in one case by negligently dumping construction debris into the river, thereby narrowing the channel and causing flooding on adjacent landowners' property, and in the other case by illegal gold mining operations that were polluting the waters. In neither of these cases, however, did the courts treat the claims any differently than they would have had they been based on the rights of land or soil.

F. HYBRIDIZED HUMAN AND ENVIRONMENTAL WATER RIGHTS

In some situations, the human and ecological interests converge, as where a polluter degrades the quality of the water to such an extent that it is neither potable for humans nor environmentally sustainable. In other cases, these are competitive interests as where the human-rights based demands on access to water derogate from the pristine condition in which environmental interests would seek to protect it.

Most courts do not distinguish between claims based on human rights and those based on environmental rights. This is the situation in Ecuador, for instance, where litigation by indigenous groups and local residents lasting almost 20 years—and ongoing—resulted, at least as of 2012, in an $18 billion judgment against Chevron for the environmental degradation and loss of access to clean water caused by its predecessor, Texaco's, activities in the region. Where the damage to one causes injury to the other, there is little need for the courts to distinguish between the two types of claims.

In India, too, the inextricability of human and environmental interests in water has been repeatedly acknowledged. "Violation of anti-pollution laws," the Court has said, "not only adversely affects the existing quality of life but the non-enforcement of the legal provisions often results in ecological imbalance and degradation of environment, the adverse effect of which will have to be borne by the future generations." In fact, a plethora of Indian cases reflects the convergence of environmental and human rights strategies, from the cases seeking to clean up the Ganges from toxins from tanneries and other pollutants, to cases concerning water storage and the use of catchment areas. Typical, too, is the Indian Supreme Court's statement in *Susetha vs. State Of Tamil Nadu And Ors.* (concerning the use of storage tanks), that the right to water is envisaged as the part of the quality of life protected under Article 21 of the Constitution, but "also in view of the fact that the same has been recognized in Articles 47 [relating to nutrition, standard of living and public health] and 48-A [relating to protecting and improving the natural environment including forests, lakes, rivers and wild life] of the Constitution of India." Rights to water are protected indistinguishably as human and environmental rights.

In 1996, the Indian Supreme Court decided a case that challenged the national and state governments' failure to develop and implement a policy that would protect or sustainably develop India's 6000 kilometers of coastline. Although there was *some* regulation and *some* implementation in *some* places, the plaintiff – an environmental NGO called the Indian Council For Enviro-Legal Action (ICELA) – argued, and the Supreme Court agreed, that there needed to be a comprehensive coastal zone plan that the government was bound to implement and enforce. The court was sympathetic, recognizing the complex web of interests that were at play in the case.

The court accepted the plaintiff's claim that the high level of pollution in the coastal waters was caused by "the stresses and pressure of high population growth, non-restrained development, [and] lack of adequate infrastructure facilities for the resident population." In particular, the harms were caused by "indiscriminate industrialisation and urbanisation, without the requisite pollution control systems." But the waters were affected differently in different places. Tidal waves and cyclones were destroying the mangrove forests, while anthropogenic but ecologically unsound development was threatening the major fishing areas in some of the coastal areas, and over-exploitation of groundwater in certain coastal areas was "stated to have resulted in growing intrusion of salt water from the sea to inland areas and fresh water aquifers previously used for drinking, agriculture and horticulture." At the same time, "unplanned urbanisation and industrialisation in the coastal belts is stated to be causing fast disappearance of fertile agricultural lands, fruit gardens and energy plantations like casuarina trees," and this can have devastating consequences for the human and natural environment because these areas "serve as windbreakers and protect inland habitations from the cyclonic damages." These causes of the damage run the gamut from intentional human causes to human causes for which no one could really be held responsible, such as population growth to entirely natural causes such as cyclones. While it is difficult to lay a claim against a public or private entity for the damage caused by extreme weather phenomena, courts are increasingly holding governments accountable for failing to protect against such harms, particularly when they are cyclical or foreseeable.

In the *Manila Bay* case, the Philippine Supreme Court went further and held the government accountable for being neglectful in failing to protect the bay. It described the Bay as "a dirty and slowly dying expanse mainly because of the abject official indifference of people and institutions that could have otherwise made a difference" and chastised the government for "[t]heir cavalier attitude towards solving, if not mitigating, the environmental pollution problem," which, it said, "is a sad commentary on bureaucratic efficiency and commitment." The court ordered the rehabilitation and restoration of the waters in Manila Bay "to make them fit for swimming, skin-diving, and other forms of contact recreation."

The Indian ICELA court's description of the actual injuries is also impressive in its breadth and sophistication. It described the injuries as being both short and long-term, and "physical, chemical and biological" in nature. They were both anthropocentric and ecocentric, as they included "damage to flora and fauna, public health and environment." The resources that were at stake included "extensive groundwater resources and sometimes mineral resources, while in other areas, there are iron ore, oil and gas resources and mangrove forests." The court was able to see that the water at issue in this case included coastal waters, groundwater, aquifers, and, in their most menacing forms, tidal waves and cyclones. But the court recognized that in any of these forms, water is part of a larger ecosystem that includes flora and fauna, mangrove forests, fishing areas, cities and towns, fruit gardens, energy plantations, and fertile agricultural lands which, in turn, protect population centers from cyclonic damage. The use to which water is put and for which it is valued was also understood to be varied and included mineral resources, fishing, drinking, agriculture, and horticulture. Water, the court was ready to appreciate, is clearly not a *single* thing that merits protection but a complex of elements and interests whose competing values needs to be carefully assessed and managed.

The case also illustrates the types of claims that are typically seen in constitutional water cases as they include—and conflate—questions of access and quality. Questions of access are typically deemed to raise human rights claims because the human use of water is so critical to life, dignity, health, and other commonly recognized human rights. Many parts of Africa, where water shortages are already evident and are likely to intensify in the coming decades, have already seen a number of constitutional cases aimed at assuring adequate access to water. These urgent and competing demands for water create a tension for the vindication of constitutional water rights: courts that are asked to vindicate the immediate human rights to water may well sacrifice the environmental interests in protecting water resources for future generations and for the benefit of the world's ecosystems.

The effect of constitutional provisions on these cases seems indirect. Courts tend to see through the text and focus instead on the actual interests at play, assessing whether the human claims to adequate access outweigh the competing corporate or political pressures. The text never determines the result of the balancing process and, given the complexity of the cases, courts often ignore the text altogether, reading environmental provisions to protect human rights and sometimes vice versa. Nonetheless, the existence in the constitution of a provision relating to water seems to encourage courts to pay more attention than they otherwise might to its importance to human life and to nature itself.

G. REMEDIES, IMPLEMENTATION & ENFORCEMENT

Like constitutional environmental adjudication generally, constitutional water cases often result in a multi-pronged remedial approach. Certainly, monetary damages and fines for harm already done are common. In *Tirupur v. Noyal*, the Indian Supreme Court allowed substantial fines against a tannery even though it had already installed remedial pollution measures such as pre-treatment plants to minimize water pollution from dyeing. In the Coca-Cola case in the Indian State of Kerala, the state legislature set up a claims court allowing claims against Coca-Cola up to $47 million. And, as noted, in the Ecuadorian case against Texaco, damages were assessed at $18 billion. And in *Mendoza Beatriz Silva et al vs. State of Argentina et al.*, the Argentine case involving the clean-up of the polluted river basin near Buenos Aires, fines against the companies were also available. However, the *amparo* nature of the cases required plaintiffs to obtain compensation only through separate civil litigation. Unfortunately, it is often the case, that payments to marginalized populations may not be forthcoming, and when they are, they are often inadequate to compensate for the many kinds of harms caused when clean water is unavailable or insufficient.

Other common remedial forms are also available, sometimes but not always in conjunction with damages. In the *Manila Bay* case, the court ordered mandamus against the government because, in its view, cleaning the bay was a non-discretionary duty. "In the light of the ongoing environmental degradation," the court said, it "wishes to emphasize the extreme necessity for all concerned executive departments and agencies to immediately act and discharge their respective official duties and obligations. Indeed, time is of the essence; hence, there is a need to set timetables for the performance and completion of the tasks, some of them as defined for them by law and the nature of their respective offices and mandates." But the court went much further and ordered a wide-ranging set of remedies, including education, inspection of commercial buildings, and reviewing licenses. In particular, the court said that the Department of Education "shall integrate lessons on pollution prevention, waste management, environmental protection, and like subjects in the school curricula of all levels to inculcate in the minds and hearts of students and, through them, their parents and friends, the importance of their duty toward achieving and maintaining a balanced and healthful ecosystem in the Manila Bay and the entire Philippine archipelago." And, as is becoming typical in these cases, the court retained jurisdiction over the case and, "in line with the principle of 'continuing mandamus,'" it required the government to submit quarterly reports showing the progress it had made in complying with the decision.

In the 2008 river basin case from Argentina, the court "established an action plan requiring the government agency responsible for the Matanza/Riachuelo basin[] to fulfill specific measures, including: a) producing and disseminating public information; b) controlling industrial pollution; c) cleaning up waste dumps; d) expanding water supply, sewer and drainage works; e) developing an emergency sanitation plan; f) adopting an international measurement system to assess compliance with the plans goals." Moreover, "In order to ensure adequate enforcement, the Court delegated the enforcement process to a federal court, [] to monitor enforcement of the decision [and it] created a working group formed by the national Ombudsman and the NGOs that had been involved in the case as non-litigant parties, seeking to strengthen and enable citizen participation in monitoring enforcement of the decision." Indeed, a major part of the decision was to encourage public awareness and discussion about the effects of decades of environmental degradation.

Ordering the creation of boards or commissions to monitor not only the parties' compliance with the court's order, but other ongoing issues relating to the particular water in controversy, is not uncommon, though it necessarily raises difficult theoretical and practical questions about political accountability and the balance of power between the courts and the other limbs of government, as well as questions about the allocation of fiscal resources. The Indian Supreme Court in the ICELA case strongly encouraged but did not require the Central Government to set up State Coastal Management Authorities in each state as well as a National Coastal Management Authority. The court urged this course in light of the fact that the existing Pollution Control Boards had limited jurisdiction over the important issues in question and, the court noted, "are ... overworked."

Ensuring compliance of remedial orders can be the most challenging part of any constitutional environmental case, and cases about water are no different. It cannot be assumed that a private party or governmental authority will automatically comply with a judicial order, particularly if it seeks to do anything more than impose a moderate fine or require the fulfillment of a non-discretionary duty with minimal political consequences. Rather, the expectation should be that restoration of access to water and repair of degradation to the environment requires an integrated response on behalf of courts, legislators, and executive actors at all levels of government. In the ICELA case, the court emphasized, moreover, the important role that state courts have in ensuring compliance with environmental norms, particularly where they are more likely to be familiar with local conditions. It is also worth remembering that those conditions, which vary from place to place as the environment itself changes, are bound to change over time. In the ICELA case, for instance, the government issued one directive in 1991, but three years later, and apparently due to political pressure particularly from developers and the tourism industry, significantly relaxed the environmental standards. Plaintiffs should be mindful to frame their claims precisely, unless they are confident that the court is committed to engaging with political actors to compel the development and ongoing implementation of a comprehensive water management plan.

In fact, many cases reflect the reality that good laws have been enacted and, in some cases, environmentally friendly administrations seek to enforce them; yet, the lure of investment and development, combined with limited fiscal and human resources thwart their best intentions, so that judicial action is required to impel action on an ongoing basis. As the ICELA court recognized:

If the mere enactment of the laws relating to the protection of [the] environment was to ensure a clean and pollution-free environment, then India would, perhaps, be the least polluted country in the world. But, this is not so. There are stated to be over 200 Central and State Statutes which have at least some concern with environment protection, either directly or indirectly. The plethora of such enactments has, unfortunately, not resulted in preventing environmental degradation which, on the contrary, has increased over the years.

The situation in Brazil is similar:

Despite an impressive set of laws and policies, the pace of implementing the modern water regime remains a challenge.... Brazilian water law—like all of Brazilian environmental law—must address the problem that its statutes are strong, but enforcement is weak. This situation is partially due to a lack of resources and an accompanying lack of political will in the face of competing development priorities. In addition, although there is no way to measure it precisely, corruption remains a factor undermining the enforcement of environmental laws in Brazil.

The Indian court went on to say, "If the people were to voluntarily respect such a law, and abide by it, then it would result in law being able to achieve the object for which it was enacted. Where, however, there is a conflict between the provision of law and personal interest, then it often happens that self-discipline and respect for law disappears."

The question then is what a court can do in these situations to compel respect for the law. One option is for the court to require the development of a water management plan that balances constitutional human rights with environmental protection and with the practical necessities of development and economic growth. Such a plan should normally be developed at the national or central level, so that water remains protected equally throughout the nation and to avoid the competitive race to the bottom that decentralization often fosters, particularly in stressed economic times. A national policy would also ensure that a national tax base is available to subsidize equitable water distribution throughout the nation. This course is essentially what courts are doing when they monitor the progressive realization of a social right, as the South African court in particular is wont to do.

Another solution, where a legislative framework already exists, is for the court to build up the administrative machinery to monitor and implement the policies already chosen either by ordering the establishment of a new administrative office or, if a relevant one exists, by expanding it to include the responsibility for water. The Nepali Supreme Court did this, for example, in the face of corporate recalcitrance. Noting that the Drinking Water Corporation "seems reluctant to perform its duties to protect public health," it "decided to alert the Ministry of Housing and Physical Development to be the contact ministry for providing necessary directions to the Drinking Water Corporation in order to make the Corporation accountable and responsible and to make proper arrangements for providing pure drinking water as per its legal obligations under the Act." If a court believes that constitutional challenges are likely to continue, then another solution is the development of specialized courts, as is happening with environmental courts in general and as has already happened in Latin America at a regional level specifically for water. Indeed, George and Catherine Pring report that water courts have existed in Europe since the early 20th century and that "water issues have been the catalyst for broader-based [environmental courts] in a number of countries."

By highlighting the importance of water, constitutional provisions can invite litigation to protect water. And the value of the litigation may extend beyond the judgment. In Argentina, the highly publicized litigation over the pollution in the Matanza-Riachuelo river basin contributed to a World Bank program to support its clean-up. Even in the South African *Mazibuko* case, where the plaintiffs' claims were rejected, and where the ruling has been roundly criticized by human rights groups and those representing poor and disenfranchised populations, one United Nations publication has indicated that there is reason to believe that "during the litigation, and perhaps because of it, the City has repeatedly reviewed and revised its policies to ensure that they did promote the progressive achievement of the right of access to sufficient water." However, this did nothing to avoid the months-long water deprivation crisis experienced subsequently elsewhere in the country.

With all these fiscal and political complexities and the challenges involved in managing the cases and in developing and enforcing effective remedies, courts might be tempted to avoid adjudicating cases involving rights to water. But, remarkably, courts have not shied away from hearing cases raising claims over water rights. In part this reflects explicit language in so many of the world's constitutions that seeks to protect and manage water resources as an incident of sovereignty, as a human right, or as an essential element of a healthy ecology. And in part, it reflects the growing muscularity of constitutional courts around the world, especially in regions like Southeast Asia and Latin America, where water resources are both threatened and scarce, along with the growing recognition in both national and international arenas of the importance of water to human life and to the world's ecosystems.

QUESTIONS

1. What are "water rights"?
2. How are water rights reflected and protected throughout the globe?
3. Does water have "rights"? Why or why not?
4. What are the implications of recognizing water rights?
5. To what extent do cultural biases affect answers to these questions?

II.   STATE WATER LAW

EXCERPT: JAMES R. MAY, WATER RIGHTS AND LAW IN DELAWARE
20 Denver L. Rev. 3 (2016)

Water law in Delaware comprises an amalgam of ordinary riparian rights and the natural flow doctrine. It combines special provisions that reflect the state's four-centuries of water law, coupled with recent legislative inventions to protect coastal areas, and a federal program designed to manage the Delaware River from the upper elevations of its headwaters in upstate New York to a submerged Cypress stand in Delaware's southernmost reach, the state's only remaining virgin forest.

Shaped like a 130-mile long, jagged isosceles triangle, the State of Delaware is small, flat, and awash in water. Delaware has a variety of plentiful water resources that belie its modest size (only Rhode Island is smaller). The northern tip of the state lies in the Piedmont region and is characterized by a bed of crystalline rock that runs from New England to Alabama. Most of the state, however, is within the Atlantic Coastal Plain province, which is typically flat.

Water is one of the state's dominant resources. More than one in every six square miles in the state is under water, which means about 540 out of a total area of approximately 2500 square miles, exclusive of the Delaware River and Bay is submerged. In addition, some 490 square miles of the Delaware River and Bay lie within the boundaries of the state. There are also large areas of fresh- and saltwater marshes and hydric soils. All in all, Delaware boasts about 3000 miles of rivers and streams, 4500 acres of lakes, reservoirs, and ponds, 130,000 acres of freshwaters wetlands, 90,000 acres of coastal and tidal wetlands, 850 square miles of estuaries and bays, and twenty-five ocean coastal miles. It is also flatter than Kansas, with a mean elevation of sixty feet, and a high point of 448 feet, which means that water flows across the state like billiards on a felt tabletop.

This article is divided into three sections. The first provides a brief introduction to the role of water resources and the evolution of water rights law in Delaware. The second surveys Delaware water rights law, focusing on the processes and standards for obtaining a permit to use, withdraw, or divert water in the state. The third is an overview of some related aspects influencing water rights in Delaware, namely the Delaware Coastal Zone Act, and the Delaware River Basin Commission.

I. INTRODUCTION TO WATER RIGHTS IN DELAWARE

Historically, water has served as the state's lifeblood. Delaware was first home to Eastern Algonquian tribes that relied on Delaware's bountiful water supply for fishing, hunting, and sustenance. Then Dutch and Swedish explorers in the early and mid-1600's settled portions of what would become Delaware, largely due to ready access and availability of intricate and connected water systems. These attributes made it valuable for ingress and egress into William Penn's Pennsylvania during English colonization. By the time Delaware became the nation's first state in 1787, it already possessed some of the most elaborate water laws in the country.

The state's special brand of water laws attracted commerce large and small, including French émigré Eleuthere Irenee duPont de Nemours. DuPont established black powder mills along the banks for the shallow but brisk-flowing Brandywine River, and with it, launched the industrial revolution. Water access remains essential to Delaware's great petrochemical, pharmaceutical, agricultural and animal farming, automotive, port, fishing, crabbing, housing, shopping, motel, restaurant, and tourism industries.

Disputes about water use in Delaware have had profound effects on water and constitutional law in the United States. There is evidence of the recognition of water rights in Delaware as early as 1658, as settlers vied for position for siting water-powered mills. Determining water rights for mill operations remained the dominant force in Delaware water law for the next two hundred and fifty years. Indeed, the colonial assembly enacted water laws to sort out use by mill operators in 1719, 1760, and 1773. Post-independence, the state's assembly enacted water laws in 1819, 1859, 1869, and 1911, some of which remain in effect even though the water-powered mills that once dominated are but memories. The idea that the Commerce Clause contains a 'dormant' or 'negative' aspect originated in a case involving water use in Delaware. Chief Justice John Marshall coined the phrase "dormant Commerce Clause" in *Willson v. Black Bird Creek Marsh Co.*, a case that allowed Delaware to issue a license to block navigation of the Blackbird Creek, absent a countervailing federal law.

Thus, reaching back four centuries, with a wildly varied colonial past and dominated by mill-races first and industry later, modern water law in Delaware is a bit of this and a bit of that, like an old house restored over time to fit new owners and new codes. While it generally favors eastern water law and its riparian flavors, water law in Delaware defies easy classification.

II. PERMITTED WATER USE IN DELAWARE

In Delaware, the Delaware Division of Natural Resources and Environmental Control (DNREC) is charged with effectuating state policy to develop, use, and control water and groundwater "to make the maximum contribution to the public benefit." Accordingly, DNREC issues permits to "construct, install, replace, modify, or use any equipment or device or other article . . . intended to withdraw ground water or surface water for treatment and supply." Moreover, DNREC must authorize any increases in water use. Applicants may appeal DNREC's decision-making to the Delaware Environmental Appeals Board and then to the Superior Court of Delaware.

Certain activities are exempt from the permit process. These include damming a stream that originates on one's property when doing so does not detrimentally affect another, damming a stream flow of less than one-half million gallons per day, or creating a pond not larger than sixty thousand square feet for conservation, recreation, propagation and protection of fish and wildlife, watering of stock, or fire protection.

As with many states in the eastern U.S. the ultimate inquiry on whether to grant a permit application is whether the requested use is "reasonable." Under this authority, DNREC ordered parties to remove docks constructed without permits, but was rebuked for its attempts to charge a lease fee for subaqueous land beneath the landholder's pier.

Much of the inquiry turns to decades-old, and sometimes century-old, precedent and persuasion. For instance, natural watercourses in Delaware—waters that flow naturally along a discrete natural channel with a bed and banks – are generally subject to the riparian rights to uses undiminished in quantity and unchanged in quality or temperature. Delaware's riparian rights approach follows the natural flow doctrine, which recognizes the "right to the stream, using it so as not to injure any others." In essence, this permits diversion and other uses, provided water flow is returned to the natural channel before reaching the next riparian owner, and so on.

Much of water law applied to natural watercourses in Delaware is hardly exceptional east of the Mississippi. First, riparian ownership in Delaware of a non-tidal stream is deed-specific, but failing that, ownership defaults to the middle of the stream. Second, in the event of erosion, rights of way are lost until restored by accretion. Third, riparian owners are entitled to both natural water quality and quantity. Fourth, riparian rights yield to those of state or federal governments with no right to perpetual flow, for instance. However, governmental takings entitle the landowner to compensation. For example, the state must compensate landowners for flooding that results from government activities, such as highway construction. Fifth, landowners have no duty to prevent natural runoff from harming adjoining land, but may not collect and direct it to a neighbor. Last, damming a stream does not create concomitant fishing rights.

Yet, in what can sometimes be quite a consequential departure from practices elsewhere, riparian ownership along tidal streams extends to the low-water mark, unlike the practice in most eastern states, which limits ownership of riparian areas of tidal waters to the high-water mark.

As with most eastern states, Delaware law protects the reasonable use and enjoyment of groundwater so as not to jeopardize common supplies for neighboring owners. What is "reasonable" is an objective inquiry, which considers the intentions of each surface owner.

III. Related Laws and Controversies that Influence Water Use in Delaware

Two laws not directly related to water rights and law in Delaware nonetheless have a profound impact upon it: The Delaware Coastal Zone Act, and the Delaware River Basin Compact. The Delaware Coastal Zone Act ("CZA") was the first comprehensive coastal land-use law in the world aimed at curbing industrial uses of a coastal area. Delaware's coastal zone—which runs from Swede's Landing in Wilmington, through the Bombay and Prime Hook National Wildlife Refuges, to the state's southern beaches, freshwater wetlands, and inland bays— stands as the state's most distinguishing feature. It serves as a primary flyway for the Northern Hemisphere's most significant avian migration. The Delaware coastal zone's wetlands are recognized under the Ramsar Convention, an international treaty that recognizes wetlands of international importance.

The coastal zone is also central to the State's multi-million dollar tourism industry. For example, tourists flock from world-round to view shore birds stopping over to fatten themselves on a banquet of horse-shoe crab eggs each spring before the birds proceed along on a grueling 5000 mile trek to northern climes.

To protect these resources, the Delaware Legislature enacted the CZA at the behest of then-governor Russell Peterson in 1971. The CZA aims to protect the "natural environment of its bay and coastal areas," for recreation, tourism, and environmental uses, and establishes that the "protection of the environment, natural beauty and recreational potential of the State is . . . of great concern."

The CZA forbids large and new industrial development in the coastal zone, regulates certain existing uses, and is agnostic about commercial and residential development. Specifically, the CZA prohibits new "heavy industry" and "bulk product transfer facilities" but "grandfathers" in existing heavy industrial uses and bulk product transfer facilities, with the exception of "abandoned" facilities.

First, the CZA prohibits "[h]eavy industry use of any kind not in operation on June 28, 1971." "Heavy industry" is defined as uses "characteristically involving more than 20 acres," and employing equipment with the "potential to pollute when equipment malfunctions or human error occurs." Prohibited new heavy industry uses also include extension or expansion of certain "non-conforming uses" beyond their footprints and other similar heavy industrial uses.

Second, the CZA prohibits "[b]ulk product transfer facilities and pipelines, which serve as bulk transfer facilities that were not in operation on June 28, 1971." Corresponding regulations define "bulk product" as "loose masses of cargo such as oil, grain, gas and minerals, which are typically stored in the hold of a vessel." In turn, a "Bulk Product Transfer Facility" includes the transfer of bulk products from vessel to vessel.

Expanded or extended "manufacturing" uses, or expansions or extensions of existing "nonconforming" uses, such as existing heavy industry, bulk product transfer facilities and other non-conforming uses within their existing footprints, require a permit. The CZA also requires a permit for "the construction of pipelines or docking facilities serving as offshore bulk product transfer facilities if such facilities serve only one on-shore manufacturing or other facility," and any "public sewage treatment plant or public recycling plant."

Permit applicants must include an "Environmental Impact Statement," that assesses whether a project "may result in any negative impact" on the coastal zone. The state's evaluation must consider the "direct and cumulative environmental impacts" of the proposal. To obtain approval, applicants "must more than offset the negative environmental impacts associated with the proposed project or activity." The extent of any negative impact and the means by which to offset them are a function of various "environmental indicators." The chosen offset project must be "clearly and demonstrably more beneficial to the environment in the Coastal Zone than the harm done by the negative environmental impacts associated with the permitting activities themselves." Past achievements of the applicant, as well as the location and timing of the proposed offset, may affect the extent of offset required, and the offset need not occur in the coastal zone. Permits are then approved contingent on the completion of the offset. Permitting decisions may be appealed to the Board.

The ultimate objective of the permitting process is "environmental improvement" in the coastal zone, considering: "(1) Environmental impact, (2) Economic effect, (3) Aesthetic effect, (4) Number and type of supporting facilities required and the impact of such facilities on all factors listed in this subsection, (5) Effect on neighboring land uses, and (6) County and municipal comprehensive plans for the development and/or conservation of their areas of jurisdiction."

Project status under the CZA need not be guesswork. Project applicants may—and under some circumstances must—seek a "status decision" to determine whether a project constitutes a prohibited use, requires a permit, or is exempted from the CZA and to receive feedback on offsets, effects, and indicators.

Additionally, the Delaware River Basin Commission (DRBC) also plays a minor role in water law in Delaware. The DRBC consists of the four Delaware River basin states (Pennsylvania, New Jersey, New York, and Delaware) and the federal government. The DRBC focuses on such issues as watershed planning, water supply allocation, regulatory review, water conservation initiatives, drought management, and flood control. Those wishing to withdraw water from the Delaware River must apply for a permit from the DRBC.

Myriad other laws and programs that influence water use in the state have been covered sufficiently elsewhere and are beyond the scope of this examination—including: the Natural Areas Preservation System Act, and the Conservation and Preservation Easements Act, as well as those that address fin fishing, erosion and sedimentation control, beach erosion control, dredging and management of lagoons, wetlands, subaqueous lands, and minerals in submerged lands. The same holds for water pollution control, including that for discharges into streams supplying drinking water, by waterborne vessels and sewage treatment plants, and for oil pollution. Further, the "border wars" between Delaware and New Jersey regarding development in and of the Delaware River, are beyond the scope of this report, as are specific issues and responses to sea-level rise in the state.

Conclusion

Water law in Delaware is an amalgam that has evolved significantly over more than four centuries. Much of it revolved around mill works until the latter half of the Twentieth Century. These days, Delaware stands as an exemplar of a combination of riparian rights, coupled with agency oversight that regulates water use, assignment, and development, with an overlaying state law that prohibits heavy industrial uses in Delaware's coastal zone, and a multi-state commission that regulates water quality and quantity for the Delaware River.

QUESTIONS

1. How are water rights reflected and protected in Delaware?
2. Is there a constitutional right to water in Delaware?
3. What are "riparian rights"? How about "prior appropriation"? What test (or version of it) applies in Delaware?

III.   DELAWARE COSTAL ZONE ACT

This chapter concludes with a local look at what many believe to be the State of Delaware's most important law. In 1971, Delaware enacted the first comprehensive coastal land use law in the world aimed at curbing industrial uses of a coastal area, known as the "Coastal Zone Act." ("CZA"). The CZA forbids new heavy industry and bulk transfer facilities, regulates new heavy manufacturing uses, and is silent about commercial and residential development.

The CZA was a controversial law. It was heavily opposed by the industrial development community in general and Shell Oil and the Nixon Administration in particular. With the endorsement of then Governor Russell Peterson, it passed in the Delaware Legislature by narrow margins.

Forty years on, the CZA continues to be what might be the state's most celebrated and controversial law. Proponents of its success point to a coastline that looks much as it did 40 years ago, boasting a 100-mile stretch that lacks industrial development from Delaware City to the southern tip of the State. The coast's quality contributes to tourism, property values and quality of life. Industrial development interests, however, contend that the CZA is unnecessarily rigid and starves the state of business and employment opportunities and tax revenues. Either way, the CZA has served as a model to be examined across the country and the world.

EXCERPT: JAMES R. MAY AND WENDY MYERS, IT IS STILL NOT A SHORE THING: ENVIRONMENTAL IMPROVEMENT AND INDUSTRIAL USES OF DELAWARE'S COASTAL ZONE
Spring DEL. LAW. 20 (1999).

An immutable characteristic of any statute is that it always begins with a story. Stories are a bit of showing and telling. The showing is the coastline itself. From Delaware City southward, the coast is clear. No heavy industry. No giant, fenced facilities offloading oil and other commodities. That's the showing. It's simple.

Now the telling, which is more complex. The story behind the Act is full of strong personalities, nuanced heroes and villains, and wide, sweeping landscapes. This story rivets. The Shell Oil Complany set out to develop parts of the western shore of the Delaware River. Zapata Norness, a bulk shipping company, wanted to build a 300 acre island in the Delaware Bay to offload huge quantities of coal, iron ore, and other raw materials.

Their plan was to use the Delaware coast for oil production, unloading, and transportation. To turn Delaware City and parts surrounding into a sort of drive-in oil gushing and gulping boomtown miniature of Houston or Galvaston, or East New Orleans, or Guadalahare, or Quinto, or Newcastle, or Aberdeen, or Riyad. A booming, bustling, seaport oil town, with satellite industries galore. Trains and trucks transporting oil and other commodities throughout the eastern seaboard. Hotels booked, restaurants and nightclubs busting at the seams. Riches. Jobs. Taxes. Wealth. Political power. Happiness. A kind of HBO Boardwalk Empire, with gasoline and methyl alcohol substituting for gambling and ethyl alcohol.

So, Shell and other companies began gobbling up land, often through midnight brokers who concealed the true buyer and its intentions, often for pennies on the dollar for what was imagined as the real marketplace to come. An oil rush, as it were.

Others, however, had a more jaundiced view. In their view, the Delaware shoreline already bustled, brimmed wealth, and provided sustenance to millions. Millions of shorebirds. Millions of horseshoe crabs. Millions of commercially serviceable shell and finfish and shore mammals, including millions of tourists from around the globe. It also bustled with the thousands of people who lived in homes along the coast who would be displaced. Land would be lost. Skylines would be altered. They viewed the plan as a – wait for it – gas-tastrophy. ☺

Shell's plan caught the attention of a relatively young chemist who had just left upper management at DuPont. He spent 20 years with the company, streamlining and economizing rayon and nylon production, often in support of the national defense, say, for reliable all-weather parachutes and ponchos. Once earning his way into in upper management, he had the courage to desegregate production and management lines at DuPont's Seaford plant and elsewhere in the company. He pursued justice in the workplace so doggedly that top brass decided that he must be crazy. They even referred him for psychiatric evaluation. Which the company physician refused to administer, calling him the sanest person he knew. He also opposed segregated schools. [He opposed the state's corrupted committee system, its criminal justice system, and its death penalty because he viewed them to be slanted against African Americans, the politically disadvantaged and the poor.] He stood for justice, though the heavens may fall.

Throughout, however, he was a stalwart of the Republican Party machinery in Delaware. He believes that a responsible and accountable free market was a social good. That economic and social Darwinism was true and best, whether in the natural world or in the marketplace.

Out of nowhere, this man ran for, and became, Governor. His name was Russell Peterson. Peterson learned to love the Delaware Coastline like so many ways love is learned, with your family, while birding with his sons. It got to the point when he and his kids had identified more birds on the coast than anyone else ever had.

Peterson was concerned about what Shell wanted and what it portended for the coast. So he worked with citizen advocates throughout the state to write, advocate for, and then pass the Delaware Coastal Zone Act into law 40 years ago.

This did not earn Governor Peterson political points. He was viewed as rambunctious and radical by Republican leadership in Washington, a turncoat by corporate Delaware and his former employer, and unpatriotic by the U.S. Chamber of Commerce. He viewed the Act as rational and reasoned, and patriotic to future generations. He lost his bid for reelection amidst his plan to raise taxes to shore up state coffers during an energy crisis embedded in the recession of 1971-2. He later served the OTA and the NAS with distinction. We became friends. He served on the Advisory Board of the Mid-Atlantic Environmental Law Center at Widener, and helped launch with a keynote address here at five years ago. Russ died in 2011, and is missed.

With this background, let's take a closer look at the statute itself.

The Act is just about as high minded as a state law can be. It says that "the protection of the environment, natural beauty and recreational potential of the State is…of great concern." It aims to protect the "natural environment of its bay and coastal areas," for recreation, tourism and environmental, uses. 7 Del. C § 7001. As such, the Act forbids some uses, allows others by permit only, and does not regulate still more.

The law Governor Peterson helped to craft does two very important things. First, it prohibits the construction of new heavy industry and new bulk transfer stations in the coastal zone. Second, it requires those seeking to build a new manufacturing facility or factory, or to change the footprint or process of an existing so called existing nonconforming use, to obtain a permit from the Delaware Division of Natural Resources and Environmental Control. The primary purpose of the permit is to measure and then offset unavoidable adverse environmental impacts from the new plant or modified existing one, considering certain environmental indicators. A developer could request a "status decision" to determine where one fit.

The statute itself is a wonder, with clear structure, reach and jurisdiction,

At the time of enacted, there was no other law like it. Not here. Not at the federal level. Not in New Jersey, or Maryland, or Pennsylvania, or Virginia, or the Carolinas, or Georgia, Florida, Mississippi, Louisiana, Texas, California, Oregon, Washington, Alaska, or in any other coastal state. Or any other country or continent.

It has served as a model, if not a blueprint, for nearly two dozen states that followed by establishing coastal laws of their own. The Act is still unique. None of these state coastal laws, however, prohibit heavy industry. None prohibit bulk transfer stations. A majority don't expressly prohibit anything. None have a permitting system as elaborate as Delaware's, requiring that adverse environmental effects be more than offset. Many, however, regulate residential and commercial development. Some regulate electricity generation, and so-called green energy. There is still no law like it. How is that for being the first state.

The Act had gaps and shortcomings, however. Those who passed the law understood the perfect was the enemy of the good. So they set up a process for DNREC to develop regulations to refine certain definitions, like "heavy industry" and "bulk transfer stations" and "environmental impact," and then how to minimize them. These regulations would then need to be approved by a quasi-administrative and adjudicative entity, known as the Coastal Zone Industrial Control Board. Tall orders, all.

The Board adopted the first set of regulations (all five pages of them, mostly procedural), in December of 1971. But principal substantive issues languished. In 1990, then-Governor Mike Castle established an Ad Hoc Committee to assist DNREC to develop more comprehensive regulations. Assisted by that Committee, DNREC transmitted a comprehensive set of proposed Regulations to the Board for its consideration in September 1992. But these regulations were dashed due to a failure to comply with the state's open government law. So in October 1997, then-Governor Carper commissioned a multidisciplinary advisory group – one which I had the pleasure to serve – to develop a memorandum of agreement about these terms. The Advisory group completed the MOA in March of 1998 (in your materials). DNREC then proposed draft regulations to the Board two months later. In May 1999, after more fits and starts, the Board adopted the proposed regulations (in your materials).

The regulations were viewed as a great compromise. The business community "won" by having regulations that are predictable and provide some relief from the need to acquire a new permit each time their facility has a production increase or creates a new product. The environmental advocates "won" by keeping the 'footprints' of the existing heavy industrial sites intact and by requiring permit applicants to establish an 'Offset Proposal' to negate any new pollution from their proposed project. This offset proposal must (in the opinion of the DNREC Secretary) clearly and demonstrably more than offset the applicant's new pollution loading based on "environmental indicators." The goal of this environmental assessment is to produce a net reduction of environmental impacts within, and possibly outside of, the Coastal Zone.

Since then, DNREC has promulgated permitting forms and environmental matrices for evaluating environmental impacts, as well as effects on economic, aesthetic, employment, and the local economy.

While a wonder it is, in retrospect, the Act is almost too true to be good, in all respects. It is far from perfect. It comes up short in coastal protection. The issue of electric power plants was not engaged because compromise seemed unlikely. It does not address residential or commercial development. It exempts sewage treatment plants. These shortcomings arguably promote dumb growth. The most significant shortcoming, in my view, is that neither it nor its implementing regulations require that offset mitigation – the very purpose of the permitting process – actually protect the coastal zone. In other words, one could export mitigation to a far flung place with dubious oversight, far from prying eyes, with no benefit to the coastal zone. This is self-defeating and raises issues of environmental justice. The poorest communities would be the least likely to keep a protected coastline. Moreover, mitigation within the zone is seldom required, and that which is required is seldom enforced.

The Act also comes up short in promoting smart development. It is a proscriptive, unyielding law. It discourages redevelopment of brownfields. It is agnostic about green energy other than solar. It discourages certain kinds of development. It has a heavy reputation.

And it is still in flux, 40 years on. Its terms have been subject to a handful and a half of court decisions, a dozen appeals, and two dozen status decisions, including a rather (in)famous one decided last year involving the Widener Environmental and Natural Resources Law Clinic, in which the CZICB ruled that hearsay evidence is inadmissible for purposes of demonstrating standing before it. (A truly bizarre ruling, since challenged). And so it goes.

QUESTIONS

1. How is the coastal zone protected in Delaware?
2. What makes the Delaware CZA unique?
3. Does the CZA regulate commercial development? Residential?
4. If not, what does it regulate?
5. Is there a constitutional right to the coastal zone in Delaware?

To summarize the Act (and finish the chapter), where it's been and what it can be, let me try with a fit of poetry:

A Sonnet to the Shore
By James R. May

The Delaware Shore
Kids, sand, cars, evermore

Owes its place to an Act
With immeasurable impact

40 years ago
Shell asked to have a go

Build a giant oceanport
A place for tankers to consort

Yet Governor Peterson
Found this troublin'

He issued a moratorium contemporaneously
To prohibit all new heavy industry

This was decried as an atrocity
By owners of a bulk transfer facility

But for others Shell's plan was the last straw
So they succeeded in making the moratorium a law

And so too new factories and existing sources
Would need a permit to protect valuable resources

But the perfect is the enemy of the good
This law does not regulate malls and neighborhoods

Or require offsets to be known
To those within the coastal zone

Now 40 years on it's hard to forgot that remarkable day
When a small wonder decided to go its own way

And Russ Peterson told the folks at Shell
We don't need you, go home, or go to hell

CHAPTER 9: INTERNATIONAL ENVIRONMENTAL LAW

"[Sustainable development] meets the needs of the present without compromising the ability for future generations to meet their own needs."

-- OUR COMMON FUTURE, The World Commission on the Environment (1987)

"[Corporate success means] fully integrating sustainability considerations into governance, performance, accountability, R&D and overall business strategy. Tracking results, analyzing data and implementing actions to increase efficiency and competitiveness are cornerstones for success."

--CERES, The 21st Century Corporation: The CERES Roadmap for Sustainability

Chapter 9 describes international environmental law. Part I takes a 30,000 foot view of its manifold manifestations, including treaties, customs and principles. Part II then focuses on the internationally unifying concept of sustainability, including how it is constitutionally recognized, and its relationship with protecting and promoting human rights, including to dignity.

I.   INTRODUCTION TO INTERNATIONAL ENVIRONMENTAL LAW

EXCERPT: JAMES R. MAY & J. PATRICK KELLY: "THE ENVIRONMENT AND INTERNATIONAL SOCIETY: ISSUES, CONCEPTS AND CONTEXT

ROUTLEDGE HANDBOOK OF INTERNATIONAL ENVIRONMENTAL LAW, Chapter 1 (Shawkat Alam et al. eds, Routledge Handbooks 2012)

The world's resources are under enormous strain. The population of the planet has eclipsed 7 billion people, many if not most of who desire a better quality of life. Population stress naturally contributes to the rising demand for food, energy, metals, and materials. These demands create enormous pressure on domestic and transboundary ecosystems.

International environmental law is the study of how treaties, principles, custom and other sources of international law can be used to address these strains. This book examines what international environmental is, and how it is or can be used to address the planet's wide array of complex and seemingly intractable challenges, including human-induced climate change, resources-based conflict, rising sea levels, loss of timber, biological and cultural diversity loss, diminution of livable land and fresh water, pollution of the oceans, seas and coastal areas, persistent organic pollutants, byproducts of technology and nanotechnology, overharvesting of forests and oceans, global disposal of chemical and hazardous wastes, trade in endangered plants and animals, minerals harvesting in the polar regions, and a human right to a quality environment.

...This section provides a brief survey of threshold principles in international law, including common issues, concepts and definitions, and associated international law constructs. In addition, it views how these concepts are shaped by external and emerging notions of global trade, economics, sustainability and environmental rights.

What is International Environmental Law? Common Issues, Concepts and Definitions

[I]nternational environmental law provides and describes the global institutional means for engaging the global ecological challenges. It is conceptually commodious, a reflection of interconnected ends that can be global, parochial, and everything in between. It consists of a loose affiliation of treaties, principles and customs that define and describe norms, relationships and responses among and between states to meet these many global ecological challenges. It can be poetic and inscrutable, as shown by the definition of "sustainable development": "development . . . that . . . meets the needs of the present without compromising the ability of future generations to meet their own needs." Regardless of whether it appears as positive hard law, normative soft law, or a hybrid of these, international environmental law is essential to the global order of environmental law.

International environmental law is also evolutionary. It reflects the confluence of 500 years of *opinio juris*, *lex suprema* and customary law coupled with more modern conventions and general principles of international environmental law, with added ingredients of environmental ethics, ecology and economics, and human rights.

Moreover ... most treaty negotiations – from climate to fish stocks -- reflect endogenous political, cultural, religious and ethnic consilience and division, and exogenous influences respecting who should pay for what and when, who participates, and who decides. It reflects the inescapable binomialism of the global age: north and south, east and west, developed and developing, financially rich and poor, biologically endowed and barren, givers and takers around the globe. ...

Skeptics argue that international environmental law is unnecessary at best and unwise at worst. This view invites political and societal backlash by trivializing huge moral and ethical challenges, engendering unnecessary counter-colonial effects, facilitating scapegoating, diluting sovereignty and autonomy, creating 'spillover' effects that curtail private property, and undermining more sensible cooperative efforts. International environmental law is also shaped by principles of geography, population distribution, engineering, land use planning, and the applied sciences.

[I]nternational environmental law also has a dizzying array of stakeholders. It is shaped by nation-states, international institutions such as the United Nations Environment Programme, non-governmental organizations such as the International Union for the Conservation of Nature, corporate associations, individuals, academics and the concern for future generations.

To complicate matters, as Chapter 4 suggests, no two countries implement international law the same way. The constitutions of some countries allow the head of state to negotiate and implement binding agreements unilaterally. Other countries require parliamentarian ratification and legislation to implement an international accord. Many countries fall somewhere in between. Domestic implementation is also complicated by domestic policies concerning the use and disposition of natural resources, energy policies, and national security. Many countries lack the resources and statutory and regulatory architectures to implement, or the wherewithal and resources to enforce, international laws. ...

The International Legal Constructs

International law constructs include principles, rules, and norms that are binding on nations and sub-national actors. Environmental legal principles and policy prescriptions emerge from the use of international sources and processes to make law and to cooperate to solve problems. While international law and legal processes may be mechanisms to address transboundary environmental problems, it is a relatively undeveloped and cumbersome system, not an integrated, hierarchical system of universal rules and principles.

International law is complex, to say the least. The international legal system is a decentralized system of independent nation-states with different histories, values, and interests. The international system lacks a legislature with the authority to make law, an authoritative court with mandatory jurisdiction to articulate norms, an executive with delegated authority to make law or execute legal norms, or an international police force to enforce norms.

Accordingly, international society has been conceived as made up of independent states that must consent to restraints on their authority. These limitations make solving problems on the basis of consent or consensus difficult and slow.

Hence, the international legal system has been criticized for its anarchic character. Critics particularly within the international legal community have called for a new sense of common humanity to transcend the limited vision of states asserting sovereignty rather than solving common problems.

The primary means of creating international environmental norms are treaty, customary law, general principles of law, and soft law processes. Under conventional theory, substantive international law is largely consensual. International law is formed by express consent in the case of treaty law and implied consent in the case of customary international law (CIL).

Treaties negotiated, signed and ratified by nations have several distinct advantages as a form of lawmaking. The norms created and nations bound are clearly identified. Nations have agreed in advance to accept such norms as law and to comply. In several cases the treaties contain the means of resolving disputes and the sanctions or procedures for encouraging or policing compliance. In some cases specific legal norms in treaties may become CIL if the requirements for customary law are met. On the other hand, treaty norms do not generally bind non-parties states that may be useful or necessary to achieve the ends of a treaty.

One of the most significant developments of the last 50 years has been the birth of Multilateral Treaty Regimes (MTR). Such MTR are not just treaties with defined norms. The treaty instruments, by their terms, create ongoing legislative and administrative bodies that expand the limited contractual nature of treaties themselves. For example, the Ozone Layer treaty regime discussed elsewhere in this book began with a Framework Convention that created an ongoing institution, a conference of parties that meets regularly, and a means for resolving disputes and/or managing compliance.

The conference of parties or another mechanism with the authority to make decision such as the Ministerial Conference of the World Trade Organization (WTO) will typically monitor new information, technology, and needs. The Conference of Parties will then assess the need for amendments or protocols that may define the standards with greater particularity or expand the subject matter of the treaty to new areas such as the expansion of the trade regime into intellectual property. As discussed in chapter 2.5, some MTR such as the WTO have formal dispute settlement bodies that adjudicate disputes and render formal opinions that become a form of precedent that creates law or at least ongoing rules of decision.

Such treaty regimes must be interpreted to clarify norms and settle disputes. There are two general approaches: (1) interpreting a treaty using the ordinary meaning and context of the treaty in light of the object and purpose at the time of the conclusion of the treaty or (2) interpreting the treaty as an evolutionary instrument in light of the contemporary principles of international law and the contemporary concerns of the international community.

This latter process of interpretation may and has lead to the expansion of norms beyond what appeared to be prior agreed principles. For example, in the *Shrimp/Sea Turtle* case discussed in chapter 3, the Appellate Body (AB) of the WTO reexamined the meaning of "conservation of exhaustible natural resources" in Article XX (g) of the general exceptions section of the GATT agreement under an "evolutionary methodology" that included the contemporary concerns of the international community and the meaning of 'natural resources' in several recent environmental treaties to conclude that 'natural resources' now included living as well as inanimate resources.

CIL norms are created by state practice generally accepted as law by the international community of states. States impliedly consent to norms by their participation in state practice and their demonstrated attitude of acceptance. Custom, then, consists of two elements: (1) the practice of states as the material element that provides evidence of customary norms, and (2) the general acceptance of a norm as a legal obligation by the world community as the attitudinal requirement. Note this is not actual consent, but rather acceptance by the community as a whole. Consent is implied from community acceptance. The great advantage of CIL is that it binds all states. Even new members of the international community of states are said to be bound by existing customary law. However, an existing state is generally said to not be bound by emerging customary law if it persistently objects during the formation of custom.

Several CIL norms, particularly in the field of international environmental law, are controversial because few states participate in the practice that may form a norm and there is no objective way to determine if the generality of states has accepted a given norm. The arbitrator in the *Trial Smelters Arbitration*, for example, invoked a general principle of international law, the *sic utere tuo* principle that states must not use their territory in a manner that injuries another state, to decide a transboundary air pollution matter without reference to state practice or proof that the principle on question had been generally accepted. Since then the *sic utere tuo* principle has been affirmed in the Stockholm and Rio Declarations and recognized by the ICJ in the *Nuclear Weapons Advisory Opinion* of 1996.

The disadvantages of CIL as a form of lawmaking include that the precise contours of CIL norms are often not clear, and require further definition in treaties or nonbinding instruments. Nor is it clear when there is sufficient general acceptance to create a legally binding norm. Many states may, for example, object to a norm because they did not specifically consent or participate in the process that created the norm and were unaware of its formation. Moreover, CIL processes do not create institutions to adjudicate disputes or provide for sanctions or other mechanisms to enforce such norms as do several MTR.

General principles of law are an exception to the consent or consensus bases of international law. The Statute of the International Court of Justice in Article 38 lists "general principles of law recognized by civilized nations" as a source of law to be applied by the Court. Putting aside the anachronism or perhaps misnomer of which are "civilized nations," the general principles referred to appear to be the rules generally accepted in the domestic laws of the major legal systems of the world. Since the international legal system is inherently incomplete, resort may be had to rules and procedures that are common to the major legal cultures as gap-fillers to this incomplete system.

There are several different theories or approaches as which principles of law are appropriate as binding rules of international law. At a minimum international tribunals have looked to common domestic doctrine when necessary to make the law of nations a viable system that can be applied in a judicial process. International tribunals have looked to domestic systems for procedural and equitable principles such as *res judicata,* laches, good faith and estoppel. This implies a limiting methodology of a systemic search through the domestic law of all the major legal systems of the world for evidence of a particular principle.

Some theorists, and at times the ICJ, have used the concept of general principles as a form of natural law to discern principles of justice. For example, the ICJ in its *Advisory Opinion on the Legality of the Threat or Use of Nuclear Weapons* indicated that there existed prior principles of law to protect nations and peoples based on usages, the laws of humanity and the dictates of public conscience.

The general principles of international environmental law have often been referred to in a similar non-consensual source of substantive principles limiting state actions. One such principle, the *Sic utere tuo* principle that a nation should not use its territory in a manner to harm the interests of another nation in its territory, was used by the ICJ to help resolve the Corfu Channel case involving the mine that destroyed a British ship.

Numerous non-binding international instruments, such as the Stockholm Declaration on Human Environment, contain norms, principles or standards that are termed "soft law." Soft law norms are non-binding social norms that may lead to binding legal norms and as an empirical matter, may create expectations of compliance that limit or influence state behavior. While States consider such instruments as political commitments and not legal norms, they nevertheless may treat political commitments as defining standards of behavior that if violated may significantly diminish a nation's reputation as a trustworthy partner and as a responsible member of the international community. In that respect, soft law can and does have real world effects.

Economics, Trade and the International Policy Process

[On] one level economic ideas and tools are a means to achieve environmental goals in an efficient manner; on the other hand, there is considerable tension between environmental goals and rapid economic development particularly in less developed countries. Many environmental problems such as air and water pollution, ozone layer protection, the protection of endangered species, the transboundary movement of toxic substances, and climate change, may be seen as the overuse of public goods. Public goods, such as the atmosphere and the oceans, are treated as the property of no one without a price to reduce their exploitation. Such resources are overused and degraded. This is the tragedy of the commons. Public resources degrade with increases in population unless there is a mechanism to regulate their use or put a price on its consumption as, for example, a carbon tax or cap and trade system would do. Economic theory suggests that the external costs of production including the effect on human and animal health should be placed on the producer as a cost of production. National and international legal institutions may place the cost back on the manufacturer or manage the externalities (emissions) by regulations to reduce the external effects of the various activities of modern life from manufacturing to residential construction to energy production. The principles of economics help shape and provide alternative approaches to achieving international policy goals. Treaty negotiators have a number of means or alternative policy tools to mandate or encourage actions to safeguard the environment. These include a tax on the damaging activity (air or water pollution) to discourage such pollution and encourage alternative less polluting processes thereby channeling the spending of resources. Command and Control regulations, including the prohibition in the Montreal Protocols on producing or consuming listed ozone-depleting chemicals, limit permissible activity and force producers to discover or invent new chemicals as substitutes for the damaging ones.

Tradable permits and permit exchanges, such as the cap and trade system, currently used under the Kyoto Protocol in Europe and the sulfur dioxide regulations within the domestic law of the U.S., provide an economic incentive to emit fewer greenhouse gases in both the production process and the consumption of energy. Under the tradable permit approach a government places a cap on permissible GHG and then grants property rights to those who emit below the cap. The more GHG efficient producers may then sell the right to emit up to their cap to other producers via commodity exchanges. This effectively places a price on pollution and encourages all to create new, less polluting processes to reduce their costs.

Subsidies may be used to encourage the development of new energy sources to reduce GHG. Similarly, the reduction of subsidies to industries that are more carbon-based may reduce the overuse of environmental resources returning the industry to the full cost of production. Several international treaties establish multilateral environmental funds to help defer or reduce the costs of technology transfer or encourage the adaptation of new less polluting production methods. The Montreal Protocol as amended in London, for example, created a Multilateral Fund to provide financial and technical assistance to developing countries in adopting ozone friendly technologies instead of ozone depleting ones. Finally sanctions or prohibitions on trade maybe a very effective means of enforcement of international agreements and norms. CITES prohibits trade in listed species thereby limiting the markets for such goods and reducing the incentive to kill such species.

[T]he rapid increase in international trade and increased economic interdependence among nations are transforming the organization of economic life placing pressure on the ecosystems of the world. ...

In general, nations with higher levels of economic development have cleaner environments, a larger middle class that puts demands on government for reduced pollution, and possess more democratic political systems. Unfortunately, not all nations and people share equally in this growth. There is evidence of increased income inequality in and among some countries even as average income rises. There is another fundamental cost: the cost of the internationalization of production. As production, goods, services, and people move from one country to another, environmental and other costs are transferred to those nations with fewer economic and political resources to internalize those costs. Rather many developing countries suffer from the increased pollution from rapid economic development with little regulation or enforcement of what environmental laws may exist ...

A question often arises as to the extent that trade sanctions used as a means to enforce multilateral treaties and domestic unilateral environmental laws may violate the World Trade Organization (WTO) agreements. The GATT and its successor, the WTO, by reducing tariffs and opening markets to trade have stimulated this globalization phenomenon. The Dispute Settlement Understanding, one of the package of WTO agreements, creates a mandatory dispute settlement system to resolve disputes about rule violations. Yet dispute settlement or treaty solutions to regional problems, for example, raise issues of festering unsettled scores, politics, population pressure, diplomacy, ongoing or potential war over resources, disaster relief, and the human condition. The solutions to environmental problems are intertwined with the old debates of north and south, east and west, rich and poor, developing and developed.

Emerging Principles

Some of the most important emerging issues in international environmental law revolve around concepts of sustainability, and environmental human rights, as Chapter 6 explores in depth.

The principle of "sustainability" is approaching its 40th anniversary. It is a concept that has experienced both evolution and stasis. It has shaken the legal foundation, and often engaged, recited, and even revered by policymakers, lawmakers and academics worldwide. Sustainability entered the general public conscience in 1972 with the Stockholm Declaration on the Human Environment. In 1987 it secured center stage when the World Commission on Environment and Development released its pioneering study, Our Common Future, which defines "sustainable development" as "development . . . that . . . meets the needs of the present without compromising the ability of future generations to meet their own needs." In 1992 the Earth Summit's Rio Declaration declared that sustainable development must "respect the interests of all and protect the integrity of the global environmental and developmental system." The Rio Declaration's blueprint document, Agenda 21, provides that sustainable development must coincidently raise living standards while preserving the environment: "[I]integration of environment and development concerns ... will lead to the fulfillment of basic needs, improved living standards for all, better protected and managed ecosystems and a safer, more prosperous future."

While disparate, the unmistakable thread that runs through threshold definitions of sustainability is the interconnectedness of living things, opportunity, and hope. Recognition of the importance of sustainability has grown exponentially since the Earth Summit. Since then, the concept of sustainability has been regularly recognized in international accords, by nations in constitutional, legislative and regulatory reform, by States, municipalities and localities in everything from policy statements to building codes, and in corporate mission statements and practices worldwide. Sustainability principles are shape-shifters, adaptive to most environmental decision making, including water and air quality, species conservation, and national environmental policy in the U.S. and around the globe. Furthermore, it has entered the bloodstream of courts around the globe as a guiding principle of judicial discretion in environmental cases.

Next ... human rights have emerged as an important area in international environmental law. Fundamental human rights to life and liberty, for example, cannot be achieved without adequate environmental conditions of clean water, air, and land. Forty years ago, the Universal Declaration of Human Rights first recognized the link between the human condition and the environment. Next were efforts to have foundational international environmental measures expressly recognize a human right to a quality environment. For the most part, domestic courts have declined to find that these normative developments in international law amount to domestically enforceable environmental human rights. Meanwhile, many countries still lack the laws, agencies, resources, or political will to protect environmental rights.

While some question whether applying existing human rights to environmental challenges is effective, most conclude the point academic because international human rights do not encompass environmental rights. To be sure, of the two human rights treaties that equate human and environmental rights, one is not in force and the other "suffers from weak institutional and compliance mechanisms." International law generally does not provide for protection of substantive environmental rights. First, there is no international 'environmental rights' treaty. International accords that bespeak environmental rights, such as the 1972 Stockholm Declaration, and the Rio Declaration, are not enforceable. Second, international legal customs and norms do not provide an enforceable right. The protection of fundamental human rights is the closest international law comes to protecting fundamental rights to the environment. Indeed, the extent to which human rights embody environmental rights has engendered ample commentary. Some contend that existing international human rights treaties include FERs. Third, general principles of international environmental law fall short of protecting fundamental environmental rights, including those involving environmental procedural rights, and notions of intergenerational equity.

Embedding environmental human rights domestically can be preferable to international, multilateral, or bilateral treaties, if for no other reason than that treaties must usually be ratified by the country's legislature, and then must often be implemented by domestic legislation. Courts worldwide are with growing frequency recognizing that human rights and the environment are inextricably intertwined. Some countries have opted to adopt constitutional protections to a quality environment. whether and the extent to which countries have entrenched environmental rights constitutionally, [C]onstitutional provisions from roughly five-dozen countries embed individualized rights to some form of healthy, adequate or quality environment. Domestic courts and international tribunals are enforcing constitutionally enshrined environmental rights with growing frequency, recognizing basic human rights to clean water, air, and land, and environmental opportunity. These provisions are inherently complex for five reasons, revolving around form, scope, parties, remedies and justiciability.

While many judicial opinions mention constitutionally embedded rights, including procedural rights, surprisingly few have reached the merits and implemented constitutionally enshrined environmental rights provisions. Regardless of the legal apparatus—international, national, or subnational—environmental rights run into some basic inertial truisms: Economic concerns usually trump environmental concerns, and property rights usually prevail over environmental rights.

Conclusion

We are amidst a period of unprecedented species and habitat loss due to accelerated climate change, continued population growth, half-lives of persistent pollution, biodiversity loss, oceanic and atmospheric acidification, habitat destruction, persistent organic pollutants, and water, air and soil pollution, to name but a few. Accelerated and decidedly non-Darwinian adaptation, then, is an inevitable condition. Humans must adapt, mitigate, or face the inevitable consequences.

International environmental law contributes some of the means to address intractable global challenges. New international treaty regimes such as the World Trade Organization, the Ozone Layer Treaty regime and the Climate Change Treaty regime are essentially specialized legislative bodies created by treaties with the ongoing capacity to react to events and create new norms generally under the principle of consent by member nations. These institutions conduct negotiations that may lead to new treaties or protocols with specific binding norms. In the case of WTO's dispute settlement system, the Appellate Body as a judicial-like body that decides specific cases, may create new norms or expand existing understandings through the process of interpretation much like domestic courts do. These structures must be used to create legal norms binding on all. One of the great challenges of the 21st century will be to develop authoritative processes for making new international law and solving common environmental problems binding on all that are viewed by nations and their peoples as legitimate. The chapters that follow examine how treaties, CIL, principles and soft law have helped to shape international environmental law for ours and future generations.

QUESTIONS

1. What is "international law"?
2. What is "international environmental law"?

II. SUSTAINABILITY

Environmental sustainability is an amorphous concept that stands for the proposition that present generations should use resources so as to preserve opportunities for future generations. It reflects the Native American proverb that "We do not inherit the Earth from our ancestors: we borrow it from our children."

'Sustainability' serves as a guiding framework for addressing the most pressing economic, social and environmental issues of our day, including climate change, poverty, equality and shale gas development. It is a central feature in international and domestic relations. The concept of sustainability has been regularly acknowledged by international accords, by the laws and regulations of nations, in local building codes, and in corporate mission statements and practices worldwide, as well as by some courts, although not in the United States, as examined below. Sustainability has a bearing on many environmental matters, including water and air quality, species conservation, and national environmental policy, including advancing green energy.

Some energy companies and venture-energy interests have embraced sustainability as a good corporate practice and have adopted sustainability in corporate mission statements and guiding standard operating procedures in manufacturing, shipping, technology, and land development worldwide. For instance, Ceres -- a non-profit organization advocating for sustainability leadership that works to accelerate and expand the adoption of sustainable business practices and solutions to build a healthy global economy with a powerful network of investors, companies and public interest groups – has 1,100 corporate members worldwide.

A. SUSTAINABILITY SYNOPSIS

The concept of sustainability recently entered its fifth decade. In 1972, the Stockholm Declaration on the Human Environment was the first international instrument to recognize a principle of sustainability. Fifteen years later, the World Commission on Environment and Development released its pioneering study, *Our Common Future*, which defines 'sustainable development' as 'development . . . that . . . meets the needs of the present without compromising the ability of future generations to meet their own needs.'

In 1992, the Earth Summit's Rio Declaration stated that sustainable development must 'respect the interests of all and protect the integrity of the global environmental and developmental system.' The Rio Declaration's blueprint document, *Agenda 21*, provides that "integration of environment and development concerns . . . will lead to the fulfilment of basic needs, improved living standards for all, better protected and managed ecosystems and a safer, more prosperous future." Parties at the Earth Summit's 20th anniversary in 2012 (Rio +20) released a follow-up document, *The Future We Want*, which underscored the import of sustainability to promote peace and prosperity and alleviate poverty.

And then in September 2015 more than 190 nations of the U.N. General Assembly issued the 2030 Agenda for Sustainable Development, which describes sustainability's role as one to "Promote peaceful and inclusive societies for sustainable development, provide access to justice for all and build effective, accountable and inclusive institutions at all levels." Effective January 1, 2016, the 2030 Agenda incorporates the UN's 17 Sustainable Development Goals (SDGs), including reflecting human dignity, adapting to climate change, ensuring clean water, air and soil, reducing poverty, promoting gender equity, and respecting sovereignty, among other ambitious objectives, by 2030.

B. INCORPORATING SUSTAINABILITY IN NATIONAL CONSTITUTIONS

Constitutionally-embedded guarantees to environmental quality, stewardship and participation – or what is known as 'environmental constitutionalism' – are thought to serve an important function in advancing sustainable environmental outcomes by embodying the recognition that the environment is a proper subject for protection in constitutional texts and for vindication by constitutional courts worldwide. Importantly, sustainability has also found footing in a growing number of national constitutions, either by advancing 'sustainable development,' 'future generations,' or some variation of these themes, discussed below.

'Sustainable Development'

Nearly 20 countries expressly recognize a constitutional goal of 'sustainability' or 'sustainable development' though most of these are in sections of the constitutions or written in language that indicates that they are not amenable to judicial enforcement. For example, Albania's constitution proclaims that the state "aims to supplement private initiative and responsibility with: Rational exploitation of forests, waters, pastures and other natural resources on the basis of the principle of sustainable development." Belgium's constitution bespeaks a commitment to "pursue the objectives of sustainable development in its social, economic and environmental aspects." Bolivia's constitution states that "the Natural assets are of public importance and of strategic character for the sustainable development of the country." Colombia's constitution requires policy makers to "plan the handling and use of natural resources in order to guarantee their sustainable development . . ." Montenegro's Preamble outlines its "conviction that the state is responsible for the preservation of nature, sound environment, sustainable development, [and] balanced development of all its region." Nepal's constitution provides that "provision shall be made for the protection of the forest, vegetation and biodiversity, its sustainable use and for equitable distribution of the benefit derived from it." The constitution of Seychelles provides that the state will "ensure a sustainable socio-economic development of Seychelles by a judicious use and management of the resources of Seychelles." Somalia's constitution provides that "Land shall be held, used and managed in an equitable, efficient, productive, and sustainable manner." Switzerland's constitution contains a specific section entitled "Sustainable Development," which provides that "The Confederation and the Cantons shall endeavor to achieve a balanced and sustainable relationship between nature and its capacity to renew itself and the demands placed on it by the population." The Ugandan constitution states that "Parliament shall, by law, provide for measures intended—to manage the environment for sustainable development." The constitutions of Greece, Mozambique, Poland, Serbia, and Thailand also expressly require that environmental policy be developed in accordance with 'sustainable development.'

'Future Generations'

Sustainability recognizes responsibilities owed to those who follow. The constitutions from about a dozen countries give at least a passing nod to 'future generations.' For example, Andorra's constitution directs policy makers to protect natural resources "for the sake of future generations." Argentina's constitution directs the state to manage resources for "a healthy and balanced environment fit for human development in order that productive activities shall meet present needs without endangering those of future generations . . ." Armenia's constitution requires that the state "pursue the environmental security policy for present and future generations." Brazil's declares that "The Government and the community have a duty to defend and to preserve the environment for present and future generations." Ethiopia's constitution provides that its natural resources are "a sacred trust for the benefit of present and succeeding generations." Papua New Guinea's constitution requires the state to hold environmental resources "in trust for future generations" and "for the benefit of future generations." The constitutions of both Niger and Vanuatu provide for protection of the environment in the "interests of future generations." Germany's constitution expresses "its responsibility toward future generations." Norway's constitution directs that natural resources be "safeguarded for future generations." The constitution of Iran provides for the "preservation of the environment, in which the present as well as the future generations have a right to flourishing social existence." Lesotho's lists a duty of the state to protect the environment "for the benefit of both present and future generations."

'Sustainable Development' and 'Future Generations'

The strongest embodiment of environmental sustainability would seem to stem from those constitutions that promote sustainable development *for the purpose of* protecting the interests of future generations. The constitutions from nearly twenty countries contain this sort of hybrid pronouncement. For example, Albania's constitution bespeaks a "healthy and ecologically adequate environment for the present and future generations." Mozambique's requires the state, "[w]ith a view to guaranteeing the right to the environment within the framework of sustainable development . . . shall adopt policies aimed at . . . guaranteeing the rational utilisation of natural resources and the safeguarding of their capacity to regenerate, ecological stability and the rights of future generations." France's amended constitution proclaims that "Care must be taken to safeguard the environment along with other fundamental interests of the Nation . . . In order to ensure sustainable development, choices designed to meet the needs of the present generation should not jeopardise the ability of future generations and other peoples to meet their own needs . . . " Eritrea's provides for state management of natural resources in a "sustainable manner" for "present and future generations." The constitutions of Namibia and Swaziland provide for the protection of the environment and natural resources "on a sustainable basis" for the benefit of "present and future" citizens and generations. Qatar's provides for protection of the environment "so as to achieve sustainable development for the generations to come." The constitution of South Sudan provides that "Every person shall have the right to have the environment protected for the benefit of present and future generations, through appropriate legislative action and other measures that . . . secure ecologically sustainable development and use of natural resources. . . ." Uganda's provides that "The State shall promote sustainable development and public awareness of the need to manage land, air and water resources in a balanced and sustainable manner for the present and future generations." In addition, the constitutions of Angola, Bhutan, Georgia, Guyana, Malawi, Maldives, Sweden, East Timor, and Zambia provide for the "sustainable development" of environmental resources in the interests of "future generations."

The constitutions of some countries require that specific resources be developed with future generations in mind. For example, the Dominican Republic provides that "nonrenewable natural resources, can only be explored and exploited by individuals, under sustainable environmental criteria . . ." and provides for the protection of the environment "for the benefit of the present and future generations . ." The Dominican Republic is the only country on the planet with a constitution to address sustainability, future generations, and climate change.

C. JUDICIAL RECEPTIVITY TO SUSTAINABILITY

The elasticity of the concept of sustainability can frustrate implementation and enforcement as a legal construct. On the other hand, sustainability has earned a foothold with some international tribunals. Outside of judicial sphere, however, sustainability serves as a remarkably influential legal norm for laws, policies and practices. For example, sustainability is a common feature of national and subnational laws around the globe. To be sure, more than three-dozen countries have incorporated sustainability in their constitutions by advancing 'sustainable development,' 'future generations,' or some combination of these themes. These include Belgium ("pursue the objectives of sustainable development in its social, economic and environmental aspects"); Dominican Republic ("nonrenewable natural resources, can only be explored and exploited by individuals, under sustainable environmental criteria . . ." and provides for the protection of the environment "for the benefit of the present and future generations ..."); France ("Care must be taken to safeguard the environment along with other fundamental interests of the Nation . . . In order to ensure sustainable development, choices designed to meet the needs of the present generation should not jeopardise the ability of future generations and other peoples to meet their own needs ..."); Nepal ("provision shall be made for the protection of the forest, vegetation and biodiversity, its sustainable use and for equitable distribution of the benefit derived from it"); and Uganda ("Parliament shall, by law, provide for measures intended—to manage the environment for sustainable development"). These constitutional provisions help bridge the gap left by international and domestic laws, even given the array of sustainability provisions already in existence. Even though the vast majority of these provisions do not create judicially enforceable rights, they nonetheless affirm national values of environmental sustainability to which courts, institutions of higher education, and others may advert.

Judicial Receptivity

There is very little jurisprudence applying constitutionally embedded provisions regarding sustainability and related provisions. In fact, there is very little jurisprudence explicitly engaging sustainability at all, even where one might expect to find it. For example, while South Africa's constitution embraced sustainable development in 1996, the provision has had little practical effect. Section 24 of its constitution provides that everyone has the right "[t]o have the environment protected, for the benefit of present and future generations, through reasonable legislative and other measures that ... [s]ecure ecologically-sustainable development and use of natural resources while promoting justifiable economic and social development."

Yet, these novel provisions hardly seem to register in everyday decision-making in environmental matters. Two decades after the end of apartheid, the provision's constitutional or normative status is unclear. Social striation, economic disparity, and despoliation of natural resources in South Africa accentuate the difficulty of breathing life into the concept of sustainable development. As Kotze reports, the constitutional court hasn't engaged the provision so as to define what it means, who can enforce it, to whom it applies, what remedies might redress infractions, or what role sustainable development could play in the broader environmental constitutionalism paradigm. The passing of President Mandela will serve to place additional strain on the implementation of cultural, social and economic rights, including environmental constitutionalism, in South Africa.

And while Section 225 of the Brazilian constitution requires that governmental policies promote ecologically sustainable development, apex courts there rarely enforce this provision.

Another leading (by way of lagging) example is the United States Supreme Court. More than four decades removed from Stockholm, the U.S. Supreme Court—and no member of it—has yet to recognize or even acknowledge the concept of sustainability. Since Stockholm, the U.S. Supreme Court has decided more than 4,000 cases, including more than 300 involving environmental matters. Yet the word "sustainability" appears not at all before the Court in any majority, concurring or dissenting opinion.

Sustainability stands very little chance of being taken seriously by the current U.S. Supreme Court. Sustainability is a guiding principle, not a constitutionally enshrined doctrine, and it is not readily shaped into a traditional legal case or controversy. No U.S. law requires or even recognizes sustainability. And, the United States has not ratified an international treaty that does so either. Moreover, no member of the Court studied environmental law. None of them has much if any practical experience with environmental law in general, and sustainability in particular. Few Supreme Court justices have held elected political office, and few have regulatory experience that would sensitize them to environmental concerns and the complexities and challenges of sustainability. Indeed, most of the current Court's legal experience has been predominantly on the business or "development" side of the sustainable development equation. Surprisingly, sustainability—even as a governing principle—has not managed to capture the imagination of litigants, who seldom if ever invoke "sustainability" in pleadings, briefs, and oral arguments.

The incorporation of sustainability into domestic constitutions has great potential to advance both sustainability and constitutionalism. Abdul Haseeb Ansari, for one, has examined the relationship among sustainable management, the utilization of the environment, and the constitutional safeguards of environmental rights. He notes how constitutional provisions help bridge the gap left by international and domestic laws, even given the array of sustainability provisions already in existence. Even though most of these provisions create no judicially enforceable rights, they nonetheless affirm national values of environmental sustainability to which courts and others may advert.

Constitutionalizing sustainability may contribute to the work that the concept can perform. The principal attraction of the 'sustainability' is its wide applicability. It can mean so many different things in so many different contexts. But when used appropriately, Dernbach maintains that it can advance passing along an environment that is as suitable for existence as what was inherited; a promise to future generations of opportunity, wealth, satisfaction, or peace; optimal sustained yields of agriculture, animals or resources; continued employment or employability; or economic development. But because it contains no limiting principle or metrics, its potential application across and even within judicial cultures may be varied and even inconsistent. The experience in the United States is typical: lacking constitutional recognition, sustainability has not yet triggered juridical engagement.

The principal strength – and some would say weakness – of 'sustainability' is its wide applicability. It can mean many different things in many different contexts. Sustainability principles are shape-shifters, adaptive to most environmental decision making, including water and air quality, species conservation, and national environmental policy in the U.S. and around the globe. But when used appropriately, sustainability can advance passing along an environment that is as suitable for existence as what was inherited; a promise to future generations of opportunity, wealth, satisfaction, or peace; optimal sustained yields of agriculture, animals or resources; continued employment or employability; or economic development and green energy.

D. SUSTAINABILITY AND HUMAN RIGHTS

EXCERPT: JAMES R. MAY & ERIN DALY, SUSTAINABILITY AND DIGNITY

International Environmental Law-making and Diplomacy Review
Tuula Honkonen and Seita Romppanen (eds) (University of Eastern Finland & UN Environment, 2020).

The 17 Sustainable Development Goals (SDGs) are often regarded as if they are stand-alone goals. For instance, the High-Level Political Forum focuses on a handful of connected SDGs at a time, such as achieving SDGs 13 (climate action) and 17 (peace, justice and strong communities). But what can be lost in conversations about the SDGs is that advancing human dignity is the thread that stitches the SDGs together. Understanding the implications of this simple recognition warrants exploration of the concept of dignity, how it has evolved in law, what it means to environmental protection, and how taking it seriously might contribute to better outcomes guided by the SDGs.

1 Introduction

'Sustainability' – the idea that those living have a responsibility to leave for future generations an environment at least as livable as presently enjoyed – has witnessed dispersive distribution, including applications to energy policy, constitutionalism, and the concept of "sustainable development," which itself has become a common if not ubiquitous feature in legal expressions at the international, national and subnational levels, culminating in the United Nations setting 17 Sustainable Development Goals (SDGs) to achieve by 2030.

The SDGs face myriad structural and other challenges, most importantly that they are often treated as if disconnected from within. For instance, the annual United Nations High Level Political Forum (formerly the UN Sustainability Commission) focuses on a few connected SDGs at a time, such as (in 2019) achieving SDGs 13 (climate action) and 17 (peace, justice and strong communities). Moreover, the concept of 'sustainability' has a growing cadre of critics who hold that the concept has reached the limits of its own utility, has not much improved environmental outcomes, is no match for the Anthropocene, and should be replaced by the goal of 'resilience.'

Yet these challenges overlook the connection between human dignity and the SDGs. This chapter posits that the SDGs should be understood as having as their purpose to advance human dignity; this thread coheres and complements them. Understanding the implications of this simple realization warrants exploration of the concept of dignity, how it has evolved in law, what it means to environmental protection, and how taking it seriously might contribute to better outcomes guided by the SDGs, discussed in the passages that follow.

Section 2 briefly summarizes how sustainability is reflected in law, primarily through the SDGs. Section 3 describes relevant legal expressions of human dignity. Section 4 then explores how human dignity informs understanding and implementation of sustainability. Section 5 concludes.

2 Sustainability and law

Sustainability has a vast reach, embodying environmental, social and economic equity in a variety of contexts, including dignity, human rights, climate change, access to and availability of fresh water, shale gas development, corporate practices, and higher education, among others.

Sustainability is also a central feature in international and domestic relations. It has long served as a general principle of international environmental law, including as an interpretive principle in international accords and by international tribunals resolving environmental disputes.

Specifically, sustainable development has served as a mostly normative concept in international, regional and domestic law. In addition to the SDGs and other mechanisms designed to advance sustainable development directly, the concept of sustainable development informs or animates international law under various international accords, including Article 12 of the Kyoto Protocol (the 'Clean Development Mechanism') and in Article 6(4) of the Paris Agreement (often called 'Sustainable Development Mechanism').

Regionally, sustainable development is also an explicit component of several bilateral and regional trade agreements under the auspices of the European Union since 2007, following the 2006 Global Europe Communication and the 2006 Renewed Sustainable Development Strategy.

Domestically, sustainability has infiltrated constitutionalism around the globe. Presently, more than three-dozen countries incorporate sustainability in their constitutions by advancing 'sustainable development,' the interests of 'future generations,' or some combination of these themes. Switzerland's constitution, for instance, contains a section entitled 'Sustainable Development', which provides that '[t]he Confederation and the Cantons shall endeavor to achieve a balanced and sustainable relationship between nature and its capacity to renew itself and the demands placed on it by the population.' Albania's constitution proclaims that the state 'aims to supplement private initiative and responsibility with: Rational exploitation of forests, waters, pastures and other natural resources on the basis of the principle of sustainable development.' Colombia's requires policy-makers to 'plan the handling and use of natural resources in order to guarantee their sustainable development...' These constitutional provisions help bridge the gap left by international and domestic laws, even given the array of sustainability provisions already in existence.

Moreover, sustainable development has played an explicit or normative role in shaping the adjudication of international law. As to the former, the World Trade Organization (WTO) Appellate Body invoked the General Agreement on Tariffs and Trade's expressed objective of sustainable development when interpreting the terms 'exhaustible natural resources' under Article XX(g) ('relating to the conservation of exhaustible natural resources if such measures are made effective in conjunction with restrictions on domestic production or consumption') as reflecting 'contemporary concerns of the community of nations about the protection and conservation of the environment.' Similarly, in *China – Raw Materials*, the Panel noted 'that the international law principles of sovereignty over natural resources and sustainable development... are relevant to our interpretive exercise in this dispute.'

The *Gabcīkovo-Nagymaros* case provides an example of the latter, where the International Court of Justice Court noted that sustainable development had 'to be taken into consideration, and [...] given proper weight, not only when States contemplate new activities but also when continuing with activities begun in the past.'

Regional adjudicative bodies have made reference to sustainable development or, at least, to integration, even in the absence of a specific treaty basis, including the *Ogoni* case, where the African Commission reasoned that Article 24 of the African Charter (the collective right to a generally satisfactory environment) required Nigeria 'to take reasonable and other measures to prevent pollution and ecological degradation, to promote conservation, and to secure an ecologically sustainable development and use of natural resources'. Domestic courts have been least receptive to sustainable development, however, including in the United States. These adjudicative developments noted, it is fair to observe that sustainable development seldom provides a 'decision-making function,' and should be 'considered a normative concept,' rather than rule.

The most significant international expression of sustainable development are the United Nations' 2015 Sustainable Development Goals, which are the culmination of four decades of multidisciplinary thinking about what sustainable development means, and grasping that, how to effectuate it. The SDGs are 17 'Goals' to achieve by 2030, including protecting biodiversity; ensuring clean water, air, land and food; ending poverty, hunger and discrimination; and providing access to justice and opportunity for the future. The SDGs "are the blueprint to achieve a better and more sustainable future for all. They address the global challenges we face, including those related to poverty, inequality, climate, environmental degradation, prosperity, and peace and justice. The Goals interconnect and in order to leave no one behind, it is important that we achieve each Goal and target by 2030.

The SDGs underscore that advancing human dignity is the core of sustainability by "envisag[ing] a world of universal respect for human rights and human dignity, the rule of law, justice, equality and non-discrimination; of respect for race, ethnicity and cultural diversity; and of equal opportunity permitting the full realization of human potential and contributing to shared prosperity." Moreover, the SDGs "[r]ecognize that the dignity of the human person is fundamental …"

Accordingly, dignity informs and influences the implementation of myriad SDGs, including water and sanitation (Goal 6), energy (Goal 7), economic growth (Goal 8), infrastructure and industrialization (Goal 9), consumption and production (Goal 12), oceans, seas and marine sources (Goal 14), terrestrial ecosystems (Goal 15), the role of the rule of law (Goal 16), and global cooperation (Goal 17). In particular, the SDGs underscore the correspondence between the poverty, hunger and dignity: 'We are determined to end poverty and hunger, in all their forms and dimensions, and to ensure that all human beings can fulfil their potential in dignity and equality and in a healthy environment,' and that "[b]illions of our citizens continue to live in poverty and are denied a life of dignity."

As this shows, sustainable practices are necessary to protect human dignity and the full achievement of human dignity for all will ensure that development will proceed sustainably. Thus, the concerns of the SDGs – poverty, hunger and lack of education, equality and access to justice – can be affronts to dignity. The dignity implications of environmental degradation are especially trenchant, including climate change and the lack of access to potable water, clean air, and safe soils. At the same time, peaceful and inclusive societies based on human dignity will conduce to sustainable development.

While the 17 Sustainable Development Goals (SDGs) are indivisible insofar as it is not possible either to realize human rights in a degraded environment or to protect the environment in the absence of human rights, the SDGs are often discussed as if they are stand-alone goals. For instance, the High Level Political Forum focuses on a handful of connected SDGs at a time, such as (in 2019) achieving SDGs 13 (climate action) and 17 (peace, justice and strong communities). But what can be lost in conversations about the SDGs is the elegant idea that dignity stitches them together.. Understanding the implications of this simple step warrants exploration of the concept of dignity, how it has evolved in law, what it means to environmental protection, and how taking it seriously might contribute to better outcomes guided by the SDGs, the subject of the next section.

3   Human dignity and law

There are good reasons for dignity's prominence in the SDGs that harken back to the dawn of both elemental philosophy and modern global governance. Dignity refers to the inherent humanness of each person; it is an elemental value that presupposes that every human being has equal worth. It emphasizes the fundamental value and equality of all members of society –

humans not only are endowed with dignity, but each is endowed with an equal quantum of dignity.

4   Dignity and sustainability

In understanding the role of dignity and sustainability, it is helpful to begin with recognizing that the concept of human dignity is no stranger to the development of environmental law. International law already acknowledges that the right to human dignity embeds a right to live in a quality environment. The 1972 Stockholm Declaration – largely viewed as the origin of modern global environmental law – recognizes the 'fundamental right to freedom, equality, and adequate conditions of life, in an environment of quality that permits a life of dignity and well-being'. The 1990 Hague Declaration expressly acknowledges 'the right to live in dignity in a viable global environment.' In 1992, Principle 1 of the 1992 Rio Declaration focused attention on the human-centered approach of environmental protection and sustainable development in particular: "Human beings are at the centre of concerns for sustainable development. They are entitled to a healthy and productive life in harmony with nature." Two years later, the United Nation's influential Ksentini Report is also explicit on the subject:

> Environmental damage has direct effects on the enjoyment of a series of human rights, such as the right to life, to health, to a satisfactory standard of living, to sufficient food, to housing, to education, to work, to culture, to non-discrimination, to dignity and the harmonious development of one's personality, to security of person and family, to development, to peace, etc.

Recently, the principal human rights organs of the United Nations have become increasingly explicit about the relationship between life, dignity, and a sustainable environment. In its General comment No. 36 (2018) on article 6 of the International Covenant on Civil and Political Rights, on the right to life the UN Human Rights Committee expressly defined the right to life as the right to live with dignity and noted in particular the need for a healthy and sustainable environment in order to ensure a life of dignity. This recognition imposes on the State parties the obligations to "take appropriate measures to address the general conditions in society that may give rise to direct threats to life or prevent individuals from enjoying their right to life with dignity [including *inter alia*] degradation of the environment [and] deprivation of land, territories and resources of indigenous peoples." Moreover, the Committee explained that "Implementation of the obligation to respect and ensure the right to life, and in particular life with dignity, depends, inter alia, on measures taken by States parties to preserve the environment and protect it against harm, pollution and climate change caused by public and private actors." This, in turn, requires a specific commitment to sustainability: "States parties should therefore ensure sustainable use of natural resources, develop and implement substantive environmental standards, conduct environmental impact assessments and consult with relevant States about activities likely to have a significant impact on the environment, provide notification to other States concerned about natural disasters and emergencies and cooperate with them, provide appropriate access to information on environmental hazards and pay due regard to the precautionary approach."

More recently, UN Human Rights Office of the High Commissioner has noted:

> All human beings depend on the environment in which we live. A safe, clean, healthy and sustainable environment is integral to the full enjoyment of a wide range of human rights, including the rights to life, health, food, water and sanitation. Without a healthy environment, we are unable to fulfil our aspirations or even live at a level commensurate with minimum standards of human dignity.

National constitutions are also beginning to appreciate the linkages between dignity and the environment. Belgium's constitution expressly entwines environmental and dignity rights constitutionally: 'Everyone has the right to lead a life worthy of human dignity ... [including] the right to enjoy the protection of a healthy environment.' South Africa's constitution is among those that echoes dignity dimensions by providing that 'everyone has the right to an environment that is not harmful to their health or wellbeing.' Yet few other constitutions directly recognize the impact of the natural environment on the quality of human life, and none yet link dignity and sustainability.

Courts sometimes turn to effects on human dignity as a basis for recognizing a right to live in a healthy environment. One of the earliest cases to connect dignity and environmental harm is from Nigeria. In *Gbemre v. Shell Petroleum Development Company Nigeria Limited and Others*, the lower court held that gas flaring violated the petitioners' constitutional 'right to respect for their lives and dignity of their persons and to enjoy the best attainable state of physical and mental health as well as [the] right to a general satisfactory environment favourable to their development' and that the gas flaring activities formed 'a violation of their said fundamental rights to life and dignity of human person and to a healthy life in a healthy environment.' Although a declaratory judgment without remedy or continuing judicial oversight, the case signals a growing appreciation of the connection between dignity and environmental conditions. For instance, in 2017, the Irish High Court held that

> [a] right to an environment that is consistent with the human dignity and well-being of citizens at large is an essential condition for the fulfilment of all human rights. It is an indispensable existential right that is enjoyed universally, yet which is vested personally as a right that presents and can be seen always to have presented, and to enjoy protection.

Human dignity also informs conversations about the disproportionate effects of environmental policies on the most vulnerable, what is generally known as 'environmental justice.' All of these developments in turn inform the role that human dignity can play in shaping narratives about implementing the SDGs.

QUESTIONS

1. What is "sustainability"?
2. How does law advance sustainability?
3. Does the U.S. constitution have anything to say about sustainability?
4. To what extent do countries around the globe recognize sustainability? How?

CHAPTER 10: ENVIRONMENTAL JUSTICE

Chapter 10 concludes the book with the concept of environmental justice, which explores the disproportionate effects of environmental policies, implementation and enforcement on vulnerable communities, and features a recent resolution of the American Bar Association to advance environmental justice in its policies, practices and procedures throughout the practice of law.

Environmental justice is the heart of environmental performance. Environmental justice explores the disproportionate effects of environmental law and policy for the most vulnerable in society. In 2021, the American Bar Association adopted a resolution "to advance environmental justice principles and considerations in its programs, policies, and activities, including advocating for legislation and policy, and work with all levels of government to establish environmental justice laws, regulations, guidelines, policies, and best practices that reflect the right of every human being to dignity and a clean and healthy environment." The report accompanying the resolution helps to put environmental justice into current context.

EXCERPT: ADVANCING ENVIRONMENTAL JUSTICE AT THE ABA (2021)

Source: Environmental Justice Task Force of the ABA Section of Environment, Energy and Resources: James R. May (chair), Daniel Appelman, Nadia B. Ahmad, Scott W. Badenoch, Jr., Stacey J. Halliday, Howard Kenison (*ex officio*), William Kinsey, and Lawrence Pittman.

> "Communities of color, indigenous communities, and low-income populations are more likely to be located near hazardous sites and exposed to toxins. Achieving environmental justice would result in the same degree of protection from environmental and health hazards for all people and equal access to the decision-making process to have a healthy environment in which to live, learn, and work."

-- *ABA President Hilarie Bass, ABA Letter in Support of Environmental Justice Act, 2017*
Introduction

This Report supports adoption and implementation of proposed Resolution 112 to advance environmental justice. The Resolution and Report recognize that a wide spectrum of organizations, including the American Bar Association, affect environmental policy and have multiple opportunities to correct the causes and consequences of the disparate adverse effects and heightened risks of environmental policies on communities of color, indigenous communities, low-income communities, and other vulnerable populations and people. The emergence and importance of environmental justice, and relevant developments at the federal, state, and local levels in litigation, legislation, and policymaking further justifies advancement of these principles by the ABA and inclusion and consideration of these principles by other legal entities.

...

Environmental justice recognizes that every person has equal dignity and equal rights to a clean and healthy environment and access to information, participation, justice and remedies in environmental matters. Environmental justice aims to address and redress the disproportionate effects of policies and practices on communities of color, indigenous communities, low-income communities, and other vulnerable populations in the United States and around the world who are adversely affected by activities in the U.S. Environmental justice is implicated at every level of decision-making, including issues related to equal protection, civil rights, Native American law, public participation, access to information, impact and risk assessments, access to courts, development and infrastructure, hazardous facility siting, brownfield remediation, citizen science, cumulative impacts, tort remedies, litigation, and citizen suits, limiting toxic exposures and releases, and enforceability and access to remedy.

Environmental injustice has been present from ancient times to the height of the transatlantic slave trade to the trans-modern era of the current global regimes. It reflects power imbalances, deeply rooted in dynamics of race, class and wealth, alongside environmental policies involving such inputs as pollution, toxic releases, environmental quality, and climate change, challenges that tend to disproportionately affect communities of color, indigenous communities, low-income communities, and other vulnerable populations the world over.

Environmental injustice is the product of historical redlining and the legacy of the failure to abide by treaties and responsibilities accorded to domestic dependent nations and land conquest with respect to American Indian tribes and indigenous communities. It is reflected at a local, national, international, and global-level, with expressions in national practices, international law, cultural practices, sustainability, climate change, land use, and facets at the intersection of environmental law and human rights. In the United States, responses to environmental justice include litigation, federal policy and advisory groups, and proposed legislation at the national and subnational levels. Environmental justice continues to face obstacles resulting from countless unequal socioeconomic and environmental impacts including access to healthy air, water and land, biodiversity, and other environmental conditions, and unintended consequences of mitigation measures. These obstacles are exacerbated by health disparities, including those revealed by the COVID-19 pandemic, and climate change.

***

I. Disproportionate Adverse Effects of Environmental Pollution

Since at least 1971, scientists and federal agencies have documented the disproportionately adverse effects of environmental pollution on low-income populations (below the U.S. poverty line). In the early 1980s, that analysis was refined to reveal that race was the controlling factor in forecasting the location of toxic waste facilities. Recent studies show that these trends have not changed. Communities of color and low-income communities continue to be subject to environmental hazards as "fenceline communities" – or communities most vulnerable to toxic releases due to proximity to industrial facilities. Moreover, these communities are often subject to the cumulative impacts arising from multiple environmental stressors and existing health vulnerabilities.

Communities of color and low-income communities are far more likely to live along the fenceline than are White communities. Black and Latino Americans are 75 and 60 percent respectively more likely to live in fenceline zones than White Americans. The imbalances affect children acutely: "Poor children of color already face financial and racial disadvantages; living alongside hazardous chemical facilities is an additional burden that may also expose them to toxic emissions daily." Studies show "that a significantly greater percentage of Blacks, Latinos, and people in poverty live near industrial facilities that use large quantities of toxic chemicals, compared to national averages ... that larger, more chemical-intensive facilities tend to be located in counties with larger black populations and in counties with high levels of income inequality." Ultimately, there is "compelling evidence that increasing social inequality is linked to environmental degradation and that the health of people of color and those living in poverty is negatively impacted by being exposed to higher levels of environmental pollution than whites or people not in poverty."

Tribal communities face unique challenges with respect to environmental justice, given their longstanding struggles for tribal sovereignty and self-determination, as well as overcoming jurisdictional obstacles to environmental protection against non-Tribal actors. In addition, the importance of land and place to tribal culture amplifies threats presented by environmental harm – such as the destruction of subsistence fishing resources due to water pollution. Efforts in federal and state courts to address environmental and other harms have largely been unsuccessful, and administrative tribal consultation efforts - while improved - still leave open questions of whether processes are sufficiently tailored to tribal government and communities, as well as effective for achieving environmental protection.

The COVID-19 pandemic underscores the disparate impacts of these disparities. COVID-19 infects and kills Black, Asian, Native American, and Hispanic patients at least 40 percent more frequently than White patients. Pandemic risk assessment has revealed clear disparate impacts of the disease on population segments including the elderly and racial minorities. A recent study found higher COVID-19 mortality rates in communities of color subject to high levels of air pollution, finding that "an increase of only 1 g/m3 in PM2.5 is associated with a 8% increase in the COVID-19 death rate." A study of 3,000 counties shows higher mortality rates from COVID-19 and long-term exposure to air pollution in communities living near heavily polluted areas. In addition, Indigenous communities have a higher mortality rate from COVID-19, in part due to inadequate access to essential services, such as sanitation. The Navajo Nation experiences among the highest per capita Covid-19 infection rates in the United States, which is in part attributed to inadequate access to potable water. The Centers for Disease Control and Prevention report, "COVID-19 in Racial and Ethnic Minority Groups" underscores the lack of information to assess how health disparities are impacted by environmental factors and living conditions.

II. Evolution of the Environmental Justice Movement

A. Civil Rights Movement and Warren County

In 1982, a majority-minority community in Warren County, North Carolina, protested the siting of a toxic waste landfill by lying in front of truckloads of incoming contaminated polychlorinated biphenyl (PCB) soil. The waste was imported from across the state to Warren County, which was the one of the poorest counties and had the highest percentage of people of color. The ensuing protest, the first such against the location of a hazardous waste facility, resulted in the arrests of more than 500 people, which included not only residents of Warren County, but civil rights, labor, environmental, and political leaders and activists.

B. Reports of Disparate Impacts

Three formative reports provided early data substantiating disparate impacts. In 1982, the U.S. General Accounting Office (now, "Government Accountability Office") (GAO) found a "correlation between the location of hazardous waste landfills and the racial and economic status of the surrounding communities." Then in 1987, the United Church of Christ Commission for Racial Justice (UCC) issued a report concluding that the racial composition of a neighborhood is the single most important factor in determining where a toxic waste facility is sited. These disparities have only increased over time. In 1992, the National Law Journal (NLJ) found that the Environmental Protection Agency (EPA) approved Superfund cleanup remedies that left contamination in-place more frequently in minority communities than in the general population.

The National Law Journal (NLJ) also found comparative under-enforcement of other federal environmental laws aimed at protecting residents from air, water, and waste pollution. The NLJ confirmed that the disparity in responding to and enforcing hazardous waste laws was based on race and not wealth or income. In 2007, the UCC updated its earlier report and found that a majority of those living in neighborhoods within 3 kilometers (1.8 miles) of the nation's hazardous waste facilities ("host neighborhoods") were people of color.

C. National People of Color Leadership Summit (1991)

In 1991, the First National People of Color Leadership Summit issued seventeen "Principles of Environmental Justice." The Principles promoted equality in access to environmental information, participation and access to justice, "demand[ing] the right to participate as equal partners at every level of decision-making, including needs assessment, planning, implementation, enforcement and evaluation." These Principles also sought reconciliation through relief; that is, to "protect[] the right of victims of environmental injustice to receive full compensation and reparations for damages as well as quality health care." A second Leadership Summit in 2002 reaffirmed these principles.

D. National Environmental Justice Advisory Council (1993 - present)

The National Environmental Justice Advisory Council (NEJAC) is a federal advisory committee to the EPA, formed on September 30, 1993. The NEJAC provides the EPA Administrator with guidance and recommendations related to environmental justice, as well as serving as a forum for discussions on environmental justice implementation among stakeholders. Efforts include the evaluation of a diverse set of strategic, scientific, technological, regulatory, community engagement and economic issues related to environmental justice. NEJAC members represent a cross-section of environmental justice stakeholders, including those from academia, community groups, industry, non-governmental and environmental organizations, state and local governments, and tribal or indigenous groups. In providing guidance and recommendations, the NEJAC prepares recommendation reports on specific topics – most recently on Superfund remediation and redevelopment for environmental justice communities in February 2020.

E. Executive Order 12898 (1994)

Executive Order 12898 directs federal executive branch agencies to make achieving environmental justice a part of their missions by "identifying and addressing, as appropriate, disproportionately high and adverse human health or environmental effects of [their] programs, policies, and activities on minority populations and low-income populations." In addition, EO 12898 established the Interagency Working Group (IWG) on environmental justice. The IWG is composed of heads of specified federal agencies and tasked with providing guidance on identifying disproportionately high and adverse human health or environmental effects on minority and low-income populations, among other responsibilities. EO 12898 signified the importance of federal executive branch agencies considering environmental justice within their various duties, and the execution of such consideration has varied among the agencies. "Integrating EJ into program design has been relatively rare, and comprehensive assessment and analysis exceedingly uncommon. Based upon the agency responses, there appears to be only a few instances in which agencies have incorporated EJ principles and protections into programmatic design."

F. Environmental Justice at the EPA (1990 - present)

The U.S. Environmental Protection Agency has various environmental justice programs. In 1990, the EPA formed an Environmental Equity Workgroup, which delivered a detailed report in June 1992. Among the major findings in its Environmental Equity report, the EPA agreed with community advocates that: "There are clear differences between racial groups in terms of disease and death rates." The EPA report further found that: "Racial minority and low-income populations experience higher than average exposures to selected air pollutants, hazardous waste facilities, contaminated fish[,] and agricultural pesticides." Following issuance of the Environmental Equity report, the EPA formed an Office of Environmental Equity, soon to be renamed the EPA Office of Environmental Justice (OEJ), as it remains today.

Through a separate office, formerly known as the EPA Office of Civil Rights, the EPA hears administrative complaints about environmental justice under Title VI of the Civil Rights Act of 1964 (Title VI), 42 U.S.C. § 2000d, which provides that: "No person in the United States shall, on the ground of race, color, or national origin, be excluded from participation in, be denied the benefits of, or be subjected to discrimination under any program or activity receiving Federal financial assistance." The EPA has long been criticized for its poor enforcement record and extreme delays in resolving Title VI administrative complaints, with some cases waiting more than ten years for resolution. Prior to 2016, the agency had neither made formal findings of discrimination nor denied or withdrawn financial assistance from a recipient, raising significant questions about the effectiveness of the program. As such, the EPA's Title VI enforcement office, now the External Civil Rights Compliance Office (ECRCO), is the subject of various critiques, including a 2016 investigation and critical report by the U.S. Commission on Civil Rights. ECRCO was reorganized in 2017, which aimed to address the Office's shortcomings by placing it under the oversight of the EPA Office of General Counsel. Yet a 2019 GAO report concluded that these changes were insufficient to resolve many longstanding ECRCO performance issues. In addition, a federal court recently ruled that the EPA violated the Civil Rights Act of 1964 by waiting a decade or more to investigate Title VI civil rights complaints filed by community groups across the country.

III. Environmental Justice Litigation

Environmental justice claimants have few footholds in federal and state law, using civil rights laws creatively in the absence of specific environmental justice legislation, which underscores the need for further ABA action on environmental justice.

A. Equal Protection Clause

The Equal Protection Clause of the 14th Amendment provides "nor shall any state deny to any person within its jurisdiction the equal protection of the laws." The Supreme Court has interpreted this to require evidence of "invidious" express or intentional racial discrimination to warrant heightened scrutiny to discriminatory governmental action. While there has been a notable lack of success so far in applying Equal Protection principles to the environmental justice context, civil rights advocates have found some success in establishing intentional race discrimination through application of the factors identified by the Supreme Court in *Village of Arlington Heights v. Metropolitan Housing Development Corp.* Among other contexts, the *Arlington Heights* factors have been used to indicate invidious intent in contexts of travel, voting, education, and even religious exercise.

B. Due Process

The Due Process Clause of the 14th Amendment provides that "nor shall any State deprive any person of life, liberty, or property, without due process of law." Courts have long recognized a substantive dimension to this clause, relying upon the concept of Substantive Due Process for securing "fundamental rights." At least one federal court so far has found "fundamental rights" to include a right to a stable climate system. Fundamental rights also include rights to "personal autonomy" and "bodily integrity." A violation of "bodily integrity" is "an egregious, nonconsensual entry into the body which was an exercise of power without any legitimate governmental objective." The Supreme Court of Michigan recently held that knowingly subjecting residents of Flint, Michigan, to contaminated drinking water violated Substantive Due Process rights to bodily integrity.

C. Civil Rights Act of 1964

Title VI prohibits recipients of federal financial assistance from discriminating on the basis of race, color, or national origin. Claims under Title VI have historically related to (1) disparate treatment (discriminatory actions with clear discriminatory intent), or (2) disparate impact (facially neutral program or policy, with discriminatory outcomes). Federal and state claims under Title VI have been filed, for example, to address concerns with state permitting of air pollution sources and state failures to provide for needs of Limited English Proficiency populations. However, in *Alexander v. Sandoval*, the SCOTUS held that intentional discrimination is a necessary component of claims under Title VI and disparate impacts were insufficient grounds for private causes of action. In *Sandoval*, the State of Alabama declared English as the official state language; when an applicant for a driver's license complained that the policy discriminated based on national origin, a 5-4 majority of the Court found that Sandoval could not maintain a private cause of action because he could not prove that the State intended to discriminate. Rather, under Title VI, the plaintiff must demonstrate intentional discrimination through disparate treatment.

D. Other Federal Civil Rights Laws

Beyond Title VI, which primarily limits environmental justice advocates to an administrative process before the EPA, the Civil Rights Act also provides environmental justice advocates with the potential for direct action in federal court for damages under 42 U.S.C. § 1983. Under this provision,

> Every person who, under color of any statute, ordinance, regulation, custom, or usage, of any State or Territory ... subjects ... any citizen of the United States ... to the deprivation of any rights, privileges, or immunities secured by the Constitution and laws, shall be liable to the party injured in an action at law....

Section 1983 also offers a potential authority for environmental justice advocates. For example, the Sixth Circuit recently sustained claims under § 1983 against state actors responsible for providing contaminated drinking water to residents of Flint, Michigan. In addition, Title VIII of the Civil Rights Act of 1968 (also known as the Fair Housing Act) has been an increasingly popular tool among environmental justice advocates, providing grounds for civil and administrative claims against federal financial recipients on grounds of discriminatory sale, rental, and financing of dwellings. For example, in 2020, several environmental justice community groups filed a Title VIII administrative complaint with the U.S. Department of Housing and Urban Development (HUD) challenging the City of Chicago's approval of permits allowing relocation of a scrap shredding facility from a largely White neighborhood to a Latino-majority neighborhood. HUD subsequently suspended the permit indefinitely.

E. At the State Level

Environmental justice claims at the state level can also play an important role in advancing environmental justice. For example, in *Friends of Buckingham v. State Air Pollution Control Board,* the U.S. Court of Appeals for the Fourth Circuit addressed a community group's challenge to the Board's grant of a permit without the Board meeting its obligations under Virginia law to consider impacts of the permitted project. Notably, the court concluded: "[E]nvironmental justice is not merely a box to be checked, and the Board's failure to consider the disproportionate impact on those closest to the [project] resulted in a flawed analysis." State courts have been receptive to environmental justice advocates advancing claims based upon theories of tort liability, including theories grounded in nuisance, negligence, and trespass. For one recent example, the state court affirmed a judgment for nuisance against industrial hog farms in rural communities in eastern North Carolina. State constitutional provisions are another potential venue for environmental justice claims.

IV. Environmental Justice Legislation and Policy

A. Federal Level

There have been various proposals to enact environmental justice legislation at the federal level. In 2017, Senator Cory Booker (D-NJ) introduced the "Environmental Justice Act" (EJA). The EJA would have, *inter alia,* overturned *Sandoval* by establishing a private cause of action on the basis of disparate impacts, as well as disparate treatment. The EJA would have also provided that affected communities have "access to public information and opportunities for meaningful public participation relating to human health and environmental planning, regulations, and enforcement," protection from exposure to a "disproportionate burden of the negative human health and environmental impacts of pollution or other environmental hazards," and legal recognition of the seventeen environmental justice Principles adopted by the National People of Color Environmental Leadership Summit. The ABA supported the bill:

> [E]nvironmental justice has its own landmark legislation, as clean air and water do. By requiring air and water permitting to look at cumulative impacts to vulnerable communities and clarifying citizens' right to sue, this legislation helps us remove barriers to justice for victims of man-made environmental disasters.

Recent legislative proposals include the Environmental Justice Mapping and Data Collection Act of 2021 (H.R. 516), which would establish an "Environmental Justice Mapping Committee" tasked with creating a tool to identify "environmental justice communities," or communities with "significant representation of communities of color, low-income communities, or tribal and indigenous communities that experience, or are at risk of experiencing, higher or more adverse human health or environmental effects, as compared to other communities." Moreover, the Environmental Justice for All Act would (S. 872) "establish[] several environmental justice requirements, advisory bodies, and programs to address adverse human health or environmental effects of federal laws or programs on communities of color, low-income communities, or tribal and indigenous," and create a private cause of action. Furthermore, the *American Rescue Plan* appropriates funds for "disproportionate environmental or public health harms and risks in minority populations or low-income populations ..." President Biden has pledged to update and strengthen EO 12898, and has issued several Environmental Justice-advancing Executive Orders, including the *Executive Order on Tackling the Climate Crisis at Home and Abroad)*(EO 14008), the *Executive Order on America's Supply Chains* (EO 14017), and, the *Executive Order on the Establishment of the Climate Change Support Office* (EO 14027)."

B. State Level

State engagement of environmental justice has set the pace for environmental justice practice nationally in multiple arenas, including via statutes, policies, data tools, and courts. For instance, in September 2020, New Jersey passed laws that require the New Jersey Department of Environmental Protection to: (1) identify "overburdened communities" across the state; and (2) consider cumulative impacts when granting new or renewed permits impacting those "overburdened communities" by considering newly required "environmental justice impacts statements" submitted by permit applicants. California has enacted laws to guarantee the Human Right to Water (AB 685) and the Safe and Affordable Drinking Water Fund (SB 200); require consideration of environmental justice in all general plans (SB 1000); establish a community air protection program (AB 617); promote sustainable communities strategies by linking planning efforts around transportation, housing, and employment (SB 375); and provide new resources for clean energy development, such as solar roofs and electric cars, in disadvantaged communities (SB 1204 and SB 1275). New York recently enacted an Environmental Justice Section (Article 48).

There are notable subnational developments elsewhere. Illinois mandates that 25% of its Solar for All program benefits environmental justice communities, including $750 million in low-income programs for solar, solar workforce, and energy efficiency. In 2019, New York's Climate Leadership and Community Protection Act mandates that 40% of the renewable energy resources involved benefit areas of environmental justice concern. Multiple states have issued environmental justice executive orders.

***

QUESTIONS

1. What is "environmental justice"?
2. How does law thwart environmental justice? Advance it?
3. What does federal law have anything to say about environmental justice?
4. How about state law(s)?

Congratulations! You've finished the book! ☺